Smart and Sustainable Interactive Marketing

Hamid Reza Irani
University of Tehran, Iran

Hamed Nozari
Department of Management, Azad University of the Emirates, Dubai, UAE

A volume in the Advances in Marketing, Customer Relationship Management, and E-Services (AMCRMES) Book Series

Published in the United States of America by
IGI Global
Business Science Reference (an imprint of IGI Global)
701 E. Chocolate Avenue
Hershey PA, USA 17033
Tel: 717-533-8845
Fax: 717-533-8661
E-mail: cust@igi-global.com
Web site: http://www.igi-global.com

Library of Congress Cataloging-in-Publication Data

Names: Irani, Hamid Reza, 1983- editor. | Nozari, Hamed, 1984- editor.
Title: Smart and sustainable interactive marketing / edited by Hamid Reza
  Irani, Hamed Nozari.
Description: Hershey, PA : Business Science Reference, [2024] | Includes
  bibliographical references and index. | Summary: "This book examines
  qualitative and quantitative approaches to show the effects of digital
  technologies such as the Internet of Things, artificial intelligence,
  and blockchain on Marketing systems"-- Provided by publisher.
Identifiers: LCCN 2023055054 (print) | LCCN 2023055055 (ebook) | ISBN
  9798369313398 (hardcover) | ISBN 9798369313404 (ebook)
Subjects: LCSH: Marketing--Technological innovations.
Classification: LCC HF5415 .S593 2024 (print) | LCC HF5415 (ebook) | DDC
  658.800285/63--dc23/eng/20231206
LC record available at https://lccn.loc.gov/2023055054
LC ebook record available at https://lccn.loc.gov/2023055055

This book is published in the IGI Global book series Advances in Marketing, Customer Relationship Management, and E-Services (AMCRMES) (ISSN: 2327-5502; eISSN: 2327-5529)

British Cataloguing in Publication Data
A Cataloguing in Publication record for this book is available from the British Library.

All work contributed to this book is new, previously-unpublished material. The views expressed in this book are those of the authors, but not necessarily of the publisher.

For electronic access to this publication, please contact: eresources@igi-global.com.

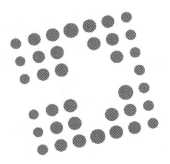

Advances in Marketing, Customer Relationship Management, and E-Services (AMCRMES) Book Series

Eldon Y. Li

National Chengchi University, Taiwan & California Polytechnic State University, USA

ISSN:2327-5502
EISSN:2327-5529

MISSION

Business processes, services, and communications are important factors in the management of good customer relationship, which is the foundation of any well organized business. Technology continues to play a vital role in the organization and automation of business processes for marketing, sales, and customer service. These features aid in the attraction of new clients and maintaining existing relationships.

The Advances in Marketing, Customer Relationship Management, and E-Services (AMCRMES) Book Series addresses success factors for customer relationship management, marketing, and electronic services and its performance outcomes. This collection of reference source covers aspects of consumer behavior and marketing business strategies aiming towards researchers, scholars, and practitioners in the fields of marketing management.

COVERAGE

- Social Networking and Marketing
- Customer Retention
- E-Service Innovation
- B2B marketing
- Cases on CRM Implementation
- Web Mining and Marketing
- Cases on Electronic Services
- Data mining and marketing
- Telemarketing
- Text Mining and Marketing

IGI Global is currently accepting manuscripts for publication within this series. To submit a proposal for a volume in this series, please contact our Acquisition Editors at Acquisitions@igi-global.com or visit: http://www.igi-global.com/publish/.

Titles in this Series

For a list of additional titles in this series, please visit: www.igi-global.com/book-series

Connecting With Consumers Through Effective Personalization and Programmatic Advertising
Jorge Remondes (Instituto Superior de Entre Douro e Vouga, Portugal & ISCAP, Instituto Politecnico do Porto, Portugal) Paulo Madeira (Instituto Superior de Entre Douro e Vouga, Portugal) and Carlos Alves (Instituto Superior de Entre Douro e Vouga, Portugal)
Business Science Reference • © 2024 • 308pp • H/C (ISBN: 9781668491461) • US $250.00

Business Drivers in Promoting Digital Detoxification
Simon Grima (Department of Insurance, Faculty of Economics Management and Accountancy, University of Malta, Msida, Malta & Faculty of Business, Management and Economics, University of Latvia, Riga, Latvia) Shilpa Chaudhary (Lovely Professional University, India) Kiran Sood (Chitkara Business School, Chitkara University, India & Research Fellow at the Women Researchers Council (WRC) at Azerbaijan State University of Economics (UNEC), Azerbaijan) and Sanjeev Kumar (Lovely Professional University, India)
Business Science Reference • © 2024 • 355pp • H/C (ISBN: 9798369311073) • US $265.00

Using Influencer Marketing as a Digital Business Strategy
Sandrina Teixeira (ISCAP, Polytechnic Institute of Porto, Portugal) Sara Teixeira (Polytechnic Institute of Porto) Zaila Oliveira (Unichristus, Brazil & Unifametro, Brazil) and Elnivan Souza (Christus University Center, Brazil)
Business Science Reference • © 2024 • 371pp • H/C (ISBN: 9798369305515) • US $265.00

The Use of Artificial Intelligence in Digital Marketing Competitive Strategies and Tactics
Sandrina Teixeira (Centre for Organizational and Social Studies (CEOS), Porto Accounting and Business School, Polytechnic of Porto, Portugal) and Jorge Remondes (Centre for Organizational and Social Studies (CEOS), Porto Accounting and Business School, Polytechnic of Porto, Portugal)
Business Science Reference • © 2024 • 318pp • H/C (ISBN: 9781668493243) • US $250.00

The Rise of Blockchain Applications in Customer Experience
Mohammed Majeed (Tamale Technical University, Ghana) Kwame Simpe Ofori (International University of Grand Bassam, Cote D'Ivoire) George Kofi Amoako (Ghana Communication Technology University, Ghana) Abdul-Raheed Alolo (Tamale Technical University, Ghana) and Gideon Awini (Business School, University of Ghana, Ghana)
Business Science Reference • © 2024 • 304pp • H/C (ISBN: 9781668476499) • US $250.00

IGI Global
PUBLISHER of TIMELY KNOWLEDGE

701 East Chocolate Avenue, Hershey, PA 17033, USA
Tel: 717-533-8845 x100 • Fax: 717-533-8661
E-Mail: cust@igi-global.com • www.igi-global.com

Editorial Advisory Board

Table of Contents

Detailed Table of Contents

Chapter 1

Ali Bakhshi Movahed, Iran University of Science and Technology, Tehran, Iran
Aminmasoud Bakhshi Movahed, Iran University of Science and Technology, Tehran, Iran
Hamed Nozari, Azad University of the Emirates, Dubai, UAE

The fifth generation of marketing is Marketing 5.0 (M 5.0). In this chapter, the opportunities and challenges of M 5.0 are defined. The main factors of M 5.0 are humans, culture, and technology. M 5.0 and business have a close connection to each other. M 5.0 is important based on creating content planning, brand awareness, and predictive marketing and has some applications in the business. The evolution of M 5.0 is defined as a long journey in marketing history. For highlighting the fifth generation of marketing, other elements of the same generation of M 5.0 such as marketing personalization and the creation of a magnificent feeling for customers are stated too. As a classic insight, exploring the challenges and opportunities is important. Finding opportunities and challenges is an attractive topic to help top management. After reviewing the literature and data analysis, finally, four opportunities and four challenges were selected with the Delphi method.

Chapter 2

Mohammadreza Nasiri Jan Agha, Islamic Azad University of Lahijan, Iran

Marketing is one of the most important organizational units and one of the most important value chain processes in organizations. Since this part of the organization shows the final output of the organization's activities, it has always been one of the strategic parts that organizations pay great attention to. In the coming era, the presence of technologies is mixed in all processes of organizations, and therefore, the processes of the marketing unit, as one of the most important parts of the organization's value chain, are also involved in technologies such as the internet of things and blockchain and artificial intelligence-based analysis. By using these growing technologies in Industry 4.0, it is possible to obtain large and efficient data that was not possible in the past. Therefore, these data, which are accurate, transparent, and based on human performance, can be used for optimal marketing and achieving brilliant organizational results. In this research, the main features of the technology-based marketing system and the future directions of using these tools are examined.

Chapter 3

Rasoul Abbasi, Hazrat-e Masoumeh University, Iran
Mohadeseh Esmaili, Hazrat-e Masoumeh University, Iran

The integration of artificial intelligence (AI) in marketing has revolutionized customer engagement, product design, advertising, pricing, and distribution. AI's diverse applications, driven by algorithms, enhance data analysis, enabling more effective marketing and sales strategies. In product design, AI creates personalized value propositions aligned with individual customer needs. In advertising, AI facilitates targeted and accurate ads, optimizing returns and reducing waste. AI transforms pricing through dynamic pricing using predictive algorithms for cost-effective and competitive strategies. In distribution and supply chain, AI enhances speed, accuracy, and efficiency through real-time monitoring and predictive modeling, ultimately improving customer satisfaction.

Chapter 4

Mohammad Nematpour, University of Tehran, Iran
Mohammad Ghaffari, University of Tehran, Iran

Smart urban tourism destinations with IoT-based devices and applications are the future of world tourism. This study identifies core factors of sustainable IoT-based interactive marketing influencing urban tourism destinations. The study adopts a systematic approach with two sides of the tourism system including supply-side and demand-side. The findings showed that factors including smart tourism ecosystems, new business approach employing multi-sided platforms, intra-organizational participative through network-based model, big data analysis, green marketing campaigns, enhance tourists' environmental knowledge and awareness, and smart CRM were determined as core factors on the use of IoT in sustainable interactive marketing. On demand side, based on the findings, perceived usefulness, perceived ease of use, trust, social influence, cyber-resilience, and perceived privacy have been determined as core indicators on the use of IoT in sustainable smart interactive marketing.

Chapter 5

Hamed Nozari, Azad University in the Emirates, UAE
Agnieszka Szmelter-Jarosz, Faculty of Economics, University of Gdańsk, Poland
Maryam Rahmaty, Department of Management, Islamic Azad University, Chalous, Iran

The use of IoT and artificial intelligence (AI) technologies and blockchain technology in the marketing field is an emerging topic in the new digitization era. The chapter aims to create a conceptual framework that describes a marketing system's main stages and dimensions based on the artificial intelligence of things (AIoT) and blockchain and evaluates the critical success factors of implementing this marketing system. This research, at first, tried to identify the most important critical success factors in these smart systems by reviewing the literature and opinions of active experts, and in the next step, these indicators were evaluated using decision-making methodology. For this purpose, a fuzzy nonlinear evaluation method has been used to examine the priorities and relationships of success factors. The results show that technology-related success factors, such as the presence of technical infrastructure and technological maturity, play the most important roles in the proper functioning of marketing based on transformational technologies.

Chapter 6

Pratap Chandra Mandal, Indian Institute of Management, Shillong, India

Companies should ensure environmental sustainability and promote sustainable marketing in their business actions. The objective of the study is to analyze environmental sustainability and sustainable marketing and business actions in the promotion of sustainable marketing. The methodology adopted is a conceptual analysis of environmental sustainability, sustainable marketing, and business actions towards promotion of sustainable marketing. Various sustainable marketing principles including consumer-oriented marketing, customer value marketing, innovative marketing, sense-of-mission marketing, and societal marketing are discussed. Companies have roles and responsibilities towards promotion of sustainable marketing. They adopt different initiatives and strategies for promotion of sustainable marketing. The discussions will help academicians and practicing managers understand their roles and responsibilities towards environmental sustainability and sustainable marketing. Companies may incorporate sustainable marketing in their processes to achieve business excellence in the long run.

Chapter 7

Bishal Poddar, Woxsen University, India
Harsh Sethia, Woxsen University, India
Atrij Jadon, Woxsen University, India
Mohd Azhar, Woxsen University, India

The chapter intends to discuss the growing significance of IoE in the realm of sustainable marketing. Nevertheless, the realm of information technology solutions within the domain of sustainable or eco-friendly marketing remains relatively underexplored within the existing literature. Therefore, this study sincerely attempts to fill this void by concerning IoE in the realm of sustainable marketing, specifically in the post-COVID-19 context. This study discusses the increasing significance of post-COVID-19 IoE in sustainable marketing practices, closely examines various constraints and prospects in the Indian context, and provides detailed implications of IoE in sustainable marketing practices. The novelty of the present study lies in the fact that IoE in the realm of sustainable marketing is a less investigated topic, and there is a dearth of literature on the subject.

Chapter 8

Subhashini Durai, Bharathiar University, India
Geetha Manoharan, SR University, India
T. Sathya Priya, Coimbatore Institute of Technology, India
R. Jayanthi, Coimbatore Institute of Technology, India
Abdul Razak, Entrepreneurship Development Institute of India, India
Sunitha Purushottam Ashtikar, SR University, India

AI will personalize marketing. Analysis of client behavior and preferences customizes product and service suggestions. AI-powered CRM solutions can automate customer service, help customers, and boost satisfaction. AI improves marketing targeting. Technology can improve client behavior targeting. AI will also impact digital marketing. Personalization boosts client engagement and sales. Virtual assistants and chat bots will increase marketing. Apps can swiftly answer customer questions, improve service, boost satisfaction, and develop brand loyalty. AI can enhance price by studying market trends, competition, and customer behaviour. Machine learning algorithms help organizations set rates, increasing sales and profit. Marketers may create more engaging content with AI. AI can analyze client data and behavior to determine which content performs best for target demographics, improving content marketing. AI marketing will develop in the future. Companies will benefit from AI-powered, tailored, and data-driven marketing that boosts customer engagement, loyalty, and revenue.

Chapter 9

In today's world and with the development of advanced industrial generations, the internet of things as an epidemic technology has caused a huge change and transformation in all aspects of daily life, including business. This technology has affected all dimensions and components of the organization's value chain, and a new concept called intelligent and interactive marketing based on the internet of things has also been formed. Considering the importance of sales and marketing in the organization's supply chain, it is necessary to understand the dimensions and components of this type of marketing. The internet of things is one of the most important sources of big data production from marketing processes and it seems that businesses' emphasis on this type of marketing can guarantee business growth.

Chapter 10

Smart marketing is a term that encompasses various forms of marketing that leverage artificial intelligence (AI) and the internet of things (IoT) to deliver personalized, relevant, and engaging experiences to customers. This research aims to provide a comprehensive literature review on smart marketing, covering its definitions, applications, advantages, disadvantages, and implications on sustainability. The chapter also discusses the benefits and challenges of smart marketing for both marketers and customers, such as improved efficiency, effectiveness, creativity, customer satisfaction, loyalty, and retention, as well as ethical, privacy, security, and social issues. Furthermore, the chapter examines the impact of smart marketing on sustainability, highlighting the potential opportunities and risks for environmental, social, and economic dimensions. The chapter concludes with some suggestions for future research directions and best practices for smart marketing.

Chapter 11

The advent of the digital age has brought about significant changes in consumer behavior, with online services becoming an integral part of everyday life. This chapter explores the consumer awareness and perception of online services, focusing on a comparative analysis of brand preferences and the decision-making process. By examining various studies and surveys, this chapter aims to shed light on the factors that influence consumer choices in the online service domain and understand how brands can enhance their strategies to attract and retain customers. The chapter concludes with actionable insights for businesses to better align their offerings with consumer expectations.

Chapter 12
Place-Based Strategies, Multichannel Merger, and Context-Driven Alerts for Engagement With Mobile Marketing 198
Anagha Kuriachan, Christ University, India
Reshma Rose Thomas, Christ University, India
R. Sukanya, Christ University, India

Mobile marketing is essential for timely, personalized communication in the digital world. Engagement is increased by location-based strategies like geofencing and context-driven notifications. Integrating social media improves ties with customers. In the digital age, multi-channel integration guarantees a smooth and personalized experience. As per the authors, this chapter explores how location-based suggestions, context-driven notifications, and multi-channel integration enhance client connections while highlighting the significance of geolocation data for targeted content. For context-driven notifications to be effective, helpfulness and privacy must be balanced. Companies create stronger relationships with their consumers and improve the customer experience, which motivates both present and new customers to engage and connect with their brand. An analysis is conducted on the changing field of mobile marketing, emphasizing the use of location-based tactics, multi-channel integration, and context-driven notifications to increase user engagement.

Chapter 13
Unveiling the Advancements and Trends in Innovative Sustainable Marketing Strategies 230
N. V. Kavimayil, School of Law, SASTRA University, India
C. Vijayabanu, School of Management, SASTRA University, India

This chapter aims to bring a crystalline understanding of trends in marketing strategies with their origin of invention. Marketing, a significant component, was incorporated following the division of the section within the chapter that encompasses the management abstract. It brings out an ocean of information on the past viability of management and marketing alignment for performance by understanding the stiff competition and predicting recent trends based on the relevant strategies. Integration into e-commerce and engaging in technologies lead an organization to get itself well-developed and managed accordingly. The chapter will facilitate traders, academicians, research scholars, government, consultants, and practicing managers through the current trends in marketing strategies.

Chapter 14
Acceptance of Digital Technologies: Empirical Evidence From Sport Marketing (or Industry) 251
Alireza NazemiBidgoli, University of Tehran, Iran
Ehsan Mohamadi Turkmani, University of Tehran, Iran
Hamid Reza Irani, University of Tehran, Iran

This study investigated the intention to use wearable sports technologies using a social-psychological approach, namely technophobia. This study was applied and correlational. The statistical population of this study included all athletes who had been insured in the current year. A non-probability sampling method was used, and 394 people were selected as the study sample using the Morgan table. The results of the study showed that expected performance and social influence have a positive and direct effect on the attitude to use. No significant negative effect of technophobia was found for the relationship between expected effort and expected performance on the attitude to use. Based on the results, it is suggested to launch different campaigns with rich content to highlight the capabilities of these technologies and the power of these devices in increasing the effectiveness of sports activities and motivating people to lead a healthier life.

Preface

Interactive marketing is one of the advertising and marketing methods that includes direct response to the actions, behaviors, demands and expectations of consumers. This method has been used in internet and digital advertising for more than a decade. Personalizing advertising messages is the priority of interactive marketing. Interactive marketing has actually moved away from traditional marketing and two-way interactions are established between the commercial brand and the target audience. In today's era, the use of transformative technologies in Various areas of business, especially in work processes and the value chain of the organization, have become very impressive. Technologies such as the Internet of Things, artificial intelligence, blockchain technology or big data analysis have all had a tremendous impact on business processes. Marketing, as one of the most important organizational units, has not been separated from this category. In addition to collecting and maintaining big data and analyzing this data, these technologies also guarantee the transparency and accuracy of the data to a great extent. By using these transformative technologies, the depth of data can be reached. Data that is based on performance. The presence of the network creates powerful communication among all actors in the marketing and sales process. With the presence of these technologies, sustainable marketing can mean creating and maintaining stable relationships with customers, social environment and natural environment. Therefore, to use these technologies in the field of marketing, in addition to guaranteeing the quality of data, it also prevents many environmental harms. In general, sustainable and interactive marketing is a key concept in the era of the fourth industrial revolution and aligned with the concepts of sustainable development and circular economy.

The purpose of this book is to express the dimensions, components, features, opportunities and challenges of intelligent interactive marketing in the new era with an emphasis on sustainable development. In addition to describing the concept of interactive marketing due to digital technologies, this book has tried to analyze the effects of technology in sustainable development. In this book, the future trends of marketing in the era of transformative technologies are discussed. Also, the role of technologies such as the Internet of Things, artificial intelligence, and blockchain have been specifically examined and analyzed. Finally, studies in a specific industry are also proposed to understand the concepts more. And. This book can be useful for researchers and researchers interested in the fields of sales and marketing in the new era.

Hamid Reza Irani
University of Tehran, Iran

Hamed Nozari
Department of Management, Azad University of the Emirates, Dubai, UAE

Chapter 1
Opportunities and Challenges of Marketing 5.0

Ali Bakhshi Movahed
Iran University of Science and Technology, Tehran, Iran

Aminmasoud Bakhshi Movahed
 https://orcid.org/0000-0003-3259-5419
Iran University of Science and Technology, Tehran, Iran

Hamed Nozari
 https://orcid.org/0000-0002-6500-6708
Azad University of the Emirates, Dubai, UAE

ABSTRACT

The fifth generation of marketing is Marketing 5.0 (M 5.0). In this chapter, the opportunities and challenges of M 5.0 are defined. The main factors of M 5.0 are humans, culture, and technology. M 5.0 and business have a close connection to each other. M 5.0 is important based on creating content planning, brand awareness, and predictive marketing and has some applications in the business. The evolution of M 5.0 is defined as a long journey in marketing history. For highlighting the fifth generation of marketing, other elements of the same generation of M 5.0 such as marketing personalization and the creation of a magnificent feeling for customers are stated too. As a classic insight, exploring the challenges and opportunities is important. Finding opportunities and challenges is an attractive topic to help top management. After reviewing the literature and data analysis, finally, four opportunities and four challenges were selected with the Delphi method.

1. INTRODUCTION

The main purpose of this section is to identify the most important opportunities and challenges of Marketing 5.0 (M 5.0). Finding significant M 5.0 opportunities and challenges is essential because researchers are interested in continuing the development way of marketing. If scholars want to carry on the way,

DOI: 10.4018/979-8-3693-1339-8.ch001

they need to be aware of the situation. So, they should find opportunities and challenges in marketing. Marketing 5.0, the fifth generation of marketing, was introduced in January 2021 by Philip Kotler, the father of marketing science, with a book under the same title. He believes that there is a wide difference between machines and humans. Marketing 5.0 focuses on the integration of culture, technology, and humans. In the new era, marketing must focus on human communication and human values to successfully respond to customer needs and expectations. In Fig. 1 the basic elements of M 5.0 have been shown. Human, technology, and culture are the three major ones that can have a mutual effect on each other through the following cycle.

Figure 1. The main factors of M 5.0

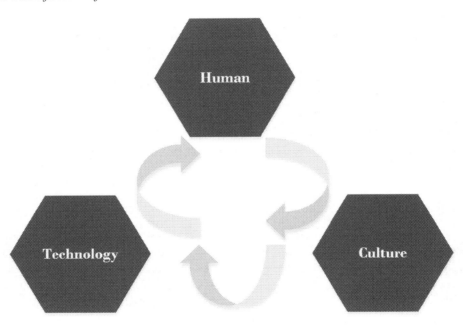

M 5.0 is a postmodern new marketing approach (Sarıoğlu, 2023). The approach of M 5.0 adds sensors, and smart objects to integrate connection with the world of physical and digital (Aytekin et al., 2020). There are some technologies like AI, Chabot's, and virtual reality in M 5.0 (Ferriz, 2022). The only goal of these technologies is to improve customer experience. M 5.0 is explained by integrating smart technology into marketing strategies such as AI, IoT, and big data analytics (Bakator et al., 2023). The era now in charge of M 5.0 is turning into an oriented topic. M 5.0 is a technological world and global social communication that can reach customers regardless of time and place (Valentino, 2022).

M 5.0 is based on data and can predict. M 5.0 is contextual, augmented, and agile too (Kotler et al., 2021). Also, it is crucial to specify the proper marketing strategy that pays attention to M 5.0 technologies and the behavior of consumers (Hermina et al., 2022). Identifying the framework and strategies of M 5.0 to increase the number of customers (Kotler et al., 2021) and service quality. the effect of M 5.0 on marketing performance (Alanazi, 2022) is undeniable. M 5.0 can affect the whole world of businesses. Truly it is necessary to provide the business needs for M 5.0 in the economy especially the digital one

(Kajale & Joshi, 2021). So, there is a mutual sense of need between business and M 5.0. Generally, the next technology is not the topic that M 5.0 is focused on. On the reverse certain principles of current marketing are the topic that M 5.0 is concentrated on (Kumar et al., 2022). As a future view, the M 5.0 strategy enables a new vision of applying the technology from the social media Instagram (Sari et al., 2023). According to the research, M 5.0 and business connect In Fig. 2 Constructing the M 5.0 paradigm (Montero et al., 2023) needs the use of new types of technologies. It can help to change the business paradigm too. On the other hand, the competition among enterprises can create an amazing atmosphere between them. Enterprise competitiveness is one of the most universal issues in marketing (Lupak et al., 2021). Surely, in enterprises based on projects, this topic is more understandable (Ni et al., 2020).

Ethical business practices (EBP) define values and ethics that manage the behavior of an organization in its communication with consumers, employees, stakeholders, and society (Rana, 2020). To better understand EBP, managers must reach a determined level of experience that many top managers have reached at the ideal level before (Hıdıroğlu, 2020). EBP is essential to making digital user experiences, especially in the designing process (Rana, 2020). Thus, EBP is important in marketing and customers' feelings. There is a close connection between science such as marketing and innovative technology (Miah et al., 2021). People may use technologies that are cutting edge, but they don't understand the effect of those on their daily lives. in modern economic activities, Innovative technology companies are known as an important element (Eliakis et al., 2020). Some new technologies are known as new techniques. Virtual Reality (VR) is one of them and can be explained as computer simulation (Sholihin et al., 2020) which in M 5.0 can provide novel experiences and several insights (Wijayanto & Putra, 2021). These can include products or services for the customers. Also, some campaigns use VR and increase marketing effectiveness (Regt et al., 2021). Also, in 2023, marketing will change with the development of AI in many ways (Varmavuo, 2020).

Figure 2. M 5.0 and businesses

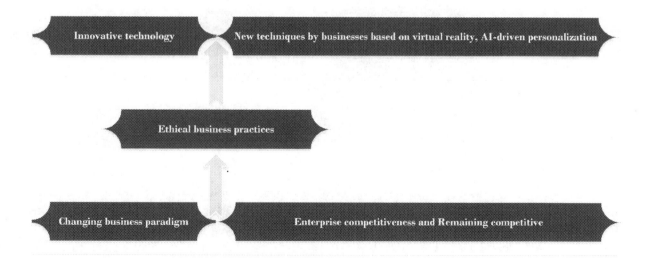

The M 5.0 is important because it opens many new doors to the world of business. Several arguments show M 5.0 is important. M 5.0 is changing the game of marketing to the new generation of marketing. Additionally, some trends are changing marketing which can be technological, socioeconomic, or geopolitical (Rust, 2020). It is important to make delightful memories for the customers of enterprises that's why for creating good user experiences the Implementation of M 5.0 puts pressure on businesses to use technological and human resources (Santoso et al., 2023).

According to the many research, the applications of M 5.0 in the tourism industry are significant. Practically, the use of social media such as Instagram by various generations in marketing from a sustainable tourism perspective (Hysa et al., 2021). From a technical view, M 5.0 plays a role in McDonald's all around the world (Sardjono et al., 2023). M 5.0 strategies will probably improve health system quality through personalized communication (Gitarja & Hariyati, 2023). Thus, there are many fields and cases in M 5.0 that researchers can observe and find the trend of this topic in developed countries. There are some significant importance and applications in M 5.0. They include creating content planning, brand awareness, and predictive marketing which is demonstrated in Fig. 3.

Figure 3. M 5.0 importance and applications

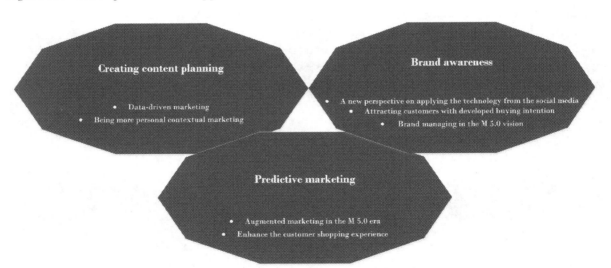

2. LITERATURE REVIEW

The trend of marketing concepts from M 1.0 to M 5.0 will be explained in the following. Generally, Marketing and especially modern marketing began from 1950 to 1970 (Khan & Arif, 2023). The focus of M 1.0 was on the product, M 2.0 was on the customer and M 3.0 was on the value and brand. Furthermore, M 4.0 adds experience and M 5.0 adds relationships, authenticity, and co-creation. The base of M 5.0 is the human centricity of M 3.0 and the technological ability of M 4.0 (Sima, 2022). Specifically, there is a trend from M 4.0 to M 5.0 and the digitization of marketing activities plays an important role in that (İnan, 2023). For better explanations, there is Fig. 4 which shows the evolution process of M 5.0.

Figure 4. The evolution to M 5.0

Also, marketers experience the sequences of generations from X to A. In addition, the Y and Z generation was discovered too. In the following, M 5.0, its Opportunities and Challenges are explained.

2.1 Marketing 5.0

To increase sustainability and value in business, it is necessary to create a beautiful relationship between the fifth generation of Industry, design, and marketing (Ribeiro & Teixeira, 2021). The impacts of new technologies are vital for new generations and M 5.0 (Kartajaya, Setiawan, & Kotler, 2021). M 5.0 has responsibility for the technology and daily life of people (Sasisuriyaphoom & Choompolsathien, 2021). Practically, using IoT technologies and marketing 5.0 in sports facilitates the determined process (Nazemi et al., 2023). For this reason, it is acceptable for related people in this field. Society 5.0 is considered at the modern social level and its vision needs the construction of a novel and innovative business model (Roblek et al., 2020). M 5.0 and Society 5.0 have a close connection (Koroglu et al., 2023). Siemens is a clear leader in tech companies and integrates the Society 5.0 concept into their marketing concepts (Banholzer et al., 2022). Technically, marketing strategy development for the Society 5.0 era by increasing the number of tourists and their satisfaction in the business sector of the lodging industry (Anggraeni et al., 2023).

Industry 5.0 shows important challenges including ability improvements and AI-assisted knowledge management (Joshi & Masih, 2023). Marketing in its new generation which is called M 5.0 includes industry 5.0 technologies such as automation and cyber technology (Jaiwant, 2023). Marketing is a member of the whole industry. So, M 5.0 is a subcategory of industry 5.0. Also, Consumer 5.0 is new in M 5.0. The fifth generation of consumers is educated at a high level to apply digital technologies (Sarıoğlu, 2023). So, they can plan to achieve their goals and provide their requirements. Fig. 5 shows the effect of the fifth generation on society, industry, marketing, and consumers.

Figure 5. The elements of fifth generation

2.2 Opportunities of Marketing 5.0

Finding opportunities and challenges is an attractive topic. For this reason, there are some review papers on Neuro-sensory marketing and the situation of opportunities and challenges in the market (Kumar et al., 2020). Also, the key performance indicators and identifying opportunities and challenges of marketing 5.0 can help top management (Phanga et al., 2020). In this section, there are 5 opportunities according to the studied articles including Customer experience improvement with AI, Marketing personalization with AI & IoT, Machines and human collaboration for customer prediction, marketing campaign simulation to detect customer emotions and interactions, and Empathetic thinking between companies and society with improving brand awareness.

2.2.1 Customer Experience Improving With AI

There are some new trends in Marketing including M 5.0 and the use of AI in marketing (Kumar et al., 2022). AI can use sensors and cameras to gauge potential customer's level of interest or emotion while using external information such as local events or weather to personalize experiences. As a practical view, AI can use sensors and cameras to track viewers' movements in exhibitions and theaters, adopting virtual principles to match real-world situations (Hutson, 2023). AI has been applied in marketing recently. It is attractive among scholars, and it can be a clear leader in some kinds of industries (Varmavuo, 2020).

2.2.2 Marketing Personalization With AI and IoT

M 5.0 presents personalized experiences (Hossain & Rahman, 2022). Creating a connected ecosystem of devices and sensors is ideal for providing personalized responses to customers. It is interesting that if there is an ecosystem of devices and sensors from different vendors, handling the device data will be an extra challenge (Márquez & Taramasco, 2023). If there is no attention, every opportunity can make challenges in the future. Marketing personalization requires enterprises to collect data and information that they can use to customize and personalize their products or services, which might expand the privacy concerns of customers (Cloarec et al., 2022). Marketing personalization endeavors increasingly exist in technologies such as AI (Peltier et al., 2023; Scarpi et al., 2022) and IoT. It happens in marketing automation too. Marketing personalization in the decision-making of Gen Z is important (McKee et al., 2023).

2.2.3 Machines and Humans Collaboration for Customer's Prediction

Furthermore, customer behavior prediction is a fundamental indicator in improving the service quality of companies and their growth (Altameem & Hafez, 2022). machine learning can solve customer behavior prediction problems. (Quynh & Dung, 2021). Steve Jobs believed that Customers are not aware of what they want until a company offers them. So, it shows that the marketing role is a presentation role. Also, retailers used different customer behavior prediction models like recommendation systems to increase consumers and sales (Murugan et al., 2022). Recently, there have been many models in articles that attempt to evaluate the behavior of consumers. M 5.0 by using machine learning and analytics can forecast results or predict the movements of the market (Polak et al., 2022). Furthermore, the concept of M 5.0 strategies develops new experiences for customers by combining some kind of technologies and human intelligence (Giner et al., 2021). As an example, predictive models and machine learning algorithms are in the field of tailoring (Rathore, 2020).

2.2.4 Marketing Campaigns Simulation to Detect Customer Emotions and Interactions

Recently, accurate analysis of customers' emotions has been faced with positive feedback (Manoharan & Sathesh, 2020). Many models have been developed for emotion detection (Bjelak & Selimović, 2023). Also, The influence of emotions of customers on their online shopping behavior and their online service quality (Golalizadeh et al., 2023). On the other hand, marketing campaign effects are measured by consumer numbers (Xiao et al., 2023). Thus, the simulation of these campaigns can help us to interact with customers.

2.2.5 Empathetic Thinking Between Companies and Society With Improving Brand Awareness

The empathy between companies and society can help the branding process. The effect of society on the brand image of companies is undeniable (Mysakova & Zakharcheva, 2023). Some studies assess the communication between social responsibility and the perception of consumers about a brand (Martínez et al., 2022). Awareness and trust in a brand have a positive influence on loyalty to the brand (Bernarto et al., 2020). Brand awareness is the first stage of making brand value for customers (Azzari & Pelissari, 2021). Activities of social media marketing influence brand awareness and brand loyalty (Fatima et al., 2022). Also, brand awareness and social media marketing play a positive and important role in brand loyalty and brand image (Heskiano et al., 2020). Practically, the application of social media, especially YouTube Ads in building brand image and brand awareness is undeniable. In addition, its influence on purchase intention is important too (Febriyantoro, 2020). Some research creates new visions that influence the field of brand in the M 5.0 world. So, enterprises and society should collaborate to improve the brand in an empathetic way.

2.3 Challenges of Marketing 5.0

As a classic insight, exploring the challenges and opportunities is important. This title especially is in micro, small, and medium enterprises (Retnawati et al., 2022). Marketing has been changed in a global measure and it made many challenges (Dubey & Sushma, 2020). Furthermore, M 5.0 can cause some other challenges including the generation gap, prosperity polarization, and digital divide (Kotler et al., 2021). In this section, there are 5 opportunities according to the studied articles including the Threat of social values with increasing penetration of technology, social polarization due to the uneven distribution of technological infrastructure affected by advertising, Consumer habits change, and Buying patterns change, increasing competition.

2.3.1 Threat of Social Values With Increasing Penetration of Technology

Social values are crucial for well-being at the offices and workplaces. (Santos & Lousã, 2022). On the other hand, increasing penetration of technology can be observed in the whole world (Dhir & Dhir, 2015). If the penetration of technology increases into society, the algorithms will be extensively used in the lives of people (Wu & Liu, 2022). Also, if the penetration of technology increases in the form of AI and IoT, it will be an opportunity for companies and organizations to understand their effect on the contemporary workforce (Vyas & Priya, 2023). So, the point of view can make a difference here. Thus, by increasing the penetration of technology, social value can be a threat.

2.3.2 Social Polarization Due to the Uneven Distribution of Technological Infrastructure Affected by Advertising

Social polarization is a very wide topic and has increased in some Asian countries. Recently, Turkey has experienced increased social polarization (Kulkul, 2020). Not only Asia experiences this but also the whole world is trying to find out whether it is a challenging issue or not (Verchere, 2022). Financially, social polarization plays an important role in public finance at the central and local levels (Nedelea et al., 2021). On the other hand, Technological infrastructure plays a key role in the developing process of the country (Elshaiekh et al., 2023). Technological infrastructure determines the management of resources of enterprises (Kilani, 2020). Furthermore, advertising affects technological infrastructure. Basic technological infrastructure is provided for computational advertising in organizations (Helberger et al., 2020). The exchange of social ratios on the global market is widely responsible for the uneven distribution of technological infrastructure (Skrbina et al., 2021). So, the uneven distribution of technological infrastructure is affected by advertising and social polarization happens because of that.

2.3.3 Consumer Habits Change

In the world, customer habits create an uncertain element (Pasha, 2022). Consumer habits and tastes change rapidly, and marketers must be able to adapt to these changes and find appropriate solutions to attract new consumers. There are some changes in consumer habits. So, organizations and companies must develop and design their strategies (David, 2021) to adapt their marketing strategies to that current situation. In addition, there is a challenge in research which shows that scholars are not sure enough about the changing customer perception over time (Morell, 2022). As a long-term insight, consumer habits will be changed in the future (Mukendi et al., 2020).

2.3.4 Buying Patterns Change

Buying patterns are changing significantly and marketers should be able to understand these changes and find a suitable solution to attract consumers. As a practical view, researchers attempt to identify specific attitudes in the car industry that can form patterns of buying (Al-Hitmi, 2020). In the same way in iPhone products, researchers assess the connection between quality and price and its impact on customer buying patterns (Hamizan et al., 2023). On the other hand, E-word of mouth as a marketing technique can affect the buying patterns of consumers in the products of Samsung (Shenoy & Rao, 2020). Some factors can affect consumer buying patterns as an internal one or external one (Al-Hitmi, 2020).

2.3.5 Increasing Competition

The final challenge is about increasing competition. With the development of technology and the improvement of access to information, the competition in the market has greatly increased, and it has become more challenging to win in a high-pressure competitive environment than in the past years. If competition increases and the sense of people communicating with each other decreases, neoliberalism will increase loneliness and decrease the welfare of people (Becker et al., 2021). It is based on the approach of social identity to the topic of health. Additionally, many cases and articles investigate the impacts of increasing competition in the whole market and delivering products (Mehdizadehrayeni et al., 2022).

3. APPROACH AND FRAMEWORK

Marketing 5.0 needs a conceptual approach to submit opportunities and challenges. The Delphi method has been used to validate the extracted indicators. In Delphi studies, feedback influences individual responses and the achievement of consensus (Barrios et al., 2021). After presenting the Delphi results, the conceptual framework is presented.

3.1 Delphi Method

The Delphi method is considered in academic research as a valuable technique for reaching consensus about specific topics when empirical evidence is scarce or contentious (Barrios et al., 2021). The Delphi technique is defined as a research approach to obtain consensus by using a series of questionnaires and providing feedback to participants who have expertise in key areas. This technique is used to screen indicators or reach an agreement on the importance of indicators (Yousuf, 2019).

3.1.1 Delphi Descriptive Statistics

A Delphi team and panel were formed to perform the Delphi method. After review, the opinions of the Delphi team were provided to the Delphi panel for aggregation. Descriptive statistics of the Delphi team and panel are given in Tables 1 and 2.

3.1.2 Delphi Results

Delphi steps were done in three rounds. Two rounds are qualitative, and one is quantitative. In two qualitative rounds, opinions about opportunities and challenges were announced. The third round was held quantitatively because no new qualitative opinion was obtained in the second round. The consensus index in the quantitative round was that 75% of the opinions were in one of the three ranges (1 to 3, 4 to 6, and 7 to 9).

Table 1. Descriptive statistics of the Delphi panel

Work Experiences	Job Career	Academic Degree	Age	
18 Years	Associate Professor	Ph.D. in Strategic Marketing	48	1.
15 Years	Associate Professor	Ph.D. in International Marketing	44	2.
10 Years	Assistant Professor	Ph.D. in Marketing Communications	41	3.
8 Years	Assistant Professor	Ph.D. in Marketing Management	38	4.
6 Years	Assistant Professor	Ph.D. in Brand Management	35	5.

Table 2. Descriptive statistics of the Delphi team

Work Experiences	Job Career	Academic Degree	Age	
15 Years	Assistant Professor	Ph.D. in Marketing Management	47	1.
13 Years	Assistant Professor	Ph.D. in Strategic Marketing	44	2.
13 Years	Chief marketing officer	Ph.D. in Strategic policy	43	3.
10 Years	Marketing Manager	Ph.D. in Strategic Marketing	41	4.
10 Years	Product Manager	Ph.D. in Marketing Management	41	5.
9 Years	Market research analyst	Master of International Marketing	40	6.
8 Years	Business Analyst	Master of Business Administration	38	7.
7 Years	Digital Marketing Strategist	Master of Marketing Communications	35	8.
5 Years	Marketing Assistant	Master of Brand Management	34	9.
5 Years	Social media Specialist	Master of Business Administration	32	10.
5 Years	Event marketing Specialist	Master of International Business	31	11.
5 Years	Marketing Assistant	Master of Business Administration	31	12.

Table 3. First-round

Explanation	Point of View	Opportunities	
Integration with 2	Integration	Customer experience improving with AI	1.
Integration with 1	Integration	Marketing personalization with AI & IoT	2.
Correction to "Evolutionary collaboration of machines and humans to customer behavior prediction"	Correction	Collaboration of Machines and humans for customer prediction	3.
Correction to "Marketing campaigns simulation to detect customer interactions"	Correction	Marketing campaign simulation to detect customer emotions and interactions	4.
Agreed by eleven experts of the Delphi team	Agreement	Empathetic thinking between companies and society with improving brand awareness	5.
Explanation	**Point of view**	**Challenges**	
Correction to "Threat of social values"	Correction	Threat of social values with increasing penetration of technology	1.
Correction to "Social polarization affected by advertising and technological infrastructure"	Correction	Social polarization due to the uneven distribution of technological infrastructure affected by advertising	2.
Integration with 4	Integration	Consumer habits change	3.
Integration with 3	Integration	Buying patterns change	4.
Agreed by eleven experts of the Delphi team	Agreement	Increasing competition	5.

3.1.2.1 First Round of Delphi

The questionnaire was given to the experts to express their opinions in step one. The opinions obtained in the first round are listed in Table 3.

The opinion of the experts includes agreement, correction, integration, or deletion. These opinions are the basis of the second round of the Delphi questionnaire.

3.1.2.2 Second Round of Delphi

In this step, no new qualitative opinions were obtained, and the experts only expressed their agreement and disagreement with the opinions of the previous round. The results are given in Table 4.

Table 4. Second-round

Explanation	Opportunities	
Ten people agreed and Two people did not answer	Customer experience improving and marketing personalization with AI & IoT	1.
Eleven people agreed and a people disagreed without declaring a qualitative opinion	Evolutionary collaboration of machines and humans to customer behavior prediction	2.
Ten people agreed without declaring a qualitative opinion and Two people did not answer	Marketing campaign simulation to detect customer interactions	3.
Twelve people agreed without declaring a qualitative opinion	Empathetic thinking between companies and society with improving brand awareness	4.
Explanation	**Challenges**	
Eleven people agreed and a people disagreed without declaring a qualitative opinion	Threat of social values	1.
Ten people agreed and Two people did not answer	Social polarization affected by advertising and technological infrastructure	2.
Ten people agreed without declaring a qualitative opinion and Two people did not answer	Changes in consumer habits and buying patterns	3.
Twelve people agreed without declaring a qualitative opinion	Increasing competition	4.

In the end, the factors were confirmed because no new qualitative opinion was obtained.

3.1.2.3 Third Round of Delphi

In this step, a quantitative questionnaire was prepared. The range of 1 to 9 is used in this questionnaire. The basis for reaching a relative opinion consensus is that 75% of the respondents mark in one of the ranges 1 to 3, 4 to 6, or 7 to 9. If 75% of the opinions are in the range of 7 to 9, the relevant factor has reached a consensus and is approved; but if 75% of the results are answered in the other intervals; the index reaches consensus and is rejected. In other cases, the index does not reach a consensus and is transferred to the next round. The results are given in Table 5.

The experts approved all the opportunities and challenges of marketing 5.0 according to Table 5.

Table 5. Third-round

Interpretation	Standard Deviation	Average	Opportunities	
Consensus and approval	0.39	2.51	Customer experience improving and marketing personalization with AI & IoT	1.
Consensus and approval	0.14	2.87	Evolutionary collaboration of machines and humans to customer behavior prediction	2.
Consensus and approval	0.77	1.67	Marketing campaign simulation to detect customer interactions	3.
Consensus and approval	0.46	2.19	Empathetic thinking between companies and society with improving brand awareness	4.
interpretation	Standard Deviation	Average	Challenges	
Consensus and approval	0.68	1.85	Threat of social values	1.
Consensus and approval	0.87	1.48	Social polarization affected by advertising and technological infrastructure	2.
Consensus and approval	0.94	1.36	Changes in consumer habits and buying patterns	3.
Consensus and approval	0.23	2.74	Increasing competition	4.

3.2 Conceptual Framework

A conceptual model of the main factors is shown in Fig. 6.

Figure 6. Opportunities and challenges of Marketing 5.0

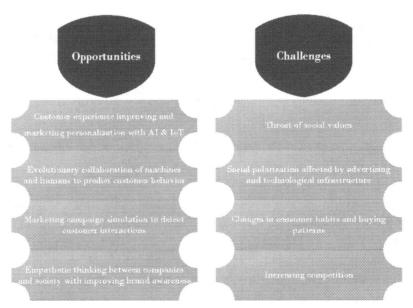

4. CONCLUSION

In this chapter Opportunities and Challenges of M 5.0 were defined in the conceptual framework. On one hand M 5.0 opportunities can help to improve the business environment, transform social conditions, and facilitate the daily lives of customers. Concentration on sustainable development and the business environment field can be an opportunity for firms (Brychko et al., 2023). the transformed social condition can improve healthcare systems eventually (Berkowitz & Orr, 2023). To sum up, the applications and definitions of nominated opportunities and challenges are explained. New technologies like AI and IoT can personalize marketing and bring delightful user experiences. One of the AI benefits is marketing personalization which can predict customers' reactions (Hopkinson et al., 2022). New technologies like AI and big data have enabled new directions to practice marketing (Varmavuo, 2020). In the future world, new technologies will probably find their applications in creating magnificent user experiences (Akhunova & Abdusattorova, 2023). Machine learning and IOT tend to personalize marketing and customize user experience (Singh, 2020). Some technologies can be used in M 5.0 (Rosário & Dias, 2023). Technologies such as using blockchain in marketing (Jain et al., 2021) are crucial. Also, the applications of AI and big data in marketing are important too (Verma et al., 2021). There is text mining in management services to increase top management awareness (Kumar et al., 2021). The future path of technology will be innovative technology which defines new ideas (Miah et al., 2021).

For predicting customers' decisions, machines and humans should collaborate. Technologies like machine learning are using data and information to predict patterns of consumers (Sap & Özdemir, 2023). From a practical view developing some models to predict the customers' status can help the banks to have an early alert to make some changes in the service process and make a new service process (Najjar et al., 2022). In addition, machine learning concentrates on predicting the decisions of customers in the banking sector, especially in the crisis (El Koufi et al., 2022). This forecasting can enable the department of marketing to aim for high-quality customers as soon as possible with very fast timing (El Koufi et al., 2022). Also, some techniques of data mining can provide new information by analyzing the data of customers (Yulianti & Saifudin, 2023). To find the actions and reactions of consumers, a marketing campaign should be simulated. If marketing campaigns want to be prosperous, they should use data mining (Huynh et al., 2023). Also, employees can use technology and conduct types of marketing, especially digital marketing (Yudhiasta & Mijiarto, 2020). Practically in the context of M 5.0, bank marketers can improve the brand of banks and increase customer satisfaction (Hafez, 2023). There are mechanisms for empathetic thinking between firms and society which lead to an increase in the awareness of the brand and employee satisfaction (Lee, 2016). Thus, if a company tends to increase the awareness of a brand in society, it should think in an empathetic way with communities.

On the other hand, M 5.0 challenges cause problems for people and businesses. cultural changes, technological advancements, political ideologies, or economic influences can be a challenge. cultural changes directly connected to the geographic location (Anghelinu et al., 2023). From a technical view, the influence of technological advancements on the shaping of children's character is proven (Tabroni et al., 2022). The nominated challenges have some applications and explanations for sure. For example, social values need society to emerge and improve. it never occurs in an empty space (Filho et al., 2022). According to the research, significant social values can be defined as efficiency, equity, and personal responsibility (Torbica et al., 2020). By increasing the penetration of technology, threats to social values will probably happen. Social polarization is a wide and broad gap (Keys, 2021) that can be influenced by technology.

Customers have an algorithm of habits that can change. Generally, humans are habit creatures (Fishman et al., 2023). Much research demonstrates that ignoring habit impacts on consumers can be incredibly costly for an enterprise (Chen et al., 2023). The challenge is changing customer's patterns and habits. Changing the consumption of customer's habits is the new status. Adapting to this new situation is necessary because of online commercial activities and changes in shopping attitudes (Afrina et al., 2020). Also, increasing the competition in this field is turning into a challenge. The competition is increased in marketing for the categories of products and services (Indiani et al., 2022). Also, there is a brand competition in the world of business.

REFERENCES

Afrina, M., Samsuryadi, Hussin, A. R. C., & Miskon, S. (2020, December). Derivation of a Customer Loyalty Factors Based on Customers' Changing Habits in E-Commerce Platform. In *International Conference of Reliable Information and Communication Technology* (pp. 879-890). Cham: Springer International Publishing.

Akhunova, S., & Abdusattorova, M. (2023). Digital Marketing: Near Future and Perspectives. *European Journal of Economics. Finance and Business Development*, *1*(2), 18–25.

Al-Hitmi, H. K. (2020). A Transition from Brick-and-Mortar to Online Stores and Its Role in Shifts in Consumer Buying Patterns. *Psychology and Education*, *57*(6), 375–381.

AL-Najjar, D., Al-Rousan, N., & AL-Najjar, H. (2022). Machine learning to develop credit card customer churn prediction. *Journal of Theoretical and Applied Electronic Commerce Research*, *17*(4), 1529–1542. doi:10.3390/jtaer17040077

Alanazi, T. M. (2022). Marketing 5.0: An Empirical Investigation of Its Perceived Effect on Marketing Performance. *Marketing and Management of Innovations*, *13*(4), 55–64. doi:10.21272/mmi.2022.4-06

Aliahmadi, A., Nozari, H., & Ghahremani-Nahr, J. (2022). A framework for IoT and Blockchain Based on Marketing Systems with an Emphasis on Big Data Analysis. *International Journal of Innovation in Marketing Elements*, *2*(1), 25-34.

Altameem, A. A., & Hafez, A. M. (2022). Behavior Analysis Using Enhanced Fuzzy Clustering and Deep Learning. *Electronics (Basel)*, *11*(19), 3172. doi:10.3390/electronics11193172

Anggraeni, T., Gaffar, V., Disman, D., Dirgantari, P. D., & Handayani, T. (2023). Tourist satisfaction in era Society 5.0 as a marketing strategy. *Journal of Eastern European and Central Asian Research*, *10*(6), 877–887. doi:10.15549/jeecar.v10i6.1509

Anghelinu, M., Niță, L., Veres, D., Hambach, U., Händel, M., Cordoș, C., Ilie, M., & Murătoreanu, G. (2021). Break vs. continuity: Techno-cultural changes across the LGM in the Eastern Carpathians. *Quaternary International*, *581*, 241–257. doi:10.1016/j.quaint.2020.08.002

Azzari, V., & Pelissari, A. (2021). Does brand awareness influence purchase intention? The mediation role of brand equity dimensions. *BBR. Brazilian Business Review*, *17*(6), 669–685. doi:10.15728/bbr.2020.17.6.4

Bakator, M., Vukoja, M., & Manestar, D. (2023). Achieving competitiveness with marketing 5.0 in new business conditions. *UTMS Journal of Economics (Skopje)*, *14*(1).

Banholzer, V. M. (2022). From Industry 4.0 to Society 5.0 and Industry 5.0: Value-and Mission-Oriented Poli-cies. *Technological and Social Innovations–Aspects of Systemic Transformation. IKOM WP*, *3*(2), 2022.

Barrios, M., Guilera, G., Nuño, L., & Gómez-Benito, J. (2021). Consensus in the Delphi method: What makes a decision change? *Technological Forecasting and Social Change*, *163*, 120484. doi:10.1016/j.techfore.2020.120484

Becker, J. C., Hartwich, L., & Haslam, S. A. (2021). Neoliberalism can reduce well-being by promoting a sense of social disconnection, competition, and loneliness. *British Journal of Social Psychology*, *60*(3), 947–965. doi:10.1111/bjso.12438 PMID:33416201

Berkowitz, S. A., & Orr, C. J. (2023). Three Lessons About Diabetes and the Social Determinants of Health. *Diabetes Care*, *46*(9), dci230045. doi:10.2337/dci23-0045 PMID:37354315

Bernarto, I., Berlianto, M. P., Meilani, Y. F. C. P., Masman, R. R., & Suryawan, I. N. (2020). The in-fluence of brand awareness, brand image, and brand trust on brand loyalty. *Jurnal Manajemen*, *24*(3), 412–426. doi:10.24912/jm.v24i3.676

Bjelak, A., & Selimović, A. (2023, June). Emotion Detection Using Convolutional Neural Networks. In *International Symposium on Innovative and Interdisciplinary Applications of Advanced Technologies* (pp. 263-279). Cham: Springer Nature Switzerland.

Brychko, M., Bilan, Y., Lyeonov, S., & Streimikiene, D. (2023). Do changes in the business environment and sustainable development really matter for enhancing enterprise development? *Sustainable Development (Bradford)*, *31*(2), 587–599. doi:10.1002/sd.2410

Chen, W., He, Y., & Bansal, S. (2023). Customized Dynamic Pricing when Customers Develop a Habit or Satiation. *Operations Research*, *71*(6), 2158–2174. doi:10.1287/opre.2022.2412

Cloarec, J., Meyer-Waarden, L., & Munzel, A. (2022). The personalization–privacy paradox at the nexus of social exchange and construal level theories. *Psychology and Marketing*, *39*(3), 647–661. doi:10.1002/mar.21587

David, J. V., Ana, M. R., Santiago, F. B., & Faustino, A. V. (2021). Aspects of industrial design and their implications for society. Case studies on the influence of packaging design and placement at the point of sale. *Applied Sciences (Basel, Switzerland)*, *11*(2), 517. doi:10.3390/app11020517

de Regt, A., Plangger, K., & Barnes, S. J. (2021). Virtual reality marketing and customer advocacy: Transforming experiences from story-telling to story-doing. *Journal of Business Research*, *136*, 513–522. doi:10.1016/j.jbusres.2021.08.004

Dhir, S., & Dhir, S. (2015). Technology Penetration and its Impact on Information Access by Customers: An Exploratory Study. *Advances in Global Business Research*, *12*(1), 361.

El Koufi, N., Belangour, A., & Sdiq, M. (2022). Research on Precision Marketing based on Big Data Analysis and Machine Learning: Case Study of Morocco. *International Journal of Advanced Computer Science and Applications*, *13*(10). Advance online publication. doi:10.14569/IJACSA.2022.0131008

Eliakis, S., Kotsopoulos, D., Karagiannaki, A., & Pramatari, K. (2020). Survival and growth in innovative technology entrepreneurship: A mixed-methods investigation. *Administrative Sciences*, *10*(3), 39. doi:10.3390/admsci10030039

Elshaiekh, N. E., Al-Hijji, K., Shehata, A., & Alrashdi, S. M. A. (2023). An Empirical Analysis of Factors Motivating Unemployed Individuals to Engage in Digital Entrepreneurship in Oman: Focus on Technological Infrastructure. *Sustainability (Basel)*, *15*(17), 12953. doi:10.3390/su151712953

Fatima, S., Alqahtani, H., Naim, A., & Alma'alwi, F. (2022). E-CRM Through Social Media Marketing Activities for Brand Awareness, Brand Image, and Brand Loyalty. In *Building a Brand Image Through Electronic Customer Relationship Management* (pp. 109–138). IGI Global. doi:10.4018/978-1-6684-5386-5.ch006

Febriyantoro, M. T. (2020). Exploring YouTube Marketing Communication: Brand awareness, brand image, and purchase intention in the millennial generation. *Cogent Business & Management*, *7*(1), 1787733. doi:10.1080/23311975.2020.1787733

Fishman, A., Hellman, Z., & Weiss, A. (2023). Habit forming consumers and firm dynamics. *Journal of Economic Dynamics & Control*, *154*, 104704. doi:10.1016/j.jedc.2023.104704

Ghahremani-Nahr, J., & Nozari, H. (2021). A Survey for Investigating Key Performance Indicators in Digital Marketing. *International Journal of Innovation in Marketing Elements, 1*(1), 1-6.

Gitarja, W. S., & Hariyati, R. T. S. (2023, November). The Influence of Marketing 5.0 and Creating Share Value on Wound Care Quality and Purchased Intention among Wound Care Professional. *Journal of International Conference Proceedings*, *6*(4), 188–199. doi:10.32535/jicp.v6i4.2609

Golalizadeh, F., Ranjbarian, B., & Ansari, A. (2023). Impact of customer's emotions on online purchase intention and impulsive buying of luxury cosmetic products mediated by perceived service quality. *Journal of Global Fashion Marketing*, *14*(4), 468–488. doi:10.1080/20932685.2023.2205869

González-Ferriz, F. (2022). Marketing 5.0 and new technologies before and after the COVID-19 pandemic. *Estudios de Economía Aplicada*, *40*(3). Advance online publication. doi:10.25115/eea.v40i3.7885

Hafez, M. (2023). The nexus between social media marketing efforts and overall brand equity in the banking sector in Bangladesh: Testing a moderated mediation model. *Journal of Internet Commerce*, *22*(2), 293–320. doi:10.1080/15332861.2022.2042968

Hamizan, M., Abu, N. H., Mansor, M. F., & Zaidi, M. A. (2023). An Analysis of the Effect of Price and Quality on Customer Buying Patterns: An Empirical Study of iPhone Buyers. *International Journal of Interactive Mobile Technologies*, *17*(18).

Helberger, N., Huh, J., Milne, G., Strycharz, J., & Sundaram, H. (2020). Macro and exogenous factors in computational advertising: Key issues and new research directions. *Journal of Advertising*, *49*(4), 377–393. doi:10.1080/00913367.2020.1811179

Hermina, N., Rahma, Y. D., & Gusnia, A. R. (2022). Marketing 5.0 and consumer behavior of the millennial (GEN Z) Generation as business performance boosting in COVID-19 pandemic (case study: SMEs in West Java). *Central Asia & the Caucasus, 23*(1).

Heskiano, H., Syah, T. Y. R., & Hilmy, M. R. (2020). Social Media Marketing Relations, Brand Awareness to Brand Loyalty Through The Brand Image. *Journal of Multidisciplinary Academic, 4*(4), 208–214.

Hopkinson, P. J., Singhal, A., Perez-Vega, R., & Waite, K. (2022, May). The Transformative Power of Artificial Intelligence for Managing Customer Relationships: An Abstract. In *Academy of Marketing Science Annual Conference* (pp. 307-308). Cham: Springer Nature Switzerland.

Hossain, M. S., & Rahman, M. F. (2022). Machine Learning and Artificial Intelligence: The New Move for Marketers. In Developing Relationships, Personalization, and Data Herald in Marketing 5.0 (pp. 215-241). IGI Global.

Hutson, J. (2023). *Shared cinematic experience and emerging technologies: Integrating mixed-reality components for the future of cinema.* Arts & Commuication.

Huynh, L. D., Duong, P. T., Bach, K. D., & Hung, P. D. (2023, February). Potential Customers Prediction in Bank Telemarketing. In *Proceedings of International Conference on Data Science and Applications: ICDSA 2022,* Volume 2 (pp. 43-50). Singapore: Springer Nature Singapore. 10.1007/978-981-19-6634-7_4

Hysa, B., Karasek, A., & Zdonek, I. (2021). Social media usage by different generations as a tool for sustainable tourism marketing in society 5.0 idea. *Sustainability (Basel), 13*(3), 1018. doi:10.3390/su13031018

İnan, Ü. S. E. (2023). Evaluation Of Digital Marketing From A Bibliometric Analysis Perspective. *Socialis Series in Social Science, 4,* 45–58. doi:10.20319/socv4.4558

Indiani, N. L., Sudiartini, N. W. A., & Utami, N. K. A. T. (2022). Pengaruh Brand Image, Awareness Dan Trust Terhadap Keputusan Pembelian Melalui Digital Marketing Pada Produk Dupa Harum Grosir. *Jurnal Valuasi: Jurnal Ilmiah Ilmu Manajemen dan Kewirausahaan, 2*(1), 152-163.

Jaiwant, S. V. (2023). The Changing Role of Marketing: Industry 5.0-the Game Changer. In Transformation for Sustainable Business and Management Practices: Exploring the Spectrum of Industry 5.0 (pp. 187-202). Emerald Publishing Limited.

Joshi, D. A., & Masih, D. J. (2023). Enhancing employee efficiency and performance in industry 5.0 organizations through artificial intelligence integration. *European Economic Letters, 13*(4), 300–315.

Kajale, P. A., & Joshi, S. (2021). Gearing up for marketing 5.0 in the digital economy: Moving from traditional to digital. *IBMRD's. Journal of Management Research, 10*(2), 79–81.

Keys, C. (2021). Social Polarization and Ghettoization: Economic and Policy-Driven Causes. In *Reduced Inequalities* (pp. 789–798). Springer International Publishing. doi:10.1007/978-3-319-95882-8_88

Kilani, Y. (2020). Cyber-security effect on organizational internal process: Mediating role of technological infrastructure. *Problems and Perspectives in Management, 18*(1), 449–460. doi:10.21511/ppm.18(1).2020.39

Koroglu, O. (2023). AI and XR (AIXR) Marketing in Industry 5.0 or Society 5.0. In Digitalization, Sustainable Development, and Industry 5.0: An Organizational Model for Twin Transitions (pp. 83-100). Emerald Publishing Limited.

Kotler, P., Kartajaya, H., & Setiawan, I. (2021). *Marketing 5.0: Technology for humanity*. John Wiley & Sons.

Kulkul, C. (2020). Public Space and Social Polarization: A case study of the New Wave Turkish Migrants with a comparative analysis of Berlin, İstanbul & Ankara. *The Journal of Public Space*, *5*(1), 111–128. doi:10.32891/jps.v5i1.1128

Kumar, A., Gawande, A., & Brar, V. (2020). Neuro-Marketing: Opportunities and Challenges in India. *Vidyabharati International Interdisciplinary Research Journal*, *10*(2), 214–217.

Kumar, S., Chawla, C., Yadav, A. K., Udaipure, P. A., & Chatley, P. (2022). Altered Consumer Behavior Paradigms and Novel Trends of Sustainable Marketing in the Next Normal. *Korea Review of International Studies*, *15*(3).

Leal Filho, W., Levesque, V., Sivapalan, S., Salvia, A. L., Fritzen, B., Deckert, R., Kozlova, V., LeVasseur, T. J., Emblen-Perry, K., Azeiteiro, U. M., Paço, A., Borsari, B., & Shiel, C. (2022). Social values and sustainable development: Community experiences. *Environmental Sciences Europe*, *34*(1), 1–13. doi:10.1186/s12302-022-00641-z PMID:35967983

Lee, E. J. (2016). Empathy can increase customer equity related to pro-social brands. *Journal of Business Research*, *69*(9), 3748–3754. doi:10.1016/j.jbusres.2015.05.018

Lupak, R., Kunytska-Iliash, M., Berezivskyi, Y., Nakonechna, N., Ivanova, L., & Vasyltsiv, T. (2021). Information and analytical support system of enterprise competitiveness management. *Accounting*, *7*(7), 1785–1798. doi:10.5267/j.ac.2021.4.018

Manoharan, D. S., & Sathesh, A. (2020). Geospatial and social media analytics for emotion analysis of theme park visitors using text mining and gis. *Journal of Information Technology and Digital World*, *2*(2), 100–107. doi:10.36548/jitdw.2020.2.003

Márquez, G., & Taramasco, C. (2023). Barriers and Facilitators of Ambient Assisted Living Systems: A Systematic Literature Review. *International Journal of Environmental Research and Public Health*, *20*(6), 5020. doi:10.3390/ijerph20065020 PMID:36981929

McKee, K. M., Dahl, A. J., & Peltier, J. W. (2023). Gen Z's personalization paradoxes: A privacy calculus examination of digital personalization and brand behaviors. *Journal of Consumer Behaviour*, cb.2199. doi:10.1002/cb.2199

Mehdizadehrayeni, M., Hamidmohammadi, H., & Dehdashti, M. (2022). Welfare effects of increasing competition in the market of export products (Case study: Saffron product). *Saffron Agronomy and Technology*, *10*(3), 287–302.

Miah, M. R., Rahman, A. A. M. S., Parisa, J. T., Hannan, M. A., Khan, M. S., Samdany, A. A., ... Chowdhury, S. H. (2021). Discovery of Coronavirus with Innovative Technology. *Science and Technology*, *11*(1), 7–29.

Montero, A. R., Álvarez, A. C., & Rubio, R. S. (2023). Inbound marketing in the hospitality industry: A systematic review in the last 12 years. *Enlightening Tourism. A Pathmaking Journal, 13*(1), 86-125.

Mukendi, A., Davies, I., Glozer, S., & McDonagh, P. (2020). Sustainable fashion: Current and future research directions. *European Journal of Marketing, 54*(11), 2873–2909. doi:10.1108/EJM-02-2019-0132

Murugan, S., Assi, S., Alatrany, A., Jayabalan, M., Liatsis, P., Mustafina, J., ... & Al-Jumeily OBE, D. (2022, December). Consumer Behavior Prediction During Covid-19 Pandemic Conditions Using Sentiment Analytics. In *The International Conference on Data Science and Emerging Technologies* (pp. 209-221). Singapore: Springer Nature Singapore.

Mysakova, A. G., & Zakharcheva, K. S. (2023). The Impact of ESG Strategy on Brand Perception of Fuel and Energy Companies. In *Smart Green Innovations in Industry 4.0 for Climate Change Risk Management* (pp. 277–285). Springer International Publishing. doi:10.1007/978-3-031-28457-1_29

Nazemi Bidgoli, A., Mohamadi Turkmani, E., & Irani, H. R. (2023). Investigating the Effect of Social Influence and Gender on the Willingness to use IOT Technology in Sports: From Consumer Perspective. *Research in Sport Management and Marketing, 4*(4), 28–41.

Nedelea, A., Çanakcı, M., & Arslan, A. (2021). Social Polarization And Its Effects On Public Investments. *The USV Annals of Economics and Public Administration, 21*(1 (33)), 153–166.

Ni, G., Xu, H., Cui, Q., Qiao, Y., Zhang, Z., Li, H., & Hickey, P. J. (2020). Influence mechanism of organizational flexibility on enterprise competitiveness: The mediating role of organizational innovation. *Sustainability (Basel), 13*(1), 176. doi:10.3390/su13010176

Nozari, H., Szmelter-Jarosz, A., & Ghahremani-Nahr, J. (2021). The Ideas of Sustainable and Green Marketing Based on the Internet of Everything—The Case of the Dairy Industry. *Future Internet, 13*(10), 266. doi:10.3390/fi13100266

Orea-Giner, A., Fuentes-Moraleda, L., Villacé-Molinero, T., Muñoz-Mazón, A., & Calero-Sanz, J. (2022). Does the implementation of robots in hotels influence the overall TripAdvisor rating? A text mining analysis from the industry 5.0 approach. *Tourism Management, 93*, 104586. doi:10.1016/j.tourman.2022.104586

Pasha, F. M. (2022). Increasing Generalizability: Naïve Bayes Vs K-Nearest Neighbors. *J Robot Auto Res, 3*(2), 178–188. doi:10.21203/rs.3.rs-1578985/v1

Phanga, G., Chanb, J. K. L., Limc, T. Y., & Fresnidod, M. B. R. (n.d.). Key Success Factors, Marketing Opportunities and Challenges: A Case Study of Bonco Virgin Coconut Oil. *Journal of Agribusiness, 9*(1), 57–71.

Polak, M., Kolić Stanić, M., & Togonal, M. (2022). Artificial Intelligence in Communication with Music Fans: An Example from South Korea. *ENTRENOVA-ENTerprise REsearch InNOVAtion, 8*(1), 48–63. doi:10.54820/entrenova-2022-0006

Quynh, T. D., & Dung, H. T. T. Prediction of customer behavior using machine learning: A case study. In *Proceedings of the 2nd International Conference on Human-centered Artificial Intelligence (Computing4Human 2021)* (pp. 168-175). Academic Press.

Rathore, B. (2020). Predictive Metamorphosis: Unveiling the Fusion of AI-Powered Analytics in Digital Marketing Revolution. *International Journal of Transcontinental Discoveries*, 7(1), 15–24.

Retnawati, B. B., Leong, H., & Irmawati, B. (2022). The Study of Natural Material Crafts MSMEs in Optimizing Digital Marketing: Opportunities and Challenges. *Sustainable Competitive Advantage (SCA), 11*(1).

Ribeiro, L. W., & Teixeira, J. M. (2021, October). *The creative industry and design 5.0: The relationship of the creative industry with proposed new execution models based on Design 5.0. 6 CIDAG.*

Roblek, V., Meško, M., Bach, M. P., Thorpe, O., & Šprajc, P. (2020). The interaction between internet, sustainable development, and emergence of society 5.0. *Data*, 5(3), 80. doi:10.3390/data5030080

Rosário, A. T., & Dias, J. C. (2023). How has data-driven marketing evolved: Challenges and opportunities with emerging technologies. *International Journal of Information Management Data Insights*, 3(2), 100203. doi:10.1016/j.jjimei.2023.100203

Rust, R. T. (2020). The future of marketing. *International Journal of Research in Marketing, 37*(1), 15–26. doi:10.1016/j.ijresmar.2019.08.002

Santos, R. S., & Lousã, E. P. (2022). Give Me Five: The Most Important Social Values for Well-Being at Work. *Administrative Sciences, 12*(3), 101. doi:10.3390/admsci12030101

Santoso, R. K., Dewi, N. F., & Anindita, C. P. (2023, October). Social Media Marketing using Buzzer on Brand Awareness at PT Telkomsel. In *The 6th International Conference on Vocational Education Applied Science and Technology (ICVEAST 2023)* (pp. 680-693). Atlantis Press. 10.2991/978-2-38476-132-6_58

Sardjono, W., Cholidin, A., & Johan, J. (2023). Applying Digital Advertising in Food and Beverage Industry for McDonald's with Marketing 5.0 Approach. In E3S Web of Conferences (Vol. 426, p. 02009). EDP Sciences.

Sari, N. N. P., Paramitha, A. I. I., & Putri, N. L. P. N. S. (2023). Augmented Reality as the Implementation of Digital Marketing 5.0 (Study Case: LPK Bali Aviation Tourism Center). *ProBisnis: Jurnal Manajemen, 14*(1), 97–107.

Sarıoğlu, C. İ. (2023). Industry 5.0, Digital Society, and Consumer 5.0. In Handbook of Research on Perspectives on Society and Technology Addiction (pp. 11-33). IGI Global.

Sasisuriyaphoom, P., & Choompolsathien, A. (2021). Marketing 5.0: how to improve user experience with digital solutions (No. 306535). Thammasat University. Faculty of Journalism and Mass Communication.

Shenoy, V., & Rao, R. (2020). E-Word of Mouth and Buying Patterns of Consumers: A Thematic Analysis. *Drishtikon: A Management Journal, 11*(2), 15.

Sholihin, M., Sari, R. C., Yuniarti, N., & Ilyana, S. (2020). A new way of teaching business ethics: The evaluation of virtual reality-based learning media. *International Journal of Management Education, 18*(3), 100428. doi:10.1016/j.ijme.2020.100428

Sima, E. (2021). Managing a brand with a vision to marketing 5.0. In *MATEC Web of Conferences* (Vol. 343, p. 07015). EDP Sciences.

Skrbina, D., Heikkurinen, P., & Ruuska, T. (2021). *Sustainability Beyond Technology*. Academic Press.

Tabroni, I., Husniyah, H., Sapitri, L., & Azzahra, Y. (2022). Impact of Technological Advancements on The Establishment of Characteristics of Children. *East Asian Journal of Multidisciplinary Research*, *1*(1), 27–32. doi:10.54259/eajmr.v1i1.453

Torbica, A., Fornaro, G., Tarricone, R., & Drummond, M. F. (2020). Do social values and institutional context shape the use of economic evaluation in reimbursement decisions? An empirical analysis. *Value in Health*, *23*(1), 17–24. doi:10.1016/j.jval.2019.11.001 PMID:31952668

Valentino, R. B. (2022). Developing Relationships, Personalization, and Data Herald in the Pandemic. In Developing Relationships, Personalization, and Data Herald in Marketing 5.0 (pp. 69-78). IGI Global.

Varmavuo, E. (2020). *Factors affecting the success of AI campaigns in marketing: data perspective.* Academic Press.

Vera-Martínez, J., Alvarado-Herrera, A., & Currás-Pérez, R. (2022). Do consumers really care about aspects of corporate social responsibility when developing attitudes toward a brand? *Journal of Global Marketing*, *35*(3), 193–207. doi:10.1080/08911762.2021.1958277

Verchere, A. (2022). Is social polarization bad for the planet? A theoretical inquiry. *Bulletin of Economic Research*, *74*(2), 427–456. doi:10.1111/boer.12303

Vyas, P. G., & Priya, S. (2023). Social Media and Gen Y at Work: The Uses and Gratifications of Technology. In 5G, Artificial Intelligence, and Next Generation Internet of Things: Digital Innovation for Green and Sustainable Economies (pp. 123-142). IGI Global.

Wijayanto, S., & Putra, J. C. P. (2021). The Effectiveness of a Virtual Reality Marketing Video on the People Desire to Buy a Product. *JOIV: International Journal on Informatics Visualization*, *5*(4), 360–365. doi:10.30630/joiv.5.4.483

Wu, D., & Liu, J. (2022). Involve Humans in Algorithmic Fairness Issue: A Systematic Review. In *International Conference on Information* (pp. 161-176). Springer. 10.1007/978-3-030-96957-8_15

Xiao, Y., Zhu, Y., He, W., & Huang, M. (2023). Influence prediction model for marketing campaigns on e-commerce platforms. *Expert Systems with Applications*, *211*, 118575. doi:10.1016/j.eswa.2022.118575

Yudhiasta, S., & Mijiarto, J. (2023). Digitalization of tourist attractions: Increasing the capacity of Sunrise Land Lombok tourism workers through digital marketing. *Journal of Community Service and Empowerment*, *4*(1), 95–103.

Yulianti, Y., & Saifudin, A. (2020, July). Sequential feature selection in customer churn prediction based on Naive Bayes. *IOP Conference Series. Materials Science and Engineering*, *879*(1), 012090. doi:10.1088/1757-899X/879/1/012090

Chapter 2
Future Direction for IoT–Blockchain–Based Marketing

Mohammadreza Nasiri Jan Agha
Islamic Azad University of Lahijan, Iran

ABSTRACT

Marketing is one of the most important organizational units and one of the most important value chain processes in organizations. Since this part of the organization shows the final output of the organization's activities, it has always been one of the strategic parts that organizations pay great attention to. In the coming era, the presence of technologies is mixed in all processes of organizations, and therefore, the processes of the marketing unit, as one of the most important parts of the organization's value chain, are also involved in technologies such as the internet of things and blockchain and artificial intelligence-based analysis. By using these growing technologies in Industry 4.0, it is possible to obtain large and efficient data that was not possible in the past. Therefore, these data, which are accurate, transparent, and based on human performance, can be used for optimal marketing and achieving brilliant organizational results. In this research, the main features of the technology-based marketing system and the future directions of using these tools are examined.

1. INTRODUCTION

Marketing and sales are one of the most important units of organizations and the ultimate organizational performance and success of the organization depends on the optimal performance of these units. A correct understanding of customers and their behaviors is an important element in increasing sales. However intelligent sales and the use of effective data can be an effective step in customer loyalty. With the advent of new e-commerce technologies, retailers and wholesalers can be more in touch with their customers than ever before. That too in a situation where the geographical dispersion of customers can be very wide. Using innovative and smart methods for sales can increase profits, increase the level of interaction with customers, and create stable relationships with them. In this way, we can expect more loyalty from our customers (Nozari et al., 2021).

DOI: 10.4018/979-8-3693-1339-8.ch002

Sales intelligence is the process of simplifying manual, tedious, and time-consuming tasks in the sales process. Sales Intelligence is a practical way to use technology to improve the sales situation. Smart sales methods can save time and money, both of which are very important for many businesses. In recent years, various sellers have used all the potential of modern technologies to increase their sales. There are various software for sales intelligence that can help in this field. This software shortens manual processes and allows customers to make their purchases faster. In the field of marketing, smart and interactive tools have grown increasingly in recent years and have given attractive functions to these functional processes. Smart sales and marketing can help you know your customers and have access to a database of customers. Access to customer data and their needs and preferences can be done through smart technologies.

One of the technologies that has grown rapidly in recent years and has become widespread is the Internet of Things. This technology gives the ability to extract and store big data to the marketing processes in organizations. Also, blockchain technology, along with the Internet of Things technology, adds accuracy and transparency to the data. The combination of these technologies with artificial intelligence technology can provide high analytical power to clear, explicit, and accurate data and double the capability of intelligent marketing systems. Today, systems based on the Internet of Things and blockchain as part of marketing provide marketers with a wide range of benefits and real opportunities. Combining these technologies with artificial intelligence such as; Forecasting using data analytics enables better experiences for customers and targeted marketing, which will undoubtedly increase ROI and sales growth for businesses (Nozari et al., 2021).

Marketing based on the Internet of Things, blockchain, and artificial intelligence uses intelligent technology for automatic decision-making, which is based on collecting and analyzing data and examining audiences or economic trends. Artificial intelligence is often used in those digital marketing activities where speed is very important and plays a key role. Marketing tools based on these technologies use their data and profiles to establish the best communication with customers and then provide them with appropriate messages at the right time without the involvement of marketing team members, which causes maximum efficiency. Most marketers in the age of digital technologies use these technologies to strengthen their marketing teams or perform more methodical tasks that require less human work. Therefore, it can be seen that these revolutionary technologies play a colorful role in the development of businesses and increasing sales (Simões et al., 2019).

This research, by examining the dimensions, components, and indicators that affect marketing systems based on the Internet of Things and Blockchain, in addition to expressing the capabilities that these technologies add to the marketing of the new era, examines the future trends of using these technologies.

In the continuation of this research, the second part constitutes the literature review. In the third part, the most important advantages and characteristics of marketing based on the Internet of Things and artificial intelligence are presented and the future trends are discussed. Finally, the discussion and conclusion will be presented in the last part.

2. LITERATURE REVIEW

In recent years, most businesses have realized that to create a competitive advantage and face strong competitors, it is necessary to update their marketing space and create effective technology-based marketing systems. Because they have realized that without getting involved in technologies and taking advantage of a lot of unstructured data, they will suffer losses compared to their competitors. Therefore, in recent years, much research has been conducted regarding the use of smart technologies in the marketing system.

For example, Khan et al. (2023) in research tried to relate e-marketing, e-commerce, e-commerce, and the Internet of Things in the field of SMEs and marketing automation by conducting a bibliometric analysis of the Scopus database and literature review. Their research helps to understand the way concepts have evolved in recent times. Mansouri et al. (2023) presented a hierarchical decentralized framework for the simultaneous management of electricity, heat and hydrogen markets among multi-energy microgrids (MEMGs) integrated with smart customers. In this research, the market strategy of MEMGs has been established using a hierarchical framework and considering the applications requested by smart customers. A deep learning-based predictor is used to predict uncertain parameters while a strategy based on risk-averse information gap theory controls the timing risk. A new prediction-based mechanism is introduced to design dynamic demand response (DR) schemes adapted to intelligent buyer behavior. Also, the results show that the introduced structure for hydrogen exchange through the transportation system can be implemented in competitive markets. Overall, the simulation results confirm that the proposed hierarchical model can optimally manage the competitive electricity, heat, and hydrogen markets by exploiting the potential of intelligent consumers.

Sehgal et al. (2022) examined the challenges that the Internet of Things brings to our lives and marketing. A sample of 393 respondents was surveyed to find out the different roles of the Internet of Things and its importance in marketing transformation. Multiple regression was used to reach the final results. This study concludes that there is a significant impact of IoT in marketing transformation. Tariq et al. (2020) examine the effectiveness of data stored from the operational use of Internet of Things (IoT) technologies to generate marketing-related outcomes, such as business intelligence for product development, product support, and customer relationship management (CRM), by examining this research. This study conducted a multidisciplinary literature review to develop a conceptual framework. In addition, a smart refrigerator was chosen as an example to show how the analysis of data stored from the operational use of IoT devices can help generate marketing results such as new product development, customer support, and CRM. The study states that IoT technology helps advance CRM goals along with other business growth and success strategies. Using a practical example underpinned by a sound theoretical framework, this study not only helps clinicians empirically test this important yet unknown issue but also helps to clarify that with the embedding of Internet device objects in their products, business managers can ensure the longevity of the business. In addition, it explains how the Internet of Things can provide support for improving the communication relationship between the product manufacturer and the consumer through product support and CRM strategies.

Najafi et al. (2022) investigated the dimensions and features of the intelligent marketing system based on the Internet of Things and other transformative technologies. They investigated the role of system stability and extracted indicators of sustainable development and the effects of the Internet of Things on this stability. Shanmuganathan and Mahendran (2021) investigated security challenges in Internet of Things marketing. Li (2022) conducted an in-depth analysis of the precision marketing approach by building an Internet of Things cloud platform and then using big data mining technology. Also, the method of storing temporary data of the Internet of Things has been optimized, and the method of storing data in time intervals is used to improve the efficiency of reading large amounts of data. For the scalability of the IoT data storage system, a MongoDB database clustering scheme is designed to ensure data storage scalability and disaster recovery capability.

Dwesar et al. (2022) examined how organizations are using the Internet of Things, which is expected to bring about significant changes in marketing and related activities. In addition, they showed how AI and IoT together can enhance their capabilities and bring potential benefits together. They presented various ways and examples in which organizations are using IoT systems and the developments that are being made. They also shared various examples of how companies develop new products and solutions using the Internet of Things. Finally, they presented a case study on how a self-driving car rental company uses the Internet of Things to improve its services and gain benefits for itself and its customers. Sachdev (2020) also investigated security and privacy issues in digital marketing research. The most important security measures have been identified and prioritized in this study. Naim et al. (2022) showed the role of the Internet of Things as an example of emerging technology in industrial transformation in general and in three areas of marketing management. In fact, their research is a sample-based qualitative analysis that explains how the Internet of Things has contributed to important areas of marketing management.

Rejeb et al. (2020) conceptualized how blockchain technology could potentially impact a company's marketing activities. In particular, they showed how blockchain technology acts as incremental innovation and enables a consumer-centric paradigm. In addition, blockchain technology reduces disintermediation, helps fight click fraud, strengthens trust and transparency, increases privacy protection, enhances security, and enables innovative loyalty programs. They presented six propositions that will guide future blockchain-related research in the field of marketing. Antoniadis et al. (2020) investigated the use of blockchain in tourism industry marketing. They identified the potential applications of blockchain in the tourism and hospitality industry in general and outlined the benefits gained and the challenges arising from the adoption of this innovative technology. Coita et al. (2019) examined the effects of blockchain on human resources and marketing. They analyzed the existing literature, experts' expectations about blockchain, and conceptualized implications for businesses, human resource management, and marketing.

Yan et al. (2021), systematically reviewed the development history of financial blockchain marketing products in financial blockchain and analyzed the gradual improvement of functions and features of financial blockchain marketing products in China. In this research, the features and shortcomings of financial blockchain marketing products were discussed in detail, and from the perspective of technological innovation, the application of emerging technologies in financial blockchain marketing was analyzed. This article analyzed the many challenges and opportunities that security companies face in the development of the Internet. They showed that in the new conditions, what kind of development model should be adopted and how to change and improve it. They also showed that, on the one hand, the use of crowdfunding by security companies can increase their direct financing capabilities, which will benefit the security industry, especially Internet security companies. On the other hand, through crowdfunding, security companies can expand direct financing channels for small, medium, and micro enterprises to promote entrepreneurship. This article promotes the development of Internet finance, thereby improving the ability of capital markets to serve the real economy.

3. INTERNET OF THINGS AND DIGITAL MARKETING

The more we move towards the era of progress, the more professional use of Internet of Things technology we see, and it becomes a part of everyday life. As with technological advances in the past, it is difficult to predict exactly what our daily activities and everyday technology will look like in the future.

However, digital marketers must do their best to understand how the current IoT market works, its risks, and how big data is changing the digital marketing industry (Nozari et al., 2022).

The rise of the Internet of Things is profitable for digital marketers; Because they can use this huge data set to analyze and analyze consumer behavior in their marketing strategy. This allows them to predict consumer behaviors to take a better step to implement their next strategy. With the Internet of Things, access to a wide range of information from different points is obtained for marketers. From a digital marketing perspective, this is extremely useful for creating a better understanding of the starting point of the customer journey from start to finish. Along this path, from the time of interest in the desired product to the end of the purchase, digital marketers will also have an opportunity to use this data to their advantage (Nozari and Aliahmadi, 2023). As the application of IoT technology allows digital marketers to see the customer along their path to purchase, they can create more touchpoints for positive customer interaction. With increased access to customer journey information, marketers will be able to find new ways to connect with them to answer questions and build brand relationships at an early stage. For digital marketers, access to information about customer lifestyles means they can see how, when, and what specific products or services are being used. Figure 1 shows the effects of Internet of Things on marketing. In general, the role of the Internet of Things in marketing can be expressed as follows:

- With the help of IoT, digital marketers can understand what customers expect from their brands, which helps improve their product quality. IoT not only helps to increase product quality but also helps in forecasting demand and planning for new products. Access to data from IoT devices helps businesses make better and faster decisions.
- IoT helps digital marketers to understand consumer buying behavior from beginning to end and also helps in analyzing consumer needs, buying pattern, and trends that affect consumer buying pattern and location. IoT can provide more detailed information about consumer preferences, allowing marketers to develop products accordingly.
- Smart devices allow marketers to collect large amounts of data about consumers that can be used for effective marketing activities. IoT devices can provide much more data from sensors related to consumers than traditional research. Big data provides more accurate insights that help marketers mitigate threats and increase opportunities.
- Tracking data from IoT devices helps marketers predict when a customer will need a particular product or service. This information is also used for sales timing and real-time customer insights help marketers to increase sales.
- Personalization is an effective way to reach and engage your audience. IoT helps marketers connect with customers in a real way. This helps target the audience more accurately and improves the effectiveness of the marketing campaign.
- Marketers usually spend a lot of time and effort collecting customer data. But IoT helps marketers save more time in collecting and analyzing data.
- In IoT, any smart device can be used as a channel to communicate with customers. So any smart product helps marketers connect with their customers, which leads to more customer acquisition.

Figure 1. The effects of the Internet of Things on marketing (Woodside & Sood, 2017)

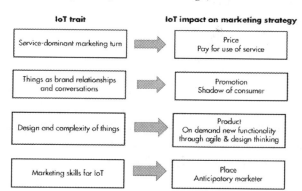

4. BLOCKCHAIN AND MARKETING

Detailed academic studies on blockchain applications in the marketplace and in support of marketing activities are scarce. Despite this, in the literature based on expertise, the advantages of blockchain in the market are undeniable. By creating immutable and shared data records, blockchain technology in the marketplace can also help improve data quality and facilitate data access. From a consumer perspective, blockchain technology has the potential to fundamentally change consumer relationships by increasing data and information transparency and improving privacy and security. It also allows for innovative forms of customer loyalty programs that help create value (Nozari & Szmelter-Jarosz, 2024).

The advent of the Internet has made intermediation possible and has drastically changed the way companies distribute products and services. New technologies have replaced traditional business mechanisms, reduced the reliance on traditional intermediaries and introduced new forms of electronic intermediaries. Businesses are highly dependent on intermediaries to identify the needs and wants of their potential customers. On the other hand, businesses seek to attract the attention of consumers, but often rely on communication channels provided by many information intermediaries because they provide a lot of information about the demand for goods and services. It may happen that these intermediaries do not allow brands to make their own decisions and therefore hinder their innovation and ability to create new perspectives and proposals to reach the goal.

To address the aforementioned concerns, blockchain technologies in the marketplace can be the right tools that enable brands and consumers to bypass disintermediation and build stronger relationships. This technology allows brands to expand their advertising campaigns, improve their customer targeting capabilities and increase service responsiveness. Its interactive and inclusive features allow marketers to effectively share their business content and reduce costs by bypassing middlemen (Aliahmadi et al., 2024).

Blockchain technology in the marketplace can also mitigate certain risks associated with the potentially devastating impact of click fraud by creating a more trusted digital marketing environment for consumers and brands. A blockchain-based platform can encourage stakeholders in the advertising industry to operate in an open and collaborative environment where each party acts with integrity.

Another point to note is that in an increasingly competitive market environment, brands strive to ensure that consumers remain loyal to their products and services. To increase customer retention, brands systematically collect and store customer data, primarily through loyalty programs. These tools serve to increase brand loyalty, reduce price sensitivity, encourage word of mouth, and increase their customer base. Blockchain technology in the marketplace has the potential to revolutionize the way loyalty programs are designed, tracked, and communicated to consumers. . In a blockchain-based marketing ecosystem, loyalty programs are fully integrated. All parties participating in such programs such as loyalty program operators, marketers, consumers, information systems managers, contact centers, sales offices and other organizations will be efficiently integrated and interconnected. Instead of being fragmented, loyalty program partners can work synergistically to improve the member experience and attract different consumer segments. The effects of blockchain on marketing are shown in Figure 2.

Through real-time access to the blockchain platform, marketers can view member profiles, points, purchase patterns, payment history, and ad responses, which helps them create more engaging, valuable, and customized loyalty programs. Additionally, the decentralized nature of blockchain technology also allows members to track their loyalty points and rewards, freeing them and marketers from physically holding coupons. Additionally, this technology can help create more value for members by enabling them to trade and exchange their loyalty points.

Figure 2. Blockchain's effects on marketing (Rejeb et al., 2020)

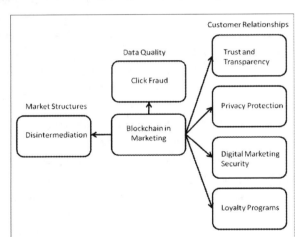

5. CONCLUSION

Rapid technological progress and the growth of e-commerce and e-commerce have significantly shaped the process of value creation. Many businesses rely heavily on technology to deliver integrated products and services to their existing customers. Emerging technologies can help better design new products and services, improve data quality, and make the manufacturing process more responsive and economical. New technologies have also significantly changed the marketing discipline and brought new marketing terms and tactics. Today, brands are increasingly using technology to leverage their global reach by penetrating new markets and creating consumer demand. In the process, the Internet enables marketers to reach consumers with advanced electronic communications and interactive media. Meanwhile, consumers have become more aware of the offers available and can make informed decisions in a convenient manner. Businesses have benefited from data mining and big data techniques to draw conclusions about consumer needs and wants. Analyzing big data sets helps businesses gain actionable insights through predictive analytics. Blockchain and IoT use cases are technological advances that can help brands better understand and target their customers.

Our goal was to present the future applications of IoT and blockchain technologies in the market and in marketing in a concise way. As a result, we were unable to explain many of the complexities and subtleties of IoT and blockchain technologies that we see as great opportunities for future research. We also recommend that future researches discuss the architecture and operating environment in detail to enhance the understanding of how the application of offline technologies in the market can contribute to the creation of organizational value. In addition, our goal was to highlight the potentials of the application of these two technologies in marketing, but we should also point out the potential challenges that may emerge from the (inter)organizational integration of these technologies. Blockchains, for example, are not silver bullets or panaceas for all contemporary marketing problems, but rather present several shortcomings and potential negative consequences. Compared to conventional databases, blockchain technology has several negative aspects. Storing information and transactions in blockchain is still complicated and expensive. The cost of blockchain security and redundancy in the marketplace may far exceed the value of its marketing applications. As such, the redundant nature of blockchain increases costs, as transactions on the blockchain take longer to process than single-source transactions. Therefore, in addition to the types of opportunities that these technologies create, their challenges should also be considered.

REFERENCES

Aliahmadi, A., Movahed, A. B., & Nozari, H. (2024). Collaboration Analysis in Supply Chain 4.0 for Smart Businesses. In Building Smart and Sustainable Businesses With Transformative Technologies (pp. 103-122). IGI Global.

Antoniadis, I., Spinthiropoulos, K., & Kontsas, S. (2020). Blockchain applications in tourism and tourism marketing: A short review. *Strategic Innovative Marketing and Tourism: 8th ICSIMAT. Northern Aegean, Greece, 2019*, 375–384.

Coita, D. C., Abrudan, M. M., & Matei, M. C. (2019). Effects of the blockchain technology on human resources and marketing: an exploratory study. In Strategic Innovative Marketing and Tourism: 7th ICSIMAT, Athenian Riviera, Greece, 2018 (pp. 683-691). Springer International Publishing. doi:10.1007/978-3-030-12453-3_79

Dwesar, R., & Kashyap, R. (2022). IOT in marketing: Current applications and future opportunities. *Internet of things and its applications*, 539-553.

Khan, S. A. (2023). E-Marketing, E-Commerce, E-Business, and Internet of Things: An Overview of Terms in the Context of Small and Medium Enterprises (SMEs). *Global Applications of the Internet of Things in Digital Marketing*, 332-348.

Li, W. (2022). Big Data precision marketing approach under IoT cloud platform information mining. *Computational Intelligence and Neuroscience, 2022*. doi:10.1155/2022/4828108 PMID:35069719

Mansouri, S. A., Jordehi, A. R., Marzband, M., Tostado-Véliz, M., Jurado, F., & Aguado, J. A. (2023). An IoT-enabled hierarchical decentralized framework for multi-energy microgrids market management in the presence of smart prosumers using a deep learning-based forecaster. *Applied Energy*, *333*, 120560. doi:10.1016/j.apenergy.2022.120560

Naim, A., Muniasamy, A., Clementking, A., & Rajkumar, R. (2022). Relevance of Green Manufacturing and IoT in Industrial Transformation and Marketing Management. In *Computational Intelligence Techniques for Green Smart Cities* (pp. 395–419). Springer International Publishing. doi:10.1007/978-3-030-96429-0_19

Najafi, S. E., Nozari, H., & Edalatpanah, S. A. (2022). Investigating the Key Parameters Affecting Sustainable IoT-Based Marketing. In *Computational Intelligence Methodologies Applied to Sustainable Development Goals* (pp. 51–61). Springer International Publishing. doi:10.1007/978-3-030-97344-5_4

Nozari, H., & Aliahmadi, A. (2023). Analysis of critical success factors in a food agile supply chain by a fuzzy hybrid decision-making method. *Iranian Journal of Management Studies*, *16*(4).

Nozari, H., Fallah, M., Kazemipoor, H., & Najafi, S. E. (2021). Big data analysis of IoT-based supply chain management considering FMCG industries. *Бизнес-информатика*, *15*(1, 1 (eng)), 78–96. doi:10.17323/2587-814X.2021.1.78.96

Nozari, H., & Szmelter-Jarosz, A. (2024). An Analytical Framework for Smart Supply Chains 5.0. In *Building Smart and Sustainable Businesses With Transformative Technologies* (pp. 1–15). IGI Global.

Nozari, H., Szmelter-Jarosz, A., & Ghahremani-Nahr, J. (2021). The Ideas of Sustainable and Green Marketing Based on the Internet of Everything—The Case of the Dairy Industry. *Future Internet*, *13*(10), 266. doi:10.3390/fi13100266

Nozari, H., Szmelter-Jarosz, A., & Ghahremani-Nahr, J. (2022). Analysis of the challenges of artificial intelligence of things (AIoT) for the smart supply chain (case study: FMCG industries). *Sensors (Basel)*, *22*(8), 2931. doi:10.3390/s22082931 PMID:35458916

Rejeb, A., Keogh, J. G., & Treiblmaier, H. (2020). How blockchain technology can benefit marketing: Six pending research areas. *Frontiers in Blockchain*, *3*, 3. doi:10.3389/fbloc.2020.00003

Sachdev, R. (2020, April). Towards security and privacy for edge AI in IoT/IoE based digital marketing environments. In *2020 fifth international conference on fog and mobile edge computing (FMEC)* (pp. 341-346). IEEE.

Sehgal, P., Kumar, B., Sharma, M., Salameh, A. A., Kumar, S., & Asha, P. (2022). Role of IoT in transformation of marketing: A quantitative study of opportunities and challenges. *Webology*, *18*(3), 1–11.

Shanmuganathan, H., & Mahendran, A. (2021, September). Current trend of IoT market and its security threats. In *2021 International Conference on Innovative Computing, Intelligent Communication and Smart Electrical Systems (ICSES)* (pp. 1-9). IEEE. 10.1109/ICSES52305.2021.9633850

Simões, D., Filipe, S., & Barbosa, B. (2019). An overview on IoT and its impact on marketing. *Smart marketing with the internet of things*, 1-20.

Tariq, B., Taimoor, S., Najam, H., Law, R., Hassan, W., & Han, H. (2020). Generating marketing outcomes through Internet of things (Iot) technologies. *Sustainability (Basel)*, *12*(22), 9670. doi:10.3390/su12229670

Woodside, A. G., & Sood, S. (2017). Vignettes in the two-step arrival of the internet of things and its reshaping of marketing management's service-dominant logic. *Journal of Marketing Management*, *33*(1-2), 98–110. doi:10.1080/0267257X.2016.1246748

Yan, C., Zhu, J., Ouyang, Y., & Zeng, X. (2021). Marketing method and system optimization based on the financial blockchain of the internet of things. *Wireless Communications and Mobile Computing*, *2021*, 1–11. doi:10.1155/2021/9354569

Chapter 3
Identifying the Applications of Artificial Intelligence in Online Marketing

Rasoul Abbasi

Hazrat-e Masoumeh University, Iran

Mohadeseh Esmaili

Hazrat-e Masoumeh University, Iran

ABSTRACT

The integration of artificial intelligence (AI) in marketing has revolutionized customer engagement, product design, advertising, pricing, and distribution. AI's diverse applications, driven by algorithms, enhance data analysis, enabling more effective marketing and sales strategies. In product design, AI creates personalized value propositions aligned with individual customer needs. In advertising, AI facilitates targeted and accurate ads, optimizing returns and reducing waste. AI transforms pricing through dynamic pricing using predictive algorithms for cost-effective and competitive strategies. In distribution and supply chain, AI enhances speed, accuracy, and efficiency through real-time monitoring and predictive modeling, ultimately improving customer satisfaction.

INTRODUCTION

Nowadays, artificial intelligence-based marketing has become highly prevalent, attracting increasing attention from researchers worldwide. Currently, research on the independent assessment of the impact of artificial intelligence functions on discrete marketing has garnered considerable attention from researchers (Prabowo et al., 2019; Hildebrand, 2019; Jarek & Mazurek, 2019). A recent study by McKinsey indicated that the most popular applications of artificial intelligence in organizations relate to optimizing marketing services and processes (McKinsey, 2022). Continuous technological advancements have brought about significant changes in the evolution of marketing, affirming that marketing can leverage artificial intelligence (AI) hand in hand to innovate and implement a new approach (Siau,

DOI: 10.4018/979-8-3693-1339-8.ch003

2017; Wirth, 2018). Thus, the marketing landscape is evolving with machine learning and artificial intelligence (Syam & Kaul, 2021).

In the contemporary era, fierce competition among global organizations underscores the need for artificial intelligence deployment to gain a competitive edge over rivals (Ransbotham et al., 2018). Intelligent solutions to enhance marketing capabilities in a complex business environment are essential and often involve dealing with complexity and extensive information requirements. In this regard, artificial intelligence facilitates quick decision-making by processing significant volumes of data and providing insightful information to key business partners and customers. Consequently, this technology holds the potential to revolutionize conventional business activities significantly (Bag et al., 2021). Indeed, a recent survey conducted by Gartner on business managers revealed that the majority believe artificial intelligence will likely be a key advancement for businesses in the coming years (Shin & Kang, 2022).

Contemporary marketing is increasingly data-driven, automated, and intelligent. The highly focused approach of modern marketing has a direct impact on marketing outcomes (Kumar et al., 2019; Paschen et al., 2019). Additionally, big data analytics in marketing has now become a primary approach for gaining marketing insights (Berger et al., 2019). Advanced and innovative marketing solutions equipped with artificial intelligence can quickly adapt to the changing needs of businesses, providing communications and solution packages that are vital and profitable for stakeholders (Epstein, 2018). Artificial intelligence represents a broad and continuous technological evolution with extensive and far-reaching consequences. Therefore, it is recommended to harness artificial intelligence in digital marketing to foster innovation and improve efficiency, with visible results expected in the future (Haleem et al., 2022).

Many businesses are deploying this technology to address various organizational challenges, with a widespread adoption of artificial intelligence in marketing. This chapter explores the comprehensive application of artificial intelligence in marketing. It begins by defining artificial intelligence and digital marketing, then delves into the importance of the role of artificial intelligence in digital marketing. Artificial intelligence marketing and its applications are discussed in detail, categorized into five sections.

The Importance of Artificial Intelligence in Marketing

In recent years, artificial intelligence (AI) has captured the attention of a wide spectrum of researchers and marketing managers (Davenport et al., 2020). The effectiveness of marketing activities heavily depends on how they are carried out. Organizations must examine industry trends, customers, competitors, and other relevant stakeholders when conducting market research. These data can be collected from various sources such as internal and external reports, social media, etc. However, the analysis of diverse data and intelligent identification from such data requires the deployment of artificial intelligence in organizations. In fact, the proficiency in using AI techniques for market research and marketing decision support can provide organizations with a multidimensional insight, leading to better decision-making (Pietronudo et al., 2022).

The trend of artificial intelligence (AI) in marketing is currently growing and expanding. The significance of this technology lies in increased computational power, lower computational costs, the availability of large datasets, and advances in machine learning algorithms and models. We witness widespread applications of artificial intelligence in various marketing areas today. Many businesses now use this technology to enhance their performance in relation to customers (Davenport et al., 2020; Rust, 2020). As discussed, artificial intelligence has a considerable impact on marketing processes, and the adoption of digitally and AI-based marketing has become a necessity for businesses today.

APPLICATIONS OF ARTIFICIAL INTELLIGENCE IN MARKETING

Product Design and Value Creation

Artificial Intelligence (AI) assists organizations in tracking heterogeneous data for analysis and prompt responses to customer needs (Wirth, 2018). AI is crucial for a better understanding of consumer insights and behaviors to attract and retain customers. It stimulates the next customer move and redefines the overall customer experience (Tjepkema, 2019). AI-based marketing analytics tools can effectively assess the alignment of product design with customer needs and satisfaction (Dekimpe, 2020). Topic modeling enhances the system's capabilities in transformation and service design (Antons & Breidbach, 2018). Giving weight to product features during product searches helps marketers understand and align marketing strategies with meaningful product management (Guo et al., 2020). AI provides capabilities for customizing recommendations to fit customer needs (Kumar et al., 2019).

AI can accelerate decision-making speed, significantly aiding in multiple marketing experiments and strategy development (Singh et al., 2022). Its ability to evaluate and execute marketing strategies contributes to continuous adaptation to the market and achieving business success. AI can enhance overall company performance in operational, financial, and market domains. With AI technologies, organizations can make quality decisions quickly, positively impacting organizational performance (Wamba-Taguimdje et al., 2020). Additionally, AI is valuable for market insights, including prediction and understanding, facilitating informed decision-making (Berger et al., 2019).

In the current era, AI allows us to analyze customer sentiments. This technology is particularly helpful for businesses in evaluating initial sample assessments in relation to customer sentiments, providing a comprehensive view in the analysis process (Kulkarni et al., 2012). AI reduces human errors and optimizes content in various email formats, ensuring relevance to recipients. AI also plays a role in preventing human interaction, thus eliminating the possibility of human errors. Given recurring data security issues, many companies are concerned about their employees' inability to protect customer data and other essential company information. AI can assist in addressing various security issues through learning, adaptation, and responding to the cybersecurity needs of an organization (Syam & Sharma, 2018; Tan & Ko, 2016; Ekramifard et al., 2020).

The insights gathered by AI for organizations are valuable resources for better understanding consumers and customer-centric choices. AI provides market knowledge by assessing extensive content on social media platforms, blogs, and more. Marketers can quickly develop personalization for consumers using billions of data points from AI systems, including interactions on websites, purchasing habits, previous interactions, referral sources, and other factors. Additionally, AI can reveal information on factors such as the stated price for customer conversion and the likelihood that customers will make multiple purchases, providing marketers with highly useful information (Feng et al., 2021; Rekha et al., 2016; Paschen et al., 2019).

Intelligent technology solutions are increasingly used by companies and their marketing departments to improve operational efficiency and consumer experience. Using these platforms, marketers may obtain a more complex and complete image of their target customers, enabling them to offer products tailored to their preferences (Dwivedi et al., 2021; Rust & Huang, 2014; Güngor, 2020).

Marketers can use AI to understand behaviors, actions, and indicators. As a result, they can adopt the right approach to the right person in a timely and effective manner, achieving targeted goals. AI in marketing allows for the rapid processing of large amounts of data from social media, emails, and the web, enabling marketers to obtain vast volumes of raw data. AI marketing helps collect data, consumer insights, predict customer next moves, and make automatic marketing decisions (Shah & Shay, 2019; Paschen et al., 2022; Syam & Sharma, 2018). As mentioned, AI plays a significant role in product design and is influential in this field.

Advertising and Informing Customers

Artificial Intelligence (AI) is employed in marketing campaigns across various industries, including finance, government, healthcare, entertainment, retail, and more. Each application yields different outcomes, such as enhancing campaign performance, improving customer experience, or increasing marketing operations efficiency. Marketers leverage AI through programmatic advertising to address various challenges. Programmatic platforms use Machine Learning (ML) to suggest relevant ad spaces to target audiences, delivering personalized advertisements (Sohrabpour et al., 2021; Grover et al., 2022; Thomassey et al., 2018).

Recommended product patterns generated by AI algorithms can lead to media bidding, essentially an automated method for online buying and selling. This program utilizes computer-based models, utilizing audience data to provide targeted advertisements to potential buyers, ultimately improving companies' marketing strategies and performance (Karimova & Goby, 2021; Thontirawong & Chinchanachokchai, 2021; Bhattacharjee, 2019).

AI is frequently employed in digital advertising to ensure maximum success; it is utilized across networks like Facebook, Google, and Instagram to offer the best possible expertise. Targeted advertisements, based on user data analysis such as gender, age, interests, and other factors, are presented. Marketers may use AI technology to identify micro-trends and even predict trends, enabling them to make strategic judgments. Consequently, companies can reduce digital advertising waste, ensuring that their investments yield the highest possible returns. AI shapes the future of digital marketing, as its ability to utilize data and algorithmic precision can significantly streamline marketing processes, emphasizing the necessity for marketers to embrace this technology as an effective team member (Alawaad, 2021; Boz & Kose, 2018; Kietzmann & Pitt, 2020).

As long as there is supervision and training, AI can perform specialized activities more effectively than humans. AI is likely to lead to higher returns on investment, significantly accelerating marketing campaign processes, reducing costs, and enhancing marketing strategy efficiency. This technology can quickly analyze tactical data and use ML to make rapid decisions based on advertisements and customer areas, freeing up time for team members to focus on strategic projects. Marketers can utilize comprehensive analyses for better media selection (Daskou & Mangina, 2003; Goyal, 2019; Sıgırcı, 2021).

AI, as the best technique for predicting customer behavior and improving customer journeys, is created by combining customer data. Advances in AI offer more ways to accomplish this task. This technology can aid in developing more successful marketing strategies, increasing customer journeys, and transforming how companies attract, nurture, and convert prospects (Ballester et al., 2021; Fredstrom et al., 2022). Marketers use AI to segment customers into key groups based on specific criteria, managing content creation automatically for customer journeys through AI-generated content. AI-powered content curation allows us to engage visitors better, positioning ourselves as industry leaders by providing relevant content and added value during industry-specific displays. Additionally, AI is used for various purposes, including delivering tailored messages and better-personalized recommendations to consumers (Neuhofer et al., 2021; Brobbey et al., 2021; Varsha et al., 2021).

AI plays a crucial role in helping businesses understand customer needs and providing a personalized user experience. Companies can target customers more effectively by collecting purchase history and social media data. AI technology plays a significant role in optimizing ad performance. AI in social media is used for automated ad guidance, suggesting optimal patterns, and highlighting performance (Singh et al., 2019; Ahmed & Ganapathy, 2021; Kaiyp & Alimanova, 2020; Haleem & Javaid, 2019). Sentiment analysis in text-based online reviews and social media content is common in marketing literature. For example, the capacity of consumer-generated content to perform with stock market performance is noteworthy (Huang & Rust, 2022).

AI solutions provide marketers with a better understanding of current and future customers, enabling them to deliver the right message to the right person at the right time. Building a comprehensive profile through consumer data collection during each interaction is key. Marketers can use AI solutions to refine marketing campaigns and create highly personalized content using the data from these profiles. AI can tap into hidden consumer data in keyword searches, social profiles, and other online data to assist in creative and effective digital advertising (Li et al., 2021; Pangkey et al., 2019; Zhao & Cai, 2021). AI in marketing is particularly beneficial in retargeting strategies. AI continually examines behavior outlooks and purchase histories, revealing patterns and informing marketers about trends (Xu et al., 2022; Wu et al., 2020; Xu et al., 2022; Vinuesa et al., 2020).

AI technologies ease the process by examining each new piece of data and providing customer-relevant information. AI undoubtedly assists marketers in combining complex technology and human ingenuity to read, understand, and interact with modern customers on a personalized, relevant, and timely level through excessive personal messaging. Algorithms successfully assess the activities of a website visitor to adjust and instantly generate individualized advertising data. Continuous data collection is used to create future changes in advertising content. AI, using personal and behavioral data, empowers sellers to focus more on results and assist their customers. Psychology provides a more comprehensive insight into the goals, desires, and purchasing patterns that significantly influence customer decisions on choosing products or services through AI (Purwanto et al., 2020; Brooks et al., 2022; Makarius et al., 2020).

With the rapid advancement of technology, customers can search and find anything at any time using fast search engines. Artificial intelligence plays a crucial role in assisting marketers in analyzing customer search patterns and identifying key areas for focused efforts. With abundant data available, marketers can execute more precise and effective online advertising. AI solutions can greatly contribute to evaluating customer keyword searches, social profiles, and assist in creating personalized advertisements, leading to success in marketing strategies. Analyzing the audience enables marketers to understand customers individually.

Artificial intelligence has the potential to offer personalized recommendations to filter potential buyers and create customized content ideal and relevant to customer groups. Retaining existing customers is as important as generating new ones, with AI acting as a primary driver for customer retention. Using robots for direct interaction with consumers allows marketers to reduce additional costs and save time (Jain & Aggarwal, 2020).

Market research is a strategic stage in the marketing process, and artificial intelligence can effectively assist marketers in this area. Artificial intelligence gathers data for market analysis and understanding customer sentiments in various fields such as markets, the environment, company, competitors, and customers. In the digital age, market data is easily traceable and monitorable, allowing marketers to gain deeper insights into consumer behavior and enhance organizational efficiency without wasting resources on ineffective efforts (Huang & Rust, 2021; Peyravi et al., 2020; Theodoridis & Gkikas, 2019).

Artificial intelligence tools are perceived as valuable in inferring customer expectations and navigating future trends. For instance, AI-based algorithms on platforms like Facebook collect a vast amount of personal data for segmentation and targeting. While concerns about the ethics of AI-driven methods have intensified in recent years, privacy threats in data handling have raised more concerns in some countries compared to others (e.g., France vs. the United States) (Trepte et al., 2017).

Advertising management encompasses media planning, scheduling, advertising tracking, search engine optimization, and more. Advertising techniques are transforming from physical to physical-digital modes. Social media campaigns are now prevalent due to the global digital transformation. In the ever-changing world of technology, customers decide on content, location, and timing. Utilizing AI in advertising processes, including consumer insight discovery, ad creation, media planning, and assessing the impact of advertisements, was examined in this study.

In consumer insight discovery, practical algorithms can be used to understand user behavior patterns. For ad creation, customer preferences can be estimated using deep semantic analysis and real-time user interactions to predict the likelihood of future acceptance of creative ideas. In media planning and buying, user touchpoints can be categorized and simulated based on behavioral paths in news media, social media, and purchase media to provide personalized ads. In evaluating the impact of advertisements, data can be collected in real-time to monitor audience responses, and machine learning can optimize real-time responses to achieve alignment between the impact of advertising and brand impact. This research demonstrates that artificial intelligence has integrated into the advertising process at various levels, and further research is essential to advance our understanding of such applications and their impact (Jiang & Qin, 2019).

Our initial analysis of some prevalent artificial intelligence applications highlights new features in intelligent advertising. For instance, Google's Assistant, launched in 2016, can extract data from all Google applications used by a user with a single sign-in, including Gmail, search, shopping, photos, calendar, calls, and more. Another example is TikTok, a short-form video platform released in 2017, utilizing AI technologies to assess user preferences through their interactions with content and provide personalized content feeds for each user (Jennings, 2019). According to ByteDance, TikTok's parent company, there's no need for users to input personal preferences or identify desired topics while using the platform.

Through large-scale machine learning algorithms and deep learning, TikTok's platform learns from user interactions with content, including clicks, time spent on each article, daily content consumption time, pauses, and more. This results in a personalized content feed for each user. Hema, a supermarket app, is a third example that allows users to order and immediately consume ready-to-eat seafood or receive free home delivery within 1.9 miles (3 kilometers) in 30 minutes for local residents (Li, 2019). According to Zhang Guohong, Hema's general manager, Hema users shop every three days, and approximately 70% of orders are placed through the app (TVBS, 2017).

Artificial intelligence can create custom simulation models and purchasing processes by providing recommendations based on machine learning technologies and interacting with virtual assistants. Many companies utilize AI to engage with their customers, with Amazon using AI to suggest products based on past purchases, reviews, and previous searches. These intelligent technologies are continually evolving and approaching a point where they can outperform humans in specific areas.

AI enhances human performance in marketing trend detection by providing superior knowledge, data analysis, and input. Therefore, it can definitively determine the effectiveness of marketing strategies (Pedersen & Duin, 2022; Khrais, 2020; Kumar, 2020). The impact of AI on the advertising process primarily increases efficiency. However, the influence of AI on the advertising industry structure remains an open question.

The proliferation of advertising apps has led to changes in relationships between customers and advertising agencies, with some consulting firms assisting clients in utilizing in-house capabilities for advertising tasks. Structural changes may accelerate with increased adoption of AI in advertising creation, potentially challenging agency businesses (Qin & Jiang, 2019).

AI is sometimes employed for branding and sales purposes. Branding refers to delayed advertising effects, usually of a cognitive nature, measured through subtle criteria or partial exchanges, such as ad views, unique views, comments, and shares. Sales, on the other hand, refer to immediate advertising effects, typically of a behavioral nature, measured through hard criteria and major conversions such as app downloads, sign-ups, and purchases (Li, 2019). Tracking hard criteria and major conversions in AI-based analyses is relatively straightforward. The challenge lies in developing new models for better measuring the effects of intelligent advertising on branding and sales, either separately or synergistically (Wang et al., 2019).

AI assists marketers in swiftly identifying qualified leads, devising better nurturing tactics, and, when integrated into automation tools, generating relevant content marketing. Dynamic content emails, especially one-to-one, prove to be the most effective as they use text emails to energize what the brand communicates and align with what subscribers are interested in hearing. Dynamic content strategies ensure that emails are relevant to the geographical location, psychographic-behavioral data, and insights of the subscribers (Alyoshina, 2019; Tanase, 2018; Jarek & Mazurek, 2019). AI methods predict individual needs and convert consumer needs, interests, preferences, and habits into intelligent advertisements. These consumer characteristics can be analyzed in real-time or utilized in creating consumer insights from vast multi-sensory data gathered everywhere, especially from virtual assistants (Li, 2019). Additionally, algorithms can be employed to suggest versions of advertisements (Wang et al., 2019). Furthermore, this technology would be highly effective for estimating and predicting a company's sales (Boone et al., 2019).

In marketing, AI can be applied in various ways, each application offering benefits such as risk reduction, increased speed, improved customer satisfaction, and enhanced revenue. AI platforms can make quick decisions regarding cost allocation in media channels, ensuring continuous customer engagement and valuable campaigns. AI can assist in delivering personalized messages to customers at the right time in their lives. This technology can also help marketers identify at-risk customers and provide information to attract them back to the business. An AI-powered dashboard provides more accurate information about what works, allowing reproduction through channels and proper budget allocation. Effective AI solutions provide marketers with a central platform to handle vast amounts of data, which, when properly analyzed, can be highly insightful (Tchelidze, 2019; Deggans et al., 2019; Popova, 2017; Sajid et al., 2021).

Marketers use AI to increase customer demand. Through unified applications utilizing AI, customers' purchasing processes, including where and when they make purchases, are monitored. This technology can analyze data and offer customized marketing messages to customers when they visit a retail store. These messages may contain special offers to improve the customer's situation, such as average order value, and can contribute to creating a positive user experience (Rizvi et al., 2021; Liu & Chen, 2021). This information can analyze data to predict the buying patterns of target customers and enhance the user experience to showcase what they truly need. AI helps marketers interact effectively with their customers, thereby increasing their profitability (Enholm et al., 2021; Bader & Kaiser, 2019; Loureiro et al., 2021). In the field of advertising, AI can be highly beneficial for companies, leading to increased productivity in this domain.

Pricing and Costs

Pricing is one of the crucial components of organizational marketing (Borden, 1964). In the present era, with the emergence of algorithms and digital economy in computer programs, it is possible to automatically synchronize prices and trade terms (Xiao & Ke, 2021). Companies increasingly delegate their pricing to algorithms utilizing precise customer preference data, sometimes employing a learning process to develop competitive pricing strategies in the presence of competitors, creating a competitive advantage (Brown & MacKay, 2021; Calvano et al., 2020; Assad et al., 2020). Artificial intelligence models, including deep learning and reinforcement learning, have been widely adopted for predicting accepted prices and have shown satisfactory results (Xiao & Ke, 2021).

Artificial intelligence technology is employed by companies for price determination (Gautier et al., 2020). This technology aids in analyzing product pricing trends in the market and can reveal competitor trends, proving crucial (Lu et al., 2020; Chow, 2020; Chiramel et al., 2020). It leads to dynamic pricing, predicting market behavior based on criteria such as demand levels, competitor performance, etc., assisting in calculating optimal product prices (Lu et al., 2020). This technology can transform into an intelligent assistant for developing customer shopping baskets within their budget, predicting products accordingly (Bleakley et al., 2020). Artificial intelligence, by collecting and analyzing unstructured customer data related to pricing, provides marketers with accurate insights for product pricing decisions (Huang & Liu, 2020).

As organizations with excellent data collection tools that significantly reduce employee needs and barriers, businesses use dynamic pricing modules to reach optimal prices for their products or services, enhancing competition and rapidly increasing profitability. AI-controlled dynamic pricing modules enable them to accurately price their services even for short periods. This is one of the most beneficial applications of AI in marketing, particularly in the pricing strategy domain, creating a vital competitive edge (Jo, 2020; Zhao et al., 2022; Rabby et al., 2021). AI may improve stock control during periods of high demand and extensive purchases, naturally discouraging customers from purchasing beyond actual and optimal amounts, creating economic benefits for both the company and the customer. Dynamic pricing for each company and predictive demand needs varies, and a custom solution created by a team or an external seller may be the best option to develop a system that meets goals and enhances marketing strategy efficiency (Wierenga, 2010; Nalini et al., 2021; Rodgers & Nguyen, 2022; Aladayleh, 2020).

Transitioning from revenue management in targeted industries (such as airlines, car rentals, etc.) to scenarios where companies simultaneously price various goods and services requires a cost-effective AI-based model, incorporating flexible demand modeling and revenue optimization algorithms (Shakya et al., 2020). With the prevalence of personalized pricing in online markets, revenue optimization necessitates considering the availability of supply (in nearby warehouses) and transportation costs to the customer's doorstep (Lei et al., 2018). Data aggregation provides an opportunity for companies to maintain a competitive advantage through the evolution from "adaptive" to "learning" pricing. Implementing a dynamic element in targeted pricing in competitive industries can lead to more significant profits (Chen & Zhang, 2009). Consumer willingness to disclose information can facilitate the design of personalized pricing, economically beneficial for both the company and the customer (Rayna et al., 2015).

Pricing involves combining various aspects in the finalization of prices and is a complex computational task. Real-time price adjustments based on demand fluctuations increase the complexity of pricing tasks. AI-based algorithmic banditry can dynamically adjust prices in real-time scenarios and suggest the best prices (Misra et al., 2019). In scenarios with variable pricing, such as in e-commerce, game inference in machine learning algorithms can quickly adapt price points to match competitor prices (Bauer & Jannach, 2018). Pricing algorithms, encompassing customer choices, competitor strategies, and supply networks, are crucial for optimizing dynamic pricing (Dekimpe, 2020). There are two approaches to AI-based pricing, including predictive algorithms and learning algorithms. Predictive algorithms are mainly used for forecasting elements related to market conditions and demand levels (Mikl´os-Thal & Tucker, 2019), while learning algorithms can identify optimal pricing rules through price testing and adaptation (Calvano et al., 2020).

Automatic pricing algorithms exhibit various degrees of complexity. Some systems based on simple rules operate according to protocols predefined by human agents. Others are more advanced and utilize Artificial Intelligence (AI) with self-learning capabilities. These advanced algorithms can independently identify optimal price points that maximize long-term profits through repetitive pricing experiments (Wang et al., 2023). In recurrent price competitions within simulated market environments, where RL algorithms are recognized for their capabilities, these algorithms employ complex pricing strategies, softening competition and enabling competitive escape. They determine prices that must be maintained in competitive markets (Calvano et al., 2020; Hansen et al., 2021; Asker et al., 2022; Johnson et al., 2023; Klein, 2021). This technology also operates dynamically in personalized pricing, playing a key role in this domain.

PRODUCT DISTRIBUTION

Artificial Intelligence, through the use of the Internet of Things, integrates intelligent logistics management systems, electronic market management, and supply chain quality control to shape comprehensive and organized information. Effective metrics are promptly adopted to meet customer needs, enhance service quality, and optimize the entire system (Wu, 2021). Real-time warehouse monitoring improves overall product profitability rates, and supply chain network management in the product space enhances inventory management information. Smart containers and product spaces can provide relevant physical and intelligent features to facilitate integrated data management (Harmel et al., 2021).

In contemporary supply chains, sensors and devices such as RFID, GPS, POS, tags, and other smart devices continuously send and receive data, enhancing the role of the Internet of Things (IoT) in shaping accurate predictions. Technologies like Big Data Analytics (BDA) and AI, however, play a crucial role in making these data streams useful, reducing risks, and overcoming challenges related to incorrect information (Roden et al., 2017). The application of AI techniques significantly improves adaptability, allowing companies to learn from the external environment, reduce complexity, and enhance the resilience of these complex systems (Belhadi et al., 2021). Additionally, AI, as a pivotal technology in the current era, can contribute to the reconstruction capacity of companies and positively impact supply chain improvement (Cavalcante et al., 2019; Modgil et al., 2021).

The flexibility of supply chain positions is vital, as the adoption of AI can act as a vital capability, enabling better control mechanisms and the identification of disturbance areas (Gupta et al., 2020; Wamba et al., 2020; Dwivedi et al., 2019). Innovations based on AI can facilitate seamless coordination and collaboration to enhance supply chain effectiveness (Wamba et al., 2020). Leveraging emerging technologies like AI, IoT, advanced robotics, etc., as part of Industry 4.0, can contribute to increased revenue through improved cost reduction, differentiation, risk optimization, innovation, and business model and process changes (Mithas et al., 2022).

Demand prediction for new products is crucial for managing the required investment level for supply. Failure to predict demand leads to potential sales loss, while overprediction results in costly excess inventory. In modern models, machine learning technology is employed for predicting demand for new products, utilizing vast data, including sales history for similar products (Hamoudia & Vanston, 2023).

AI-based supply chain systems lead to accurate demand predictions, reducing the bullwhip effect (Sing & Challa, 2016). Additionally, AI can focus on post-processing monitoring, improving the accuracy of AI-based quality assessments (Kousiouris et al., 2019). AI's capabilities extend to supplier or partner selection (Cavalcante et al. 2019; Soleimani, 2018). It can minimize supplier risk/credit risk prediction for SMEs in the financial supply chain (Zhu et al. 2019; Soleimani 2018). Other AI capabilities include chatbots and smart assistants for operational procurement, playing a pivotal role in this domain (Davenport, 2018). Considering the above, it is evident that AI technology will be instrumental in the field of product distribution, playing a decisive role.

CONCLUSION

The integration of artificial intelligence (AI) in marketing has transformed the landscape of customer engagement, product design, advertising, pricing and distribution. The multifaceted applications of AI have proven to be instrumental in reshaping traditional marketing strategies and creating new avenues for businesses to connect with their target audiences. Artificial intelligence (AI) stands out as one of the most advanced technologies of the present era, significantly impacting various businesses. Utilizing algorithms, AI can create new capabilities and tools, enabling businesses to market more effectively. A crucial impact of AI is the improvement of data analysis processes. With AI algorithms, large and complex datasets can be easily and rapidly analyzed, identifying various patterns. This assists businesses in providing more effective marketing and sales strategies. AI's influence on product design and value creation is paramount, enabling organizations to analyze heterogeneous data for prompt responses to customer needs. The technology enhances customer understanding, stimulates personalized recommendations, and accelerates decision-making processes. Moreover, AI facilitates the extraction of valuable insights from social media, blogs, and other platforms, allowing marketers to develop personalized strategies based on billions of data points. The ability to understand behaviors, actions, and indicators enables marketers to adopt the right approach at the right time, achieving targeted goals. The integration of AI in marketing analytics tools ensures alignment with customer needs and satisfaction, fostering continuous adaptation to the market. AI-based market analysis tools can examine product design alignment with customer needs and assess customer satisfaction. In product design, AI can contribute significantly to creating and discovering personalized value propositions, ensuring that the offered value aligns proportionally with individual customer needs.

In the advertising domain, AI plays a vital role. AI algorithms enable targeted and highly accurate advertising to specific audiences. AI also aids businesses in identifying appropriate audiences and analyzing advertising performance. AI is one of the best techniques for customer prediction and improving the customer journey by integrating customer data. Companies can effectively target customers by collecting purchase histories and social media data, creating personalized advertisements. Essentially, this technology delivers the right message to the right individual at the right time, enhancing advertising efficiency. AI plays a pivotal role in programmatic advertising, recommending relevant ad spaces to target audiences. The use of AI algorithms in digital advertising platforms has revolutionized the way ads are targeted. Targeted advertisements based on user data analysis contribute to reducing digital advertising waste and optimizing returns on investment.

Pricing is a crucial component of organizational marketing. AI has transformed this area, leading to dynamic pricing. This technology assists in analyzing product pricing trends in the market and can reveal competitor trends, vital for strategic decision-making. In the domain of pricing, AI offers significant advancements by automating price synchronization, predicting market behavior, and enabling dynamic pricing. The technology employs predictive algorithms and learning algorithms to forecast market conditions, demand levels, and optimal pricing rules. AI-driven pricing models contribute to cost-effective and competitive pricing strategies, ensuring optimal prices for products and services. This application of AI in pricing not only increases efficiency but also enhances profitability through personalized and adaptive pricing approaches. AI can lead to dynamic pricing to achieve optimal prices for products or services, ensuring competitiveness and rapid profitability growth. AI can even facilitate personalized pricing design, economically beneficial for both the company and the customer.

In product distribution and supply chain management, AI plays a vital role. Real-time warehouse monitoring improves the speed of product circulation. AI-based supply chain systems lead to accurate demand predictions, particularly useful in product distribution. AI's impact on product distribution is evident through the integration of the Internet of Things (IoT) in intelligent logistics management systems. Real-time monitoring, data analytics, and predictive modeling contribute to more efficient supply chain operations. AI's role in demand prediction for new products and quality assessment further strengthens its influence on product distribution. Today, companies can understand customer behavior, enhance customer experience, and make marketing systems more efficient using AI algorithms. AI can precisely analyze customer experiences and offer appropriate strategies for improvement. Furthermore, AI can automatically provide suitable responses to customer questions and needs, contributing to improved customer satisfaction.

In conclusion, the use of AI techniques has a significantly positive impact on a company's adaptive capabilities. Considering the continuous growth of AI technology, these effects are likely to expand further. Overall, AI, as a powerful tool in marketing, has extensive effects, helping businesses improve strategies, enhance customer experiences, and increase sales. With the continuous growth of this technology, the future impact of AI on marketing is expected to be even more significant, emphasizing the importance for businesses to take it seriously for performance improvement.

REFERENCES

Ahmed, A. A. A., & Ganapathy, A. (2021). Creation of automated content with embedded artificial intelligence: A study on learning management system for educational entrepreneurship. *Academy of Entrepreneurship Journal, 27*(3), 1–10.

Aladayleh, K. (2020). A framework for integration of artificial intelligence into digital marketing in Jordanian commercial banks. *Journal of Innovations in Digital Marketing, 1*(1), 32–39. doi:10.51300/jidm-2020-10

Alawaad, H. A. (2021). The role of artificial intelligence (AI) in public relations and product marketing in modern organizations. *Turkish Journal of Computer and Mathematics Education, 12*(14), 3180–3187.

Allal-Chérif, O., Simón-Moya, V., & Ballester, A. C. C. (2021). Intelligent purchasing: How artificial intelligence can redefine the purchasing function. *Journal of Business Research, 124,* 69–76. doi:10.1016/j.jbusres.2020.11.050

Alyoshina, I. V. (2019). Artificial intelligence in an age of digital globalization. In *International Conference Technology & Entrepreneurship in Digital Society* (pp. 26-30). Academic Press.

Antons, D., & Breidbach, C. F. (2018). Big data, big insights? Advancing service innovation and design with machine learning. *Journal of Service Research, 21*(1), 17–39. doi:10.1177/1094670517738373

Aphirakmethawong, J., Yang, E., & Mehnen, J. (2022, September). An overview of artificial intelligence in product design for smart manufacturing. In *2022 27th International Conference on Automation and Computing (ICAC)* (pp. 1-6). IEEE. 10.1109/ICAC55051.2022.9911089

Asker, J., Fershtman, C., & Pakes, A. (2022, May). Artificial intelligence, algorithm design, and pricing. *AEA Papers and Proceedings. American Economic Association, 112,* 452–456. doi:10.1257/pandp.20221059

Bader, V., & Kaiser, S. (2019). Algorithmic decision-making? The user interface and its role for human involvement in decisions supported by artificial intelligence. *Organization, 26*(5), 655–672. doi:10.1177/1350508419855714

Bag, S., Gupta, S., Kumar, A., & Sivarajah, U. (2021). An integrated artificial intelligence framework for knowledge creation and B2B marketing rational decision making for improving firm performance. *Industrial Marketing Management, 92,* 178–189. doi:10.1016/j.indmarman.2020.12.001

Bassano, C., Barile, S., Saviano, M., Pietronudo, M. C., & Cosimato, S. (2020). *AI technologies & value co-creation in luxury context.* Academic Press.

Bauer, J., & Jannach, D. (2018). Optimal pricing in e-commerce based on sparse and noisy data. *Decision Support Systems, 106,* 53–63. doi:10.1016/j.dss.2017.12.002

Belhadi, A., Mani, V., Kamble, S. S., Khan, S. A. R., & Verma, S. (2021). Artificial intelligence-driven innovation for enhancing supply chain resilience and performance under the effect of supply chain dynamism: An empirical investigation. *Annals of Operations Research,* 1–26. doi:10.1007/s10479-021-03956-x PMID:33551534

Berger, J., Humphreys, A., Ludwig, S., Moe, W. W., Netzer, O., & Schweidel, D. A. (2020). Uniting the tribes: Using text for marketing insight. *Journal of Marketing, 84*(1), 1–25. doi:10.1177/0022242919873106

Bhattacharjee, S. (2019). Metamorphic transformation: Critically understanding Artificial Intelligence in marketing. Bhattacharjee, Sandeep.(2019)."Metamorphic Transformation: Critically Understanding Artificial Intelligence in Marketing. *Asia Pacific Journal of Multidisciplinary Research, 7,* 61.

Bleakley, D. O., Demmler, L. M., Desai, A. A., Etgen, M. P., & Kenna, S. (2020). *U.S. Patent Application No. 16/681,798*. US Patent Office.

Boone, T., Ganeshan, R., Jain, A., & Sanders, N. R. (2019). Forecasting sales in the supply chain: Consumer analytics in the big data era. *International Journal of Forecasting, 35*(1), 170–180. doi:10.1016/j.ijforecast.2018.09.003

Borden, N. H. (1964). The concept of the marketing mix. *Journal of Advertising Research, 4*(2), 2–7.

Boz, H., & Kose, U. (2018). Emotion extraction from facial expressions by using artificial intelligence techniques. BRAIN. *Broad Research in Artificial Intelligence and Neuroscience, 9*(1), 5–16.

Brobbey, E. E., Ankrah, E., & Kankam, P. K. (2021). The role of artificial intelligence in integrated marketing communications. A case study of Jumia Online Ghana. Inkanyiso. *Journal of the Humanities and Social Sciences, 13*(1), 120–136.

Brooks, R., Nguyen, D., Bhatti, A., Allender, S., Johnstone, M., Lim, C. P., & Backholer, K. (2022). Use of artificial intelligence to enable dark nudges by transnational food and beverage companies: analysis of company documents. *Public Health Nutrition, 25*(5), 1291-1299.

Brown, Z. Y., & MacKay, A. (2021). *Competition in pricing algorithms (No. w28860)*. National Bureau of Economic Research. doi:10.3386/w28860

Calvano, E., Calzolari, G., Denicolo, V., & Pastorello, S. (2020). Artificial intelligence, algorithmic pricing, and collusion. *The American Economic Review, 110*(10), 3267–3297. doi:10.1257/aer.20190623

Cavalcante, I. M., Frazzon, E. M., Forcellini, F. A., & Ivanov, D. (2019). A supervised machine learning approach to data-driven simulation of resilient supplier selection in digital manufacturing. *International Journal of Information Management, 49,* 86–97. doi:10.1016/j.ijinfomgt.2019.03.004

Chen, X., & Zhang, Y. (2009). Uncertain linear programs: Extended affinely adjustable robust counterparts. *Operations Research, 57*(6), 1469–1482. doi:10.1287/opre.1080.0605

Chiramel, S., Logofătu, D., Rawat, J., & Andersson, C. (2020). Efficient Approaches for House Pricing Prediction by Using Hybrid Machine Learning Algorithms. In Intelligent Information and Database Systems: 12th Asian Conference, ACIIDS 2020, Phuket, Thailand, March 23–26, 2020 [Springer Singapore]. *Proceedings, 12,* 85–94.

Chow, V. (2020). Predicting auction price of vehicle license plate with deep recurrent neural network. *Expert Systems with Applications, 142,* 113008. doi:10.1016/j.eswa.2019.113008

Daskou, S., & Mangina, E. E. (2003). Artificial intelligence in managing market relationships: The use of intelligence agents. *Journal of Relationship Marketing, 2*(1-2), 85–102. doi:10.1300/J366v02n01_06

Davenport, T., Guha, A., Grewal, D., & Bressgott, T. (2020). How artificial intelligence will change the future of marketing. *Journal of the Academy of Marketing Science, 48*(1), 24–42. doi:10.1007/s11747-019-00696-0

Davenport, T. H. (2018). From analytics to artificial intelligence. *Journal of Business Analytics, 1*(2), 73–80. doi:10.1080/2573234X.2018.1543535

Deggans, J., Krulicky, T., Kovacova, M., Valaskova, K., & Poliak, M. (2019). Cognitively enhanced products, output growth, and labor market changes: Will artificial intelligence replace workers by automating their jobs? Economics. *Management and Financial Markets*, *14*(1), 38–43.

Dekimpe, M. G. (2020). Retailing and retailing research in the age of big data analytics. *International Journal of Research in Marketing*, *37*(1), 3–14. doi:10.1016/j.ijresmar.2019.09.001

Deng, S., Tan, C. W., Wang, W., & Pan, Y. (2019). Smart generation system of personalized advertising copy and its application to advertising practice and research. *Journal of Advertising*, *48*(4), 356–365. doi:10.1080/00913367.2019.1652121

Dwivedi, Y. K., Hughes, L., Ismagilova, E., Aarts, G., Coombs, C., Crick, T., Duan, Y., Dwivedi, R., Edwards, J., Eirug, A., Galanos, V., Ilavarasan, P. V., Janssen, M., Jones, P., Kar, A. K., Kizgin, H., Kronemann, B., Lal, B., Lucini, B., ... Williams, M. D. (2021). Artificial Intelligence (AI): Multidisciplinary perspectives on emerging challenges, opportunities, and agenda for research, practice and policy. *International Journal of Information Management*, *57*, 101994. doi:10.1016/j.ijinfomgt.2019.08.002

Ekramifard, A., Amintoosi, H., Seno, A. H., Dehghantanha, A., & Parizi, R. M. (2020). A systematic literature review of integration of blockchain and artificial intelligence. *Blockchain Cybersecurity, Trust and Privacy*, 147-160.

Enholm, I. M., Papagiannidis, E., Mikalef, P., & Krogstie, J. (2022). Artificial intelligence and business value: A literature review. *Information Systems Frontiers*, *24*(5), 1709–1734. doi:10.1007/s10796-021-10186-w

Epstein, M. J. (2018). Adapting for digital survival. *Strategic Finance*, *99*(8), 26–33.

Ezrachi, A., & Stucke, M. E. (2016). *Is Your Digital Assistant Devious?* Oxford Legal Studies Research Paper No. 52/2016, University of Tennessee Legal Studies Research Paper No. 304. Available at https://ssrn.com/abstract=2828117 doi:10.2139/ssrn.2828117

Fang, C., Lu, H., Hong, Y., Liu, S., & Chang, J. (2020). Dynamic pricing for electric vehicle extreme fast charging. *IEEE Transactions on Intelligent Transportation Systems*, *22*(1), 531–541. doi:10.1109/TITS.2020.2983385

Farrokhi, A., Shirazi, F., Hajli, N., & Tajvidi, M. (2020). Using artificial intelligence to detect crisis related to events: Decision making in B2B by artificial intelligence. *Industrial Marketing Management*, *91*, 257–273. doi:10.1016/j.indmarman.2020.09.015

Feng, C. M., Park, A., Pitt, L., Kietzmann, J., & Northey, G. (2021). Artificial intelligence in marketing: A bibliographic perspective. *Australasian Marketing Journal*, *29*(3), 252–263. doi:10.1016/j.ausmj.2020.07.006

Fosso Wamba, S., Gunasekaran, A., Dubey, R., & Ngai, E. W. (2018). Big data analytics in operations and supply chain management. *Annals of Operations Research*, *270*(1-2), 1–4. doi:10.1007/s10479-018-3024-7 PMID:36687515

Fosso Wamba, S., Queiroz, M. M., Wu, L., & Sivarajah, U. (2020). Big data analytics-enabled sensing capability and organizational outcomes: assessing the mediating effects of business analytics culture. *Annals of Operations Research*, 1-20. doi:10.1007/s10479-020-03812-4

Fredström, A., Parida, V., Wincent, J., Sjödin, D., & Oghazi, P. (2022). What is the market value of artificial intelligence and machine Learning? The role of innovativeness and collaboration for performance. *Technological Forecasting and Social Change*, *180*, 121716. doi:10.1016/j.techfore.2022.121716

Gautier, A., Ittoo, A., & Van Cleynenbreugel, P. (2020). AI algorithms, price discrimination and collusion: A technological, economic and legal perspective. *European Journal of Law and Economics*, *50*(3), 405–435. doi:10.1007/s10657-020-09662-6

Giri, A., Chatterjee, S., Paul, P., & Chakraborty, S. (2019). Determining the impact of artificial intelligence on'developing marketing strategies' in organized retail sector of West Bengal, India. *International Journal of Engineering and Advanced Technology*, *8*(6), 3031–3036. doi:10.35940/ijeat.F9030.088619

Giroux, M., Kim, J., Lee, J. C., & Park, J. (2022). Artificial intelligence and declined guilt: Retailing morality comparison between human and AI. *Journal of Business Ethics*, *178*(4), 1027–1041. doi:10.1007/s10551-022-05056-7 PMID:35194275

Goyal, M. (2019). Artificial intelligence: A tool for hyper personalization. International Journal of 360. *Management Review*, *7*(01).

Grover, P., Kar, A. K., & Dwivedi, Y. K. (2022). Understanding artificial intelligence adoption in operations management: Insights from the review of academic literature and social media discussions. *Annals of Operations Research*, *308*(1-2), 177–213. doi:10.1007/s10479-020-03683-9

Güngör, H. (2020). Creating value with artificial intelligence: A multi-stakeholder perspective. *Journal of Creating Value*, *6*(1), 72–85. doi:10.1177/2394964320921071

Guo, H., Woodruff, A., & Yadav, A. (2020, April). Improving lives of indebted farmers using deep learning: Predicting agricultural produce prices using convolutional neural networks. *Proceedings of the AAAI Conference on Artificial Intelligence*, *34*(08), 13294–13299. doi:10.1609/aaai.v34i08.7039

Gutierrez, N. (2006). *Demystifying market basket analysis*. DM Review Special Report.

Haleem, A., Javaid, M., Qadri, M. A., Singh, R. P., & Suman, R. (2022). Artificial intelligence (AI) applications for marketing: A literature-based study. *International Journal of Intelligent Networks*.

Haleem, A., & Javaid, M. (2019). Additive manufacturing applications in industry 4.0: a review. *Journal of Industrial Integration and Management, 4*(4), 1930001.

Hamoudia, M., & Vanston, L. (2023). Machine Learning for New Product Forecasting. In *Forecasting with Artificial Intelligence: Theory and Applications* (pp. 77-104). Cham: Springer Nature Switzerland.

Han, R., Lam, H. K., Zhan, Y., Wang, Y., Dwivedi, Y. K., & Tan, K. H. (2021). Artificial intelligence in business-to-business marketing: A bibliometric analysis of current research status, development and future directions. *Industrial Management & Data Systems*, *121*(12), 2467–2497. doi:10.1108/IMDS-05-2021-0300

Hansen, K. T., Misra, K., & Pai, M. M. (2021). Frontiers: Algorithmic collusion: Supra-competitive prices via independent algorithms. *Marketing Science*, *40*(1), 1–12. doi:10.1287/mksc.2020.1276

Harmel, R. D., Kleinman, P., Eve, M., Ippolito, J. A., Beebout, S., Delgado, J., Vandenberg, B., & Buser, M. (2021). The Partnerships for Data Innovations (PDI): Facilitating data stewardship and catalyzing research engagement in the digital age. *Agricultural & Environmental Letters*, *6*(4), e20055. doi:10.1002/ael2.20055

Hernández-Nieves, E., Hernández, G., Gil-González, A. B., Rodríguez-González, S., & Corchado, J. M. (2020). Fog computing architecture for personalized recommendation of banking products. *Expert Systems with Applications*, *140*, 112900. doi:10.1016/j.eswa.2019.112900

Hildebrand, C. (2019). The machine age of marketing: How artificial intelligence changes the way people think, act, and decide. *NIM Marketing Intelligence Review*, *11*(2), 10–17. doi:10.2478/nimmir-2019-0010

Huang, J. Y., & Liu, J. H. (2020). Using social media mining technology to improve stock price forecast accuracy. *Journal of Forecasting*, *39*(1), 104–116. doi:10.1002/for.2616

Huang, M. H., & Rust, R. T. (2021). A strategic framework for artificial intelligence in marketing. *Journal of the Academy of Marketing Science*, *49*(1), 30–50. doi:10.1007/s11747-020-00749-9

Huang, M. H., & Rust, R. T. (2022). A framework for collaborative artificial intelligence in marketing. *Journal of Retailing*, *98*(2), 209–223. doi:10.1016/j.jretai.2021.03.001

Humphreys, A., & Wang, R. J. H. (2018). Automated text analysis for consumer research. *The Journal of Consumer Research*, *44*(6), 1274–1306. doi:10.1093/jcr/ucx104

Iafrate, F. (2018). *Artificial intelligence and big data: The birth of a new intelligence.* John Wiley & Sons. doi:10.1002/9781119426653

Jarek, K., & Mazurek, G. (2019). Marketing and Artificial Intelligence. *Central European Business Review*, *8*(2), 46–55. doi:10.18267/j.cebr.213

Jarrahi, M. H. (2018). Artificial intelligence and the future of work: Human-AI symbiosis in organizational decision making. *Business Horizons*, *61*(4), 577–586. doi:10.1016/j.bushor.2018.03.007

Jatobá, M., Santos, J., Gutierriz, I., Moscon, D., Fernandes, P. O., & Teixeira, J. P. (2019). Evolution of artificial intelligence research in human resources. *Procedia Computer Science*, *164*, 137–142. doi:10.1016/j.procs.2019.12.165

Javaid, M., Haleem, A., Singh, R. P., & Suman, R. (2022). Artificial intelligence applications for industry 4.0: A literature-based study. *Journal of Industrial Integration and Management*, *7*(01), 83–111. doi:10.1142/S2424862221300040

Jennings, R. (2019). *TikTok, explained.* Vox.Retrieved from https://www.vox.com/culture/2018/12/10/18129126/tiktok-app-musically-meme-cringe

Jo, J. W. (2020). Case Studies for Insurance Service Marketing Using Artificial Intelligence (AI) in the InsurTech Industry. *Journal of Digital Convergence*, *18*(10), 175–180.

Johnson, J. P., Rhodes, A., & Wildenbeest, M. (2023). Platform design when sellers use pricing algorithms. *Econometrica, 91*(5), 1841–1879. doi:10.3982/ECTA19978

Kaiyp, K., & Alimanova, M. (2020). Improving indicators of digital marketing using artificial intelligence. *Suleyman Demirel University Bulletin: Natural and Technical Sciences, 52*(1). Available at: https://journals.sdu.edu.kz/index.php/nts/article/view/71

Karimova, G. Z., & Goby, V. P. (2021). The adaptation of anthropomorphism and archetypes for marketing artificial intelligence. *Journal of Consumer Marketing, 38*(2), 229–238. doi:10.1108/JCM-04-2020-3785

Khokhar, P. (2019). Evolution of artificial intelligence in marketing, comparison with traditional marketing. *Our Heritage, 67*(5), 375–389.

Khrais, L. T. (2020). Role of artificial intelligence in shaping consumer demand in E-commerce. *Future Internet, 12*(12), 226. doi:10.3390/fi12120226

Kietzmann, J., & Pitt, L. F. (2020). Artificial intelligence and machine learning: What managers need to know. *Business Horizons, 63*(2), 131–133. doi:10.1016/j.bushor.2019.11.005

Klein, T. (2021). Autonomous algorithmic collusion: Q-learning under sequential pricing. *The RAND Journal of Economics, 52*(3), 538–558. doi:10.1111/1756-2171.12383

Kousiouris, G., Tsarsitalidis, S., Psomakelis, E., Koloniaris, S., Bardaki, C., Tserpes, K., Nikolaidou, M., & Anagnostopoulos, D. (2019). A microservice-based framework for integrating IoT management platforms, semantic and AI services for supply chain management. *Ict Express, 5*(2), 141–145. doi:10.1016/j.icte.2019.04.002

Kulkarni, G., Kannan, P. K., & Moe, W. (2012). Using online search data to forecast new product sales. *Decision Support Systems, 52*(3), 604–611. doi:10.1016/j.dss.2011.10.017

Kumar, D. T. S. (2020). Data mining based marketing decision support system using hybrid machine learning algorithm. *Journal of Artificial Intelligence and Capsule Networks, 2*(3), 185–193. doi:10.36548//jaicn.2020.3.006

Kumar, V., Rajan, B., Venkatesan, R., & Lecinski, J. (2019). Understanding the role of artificial intelligence in personalized engagement marketing. *California Management Review, 61*(4), 135–155. doi:10.1177/0008125619859317

Li, C., McMahon, C., & Newnes, L. (2009, January). Annotation in product lifecycle management: a review of approaches. In *International Design Engineering Technical Conferences and Computers and Information in Engineering Conference* (Vol. 48999, pp. 797-806). 10.1115/DETC2009-86624

Li, H. (2019). Special section introduction: Artificial intelligence and advertising. *Journal of Advertising, 48*(4), 333–337. doi:10.1080/00913367.2019.1654947

Li, R., Cao, Z., Ye, H., & Yue, X. (2021, April). Application and development trend of artificial intelligence in enterprise marketing. *Journal of Physics: Conference Series, 1881*(2), 022032. doi:10.1088/1742-6596/1881/2/022032

Liu, Y., & Chen, W. (2021). Optimization of brand marketing strategy of intelligent technology under the background of artificial intelligence. *Mobile Information Systems*, *12*, 1–8. doi:10.1155/2021/9507917

Loureiro, S. M. C., Guerreiro, J., & Tussyadiah, I. (2021). Artificial intelligence in business: State of the art and future research agenda. *Journal of Business Research*, *129*, 911–926. doi:10.1016/j.jbusres.2020.11.001

Lu, H., Ma, X., Huang, K., & Azimi, M. (2020). Carbon trading volume and price forecasting in China using multiple machine learning models. *Journal of Cleaner Production*, *249*, 119386. doi:10.1016/j.jclepro.2019.119386

Maedche, A., Legner, C., Benlian, A., Berger, B., Gimpel, H., Hess, T., Hinz, O., Morana, S., & Söllner, M. (2019). AI-based digital assistants: Opportunities, threats, and research perspectives. *Business & Information Systems Engineering*, *61*(4), 535–544. doi:10.1007/s12599-019-00600-8

Makarius, E. E., Mukherjee, D., Fox, J. D., & Fox, A. K. (2020). Rising with the machines: A sociotechnical framework for bringing artificial intelligence into the organization. *Journal of Business Research*, *120*, 262–273. doi:10.1016/j.jbusres.2020.07.045

McKinsey. (2022). *The state of AI in 2022—and a half decade in review*. https://www.mckinsey.com/capabilities/quantumblack/our-insights/the-state-of-ai-in-2022-and-a-half-decade-in-review

Miklós-Thal, J., & Tucker, C. (2019). Collusion by algorithm: Does better demand prediction facilitate coordination between sellers? *Management Science*, *65*(4), 1552–1561. doi:10.1287/mnsc.2019.3287

Mithas, S., Chen, Z. L., Saldanha, T. J., & De Oliveira Silveira, A. (2022). How will artificial intelligence and Industry 4.0 emerging technologies transform operations management? *Production and Operations Management*, *31*(12), 4475–4487. doi:10.1111/poms.13864

Modgil, S., Singh, R. K., & Hannibal, C. (2022). Artificial intelligence for supply chain resilience: Learning from Covid-19. *International Journal of Logistics Management*, *33*(4), 1246–1268. doi:10.1108/IJLM-02-2021-0094

Murgai, A. (2018). Transforming digital marketing with artificial intelligence. International Journal of Latest Technology in Engineering, Management &. *Applied Sciences (Basel, Switzerland)*, *7*(4), 259–262.

Nalini, M., Radhakrishnan, D. P., Yogi, G., Santhiya, S., & Harivardhini, V. (2021). Impact of artificial intelligence (AI) on marketing. *International Journal of Aquatic Science*, *12*(2), 3159–3167.

Neuhofer, B., Magnus, B., & Celuch, K. (2021). The impact of artificial intelligence on event experiences: A scenario technique approach. *Electronic Markets*, *31*(3), 601–617. doi:10.1007/s12525-020-00433-4

Pangkey, F. M., Furkan, L. M., & Herman, L. E. (2019). Pengaruh artificial intelligence dan digital marketing terhadap minat beli konsumen. *Jurnal Magister Manajemen Unram*, *8*(3), 21–25. doi:10.29303/jmm.v8i3.448

Paschen, J., Kietzmann, J., & Kietzmann, T. C. (2019). Artificial intelligence (AI) and its implications for market knowledge in B2B marketing. *Journal of Business and Industrial Marketing*, *34*(7), 1410–1419. doi:10.1108/JBIM-10-2018-0295

Paschen, J., Paschen, U., Pala, E., & Kietzmann, J. (2021). Artificial intelligence (AI) and value co-creation in B2B sales: Activities, actors and resources. *Australasian Marketing Journal, 29*(3), 243–251. doi:10.1016/j.ausmj.2020.06.004

Pedersen, I., & Duin, A. (2022). AI agents, humans and untangling the marketing of artificial intelligence in learning environments. *Conference: 55th Hawaii International Conference on System Sciences.* 10.24251/HICSS.2022.002

Peyravi, B., Nekrošienė, J., & Lobanova, L. (2020). Revolutionised technologies for marketing: Theoretical review with focus on artificial intelligence. *Business: Theory and Practice, 21*(2), 827–834. doi:10.3846/btp.2020.12313

Phan, M., Thomas, R., & Heine, K. (2011). Social media and luxury brand management: The case of Burberry. *Journal of Global Fashion Marketing, 2*(4), 213–222. doi:10.1080/20932685.2011.10593099

Pietronudo, M. C., Croidieu, G., & Schiavone, F. (2022). A solution looking for problems? A systematic literature review of the rationalizing influence of artificial intelligence on decision-making in innovation management. *Technological Forecasting and Social Change, 182*, 121828. doi:10.1016/j. techfore.2022.121828

Popova, E. A. (2018). Using artificial intelligence in marketing. *Современные научные исследования и разработки, 2*(11), 31-32.

Prabowo, S. H. W., Murdiono, A., Hidayat, R., Rahayu, W. P., & Sutrisno, S. (2019). Digital marketing optimization in artificial intelligence era by applying consumer behavior algorithm. *Asian Journal of Entrepreneurship and Family Business, 3*(1), 41–48.

Purwanto, P., Kuswandi, K., & Fatmah, F. (2020). Interactive applications with artificial intelligence: The role of trust among digital assistant users. *Форсайт, 14*(2, 2 (eng)), 64–75. doi:10.17323/2500-2597.2020.2.64.75

Qin, X., & Jiang, Z. (2019). The impact of AI on the advertising process: The Chinese experience. *Journal of Advertising, 48*(4), 338–346. doi:10.1080/00913367.2019.1652122

Rabby, F., Chimhundu, R., & Hassan, R. (2021). Artificial intelligence in digital marketing influences consumer behaviour: A review and theoretical foundation for future research. *Academy of Marketing Studies Journal, 25*(5), 1–7.

Rai, Y., Raj, A., Sah, K. S., & Sinha, A. (2020). AIRUYA-A Personal Shopping Assistant. In *International Conference on Innovative Computing and Communications: Proceedings of ICICC 2019,* Volume 1 (pp. 435-442). Springer. 10.1007/978-981-15-1286-5_37

Raiter, O. (2021). Segmentation of bank consumers for artificial intelligence marketing. *International Journal of Contemporary Financial Issues, 1*(1), 39–54.

Ransbotham, S., Gerbert, P., Reeves, M., Kiron, D., & Spira, M. (2018). Artificial intelligence in business gets real. *MIT Sloan Management Review.* Retrieved from: https://sloanreview.mit.edu/projects/artificial-intelligence -in-business-gets-real/

Rayna, T., Darlington, J., & Striukova, L. (2015). Pricing music using personal data: Mutually advantageous first-degree price discrimination. *Electronic Markets, 25*(2), 139–154. doi:10.1007/s12525-014-0165-7

Rekha, A. G., Abdulla, M. S., & Asharaf, S. (2016). Artificial intelligence marketing: An application of a novel lightly trained support vector data description. *Journal of Information and Optimization Sciences, 37*(5), 681–691. doi:10.1080/02522667.2016.1191186

Rizvi, A. T., Haleem, A., Bahl, S., & Javaid, M. (2021). Artificial intelligence (AI) and its applications in Indian manufacturing: a review. *Current Advances in Mechanical Engineering: Select Proceedings of ICRAMERD 2020,* 825-835.

Roden, S., Nucciarelli, A., Li, F., & Graham, G. (2017). Big data and the transformation of operations models: A framework and a new research agenda. *Production Planning and Control, 28*(11-12), 929–944. doi:10.1080/09537287.2017.1336792

Rodgers, W., & Nguyen, T. (2022). Advertising benefits from ethical artificial intelligence algorithmic purchase decision pathways. *Journal of Business Ethics, 178*(4), 1043–1061. doi:10.1007/s10551-022-05048-7

Rust, R. T. (2020). The future of marketing. *International Journal of Research in Marketing, 37*(1), 15–26. doi:10.1016/j.ijresmar.2019.08.002

Rust, R. T., & Huang, M. H. (2014). The service revolution and the transformation of marketing science. *Marketing Science, 33*(2), 206–221. doi:10.1287/mksc.2013.0836

Sahai, S., & Goel, R. (2021). Impact of artificial intelligence in changing trends of marketing. *Applications of Artificial Intelligence in Business and Finance: Modern Trends,* 221.

Sajid, S., Haleem, A., Bahl, S., Javaid, M., Goyal, T., & Mittal, M. (2021). Data science applications for predictive maintenance and materials science in context to Industry 4.0. *Materials Today: Proceedings, 45,* 4898–4905. doi:10.1016/j.matpr.2021.01.357

Shabbir, J., & Anwer, T. (2018). *Artificial intelligence and its role in near future.* arXiv preprint arXiv:1804.01396.

Shah, D., & Shay, E. (2019). How and why artificial intelligence, mixed reality and blockchain technologies will change marketing we know today. Handbook of advances in marketing in an era of disruptions: Essays in honour of Jagdish N. Sheth, 377-390. doi:10.4135/9789353287733.n32

Shahid, M. Z., & Li, G. (2019). Impact of artificial intelligence in marketing: A perspective of marketing professionals of Pakistan. *Global Journal of Management and Business Research, 19*(2), 27–33.

Shin, S., & Kang, J. (2022). Structural features and Diffusion Patterns of Gartner Hype Cycle for Artificial Intelligence using Social Network analysis. *Journal of Intelligent Information Systems, 28*(1), 107–129.

Shukla, A., Gullapuram, S. S., Katti, H., Kankanhalli, M., Winkler, S., & Subramanian, R. (2020). Recognition of advertisement emotions with application to computational advertising. *IEEE Transactions on Affective Computing, 13*(2), 781–792. doi:10.1109/TAFFC.2020.2964549

Siau, K. L., & Yang, Y. (2017). Impact of artificial intelligence, robotics, and machine learning on sales and marketing. *Conference: MWAIS.*

Sığırcı, Ö. (2021). Artificial Intelligence in Marketing: A Review of Consumer-AI Interactions. Handbook of Research on Applied Data Science and Artificial Intelligence in Business and Industry, 342-365. doi:10.4018/978-1-7998-6985-6.ch016

Singh, J., Flaherty, K., Sohi, R. S., Deeter-Schmelz, D., Habel, J., Le Meunier-FitzHugh, K., & Onyemah, V. (2019). Sales profession and professionals in the age of digitization and artificial intelligence technologies: Concepts, priorities, and questions. *Journal of Personal Selling & Sales Management, 39*(1), 2–22. doi:10.1080/08853134.2018.1557525

Singh, L. P., & Challa, R. T. (2016). Integrated forecasting using the discrete wavelet theory and artificial intelligence techniques to reduce the bullwhip effect in a supply chain. *Global Journal of Flexible Systems Managment, 17*(2), 157–169. doi:10.1007/s40171-015-0115-z

Sohrabpour, V., Oghazi, P., Toorajipour, R., & Nazarpour, A. (2021). Export sales forecasting using artificial intelligence. *Technological Forecasting and Social Change, 163*, 120480. doi:10.1016/j.techfore.2020.120480

Soleimani, S. (2018). A perfect triangle with: Artificial intelligence, supply chain management, and financial technology. *Archives of Business Research, 6*(11). Advance online publication. doi:10.14738/abr.611.5681

Syam, N., & Kaul, R. (2021). *Machine Learning and Artificial Intelligence in Marketing and Sales: Essential Reference for Practitioners and Data Scientists.* Emerald Publishing Limited. doi:10.1108/9781800438804

Syam, N., & Sharma, A. (2018). Waiting for a sales renaissance in the fourth industrial revolution: Machine learning and artificial intelligence in sales research and practice. *Industrial Marketing Management, 69*, 135–146. doi:10.1016/j.indmarman.2017.12.019

Tan, T. F., & Ko, C. H. (2016, November). Application of artificial intelligence to cross-screen marketing: a case study of AI technology company. In *2016 2nd International Conference on Artificial Intelligence and Industrial Engineering (AIIE 2016)* (pp. 517-519). Atlantis Press.

Tanase, G. C. (2018). Artificial intelligence: Optimizing the experience of digital marketing. *Romanian Distribution Committee Magazine, 9*(1), 24–28.

Tchelidze, L. (2019). Potential and skill requirements of artificial intelligence in digital marketing. *Calitatea, 20*(S3), 73–78.

Theodoridis, P. K., & Gkikas, D. C. (2019). How artificial intelligence affects digital marketing. In Strategic Innovative Marketing and Tourism: 7th ICSIMAT, Athenian Riviera, Greece, 2018 (pp. 1319-1327). Springer International Publishing. doi:10.1007/978-3-030-12453-3_151

Thiraviyam, T. (2018). Artificial intelligence marketing. *International Journal of Recent Research Aspects, 4*, 449–452.

Thomassey, S., & Zeng, X. (2018). *Introduction: artificial intelligence for fashion industry in the big data era.* Springer Singapore.

Thontirawong, P., & Chinchanachokchai, S. (2021). Teaching artificial intelligence and machine learning in marketing. *Marketing Education Review*, *31*(2), 58–63. doi:10.1080/10528008.2021.1871849

Tjepkema, L. (2019). *What Is Artificial Intelligence Marketing & Why Is It So Powerful*. Emarsys: https://www. emarsys. com/resources/blog/artificial-intelligence-marketing-solutions/03.05

Varsha, P. S., Akter, S., Kumar, A., Gochhait, S., & Patagundi, B. (2021). The impact of artificial intelligence on branding: A bibliometric analysis (1982-2019). *Journal of Global Information Management*, *29*(4), 221–246. doi:10.4018/JGIM.20210701.oa10

Verma, S., Sharma, R., Deb, S., & Maitra, D. (2021). Artificial intelligence in marketing: Systematic review and future research direction. *International Journal of Information Management Data Insights*, *1*(1), 100002. doi:10.1016/j.jjimei.2020.100002

Vinuesa, R., Azizpour, H., Leite, I., Balaam, M., Dignum, V., Domisch, S., Felländer, A., Langhans, S. D., Tegmark, M., & Fuso Nerini, F. (2020). The role of artificial intelligence in achieving the Sustainable Development Goals. *Nature Communications*, *11*(1), 1–10. doi:10.1038/s41467-019-14108-y PMID:31932590

Von Pape, T., Trepte, S., & Mothes, C. (2017). Privacy by disaster? Press coverage of privacy and digital technology. *European Journal of Communication*, *32*(3), 189–207. doi:10.1177/0267323117689994

Wamba, S. F., Bawack, R. E., Guthrie, C., Queiroz, M. M., & Carillo, K. D. A. (2021). Are we preparing for a good AI society? A bibliometric review and research agenda. *Technological Forecasting and Social Change*, *164*, 120482. doi:10.1016/j.techfore.2020.120482

Wamba-Taguimdje, S. L., Wamba, S. F., Kamdjoug, J. R. K., & Wanko, C. E. T. (2020). Impact of artificial intelligence on firm performance: exploring the mediating effect of process-oriented dynamic capabilities. In Digital Business Transformation: Organizing, Managing and Controlling in the Information Age (pp. 3-18). Springer International Publishing. doi:10.1007/978-3-030-47355-6_1

Wierenga, B. (2010). Marketing and artificial intelligence: Great opportunities, reluctant partners. In *Marketing intelligent systems using soft computing: Managerial and research applications* (pp. 1–8). Springer Berlin Heidelberg. doi:10.1007/978-3-642-15606-9_1

Wirth, N. (2018). Hello marketing, what can artificial intelligence help you with? *International Journal of Market Research*, *60*(5), 435–438. doi:10.1177/1470785318776841

Wu, F., Lu, C., Zhu, M., Chen, H., Zhu, J., Yu, K., Li, L., Li, M., Chen, Q., Li, X., Cao, X., Wang, Z., Zha, Z., Zhuang, Y., & Pan, Y. (2020). Towards a new generation of artificial intelligence in China. *Nature Machine Intelligence*, *2*(6), 312–316. doi:10.1038/s42256-020-0183-4

Wu, G. (2021, March). Research on the development path of logistics management innovation in e-commerce environment. *IOP Conference Series. Earth and Environmental Science*, *714*(4), 042022. doi:10.1088/1755-1315/714/4/042022

Xiao, F., & Ke, J. (2021). Pricing, management and decision-making of financial markets with artificial intelligence: Introduction to the issue. *Financial Innovation, 7*(1), 1–3. doi:10.1186/s40854-021-00302-9 PMID:35024295

Xu, Z., Lv, Z., Li, J., & Shi, A. (2022). A novel approach for predicting water demand with complex patterns based on ensemble learning. *Water Resources Management, 36*(11), 4293–4312. doi:10.1007/s11269-022-03255-5

Xu, Z., Lv, Z., Li, J., Sun, H., & Sheng, Z. (2022). A novel perspective on travel demand prediction considering natural environmental and socioeconomic factors. *IEEE Intelligent Transportation Systems Magazine, 15*(1), 136–159. doi:10.1109/MITS.2022.3162901

Yang, Y., Liu, Y., Lv, X., Ai, J., & Li, Y. (2022). Anthropomorphism and customers' willingness to use artificial intelligence service agents. *Journal of Hospitality Marketing & Management, 31*(1), 1–23. doi:10.1080/19368623.2021.1926037

Yeğin, T. (2020). The place and future of artificial intelligence in marketing strategies. *Ekev Akademi Dergisi,* (81), 489–506.

Yoo, S., Lee, S., Kim, S., Hwang, K. H., Park, J. H., & Kang, N. (2021). Integrating deep learning into CAD/CAE system: Generative design and evaluation of 3D conceptual wheel. *Structural and Multidisciplinary Optimization, 64*(4), 2725–2747. doi:10.1007/s00158-021-02953-9

Zhang, Z., Wang, R., Zheng, W., Lan, S., Liang, D., & Jin, H. (2015, November). Profit maximization analysis based on data mining and the exponential retention model assumption with respect to customer churn problems. In *2015 IEEE International Conference on Data Mining Workshop (ICDMW)* (pp. 1093-1097). IEEE. 10.1109/ICDMW.2015.84

Zhao, H., Lyu, F., & Luo, Y. (2022). Research on the effect of online marketing based on multimodel fusion and artificial intelligence in the context of big data. *Security and Communication Networks, 2022,* 1–9. doi:10.1155/2022/1516543

Zhao, R., & Cai, Y. (2021). Research on online marketing effects based on multi-model fusion and artificial intelligence algorithms. *Journal of Ambient Intelligence and Humanized Computing,* 1–17.

Zhu, Y., Zhou, L., Xie, C., Wang, G. J., & Nguyen, T. V. (2019). Forecasting SMEs' credit risk in supply chain finance with an enhanced hybrid ensemble machine learning approach. *International Journal of Production Economics, 211,* 22–33. doi:10.1016/j.ijpe.2019.01.032

Chapter 4
Examining the Core Factors Influencing Sustainable IoT–Based Interactive Marketing in Smart Urban Tourism Destinations

Mohammad Nematpour
 https://orcid.org/0000-0002-0766-2010
University of Tehran, Iran

Mohammad Ghaffari
University of Tehran, Iran

ABSTRACT

Smart urban tourism destinations with IoT-based devices and applications are the future of world tourism. This study identifies core factors of sustainable IoT-based interactive marketing influencing urban tourism destinations. The study adopts a systematic approach with two sides of the tourism system including supply-side and demand-side. The findings showed that factors including smart tourism ecosystems, new business approach employing multi-sided platforms, intra-organizational participative through network-based model, big data analysis, green marketing campaigns, enhance tourists' environmental knowledge and awareness, and smart CRM were determined as core factors on the use of IoT in sustainable interactive marketing. On demand side, based on the findings, perceived usefulness, perceived ease of use, trust, social influence, cyber-resilience, and perceived privacy have been determined as core indicators on the use of IoT in sustainable smart interactive marketing.

DOI: 10.4018/979-8-3693-1339-8.ch004

1. INTRODUCTION

Technologies, as one of the factors of smart management, play a vital role in the development of smart tourism. The vision of the World Tourism Organization (WTO) is to embrace our world's tourism digital future as sustainable and reliable (Ordóñez et al., 2021). The level of sustainability in smart tourism is one of the core aspects resulting in the growth of the urban tourism destinations. The increased demand for smart tourism in urban communities means that these destinations should adopt rapid technological changes and strategies based on evolving global marketing techniques to be able to employ its sustainable competitive advantages (Shafiee et al., 2022). Internet of Things (IoT) relates to numerous physical objects such as wireless networks and cheap processors which are wirelessly linked to each other and the internet in order to gather and share data. IoT is a technology that could play a critical role in smartening urban tourism destinations (Novera et al., 2022).

Smart urban tourism destinations are aimed to increase competition, enhance the quality of life of local and guest communities, transform tourist's experience and marketing strategies. The IoT as an evolving technology can help Destination Management Organizations (DMOs) and Small and medium-sized tourism enterprises (SMTEs) by employing in developing an integrated marketing management and sustainable competitive identity. Rapid development of smart urban tourism destinations has presented a better opportunity for evolving destinations' marketing under a smart sustainable approach (Shafiee et al., 2022). Nowadays, urban destinations are faced with numerous challenges, especially sustainability (Faraji et al., 2021). Despite the effects of smart technologies on sustainable urban destinations, the employment of smart technologies and devices has not yet been pertinently investigated by scholars (like smart sustainability) and study regarding smart technologies on sustainable smart destination marketing still suffers major conceptual and empirical shortcomings. Sustainable marketing refers to promoting products and services which are socially and environmentally conscious. It aims to be more ethical, responsible, and environmentally conscious activities for marketing and promoting products and services (Nozari et al., 2021).

In this regard, the IoT-based marketing provides new opportunities for the urban tourism destinations by facilitating information access and integrating big data, content marketing, social media and other tools. The interaction of tourists with IoT-based devices and applications would enable to transform the tourist's experience, to produce and exchange knowledge (Wise & Heidari, 2019). The new paradigm of smart marketing known as smart interactive marketing is parallelly in line with IoT-based marketing and involves marketing efforts that are generated by tourists' behavior and preferences. Products and services are directly linked to the internet and report directly the performance and capabilities in a social network. This type of marketing can find solutions to facilitate more application of the resources and improve the stakeholders' quality of life and guest communities' (tourists) sustainability (Shafiee et al., 2022). In this regard, this study aimed to have a sustainable approach in defining and presenting IoT-based interactive marketing for urban tourism destinations. To have a sustainable approach we should have a systematic perspective including the supply to demand side of the tourism system (Nematpour et al., 2022). On one hand, the present study provides valuable insights for DOMs, SMTEs, destination managers and practitioners to provide effective sustainable marketing strategies for smartening urban tourism destinations through IoT-based smartness. On the other hand, the study presents insights from customers' (tourists) perspectives by determining key factors influencing customer acceptance of IoT technology to show how potential tourists perceive IoT products and applications and how the technology accelerates their acceptance?

2. SMART URBAN TOURISM DESTINATION

Smart urban destinations aim to provide an integrated technological infrastructures to create perceived value for tourists, enhance the residents' quality of life, increase destination competitiveness, and support tourism development projects (Sorokina et al., 2022). In recent years, urban tourism destinations have focused on the role of innovation in promoting tourism products and services and have considered new technologies as the main tools of developing marketing activities. In fact, smart urban destinations focus on taking care of the needs of tourists by combining information and communication technology and customer culture. This ultimately increases the quality of tourism products and services at a particular destination and improves the specific process of the marketing management of the destination (Zhang et al., 2022). According to Gelter et al. (2021) a smart tourism destination should contain three components of Internet of Things (IoT), cloud computing services, and end system. In this direction, many researchers have promoted the IoT as a fundamental part of the smart ecosystem in tourism destinations (Wang et al., 2013). Inanimate smart objects i.e. RFID tags (Radio-frequency identification), sensors, and mobiles as IoT devices and features aim to achieve shared goals in a smart tourism ecosystem (Gretzel, 2018). During COVID-19 pandemic the role of smartness in tourism destinations have been noticeably increased and due to this fast-paced emergency the necessity of accessibility for consumers' data for providing appropriate and well-structure services such as positioning and tracking has become a static rule for ecosystems in order to providing a better structure and context for managing the space and services. The COVID-19 pandemic has acted as an impetus that may induce tourism and hospitality to further advance of the use of emerging technologies (Nematpour et al., 2022) and IoT is introduced as one of highlighted technologies in this direction (Nasajpour et al. 2020). With the increase of global changes and transformations towards smartness, DMOs and SMTEs strongly need to employ new technologies in the tourism and hospitality marketing, and many tourist destinations, even in developing countries, are trying to welcome such changes and use these smart technologies (Nematpour et al., 2022). In order to become a smart tourism destination, destinations need to integrate, coordinate, and support tourism products and services with the comprehensive and in-depth use of technology. This smartness includes enhancing the quality of tourist experience, adopting innovative and consistent technologies that facilitate access to tourism and hospitality based services and facilitate faster data sharing, meeting the needs of stakeholders (citizens, tourists, government, DMOs, SMTEs, etc.), reducing the extra usage of environmental resources, developing a sustainable urban society and destination, and enhancing the quality of the travel experience for tourists and local community's quality of life. One of the most important aspects of using IoT-based marketing in tourism destinations is the possibility of personalizing the travel services, based on the data collected from tourists. In particular, IoT creates great opportunities in urban destinations by enabling new applications for customization and personalization of services (Shafiee et al., 2022). The fact that tourists know what they like and what they don't like helps them to get "custom" information. Therefore, it meets their expectations and subsequently turns them into loyal customers. In short, with the support of the IoT, everything will become easier.

3. SUSTAINABLE MARKETING FOR URBAN DESTINATIONS

Destination sustainability refers to the comprehensive goals that include the philosophical approaches, theoretical perspectives, and practical insights for driving positive change in DMOs, SMTEs, and local governmental organizations (Low et al., 2022). The sustainability in urban destinations is continuum process including strategic vision, planning, and implementation that is internally led by insightful strategic management based on external realities for providing solutions, realizing positive outcomes, and sustainable success (Tariq et al., 2022). From a marketing perspective, a sustainable approach calls for holistic, integrated, unbiased, and responsible functions of marketing (Nematpour et al., 2022). Sustainability refers to sustaining a customer centric value and this achieved by process including generating, improving, developing, deploying, and finally sustaining activities (Rainey, 2015). DOMs and SMTEs try to initiate sustainability by building perceived trust and enhancing brand image and reputation, creating integrated marketing and sales systems, and developing smart CRM. These practices have best solutions for preserving the natural environment, improving local and guest communities' quality of life, and ensuring socio-economic stability (Chhabra, 2009). Specifically, sustainability in destination marketing refers to transformation to a high degree of complexity in how marketing managers and practitioners develop and implement marketing strategies, policies, and plans to achieve favorable and stable outcomes (Shafiee et al., 2022). In the light of the emerging importance of an integrated approach of sustainability in urban tourism destinations, and additionally, for viable development of urban tourism destinations, it is therefore vital that smart sustainable marketing strategies should be formulated. Thus, marketing efforts should utilize urban destination resources based on a preordained set of sustainable indicators (Choi & Sirakaya, 2006). In addition to providing new insights for DMOs and SMTEs, a smart sustainable marketing agenda should turn to be all the more vital to address the concerns and needs of destination stakeholders regarding improving destination identity by formulating strategies to increase tourists' visitation and spending. In sum, urban governmental organizations and DMOs should accomplish an integrated sustainable marketing plan to promote environmental, socio-cultural, economic integrity of destination resources and managing demand side of the tourism system. Furthermore, urban destinations should adopt a smart sustainable marketing perspective with retro-branding approaches for commodification of destination resources (attractions and sites) to attract more domestic and international tourists.

In short, for smart sustainable marketing, destination local governments, DMOs and SMTEs need to have a systematic approach to understand current state and future plausible states of complex systems. Systematic approach is a relatively integrated and comprehensive way to identify, analyze, and plan tourism in urban destinations; and the approach can well assess destination actors and components, such as relevant environment, local community, destination's organizations and companies, and tourists (Nematpour et al., 2021). The systematic approach illustrates the nature, reality, and foundation of sustainable marketing in a coherent whole or at different local, regional, national, and global scale and the connection between the actors of the tourism supply side including accommodations, attractions, ancillary services, gastronomy, transportations, local organizations, etc.

4. IoT BASED INTERACTIVE MARKETING TO PROMOTE URBAN TOURISM DESTINATION

Interactive marketing is a modern form of direct marketing which focuses on two-way communications in technological ecosystem. Core feature of interactive marketing mutual communications between companies and companies with its targeted touristic consumers. Interactive marketing refers to serving better experience and long-term communications for touristic consumers with providing personalized features and more engagement. This kind of marketing is pertaining to participatory activities of touristic consumers which interact a user-driven dialogue between touristic consumers and the product and service supplier with providing an instant feedback (Stone & Woodcock 2013). One of the core features of interactive marketing is "the opportunity to go from product interest to product order in a matter of seconds" (Ryan, 2004: 5-8). According to Spiller & Baier (2005), interactive marketing can employ different but modern types of digital based channels and media to serve better experience for potential touristic consumers.

DMOs, SMTEs, and other companies in urban destinations could transform data into beneficial information that can outline tourists' behavior, preferences, and expectations. IoT technologies evolve destination marketing to make a difference and fomented marketing activities to act based on big data (Chintalapati & Pandey, 2022). IoT technologies allow devices and services to be linked with smart phones and sensors in a common network. The network enables the service suppliers to provide value proposals to tourists (users) via the internet and the capability of artificial intelligence to constantly interpret and predict tourists' behavioral intentions, and in addition, the IoT technologies could facilitate the personalization and automation of marketing (Ryan, 2004). The bellow we summarized the benefits of IoT technologies that can employ in interactive marketing:

- Smart tourism ecosystems
- New business approach employing multi-sided platforms
- Intra-organizational participative through network-based model
- Big data analysis
- Green marketing campaigns
- Enhance tourists' environmental knowledge and awareness
- Smart CRM
- Perceived usefulness
- Perceived ease of use
- Perceived trust
- Cyber resilience
- Social influence
- Perceived privacy

5. SUSTAINABLE IoT-BASED MARKETING FOR TOURISM DESTINATIONS

Sustainability is a broad concept and should be realized in sustainable development. Previous studies considered the tourism industry as a system including supply-side and demand-side. In fact, both sides of the tourism system should mutually pay attention to sustainability. From a supply-side perspective, DMOs and SMTEs should have particular concentration on sustainability and be faced by environmental, social, and economic challenges and predicaments which exist in the world communities (Nematpour et al., 2021). On the other hand, from a demand-side perspective, tourists should have sustainable behavior. In this connection, if the potential tourists want sustainable tourism products and services in urban destinations, they should accept sustainable marketing (Nozari et al., 2021). The purpose of sustainable destination marketing (as subset of sustainable development) is to enhance DMOs and SMTEs' productivity and meet the marketing' original goals (economic), and simultaneously to prevent destruction of ecosystems and degradation of environmental resources (Najafi et al., 2022). Sustainable destination marketing develops and promotes tourism products and services that meet tourists' needs and expectations besides required accessibility, quality, affordability, efficiency, and convenience without inciting negative and detrimental unintended environmental consequences (Sharmin et al., 2021). Sustainable destination marketing basically focused on three main dimensions of sustainable development but in other form of concentration; in terms of environmental, the destination marketers aims to decrease waste and hazards (e.g., green consumptions, sustainable packaging, and effective recycling of tourism products, advertising solutions for eco-friendly initiatives, promoting responsible travel behaviors). In terms of social dimensions, DMOs and SMTEs should aim to prioritize social values through CSR (Corporate Social Responsibility) to benefit the destination community by influencing the behavior directly. In addition, sustainable social marketing can encourage potential tourists to learn how to be responsibly participating and engaged in destination and how to have high-quality interaction with promoting and sharing information through social communities. Finally, from an economic perspective, sustainable marketing should support local governments, municipalities, DMOs, and SMTEs' long range planning (mission, goals, policies, strategies, and implementation measures).

Since digital transformation currently influences different types of tourism destinations, they go beyond transforming or updating technologies and destination marketing go to be re-determined and employ digital solutions especially in the era of post-COVID-19 pandemic (Nematpour et al., 2022). Urban tourism destinations are experiencing a digital revolution via technologies such as AI, Blockchains, and IoT which will have massive impacts on the tourism and hospitality industry (Faraji et al., 2021). The IoT relies on the independent communication of physical objects in Internet context which are in the form of interconnected applications, devices, services, or systems (Nguyen & Simkin, 2017). There are mutual flows of implications between marketing and IoT, in this direction, destination marketing may beneficially adopt the IoT and, in turn, the IoT might constructively shape marketing in urban destinations. The IoT applications, devices, and systems has been proclaimed as requisite for destination innovation, adaptation and success, especially for DMOs and SMTEs with high amounts of data, network, and connectivity (Nguyen, & Chen, 2016). However, more studies are necessary to determine the capabilities necessary to employ the IoT in the DMOs and SMTEs and how these are associated with different aspects of destination marketing, particularly by considering changing rules of marketing which are introduced by new technologies like the IoT era. IoT based marketing can evolve and develop DMOs and SMTEs' marketing management in urban destinations by focusing on relationship-oriented organizations which can contribute in CRM, joint ventures, partnerships, and alliances. Due to increasing use of social media, tourists' experiences with the use of tourism products and services have become very vital. The data of tourists' experiences are integrated with the information gathered from tourists' searching behavior, engaging, decision making, and purchasing to predict future intentions and potential behavior of tourists (Tiwari et al., 2023).

In the following subsections we discussed regarding sustainable interactive IoT-based marketing form a systematic view including supply-side and demand-side perspective.

5.1 Supply-Side Core Factors Influencing Sustainable IoT-Based Interactive Marketing

To develop sustainable interactive IoT-based marketing from supply-side perspectives, it is necessary to determine key factors influencing urban destination marketing. These core factors should be considered in decision-making processes and adopting strategies of practitioners, planners, managers, and decision-makers. Supply-side view refers to the all IoT-based marketing activities that are measured by local governments, DMOs, and SMTEs in urban tourism destinations. In this direction, the core factors of sustainable IoT-based interactive marketing from supply-side view separately explained as below:

1. Smart tourism ecosystems: Urban destinations should obviously distinguish the components of a smart tourism system (users, intermediaries, and producers) and their hierarchical relationships. Tourism producers, suppliers or business-concentrated species should connect through smart IoT-based systems and devices by developing new products and services in the destination. Data should be the main source in the smart urban ecosystems which DMOs and SMTEs efficiently and effectively and transformed the ecosystem into an enriched tourism system ensure longevity. It is necessary that the system should be open, and the actors of other ecosystems (medical, insurance, transportation, etc.) being able to use resources or develop beneficial relationships. By establishing the IoT-based smart ecosystem and defining mechanisms to resources integration, the DMOs, SMTEs, and local administrations develop over time both actual and representative social rules and develop value co-creation in order to bring advantages in terms of: environmentally as marketing network involves the development of the whole system; socially as strengthen the relationships between system actors to increase social well-being; and finally economic as suppliers develop innovation to improve tourism products and services (Shafiee et al., 2022).

2. New business approach employing multi-sided platforms: Multi-sided business ecosystems reveals DMOs and SMTEs should adopt IoT-based marketing to understand more effectively regarding the tourism market and to employ IoT technologies in the value chain and smart ecosystem. In this direction, several suppliers can take part in the preparation of tourism and hospitality services via one combined business platform or make a value added in any way, and this leads the platform to develop to a multi-sided one. In other words, several suppliers integrate their value propositions to digital platform customers (OECD, 2020).

3. Intra-organizational participative through network-based model: All of the DMOs and SMTEs in urban tourism destinations should be placed in one or multiple networks in order to cooperate with each other and to create value. Indeed, DMO or SMTE is not big enough to be completely independent. The intra-organizational participative through network-based model can create a consistent and sustainable relationship between destination actors (business partners) to facilitate exchange of the IoT resources (Chen & Chen, 2002). Network-based participative strategy is a process in which dynamic changes of IoT tools are magnified. Therefore, the strategic partnerships and sustainable marketing efforts in urban tourism destinations need to go through long-term processes rather than addressing short-term issues.

4. Big data analysis: The IoT-based interactive marketing provides a wide range of compatible sources of big data regarding time, geographical information, behavioral outputs, speed, demographic characteristics, etc. The availability and accessibility of the big data make the provision for DMOs and SMTEs to develop the general frameworks of predictive behavioral models for their future marketing efforts in testing out new ideas and tools for the target market (Tsourela & Nerantzaki, 2020).

5. Green marketing campaigns: Integrating green marketing and IoT devices and applications can make the touristic customers satisfied with green ways (promotion, distribution, etc.) of visiting the urban destinations. Local administrations, DMOs, should take into account to bring innova-

tive green and sustainable concepts into the entire businesses to develop new markets and fortunes (Najafi et al., 2022).

6. Enhance tourists' environmental knowledge and awareness: DMOs and SMTEs use IoT-based interactive marketing to provide information that influence tourist behavior to be more eco-friendly by visiting a green attraction or purchasing a green service or product. DMOs and SMTEs should focus on presenting an environmentally friendly brand using IoT-based devices and applications to engage in marketing initiatives in order to attract touristic consumers and this leads to improve tourists' awareness by giving enough information regarding the destination's environmental challenges. DMOs and SMTEs should employ IoT-based devices and applications to focus on green communication, such as sustainability reports, eco-labeling, and green designing because these measures can increase tourists' trust in a destinations' environmental commitment (Tiwari et al., 2023).

7. Smart CRM: CRM (customer relationship management) puts the tourists at the center of the business process. DMOs and SMTEs aim to provide a superior and optimal tourist experience regardless of the communication channel they use. The close interaction of devices with intelligent systems creates a new space for offering suggestions, personalized and contextual services and superior support, while continuously innovating products and services in urban destinations (Nozari et al., 2021).

5.2 Demand-Side Core Factors Influencing Sustainable IoT-Based Interactive Marketing

To develop sustainable interactive IoT-based marketing from demand-side perspectives, marketers need to identify influential factors affecting tourists' behavior in urban destination marketing. Marketing practitioners, managers, and decision-makers should consider the factors in decision-making processes and adopting strategies in marketing initiatives. Demand-side view refers to factors manipulating touristic consumers' sustainable behavior which local governments, DMOs, and SMTEs in urban tourism destinations should consider all of them in IoT-based marketing activities. In this direction, the following section explained the core factors as below:

1. Perceived usefulness: According to Davis (1989) Perceived usefulness is defined "as the extent to which a technology is expected to improve a potential user's performance." This factor indicates the degree of usefulness which a touristic user/consumer finds out that employing a specific IoT system, device or application is beneficial and useful. Using IoT devices and technologies while traveling can provide tourists a better understanding and access to beneficial information and save their cost in travel related activities such as information seeking, planning, booking tourism products and services, and (Pradhan et al., 2018). In short, potential tourists should realize that employing IoT devices and applications will improve their performance of on-site activities and make it easier for them (Tripathy et al., 2018).

2. Perceived ease of use: Perceived ease of use refers to the degree to which a tourist believes that employing IoT technologies would be easy without much attempt to carry it, to install it, to start it, to know its usage, to acquire knowledge of its usage. Furthermore, without much effort to access, employ, maintain, pay, and bring to end it (Davis, 1989). Using IoT devices and applications for online reserve or purchase of tourism products and services should not require great mental effort

for potential tourists. The function of using the IoT applications and devices should be simple, clear, and understandable for potential tourists (Hatamifar et al., 2021).

3. Perceived trust: Perceived trust is defined as the tourist mindset to reduce potential risks when they experience through using IoT-based devices and applications (Akroush & Al-Debei, 2015). Perceived trust would be enhanced over time through the interactions and experience. Using IoT-based devices and applications should be reliable, trustworthy, and persuade tourists to use in future behavioral intentions (Yoon et al., 2002).

4. Cyber resilience: Cyber resilience is the "ability to continuously deliver the intended outcome despite adverse cyber events" (Björck, 2015). Tourists with a high level of cyber resilience do not easily lean into negative emotions and challenge or demotivate to employ IoT devices and applications and return back to offline mode of the real world. Thus, potential tourists should be able to adapt themselves to change and cope with stress and pressure concerning IoT technologies.

5. Social influence: Social influence refers to the potential tourist's intention to adopt IoT technologies in urban tourism destinations. It defines the degree of effect from third parties for potential tourists toward IoT devices and applications usage in destination (Tsourela & Nerantzaki, 2020). In the digitally transformed era, the impact of social influence in IoT interactive marketing cannot be neglected. As a result, social influence may be a substantial tool in destination marketing which can shape tourists' opinion regarding IoT devices and applications positively (Chang et al., 2016).

6. Perceived privacy: Perceived privacy is defined as 'an individual's self-assessed state in which external agents have limited access to information about him or her' (Dinev et al. 2013). Perceived safety-security and privacy risks are considered as key concerns that influence the tourists' level of trust in the urban technology, which impacts perceived ease of use, perceived usefulness, attitudes, and future behavioral intention. Lack of privacy and safety leads potential tourists to fear that their personal information might be manipulated or stolen by third parties. In short, tourists are generally deeply concerned about the safety and security of the shared data on IoT-enabled technologies (Tiwari et al., 2023).

6. CONCLUSION

IoT-based technologies help to automatically, intelligently, and collaboratively improve the quality of urban tourist experiences through ongoing data collection and assessing. For smart urban destinations, IoT plays a vital role in the design and smartening of an urban environment. IoT-based devices and applications are designed to link and communicate with each other through network and collected data. Increasing the perceived benefit of employing the IoT-enables marketing in urban destination competitive intelligence among destination managers and practitioners should be deemed as one of the strategic goals of DMOs, SMTEs, and local government by marketers. Because the perceived benefit will enhance tourists' satisfaction and will establish a sustainable and powerful intelligent system. This chapter aimed to provide the latest and most innovative contributions regarding the sustainable IoT-based interactive marketing core factors in smart urban tourism destinations. In line with the digital revolution on a global scale, competitive intelligence is considered as a vital marketing management concept in leading DMOs, SMTEs, and local governments in urban tourism destinations. Developing competitive intelligence empowers DMOs and SMTEs to assess environmental information more accurately, and make valuable knowledge and insights for future marketing directions.

Findings of this chapter are presented as guidelines for smart urban destination actors, more specifically to local governments, DMOs, and SMTEs in the area of IoT with providing a wider knowledge of how IoT could change urban destinations by adopting smart urban planning. Managers and practitioners working in the field of IoT around smart urban destinations should link IoT to smart urban destination discussions automatically. The initiating step for any IoT-based application in urban tourism destination is developing a platform. The platform refers to developing hub technology networks, which can then work as integrated platform for other smart application and devices. One theme should catch more concentration is the sustainability of IoT-based interactive marketing. Sustainability should happen with creating value and smart solutions for IoT oriented ecosystems and touristic consumers in smart urban destinations regarding reducing costs, saved human and environmental resources, and enhanced tourists' experience and well-being of local communities. Managers and practitioners should adopt key efforts and essential parts in preparing IoT-based ecosystem for urban destinations encompassing smart devices, connectivity requirements, back-end systems, solution providers and end touristic consumers. In brief, urban ecosystem consists of key actors that are working together towards developing smart urban tourism destinations.

REFERENCES

Akroush, M. N., & Al-Debei, M. M. (2015). An integrated model of factors affecting consumer attitudes towards online shopping. *Business Process Management Journal*, *21*(6), 1353–1376. doi:10.1108/BPMJ-02-2015-0022

Björck, F., Henkel, M., Stirna, J., & Zdravkovic, J. (2015). Cyber resilience–fundamentals for a definition. In *New Contributions in Information Systems and Technologies* (pp. 311–316). Springer. doi:10.1007/978-3-319-16486-1_31

Chang, I. C., Chou, P. C., Yeh, R. K. J., & Tseng, H. T. (2016). Factors influencing Chinese tourists' intentions to use the Taiwan Medical Travel App. *Telematics and Informatics*, *33*(2), 401–409. doi:10.1016/j.tele.2015.09.007

Chen, H., & Chen, T. J. (2002). Asymmetric strategic alliances: A network view. *Journal of Business Research*, *55*(12), 1007–1013. doi:10.1016/S0148-2963(02)00284-9

Chhabra, D. (2009). Proposing a Sustainable Marketing Framework for Heritage Tourism. *Journal of Sustainable Tourism*, *17*(3), 313–320. doi:10.1080/09669580802495758

Chintalapati, S., & Pandey, S. K. (2022). Artificial intelligence in marketing: A systematic literature review. *International Journal of Market Research*, *64*(1), 38–68. doi:10.1177/14707853211018428

Choi, H., & Sirakaya, E. (2006). Sustainability Indicators for Managing Community Tourism. *Tourism Management*, *27*(6), 1274–1289. doi:10.1016/j.tourman.2005.05.018

Colabi, A. M. (2020). Modeling Factors Affecting the Sustainability of Business model. *Public Management Researches*, *13*(47), 111–134. doi:10.22111/jmr.2020.32518.4901

Davis, F. D. (1989). Perceived usefulness, perceived ease of use, and user acceptance of information technology. *Management Information Systems Quarterly*, *13*(3), 319–340. doi:10.2307/249008

Dinev, T., Xu, H., Smith, J. H., & Hart, P. (2013). Information privacy and correlates: An empirical attempt to bridge and distinguish privacy-related concepts. *European Journal of Information Systems*, *22*(3), 295–316. doi:10.1057/ejis.2012.23

Faraji, A., Khodadadi, M., Nematpour, M., Abidizadegan, S., & Yazdani, H. R. (2021). Investigating the positive role of urban tourism in creating sustainable revenue opportunities in the municipalities of large-scale cities: The case of Iran. *International Journal of Tourism Cities*, *7*(1), 177–199. doi:10.1108/IJTC-04-2020-0076

Gelter, J., Lexhagen, M., & Fuchs, M. (2021). A meta-narrative analysis of smart tourism destinations: Implications for tourism destination management. *Current Issues in Tourism*, *24*(20), 2860–2874. doi:10.1080/13683500.2020.1849048

Gretzel, U. (2018). From smart destinations to smart tourism regions, Investigaciones Regionales. *Journal of Regional Research*, *42*, 171–184. https://investigacionesregionales.org/wp-content/uploads/sites/3/2019/01/10-GRETZEL.pdf

Hatamifar, P., Ghaderi, Z., & Nikjoo, A. (2021). Factors affecting international tourists' intention to use local mobile apps in online purchase. *Asia Pacific Journal of Tourism Research*, *26*(12), 1285–1301. doi:10.1080/10941665.2021.1983626

Low, S., Ullah, F., Shirowzhan, S., Sepasgozar, S. M., & Lin Lee, C. (2020). Smart digital marketing capabilities for sustainable property development: A case of Malaysia. *Sustainability (Basel)*, *12*(13), 5402. doi:10.3390/su12135402

Najafi, S. E., Nozari, H., & Edalatpanah, S. A. (2022). Investigating the Key Parameters Affecting Sustainable IoT-Based Marketing. In *Computational Intelligence Methodologies Applied to Sustainable Development Goals* (pp. 51–61). Springer International Publishing. doi:10.1007/978-3-030-97344-5_4

Nasajpour, M., Pouriyeh, S., Parizi, R. M., Dorodchi, M., Valero, M., & Arabnia, H. R. (2020). Internet of Things for Current COVID-19 and Future Pandemics: An Exploratory Study. *Journal of Healthcare Informatics Research*, *4*(4), 325–364. doi:10.1007/s41666-020-00080-6 PMID:33204938

Nematpour, M., Khodadadi, M., Makian, S., & Ghaffari, M. (2022). Developing a competitive and sustainable model for the future of a destination: Iran's tourism competitiveness. *International Journal of Hospitality & Tourism Administration*, 1–33. doi:10.1080/15256480.2022.2081279

Nematpour, M., Khodadadi, M., & Rezaei, N. (2021). Systematic analysis of development in Iran's tourism market in the form of future Study: A new method of strategic planning. *Futures*, *125*, 102650. doi:10.1016/j.futures.2020.102650

Nguyen, B., & Simkin, L. (2017). The Internet of Things (IoT) and marketing: The state of play, future trends and the implications for marketing. *Journal of Marketing Management*, *33*(1-2), 1–6. doi:10.1080/0267257X.2016.1257542

Novera, C.N., Ahmed, Z., Kushol, R., Wanke, P. and Azad, M.A.K. (2022). Internet of Things (IoT) in smart tourism: a literature review. *Spanish Journal of Marketing - ESIC, 26*(3), 325-344. doi:10.1108/SJME-03-2022-0035

Nozari, H., Szmelter-Jarosz, A., & Ghahremani-Nahr, J. (2021). The Ideas of Sustainable and Green Marketing Based on the Internet of Everything—The Case of the Dairy Industry. *Future Internet, 13*(10), 266. doi:10.3390/fi13100266

OECD. (2020). *OECD Tourism Trends and Policies 2020*. OECD Publishing. doi:10.1787/6b47b985-

Ordóñez, M. D., Gómez, A., Ruiz, M., Ortells, J., Niemi-Hugaerts, H., Juiz, C., Jara, A., & Butler, T. (2021). *IoT Technologies and Applications in Tourism and Travel Industries*. https://www.riverpublishers.com

Pradhan, M. K., Oh, J., & Lee, H. (2018). Understanding travelers' behavior for sustainable smart tourism: A technology readiness perspective. *Sustainability (Basel), 10*(11), 4259. doi:10.3390/su10114259

Rainey, D. L. (2015). A Holistic Model for Linking Sustainability, Sustainable Development, and Strategic Innovation in the Context of Globalization. In *Handbook of Research on Sustainable Development and Economics* (pp. 222–247). IGI Global. doi:10.4018/978-1-4666-8433-1.ch010

Ryan, C. (2004). *High Performance Interactive Marketing*. Viva Books Private Limited.

Shafiee, S., Jahanyan, S., Ghatari, A. R., & Hasanzadeh, A. (2023). Developing sustainable tourism destinations through smart technologies: A system dynamics approach. *Journal of Simulation, 17*(4), 477–498. doi:10.1080/17477778.2022.2030656

Sharmin, F., Sultan, M. T., Badulescu, D., Badulescu, A., Borma, A., & Li, B. (2021). Sustainable destination marketing ecosystem through smartphone-based social media: The consumers' acceptance perspective. *Sustainability (Basel), 13*(4), 2308. doi:10.3390/su13042308

Sorokina, E., Wang, Y., Fyall, A., Lugosi, P., Torres, E., & Jung, T. (2022). Constructing a smart destination framework: A destination marketing organization perspective. *Journal of Destination Marketing & Management, 23*, 100688. doi:10.1016/j.jdmm.2021.100688

Spiller, L., & Baier, M. (2005). *Contemporary Direct & Interactive Marketing*. Pearson Education Inc.

Stone, M. D., & Woodcock, N. D. (2014). Interactive, direct and digital marketing: A future that depends on better use of business intelligence. *Journal of Research in Interactive Marketing, 8*(1), 4–17. doi:10.1108/JRIM-07-2013-0046

Tan, Z., Sadiq, B., Bashir, T., Mahmood, H., & Rasool, Y. (2022). Investigating the impact of green marketing components on purchase intention: The mediating role of brand image and brand trust. *Sustainability (Basel), 14*(10), 5939. doi:10.3390/su14105939

Tariq, B., Taimoor, S., Najam, H., Law, R., Hassan, W., & Han, H. (2020). Generating marketing outcomes through Internet of things (Iot) technologies. *Sustainability (Basel), 12*(22), 9670. doi:10.3390/su12229670

Tiwari, V., Mishra, A., & Tiwari, S. (2023). Role of data safety and perceived privacy for acceptance of IoT-enabled technologies at smart tourism destinations. *Current Issues in Tourism*, 1–16. doi:10.1080/13683500.2023.2247534

Tripathy, A. K., Tripathy, P. K., Ray, N. K., & Mohanty, S. P. (2018). iTour: The future of smart tourism: An IoT framework for the independent mobility of tourists in smart cities. *IEEE Consumer Electronics Magazine*, *7*(3), 32–37. doi:10.1109/MCE.2018.2797758

Tsourela, M., & Nerantzaki, D. M. (2020). An internet of things (Iot) acceptance model. Assessing consumer's behavior toward iot products and applications. *Future Internet*, *12*(11), 191. doi:10.3390/fi12110191

Wang, D., Li, X., & Li, Y. (2013). China's "smart tourism destination" initiative: A taste of the service-dominant logic. *Journal of Destination Marketing & Management*, *2*(2), 59–61. doi:10.1016/j.jdmm.2013.05.004

Yoon, S.-J. (2002). The antecedents and consequences of trust in online-purchase decisions. *Journal of Interactive Marketing*, *16*(2), 47–63. doi:10.1002/dir.10008

Zhang, Y., Sotiriadis, M., & Shen, S. (2022). Investigating the Impact of Smart Tourism Technologies on Tourists' Experiences. *Sustainability*, *14*(5), 30–48. doi:10.3390/su15010030

Chapter 5
Smart Marketing Based on Artificial Intelligence of Things (AIoT) and Blockchain and Evaluating Critical Success Factors

Hamed Nozari
(iD) https://orcid.org/0000-0002-6500-6708
Azad University in the Emirates, UAE

Agnieszka Szmelter-Jarosz
(iD) https://orcid.org/0000-0002-6183-6114
Faculty of Economics, University of Gdańsk, Poland

Maryam Rahmaty
Department of Management, Islamic Azad University, Chalous, Iran

ABSTRACT

The use of IoT and artificial intelligence (AI) technologies and blockchain technology in the marketing field is an emerging topic in the new digitization era. The chapter aims to create a conceptual framework that describes a marketing system's main stages and dimensions based on the artificial intelligence of things (AIoT) and blockchain and evaluates the critical success factors of implementing this marketing system. This research, at first, tried to identify the most important critical success factors in these smart systems by reviewing the literature and opinions of active experts, and in the next step, these indicators were evaluated using decision-making methodology. For this purpose, a fuzzy nonlinear evaluation method has been used to examine the priorities and relationships of success factors. The results show that technology-related success factors, such as the presence of technical infrastructure and technological maturity, play the most important roles in the proper functioning of marketing based on transformational technologies.

DOI: 10.4018/979-8-3693-1339-8.ch005

1. INTRODUCTION

Today the fourth industrial revolution changes the world – operation of organizations and life of people. It affects almost every aspect of life. The most disruptive technologies changing the traditional management paradigms are 3D printing, Internet of Things and blockchain technology (Hopkins, 2021).

With the overgrowth of industries, one of the most important basic requirements of managers to develop and increase profitability is the sale of products in urgent need of marketing. As both vendors and consumers change over time in line with new trends and technologies, marketing science needs to keep up with these changes. The increasing impact of innovative marketing strategies on creating a competitive advantage and business performance has led businesses always to seek to use new digital technologies to improve marketing activities. Artificial intelligence, Internet of Things, and blockchain technologies have led to extensive marketing innovations (Simões et al., 2018).

The growth of the Internet and emerging technologies has significantly impacted the composition of traditional marketing. Traditional marketing has given way to digital marketing. This model of marketing has its details. Each component is briefly defined and together constitutes digital marketing. The Internet of Things is the product of the fourth industrial revolution (Hahn, 2020). This technology creates real-time insights with its ability to connect acquired data and processes with business infrastructure (Lo and Campos, 2018). The IoT is a leading digital transformation technology that combines smart devices with business-to-business analytics and big data analytics (e.g. using Business Intelligence) to provide solutions that have never been possible. All of this stems from the simple idea of using sensors and wearables to monitor processes. The implications of digital marketing are the maintenance and complete tracing and tracking of assets at the top of a customer's broad insights. As a result, technology is shifting business to the personalization of product while greater efficiency (Dwesar and Kashyap, 2022). Understanding the movement of the IoT is crucial for digital marketers who want to stay ahead of the competition in the future. The Internet of Things is constantly evolving in supply chains and product lifecycles. Devices connected to sensors, processors and monitors produce accurate, real-time, reliable data that provides unparalleled insight into the market (Badica et al., 2021).

The presence of artificial intelligence technology alongside the Internet of Things creates things and gives analytical power to data from the Internet of Things. Therefore, learning-based data can be used to discover the characteristics of the open space of customer preferences. Furthermore, since the presence of the Internet and the network can always brings many concerns, such as security and privacy, so with the rise of blockchain, the use of it in the marketing space can instill trust and credibility in the customer without the need for anything else; because all payments, transactions and system activities are regularly recorded and stored in decentralized sources (Nozari et al., 2021).

Therefore, it can be seen that the simultaneous presence of these technologies can enhance the understanding of the market differently. This can increase the ability of marketers to understand the depth of data and pave the way for creating customer value (Mariani et al., 2022).

Considering the above advantages and challenges, this study seeks to establish a marketing system based on artificial intelligence technologies, IoT, and blockchain and design an approach to evaluate the critical factors of project success through the opinions of various experts. For this reason, in this study, a system of hierarchical criteria was identified that includes success factors. At the same time, the flow of literature in various fields such as artificial intelligence, the Internet of Things, and blockchain technology, and their role in modern marketingwas sought to determine the criteria for success. An integrated framework for a marketing system based on these technologies has also been developed.

This study aims to apply multi-criteria decision making (MCDM) approaches using a panoramic view to assist marketing managers in implementing an AIoT and blockchain-based marketing system. The research framework is shown in Figure 1.

The rest of this paper is organized as follows. In section 2, a review of the literature is provided and the relevant factors are identified. The proposed method for ranking the critical success factors is described in Section 3. Section 4 provides data collection and analysis. Finally, Section 5 presents the conclusions of this study and describes future research directions.

Figure 1. Research framework

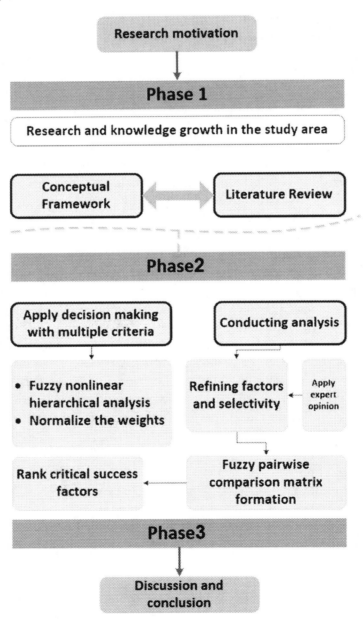

2. LITERATURE REVIEW

2.1 Artificial Intelligence of Things (AIoT)

Today's business world is changing with the advent of the Internet of Things (IoT) and artificial intelligence. The Internet of Things is helping to gather vast amounts of data from several sources. However, collecting large amounts of data and change them to valuable information while they are obtained through the myriad of IoT devices complicates data processing and analysis is a true challenge (Guo et al., 2022). The convergence and synergy effects of artificial intelligence (AI) and the Internet of Things (IoT) can redefine how industries, jobs and the economy work. Artificial intelligence uses the Internet of Things to create intelligent machines that simulate intelligent behavior and support decisions with little or no human intervention (Chen et al., 2022).

While the Internet of Things deals with devices that interact with each other using the Internet, artificial intelligence lets devices learn from their data and experiences. At its core, the IoT is about sensors embedded in machines, which provide data streams over an Internet connection (Dong et al., 2021). All IoT-related services inevitably follow five basic steps: creation, communication, aggregation, analysis, and action. Undeniably, the value of "action" depends on the penultimate analysis. Hence, the exact value of the Internet of Things is determined in the analysis phase. This is where artificial intelligence technology comes into play. Machine learning and artificial intelligence allow to understand and improve the data collected from physical devices. Expert systems in the IoT are used to add more value to the IoT by better understanding and explaining the results obtained from the analysis. When a group of connected devices collects and integrates raw data, software programs with machine intelligence capabilities analyze the data. After a thorough review, the final result contains useful information (Sun et al., 2021), the right information provided at the right time and place, and the right receiver (Barreto et al., 2017).

Artificial intelligence in the IoT breaks down continuous data streams and discovers patterns that cannot be detected by traditional measurement systems based on measuring separately different processes. In addition, machine learning with artificial intelligence can predict operating conditions and identify parameters that must be changed to achieve the desired results(Chiu et al., 2020). As a result, the IoT can indicate which data and processes are redundant and time-consuming and identify tasks that are well-tuned to increase performance. Therefore, combining these two technologiescan increase the analytical value of data and create a more accurate and agile supply chain system (Zhu et al., 2021).

In recent years, numerous studies have been conducted on combining these technologies. Wang et al.(2021) examined customer acceptance in AIoT-based stores. They examined perceived risks and technolog, acceptance models. In their research, Nahr et al.(2021) provided a conceptual framework for a green supply chain based on AIoT technology. This study showed the path of implementing a supply chain with emphasis on transformational technologies. In the other study, Jain et al. (2021) investigated the role of AIoT in countering the COVID-19 epidemic and identified the effects of this technology. Finally, Mamza (2021) discusses the role of AIoT technology in healthcare systems and identifies critical dimensions, components, and indicators influencing the industry.

2.2 Blockchain Technology

Blockchain technology is a topic that is almost in the discourse of most people today. This technology, which has grown steadily over the past decade and is increasingly recognized by more and more people, has a history of more than a decade (Sobb et al., 2020). Blockchain is a type of database gathering data from dispersed data sources. The main difference between blockchain technology and regular databases is how information is stored (Harvey et al., 2018). In the blockchain, the data is first stored in a block and then connected to each other. Once the information is entered, they are moved to a new block. Finally, when the block is filled with data, the new block is connected to the previous block. This will eventually lead to the data being chained to each other in a certain chronological order. Blockchain technology is a structure that stores transaction records, also known as blocks, in several databases known as "chains", in a network connected through peer-to-peer nodes. This memory is commonly referred to as a "ledger".Blockchain technology creates an irreversible timeline to implement data in a decentralized manner (Coita et al., 2019).

Technological readiness is the basis for developing and implementing China Blockchain technology (Hastig & Sodhi, 2020). Types of blockchain networks are divided into at least four categories: public blockchain, private blockchain, consortium blockchain, and hybrid blockchain. A public blockchain network is an unlicensed distributed head office technology that anyone can access, trade, and participate in online validations (Varma et al., 2022). A private blockchain network is a blockchain operating in a restricted environment and requires membership to be licensed and controlled by an organization, group or individual. A consortium blockchain is a type of blockchain that meets the need for both public and private blockchain features. A hybrid blockchain is a combination of two different types. . Although this type of blockchain may look like a consortium blockchain; their nature is fundamentally different. Users on this network can control people's access to data stored in the Chinese blockchain (Yadav et al., 2021). In recent years, numerous studies have been conducted in various fields emphasising blockchain technology. Antoniadis et al. (2020) examined blockchain technology's role in tourism industry's marketing. They explored the potential of this technology in retaining tourists. In the other study, Liu et al. (2019) examined the challenges of using blockchain technology in the marketing of the retail industry. They measured performance on the chain with a scalability discussion to demonstrate the feasibility of the proposed system. Garg et al. (2021) also examined the benefits of using blockchain technology in banking and provided a framework for using this technology in banking. Rabby et al. (2022) examined the composition of customer trust under the influence of blockchain and extracted key indicators. This was very valuable in building the list of KPIs in this very study.

2.3 AIoT and Blockchain-Based Marketing

The world of marketing pays special attention to the evolution of human life because it is possible to choose effective marketing methods according to the information obtained from the customer and identify the needs and finally meet his needs by using this information. The most valuable information in the world of marketing is the information of the audience and the IoT is one of the most important sources of data production of high accuracy and precision(Mohanty and Vyas, 2018).

The ability of companies to obtain useful customer information through the Internet of Things provides them with a significant competitive advantage. In the past, customer data was collected through surveys or customer complaints. These methods are not wrong, but they rely on the customer's desire to provide, and therefore can always question the purity of the data. Connecting smart devices, including smartphones, laptops, TVs, and smart voice assistants to cloud solutions, makes data collection and accuracy more accurate. Smart devices provide more accurate information and therefore can help marketers offer more attractive products and services to customers(Stallone et al., 2021). To avoid security challenges and protect the privacy of the audience, blockchain technology can help with the ability to maintain data records in a decentralized manner. In addition, using artificial intelligence with learning capabilities allows marketers to accurately analyze data collected by the Internet of Things and stored by blockchain. In this case, the depth of data can be analyzed and the customer's specific value for customers(Liu et al., 2021).

By connecting all objects to the Internet through IoT technology, data tracking has become much easier, more realistic and of better quality, allowing marketers to better understand customer behavior and needs. This understanding allows such professionals to quickly change their marketing campaigns and offer more personalized product ads. In this case, multidimensional connections are formed between products, Internet-connected devices, and information received from social platforms and manufacturers, which allows us to move more accurately and quickly to create customer value(Le et al., 2021). Figure 2 provides a framework for an AIoT and blockchain-based marketing system.

Figure 2. AIoT and blockchain-based marketing system

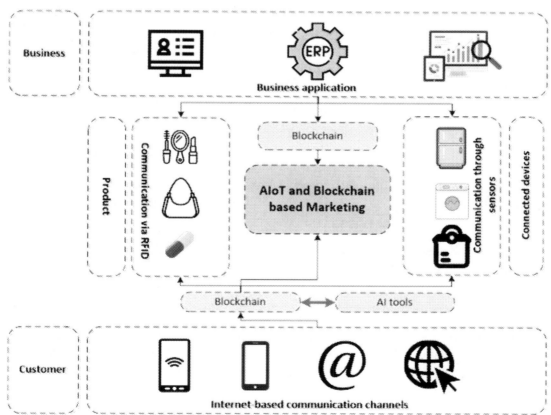

2.4 Criteria and Critical Success Factors

This research can be classified as descriptive survey research regarding data collection method and nature. The required data and information were collected to formulate theoretical foundations of research through library resources and dissertations, books, texts indexed in databases and Internet resources. In order to extract the key factors of success in marketing based on transformational technologies, first by reviewing the articles in scientific databases such as Google Scholar and Scopus, these key indicators were extracted. Then, the experts made these factors available to select the most important criteria and factors with their opinion for the final review. Industrial experts were selected from among managers active in the field of marketing and familiar with the concepts of technology, and academic reporters were selected from among professors who had research backgrounds in the field of study. The additional selection criteria were the experience in marketing (minimally 10 years) and experience as a manager (minimally 3 years). In order to evaluate the opinions of experts, a questionnaire with a 5-level Likert scale was used.

Finally, as shown in Table 1, the key metrics and success factors for successfully implementing an AIoT-based marketing system and blockchain for market management and growth are listed. Codes and literature sources are listed in Table 1 for criteria and success factors.

Table 1. Critical factors for the success of an AIoT and blockchain-based marketing system

Criteria	Code	Success Factors	Code	Reference
Credibility and trust	C_1	Partnership trust	C_{11}	Cao et al. (2021)
		Message validity	C_{12}	Ahmed et al. (2022)
		Privacy	C_{13}	Hasan et al. (2022)
Technological readiness	C_2	Data security	C_{21}	Esposito et al. (2018)
		Technology maturity	C_{22}	Wang et al. (2016)
		Technical infrastructure	C_{23}	Huang et al. (2022)
Target	C_3	Target community	C_{31}	Wu et al. (2021)
		Access to the audience	C_{32}	Schlegel et al. (2018)

As can be seen from Table 1, after identifying the key factors of marketing success based on transformational technologies and the sub-factors of each, a decision hierarchy tree will be created that has three levels. The first level is the goal, which is to prioritize the key factors of marketing success with an emphasis on technology. The second level is the criteria and the third level is the critical factors of success. As can be seen, the factors are categorized with emphasis on three criteria: reliability, technological readiness and marketing target.

3. RESEARCH METHOD

This research with a quantitative approach seeks to investigate the critical factors of marketing success based on AIoT and blockchain technologies for successful and effective implementation. In this study, to investigate the challenges, first by examining the subject literature and opinions of active experts and using the distribution of questionnaires, 8 factors were extracted as the most important factors. Fuzzy hierarchical analysis was used. In this study, firstly Cronbach's alpha method was used to assess the reliability of the relevant questionnaires using SPSS software. The Cronbach's alpha value of all questionnaires was 0.853, which is considered desirable. Considering that in this study, 8 factors have been selected as the most important factors, so for each factor, a separate factor analysis has been performed.

3.1 Mikhailov Nonlinear Fuzzy Ranking Method

In this research, a fuzzy nonlinear hierarchical analysis method, which is represented by the Mikhailov method (Nozari et al. 2022), has been used to prioritize the most critical success factors in marketing based on digital technologies. The steps for using this method are as follows:

1. Drawing the hierarchical structure: shown in Table 1.
2. Formation of fuzzy pairwise comparison matrix: Fuzzy judgment agreement matrices are formed based on experts' opinions. For this reason, fuzzy numbers have been used to express the preferences of experts in this study. Linguistic variables and their fuzzy scale are presented in Table 2.

Table 2. Linguistic variables for pairwise comparisons

Language Variable	Triangular Fuzzy Scale
Very Low	(1,2,3)
Low	(2,3,4)
Medium	(3,4,5)
High	(4,5,6)
Very High	(5,6,7)

3. Modeling and Problem Solving: In this method, fuzzy even comparisons are assumed to be fuzzy triangular numbers. The definite weight vectors $w = (w_1, w_2, \ldots, w_n)$ are extracted in such a way that the priority rate is approximately within the range of the initial fuzzy judgments. In other words, the weights are determined so that relation (1) is established:

$$l_{ij} \leq \frac{w_i}{w_j} \leq u_{ij} \tag{1}$$

Each definite weight vector (w) holds with a degree in the above fuzzy inequalities that can be measured by the linear membership function of Equation (2):

$$\mu_{ij}\left(\frac{w_i}{w_j}\right) = \begin{cases} \dfrac{(w_i / w_j) - l_{ij}}{m_{ij} - l_{ij}} & \dfrac{w_i}{w_j} \leq m_{ij} \\ \dfrac{u_{ij} - (w_i / w_j)}{u_{ij} - m_{ij}} & \dfrac{w_i}{w_j} \leq m_{ij} \end{cases} \tag{2}$$

Given the specific form of membership functions, the fuzzy prioritization problem becomes a non-linear optimization problem in the form of model (3):

max λ
subject to:

$$(m_{ij} - l_{ij})\lambda w_j - w_i + l_{ij}w_j \leq 0$$
$$(u_{ij} - m_{ij})\lambda w_j + w_i - u_{ij}w_j \leq 0$$
$$i = 1, 2, ..., n-1, \quad j = 2, 3, ..., n, \quad j > i \tag{3}$$
$$\sum_{k=1}^{n} w_k = 1 \qquad w_k > 0, \qquad k = 1, 2, ..., n$$

Positive optimal values for the λ index (objective function) indicate that all weight ratios are entirely true in the initial judgment, but if this index is negative, it can be seen that the fuzzy judgments are strongly inconsistent and the weight ratios are almost true in these judgments.

4. RESEARCH FINDINGS

The stages of evaluating and ranking critical success factors in marketing based on transformational technologies in this study are divided into two main parts:

1. Determining the matrix of pairwise comparisons based on the integration of experts' opinions.
2. Using mathematical modeling to rank and obtain the weight of factors in the research model.

In order to evaluate and prioritize the factors extracted in this study, fuzzy questionnaires using language variables were sent to 13 experts in the industry as well as 8 academic experts. 21 questionnaires were completed and received. These pairwise comparison tables are shown in Tables 3 to 6. These tables are used for calculations by the Mikhailov method.

Table 3. Paired comparison matrix for criteria

	C_1			C_2			C_3		
C_1	-	-	-	-	-	-	-	-	-
C_2	2.5	2.7	3.1	-	-	-	-	-	-
C_3	2.1	3.1	4.5	3.1	4.0	5.21	-	-	-

Table 4. Paired comparison matrix for credibility and trust criteria

	C_{11}			C_{12}			C_{13}		
C_{11}	-	-	-	-	-	-	-	-	-
C_{12}	2.25	4.2	5.1	-	-	-	-	-	-
C_{13}	2.12	2.8	4.95	1.98	3.1	4.5	-	-	-

Table 5. Paired comparison matrix for technological readiness criteria

	C_{21}			C_{22}			C_{23}		
C_{21}	-	-	-	-	-	-	-	-	-
C_{22}	1.25	3.75	4.2	-	-	-	-	-	-
C_{23}	2.5	3.1	5.21	2.4	3.25	4.96	-	-	-

Table 6. Paired comparison matrix for target criteria

	C_{31}			C_{32}		
C_{31}	-	-	-	-	-	-
C_{32}	2.11	3.25	5.11	-	-	-

By placing the data from Tables 3 to 6 in the nonlinear model (3) as a model providing weights and rankings based on hierarchical analysis and model equation, the weight and rank of each criterion as well as critical success factors can be obtained. Brought. The computational results related to solving the nonlinear model are shown in Tables 7 to 10.

Table 7. Weight and ranking of criteria

Criterion	Code	Weight	Rank	Objective Function(λ)
Credibility and trust	C_1	0.345241	2	
Technological readiness	C_2	0.453564	1	0.521
Target	C_3	0.206221	3	

Table 8. Weight and ranking of credibility and trust factors

Key Success Factor	code	Weight	Rank	Objective Function(λ)
Partnership trust	C_{11}	0.337421	2	
Message validity	C_{12}	0.240032	3	0.374
Privacy	C_{13}	0.423211	1	

Table 9. Weight and ranking of technological readiness factors

Key Success Factor	Code	Weight	Rank	Objective Function(λ)
Data security	C_{21}	0.183214	3	
Technology maturity	C_{22}	0.330032	2	0.454
Technical infrastructure	C_{23}	0.492145	1	

Table 10. Weight and ranking of target factors

Key Success Factor	Code	Weight	Rank	Objective Function(λ)
Target community	C_{31}	0.442104	2	
Access to the audience	C_{32}	0.550147	1	0.514

As can be seen in Tables 7 to 10, a positive value for the compatibility index indicates the acceptable compatibility of the matrices. Also, it was possible to get their overall ranking. The normalized computational results are shown in Table 11.

Table 11. Normal weight and rank of critical success factors in AIoT and blockchain-based marketing

Criterion	Weight	Key Success Factor	Weight	Normalized Weight	Rank
Credibility and trust	0.345241	Partnership trust	0.337421	0.1164	4
		Message validity	0.240032	0.0828	8
		Privacy	0.423211	0.1461	3
Technological readiness	0.453564	Data security	0.183214	0.0830	7
		Technology maturity	0.330032	0.1496	2
		Technical infrastructure	0.492145	0.2232	1
Target	0.206221	Target community	0.442104	0.0911	6
		Access to the audience	0.550147	0.1134	5

As can be seen in Figure 3 and Table 11, technical infrastructure and technology maturity are the most important critical factors for success in implementing a smart marketing system in the new digital era.

5. CONCLUSION AND SUGGESTIONS

Competitive pressures in today's world on firms, has caused them to understand the importance of knowledge in competitive areas and try to use it to achieve their competitive goals. Such a phenomenon has led to the emergence of a new concept called intelligent marketing, meaning the combination of machine-learning – based and Internet-based technologies. It aims to collect and use this data about

Figure 3. Rank of critical success factors in implementing an AIoT and blockchain-based marketing system

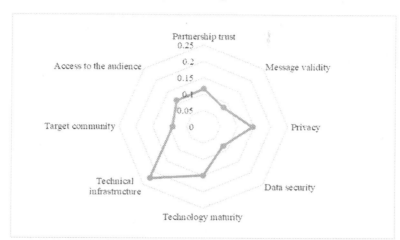

competitive areas by processing information on time meaning so soon to be able to respond to the market requirements and changes efficiently. Customer data is traditionally collected and interpreted through marketing research and management information systems. Nevertheless, in the present digital era, relying on new technologies, access to data can be taken out of the monopoly of individuals and in addition to producing high-volume data, the accuracy of the data can also be increased. IoT technology is one of the most important sources of big data production and with its online connectivity and data capture can increase the amount of quality data received. Combining this technology with artificial intelligence technology has led to the creation of AIoT technology and increases the analytical power of data, and keeping records of this analytical data with emphasis on blockchain technology can increase the security and transparency of analytical output. Therefore, the combined use of IoT, artificial intelligence and blockchain technologies can provide a valuable solution for attracting, maintaining and analyzing customer data that can be used to understand customers' real needs and thus propose the tailored products (goods or services or both). Given the above, our study aims to investigate and evaluate the critical success factors in an AIoT and blockchain-based marketing system. Therefore, the most important factors were extracted after introducing a conceptual framework for the system using the literature review and receiving the opinions of industrial and academic experts. Fuzzy and nonlinear measurements should be used to prioritize these factors. The ranking results show that technical infrastructure and technology maturity are the most critical success factors in a marketing system based on intelligent technology. Therefore, to succeed in implementing this system. Smart marketing should place special emphasis on these factors.

Despite the valuable results this study has for managers, it should be noted that it also faces limitations. The basic limitation of this research is that the decision-making method used, which is based on fuzzy hierarchical analysis, integrates the opinions of experts in many fields. So there are limitations to generalization – it is not possible - although experts came from academia and industry, not all disciplines were represented. People may have different preferences for research in technology fields such as artificial intelligence, IoT, and blockchain. However, the results provide insight in the studied topic, show that some factors are more important than others and add some new input to the literature. Future research should therefore confirm through empirical studies whether these can serve as practical guidance in integrating marketing and smart technologies such as AIoT and blockchain.

REFERENCES

Ahmed, W., Wu, D., & Mukathie, D. (2022). Blockchain-Assisted Trust Management Scheme for Securing VANETs. *KSII Transactions on Internet and Information Systems, 16*(2), 609–631.

Antoniadis, I., Spinthiropoulos, K., & Kontsas, S. (2020). Blockchain applications in tourism and tourism marketing: A short review. *Strategic innovative marketing and tourism*, 375-384.

Barreto, L., Amaral, A., & Pereira, T. (2017). Industry 4.0 implications in logistics: An overview. *Procedia Manufacturing, 13*, 1245–1252. Advance online publication. doi:10.1016/j.promfg.2017.09.045

Cao, S., Powell, W., Foth, M., Natanelov, V., Miller, T., & Dulleck, U. (2021). Strengthening consumer trust in beef supply chain traceability with a blockchain-based human-machine reconcile mechanism. *Computers and Electronics in Agriculture, 180*, 105886. doi:10.1016/j.compag.2020.105886

Chen, S. W., Gu, X. W., Wang, J. J., & Zhu, H. S. (2021). AIoT Used for COVID-19 Pandemic Prevention and Control. *Contrast Media & Molecular Imaging, 2021*. doi:10.1155/2021/3257035 PMID:34729056

Chiu, T. C., Shih, Y. Y., Pang, A. C., Wang, C. S., Weng, W., & Chou, C. T. (2020). Semisupervised distributed learning with non-IID data for AIoT service platform. *IEEE Internet of Things Journal, 7*(10), 9266–9277. doi:10.1109/JIOT.2020.2995162

Coita, D. C., Abrudan, M. M., & Matei, M. C. (2019). Effects of the blockchain technology on human resources and marketing: an exploratory study. In *Strategic Innovative Marketing and Tourism* (pp. 683–691). Springer. doi:10.1007/978-3-030-12453-3_79

Dong, B., Shi, Q., Yang, Y., Wen, F., Zhang, Z., & Lee, C. (2021). Technology evolution from self-powered sensors to AIoT enabled smart homes. *Nano Energy, 79*, 105414. doi:10.1016/j.nanoen.2020.105414

Dwesar, R., & Kashyap, R. (2022). IOT in Marketing: Current Applications and Future Opportunities. In *Internet of Things and Its Applications* (pp. 539–553). Springer. doi:10.1007/978-3-030-77528-5_29

Esposito, C., De Santis, A., Tortora, G., Chang, H., & Choo, K. K. R. (2018). Blockchain: A panacea for healthcare cloud-based data security and privacy? *IEEE Cloud Computing, 5*(1), 31–37. doi:10.1109/MCC.2018.011791712

Garg, P., Gupta, B., Chauhan, A. K., Sivarajah, U., Gupta, S., & Modgil, S. (2021). Measuring the perceived benefits of implementing blockchain technology in the banking sector. *Technological Forecasting and Social Change, 163*, 120407. doi:10.1016/j.techfore.2020.120407

Guo, T., Yu, K., Aloqaily, M., & Wan, S. (2022). Constructing a prior-dependent graph for data clustering and dimension reduction in the edge of AIoT. *Future Generation Computer Systems, 128*, 381–394. doi:10.1016/j.future.2021.09.044

Hahn, G. J. (2020). Industry 4.0: A supply chain innovation perspective. *International Journal of Production Research, 58*(5), 1425–1441. doi:10.1080/00207543.2019.1641642

HarveyC. R.MoormanC.ToledoM. (2018). How blockchain will change marketing as we know it. *Available at* SSRN 3257511. doi:10.2139/ssrn.3257511

Hasan, O., Brunie, L., & Bertino, E. (2022). Privacy-Preserving Reputation Systems Based on Blockchain and Other Cryptographic Building Blocks: A Survey. *ACM Computing Surveys*, *55*(2), 1–37. doi:10.1145/3490236

Hastig, G. M., & Sodhi, M. S. (2020). Blockchain for supply chain traceability: Business requirements and critical success factors. *Production and Operations Management*, *29*(4), 935–954. doi:10.1111/poms.13147

Hopkins, J. L. (2021). An investigation into emerging industry 4.0 technologies as drivers of supply chain innovation in Australia. *Computers in Industry*, *125*, 103323. doi:10.1016/j.compind.2020.103323

Huang, L., Zhen, L., Wang, J., & Zhang, X. (2022). Blockchain implementation for circular supply chain management: Evaluating critical success factors. *Industrial Marketing Management*, *102*, 451–464. doi:10.1016/j.indmarman.2022.02.009

Jain, A., Kushwah, R., Swaroop, A., & Yadav, A. (2021). Role of Artificial Intelligence of Things (AIoT) to Combat Pandemic COVID-19. In Handbook of Research on Innovations and Applications of AI, IoT, and Cognitive Technologies (pp. 117-128). IGI Global.

Le, D., Nguyen, T. M., Quach, S., Thaichon, P., & Ratten, V. (2021). The Development and Current Trends of Digital Marketing and Relationship Marketing Research. In *Developing Digital Marketing*. Emerald Publishing Limited. doi:10.1108/978-1-80071-348-220211001

Liu, D., Alahmadi, A., Ni, J., Lin, X., & Shen, X. (2019). Anonymous reputation system for IIoT-enabled retail marketing atop PoS blockchain. *IEEE Transactions on Industrial Informatics*, *15*(6), 3527–3537. doi:10.1109/TII.2019.2898900

Liu, Y., Tang, Z., Chandu, T., & Joghee, S. (2021). Risk Handling and Vulnerability Assessment in IoT-Enabled Marketing Domain of Digital Business System. *Arabian Journal for Science and Engineering*, 1–13.

Lo, F. Y., & Campos, N. (2018). Blending Internet-of-Things (IoT) solutions into relationship marketing strategies. *Technological Forecasting and Social Change*, *137*, 10–18. doi:10.1016/j.techfore.2018.09.029

Mamza, E. S. (2021). Use of AIOT in Health System. *International Journal of Sustainable Development in Computing Science*, *3*(4), 21–30.

Mariani, M. M., Perez-Vega, R., & Wirtz, J. (2022). AI in marketing, consumer research and psychology: A systematic literature review and research agenda. *Psychology and Marketing*, *39*(4), 755–776. doi:10.1002/mar.21619

Mohanty, S., & Vyas, S. (2018). Decentralized autonomous organizations= blockchain+ AI+ IoT. In *How to Compete in the Age of Artificial Intelligence* (pp. 189–206). Apress. doi:10.1007/978-1-4842-3808-0_9

Nahr, J. G., Nozari, H., & Sadeghi, M. E. (2021). Green supply chain based on artificial intelligence of things (AIoT). *International Journal of Innovation in Management. Economics and Social Sciences*, *1*(2), 56–63.

Nozari, H., Ghahremani-Nahr, J., Fallah, M., & Szmelter-Jarosz, A. (2022). Assessment of cyber risks in an IoT-based supply chain using a fuzzy decision-making method. *International Journal of Innovation in Management, Economics and Social Sciences, 2*(1).

Nozari, H., Szmelter-Jarosz, A., & Ghahremani-Nahr, J. (2021). The Ideas of Sustainable and Green Marketing Based on the Internet of Everything—The Case of the Dairy Industry. *Future Internet, 13*(10), 266. doi:10.3390/fi13100266

Rabby, F., Chimhundu, R., & Hassan, R. (2022). Blockchain technology transforms digital marketing by growing consumer trust. *Transformations Through Blockchain Technology*, 265-289.

Schlegel, M., Zavolokina, L., & Schwabe, G. (2018, January). Blockchain technologies from the consumers' perspective: What is there and why should who care? *Proceedings of the 51st Hawaii international conference on system sciences.* 10.24251/HICSS.2018.441

Simões, D., Barbosa, B., & Filipe, S. (Eds.). (2018). *Smart marketing with the Internet of Things.* IGI Global.

Sobb, T., Turnbull, B., & Moustafa, N. (2020). Supply chain 4.0: A survey of cyber security challenges, solutions and future directions. *Electronics (Basel), 9*(11), 1–31. doi:10.3390/electronics9111864

Stallone, V., Wetzels, M., & Klaas, M. (2021). Applications of Blockchain Technology in marketing systematic review of marketing technology companies. *Blockchain: Research and Applications*, 100023.

Sun, Z., Zhu, M., Zhang, Z., Chen, Z., Shi, Q., Shan, X., Yeow, R. C. H., & Lee, C. (2021). Artificial Intelligence of Things (AIoT) Enabled Virtual Shop Applications Using Self-Powered Sensor Enhanced Soft Robotic Manipulator. *Advancement of Science, 8*(14), 2100230. doi:10.1002/advs.202100230 PMID:34037331

Varma, P., Nijjer, S., Kaur, B., & Sharma, S. (2022). Blockchain for transformation in digital marketing. In *Handbook of Research on the Platform Economy and the Evolution of E-Commerce* (pp. 274–298). IGI Global.

Wang, H., Chen, K., & Xu, D. (2016). A maturity model for blockchain adoption. *Financial Innovation, 2*(1), 1–5. doi:10.1186/s40854-016-0031-z

Wang, I., Liao, C. W., Lin, K. P., Wang, C. H., & Tsai, C. L. (2021). Evaluate the Consumer Acceptance of AIoT-Based Unmanned Convenience Stores Based on Perceived Risks and Technological Acceptance Models. *Mathematical Problems in Engineering, 2021*, 2021. doi:10.1155/2021/4416270

Wu, S. X., Wu, Z., Chen, S., Li, G., & Zhang, S. (2021). Community detection in blockchain social networks. *Journal of Communications and Information Networks, 6*(1), 59–71. doi:10.23919/JCIN.2021.9387705

Yadav, J., Misra, M., & Goundar, S. (2021). Autonomous agriculture marketing information system through blockchain: a case study of e-NAM adoption in India. In Blockchain Technologies, Applications and Cryptocurrencies: Current Practice and Future Trends (pp. 115-138). Academic Press.

Zhu, H., Tiwari, P., Ghoneim, A., & Hossain, M. S. (2021). A collaborative ai-enabled pretrained language model for aiot domain question answering. *IEEE Transactions on Industrial Informatics.*

Chapter 6
Business Involvements in Promotion of Sustainable Marketing:
Strategies and Initiatives

Pratap Chandra Mandal

Indian Institute of Management, Shillong, India

ABSTRACT

Companies should ensure environmental sustainability and promote sustainable marketing in their business actions. The objective of the study is to analyze environmental sustainability and sustainable marketing and business actions in the promotion of sustainable marketing. The methodology adopted is a conceptual analysis of environmental sustainability, sustainable marketing, and business actions towards promotion of sustainable marketing. Various sustainable marketing principles including consumer-oriented marketing, customer value marketing, innovative marketing, sense-of-mission marketing, and societal marketing are discussed. Companies have roles and responsibilities towards promotion of sustainable marketing. They adopt different initiatives and strategies for promotion of sustainable marketing. The discussions will help academicians and practicing managers understand their roles and responsibilities towards environmental sustainability and sustainable marketing. Companies may incorporate sustainable marketing in their processes to achieve business excellence in the long run.

1. INTRODUCTION

Businesses should be responsible towards customers and the society at large (Zaman, Jain, Samara, & Jamali, 2022). Businesses should meet the needs of customers and the society – now and in the future – through socially and environmentally responsible marketing actions (Kashif & Udunuwara, 2022). Companies themselves can benefit from proactively pursuing sustainable marketing practices that bring value to not only individual customers but also to the society at large (Khandai, Mathew, Yadav, Kataria,

DOI: 10.4018/979-8-3693-1339-8.ch006

& Kohli, 2022). Companies should realize that sustainable marketing actions are more than just the right thing to do. Sustainable marketing actions are also good for business (Calvo-Porral, 2021).

Sustainable marketing calls for socially and environmentally responsible actions that meet the present needs of customers and businesses while also preserving or enhancing the ability of future generations to meet their needs (Au-Yong-Oliveira & Sousa, 2022). Companies and businesses should not be confined to generating revenues and profits for themselves. Companies and businesses should understand and internalize the importance of environmental sustainability. They should have the broader objective of sustainability in mind in all their business actions and when they develop strategies and adopt initiatives (Soliman, 2021). Now-a-days, many companies understand the necessity of sustainability and aim to incorporate sustainability in all their business actions (Al-Shaer & Hussainey, 2022). Companies adopt sustainable marketing, practice sustainable marketing principles, and do promotion of sustainable marketing. There are also consumer and grassroot organizations that exist to keep businesses in line.

The importance of environmental sustainability and the responsibilities of companies and businesses working for a sustainable environment cannot be overemphasized. Initially, companies and businesses were not serious about environmental sustainability and sustainable marketing. Businesses even opposed the idea of social and sustainable marketing. Consumer and environmental activists criticized the various activities of businesses. However, companies were of the opinion that such criticisms were either unfair or unimportant (Yılmaz & Baybars, 2022). At present, companies realize the importance of environmental sustainability. They understand and realize the importance of creating and maintaining a sustainable environment. They understand the consumer rights related to environmental sustainability and sustainable marketing. They embrace the new consumer rights, at least in principle (Zaman, 2021).

From the discussions, it is evident that companies and businesses should have a focus on environmental sustainability. They should aim to create and maintain a sustainable environment. Companies and businesses have started realizing their roles and responsibilities towards creating and maintaining a sustainable environment. However, the realization is in a nascent stage. Although the topics of environmental sustainability and sustainable marketing are important, there are few studies which address the issue. The study aims to address this research gap.

The objective of the study is to investigate and to analyze the roles and responsibilities of companies and businesses towards creating and maintaining environmental sustainability. The study deals with the involvements of businesses and companies in promotion of sustainable marketing. The study also focuses on the various business actions towards promotion of sustainable marketing.

The methodology adopted is a conceptual analysis of the various aspects of environmental sustainability, sustainable marketing and its promotion, and the roles and responsibilities of companies and businesses. Research studies from reputed academic journals are referred to for understanding the various aspects. Primary data is not collected and empirical analysis is not done.

The novelty and the contributions of the study lie in the fact that an in-depth discussion about environmental sustainability, sustainable marketing, and business actions towards promotion of sustainable marketing is done. The study focuses on the roles and responsibilities of companies and businesses towards promotion of sustainable marketing. It also highlights the initiatives and strategies adopted by companies for promotion of sustainable marketing. Both academicians and practitioners may benefit from the discussions. Academicians may study and analyze the various aspects of environmental sustainability and sustainable marketing and the roles and responsibilities of companies and businesses in ensuring environmental sustainability and in promoting sustainable marketing. They may suggest better measures and initiatives. Practicing managers may analyze the various strategies and initiatives adopted in their organizations. They may suggest strategies and initiatives which are more effective in ensuring environmental sustainability and in promotion of sustainable marketing.

The study is structured as follows.

The connections between business actions and sustainable marketing are highlighted in section 2. Various sustainable marketing principles including consumer-oriented marketing, customer value marketing, innovative marketing, sense-of-mission marketing, and societal marketing are highlighted in section 3 and its sub-sections. Companies have responsibilities towards promotion of sustainable marketing and this aspect is discussed in section 4. The initiatives and strategies adopted by companies for promotion of sustainable marketing are discussed in section 5 with sub-sections 5.1, 5.2, and 5.3 highlighting the initiatives adopted by McDonald's, CVS Health, and Method respectively. The salient points of the study are discussed in section 6 with sub-sections 6.1 and 6.2 highlighting the theoretical implications and the managerial implications of the study respectively. Section 7 concludes the study with sub-sections 7.1 and 7.2 highlighting the limitations of the study and the avenues of future research respectively.

2. BUSINESS ACTIONS AND SUSTAINABLE MARKETING

Many companies opposed consumerism, environmentalism, and other elements of sustainable marketing in the beginning (Yılmaz & Baybars, 2022). They thought that the criticisms were either unfair or unimportant. However, companies and businesses have started realizing the importance of sustainability and have started embracing sustainability principles (Zaman, 2021). They abide by sustainability principles to create immediate and future customer value and to strengthen customer relationships (Lukin, Krajnović, & Bosna, 2022). Marketers themselves must take responsibility for sustainable marketing.

Companies follow a number of concepts. These include marketing concept, societal marketing concept, strategic planning concept, and sustainable marketing concept (Peterson, 2021). The marketing concept recognizes that organizations thrive by determining the current needs and wants of target customers and fulfilling them more effectively and efficiently than competitors do (Bešić, 2019). Companies focus on meeting short-term sales, growth, and profits. They engage with customers and give them what they want now. However, satisfying the present needs and preferences of customers may not always serve the future best interests of either customers or the business (Hanifah & Ismawati, 2022).

Societal marketing considers the requirements of customers and of the society (Milman, 2022). Strategic planning concept considers future needs of the company (Teixeira & Junior, 2019). Sustainable marketing concept considers the requirements of the society, customers, and of the company (Sheth & Parvatiyar, 2021). Sustainable marketing calls for socially and environmentally responsible actions that meet both the immediate and future needs of customers and the company (Sheth & Parvatiyar, 2021).

Companies should have an effective marketing system in which consumers, companies, public policy makers, and others work together to ensure socially and environmentally responsible marketing actions (Sheth & Parvatiyar, 2021). However, the marketing system does not always work smoothly. Along with businesses, legislators and government agencies also adopt steps to promote sustainable marketing. Enlightened companies adopt a number of steps to carry out socially responsible and ethical marketing that creates sustainable value for both individual customers and the society as a whole.

3. SUSTAINABLE MARKETING PRINCIPLES

Companies and businesses should support the best long-run performance of the marketing system (Peterson, 2021). Sustainable marketing is guided by five sustainable marketing principles which include consumer-oriented marketing, customer value marketing, innovative marketing, sense-of-mission marketing, and societal marketing.

3.1 Consumer-Oriented Marketing

Companies should understand their customers and should view and organize their marketing activities from the viewpoints of consumers (Ramazonovma, 2022). Companies should strive hard to sense, serve, and satisfy the requirements and preferences of a defined group of customers – both now and in the future. Enlightened marketing companies possess a passion for delivering superior value to carefully chosen customers (Hohenberg & Taylor, 2022). Companies need to understand customers well so that they can build sustainable and profitable customer relationships.

3.2 Customer Value Marketing

Companies should create value for their customers. They should invest their resources in customer value-building marketing investments (Rroy, Gulati, Sagi, & Gowda, 2022). Marketers do a number of activities to raise sales in the short run. These activities include one-shot sales promotions, cosmetic product changes, and direct-response advertising. However, in the long run, customer value is added with actual improvements in the product's quality, features, or convenience (Owolabi & Okegbade, 2015). Enlightened marketing calls for building long-term consumer engagement, loyalty, and relationships by continually improving the value which customers receive from the firm's market offering (Muninger, Mahr, & Hammedi, 2022). Companies receive value in return from customers when customers perceive to receive value from companies.

3.3 Innovative Marketing

Companies should do continual improvements in their offerings. Companies which do not focus on innovation ultimately lose customers to competitors which focus on innovation (Malik & Aggarwal, 2022).

Innovative marketers incorporate substantial innovation in all their activities to create value for their customers (Su, Fang, Kim, & Park, 2022). For example, online shoppers desire fast and dependable delivery of products. Amazon understood the importance of superior product delivery for online shoppers. It delighted customers by being the first to innovate with free shipping on orders over $50 (Ağlargöz, 2021). Amazon also launched Amazon Prime by which customers could receive their packages within only two days for no extra charge or in one day for a small additional free (Baranidharan, Yuvarani, Sthapit, & Thiyagarajan Sr., 2020). Still further, Amazon introduced Amazon Prime Now which offers super-fast delivery on the same day. In cases of emergency, it even offered delivery within one hour on tens of thousands of items in major metropolitan areas (Ağlargöz, 2021). Amazon invests heavily in order to shorten delivery times. It invests in research on drones, driverless vehicles, and robots. Amazon has a seemingly endless list of other innovations over the years. These include *Recommendations for You*, *Customer Reviews*, *1-Click Ordering features*, *Amazon Marketplace*, *Kindle e-readers*, and *Amazon*

Cloud services (Gburova & Fedorko, 2018). All these initiatives and innovations have helped Amazon to enhance the shopping experience for customers and to dominate online retailing.

3.4 Sense-of-Mission Marketing

Sense-of-mission marketing suggests that companies should define its mission in broad social terms rather than in narrow product terms (Attia, 2018). Employees feel that they are helping a social cause when companies have a social mission. Employees feel better about their work and have a clearer sense of direction. Brands are able to serve the long-run interests of both the brand and the consumers when they are linked with broader missions (Attia, 2018).

Pedigree is known for making good dog food (Lerch, 2020). However, the brand is about much more. At the core, the brand is about loving and caring for dogs. "Dogs bring out the good in us. Pedigree brings out the good in us. Pedigree brings out the good in them. Feed the good," says Pedigree. "The lovable innocence found in every dog helps us reconnect with our true selves and teaches us valuable life lessons. Simply put, dogs make us better people. And that has a profound impact on the world in which we live" (Lerch, 2020). Pedigree strives hard to support its sweeping brand philosophy. The philosophy goes beyond making nutritious dog food. Pedigree puts in substantial effort in supporting dogs in need. Pedigree introduced its *"You buy. We give."* Program to take care of shelter dogs. The brand donates healthy meals to shelter dogs (Lerch, 2020). The company created the Pedigree Foundation to fulfill its brand promise. The foundation has raised millions of dollars for helping *shelter dogs* find homes (Lerch, 2020). Sense-of-mission marketing has helped Pedigree to become the number one dog food brand in the world (Lerch, 2020).

Companies define their corporate missions in broad societal terms. For example, shoemaker TOMS has introduced its *buy-one-give-one* model. Under this model, TOMS seeks both profits and to make the world a better place (Voegtlin, Scherer, Stahl, & Hawn, 2022). TOMS aims at *doing good* and *doing well* at the same time. On the other hand, TOMS needs to earn revenue to achieve its social-change mission (Ali, Balta, & Papadopoulos, 2022). The initiatives of the company and its social mission provide the customers with a powerful reason to buy.

The *double bottom line* of values and profits is difficult for companies to maintain. Over the years, brands such as Ben & Jerry's, Timberland, The Body Shop, and Burt's Bees – all known and respected for putting *principles before profits* – have at times struggled with less-than-stellar financial returns (Armstrong & Grobbelaar, 2022). In recent years, a new generation of social entrepreneurs has emerged. They believe that to *do good*, they must first *do well* in terms of profitable business operations.

All businesses should be socially responsible. Social responsibility is not the responsibility of only small and socially conscious entrepreneurs. Many large and established companies and brands – from Walmart and Nike to Starbucks, Coca-Cola, and CVS Health – have adopted substantial social and environmental responsibility missions (Fowler, 2017). Companies should develop social missions which are driven by purpose. Purpose-driven social missions help companies to achieve the objectives of generating revenues and profits. For example, CVS is able to become the largest healthcare company in the United States because of its sense-of-mission marketing. CVS also focuses on doing what is right for customers (Fitzsimmons, Qin, & Heffron, 2022).

3.5 Societal Marketing

Societal marketing suggests that companies should make marketing decisions after considering and evaluating consumers' wants, the company's requirements, long-run interests of consumers, and long-run interests of the society (Kurniawan, 2022). Companies should be aware about customer requirements and preferences and the long-run interests of the society. Enlightened companies consider societal problems and issues as opportunities.

Sustainable marketing calls for products that are not only pleasing but also beneficial (Frempong, Mu, Adu-Yeboah, Hossin, & Amoako, 2022). Products are classified based on the degree of immediate customer satisfaction provided and the benefits in the long run perceived to be received by customers. The products are classified as deficient products, pleasing products, salutary products, and desirable products.

Deficient products are those products which have neither immediate appeal nor benefits in the long run. Bad-tasting and ineffective medicine is an example of deficient product (Blythe & Martin, 2019). Pleasing products are those products which give high immediate satisfaction but may hurt customers in the long run. Examples of pleasing products include cigarettes and junk food (Blythe & Martin, 2019). Salutary products are those products which do not have immediate appeal but may benefit customers in the long run. Examples of salutary products include some insurance products and bicycle helmets (Mohamed, 2013). Desirable products are those products which give both high and immediate satisfaction and high benefits in the long run. Examples of desirable products include a tasty and nutritious breakfast food (Sheth & Parvatiyar, 2021).

The discussions indicate that companies should try to convert all of their products into desirable products. The issue with pleasing products is that the products sell well. However, the products may end up hurting the customers. Companies should try to add benefits in the long run to such products without reducing or eliminating the pleasing qualities of the products. The challenge posed by salutary products is to add some pleasing qualities so that they will become more desirable in the minds of consumers.

4. RESPONSIBILITIES OF COMPANIES TOWARDS PROMOTION OF SUSTAINABLE MARKETING

Companies originally resisted the social movements and laws related to environmental sustainability and promotion of sustainable marketing (Yılmaz & Baybars, 2022). However, now companies recognize and acknowledge a need for positive consumer information, education, and protection. Under the sustainable marketing concept, the marketing function of a company should support the best performance of the marketing system in the long run (Sharma, Kaur, & Syan, 2021).

Sustainable marketing calls for socially and environmentally responsible actions that meet the present needs of customers and businesses without compromising with the ability of future generations to meet their needs (Sheth & Parvatiyar, 2021). The primary responsibility of companies is to satisfy the immediate requirements and preferences of customers. However, only satisfying the immediate requirements and preferences of customers in the short run may not always satisfy the best interests of either the consumers or of the business in the long run. The interests of the society at large in the long run may also not be served (Calvo-Porral, 2019).

Strategic planning considers only the needs of the company in future. However, societal marketing considers the future welfare of consumers and of the society (Handler & Chang, 2015). Sustainable marketing integrates both strategic planning and societal marketing.

Companies which are serious about sustainable marketing should incorporate a marketing system which functions smoothly. Customers, companies, public policy makers, and others work together to ensure socially and environmentally responsible marketing actions. However, there might be issues with marketing systems. Marketing systems may not always function smoothly and consequently, may face social criticisms. Different parties have different expectations from companies. Private citizens expect that companies and businesses will take actions that reduce marketing ills. Legislators and government agencies want that companies adhere to the rules and regulations. Legislators and government agencies adopt steps to promote sustainable marketing. The concerns raised by customers, the general public, and critics are acknowledged by motivated and enlightened companies. They adopt steps to carry out socially responsible and ethical marketing that create sustainable value for both individual customers and the society at large.

5. INITIATIVES BY COMPANIES FOR PROMOTION OF SUSTAINABLE MARKETING

Enlightened companies understand and realize their responsibilities towards their customers and towards the society at large. They adopt a number of initiatives to promote environmental sustainability and sustainable marketing (Buswari, Setiawan, & Khusniyah, 2021).

5.1 Initiatives by McDonald's

McDonald's is a company which was criticized for its early decisions to market tasty but fat- and salt-laden fast foods. Such products created immediate satisfaction for customers as well as sales and profits for the company (Ali, Danni, Latif, Kouser, & Baqader, 2021). Critics accused McDonald's and other fast-food chains of causing a national obesity epidemic in the long run. Consumer health was damaged and the national health system was burdened (Lewis, Huang, Merkel, Rhee, & Sylvetsky, 2020). Critics were also worried that the *Happy Meals* initiative of McDonald's created poor eating habits in children that remained with them in their later years (Singireddy, 2020). Consequently, many customers started looking for healthier options, causing a slump in the sales and profits of the fast-food industry (No, Kelly, Devi, Swinburn, & Vandevijvere, 2014).

Critics were of the opinion that the initiative of McDonald's raised issues of ethical behavior and social welfare (Singireddy, 2020). The company was criticized for the sizable environmental footprint of its vast global operations. Such operations included wasteful packaging and solid waste creation to inefficient energy use in its stores (Topley, 2020). Consequently, critics believed that the strategy adopted by McDonald's was not sustainable in the long run with respect to consumer welfare, company benefits, and of the society at large (Nizam, AlKaabi, & Husseini, 2022).

McDonald's tried to respond to these challenges with more sustainable energy options. It diversified into salads, fruits, grilled chicken, low-fat milk, and various other types of healthy food (Langert, 2019). The company tries to fulfill its social responsibility by sponsoring major education campaigns to help consumers better understand the keys to living balanced and active lifestyles. McDonald's announced an initiative which included a list of *Commitments to Offer Improved Nutrition Choices* (Wescott, Fitzpatrick, & Phillips, 2015). It works with Alliance for a Healthier Generation to make improvements to the *Happy Meal*. The initiative offers more balanced meals and simpler ingredients (Ponte, 2020). McDonald's claims that 80 percent of the items on its national menu fall into its *favorites under 400 calories* category. The items include from a basic cheeseburger to products such as Fruit & Maple Oatmeal and the Egg White Delight McMuffin, made with eight grams of whole grain, 100 percent egg whites, and extra-lean Canadian bacon (Wescott et al., 2015).

McDonald's addresses environmental issues in its various sustainability initiatives (Langert, 2019). The company focuses on food-supply sustainability, reduced and environmentally sustainable packaging, reuse and recycling, and more responsible store designs. For example, McDonald's aims to make recycling an option at all locations by 2025. It has also made the commitment to source all packaging from renewable or certified sources (Nguyen, 2021). All these efforts and initiatives suggest that McDonald's is serious about sustainability and is well positioned for a sustainably profitable future.

5.2 Initiatives by CVS Health

CVS Health is a company which balances purpose with profit (Grossmeier, 2018). CVS was in the business of selling cigarettes and other tobacco products. However, in 2014, CVS made the bold decision of discontinuing the selling of cigarettes and other tobacco products (Liu, Li, & Opara, 2018). It was a risky decision because although critics, health advocates, and public officials praised the initiative, CVS incurred an immediate loss of $2 billion in annual tobacco sales. The initiative also meant that many smoking customers of CVS shifted to competitors such as Walgreens, Walmart, or Kroger. All these companies continued selling cigarettes (Montgomery, 2019).

CVS believed that dropping tobacco was a wise decision. CVS works on the important mission: "Millions of times a day, close to home and across the country, we're helping people on their path to better health" (Quint, 2019). CVS believed that selling cigarettes and helping people to ensure better health are contradictory. So, CVS decided that tobacco products do not fit into its mission in the long run. The company announced, "CVS quits for good. This is the right thing to do" (Quint, 2019).

The decision of stopping tobacco sales was a landmark decision for CVS. The decision also grabbed headlines (Carey, Dumaine, Useem, & Zemmel, 2018). However, the decision was only one step in a more sweeping purpose-driven transformation. CVS focused on its broader mission and shifted from its decade-long traditional mission of *drug store on the corner* to becoming a *multi-spectrum healthcare company* (Fitzsimmons et al., 2022). CVS views itself not as another retail pharmacy. Rather, it considers itself as a pharmacy innovation company. The company says, "We're reinventing pharmacy to have a more active, supportive role in each person's unique health experience and in the greater healthcare environment" (Miller, 2015).

CVS reinforced its commitment towards sustainability by not only suspending tobacco sales but also by changing its name from CVS Caremark to CVS Health (Kandemir, 2021). CVS supports its mission of true health by offering a full range of products and services that help people on their path to better health. CVS Health has a network of 9800 retail pharmacies which sell an extensive assortment of prescription and non-prescription pharmaceuticals, personal care products, health and beauty aids, and general merchandize. CVS dispenses more prescriptions than any other drugstore chain. More than 71 percent of retail sales of the chain come from prescriptions (Wen, Wang, Taveira, & Akhlaghi, 2021).

Medical professionals offer treatment and care for minor health conditions and walk-in care in more than 1100 CVS locations which also house a CVS MinuteClinic (Carey et al., 2018).

CVS Health extends its mission of *path to better health* beyond retail pharmacies. For example, CVS Caremark division of the company provides Pharmacy Benefits Management (PBM) services. The services help big companies and insurers manage their prescription-drug programs (Carey et al., 2018). CVS Caremark also helps clients to cut down costs while improving health outcomes for 94 million Caremark members (Howell, Yin, & Robinson, 2021). CVS Health acquired Coram, which provides home infusion services to homebound patients, and Omnicare, a distributor of prescription drugs to nursing homes and assisted-living facilities (Reimsbach, Hahn, & Gürtürk, 2018). The company broadened its range of customer contact services. The new services include tailored in-store and phone advising to customers who manage chronic and specialty health conditions. CVS believes itself to be one-stop shop for all solutions related to healthcare. Also, retail sales contribute only 43 percent of the annual revenue for the company (Lee, Schleicher, & Henriksen, 2019).

CVS Health plays an active role in healthcare management through research, consumer outreach, and education, and support of health-related programs and organizations (Thakur & Kumar, 2022). For example, it collaborates with a number of organizations in the United States in an effort to curb the use of tobacco. It has partnered with the American Cancer Society and the National Urban League to lobby for anti-tobacco legislation. It also partners with American Academy of Pediatrics, the Campaign for Tobacco-Free Kids, and Scholastic Inc. to impart tobacco-related education (York, Lugo, Jarosz, & Toscani, 2021).

CVS launched a five-year, $50 million *Be the First* campaign. In the campaign, CVS works with national health organizations and youth groups to combat smoking through education, advocacy, tobacco control, and healthy behavior programming (Ward, Roy, & Edmondson, 2016). The chief medical officer of CVS Health says, "We are at a critical moment in our nation's efforts to end the epidemic of tobacco use that … threatens the health and well-being of our next generation. We're partnering with experts across the public health community … to move us one step closer to delivering the first tobacco-free generation" (Ward et al, 2016).

CVS Health strongly believes in sense-of-mission marketing. This is evident in the fact that even after the company stopped selling tobacco products and even after front-of-store sales dropped that year, overall revenues of CVS increased nearly by 10 percent (Neck, Houghton, & Murray, 2018). It further increased by another 10 percent in the following year. This indicates that the loss in sales from cigarettes was more than compensated by revenues from new sources, including those resulting from the decision to quit selling cigarettes (Neck et al., 2018).

CVS benefited from the fact that one source of new sales is the smokers themselves. More than 70 percent of smokers want to quit smoking themselves. At the same time that CVS Health pulled cigarettes off its shelves, it launched a *Let's Quit Together* assistance program (Garber & Downing, 2021). The program helped smokers to kick the habit. In the program, CVS offered a website complete with information offering tips, testimonials, and a website complete with information offering tips, testimonials, and other resources (Garber & Downing, 2021). By the end of the first year of its launch, CVS prescriptions for smoking cessation products grew by 63 percent. CVS Smoking Cessation Hubs also received nearly one million visits (Garber & Downing, 2021). Individuals who wish to quit smoking and seek smoking cessation products and services prefer CVS as the retailer of choice. The MinuteClinic *Start to Stop* program of CVS provides in-store personal counseling with a nurse practitioner and other services to help smokers quit (York et al., 2021).

The decision of CVS to discontinue tobacco products improved its reputation and brand image. The initiative allowed CVS to take non-smoking customers into confidence. It generated new business from non-smoking customers on one hand and PBM partners on the other (Pellegrin, 2017). It is difficult to understand the magnitude of benefits received from such initiatives. Nevertheless, in the months following the elimination of tobacco from its shelves, revenues from benefits services of its pharmacy increased by 12 percent and the company lined up $11 billion worth of new contracts for its PBM business (Pellegrin, 2017).

Exciting opportunities emerged for CVS based on the decision to quit tobacco. About a year later, CVS was an automatic choice for Target when Target was looking for a partner to buy and to operate the pharmacies in 1700 of its stores (Yap, 2018). Target had stopped selling cigarettes and tobacco products almost a decade earlier. Target and its customers had a *no tobacco* mentality. The image and sense-of-mission strategy of CVS fit into that mentality (Pellegrin, 2017).

The genuine concern of CVS Health for *helping people on their path to better health* goes beyond only revenues and profits. Success of CVS proves that earning revenues and profits can go hand in hand with social welfare. The initiatives adopted by CVS allows it to achieve high sales while fulfilling its mission of *doing good*. CVS is no longer just the *drugstore on the corner*. It is now a $185 billion healthcare organization and is number seven among the *Fortune 500* and the largest healthcare-related company in the United States (Ersoy, 2022). The transformation of CVS Health is still a work in progress. It purchased managed-healthcare company Aetna for $69 billion. Consequently, CVS Health has become the largest healthcare company in the world (Quint, 2019).

Regarding the decision to quit tobacco, the chief marketer of CVS says, "I cannot think of another example in corporate America where a company sacrificed $2 billion of revenue for what they felt was the right thing to do. It's a stunning thing, (and) it proved out for us in (so many) ways". For CVS Health, he says, success means "delivering what's right for people every day in a way that creates economic value for the business" (Grewal, 2018).

5.3 Initiatives by Method

Method is another company which is serious about sustainability. Method is the *people against dirty* brand of household and personal cleaning products (Ryan, 2012). In general, effective household cleaning products contain chemicals or even toxic ingredients that can be harmful to people and to the environment. However, Method sells products which are formulated with naturally derived, biodegradable, non-toxic ingredients. The brand says, "We prefer ingredients that come from plants, not chemical plants" (Ryan, 2012). Recyclable and recycled packaging is used. Method works with suppliers to reduce the carbon intensity of producing its products. Method supports environmental sustainability by using renewable energy sources such as wind turbines and solar trees to help power its Chicago manufacturing facility (Ryan, 2012). The company says, "Method cleaners put the hurt on dirt without doing harm to people, creatures, or the planet." The co-founder and *chief greenskeeper* summarizes the activities of Method as: "Beautiful design and environmental responsibility are equally important when creating a product and we shouldn't have to trade functionality for sustainability" (Ryan, 2012).

6. DISCUSSIONS

Business actions and activities of companies create impact on consumers, other businesses, and the society at large. So, businesses and companies should have a focus on environmental sustainability. Sustainability should be incorporated in the marketing actions of companies. Sustainable marketing requires socially, environmentally, and ethically responsible actions that bring value to not only present-day consumers and businesses but also to future generations and the society as a whole. Sustainable companies are those that act responsibly to create value for customers in order to capture value from customers in return – now and in the future.

Sustainable marketing suggests that marketing should be done by companies and businesses such that the present needs of customers and businesses are met while also preserving or enhancing the ability of future generations to meet their needs. Truly sustainable marketing requires a smooth-functioning marketing system in which consumers, companies, public policy makers, and others work together to ensure responsible marketing actions.

Companies originally resisted the social movements and laws regarding consumers. However, companies and businesses now recognize and acknowledge a need for positive consumer information, education, and protection. Sustainable marketing concept suggests that the marketing function of a company should support the best long-run performance of the marketing system. It should be guided by five sustainable marketing principles which include consumer-oriented marketing, customer value marketing, innovative marketing, sense-of-mission marketing, and societal marketing. All these aspects are discussed in the study. The study has both theoretical and managerial implications.

6.1 Theoretical Implications

Academicians may study the various aspects of environmental sustainability, sustainable marketing, and the promotion of sustainable marketing. They may study and analyze the necessity of marketing systems for the superior performance of marketing functions of companies and for ensuring sustainable marketing. They may suggest improvements in marketing systems. They may analyze the responsibilities of companies towards promotion of sustainable marketing and the initiatives of companies for promotion of sustainable marketing. They may suggest initiatives and strategies which will be effective for companies in promotion of sustainable marketing.

6.2 Managerial Implications

Companies and practicing managers may study and analyze the necessity of environmental sustainability, sustainable marketing, and the promotion of sustainable marketing. They should understand their roles and responsibilities towards ensuring environmental sustainability and promotion of sustainable marketing. They should analyze various strategies and initiatives which are already in place in their organizations for environmental sustainability and sustainable marketing. They should incorporate strategies and initiatives which will help companies to maintain environmental sustainability and sustainable marketing. Finally, companies should realize that they have the responsibilities of ensuring not only the welfare of their customers but also of the society at large.

7. CONCLUSION

Various aspects of environmental sustainability, sustainable marketing, and promotion of sustainable marketing by companies and businesses are discussed in the study. Various sustainable marketing principles viz. consumer-oriented marketing, customer value marketing, innovative marketing, sense-of-mission marketing, and societal marketing are discussed. Companies and businesses have roles and responsibilities towards promotion of sustainable marketing. They adopt various initiatives and strategies for promotion of sustainable marketing. All these aspects are discussed in the study.

7.1 Limitations

The study conducted a conceptual analysis of the various aspects of environmental sustainability, sustainable marketing, and business actions towards promotion of sustainable marketing. Primary data is not collected and empirical analysis is not done. Also, the study focused on conducting an analysis of mainly the markets in the United States.

7.2 Avenues of Future Research

Environmental sustainability and sustainable marketing are important issues in the present-day business scenario. Companies and businesses should realize the importance of environmental sustainability and sustainable marketing, and incorporate these aspects in all their business actions. Researchers should collect primary data related to various aspects of environmental sustainability and sustainable marketing and conduct empirical analysis. Researchers may conduct analysis in markets other than that of the United States and investigate whether the research results can be extended to other countries and markets.

REFERENCES

Ağlargöz, F. (2021). Enforcing Brands to Be More Sustainable: The Power of Online Consumer Reviews. *Social and Sustainability Marketing: A Casebook for Reaching Your Socially Responsible Consumers through Marketing Science*, 387.

Al-Shaer, H., & Hussainey, K. (2022). Sustainability reporting beyond the business case and its impact on sustainability performance: UK evidence. *Journal of Environmental Management, 311*, 114883. doi:10.1016/j.jenvman.2022.114883 PMID:35287071

Ali, I., Balta, M., & Papadopoulos, T. (2022). Social media platforms and social enterprise: Bibliometric analysis and systematic review. *International Journal of Information Management*, 102510.

Ali, W., Danni, Y., Latif, B., Kouser, R., & Baqader, S. (2021). Corporate social responsibility and customer loyalty in food chains—Mediating role of customer satisfaction and corporate reputation. *Sustainability (Basel), 13*(16), 8681. doi:10.3390/su13168681

Armstrong, R. M., & Grobbelaar, S. S. S. (2022). Sustainable business models for social enterprises in developing countries: a conceptual framework. *Management Review Quarterly*, 1-54.

Attia, Y. A. E. M. (2018). A Proposed Model for applying sustainable marketing strategy as a tool to improve the marketing performance Field study: Egypt air training academy. *Journal of Association of Arab Universities for Tourism and Hospitality*, *15*(2), 29–44. doi:10.21608/jaauth.2018.47934

Au-Yong-Oliveira, M., & Sousa, M. J. (2022). Sustainable Marketing and Strategy. *Sustainability (Basel)*, *14*(6), 3642. doi:10.3390/su14063642

Baranidharan, & Yuvarani, Sthapit, & Thiyagarajan. (2020). Customer Satisfaction with Special Reference to E-Business. *Ilkogretim Online*, *19*(4), 6481–6489.

Bešić, S. (2019). The Application of Contemporary Marketing Concept in the Sense of the Improvement of Business Subject Competitiveness. *Tehnicki Vjesnik (Strojarski Fakultet)*, *26*(2), 441–448.

Blythe, J., & Martin, J. (2019). Essentials of marketing. Academic Press.

Buswari, M., Setiawan, M., & Khusniyah, N. (2021). The Effect between Green Product Innovation and Green Marketing on Competitive Advantage and Business Performance. *PalArch's Journal of Archaeology of Egypt/Egyptology, 18*(2), 47-63.

Calvo-Porral, C. (2019). The role of marketing in reducing climate change: an approach to the sustainable marketing orientation. In *Climate Change and Global Development* (pp. 261–283). Springer. doi:10.1007/978-3-030-02662-2_13

Carey, D., Dumaine, B., Useem, M., & Zemmel, R. (2018). *Go long: Why long-term thinking is your best short-term strategy*. University of Pennsylvania Press. doi:10.2307/j.ctv2hdrfdx

Ersoy, N. (2022). The Influence of Statistical Normalization Techniques on Performance Ranking Results: The Application of MCDM Method Proposed by Biswas and Saha. *International Journal of Business Analytics*, *9*(5), 1–21. doi:10.4018/IJBAN.298017

Fitzsimmons, A. B., Qin, Y. S., & Heffron, E. R. (2022). Purpose vs mission vs vision: persuasive appeals and components in corporate statements. *Journal of Communication Management*, (ahead-of-print).

Fowler, M. D. (2017). Linking the public benefit to the corporation: Blockchain as a solution for certification in an age of do-good business. *Vand. J. Ent. & Tech. L.*, *20*, 881.

Frempong, M. F., Mu, Y., Adu-Yeboah, S. S., Hossin, M. A., & Amoako, R. (2022). Corporate sustainability and customer loyalty: The role of firm's green image. *Journal of Psychology in Africa*, *32*(1), 1–7. doi:10.1080/14330237.2021.2017153

Garber, J., & Downing, D. (2021). Perceptions, Policy, and Partnerships: How Pharmacists Can Be Leaders in Reducing Overprescribing. *The Senior Care Pharmacist*, *36*(3), 130–135. doi:10.4140/TCP.n.2021.130 PMID:33662235

Gburova, J., & Fedorko, R. (2018). Online shops and online shopping from the point of view of the Slovak consumer. *Economic And Social Development: Book of Proceedings*, 134-140.

Grossmeier, J. (2018). The Art of Health Promotion: Ideas for improving health outcomes. *American Journal of Health Promotion*, *32*(4), 1145–1156. doi:10.1177/0890117118765037 PMID:29667500

Handler, I., & Chang, W. (2015). Social Attributes of a Smartphone and their importance to young Taiwanese consumers: An explorative study. *source. International Journal of Arts and Commerce, 4*, 16–29.

Hanifah, I. A., & Ismawati, I. (2022). The effect of business strategy, innovation, organizational culture on the performance of micro small medium enterprises (MSMES) moderated by financial literature. *Fair Value: Jurnal Ilmiah Akuntansi dan Keuangan, 4*(10), 4416-4426.

Hohenberg, S., & Taylor, W. (2022). Measuring customer satisfaction and customer loyalty. Handbook of Market Research, 909.

Howell, S., Yin, P. T., & Robinson, J. C. (2021). Quantifying The Economic Burden Of Drug Utilization Management On Payers, Manufacturers, Physicians, And Patients: Study examines the economic burden of drug utilization management on payers, manufacturers, physicians, and patients. *Health Affairs, 40*(8), 1206–1214. doi:10.1377/hlthaff.2021.00036 PMID:34339243

Kandemir, H. K. (2021). Duties and Responsibilities of Directors of Joint Stock Companies on Corporate Social Responsibility: An Evaluation with Respect to Turkish Company Law. *Selcuk Universitesi Hukuk Fakultesi Dergisi, 29*, 2209.

Kashif, M., & Udunuwara, M. (2022). Guest editorial: Socially responsible marketing: a transformative agenda. *Asia-Pacific Journal of Business Administration, 14*(2), 161–165. doi:10.1108/APJBA-05-2022-566

Khandai, S., Mathew, J., Yadav, R., Kataria, S., & Kohli, H. (2022). Ensuring brand loyalty for firms practising sustainable marketing: a roadmap. *Society and Business Review*, (ahead-of-print).

Kurniawan, G. (2022). Social Marketing and Corporate Social Responsibility on the Brand Image of Lifebuoy Bath Soap Products. *Enrichment: Journal of Management, 12*(2), 1275–1279.

Langert, B. (2019). *The battle to do good: Inside McDonald's sustainability journey*. Emerald Group Publishing. doi:10.1108/9781787568150

Lee, J. G., Schleicher, N. C., & Henriksen, L. (2019). Sales to minors, corporate brands, and assurances of voluntary compliance. *Tobacco Regulatory Science, 5*(5), 431–439. doi:10.18001/TRS.5.5.3

Lerch, M. (2020). *Green marketing* [Doctoral dissertation]. Masarykova univerzita, Ekonomicko-správní fakulta.

Lewis, N., Huang, Q., Merkel, P., Rhee, D. K., & Sylvetsky, A. C. (2020). Differences in the sugar content of fast-food products across three countries. *Public Health Nutrition, 23*(16), 2857–2863. doi:10.1017/S136898002000110X PMID:32576300

Liu, L., Li, S., & Opara, M. (2018). Corporate social responsibility and strategic company behaviour: CVS Health's discontinuation of tobacco products. *Corporate Social Responsibility and Environmental Management, 25*(6), 1293–1305. doi:10.1002/csr.1639

Lukin, E., Krajnović, A., & Bosna, J. (2022). Sustainability Strategies and Achieving SDGs: A Comparative Analysis of Leading Companies in the Automotive Industry. *Sustainability (Basel), 14*(7), 4000. doi:10.3390/su14074000

Malik, R., & Aggarwal, R. (2022). Innovative Marketing and Consumer Behavior: A Systematic Literature Review. *SAMVAD*, *23*(0), 87–93. doi:10.53739/samvad/2021/v23/165188

Miller, R. P. (2015). Virtua and CVS Health: Partnering Within a Population Health Delivery Model. *Frontiers of Health Services Management*, *31*(3), 32–37. doi:10.1097/01974520-201501000-00004 PMID:26495552

Milman, A. (2022). Attraction Marketing Strategies. In *Managing Visitor Attractions* (pp. 271–288). Routledge. doi:10.4324/9781003041948-19

Mohamed, K. (2013). Evaluation of societal marketing (sustainable marketing) in maintaining ethics in marketing goods or services to the customers. *International Journal of Management Research and Reviews*, *3*(11), 3703.

Montgomery, N. (Ed.). (2019). *Perspectives on Purpose: Leading Voices on Building Brands and Businesses for the Twenty-first Century*. Routledge. doi:10.4324/9781351173568

Muninger, M. I., Mahr, D., & Hammedi, W. (2022). Social media use: A review of innovation management practices. *Journal of Business Research*, *143*, 140–156. doi:10.1016/j.jbusres.2022.01.039

Neck, C. P., Houghton, J. D., & Murray, E. L. (2018). *Organizational behavior: A skill-building approach*. Sage Publications.

Nguyen, L. (2021). *Developing sustainable marketing plan for plant-based products*. LAB University of Applied Sciences.

Nizam, N. Z., AlKaabi, M. R. A. Z., & Husseini, S. A. (2022). Customer service quality assessment and customers' satisfaction in food and beverage in McDonald's restaurant in United Arab Emirates. *Journal of Positive School Psychology*, *6*(3), 4684–4693.

No, E., Kelly, B., Devi, A., Swinburn, B., & Vandevijvere, S. (2014). Food references and marketing in popular magazines for children and adolescents in New Zealand: A content analysis. *Appetite*, *83*, 75–81. doi:10.1016/j.appet.2014.08.013 PMID:25128834

Owolabi, A. O., & Okegbade, I. Y. (2015). The impact of promotional tools on the sale of insurance products in Nigeria. *International Journal of Management. IT and Engineering*, *5*(6), 26–44.

Pellegrin, K. L. (2017). CVS Health: Checking the Vital Signs of the Largest Pharmacy Company in the US. In SAGE Business Cases. SAGE Publications.

Peterson, M. (2021). Sustainable marketing: A holistic approach. *Sustainable Marketing*, 1-100.

Ponte, S. (2020). Green capital accumulation: Business and sustainability management in a world of global value chains. *New Political Economy*, *25*(1), 72–84. doi:10.1080/13563467.2019.1581152

Quint, M. (2019). Measuring purpose: From organizational commitments to social impact. In *Perspectives on Purpose* (pp. 35–47). Routledge. doi:10.4324/9781351173568-5

Ramazonovma, M. D. (2022). Development of Marketing in the Context of A Tourism Pandemic in Uzbekistan. *Indonesian Journal of Innovation Studies*, *17*, 10–21070. doi:10.21070/ijins.v17i.577

Reimsbach, D., Hahn, R., & Gürtürk, A. (2018). Integrated reporting and assurance of sustainability information: An experimental study on professional investors' information processing. *European Accounting Review*, *27*(3), 559–581. doi:10.1080/09638180.2016.1273787

Rroy, A. D., Gulati, U., Sagi, S. G. K., & Gowda, K. R. (2022). Sustainability for Businesses: Marketing and Finance Perspective. *Academy of Marketing Studies Journal*, *26*, 1–7.

Ryan, T. A. (2012). Understanding green marketing and advertising in consumer society: An analysis of method cleaning products. *Journal of Research for Consumers*, *22*, 18–24.

Sharma, R. R., Kaur, T., & Syan, A. S. (2021). *Sustainability Marketing: New directions and practices.* Emerald Group Publishing. doi:10.1108/9781800712447

Sheth, J. N., & Parvatiyar, A. (2021). Sustainable marketing: Market-driving, not market-driven. *Journal of Macromarketing*, *41*(1), 150–165. doi:10.1177/0276146720961836

Singireddy, M. (2020). Mcdonald's: Global Marketing. *International Journal of Health and Economic Development*, *6*(2), 16–27.

Soliman, A. M. (2021). Governance and Sustainability Transitions in Urban Informality. In *Urban Informality* (pp. 51–83). Springer. doi:10.1007/978-3-030-68988-9_2

Su, M., Fang, M., Kim, J., & Park, K. S. (2022). Sustainable marketing innovation and consumption: Evidence from cold chain food online retail. *Journal of Cleaner Production*, *340*, 130806. doi:10.1016/j.jclepro.2022.130806

Teixeira, G. F. G., & Junior, O. C. (2019). How to make strategic planning for corporate sustainability? *Journal of Cleaner Production*, *230*, 1421–1431. doi:10.1016/j.jclepro.2019.05.063

Thakur, A., & Kumar, A. (2022). Role of Artificial Intelligence-Based Technologies in Healthcare to Combat Critical Diseases. In *Digital Health Transformation with Blockchain and Artificial Intelligence* (pp. 195–218). CRC Press. doi:10.1201/9781003247128-11

Topley, M. (2020). Keeping up with patient expectations. *BDJ In Practice*, *33*(2), 23–25. doi:10.1038/s41404-020-0298-7

Voegtlin, C., Scherer, A. G., Stahl, G. K., & Hawn, O. (2022). Grand societal challenges and responsible innovation. *Journal of Management Studies*, *59*(1), 1–28. doi:10.1111/joms.12785

Ward, C. B., Roy, D. P., & Edmondson, D. R. (2016). Is CVS Just 'Blowing Smoke?': Evaluating the CVS Decision to Ban Tobacco Products. *Case Studies in Strategic Communication*, *5*(1), 249–264.

Wen, X., Wang, S., Taveira, T. H., & Akhlaghi, F. (2021). Required warfarin dose and time in therapeutic range in patients with diagnosed Nonalcoholic Fatty Liver Disease (NAFLD) or Nonalcoholic Steatohepatitis (NASH). *PLoS One*, *16*(9), e0251665. doi:10.1371/journal.pone.0251665 PMID:34525124

Wescott, R. F., Fitzpatrick, B., & Phillips, E. (2015). *McDonald's–Alliance for a Healthier Generation Partnership: Clinton Global Initiative Commitment to Action.* Academic Press.

Yap, D. (2018). CVS Pharmacy rolls out new prescription management system. *Pharmacy Today*, *24*(5), 46–47. doi:10.1016/j.ptdy.2018.04.027

Yılmaz, M. B., & Baybars, B. (2022). A Critical Perspective on Greenwashing Under the Roof of Corporate Environmentalism. In *Green Marketing in Emerging Economies* (pp. 119–140). Palgrave Macmillan. doi:10.1007/978-3-030-82572-0_6

York, J., Lugo, K., Jarosz, L., & Toscani, M. (2021). CVS health faces a new wave of disruption. *International Journal of Pharmaceutical and Healthcare Marketing*, *15*(3), 333–353. doi:10.1108/IJPHM-01-2020-0008

Zaman, M. M. U. (2021). A Critical Review and Directions for the Use of Eco-Friendly Products in Bangladesh. *International Journal of Progressive Sciences and Technologies*, *27*(1), 67–75.

Zaman, R., Jain, T., Samara, G., & Jamali, D. (2022). Corporate governance meets corporate social responsibility: Mapping the interface. *Business & Society*, *61*(3), 690–752. doi:10.1177/0007650320973415

Chapter 7
Internet of Everything in the Realm of Sustainable Marketing Post COVID-19:
Constraints, Prospects, and Implications

Bishal Poddar
Woxsen University, India

Harsh Sethia
Woxsen University, India

Atrij Jadon
Woxsen University, India

Mohd Azhar
https://orcid.org/0000-0003-3222-5565
Woxsen University, India

ABSTRACT

The chapter intends to discuss the growing significance of IoE in the realm of sustainable marketing. Nevertheless, the realm of information technology solutions within the domain of sustainable or eco-friendly marketing remains relatively underexplored within the existing literature. Therefore, this study sincerely attempts to fill this void by concerning IoE in the realm of sustainable marketing, specifically in the post-COVID-19 context. This study discusses the increasing significance of post-COVID-19 IoE in sustainable marketing practices, closely examines various constraints and prospects in the Indian context, and provides detailed implications of IoE in sustainable marketing practices. The novelty of the present study lies in the fact that IoE in the realm of sustainable marketing is a less investigated topic, and there is a dearth of literature on the subject.

DOI: 10.4018/979-8-3693-1339-8.ch007

INTRODUCTION

Environmental awareness is growing and is spreading over the world (Yu *et al.*, 2021; Han, 2020). As a result, companies have started employing green and sustainable marketing techniques to address various environmental issues as sustainable development strategies. Since the 1980s, there have been issues closely linked to industrial output like global warming, greenhouse effects, climate change, and pollution (Hamid & Jameel, 2019). Thus, it is only reasonable to expect that virtually every sector has now started incorporating sustainable practices into their business operations. Sustainable marketing involves producing and promoting products that consumers can easily access due to low cost, maximum satisfaction, and great benefits but have few negative impacts on both the environment and the social economy. High-end tech tools are used to advertise the offer and support sustainable operations and lifestyles in companies (Nosratabadi *et al.*, 2019). Technology in the modern age helps to create value for the customer (Seretny & Gaur, 2020). One of the most important components in enhancing the environment for marketing is data, and technology has produced a variety of methods for gathering data (Mohanraj & Karthikeyan, 2016). Utilising this data helps customers meet their needs and get the finest products and services, which benefits company activity growth. The Internet of Things (IoT) is a major contributor to large data and therefore forms a valuable tool for fulfilling marketing goals. As IoT emerges, it may also greatly impact the very business models of certain firms, significantly changing their relationships both with their clients and other constituents (Fredette *et al.*, 2012). IoT is an arrangement of connected components (internet-connected components) that can be identified separately like an internet-based infrastructure giving way for remote identification, sensing, and operation of these components with real-time flow of data or information between the components (Ng & Wakenshaw, 2017). The IoT concept is expanded by the Internet of Everything (IoE) by including connections to people, data, and processes. It also involves other connectivity-oriented frameworks like the Internet of Things (IoT), Internet of People (IoP), Industrial Internet (II), etc. (Yang *et al.*, 2017). Therefore, IoE refers to a network of connections among smart things, people, enterprises, and data that enables the near instantaneous exchange of data and information. So far as it is known, this technology integrates all sorts of technologies to make ever-improving marketing communication.

Creating and promoting goods and services that are socially and environmentally responsible is the emphasis of sustainable marketing. It seeks to maximize positive environmental effects while minimizing resource consumption, generating social benefits, and maintaining profitability. The IoE and sustainable marketing strategies have gained popularity because of the COVID-19 pandemic. People are looking for sustainable goods and services as they spend more time at home and are more conscious of their impact on the environment. IoE can assist businesses in meeting this expanding need by enabling them to create and provide more sustainable goods and services as well as more effectively engage consumers in their sustainability initiatives.

In terms of sustainability and sustainable development, IoE technology can be very helpful. Therefore, knowing how to use this technology to generate sustainable marketing and its implications for sustainable development can be crucial for streamlining procedures and enabling marketing efforts. It might even be a step in the direction of environmental sustainability. Digital innovations go beyond modernizing or transforming technology. Businesses that embrace digital solutions have a greater chance of winning over customers, especially in the COVID-19 period (Rowan & Galanakis, 2020). Digital tools are therefore more important than ever in marketing (Eze & Cherish, 2019). Sustainable marketing has the potential to be completely transformed by the IoE. IoE may assist organizations in developing more sustainable products and services, communicating their sustainability efforts to customers more effectively, and developing new business models by connecting items and devices to the internet. The use of IoE for sustainable marketing is however also subject to several limitations and difficulties. The expense of putting IoE solutions into practice is one of the main obstacles. Additionally, IoE systems and devices are frequently targets of cyberattacks, so companies must put strong security measures in place to safeguard customer data. Finally, the potential advantages of IoT for sustainable marketing are not well known, which could impede adoption.

Despite the limitations and difficulties, IoE has a promising future in sustainable marketing. IoE can assist companies in more effectively communicating with customers about their sustainability initiatives. Businesses can, for instance, employ IoE sensors to gather information about how their goods and services affect the environment, and then share that information with customers through their websites or social media accounts. This might aid customers in selecting goods and services with greater knowledge.

Nevertheless, the realm of information technology solutions within the domain of sustainable or eco-friendly marketing remains relatively underexplored within the existing literature. Therefore, this study sincerely attempts to fill this void by concerning IoE in the realm of sustainable marketing, specifically in the context of post-COVID-19. This study discusses the increasing significance of IoE post-COVID-19 in sustainable marketing practices, closely examines various constraints and prospects in the Indian context and provides detailed implications of IoE in sustainable marketing practices. The novelty of the present study lies in the fact that IoE in the realm of sustainable marketing is a very less investigated topic, and there is a dearth of literature on the subject concern. In addition, to the best of researchers' knowledge, no single study has been undertaken in the Indian context that has talked about IoE in the realm of sustainable marketing post-COVID-19. Hence, the present study is a sincere attempt in this direction.

In pursuit of the research objective, this chapter is organized as follows: Section 1 presents the introduction. Section 2 offers an extensive review of the literature encompassing sustainable marketing, green marketing, and the IoE. The subsequent sections elucidate IoT and IoE and their role in sustainable marketing. Section 5 expounds upon the post-COVID-19 scenario and IoE in green marketing, grounded in IoE principles, elucidating the associated technologies, opportunities, and challenges. In the subsequent sections, constraints, prospects, implications and, at last, conclusion are discussed.

FRAMEWORK

The intent of this chapter is to provide light on COVID-19-related barriers, opportunities, and repercussions related to the Internet of Everything in the context of environmentally conscious marketing. To methodically gather, assess, and synthesize pertinent research papers on the Internet of Everything (IoE) in the context of environmentally friendly advertising after COVID-19, this study uses a methodical review of literature technique. The methodical methodology guarantees a thorough and repeatable procedure for locating and evaluating academic contributions, mostly from the last ten years. This timeline makes absolutely certain that the assessment includes the most current advancements in the Internet of Everything (IoE) and environmentally conscious marketing, particularly after the COVID-19 pandemic disrupted the world. The contribution of this chapter explicitly address how IoE and sustainable marketing coincide in the post-COVID-19 age. Journal articles, conference papers, and reports from reliable sources are the main subjects of the evaluation. The significance of learned reputation and rigor in the selected literature is emphasized by the aforementioned selection criterion.

LITERATURE REVIEW

Sustainable Marketing

Sustainable marketing refers to creating and promoting products that meet customer requirements concerning efficiency, price, and accessibility without detrimentally affecting the society, the environment, or the economy (Nosratabadi *et al.*, 2019). Fortunately, when shopping for various kinds of products, sustainability has increased in importance over the past few years. According to the global sustainability report, nearly three-quarters of consumers indicated that they would either change their purchasing habits or make a difference in their environmental impact (Nielsen, 2020). Close to half expressed that they were open to buying organic products at higher prices (Nielsen, 2020).

Since many businesses are being affected by digital transformation (Fonseca & Azevedo, 2020; Bamberger *et al.*, 2017; Bechtold *et al.*, 2021), we should reconsider the value chains (Wilkinson *et al.*, 2015). Whatever the level of transformation, it can be quite important in practically every industry branch (Seretny & Gaur, 2020). Digital innovations, however, go beyond simply modernising or altering technology. Businesses that embrace digital solutions have a greater chance of winning over customers, especially in the COVID-19 pandemic period (Rowan, 2020).

One of the serious commencements that a company or an organization has to make towards the society in which it operates includes the environmental, social, and economic commitments (Saura *et al.*, 2020). These three mentioned aspects build sustainability (Suchanek & Szmelter, 2019). Customers need sustainable marketing if they desire sustainable enterprises (and products or services). This idea includes standard economic marketing, social marketing, and environmental (green) marketing (Andronie *et al.*, 2019). Sustainable marketing includes creating and promoting goods and services that satisfy client demands without sacrificing the necessary standards of quality, effectiveness, affordability, and convenience.

Besides, sustainable marketing has an additional dimension other than its traditional division into the commercial, social, and environmental aspects. Recognizing this, for instance begins with reducing waste and hazards such as the reuse of carrier packaging and advertisement alternatives. To begin with, consumer motivation in sustainable marketing is created by the interaction of consumers and clients' interests with those of NGOs and state institutions- a social dimension. There are instances where they can use loyal users as informal sales agents in promoting products on social networks. Thirdly it should help in long-range planning (involving the organisations mission, objectives, and plans or programmes of growth along with marketing communication messages).

Internet of Things (IoT) and Internet of Everything (IoE)

The internet can be segmented into two, the IoT and the IoE. The concept of IoT is quite baffling. A concept saying that there are ways possible, through which ordinary physical objects can be interfaced with the internet and their data exchanged. By some observers, the IoT is conceived as wireless connectivity, sensors, or codes. It is also able to connect with other databases as well as technologies. "IoT refers to a world in which almost anything can be connected and have intelligent communication" (Internet of Things, 2017). Home appliances can be configured to 'smart' and enable it to comprehend human voice and respond accordingly as we desire (Wright, 2016).

The literature frequently views the IoT as a pillar of Industry 4.0 and its offshoots (Rejeb *et al.*, 2020). This concept is based on the idea that items can communicate with each other by sending and receiving messages over the internet. Its growth led to the emergence of "smart" objects including machinery, homes, factories, etc. Naturally, this communication generates a lot of data that may be used to study how individuals behave (Tariq *et al.*, 2020). One marketing strategy to optimize the company's actions and strengthen its competitive edge is to utilize those datasets. However, since 2010, the IoT has evolved, and today's methods of linking items are considerably more advanced than they were at the dawn of the Industry 4.0 era.

A more sophisticated version of IoT is the IoE. Its premise assumes relationships between individuals, processes, data, and objects (Da Costa *et al.*, 2021). In 2012, CISCO defined IoE as "a network of networks that reunites people, processes, data, and things in network connections more significant and valuable than ever" (Auger *et al.*, 2018; Ilyas, 2019). So, IoE builds an advanced network of objects and it supports creating new capacities for the benefit of both businesses and society (Xu *et al.*, 2014).

The IoE attaches digital elements to consumer electronics and connects them to the web. It is a concept based on the future of technology, which consists of a wide variety of appliances, devices, and apps connected to the global internet. Data processing is not limited to laptops, desktop computers, or tablets since devices are more intelligent and widely linked. Everything around us will be smarter and interconnected for better work. The IoE will employ an input-output structure.

IoE is a combination of the IoT, which includes radio-frequency identification (RFID), ordinary things equipped with sensors, and applications enabling users to control their house, to measure their body parameters, as well as to check household equipment's state by means of mobile (Ng & Wakenshaw, 2017; Adams, 2017; Peppet, 2014; Nguyen & Simkin, 2017). IoE differs from IoT as it is about smart interaction among physical objects and things. In contrast, an IoE is a single system that handles all of them by using internet intelligence.

The IoE follows an input/output framework that extends beyond pure machine communication towards humans as well (Tucker *et al.*, 2018; Khvoynitskaya, 2019). Big data emerges from the development of RFID technology; that is, the application of barcode tags with scanning devices to SKU tracking, telemetry, and other advancement techniques. Contemporary technological advancement has allowed businesses to be able to deal with big data systems which can be used in the creation of consumer value through marketing analytics due to the availability of state-of-the-art hardware and software solutions.

Internet of Things vs. Internet of Everything

The difference between IoT and IoE is not very clear because the term "Internet of Everything" is rather recent. Hence, a distinction between both the terms is highlighted here. IoT is focused on things, or the network of physical objects and things accessed via the internet. These items could have inbuilt technology that interacts with internal states or outside conditions. In other words, it alters who, where, and how decisions are made when things have the capacity to perceive and communicate. IoE, on the other hand, is the driving force of IoT, which aims at merging individuals, corporate practices, information, and gadgets to turn networked relationships into something even more meaningful and beneficial. This leads to the creation of new capabilities, making a better user environment, and previously unknown economic chances for organisations, people, and countries (Bojanova et al., 2014).

IoE depicts a world in which billions of goods each have a sensor to identify, gauge, and assess their current condition. These items are all connected to open or private networks that employ common and unique protocols. At three different levels- business process, action plan, and business minute- the IoE will reimagine businesses. Over the world, IoE adjustment has enormous value. IoE aims to provide an environment of availability from beginning to end that includes innovations, practices, and concepts applied to all network use cases.

IoE and Marketing

By 2020, there will be 50 billion devices with connectivity to the internet and electronics on the entire globe, which is more than there are people on it (Ahmed *et al.,* 2017; Weinberg *et al.,* 2015). Examples of these devices and technology include devices that are used, computerized home systems, mobile phones, and specialized technology. In order to create environmentally conscious communications and services, the Internet of Everything (IoE) integrates subjects, information, individuals and tactics (Cisco, 2015).

However, sensitive information and data about eating habits, respiration rate, and daily workstation also gets transmitted over the World Wide Web in the modern virtual environment where indicators help individuals feel better through minimizing their everyday strain (Bui & Namin, 2019). Inspired by the concept of "bringing together the unattached" (people to people, people to machines, machines to machines, and so on), Cisco, for instance, projects that over the next 10 years, the Internet of Everything (IoE) might cost "at stake" $14.4 trillion. 2015, Cisco). Over 60% of the economic improvement that takes place in the next ten years will come from these sectors: retail sales, production, banking and financial information, insurance, and health care.

Rise in confidentiality literacy among consumers is necessary for safeguarding the confidential nature of knowledge because customers' continued dependence on increased virtual connection to the internet and universal Wi-Fi frequently allow breaches of confidentiality (Gabisch & Milne, 2014; Gurau *et al.,* 2003; Milne *et al.,* 2009; Singh & Hill, 2003). Regulations concerning privacy of consumers, historical data, and/or "internet-based consumerism" should not be disregarded by policymakers in the public eye (Akhter, 2014; Miedema, 2018); in furthermore, companies should take into account the impact of the promotions, advertisements, and metrics they acquire, hold, and use to guide their choices (Petrescu & Krishen, 2018).

Research have shown, for instance, that consumers usually are unaware that their personal information is being gathered (Milne *et al.,* 2008). Such consumer data may be utilized to create adjustable sets of options or categorized advertisements (Krishen *et al.,* 2011), target clients with individualized promotions (Zahay *et al.,* 2012), or provide geographically based products and services in additional to mileage monitoring (Krishen e*t al.,* 2010). The Internet of Everything (IoE) has problems with gathering information, effectiveness, interpreting, assessment, its preservation, as well as security when it comes to non-anonymized information.

The Internet of Everything (IoE) has the ability to revolutionize a number of industries, including manufacturing, public transportation, medical treatment, and academia; but, it will additionally bring many novel and challenging situations, especially in the areas of data safety and privacy. Corporations must show guidance in the ethical and unlawful use of confidential information as well as its safety considering modern technology and better packaging (Cisco, 2015). Consumer complaints about data sets, misuse, and incorrect access and admitting are primarily divided into two categories: confidentiality ideals and confidentiality precautions values (Raschke *et al.,* 2014). User views concerning confidentiality have been linked to instances of factual distortion, unfair treatment, falsification, and improper use, in accordance to studies (Ahmed *et al.,* 2017; De Cremer *et al.,* 2017; FTC, 2015).

Protection, confidentiality, accountability, and record ownership are important concerns for both IoE agencies and their clients (Tucker *et al.*, 2018). In addition to this, an increasing amount of investigation has looked at the relationships amongst client vulnerabilities and online and technological consumerism (Miedema, 2018). Consequently, using advertisement analytics to assess how the Internet of Everything (IoE) might impact legislation from governments, regulations, and employer control may be beneficial. The aim of this research aims to provide an exploratory and qualitative investigation of the influence of IoE on sustainable marketing. These concerns involve database confidentiality and security, as well as the advantages and difficult situations that come with it. They additionally cover the effects of its safety and forgery frameworks. It looks at the main insurance-related concerns as well as the modern world of laws, regulations, and independent of regulation structures to offer suggestions for legislators and marketers.

Marketing's Role in Networks

Interchangeability is necessary for IoEs since they include several equipment and gadgets. For interoperability to become a reality, many parties must collaborate. In an IEEE publication, Bandyopadhyay and Sen mentioned that "the central issues are how to guarantee trust, security, and privacy of the users and their data while guaranteeing full interoperability between interconnected devices, and how to provide them with a high degree of smartness by enabling their adaptation and autonomous behavior" (Bandyopadhyay & Sen, 2011).

Furthermore, ambassadors from over one hundred different countries will discuss United Nations authority over the online at a summit starting this week in Tunisia, where the long-term viability of online communication might be at stake, according to McDowell and Goldstein's Wall Street Journal article." The choices that are made by the World Telecommunications Standardization Assembly will affect global politics, the growth of the global economy, and maybe even the liberty of internet access for billions of individuals.

A recently developed guidance and communication technique called Digital Object Architecture (DOA) could potentially make it feasible to watch and follow everyone and any gadget online in actual time. Some nations are advocating that DOA be the sole referencing system needed for the Internet of Things. They also want centralized control across the network to reside with the United Nations International Telecommunication Union, because it holds legal title to the underneath proprietary information (McDowell & Goldstein, 2016).

While architects and CEOs will be actively participating in the deliberation and discussion concerning interconnection requirements, Markcom has a significant role to play. Management of marketing will be accountable through Markcom to ensure that the companies they represent play a part in the IoEs standards and requirements and that their views are recognized enough.

Organizations (rules and norms) are established by structural events (Giddens, 1977, 1984). Recognizing the distinct role marcom has had in the growth and advancement of IoEs is equally crucial. It does this via affecting the company and organizational decision-making processes of companies to consumers marcom as well as the individual emotional processes of b-b marcom, all of which impact (a) structural processes.

One advantage of applying displaying assessment in connection to IoE is the capacity to transform a huge amount of sensor-assembled information into substantial company paperwork. Prolonged pay, lower expenses, greater responder prices, and increased levels of competency in favor development are further advantages (Ahmed *et al.*, 2017; Weinberg *et al.*, 2015). Every community gathering that the framework draws advantages fairly since both consumers and sponsors gain from the opportunity to delegate duties and adjust enterprises. Redid correspondence rises, advent's worth falls, and organization expenses could decline as incredible gadgets and internet-connected equipment grow to become increasingly ingrained in customers' lifestyles and working environments (Tucker *et al.,* 2018).

Today's organizations can employ data to seek for continual judgments thanks to technical developments in detectors and intelligent gadgets. Fact evaluations, for instance, enables businesses to deliver complex models of extraordinary valuing or to combine and disseminate information in an intra-legitimate way. The growth of authorized firms, skill improvements, exploitation recognition, and sample weighing are all supported by IoE analyses of marketing (Ahmed *et al.,* 2017; Breur, 2015; Iacobucci *et al.,* 2019). IoE considers continuous evaluation and rapid choice-making while facts can be obtained rapidly. This can aid in identifying and evaluating top businesses (Weinberg *et al.,* 2015). The cloud's capacity to exchange data reduces expenses related to data collaboration among various collaborators and organizations and allows licensing for condition-based reconfiguration of frameworks, which in turn promotes cycles within the Internet of Everything ecosystem.

PILLARS OF IoE

People

IoE connects people in significant and relevant ways to each other across all types of interactions ranging from B2B, B2C, and C2C. By analysing all customer data transmitted over the IoE, it would be possible for marketers to comprehend consumer behavior trends and patterns and come up with advanced products aimed at fulfilling the needs of consumers. This mechanism involves importantly marketing professionals. In addition to the users, there is an array of companies that participate actively in the process referred to as the IoE. There are several stakeholders who benefit directly or indirectly from such transactions- companies whose devices make it possible for people to get online (Chouk & Mani, 2019). Other important players involved in the development of policies comprise of regulatory agencies, business groups, consumer associations, pressures, policy-makers/influencers as well as other policymakers.

Process

The right information must be provided to the right person at the right time, or machine in order for this purpose. Smart devices track consumers as they go about their daily lives without any active involvement of the consumer in providing data, for instance in the physical world (Verhoef *et al.,* 2017; Woodside & Sood, 2017). The second set of processes covers all the stages including the first phase of data gathering up to the post-acquisition where data processing is carried out as an element in machine integration within IoE during their interactions with fellow machines/humans. However, these processes entail attempts to regulate the process of data gathering and utilization in decision making.

Data

The smart gadgets and sensors of the IoE collect massive amounts of information about customers' use of the product and services, sometimes while using it and others, not using them as well. Market analytics also employs a significant amount of these data for forecasting consumer behavior and trends as well to acquire knowledge (Kakatkar & Spann, 2019).

Things

The IoT consists of actual physical things and gadgets linked to the internet and to one another for the benefit of customers and to encourage wise decision-making. The term IoT describes a vast array of internet-connected gadgets that detect and share data without directly engaging humans (Khvoynitskaya, 2019). It consists of appliances, electronics, wearables, medical gear, and mobile gadgets. These gadgets engage in machine-to-machine communication as well as interactions with users (Woodside & Sood, 2017).

THE POSITION OF IoE AFTER COVID-19

IoE aided in transforming itself into remarkable identity for its large-scale concept, which includes smart cities, intelligent vehicles, and many others. We examine how many companies that were previously ignorant of IoE are benefitting from IoE after COVID-19. Because they wish to regulate and adapt to the COVID-19 outbreak as well as track and recognize those who have been infected by this disease, distinct periods of IoE usage will be most successfully encouraged. Interoperability is made possible by the IoE and precision technology, which includes cloud computing, actuators, and smart sensors, granting quick access to several locations, improving knowledge, and altering overall performance (Kibria *et al.*, 2017). The usage of touch monitoring has been confirmed to be suitable due to the COVID-19 pandemic simple IoE gadgets along with Trial Proximity trace by using touch tracking can help us cope with social distancing by warning people when they are too close to each other (Crnovrsanin *et al.*, 2009; Shigeta *et al.*, 2018).

In order to protect our programme, privacy, and safety are required given the rising usage of IoE during the pandemic and the anticipated expansion of COVID-19. Given the increasing number of IoE applications, studies that discuss the implications of privacy and safety on IoE capabilities and the risks they face have an increased risk of cyberattacks, privacy threats, and protection threats. Physical disruptions of the sensor and the sense layer may entail a change to the way the link and the device exist. The sensor may also pose a threat to the network because it can do Distributed Deniel of Service attacks (DDoS) (Dong *et al.*, 2019). Any network impact in IoE automation might be risky since real-time data is required.

SUSTAINABLE MARKETING BASED ON IoE

Data are now all pervasive and may be found anywhere. The design of goods may provide value for the consumer by collecting data from several scattered sources and performing sophisticated analysis, Therefore, this has provided a basis for an assessment of the role of IoT and subsequently the IoE in sustainable/green marketing because of the significance of the IoE in sustainable marketing.

Green marketing focuses on activities in a green way to protect the environment (Agustini *et al.*, 2019). Traditional marketing activities such as modifying product features, packaging, or labelling, and creating marketing campaigns should be also considered. However, the emphasis on nature-driven marketing goes beyond that. Consumers desire to spend more to live sustainably, which is both the cause and the result of businesses' efforts (Nieuwenhuijsen, 2016). Consequently, firms need to develop green marketing strategies through a marketing mix that targets customer's preferences and individuality as is commonly practiced in normal marketing (Cabato *et al.,* 2020).

Kotler and Zaltman (1971) realized that marketing strategies typically used to promote goods and services could also be used to promote concepts. Social marketing was developed as a result of this appreciation. The other way includes the promotion of green behavior – lifestyle of consuming less and waste lifestyle, marketing techniques and communication channels. In addition, creation of loyal consumer basis that shares a sustainable development viewpoint, sustainable lifestyle, and sustainable consumption. Businesses, third-sector organisations, and organisations that are critical of markets, processes, institutions, and the government make up the majority of the significant players in green marketing. The growth of sustainable marketing is facilitated by the significance of IoT and IoE tools. The following outcomes are therefore produced by the development of sustainable marketing (Gordon *et al.,* 2011):

- Community development entails creating new communities cantered on users of certain devices to enable social media content creation. It makes it easier to focus the marketing materials to those demographics.
- The emergence of conversational commerce uses chatbots, intelligent assistants, and smart speakers to communicate with potential consumers. They enable online buying, order tracking, and the location of businesses like restaurants and events.
- Real time data is generated by IoE devices in significant volumes from diverse sources. Availability of this data would grant marketers an opportunity to test new ideas, use Big Data analysis tools, among others.
- IoE enables advertisers to present their audience with material that is extremely relevant. Throughout the day, people are inundated with information from both online and offline sources. The majority of the adverts are then naturally disregarded. With the use of IoE devices, marketers may be able to better understand their target market and effectively reach out to them.

PROSPECTS

IoE stands for the Internet of Everything which consists of all the things in place and that can communicate and share data with other devices or even systems on the net. The sensors, software, and hardware are used in these objects. Sustainability is one of the many areas of our lives and industries that IoE has the potential to revolutionise. Initiatives for sustainability driven by data are possible because to the Internet of Everything (IoE). Marketing that is individualised and focused: IoE enables businesses to examine user data and modify messaging and product suggestions. Cost savings and improved operational effectiveness: IoE can optimise processes to use resources more efficiently. IoE may be utilised to create more immersive and captivating marketing experiences for customers, increasing their level of engagement. Decision-making that is sustainable and predictive analytics. Predictive analytics, which are made possible by IoE, may assist firms in making ethical decisions based on trends and projections:

1. Data-Driven Sustainability Initiatives: Argue that IoE facilitates immediate collection of consumer behaviour and resource use data. Such data could support, in fact improve sustainability efforts and product designing (Gupta *et al.,* 2020).

2. Personalized and Targeted Marketing: Underline the possible of very individual marketing programs based on the Internet of Things (IoE). By analyzing user data, organizations can create customized message and product recommendation (Gupta & Malhotra, 2021).

3. Operational Efficiency and Cost Reduction: Exploring How IoE Optimizes Operations, Cutting Waste and Resource Consumption. Not only does it promote sustainability, but it also brings cost savings to businesses (Rüütmann *et al.,* 2019).

4. Enhanced Consumer Engagement: Investigate the application of AR/VR in IoE for marketing. This leads to a heightened sense of marketing experience (Jung & Yoon, 2021).

5. Predictive Analytics and Sustainable Decision-Making: Understand how IoE contributes towards Predictive Analytics; helping Businesses make intelligent forecast and trend based decision-making processes (Barnaghi *et al.,* 2019).

6. IoE-Enabled Sustainable Product Innovation: Show how IoE assists in product innovation being sustainable through tracking of product performance, use and result into environmentally friendly designs (Makvandi *et al.,* 2020).

7. IoE for Sustainable Supply Chain Management: Investigate the role of IoE technologies in improving transparency and sustainability within a company's supply-chain management so that it is possible for a company to track the environmental impact of its goods (Cui *et al.,* 2021).

8. IoE-Enhanced Customer Engagement Strategies: Talk about creative methods of involving customers in business driven by IoE which entail among other things interactive showcases and loyalty programs aided by IoT (Agrawal & Joshi, 2020).

9. IoE for CSR (Corporate Social Responsibility): Investigate how IoE can help companies implement CSR projects by offering tools for measurement and communication of the company's social and environmental footprints (Sawy *et al.,* 2020).

CONSTRAINTS

IoE has the potential to significantly contribute to the cause of sustainability, but it is necessary to be aware of its limitations. These limitations can be generally divided into three categories: technical, moral, and environmental difficulties. For the limitations of IoT and IoE, it is necessary to solve technological issues, ethical challenges, environmental challenges, and the environmental sustainability of IoE devices. In order to maximise IoE's potential for sustainability, it is crucial to solving these limitations. There is a great need for example for companies to have secure and privacy-preserving ways of collecting and dealing with IoE data. Furthermore, they need to ensure that IoE technologies are brought within the reach and means of everybody in any place at any time. Moreover, companies should develop eco-friendly and energy-efficient tools for IoE. With the development of the Internet of Everything (IoE integrating the Internet of Things), sustainable marketing practices are set to come transformatively after the COVID-19 period.

1. Technological Complexity and Integration Challenges: Marketers should recognize that many IoE devices and systems are complex when it comes to integration with diverse units (Smith *et al.,* 2020).

2. Data Privacy and Security Concerns: Highlight the increasing worries on data privacy and security of the IoE environments. Moreover, this raises concerns of data sharing that may expose the consumers' privacies (Rocha *et al.,* 2019).

3. Digital Divide and Accessibility Issues: Explain what some consider to be 'The Digital Divide' with emphasis on how uneven access to some technologies underlying IoE may undermine sustainable marketing potential (Chen & Xu, 2020).

4. Environmental Sustainability of IoE Devices: Investigate the effect of the production and disposal of IOE devices on the environment. These include worries raised about electronic waste and energy consumption concerning these technologies (Zhang *et al.,* 2018).

5. Data Management and Analytics Challenges: Overwhelming is one major headache associated with the management and analysis of a wealth of data that comes along with IoE devices. This is an area that requires the advanced analytics of data processing (Verma & Rai, 2019).

6. Consumer Skepticism and Trust Issue: Exploring Consumer Skepticism on Data Collection by IOE Devices. Trust is built and maintained by the use of transparency in data practices (Moraes *et al.,* 2021).

7. Energy Consumption of IoE Devices: Present the challenges of energy consumption regarding IoE devices and the need for energy-efficient technology to reduce environmental impact (Sookhak *et al.,* 2019).

8. Data Ownership and Governance: Scrutinize the intricacies of data ownership, governance, and rights in the IoE environments, pointing out possible conflicts and legal problems (Tsai *et al.,* 2020).

IMPLICATIONS

Sustainability might undergo a significant change because of the Internet of Everything (IoE). The Internet of Things (IoE) could benefit organizations, consumers, and governments in decreasing the impact they have on the environment as well as creating a future that is more sustainable by allowing real-time data gathering, predictive analytics, and personalized interaction. IoE's capacity to provide real-time input and understanding of how resources are used, and environmental effects can help both customers and businesses adopt sustainable practices. Eco-friendly decisions and supply chain transparency: IoE can increase supply chain transparency, enabling customers to make sound choices regarding eco-friendly goods and services. The reduction of waste and the circular economy. IoE can assist with the transition to a circular economy by enabling improved tracking and recycling programs.

1. Behavioural Change and Sustainability Adoption: Highlighting the potential of IoE to significantly influence behaviour among consumers. As an example, real-time feedback on the consumption of energy might encourage environmentally friendly behaviours (Lu & Wei, 2018).

2. Eco-friendly Decisions and Supply Chain Transparency: Consider how IoE could boost supply chain visibility. This enables customers to make decisions regarding items that are environmentally friendly with expertise (Wang & Zhang, 2019).

3. Circular Economy and Waste Reduction: Investigate how the Internet of Everything (IoE) will assist with the transition to a circular economy. Waste may be diminished by means of initiatives for enhanced monitoring and disposal (Geng *et al.,* 2017).

4. Competitive Advantage and Consumer Trust: Provide evidence of how companies using IoE for sustainable advertising can acquire an edge over competitors by adhering to customer values and fostering a sense of trust (Xu & Chen, 2020).

5. Regulatory Landscape and Compliance: As IoE technologies proliferate, highlight the value of maintaining an eye on and reacting to fluctuating regulatory regimes (Lee *et al.,* 2021).

6. Collaborations and Partnerships: To completely realize the enormous potential of IoE in sustainable marketing, it is necessary to emphasize the significance of collaboration among enterprises, governments, and NGOs (Heppelmann & Porter, 2014).

7. IoE for Sustainable Urban Development: Illustrate how IoE might be applied to encourage environmentally conscious cities for growth and development, which may result in significant ramifications for companies that conduct business in densely populated environments (Kummitha *et al.,* 2021).

8. Quantifying the Impact of IoE-Based Sustainable Marketing Initiatives on Environmental and Social Goals: Offer techniques for calculating the impact of IoE-Based Sustainable Marketing Initiatives on Environmental and Social Goals (Zhang & Wang, 2020).

9. Consumer Empowerment and Advocacy: Highlight how the Internet of Everything (IoE) might enable consumers to take an active role in sustainable movements and promote ethical corporate practices (Chen & Zhang, 2021).

10. Ethical Considerations and Responsible AI: In the context of AI–driven decision–making, the ethical ramifications of the Internet of Everything need to be explored. Ethical use is considered the most important aspect of sustainable marketing Initiatives (Floridi *et al.,* 2018).

11. IoE in Sustainable Marketing: How IoT sensors and data analytics improve resource efficiency for demonstrating that a case study on the use of IoE in sustainable agriculture needs to be presented (Liu *et al.,* 2019).

12. Smart Cities and Sustainable Urbanization: Providing practical examples of how connected devices support sustainability in urban environments and provide information about Internet of Everything (IoE), applications in Smart cities (Al-Fuqaha *et al.,* 2015).

13. IoE in Retail Sustainability: Explaining how IoE is being used in the retail industry, cutting down on waste, and improving the shopping experience by just paying particular attention to IoT devices (Dimitrov & Zhelev, 2020).

REFERENCES

Adams, M. (2017). Big data and individual privacy in the age of the internet of things. *Technology Innovation Management Review, 7*(4), 12–24. doi:10.22215/timreview/1067

Agrawal, S., & Joshi, M. (2020). Internet of Things (IoT) in customer engagement: A comprehensive review of the literature. *International Journal of Information Management, 54,* 102000.

Agustini, D. H., Athanasius, S. S., & Retnawati, B. B. (2019). Identification of green marketing strategies: Perspective of a developing country. *Innovative Marketing., 15*(4), 42–56. doi:10.21511/im.15(4).2019.04

Ahmed, E., Yaqoob, I., Abaker, I., Hashem, T., Khan, I., Ibrahim, A., Ahmed, A., Imran, M., & Vasilakos, A. V. (2017). The role of big data analytics in internet of things. *Computer Networks*, *129*, 459–471. doi:10.1016/j.comnet.2017.06.013

Akhter, S. H. (2014). Privacy concern and online transactions: The impact of internet self-efficacy and internet involvement. *Journal of Consumer Marketing*, *31*(2), 118–125. doi:10.1108/JCM-06-2013-0606

Al-Fuqaha, A., Guizani, M., Mohammadi, M., Aledhari, M., & Ayyash, M. (2015). Internet of Things: A survey on enabling technologies, protocols, and application issues. *IEEE Communications Surveys and Tutorials*, *17*(4), 2347–2376. doi:10.1109/COMST.2015.2444095

Andronie, M., Gârdan, D. A., Dumitru, I., Gârdan, I. P., Andronie, I. E., & Uță, C. (2019). Integrating the principles of green marketing by using big data. Good practices. *Amfiteatru Economic*, *21*(50), 258–269. doi:10.24818/EA/2019/50/258

Auger, A., Exposito, E., & Lochin, E. (2018). Towards the internet of everything: Deployment scenarios for a QoO-aware integration platform. In *2018 IEEE 4th World Forum on Internet of Things (WF-IoT)* (pp. 499-504). IEEE.

Bamberger, V., Nansé, F., Schreiber, B., & Zintel, M. (2017). Logistics 4.0–Facing digitalization-driven disruption. *Prism*, *38*, 39.

Bandyopadhyay, D., & Sen, J. (2011). Internet of Things: Applications and challenged in technology and standardization. *Wireless Personal Communications*, *58*(1), 49–69. doi:10.1007/s11277-011-0288-5

Barnaghi, P., Sheth, A., & Henson, C. (2019). From the Internet of Things to the Internet of Everything. *Future Generation Computer Systems*, *91*, 993–997.

Bechtold, J., Lauenstein, C., Kern, A., Bernhofer, L. (2011). Industry 4.0: The capgemini consulting view. *Capgemini Consult. Digit. Transform. Supply Chain,* 1–36.

Bojanova, I., Hurlburt, G., & Voas, J. (2014). Imagineering an internet of anything. *Computer*, *47*(6), 72–77. doi:10.1109/MC.2014.150

Breur, T. (2015). Big data and the internet of things. *Journal of Marketing Analytics*, *3*(1), 1–4. doi:10.1057/jma.2015.7

Bui, M., & Namin, A. (2019). Digital technology disrupting health: Reviewing key components of modern healthcare. In A. S. Krishen & O. Berezan (Eds.), *In Marketing and Humanity: Discourses in the Real World* (pp. 148–169). New Castle.

Cabato, M. G., Macadat, Y., & Bronola, F. B. (2020). Green marketing: A study on the perception of CBA students in PUP Manila. Polytechnic University of the Philippines, College of Business Administration.

Chen, Y.-S., & Xu, Z. (2020). Sustainable marketing in the era of Internet of Everything (IoE): Opportunities, challenges, and strategies. *Journal of Business Research*, *117*, 535–546.

Chouk, I., & Mani, Z. (2019). Factors for and against resistance to smart services: Role of consumer lifestyle and ecosystem related variables. *Journal of Services Marketing*, *33*(4), 449–462. doi:10.1108/JSM-01-2018-0046

Cisco. (2015). *The internet of everything*. Available at: https:// newsroom.cisco.com/ioe

Crnovrsanin, T., Muelder, C., Correa, C., & Ma, K. (2009). *Proximity-based visualization of movement trace data. In 2009 IEEE symposium on visual analytics science and technology*. IEEE.

Cui, H., Shen, L., & Li, H. (2021). IoE-enabled supply chain management for transparency and sustainability. *Journal of Cleaner Production*, *280*, 124387.

De Cremer, D., Nguyen, B., & Simkin, L. (2017). The integrity challenge of the internet-of-Things (IoT) on understanding its dark side. *Journal of Marketing Management*, *33*(1-2), 145–158. doi:10.1080/02 67257X.2016.1247517

Dimitrov, D., & Zhelev, C. (2020). Internet of Things (IoT) technologies for waste reduction and enhanced shopping experience in the retail sector. *Sustainability*, *12*(24), 10355.

Dong, S., Abbas, K., & Jain, R. (2019). A survey on distributed denial of service (DDoS) attacks in SDN and cloud computing environments. *IEEE Access : Practical Innovations, Open Solutions*, *7*, 80813–80828. doi:10.1109/ACCESS.2019.2922196

El Sawy, O. A., Gomaa, M. H., & Kamel, M. S. (2020). Internet of Things (IoT) for corporate social responsibility: A comprehensive review of the literature. *International Journal of Information Management*, *55*, 102091.

Eze, O., & Cherish, O. C. (2019). Achieving customer satisfaction through sustainable marketing strategies: A Qualitative analysis of three bread industries in Abakaliki Ebonyi State. Nigeria. *American Journal of Multidisciplinary Research & Development, 1*(4), 1-7.

Farias da Costa, V. C., Oliveira, L., & de Souza, J. (2021). Internet of everything (IoE) taxonomies: A survey and a novel knowledge-based taxonomy. *Sensors (Basel)*, *21*(2), 568. doi:10.3390/s21020568 PMID:33466895

Floridi, L., Cowls, J., Beltrametti, M., Chatila, R., Chazerand, P., Dignum, V., ... & Vayena, E. (2021). An ethical framework for a good AI society: Opportunities, risks, principles, and recommendations. *Ethics, Governance, and Policies in Artificial Intelligence*, 19-39.

Fonseca, L. M., & Azevedo, A. L. (2020). COVID-19: Outcomes for global supply chains. *Management & Marketing. Challenges for the Knowledge Society*, *15*(s1), 424–438. doi:10.2478/mmcks-2020-0025

Fredette, J., Marom, R., Steinert, K., & Witters, L. (2012). *The promise and peril of hyperconnectivity for organizations and societies*. The Global Information Technology Report. World Economic Forum. https://www3.weforum.org/docs/GITR/2012/ GITR_Chapter1.10_20 12.pdf

FTC. (2015). *IoT privacy & security in a connected world*. FTC Staff Report.

Gabisch, J. A., & Milne, G. R. (2014). The impact of compensation on information ownership and privacy control. *Journal of Consumer Marketing*, *31*(1), 13–26. doi:10.1108/JCM-10-2013-0737

Geng, Y., Liu, Y., Zhang, J., Xue, B., & Chu, K. W. (2017). Internet of Things (IoT) applications in a circular economy: A review. *Journal of Cleaner Production*, *168*, 591–604.

Giddens, A. (1977). *Studies in social and political theory.* Basic Books.

Giddens, A. (1984). *The constitution of society: Outline of the theory of structuration.* Polity Press.

Gordon, R., Carrigan, M., & Hastings, G. (2011). A framework for sustainable marketing. *Marketing Theory, 11*(2), 143–163. doi:10.1177/1470593111403218

Gupta, P., & Malhotra, N. K. (2021). Internet of Things (IoT) and marketing: A review of opportunities and challenges. *Journal of Business Research, 129,* 122–138.

Gurau, C., Ranchhod, A., & Gauzente, C. (2003). To legislate or not to legislate': A comparative exploratory study of privacy/personalisation factors affecting French, UK and US web sites. *Journal of Consumer Marketing, 20*(7), 652–664. doi:10.1108/07363760310506184

Hamid, S., & Jameel, S. T. (2020). A Study of Green Marketing Practices in the Selected Ayurvedic Resorts of Kerala. In *Global Developments in Healthcare and Medical Tourism* (pp. 176–187). IGI. doi:10.4018/978-1-5225-9787-2.ch010

Iacobucci, D., Petrescu, M., Krishen, A., & Bendixen, M. (2019). The state of marketing analytics in research and practice. *Journal of Marketing Analytics, 7*(3), 152–181. doi:10.1057/s41270-019-00059-2

Ilyas, M. (2019). Determining Critical Success Factors for Quality and Accreditation through Delphi Technique. *International Journal of Higher Education, 8*(3), 148–158. doi:10.5430/ijhe.v8n3p148

Jung, S. Y., & Yoon, S. J. (2021). Augmented reality and virtual reality in the Internet of Things (IoE) for marketing: Opportunities and challenges. *Technological Forecasting and Social Change, 172,* 120994.

Kakatkar, C., & Spann, M. (2019). Marketing analytics using anonymized and fragmented tracking data. *International Journal of Research in Marketing, 36*(1), 117–136. doi:10.1016/j.ijresmar.2018.10.001

Khvoynitskaya, S. (2019). *Internet of everything vs internet of things: what is the difference?* Available at: www.itransition. com/blog/internet-of-everything-vs-internet -of-things-what-is-the-difference

Kibria, M. G., Ali, S., Jarwar, M. A., & Chong, I. (2017, October). A framework to support data interoperability in web objects based IoT environments. In *2017 International Conference on Information and Communication Technology Convergence (ICTC)* (pp. 29-31). IEEE. 10.1109/ICTC.2017.8190935

Kim, H.-M., Lee, I., & Kaminsky, P. (2021). Regulatory frameworks for the Internet of Everything (IoE): A review of opportunities and challenges. *Journal of Business Research, 126,* 101–113.

Kotler, P., & Zaltman, G. (1971). Social marketing: An approach to planned social change. *Journal of Marketing, 35*(3), 3–12. doi:10.1177/002224297103500302 PMID:12276120

Krishen, A. S., Raschke, R. L., & Kachroo, P. (2011). A feedback control approach to maintain consumer information load in online shopping environments. *Information & Management, 48*(8), 344–352. doi:10.1016/j.im.2011.09.005

Krishen, A. S., Raschke, R. L., & Mejza, M. (2010). Guidelines for shaping perceptions of fairness of transportation infrastructure policies: The case of vehicle mileage tax. *Transportation Journal, 49*(3), 24–38. doi:10.2307/40904902

Kummitha, R., Krishna Reddy, M., & Rao, S. S. (2021). Internet of Things (IoT) for sustainable city planning: Opportunities and challenges. *Journal of Cleaner Production, 286*, 125592.

Lee, J., Kim, H., & Kaminsky, P. (2020). Internet of Everything (IoE) for sustainability: A review of opportunities and challenges. *Journal of Cleaner Production, 253*, 119994.

Liu, Y., Li, Y., & Yu, S. (2019). Internet of Things (IoT) for sustainable agriculture: A case study of precision irrigation. *Computers and Electronics in Agriculture, 163*, 104831.

Lu, W., & Wei, L. (2018). Internet of Things (IoT) for sustainable development: A review on enabling technologies, applications, and challenges. *Journal of Cleaner Production, 174*, 442–458.

Makvandi, P., Zarrabi, A., Ashrafizadeh, M., & Samarghandian, S. (2020). Technological complexity and integration challenges: Metal-based nanomaterials in biomedical applications: antimicrobial activity and cytotoxicity aspects. *Advanced Functional Materials, 30*(28), 2000459.

McDowell, R. M., & Goldstein, G. M. (2016, October 25). The authoritarian internet power grab: The internet of things will be worth trillions by 2025. China wants centralized control. *The Wall Street Journal.* Retrieved from http://www.wsj.com/ articles/the-authoritarian-internet-power-grab-477436573?mod5rss_opinion_main

Miedema, T. E. (2018). Consumer protection in cyberspace and the ethics of stewardship. *Journal of Consumer Policy, 41*(1), 55–75. doi:10.1007/s10603-017-9364-x

Milne, G. R., Bahl, S., & Rohm, A. J. (2008). Toward a framework for assessing covert marketing practices. *Journal of Public Policy & Marketing, 27*(1), 57–62. doi:10.1509/jppm.27.1.57

Milne, G. R., Labrecque, L. I., & Cromer, C. (2009). Toward an understanding of the online consumer's risky behavior and protection practices. *The Journal of Consumer Affairs, 43*(3), 449–473. doi:10.1111/ j.1745-6606.2009.01148.x

Mohanraj, G., & Karthikeyan, P. (2016). Green Marketing-New Opportunities and Challenges. *Asian Journal of Research in Social Sciences and Humanities, 6*(7), 1238–1244. doi:10.5958/2249-7315.2016.00508.6

Moraes, D. P., de Oliveira, F. R., & da Silva, V. A. (2021). Consumer skepticism towards data collection by IoT devices: A systematic review. *Journal of Business Research, 135*, 1–17.

Ng, I. C. L., & Wakenshaw, S. Y. L. (2017). The Internet-of-Things: Review and research directions. *International Journal of Research in Marketing, 34*(1), 3–21. doi:10.1016/j.ijresmar.2016.11.003

Nguyen, B., & Simkin, L. (2017). The Internet of Things (IoT) and marketing: The state of play, future trends and the implications for marketing. *Journal of Marketing Management, 33*(1-2), 1–6. doi:10.10 80/0267257X.2016.1257542

Nielsen, A. (2019). *Natural' Rise in Sustainability around the World.* Nielsen.Available online: https:// www.nielsen.com/insights/

Nieuwenhuijsen, M. J. (2016). Urban and transport planning, environmental exposures and health-new concepts, methods and tools to improve health in cities. *Environmental Health, 15*(S1), 161–171. doi:10.1186/s12940-016-0108-1 PMID:26960529

Nosratabadi, S., Mosavi, A., Shamshirband, S., Zavadskas, E. K., Rakotonirainy, A., & Chau, K. W. (2019). Sustainable business models: A review. *Sustainability (Basel)*, *11*(6), 1663. doi:10.3390/su11061663

Peppet, S. R. (2014). Regulating the internet of things: First steps toward managing discrimination, privacy, security and consent. *Texas Law Review*, *93*, 85.

Petrescu, M., & Krishen, A. S. (2018). Analyzing the analytics: Data privacy concerns. *Journal of Marketing Analytics*, *6*(2), 41–43. doi:10.1057/s41270-018-0034-x

Porter, M. E., & Heppelmann, J. E. (2014). How smart, connected products are transforming competition. *Harvard Business Review*, *92*(11), 64–88.

Raschke, R., Krishen, A. S., & Kachroo, P. (2014). Understanding the components of information privacy threats for location-based services. *Journal of Information Systems*, *28*(1), 227–242. doi:10.2308/isys-50696

Rejeb, A., Simske, S., Rejeb, K., Treiblmaier, H., & Zailani, S. (2020). Internet of Things research in supply chain management and logistics: A bibliometric analysis. *Internet of Things : Engineering Cyber Physical Human Systems*, *12*, 100318. doi:10.1016/j.iot.2020.100318

Rocha, A., Silva, V. A., & Oliveira, F. R. (2019). Internet of Things for sustainable marketing: A systematic review of opportunities and challenges. *Journal of Cleaner Production*, *220*, 862–872.

Rowan, N. J., & Galanakis, C. M. (2020). Unlocking challenges and opportunities presented by COVID-19 pandemic for cross-cutting disruption in agri-food and green deal innovations: Quo Vadis? *The Science of the Total Environment*, *748*, 141362. doi:10.1016/j.scitotenv.2020.141362 PMID:32823223

Rüütmann, A., Perens, R., & Raud, K. (2019). Internet of Things for optimizing business operations: A review of opportunities and challenges. *Journal of Business Research*, *109*, 101–114.

Saura, J. R., Palos-Sanchez, P., & Rodríguez Herráez, B. (2020). Digital marketing for sustainable growth: Business models and online campaigns using sustainable strategies. *Sustainability (Basel)*, *12*(3), 1003. doi:10.3390/su12031003

Seretny, M., & Gaur, D. (2020). The model of sustainable marketing as a responsible approach to marketing in the era of industry 4.0. *Advances in Science. Technology and Innovation*, 1.

Shigeta, R., Kawahara, Y., Goud, G. D., & Naik, B. B. (2018). *Capacitive-touch-based soil monitoring device with exchangeable sensor probe. In 2018 IEEE SENSORS*. IEEE.

Singh, T., & Hill, M. E. (2003). Consumer privacy and the internet in Europe: A view from Germany. *Journal of Consumer Marketing*, *20*(7), 634–651. doi:10.1108/07363760310506175

Smith, P., Watson, J., & Geuens, M. (2020). Technological complexity and integration challenges: Marketing in the Internet of Everything era. *Journal of Marketing Management*, *36*(11-12), 916–937.

Sookhak, M., Gani, A., Shiraz, M., & Buyya, R. (2019). Energy efficiency and renewable energy in the Internet of Things: A review. *IEEE Communications Surveys and Tutorials*, *21*(2), 1718–1747. doi:10.1109/COMST.2018.2867288

Suchanek, M., & Szmelter-Jarosz, A. (2019). Environmental aspects of generation Y's sustainable mobility. *Sustainability (Basel)*, *11*(11), 3204. doi:10.3390/su11113204

Tariq, B., Taimoor, S., Najam, H., Law, R., Hassan, W., & Han, H. (2020). Generating marketing outcomes through Internet of things (Iot) technologies. *Sustainability (Basel)*, *12*(22), 9670. doi:10.3390/su12229670

Tsai, W.-H., Wang, Y.-F., & Chen, Y.-C. (2020). Data ownership, governance, and rights in Internet of Things (IoT) ecosystems: Complexities, conflicts, and legal issues. *Telecommunications Policy*, *44*(6), 101938.

Tucker, K., Bulim, J., Koch, G., North, M., Nguyen, T., Fox, J., & Delay, D. (2018). Internet industry: A perspective review through internet of things and internet of everything. *International Management Review*, *14*(2), 26–38.

Verhoef, P. C., Stephen, A. T., Kannan, P. K., Luo, X., Abhishek, V., Andrews, M., Bart, Y., Datta, H., Fong, N., Hoffman, D. L., Hu, M. M., Novak, T., Rand, W., & Zhang, Y. (2017). Consumer connectivity in a complex, technology-enabled, and mobile-oriented world with smart products. *Journal of Interactive Marketing*, *40*(1), 1–8. doi:10.1016/j.intmar.2017.06.001

Verma, S., & Rai, A. (2019). Internet of things (IoT) for marketing: A review of opportunities and challenges. *Journal of Business Research*, *116*, 598–613.

Wang, W., & Zhang, J. (2019). Internet of Everything (IoE) for supply chain sustainability: A review of opportunities and challenges. *Sustainability*, *11*(9), 2508.

Weinberg, B. D., Milne, G. R., Andonova, Y. G., & Hajjat, F. M. (2015). Internet of things: Convenience vs privacy and secrecy. *Business Horizons*, *58*(6), 615–624. doi:10.1016/j.bushor.2015.06.005

Wilkinson, R., Black, J., Agnew, A., Arnold, J., Francolini, A., Gardner, M., & Harder, A. (2015). Rethinking the value chain. *Consum. Goods Forum*, *1*, 48.

Woodside, A. G., & Sood, S. (2017). Vignettes in the two-step arrival of the internet of things and its reshaping of marketing management's service-dominant logic. *Journal of Marketing Management*, *33*(1-2), 98–110. doi:10.1080/0267257X.2016.1246748

Wright, L. W. L. (2016, July 15). *5 ways the Internet of Things is already affecting you*. Retrieved October 17, 2023, from https://www.saga.co.uk/magazine/technology/Internet/communications/5-ways-theInternet-of-things-affects-yo

Xu, L. D., He, W., & Li, S. (2014). Internet of things in industries: A survey. *IEEE Transactions on Industrial Informatics*, *10*(4), 2233–2243. doi:10.1109/TII.2014.2300753

Yang, L. T., Di Martino, B., & Zhang, Q. (2017). Internet of everything [editorial]. *Mobile Information Systems*, 1–3.

Yu, J., Park, J., Lee, K., & Han, H. (2021). Can environmentally sustainable development and green innovation of hotels trigger the formation of a positive brand and price premium? *International Journal of Environmental Research and Public Health*, *18*(6), 3275. doi:10.3390/ijerph18063275 PMID:33809991

Zahay, D., Peltier, J. J., & Krishen, A. S. (2012). Building the foundation for customer data quality in CRM systems for financial services firms. *Journal of Database Marketing & Customer Strategy Management, 19*(1), 5–1. doi:10.1057/dbm.2012.6

Zhang, J., & Wang, Y. (2020). Quantifying the impact of IoE-based sustainable marketing initiatives on environmental and social goals. *Journal of Cleaner Production, 259*, 120740.

Zhang, T. H., & Chen, Y. (2021). The role of Internet of Things (IoT) in empowering consumers to participate in sustainable movements and advocate for responsible business practices. *Journal of Cleaner Production, 280*, 124385.

Zhang, Y., Zhang, X., & Zhao, C. (2018). Environmental impact of internet of things devices: A review. *Journal of Cleaner Production, 198*, 1222–1237.

Chapter 8
Quantifying the Impacts of Artificial Intelligence Implementations in Marketing

Subhashini Durai
Bharathiar University, India

Geetha Manoharan
ⓘD https://orcid.org/0000-0002-8644-8871
SR University, India

T. Sathya Priya
Coimbatore Institute of Technology, India

R. Jayanthi
Coimbatore Institute of Technology, India

Abdul Razak
ⓘD https://orcid.org/0000-0003-2553-4992
Entrepreneurship Development Institute of India, India

Sunitha Purushottam Ashtikar
SR University, India

ABSTRACT

AI will personalize marketing. Analysis of client behavior and preferences customizes product and service suggestions. AI-powered CRM solutions can automate customer service, help customers, and boost satisfaction. AI improves marketing targeting. Technology can improve client behavior targeting. AI will also impact digital marketing. Personalization boosts client engagement and sales. Virtual assistants and chat bots will increase marketing. Apps can swiftly answer customer questions, improve service, boost satisfaction, and develop brand loyalty. AI can enhance price by studying market trends, competition, and customer behaviour. Machine learning algorithms help organizations set rates, increasing sales and profit. Marketers may create more engaging content with AI. AI can analyze client data and behavior to determine which content performs best for target demographics, improving content marketing. AI marketing will develop in the future. Companies will benefit from AI-powered, tailored, and data-driven marketing that boosts customer engagement, loyalty, and revenue.

DOI: 10.4018/979-8-3693-1339-8.ch008

INTRODUCTION TO ARTIFICIAL INTELLIGENCE IN MARKETING

A lot of the recent big changes in the marketing industry have happened much faster since artificial intelligence has been used in marketing tactics. The way companies promote their products has changed a lot because of artificial intelligence, which is a branch of computer science. By looking at the different ways that AI technologies are changing marketing tactics, this article aims to show how complicated the relationship is between AI and marketing. Understand what artificial intelligence (AI) is and how it works in marketing before looking into the magazine's goals and structure. "Artificial intelligence" is the general term for using computer programmes and machine learning methods in marketing. In this case, huge amounts of data need to be analysed, predictions made based on the data need to be made, and many different marketing chores need to be automated. AI can improve the targeting of ads, personalise marketing efforts, and make exchanges between businesses and customers more efficient. For businesses to stay competitive in a digital world that is changing quickly, AI technology has led to more complicated marketing apps.

STATEMENT OF THE PROBLEM

Science fiction offers many scenarios where technology takes away all of the human jobs, and robots take over the world. The good news for us is that humans will always be necessary when it comes to marketing jobs. Computers can't change their minds, make creative decisions, or use their imaginations especially in marketing field. Creativity and cultural reference will be sorely lacking if a company only uses AI for content creation. In such a case, Artificial Intelligence may offer certain solutions and efficiencies but, ultimately, humans are still the epicentre of the marketing world. Secondly, it's hard to imagine that a computer could be wrong. And mathematically or formulaically they might always be "right" but humans are comprised of so much more than simply formulas and statistics. Humans are unique and have many varieties of tastes and preferences that cannot be restricted to a formula. Ultimately, AI content tools must be implemented thoughtfully across your inbound marketing program. Understand how AI tactics will help you guide prospects to solving their pain points. Don't turn to AI because it's the hot new thing but rather because it will help you help your customers more efficiently and turn leads into customers quicker. The next problem is that the companies find it difficult to analyse the consumer behaviour to fix up their marketing strategies. Deep learning through Artificial Intelligence allows computers to more accurately identify user behaviour and predict which segments are more likely to become customers. Programs can provide specific information related to which leads will probably convert, allowing marketers to target their efforts based on detailed demographics – without wasting time on less probable leads. In marketing field it is very important that the company have to promote personalization of their products as per the customers' needs. This includes identifying possible potential customers based on data like purchase demographics, location, purchase history, etc. It also includes tracking and customer data with the products themselves. Thus to address these challenges, artificial intelligence is the only solution and is being discussed below.

PURPOSE OF THE RESEARCH

The purpose of the research is to make the readers understand what is artificial intelligence; how it is used in digital platform; its importance in marketing field; its impact on the consumer buying behaviour; etc. It also shows how AI supports the marketing function in attracting and gaining customers. The outcome of this research helps the readers to understand completely about the adaptation of AI in marketing field and how it supports the business by increase in satisfied customers.

ARTIFICIAL INTELLIGENCE

Artificial intelligence in computer science creates machines that can perform human tasks.. Many skills include learning, problem-solving, thinking, knowing natural language, and perceiving. As technology has gotten better, artificial intelligence (AI) has become more common in all fields, including marketing. AI is roughly classified into two types:

- Narrow AI (Failure AI): The limited AI's purpose-built nature. It thrives in performing predefined tasks, such as speech recognition or recommendation systems. Narrow artificial intelligence is demonstrated by virtual personal assistants such as Siri and Alexa.
- General AI (Powerful AI): General artificial intelligence is intelligent in the same way that people are and is capable of doing a wide range of jobs that humans can. However, we are still in the early phases of developing an AI, and it is purely speculative at the moment.

MARKETING APPLICATIONS OF ARTIFICIAL INTELLIGENCE

AI has several uses in marketing, revolutionising how firms interact with their customers. The following are some major applications and examples:

- Engines for Personalization and Recommendation: Personalization and recommendation engines are technologies and tactics used to personalise and improve user experiences in various applications and services by delivering content, commodities, or ideas tailored to individual tastes and behaviour. These engines use data analysis and algorithms to generate personalised suggestions that improve user engagement, client satisfaction, and company outcomes.
- Personalization: Personalization refers to the systematic adaptation of content, services, or user interfaces in order to cater for individual needs and choices for every user. It seeks to create a more relevant and engaging experience by delivering information or options that are most likely to resonate with each user. Personalization can be used in a range of industries, including e-commerce, content delivery, advertising, healthcare, and others.
- Engines of Recommendation: Recommender systems, often known as recommendation engines, are a subset of personalization that focuses on offering certain goods or actions to users based on their past behaviour, preferences, or demographic data. These engines examine user data using algorithms and data analysis techniques to detect trends and connections in order to offer ac-

curate suggestions. Social media content suggestions, product recommendations on e-commerce websites, and movie recommendation systems on streaming platforms are all common instances.

- Segmentation of customers: Customer segmentation refers to a strategic marketing approach and analytical procedure employed by companies to categorise users based on varied factors. This categorization is based on same features, behaviours, or traits exhibited by the clients. Consumer segmentation aims to enhance comprehension and effectively target distinct consumer segments by employing specialised marketing techniques, tailored product offerings, and communication tactics.

- Organising Customers: Customer segmentation is the process of grouping or segmenting customers. These groups are often defined by a variety of variables such as demographics, psychographics, location, purchasing behaviours, preferences, and customer lifecycle stages.

CUSTOMER SEGMENTATION TYPES

- Demographic classification: Customers are categorised based on demographic factors, including age, gender, income, education, and marital status.
- Psychographic classification: This method categorises clients based on psychological and lifestyle factors like as values, interests, attitudes, and hobbies.
- Geographic division: Customers are classified geographically, such as by nation, city, or region.
- Segmentation of Behaviour: Customer behaviours like as purchase frequency, product usage, brand loyalty, and response to marketing initiatives are used to segment customers.
- Segmentation of the Customer Lifecycle: Customers are classified based on their status with the company (e.g., new customers, loyal customers, at-risk consumers).
- Analytics Predictive: Predictive analytics enabled by AI assist marketers in forecasting future trends, customer behaviour, and market demand.Predictive models improve inventory management, forecasting demand, and campaign optimisation.
- NLP: Sentiment analysis of social media posts and consumer reviews is possible with NLP.

Marketers may assess public sentiment towards their brand and products, allowing them to respond to negative criticism quickly and capitalise on positive feelings.

- Virtual Assistants and Chatbots: Chatbots respond instantly to consumer requests, hence increasing customer service.Google Assistant and Apple's Siri, for example, can be linked into marketing campaigns to provide interactive experiences.
- Curation and creation of content: GPT-3 and similar artificial intelligence (AI) algorithms possess the capability to produce content that closely resembles human-generated text, including many forms such as articles, product descriptions, and social media posts.AI is used by content curation systems to sift through massive amounts of content and recommend the most relevant articles for a specific audience.
- Optimisation and A/B testing: In real-time, AI algorithms assess A/B test results, identifying winning variations and optimising marketing campaigns.

As a result, ad performance and conversion rates improve.

- Automated Marketing: Email, lead scoring, and social media publishing are automated by AI. It lets marketers focus on strategy and innovation.

THE AI'S OBJECTIVES

Its main objective is to offer an in-depth look at how artificial intelligence has affected current marketing strategies. To reach our goal, we've set the following guiding principles:

- Understanding AI's Impact: We will cover case studies, success stories, and real-world applications that showcase AI's revolutionary potentialto understand how AI is transforming marketing practises across industries.
- AI in Customer Insights: We will look at how AI-powered analytics help businesses understand consumer preferences, behaviour patterns, and sentiment analysis. This will aid in the development of highly targeted and personalised marketing efforts.
- Marketing Automation: Investigate AI's marketing automation capabilities, such as chatbots, email marketing automation, and programmatic advertising. We will examine how AI-powered automation improves efficiency, lowers costs, and increases consumer engagement.Investigate how AI-generated material, such as product descriptions, blog articles, and social media posts, might supplement content marketing efforts and ensure messaging consistency.Examine the ethical aspects of AI in marketing, such as data privacy problems, algorithm bias, and the responsible use of AI to minimise unforeseen repercussions.In the ever-changing world of marketing, where strategies and tactics are constantly changing, one technological (Geetha M, Ramachandran K K, et al., 2022) development has sprung to the fore, promising to transform the landscape like never before: Artificial Intelligence (AI). This chapter will take you on a tour through the astonishing integration of AI and marketing, examining how this revolutionary synergy has revolutionised the way businesses communicate with their consumers, make data-driven decisions, and optimise their operations.

LITERATURE REVIEW

This 2023 study by Rajesh Rajaguru examines the potential benefits of using blockchain and artificial intelligence to boost consumers' trust in online travel and hotel evaluations. Based on the findings of the research, it has been determined that the three fundamental attributes of blockchain technology, namely decentralisation, immutability, and timestamping, play a crucial role in ensuring transparency within the context of the online review process. This study examines blockchain technology, AI agents, and human characteristics using a socio-technical systems approach. It shows how these aspects combine to increase transparency, making online reviews more trustworthy and affecting customers' decisions. The study reveals that transparency affects the relationship between blockchain's three features and online evaluation accuracy.. This study underscores the importance for researchers and practitioners to focus on a particular aspect of modern technologies in order to harness potential advantages. It advocates for an examination of the characteristics of blockchain (Kumari, S., Kumar, V., et al., 2023) and its interplay with artificial intelligence in the context of online reviews.

According to the most recent study by Dogan Gursoy, Lu Lu, Robin Nunkoo, and Demi Deng (2023), the Metaverse is likely to disrupt present corporate strategies, consumer standards, and marketing practises, as well as reinvent service marketing and management, despite its immaturity. However, the majority of current research has been on the interaction-based co-creation of metaverstic experiences rather than the way of producing actual purchases of products and services. This research provides a conceptual framework that illustrates how and why the Metaverse will have a substantial impact on the creation and delivery of service experiences, as well as their marketing and the process of co-creating the purchasing experience. It accomplishes this by providing multiple stakeholders with functional and hedonic benefits. Furthermore, this paper analyses Metaverse's potential for minimising choice risks related with uncertainty in service experience offerings, information overload, and uncertainty in marketing ecosystems and customers' service experience journeys. Its ramifications and difficulties are examined because the Metaverse's adoption will have a substantial impact on all stakeholders while also providing challenges. Use the research agenda offered in this study to evaluate potential Metaverse effects on service businesses.

N. Maranchak wrote the article. (2023) aims to analyse foreign experience with artificial intelligence in library digital marketing, outline the main directions, prospects, and issues of applying these technologies in Ukraine, and formulate recommendations for the successful implementation of AI in Ukrainian library digital marketing. ways for performing research. To attain our goal, we used a variety of scientific procedures such as analysis, substantiation, systematisation, comparison, and generalisation. In order to collect empirical data, we did a content analysis of relevant literature and case studies of international libraries who have implemented AI into their digital marketing campaigns. We used the findings from statistical research to generate advice for Ukrainian libraries on how to properly integrate artificial intelligence into their digital marketing strategy. Science is novel. The paper provides a unique perspective on how to use artificial intelligence to apply digital marketing tactics in libraries. By reviewing foreign experiences, the paper provides important techniques and tools for promoting library services in the digital age. The essay also discusses the potential of artificial intelligence technology to address difficulties in the Ukrainian library industry and offers implementation tips. Conclusions. The five main uses of artificial intelligence in the digital promotion of foreign libraries are chatbots, recommendation systems, smart libraries, digital archives, and user behaviour analysis. Personalising the user experience through content recommendations based on the user's preferences and search history; improving search functionality by providing more accurate and relevant results; increasing user engagement through real-time chatbot interaction; analysing user behaviour to develop targeted marketing campaigns; simplifying the analysis of large amounts of data and identifying patterns and trends are all possibilities for AI implementation. Because of a lack of finances, technological assistance, knowledge, and other issues, implementing AI technology might be problematic. Libraries can collaborate with AI experts or other libraries that have already implemented AI fragments; identify areas that need improvement and investment; identify staff with the necessary knowledge and skills to manage and support smart technologies; consider ICT gadgets as a means of efficiently providing information services; work to improve the efficiency of information and communication technologies; and constantly improve their skills and evaluation.

In recent years, digital marketing has increasingly used AI. Companies want to maximise client engagement and revenue using this technology, which explains this trend. Kumar, Tomar, Bharti, Naredla, Ibrahim, R.K., and Bader Alazzam, M. studied. Despite its potential, many companies are struggling to use AI in their digital marketing (2023). This study addresses this gap by exploring how companies might use AI in digital marketing. The authors analyse existing literature and empirical data to highlight the main concerns and potential consequences of AI in digital marketing. Organizations aiming to improve their artificial intelligence efforts receive helpful tips. This study examines AI's potential benefits in digital marketing. It examines AI's ability to personalise consumer experiences, improve marketing, and increase customer engagement. However, implementing artificial intelligence (AI) raises worries about data privacy and algorithm bias. The analysis offers practical advice for digital marketers looking to maximise AI use. A well-defined artificial intelligence (AI) strategy, resources for high-quality data, and AI model transparency and comprehensibility are important. This study advances digital marketing by showing how organisations may use AI to boost consumer engagement and revenue. This report can help companies position themselves for digital marketing success by following its helpful advice.

A study by Abrokwah-Larbi and Awuku-Larbi (2023) experimentally examines the relationship between organisational success and marketing AI use, utilising a resource-based perspective (RBV). This section describes the study's design and methods. 225 SMEs were surveyed for this study. These Ghana Enterprise Agency Eastern Region responders were selected from their list. The influence of AIM (Advanced Information Management) on SMEs' operational outcomes was studied using structural equation modelling and path analysis. Data research shows that AIM (Advanced Information Management) deployment affects numerous areas of Ghanaian SMEs' operations. These include financial performance, customer happiness, internal business process efficiency, and learning and growth efficiency. In this study, AIM determinants including the Internet of Things (IoT), collaborative decision-making systems (CDMS), virtual and augmented reality (VAR), and customization improve financial, customer, internal business process, and learning and growth performance. Research drawbacks and implications Furthermore, the research study's shortcomings must be acknowledged. Adding subject matter expert (SME) participants from understudied regions could increase the sample size of this research project. Future research should examine how Artificial Intelligence in Marketing (AIM) may evaluate consumer discussions and data, such as social media posts, to create message strategies that boost customer engagement. The effects on daily life Practical consequences fall into two categories. This report advises small and medium-sized firm (SME) owners and managers to build an AIM (Artificial Intelligence and Machine Learning) strategy to improve SME performance. This study suggests that small and medium-sized firm (SME) owners and managers use four AIM determinants—Information Overload Tolerance, Change-Driven Mindset, Value-Added Relationships, and Customization—to build the resources needed for effective AIM implementation. This study supports the Resource-Based View (RBV) theory and the idea that Adoption of Information Management (AIM) and its determinants—IOT, CDMS, VAR, and personalization—are strategic assets for improving Small and Medium Enterprises (SMEs) performance (SMEs). This enhanced performance includes SMEs' ability to produce income, satisfy customers, manage internal business processes, and promote learning and growth. This research adds to the knowledge of AIM and its administration in a rising economy.

Because of the pandemic's broad digitization, firms were able to automate business procedures, enhancing customer-brand relationships, according to S. Zhang (2022). The next stage for businesses implementing AI in emergency scenarios is to be proactive and go a step further. Despite this, the vast majority of organisations continue to address this expanding problem insufficiently. Covid outbreaks are unlikely to cause consumer behaviour to recover to pre-pandemic levels. Remote work will increase, as will online purchases. As economies reopen post-Covid-19, AI will help firms adapt. As with previous worldwide crises, the pandemic may worsen several crucial developments that began before Covid. Business AI investments must continue during recovery. This article merges traditional marketing approaches into a comprehensive framework that structured artificial intelligence can execute, using automation and AI in user-centric ways. Artificial intelligence, automation, and embedded technology will continue to disrupt the four Ps of marketing.

In 2022, Cui, H., Nie, Y., Li, and Zeng found that artificial intelligence technology is growing more widespread. The brand marketing artificial intelligence age has begun because brand marketing, a new concept and method of thinking, uses AI extensively. Given this environment, artificial intelligence in brand marketing management and implementation methods must be examined. With AI, we can capture customer demand, precisely portray consumer groups, and create high-quality brand marketing. Brand value underpins strategic brand management. Brand management integrates and directs all business processes using company content. The company's brand plan and framework are also updated to maintain the brand's value and promote long-term growth. Modern organisations use a number of brand marketing management modes and countermeasures to boost enterprise brand marketing promotion and long-term company success. Current enterprise brand marketing management difficulties and optimization options are also discussed.

This 2022 paper by Malthouse, E.C., and Copulsky, J.R. helps researchers, students, and advertising professionals comprehend and predict the effects of AI and ML on advertising and marketing communications (Marcom). AI arguments usually centre on algorithms and models, but to understand AI in Marcom, one must also analyse the ecosystem in which these algorithms work. This article frames the Marcom-AI environment and results. Customer data, algorithms and models, digital environments (like mobile devices and digital signage), digital content assets (including photos, videos, and writing), and IT infrastructure are its five interconnected components. AI uses in marketing communications are briefly discussed. To manage Marcom opportunities and difficulties, AI needs most ecosystem components. Along with consumers, influencers, brands/advertisers, media and messaging platforms, data platforms, publishers and content producers, MarTech/AdTech vendors, AI/ML service providers, device makers, and regulators, the ecosystem includes many players. Targeting, option structures, testing platforms, data-driven insights, and marketing workflow assistance help marketers optimise touchpoints. Based on the paradigm, we conclude that academics studying advertising may study consumer reactions to AI touchpoints, privacy, stakeholder interactions, and ecosystem changes..

As artificial intelligence has improved, traditional techniques to agricultural product production, marketing, and management have experienced substantial changes, necessitating more optimisation. Agricultural product manufacturers have begun to incorporate artificial intelligence (AI) technology into their manufacturing, marketing, and distribution processes. Article by Wang, H., Jing, G., Bohan, K., Peng, and Shi, Y. (2022) examine agricultural product management as it is currently done and investigate using artificial intelligence to merge production, marketing, and distribution. A classification model that combines factor analysis with an updated support vector machine (SVM) based on genetic algorithms (GAs) addresses the inadequacies of standard agricultural item categorization methods. The trials show that the modified method can quickly and accurately distinguish between agricultural product quality categories, boosting classification accuracy and making it widely relevant to quality evaluation.

THE MARKETING AI REVOLUTION

The broad strokes and educated judgements that once defined marketing have been transformed by AI's intelligent powers. Precision-guided AI-powered harpoons that target the proper fish with incredible accuracy are replacing traditional techniques of casting enormous nets in the hope of catching a few fish. But what exactly is artificial intelligence, and why is it viewed as a game changer in the marketing industry? AI is primarily a collection of tools and techniques that enable computers to replicate cognitive processes such as learning, reasoning, problem solving, and decision making. It enables computers to process massive datasets, detect patterns, and make predictions, which were previously the sole domain of humans. The convergence of artificial intelligence and marketing is not by chance; rather, it is a response to the changing consumer landscape and the data-driven age. Customers leave digital traces across websites, social media platforms, and online marketplaces, necessitating real-time, data-driven marketing methods. Enter artificial intelligence (AI), which can sift this deluge of data, extract meaningful insights, and plan extremely successful, personalised, and targeted marketing campaigns.

ARTIFICIAL INTELLIGENCE IN CUSTOMER RELATIONSHIP MANAGEMENT

The use of artificial intelligence technologies and techniques to improve and optimise various areas of customer relationship management (CRM) is referred to as AI in CRM. CRM refers to all of the strategies, processes, and technology that businesses employ to engage with customers, analyse customer data, and improve the overall customer experience. AI plays a critical role in CRM process enhancement by employing advanced algorithms and machine learning to automate and expedite operations, make data-driven choices, and personalise customer interactions.

Here are some significant AI components in CRM:

1. Data Analysis: Artificial intelligence can analyse and analyse enormous amounts of client data, including as purchase history, behaviour trends, social media interactions, and more. This analysis provides firms with significant insights into customer preferences, allowing them to modify their marketing and sales activities accordingly.

2. Customer Segmentation: AI algorithms can automatically categorise clients based on their attributes and behaviours. This segmentation assists businesses in developing targeted marketing campaigns and personalised offerings for various client categories.

3. Predictive Analytics: AI enables predictive analytics, which entails forecasting customer behaviour, such as predicting when a client will buy or churn. This data enables firms to take proactive steps to retain clients and increase sales.

4. Chatbots and Virtual Assistants: Chatbots and virtual assistants can handle client requests, schedule appointments, and track orders.. They increase the efficiency and availability of client assistance.

5. Sales Automation: Artificial intelligence can automate a variety of sales-related operations, including lead scoring, lead nurturing, and sales forecasting. This assists sales teams in prioritising leads and concentrating on the most attractive opportunities.

6. Personalization: AI-powered personalization enables businesses to give clients with highly individualised experiences. Personalised product recommendations, content recommendations, and email marketing campaigns tailored to individual tastes are examples of this.

7. Sentiment Analysis: Artificial intelligence-powered sentiment analysis systems can monitor social media and customer feedback to determine public attitude towards a firm or its products. This enables businesses to recognise and handle client complaints, as well as capitalise on favourable attitudes.

8. Voice Assistants: AI assistants that can be operated by voice, such as Amazon's Alexa or Apple's Siri, can be incorporated with CRM systems to offer voice-based interactions and assistance. This improves client comfort and accessibility.AI can assess CRM workflows and processes to identify areas for optimisation and automation. As a result, operational efficiency improves and manual tasks are decreased.

AI IMPROVES CRM PROCESSES

AI improves CRM operations in a variety of ways, increasing their effectiveness and efficiency:

- Data Enrichment: Explain how AI can automatically collect and enhance customer data, offering a complete picture of each client's preferences, habits, and history.
- Predictive Analytics: Describe how AI-driven predictive analytics can foresee customer behaviour, allowing organisations to anticipate demands and solve difficulties proactively.
- Lead Scoring: Explain how artificial intelligence may award lead ratings based on the possibility of conversion, assisting sales teams in prioritising leads.

Discuss the role of AI chatbots and virtual assistants in addressing mundane customer inquiries, freeing up human agents for more complicated duties.

ARTIFICIAL INTELLIGENCE IN DIGITAL MARKETING STRATEGIES

In recent years, digital marketing has advanced tremendously, thanks in large part to the use of artificial intelligence technologies. As businesses battle for the attention and allegiance of online consumers, artificial intelligence has emerged as a valuable tool for gaining a competitive advantage, optimising marketing strategies, and improving customer experiences. This introduction highlights artificial intelligence in digital marketing and its impact on modern marketing practises.

THE ADVANCEMENT OF DIGITAL MARKETING

The proliferation of digital gadgets and the rise of the internet have revolutionised how businesses communicate with their target customers. Social media marketing, email marketing, search engine optimisation (SEO), pay-per-click advertising, content marketing, and other channels are all part of digital marketing. However, the sheer number of data created by online interactions, as well as the complexity of customer behaviour, presented marketers with new challenges and opportunities.

AI'S ROLE IN DIGITAL MARKETING

With its ability to process massive quantities of data, learn from trends, and make data-driven judgements, artificial intelligence has revolutionised the digital marketing landscape. AI technologies are being integrated into numerous parts of digital marketing in order to improve performance, boost efficiency, and provide personalised experiences.

MARKETING APPLICATIONS OF AI

AI has various marketing uses.

The practise of promoting and selling products or services via digital platforms and technologies, commonly referred to as internet marketing, has gained significant prominence in recent years. This approach leverages the vast reach and accessibility of the internet. Digital marketing is heavily influenced by AI. AI can help marketers understand their target audience's actions, signs, and behaviours. Through a suitable strategy, people can quickly locate and engage with the right person. Marketing can benefit from using artificial intelligence (AI) to analyse and manage large amounts of data from social media, emails, and the Internet. It can be used with marketing automation to turn data into educated decisions, meaningful interactions, and positive organisational consequences. AI helps gather data, get consumer insights, predict customer behaviour, and automate marketing decision-making.

There has been a decrease in human errors.

Artificial intelligence (AI) has effectively mitigated human errors, particularly within very crucial sectors. This system has the capability to generate and optimise content for various email formats in a manner that is visually pleasing to recipients. Undoubtedly, the purpose of AI is to minimise human involvement and mitigate the possibility of human fallibility. Due to recurring data security issues, numerous organisations express apprehension regarding their employees' ability to safeguard client information and other essential corporate data. Artificial intelligence (AI) has the potential to assist organisations in managing various challenges by acquiring knowledge, adjusting its behaviour, and effectively fulfilling cybersecurity requirements. AI has the potential to replace many of the conventional slash-and-burn resources that are typically employed in the establishment and execution of a marketing strategy.

Establishing Connections Between Corporate Processes

Through the utilisation of information systems, artificial intelligence (AI) facilitates the seamless integration of corporate operations, hence delivering a flawless user experience. Businesses that harness the potential of artificial intelligence (AI) are able to generate notable marketing results. AI applications in marketing could help marketers create and implement more personalised and consumer-focused marketing programmes.. These strategies typically bring satisfaction to customers, leading to their transformation into enthusiastic advocates of the brand. The integration of technology such as artificial intelligence (AI) and the empowerment of individuals to exert control over micro-moments have the potential to enhance the appeal of interaction designs. As the advantages of artificial intelligence (AI) continue to expand, businesses are actively reimagining their marketing strategies in order to enhance client service.

Conduct a Comprehensive Analysis of Substantial Quantities of Market Data

Artificial intelligence has the capability to assess vast quantities of market data and make predictions on the probable future actions of a user. The system possesses the capability to analyse an extensive volume of search queries, reaching into the trillions, and has the ability to forecast the probability of a user engaging in a transaction. Artificial intelligence (AI) also plays a crucial role in the identification of issues and the implementation of appropriate remedial measures. The impact of artificial intelligence (AI) and machine learning (ML) transcends the mere creation of rudimentary instruments. It has a profound impact on the manner in which we engage in commercial activities. Businesses experience a significant increase in productivity, resulting in approximately a threefold improvement.

Please Provide Relevant and Informative Content

AI technologies streamline processes by systematically assessing incoming data and providing clients with tailored information that aligns with their individual preferences. The aforementioned technology should be seen as a means to direct marketing initiatives towards more ambitious goals. Artificial intelligence (AI) is expected to play a significant role in enabling marketers to effectively integrate advanced technology with human cognitive abilities. This integration will facilitate the ability to comprehend, analyse, and engage with contemporary clients on a personalised basis through the use of highly tailored, pertinent, and timely communication. Algorithms accurately assess the actions of a website visitor with the purpose of promptly modifying and displaying tailored advertising content. Data is continuously gathered and employed to influence subsequent adjustments in advertising material. Using artificial intelligence (AI) in marketing could help marketers create and implement more personalised and targeted consumer marketing programmes. It delves into customers' aspirations, motivations, and purchasing patterns, providing in-depth insights into the factors that shape their choices.

Facilitate the Provision of Customer Service That is Convenient for Customers

The integration of artificial intelligence (AI) enables the provision of intelligent, seamless, and user-friendly customer service to clients at every stage of their interaction. Ensuring a seamless and exceptional client experience is crucial. Marketing automation approaches are built upon the fundamental concept of automating normal marketing procedures and operations. The utilisation of artificial intelligence (AI) holds significant advantages for the field of marketing automation, specifically. Artificial intelligence (AI) leverages machine learning techniques to collect and analyse customer data in real-time, and subsequently applies the insights obtained on a large scale. Artificial intelligence (AI) streamlines the process of segregating, categorising, and assigning priority to the aforementioned data. The implementation of artificial intelligence (AI) in marketing automation technologies is significantly transforming the approach to marketing automation strategy. The forthcoming platforms hold the potential to enhance marketing strategies by catering to the changing demands, including the requirement for customers to acquire highly personalised solutions.

A Marketing Automation Tool With Enhanced Efficacy

The integration of artificial intelligence (AI) with marketing automation systems facilitates expedited lead identification for marketers, enhances lead nurturing strategies, and enables the creation of tailored content. Dynamic content emails, specifically individualised emails, have shown to be highly effective since they utilise contextual emails to enhance the company's messaging and cater to the specific interests of subscribers. Dynamic content strategies are employed to maintain the relevance of emails to subscribers by taking into account their geolocations, psychographics, behavioural data, and insights.

Minimise the Amount of Work Assigned or Required

While a considerable number of individuals has the skill to derive valuable insights from extensive datasets, a significant portion of the population tends to waste a substantial amount of time in their endeavours to extract pertinent information from complex data. Artificial intelligence (AI) has the potential to assist in these scenarios by reducing workload and optimising time efficiency. The application of predictive analysis within the field of marketing, as a manifestation of artificial intelligence, has the potential to exert a significant impact on our overall marketing endeavours. The application of AI-powered predictive analysis has the potential to yield significant value from existing data. Predictive lead score is a widely employed artificial intelligence marketing tool. The innovative approach to evaluating and categorising leads in this context is deserving of attention. It is anticipated that marketers will persist in adopting the predictive algorithm-based lead scoring technique.

The Utilisation of Acceleration Techniques Enhances the Efficiency of Data Processing

To effectively develop AI-powered campaigns, it is imperative to leverage artificial intelligence (AI) technology, which offers several advantages. Firstly, AI guarantees enhanced accuracy and security in campaign design. Secondly, AI facilitates expedited data processing when compared to human involvement. Lastly, AI enables the campaign team to allocate their resources towards strategic objectives, hence increasing overall efficiency. Marketing plans can be more personalised and tailored to particular consumers by using artificial intelligence (AI) solutions.. By utilising data-driven reports, individuals can make more educated and unbiased decisions, enabling them to determine their subsequent course of action. Artificial intelligence has the potential to provide assistance in tasks that are characterised by being time-consuming and repetitive in nature. The number of personnel necessary to execute these actions is reduced, and no mistakes are made. Hiring costs can be considerably minimised by employing the personnel currently on hand to fulfil more vital jobs.

Make Customer-Centric Decisions

AI gives companies valuable information into their customers and helps them make informed decisions. AI analyses vast amounts of blog, social media, and other web content to provide external market intelligence. AI technologies can help marketers create consumer profiles from billions of data points. In-person interactions, local promotions, spending patterns, past communications, referral sources, and other factors are examined.

Examine Customer Information

ML can analyse millions of data points about a consumer to determine the best times and days to contact them, the recommended frequency, the information that draws them, and the most clicked email themes and headers. Complex algorithms can customise website experiences. After analysing hundreds of data points on a person, AI can tailor offers and information to each type. Many industries use predictive models, including marketing. These models can predict a prospect's clientship. They can also disclose the cost to convert a customer or which consumers are more likely to buy again.

Increase Stock Control

AI may improve stock control during peak demand and purchasing, preventing customers from making foolish purchases and maximising firm revenue. Companies have different demand forecasting and dynamic pricing needs. Depending on the activities and clients served, a team-created or bespoke solution from an external vendor may be best for developing a goal-achieving system.

Digital Marketing

Digital advertising platforms like Facebook, Google, and Instagram use AI to give the best expert for maximum efficiency. Ads are tailored to user data like gender, age, hobbies, and more. Marketers might use AI to find microtrends and predict trends. They can then make strategic decisions. Thus, firms can reduce digital advertising (Shameem, A., Ramachandran, K. K., et al., 2023) waste and maximise ROI. Since it uses IoT and connected devices, AI affects digital marketing.

Enhanced Customer Service

Businesses and marketing departments are increasingly turning to intelligent technology solutions to boost operational efficiency and the customer experience. Marketers can acquire a more nuanced and comprehensive image of their target audience by employing these channels. The data from this method can be used to increase conversions and reduce marketing staff work.

Providing Aid to Marketers

AI helps advertisers communicate with customers. AI marketing components include cutting-edge technologies to bridge the gap between large customer data and likely future actions. Digital media has spawned big data (Tripathi, M. A., Tripathi, R. et al., 2023), which helps marketers evaluate campaigns and transfer value across channels. Successful AI-powered systems give marketers a central hub for massive data.

Marketing Income and Consumer Happiness Have Increased

Application of AI is varied. Each application reduces risk, speeds up, makes customers happier, and boosts income. AI technologies can quickly allocate spending across channels to keep customers engaged and campaigns appreciated. Customers can receive tailored messaging at the right time with AI. This technology may help marketers detect at-risk customers and provide information to entice them back. AI-powered dashboards provide more specific data on what works, enabling channel replication and efficient spending.

Creation of a Prediction Model

Data collection, predictive modelling, and client validation can be made easier with AI. AI sends customised emails to customers. Machine-learning algorithms may potentially identify disenchanted consumers about to switch brands. AI-powered churn prediction analyses omnichannel events and detects consumer disinterest. It may send relevant emails, push notifications, and offers to engage users. AI-powered churn prediction and tailored content development engage more customers, increasing lifetime value and income.

Understanding Customer Preferences

AI can help marketing teams understand client preferences and demographics in detail. Marketers can customise experiences based on client choices. This information can help marketing teams understand clients, such as whether they would have seen a title without the image and how it affects future messaging.

Make Better Decisions

By examining quantitative and qualitative data, AI helps humans learn and make better decisions. Google Ads AI helps account managers and marketers focus on campaign planning. Deep learning complicates machine learning. It involves processing large amounts of data, especially abstract and scattered data, to identify complicated patterns and correlations that can be used to understand consumer engagement and improve targeted advertising and ROI. As artificial intelligence becomes more accessible, agencies can use it to research data, predict trends, and improve brand quality. A company's digital marketing strategy is changing quickly. Companies can create more creative, targeted marketing with AI. Artificial intelligence in the agency's digital marketing can boost sales and cut costs.

The Intended Audience

Companies must know and address client needs. AI marketing helps companies identify their target audience to provide a more personalised experience. AI elevates conversion management solutions. Comparisons of smart inbound communication to standard KPIs can help marketers address complex strategic problems. In e-commerce, retail, and corporate settings, technology is changing customer expectations, driving demand for more personalised and customised experiences.

Deliver the Proper Message on Time

Because AI technologies help marketers understand their clients and prospects, they can send the appropriate message to the right person at the right time. Data from each consumer interaction is essential for a complete picture. Expanding these profiles can help marketers use AI to create highly personalised content. AI may use customer data from keyword searches, social profiles, and other online sources to improve digital marketing (Geetha M, Harish P, et al., 2022).

Helping Businesses

AI can help organisations better understand their users' wants and create a more personalised user experience. Companies may more effectively target and contact customers by acquiring their purchase history and social media data. AI technology is vital in ad performance optimisation. In social media, AI technology is utilised to generate automated marketing, advise best practises, and expose performance flaws. AI systems may alter targeting and ad budget at the same time, boosting performance even in complex campaigns.

Personalization

By studying customer behaviour and preferences, AI may assist organisations in developing tailored experiences for their customers. AI systems assess browsing and buying histories, as well as other behavioural data points, to develop an individual profile. These software can then curate material, ads, and recommendations based on the user's interests. While this may appear to be a minor convenience, it has the potential to alter how we engage with technology by giving a more intuitive and tailored experience. However, it's vital to highlight that this level of personalization poses privacy and security risks surrounding how data is gathered and used.

Analytics for Prediction

Artificial intelligence can forecast client behaviour and identify chances for organisations to target certain populations. Predictive analytics using artificial intelligence (AI) refers to the process of analysing data, identifying trends, and forecasting future outcomes using AI algorithms and methodologies. Predictive analytics has grown in popularity among businesses across a wide range of industries because it enables them to make data-driven choices with higher precision and efficiency. The capacity to optimise company processes, cut expenses, improve customer experience, and increase income are all advantages of predictive analytics using AI. However, applying this technology necessitates the use of qualified individuals who can create efficient machine learning models and understand large amounts of data. Furthermore, in order to minimise biases or unforeseen repercussions, firms must follow ethical principles while utilising predictive analytics. Predictive analytics is poised to become an even more effective tool for enhancing corporate performance and generating innovation in a variety of industries as AI continues to grow.

Chatbots

AI-powered chatbots may respond to consumer inquiries quickly and accurately, increasing the customer experience. Chatbots are one of the most common forms of artificial intelligence in use today. These digital assistants reply to user inquiries and simulate human conversations, thereby increasing user engagement, customer assistance, and overall corporate productivity. Chatbot technology combines natural language processing (NLP), machine learning, and other AI principles to interpret human requests and answer correctly with pre-programmed responses. As these bots improve, they will be able to combine voice commands, emotion recognition, and context-awareness capabilities to offer more accurate responses while also becoming more pleasant and empathetic towards people. This technology has reduced the workload of customer service agents since it allows for quick communication amongst stakeholders while also saving businesses time and improving their entire customer service experience through enhanced accessibility.

NEW TRENDS IN AI MARKETING

Discuss some of the developing AI marketing themes that are likely to acquire traction in the near future:

- Hyper-Personalization: AI will continue to improve customization by assessing large datasets to provide personalised content, product recommendations, and pricing for each client. As a result of this trend, interactions will become more meaningful and relevant.
- Optimisation of Voice Search: As voice-activated devices such as smart speakers grow more common, optimising material for voice search will become increasingly important. Voice search algorithms powered by AI will transform SEO strategy.
- Visual Lookup: AI-powered visual search will allow consumers to search for products by uploading photographs. To capitalise on this trend, businesses will need to optimise their photos and product listings.
- Content Created by AI: AI-powered content generating systems will improve in sophistication, providing high-quality textual and graphic material for marketing campaigns while minimising the need for manual content development.
- Augmented Reality (AR) with Artificial Intelligence (AI): AI will improve AR experiences by analysing and personalising data in real time within AR applications. This can be used by brands for interactive marketing efforts.
- Predictive Analytics with AI: AI will continue to improve predictive analytics, allowing organisations to more accurately predict market trends, customer behaviour, and campaign outcomes.

AI MARKETING ETHICAL CONSIDERATIONS

1. Transparency: Companies must disclose their AI marketing use. Customers should be advised about AI-made price or content recommendations. AI can create simulation models and personalise shopping experiences using machine learning and virtual assistants. AI is used by many companies to communicate with customers. Amazon recommends products using AI based on purchases, views, and searches. Advanced technologies are evolving and may outperform humans in several areas. AI can recognise marketing trends better than humans due to its knowledge, data analysis, and input. These can analyse data to predict target consumers' purchase patterns and decisions and optimise user experience to meet their needs.
2. Privacy and Consent: It is critical to obtain informed consent from customers for data collection and utilisation. Customers should be able to govern their data and opt out of personalised marketing initiatives.
3. Fairness and bias: It is a moral imperative to address algorithmic bias. Businesses should audit AI systems on a regular basis to discover and correct biases that could lead to discriminatory practises.

4. Deception: Using artificial intelligence to create false material or to simulate human interactions can erode trust and harm a brand's reputation. Businesses must employ AI in an ethical manner to prevent misleading customers.

5. Personalization gone too far: The line between personalization and invasion of privacy is thin. Overly personalised material can be obtrusive and harmful to clients.Compliance with regulations and accountabilityDiscuss the need of legislation and accountability in AI marketing:

6. Regulatory Structures: Many countries are establishing or discussing AI and data privacy rules, such as the GDPR in Europe. Businesses must follow these standards to avoid legal ramifications.

7. Accountability: It is critical to establish clear lines of accountability within an organisation. Responsible AI governance should be in place in businesses to manage AI developments and ensure ethical practises.

8. Consumer Protection: Consumer advocacy groups and watchdog organisations can help firms hold themselves accountable for ethical AI practises. Negative publicity caused by improper AI use might harm a brand's reputation.

9. Standards for the Industry: Industry collaboration to set ethical AI standards and best practises can assist ensure that organisations are held to a high ethical standard in their marketing initiatives.While AI has enormous potential for marketing, it is not without problems and ethical considerations. To use AI's power ethically and responsibly, businesses must handle these problems carefully, prioritise transparency, accountability, and customer privacy, and remain adaptive to evolving rules and consumer expectations.

THE ADVANTAGES OF ARTIFICIAL INTELLIGENCE IN MARKETING

1. Increased Productivity and Efficiency: Artificial intelligence in marketing has the potential to automate monotonous jobs and processes, freeing up time for firms to focus on strategic projects. The end result is cost savings as well as increased production and efficiency. As a result of the impact of advanced artificial intelligence (AI) on enhancing production and efficiency, a number of industries have seen drastic transformations. AI-powered systems can do jobs that would normally require human intervention, such as customer support and data processing and analysis. Furthermore, these approaches enable the production of highly personalised and one-of-a-kind goods, which ultimately improves consumer pleasure while lowering business expenses associated with manual labour. By analysing customer activity patterns, AI supports businesses in trend forecasting and inventory optimisation decision-making. Businesses may boost overall efficiency while increasing the quality of their products and services by incorporating artificial intelligence into crucial operational operations. As artificial intelligence advances, there are more chances than ever for seamless integration into company operations to increase performance across all industries.

2. Improved Customer Service: Customers' satisfaction and loyalty can be increased by providing them with unique experiences. Because of the fast increasing field of artificial intelligence, firms in a variety of industries are focussing on delivering the best customer journeys. Businesses can now change everything from product recommendations to targeted marketing that is tailored to each customer's preferences and interests thanks to AI algorithms and technology. Businesses can now build highly personalised consumer experiences at scale because to advances in natural language processing, automation, and machine learning (Barinderjit S, Geetha M, et al., 2022) technology.

Some of these channels of communication include email, social media, phone calls, and chatbots. Incorporating excellent customer experience approaches into business operations provides two benefits: increased customer satisfaction and long-term client retention.

3. Revenue and profitability have increased: Businesses may design more successful marketing strategies that boost revenue and profitability by utilising AI to examine data and make informed decisions. Because of artificial intelligence, the way organisations approach marketing has fundamentally changed. AI algorithms can accurately predict what customers will buy by studying data sets and user activity patterns. They can then tailor advertisements to those purchases, dramatically improving sales and profitability. Automation tools reduce human expenses while enhancing lead generating strategies to increase ROI. These developments enable organisations to obtain exact client data in real-time, resulting in customised marketing activities, improved customer experiences, higher retention rates, and a lower rate of churn owing to unpleasant or inappropriate advertising. Organisations that have used these components have achieved revenue growth that is up to three times that of traditional strategies that rely just on intuition. Integrating AI-powered solutions into our digital marketing environment allows for improved market penetration, revenue growth, and operational efficiency, offering businesses a competitive advantage in today's business world.

DIFFICULTIES IN APPLYING ARTIFICIAL INTELLIGENCE IN MARKETING

1. Inadequate Skilled Personnel: Artificial intelligence applications in marketing necessitate qualified professionals who can build and manage the technology. Businesses may face difficulties due to a lack of qualified labour in this area. The use of artificial intelligence (AI) into marketing has transformed the industry with previously unheard-of accuracy and efficiency. One of the most serious difficulties confronting marketers is a lack of educated individuals to run AI systems. AI marketing integration necessitates qualified people that are familiar with data analysis, programming, and machine learning (Lourens, M., Sharma, S., et al., 2023) approaches. Businesses must spend in training programmes and certification courses to ensure that their staff have the requisite skill set. However, because there is considerable rivalry for professionals with experience in these sectors, hiring suitable staff can be challenging for organisations without solid reputations or large financial resources. To address this issue, corporations may collaborate with academic institutions and technology firms to train data scientists expressly for marketing objectives. Businesses must carefully navigate the challenges posed by the current skills shortage until then, while integrating AI in the market.

2. High Implementation Costs: Businesses must assess the return on investment before making a decision due to the initial cost of deploying the technology, which can be large. Many businesses want to use artificial intelligence in marketing to gain a competitive advantage. However, the hefty implementation costs may be a substantial hurdle for smaller businesses. AI systems have significant hardware, software, people training, and maintenance costs. Furthermore, as technology evolves, more funds must be spent on system upgrades and employee training. In addition to these expenditures, businesses must evaluate the hazards associated with AI, such as data privacy violations, moral quandaries with biassed algorithms, or automation replacing human personnel. Firms must carefully assess the potential financial risks against the advantages before deciding to

deploy AI marketing solutions. Firms must also carefully study dependable suppliers and standard operating practises.

3. Concerns about data security and privacy: Concerns have been raised about the use of artificial intelligence (AI) in marketing in terms of data security and privacy. Businesses must protect customer data and follow data protection regulations. Because of its ability to personalise and tailor customer experiences, artificial intelligence (AI) in marketing has risen fast in recent years. One of the most pressing concerns confronting marketers today is how to protect data security and privacy while embracing AI. Personal information, including as purchase history, browsing behaviours, and social media activity, is routinely collected and analysed in order to generate consumer profiles that may be used for targeted advertising. If this data is handled incorrectly or comes into the wrong hands, users' privacy could be severely violated. As a result, marketers must guarantee that their AI platforms comply with data protection rules and that their systems are secure from online threats like as hacking and identity theft. To gain the trust of customers, businesses must prioritise transparency in their data collecting methods and provide them complete control over how AI systems will use their personal data for marketing purposes.

4. Best Practises for Artificial Intelligence Implementation in Marketing: Artificial intelligence, or AI, is altering the way firms approach marketing. As data-driven decision-making becomes more ubiquitous, artificial intelligence (Manoharan, G., Durai, S. et al., 2024) may be used to automate jobs, improve marketing, and discover trends that humans would never have the time or skill to perform. But, creating artificial intelligence is not as basic as flipping a switch. The best practices for adopting artificial intelligence (AI) in marketing must include preparing and strategizing the use cases for AI. It's vital to discover areas where AI may be applied to optimise efficiency, enhance customer experience, and boost income. Predictive analytics can be used to automate repetitive operations like lead qualifying and lead scoring, correctly target the right audience with tailored content, and detect data trends that may not be immediately evident to human analysts. Also, firms must invest extensively in developing a strong foundation of dependable and accurate data in order to support effective AI decision-making. Organizations must prioritise continual training and education for this team in order to assure that people employing AI systems have the technical know-how necessary to properly capitalise on its potential. By following these best practises, organisations can make the most of AI technology, stay one step ahead of the competition, and enhance consumer experiences.

5. Start small and Scale Up gradually: Using artificial intelligence could be intimidating, especially if it entails major changes to your business's operations or marketing approach. Instead of rushing in headfirst, it's advisable to start with a tiny initiative or pilot plan to test the waters. After you thoroughly know how artificial intelligence works, you can slowly enhance your efforts. With artificial intelligence, it is vital to start small and develop up gradually in the current technological setting. Instead of investing all of their resources at once, organisations can test and update AI systems over time. This method also supports organisations in identifying the portions of their operations that could benefit most from a progressive AI automation. By doing this, firms lower the likelihood of implementation failure and increase the return on their AI investment. The rising introduction of AI also makes system development and training more efficient, and it promotes employee learning retention. Because of this, employing artificial intelligence (Abdulwahid, A. H., Pattnaik, M., et al., 2023) to start small and ramp up progressively offers organisations with a robust framework that not only enhances productivity but also guarantees high accuracy throughout all organisational

tasks. Businesses could foster competition in the contemporary, data-driven business atmosphere and enhance stakeholder confidence in AI technologies by utilising this strategy.

6. Invest in Training and Development: This necessitates investing in your marketing team's training and development. You may need to hire new staff with programming, machine learning, or data analysis knowledge. You might also teach your present team members new technical skills. Businesses must invest in artificial intelligence education (Razak, A., Nayak, M. P., et al., 2023) and advancement in order to compete in today's market. As the demand for automation and intelligent systems develops, AI has emerged as a critical technology that might benefit businesses in a variety of industries. To fully exploit AI's capabilities, qualified individuals must give enough training and programming. Businesses can design bespoke solutions based on their particular demands and processes by investing in competent staff with AI competence. Training and development programmes that keep firms up to date on new developments and improve their grasp of how AI might improve ongoing operations may be valuable. AI's ability to evaluate huge volumes of data, find trends, and make conclusions that influence corporate strategy might benefit businesses. Finally, investing in training and development assists businesses in lowering costs, advancing market trends, expediting procedures, improving accuracy, and improving customer experience.

THE FUTURE OF ARTIFICIAL INTELLIGENCE MARKETING

1. Draw an image of how AI marketing might appear in the future: AI-Assisted Creativity: AI will help marketers with creative chores such as offering new concepts, ad language, and design aspects, resulting in more engaging and effective campaigns.
2. Artificial Intelligence in Content Marketing: AI will play a larger role in content marketing, assisting firms in creating highly targeted, data-driven content that resonates with certain audiences.
3. AI Marketing Ethics: As consumers expect responsible and fair marketing practises, the necessity of ethical AI practises, such as transparency in data utilisation and algorithms, will grow.
4. Artificial Intelligence in Customer Insights: Deeper insights into client emotions (Shaikh, I. A. K., Kumar, C. N. S., et al., 2023) and sentiment will be provided by AI, allowing firms to assess customer contentment and modify strategy accordingly.
5. Customer Journeys Enhanced by AI:AI will improve consumer journeys by anticipating their demands and delivering seamless, personalised experiences across all touchpoints.
6. AI-Powered Sustainability: AI will assist businesses in optimising their marketing efforts to promote sustainability and environmental responsibility, appealing to a growing consumer base that is environmentally concerned.
7. Privacy and AI Regulation: Governments and regulatory bodies may implement stricter standards governing the use of artificial intelligence in marketing, with a focus on data privacy and consumer protection. AI in marketing has a promising and diverse future. As a result of new trends and technology, the sector will continue to evolve, improving the personalization, effectiveness, and efficiency of marketing campaigns. Companies that stay on top of these advances and adapt their strategies as needed will have a competitive advantage in the continually changing field of AI marketing.

CONCLUSION

The application of Artificial Intelligence, Machine Learning, Data Science (Manoharan, G., & Ashtikar, S. P, 2023) and other cutting-edge technology to automate and improve various marketing processes is known as artificial intelligence in marketing. Its goal is to improve the effectiveness, efficiency, and productivity of marketing initiatives. Many advantages exist for using artificial intelligence in marketing, including greater revenue and profitability. Another benefit is the ability to personalise marketing messages, automate time-consuming tasks, and make data-driven decisions. Using artificial intelligence in marketing involves a variety of problems, including a scarcity of experienced workers, significant implementation costs, and data security and privacy concerns. Starting small and gradually scaling up are best practises for utilising AI in marketing, as are investing in training and development, engaging with experts and business leaders, and assuring ethical and responsible AI use. The performance of artificial intelligence must also be constantly evaluated and analysed in order to alter methods as needed.

LIMITATIONS

On a practical level, artificial intelligence is limited only by the availability of data. Because there's a direct relationship between the richness of data and the capability of an artificial intelligence application, data becomes the key to an AI system. Sometimes the reliability of predictions and analysis done using AI can be uncertain in the long run of a business. The main limitation is that building systems where AI replaces humans 100% is really hard. Those constraints primarily come from the inputs into the model, the algorithms available to the model and/or the actions the model is capable of driving. One another limitation is that AI lack in connecting emotionally because Humans are unique in their ability to feel in a very complex way and translate those feelings into emotional connections. In today's technology driven world, AI has come a long way in dealing with unstructured data as it applies to real-world use cases and again it becomes difficult in handling.

FUTURE SUGGESTIONS

The future of AI in marketing includes excitement over the potential for AI to enhance customer experience through AI agents that engage in human like conversations by handling routine client inquiries and providing 24/7 support. Using AI in campaign management and content marketing can help marketers deliver more personalized and engaging messaging that resonates with their target audience. Also the integration of AI agents into marketing operations has the potential to revolutionize client engagement and campaign management. AI also used to process large amounts of data and generate insights while leaving the final decision making to human marketers who have the contextual knowledge and creativity needed to develop effective marketing strategies.

REFERENCES

Abdulwahid, A. H., Pattnaik, M., Palav, M. R., Babu, S. T., Manoharan, G., & Selvi, G. P. (2023, April). Library Management System Using Artificial Intelligence. In *2023 Eighth International Conference on Science Technology Engineering and Mathematics (ICONSTEM)* (pp. 1-7). IEEE.

Abrokwah-Larbi, K., & Awuku-Larbi, Y. (2023). The impact of artificial intelligence in marketing on the performance of business organizations: evidence from SMEs in an emerging economy. *Journal of Entrepreneurship in Emerging Economies*.

Cui, H., Nie, Y., Li, Z., & Zeng, J. (2022). Construction and Development of Modern Brand Marketing Management Mode Based on Artificial Intelligence. *Journal of Sensors*, *2022*, 1–11. doi:10.1155/2022/9246545

Gursoy, D., Lu, L., Nunkoo, R., & Deng, D. (2023). Metaverse in services marketing: An overview and future research directions. *Service Industries Journal*, *43*(15-16), 1140–1172. Advance online publication. doi:10.1080/02642069.2023.2252750

Krishna, Sheoliha, Ghildiyal, Reddy, Manoharan, & Purohit. (2022). An overview of exploring the potential of artificial intelligence approaches in digital marketing. *The British Journal of Administrative Management*. https://tbjam.org/vol58-special-issue-06/

Kumar, P., Tomar, P. K., Bharti, S., Naredla, S. K., Ibrahim, R. K., & Bader Alazzam, M. (2023). Maximizing the Potential of Artificial Intelligence in Digital Marketing. *2023 3rd International Conference on Advance Computing and Innovative Technologies in Engineering (ICACITE)*, 2736-2741.

Kumari, S., Kumar, V., Sharmila, A., Murthy, C. R., Ahlawat, N., & Manoharan, G. (2023, August). Blockchain-Based E-Analysis of Social Media Forums for Crypto Currency Phase Shifts. In *2023 5th International Conference on Inventive Research in Computing Applications (ICIRCA)* (pp. 1222-1225). IEEE.

Kumari, Dawra, Jaiswal, Raj, Manoharan, & Singh. (2022). An evaluation of machine learning techniques and how they affect human resource management and sustainable development. *The British Journal of Administrative Management*. https://tbjam.org/vol58-special-issue-06/

Lourens, M., Sharma, S., Pulugu, R., Gehlot, A., Manoharan, G., & Kapila, D. (2023, May). Machine learning-based predictive analytics and big data in the automotive sector. In *2023 3rd International Conference on Advance Computing and Innovative Technologies in Engineering (ICACITE)* (pp. 1043-1048). IEEE. 10.1109/ICACITE57410.2023.10182665

Malthouse, E. C., & Copulsky, J. R. (2022). Artificial intelligence ecosystems for marketing communications. *International Journal of Advertising*, *42*(1), 128–140. doi:10.1080/02650487.2022.2122249

Manoharan, G., & Ashtikar, S. P. (2023). A review on the role of statistical tools in effective functionality of data science. *Journal of Pharmaceutical Negative Results*, *14*(2).

Manoharan, G., Durai, S., Ashtikar, S. P., & Kumari, N. (2024). Artificial Intelligence in Marketing Applications. In Artificial Intelligence for Business (pp. 40-70). Productivity Press.

Manoharan, G., Durai, S., Rajesh, G. A., & Ashtikar, S. P. (2023) A Study on the Application of Natural Language Processing Used in Business Analytics for Better Management Decisions: A Literature Review. *Artificial Intelligence and Knowledge Processing*, 249-261.

Manoharan, G., Durai, S., Rajesh, G. A., & Ashtikar, S. P. (2024). A Study on the Application of Expert Systems as a Support System for Business Decisions: A Literature Review. *Artificial Intelligence and Knowledge Processing*, 279-289.

Manoharan, G., Durai, S., Rajesh, G. A., Razak, A., Rao, C. B., & Ashtikar, S. P. (2023a). An investigation into the effectiveness of smart city projects by identifying the framework for measuring performance. In *Artificial Intelligence and Machine Learning in Smart City Planning* (pp. 71–84). Elsevier. doi:10.1016/B978-0-323-99503-0.00004-1

Manoharan, G., Durai, S., Rajesh, G. A., Razak, A., Rao, C. B., & Ashtikar, S. P. (2023b). A study of postgraduate students' perceptions of key components in ICCC to be used in artificial intelligence-based smart cities. In *Artificial Intelligence and Machine Learning in Smart City Planning* (pp. 117–133). Elsevier. doi:10.1016/B978-0-323-99503-0.00003-X

Maranchak, N. (2023). The Use of Artificial Intelligence in Digital Marketing of the Library Industry in Ukraine: Foreign Experience and Prospects. *Digital Platform: Information Technologies in Socio-cultural Sphere*.

Mishra, Pant, Pant, Kumar, Kundu, & Manoharan. (2022). Integrating the principle of strategic human resource management to improve organisational performance. *The British Journal of Administrative Management*. https://tbjam.org/vol58-special-issue-06/

Palagiri, Mogre, Rawa, Manoharan, Singh, & Jaiswal. (2022). An investigation on the use of machine learning methods for predicting employee performance. *The British Journal of Administrative Management*. https://tbjam.org/vol58-special-issue-06/

Paschen, J., Paschen, U., Pala, E., & Kietzmann, J. (2021). Artificial intelligence (AI) and value co-creation in B2B sales: Activities, actors and resources. *Australasian Marketing Journal*, 29(3), 243–251. doi:10.1016/j.ausmj.2020.06.004

Rajaguru, R. (2023). Effects of contemporary technologies, such as blockchain and artificial intelligence (AI) in enhancing consumers' trustworthiness of online reviews. *Journal of Hospitality Marketing & Management*, 1–9. Advance online publication. doi:10.1080/19368623.2023.2258522

Ramachandran, K. K., Mary, S. S. C., Painoli, A. K., Satyala, H., Singh, B., & Manoharan, G. (2022). Assessing the full impact of technological advances on business management techniques. *The British Journal of Administrative Management*. https://tbjam.org/vol58-special-issue-06/

Razak, A., Nayak, M. P., Manoharan, G., Durai, S., Rajesh, G. A., Rao, C. B., & Ashtikar, S. P. (2023). Reigniting the power of artificial intelligence in education sector for the educators and students competence. In *Artificial Intelligence and Machine Learning in Smart City Planning* (pp. 103–116). Elsevier. doi:10.1016/B978-0-323-99503-0.00009-0

Shah, D., & Shay, E. (Eds.). (2019). *How and why artificial intelligence, mixed reality and blockchain technologies will change marketing we know today.* SAGE Publications Pvt Ltd. doi:10.4135/9789353287733. n32

Shaikh, I. A. K., Kumar, C. N. S., Rohini, P., Jafersadhiq, A., Manoharan, G., & Suryanarayana, V. (2023, August). AST-Graph Convolution Network and LSTM Based Employees Behavioral and Emotional Reactions to Corporate Social Irresponsibility. In *2023 Second International Conference on Augmented Intelligence and Sustainable Systems (ICAISS)* (pp. 966-971). IEEE. 10.1109/ICAISS58487.2023.10250754

Shameem, A., Ramachandran, K. K., Sharma, A., Singh, R., Selvaraj, F. J., & Manoharan, G. (2023, May). The Rising Importance of AI in Boosting the Efficiency of Online Advertising in Developing Countries. In *2023 3rd International Conference on Advance Computing and Innovative Technologies in Engineering (ICACITE)* (pp. 1762-1766). IEEE. 10.1109/ICACITE57410.2023.10182754

Syam, N., & Sharma, A. (2018). Waiting for a sales renaissance in the fourth industrial revolution: Machine learning and artificial intelligence in sales research and practice. *Industrial Marketing Management, 69,* 135-146. doi:10.1016/j.indmarman.2017.12.019

Tripathi, M. A., Tripathi, R., Effendy, F., Manoharan, G., Paul, M. J., & Aarif, M. (2023, January). An In-Depth Analysis of the Role That ML and Big Data Play in Driving Digital Marketing's Paradigm Shift. In *2023 International Conference on Computer Communication and Informatics (ICCCI)* (pp. 1-6). IEEE. 10.1109/ICCCI56745.2023.10128357

Wang, H., Jing, G., Bohan, K., Peng, L., & Shi, Y. (2022). Analysis and Research on the Marketing Strategy of Agricultural Products Based on Artificial Intelligence. *Mathematical Problems in Engineering.*

Yang, Y., Liu, Y., Xingyang, L., Ai, J., & Li, Y. (2022). Anthropomorphism and customers' willingness to use artificial intelligence service agents. *Journal of Hospitality Marketing & Management, 31*(1), 1–23. doi:10.1080/19368623.2021.1926037

Zhang, S. (2022). Artificial intelligence and marketing intersection post-COVID-19: A conceptual framework. *International Journal of Innovative Technologies in Social Science.*

Chapter 9
Smart Interactive Marketing Based on Internet of Things:
Characteristics and Effects

Mohanna Hasanzadeh

Shomal University, Amol, Iran

ABSTRACT

In today's world and with the development of advanced industrial generations, the internet of things as an epidemic technology has caused a huge change and transformation in all aspects of daily life, including business. This technology has affected all dimensions and components of the organization's value chain, and a new concept called intelligent and interactive marketing based on the internet of things has also been formed. Considering the importance of sales and marketing in the organization's supply chain, it is necessary to understand the dimensions and components of this type of marketing. The internet of things is one of the most important sources of big data production from marketing processes and it seems that businesses' emphasis on this type of marketing can guarantee business growth.

1. INTRODUCTION

Interactive marketing is a very practical method to attract target audiences through two-way communication between the customer and the owner of the product or service. In this way, by knowing the needs and interests of the audience and responding to these demands, business owners can increase their satisfaction and, as a result, increase profitability and sales. Interactive marketing, unlike traditional marketing in which there is no possibility of two-way interaction between the customer and the supplier of the product or service, has created this space so that there is a communication bridge for the exchange of ideas where users can easily share opinions, suggestions, criticisms, etc. The site manager or the owner of the ad should communicate and receive the desired answer or the necessary guidance as soon as possible (Nagaty, 2023).

DOI: 10.4018/979-8-3693-1339-8.ch009

Interactive marketing is a one-to-one marketing tactic that actually modulates and responds to customer actions. This gives the customer a more personal online interaction with a brand. Interactive marketing has many advantages over traditional marketing. First of all is the cost. Online advertising costs significantly less than television, print or radio advertising and often has a higher rate of return. Companies should always be interested in producing the same results at a lower cost. For customers, an interactive marketing strategy provides opportunities for them to help evolve and grow their favorite products and brands. The more these customers talk about a company in online forums, social networking sites, emails, and videos, the more their hopes and ideas drive understanding and awareness of the company. Businesses can use this information to develop products that their customers are excited to buy, increasing customer loyalty as well as potential sales (Abdulla & Hussain, 2023).

Over the past years, Internet technology has brought changes in the way marketing is done, and the Internet of Things has also caused fundamental changes in Internet marketing and traditional marketing due to some of its special features. Since the main strength of the Internet of Things is in receiving and analyzing environmental data, and considering the importance of environmental information in innovation, the data obtained from the Internet of Things can be an important source for innovation in the organization and innovation in marketing activities (Aliahmadi et al., 2023). In addition, marketing capabilities can add value to the market by incorporating an innovative attitude. The use of Internet of Things in marketing is a new category, therefore most of the researches are of the engineering type and case studies, and this has caused the researches conducted in this field to be highly scattered. Therefore, until now, a comprehensive and clear view of the various applications of the Internet of Things technology in the digital market has not been presented in a coherent and integrated manner.

Therefore, in this research, it is tried to examine the dimensions, components and key features of intelligent interactive marketing systems based on the Internet of Things and provide a comprehensive insight for the implementation of these systems.

2. LITERATURE REVIEW

The use of Internet of Things in marketing is a new category, therefore, most of the researches are of the engineering type and case studies, and this has caused the researches conducted in this field to be highly scattered. Therefore, so far, a comprehensive and clear view of the various applications of Internet of Things technology in digital marketing has not been presented in a coherent and integrated manner. But in the following, we will examine the researches that have been done in this field in recent years (Kumar et al., 2023).

The increasing presence of IoT is profitable for digital marketers. Because they can use this huge data set to analyze and analyze consumer behavior in their marketing strategy. This allows them to even predict consumer behaviors to take a better step to implement their next strategy. With the Internet of Things, access to a wide range of information from different points is obtained for marketers. From a digital marketing perspective, this is extremely useful for creating a better understanding of the starting point of the customer journey from start to finish.

Along this path, from the time of interest in the desired product to the end of the purchase, digital marketers will also have an opportunity to use this data to their advantage. As the application of IoT technology allows digital marketers to see the customer along their path to purchase, they can create more touchpoints for positive customer interaction. With increased access to customer journey information, marketers will be able to find new ways to connect with them to answer questions and build brand relationships at an early stage. For digital marketers, access to information about customer lifestyles means they can see how, when, and what specific products or services are being used (Cai et al., 2023).

In recent years, there have been several studies on the effects of Internet of Things technology on marketing processes. Ajeng and Marsasi (2023) investigated integrated marketing communications based on the Internet of Things in closing the quality factor marketing program in a manufacturing company. This research led to the evaluation of the program using the theory of integrated marketing communications with the implementation of the Internet of Things. It is expected to be implemented in the company's system in support of the package quality agent program. Mohammed and Syed (2023), investigated the applications and effects of Internet of Things on digital marketing. They show how the continued use of IoT technologies leads to significant organizational competition and explain how IoT can be called a new component of business analytics and digital marketing. Remadna (2023) examined the effects of the Internet of Things on consumer behavior. The findings of this research provide insights into the potential impact of the Internet of Things and its components on theories of consumer behavior through all its different dimensions. The results provide a broad understanding of IoT antecedents and outcomes and their impact on consumer behavior and intentions. The findings also show that what has been achieved in IoT in different disciplines of literature (social psychology, technology, business, economics, management, etc.) can be easily applied in marketing.

AliAhmadi et al. (2022) presented a framework for intelligent marketing systems based on the Internet of Things and Blockchain. They investigated the implementation path of interactive intelligent systems by drawing the causal and causal relationships of all actors. The results of their research create a clear path for the creation of these systems. Naim et al. (2022) presented the relationship between green production and the Internet of Things in industrial transformation and marketing management. They also explored how the Internet of Things has contributed to important areas of Marketing Management. These areas include customer relationship management (CRM), building advanced business process models (BPM) and product life cycle (PLC). This article also covers the overall impact and benefits of green manufacturing in BPM and PLC. The results show that Green Manufacturing and IoT are well integrated for industrial transformation and marketing management. Also, industrial transformation and marketing management became effective and contributed to social benefits with Green Manufacturing and IoT applications.

Reis et al. (2021) examined the effects of transformative technologies on marketing and especially digital marketing. They also analyzed the effects of green technologies on customer behavior. Nozari et al. (2021) examined green and sustainable Internet-based marketing of all things. In addition to presenting a conceptual model, they showed that the comprehensive presence of Internet networks can help the sustainable development of businesses in this era and have a tremendous impact on green businesses and attracting customers. Joghee et al. (2021) proposed a framework of e-marketing and distribution with the help of Internet of Things to improve marketing strategies in different stages of distribution, logistics and e-marketing advertising process. They showed that the Internet of Things provides a unique way to collect data through customer support. The results of their research showed that top management's focus on e-marketing contributes to e-marketing adoption. Jayadeva et al. (2022) investigated and analyzed the oles of Cloud Computing and Internet of Things in Marketing Management. They also explore future trends. In this research, they analyze several areas of cloud computing that dominate the Internet of Things and highlight open challenges and possible answers for the future Internet in cloud computing. Zhang (2024), analyzed the revolution in digital marketing, industrial supply chain management based on the Internet of Things in smart manufacturing. In this research, he evaluated the dimensions and characteristics of the Internet of Things on industrial production.

Sehgal et al. (2022) analyzed the opportunities and challenges of using the Internet of Things in digital marketing. In this research, 393 respondents were surveyed to find out the different roles of the Internet of Things and its importance in the evolution of marketing. Multiple regression was used to reach the final results. This study concludes that there is a significant impact of IoT in marketing transformation. Najafi et al. (2022) investigated and prioritized parameters affecting sustainable development in intelligent marketing systems based on the Internet of Things. In their research, they used a fuzzy non-linear prioritization method. Finally, in this research, a framework has been presented to express the situations of the impact of the Internet of Things on sustainable marketing.

3. INTERACTIVE MARKETING SYSTEM FRAMEWORK BASED ON INTERNET OF THINGS

Innovation has now become an undeniable aspect of any business, without which it is very difficult to survive in the market. With each passing day, businesses are experiencing changes in the drive to improve. However, not all results are reliable. And this is exactly what leads to innovation, where a mistake can be corrected with a new approach. In fact, the various technologies we have today are all the result of the experiences of various innovators that have brought a significant difference in business operations (Nozari et al., 2022).

With IoT, organizations can expand their marketing reach abroad. It enables a channel to share data without the need for human interaction. Predictive analytics helps in learning the market behavior and makes better decision making accordingly. They can get real data about their product and service usage to plan their strategies well to enhance the customer experience. In addition, data-driven marketing approaches can analyze user behavior using web-connected platforms. Instead of relying on advertising media to convey your message, it maximizes the possibility of reaching your target audience directly (Nozari et al., 2021).

Marketing in the world of Internet of Things or IoT Marketing means using Internet of Things technology to attract customers and increase sales. Due to the ever-increasing advancement of technology, various devices such as smartphones, smart TVs, smart watches, and home devices connect to the Internet, making it possible for companies to use these devices for marketing and sales. The rise of the Internet of Things is profitable for digital marketers; Because they can use this huge data set to analyze and analyze consumer behavior in their marketing strategy. This allows them to even predict consumer behaviors to take a better step to implement their next strategy. With the Internet of Things, access to a wide range of information from different points is obtained for marketers. From a digital marketing perspective, this is extremely useful for creating a better understanding of the starting point of the customer journey from start to finish (Nozari et al., 2023).

In general, the roles of the Internet of Things in the marketer can be summarized as follows:

1. Real data collection: IoT allows companies to collect accurate and real data about their products and customers. This data helps to make better decisions and optimize marketing campaigns.

2. Better customer experience: By using things connected to the Internet, companies can improve the experience of their customers. For example, AI objects can provide specific recommendations to customers or allow customers to interact with products remotely.

3. Optimal allocation of resources: IoT helps companies to optimize their resources. For example, by using sensors and collected data, traffic density in shopping centers can be adjusted or product inventory can be managed optimally.

4. Marketing of artificial intelligence products: Internet of Things allows businesses to market artificial intelligence products. These products often use big data analysis and artificial intelligence to make decisions and provide better services to customers.

The presence of the Internet of Things itself can be the cause of many innovations in marketing. Some of these innovations include:

- Artificial intelligence advertising: By analyzing data collected from Internet-connected objects, artificial intelligence advertising can accurately present a mix of content and products to customers, so that it matches their tastes and needs.

- Multi-channel interactions: IoT provides the possibility for companies and businesses to interact with their customers in several different channels such as mobile web applications, social media and email and help improve their experience.

- Augmented reality (AR) and virtual reality (VR) experience: IoT in AR and VR has helped to develop digital marketing applications. For example, customers can use augmented reality virtual devices to experience products realistically and make a purchase decision.

It should be noted that the successful use of IoT in digital marketing requires data management and protection of customer privacy. Appropriate security technologies and solutions should also be used to protect sensitive information against unauthorized access (Niu et al., 2023).

IoT applications in digital marketing help to improve customer experience, improve advertising and optimize marketing processes. Some of the most important applications of IoT in digital marketing are:

- Anticipation of needs: By analyzing IoT data, it is possible to identify customer behavior patterns and predict their future needs.

- Determining the location of customers: Using devices connected to the Internet, such as smartphones, it is possible to determine the location of customers.

- Improved logistics and supply: IoT can help improve logistics operations and supply chain management from accurate product tracking to inventory management.

- Increased security: The Internet of Things can help businesses maintain the security of customer data, so that sensitive customer information is best taken care of and security threats are prevented.

The applications of Internet of Things in marketing systems are shown in Figure 1.

In general, IoT offers a wide range of possibilities in digital marketing and can help improve all aspects of customer relations and business performance. Considering all the mentioned features, it can be said that the Internet of Things, in addition to creating many opportunities, also has various advantages for the intelligent marketing system. Understanding these benefits makes marketers pay deeper attention to the applications of this technology (Moedt et al., 2023).

Figure 1. Model of IoT applications in marketing (Bhusan et al., 2022; Pizlo et al., 2022)

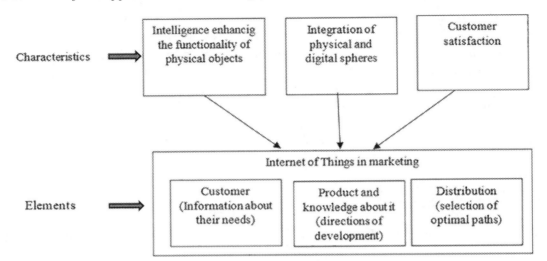

- Better understanding of customers: By accessing more information about the habits and preferences of customers, it is possible to get to know them better and provide customers with more suitable offers.
- More communication: The Internet of Things makes it possible to communicate directly with customers. This increased communication can lead to more targeted advertising and more active interactions with customers.
- Improving the performance of systems; By using IoT in supply chain and production processes, performance improvements can be made in marketing and production systems.
- Customization of products and services: IoT helps to produce customized products and services based on the needs and preferences of customers. In other words, customers can customize products using IoT.
- Inventory and supply chain management: IoT in digital marketing can help improve inventory management and supply chain monitoring. This enables timely delivery of products to customers.

4. CONCLUSION

The Internet of Things is no longer in its infancy. These days many people are using this fascinating technology without even knowing it. That's why marketers are slowly entering this field and trying their luck. Overall, IoT has improved digital marketing by interacting with Internet-connected objects and the data collected from them, allowing businesses to improve customer experience and optimize marketing processes.

The use of Internet of Things in digital marketing is a new phenomenon in the world of e-commerce and communication. This technology enables the accurate collection of data from objects connected to the Internet, which is transformed into useful information for marketing decisions with the help of detailed analysis and artificial intelligence. From AI ads to virtual shopping experience and product customization, it not only helps improve marketing strategies, but also improves the customer experience.

In addition to increasing efficiency in the supply chain, this technology allows businesses to establish a closer and more effective relationship with customers. Finally, as a key element in the world of digital marketing, IoT helps businesses take their marketing to a higher level of precision and effectiveness.

According to the mentioned materials, it can be seen that understanding the cause and effect relationships of all actors in the processes of the smart marketing system based on the Internet of Things is necessary for the growth of marketing in today's world.

REFERENCES

Abdulla, A., & Hussain, O. B. (2023). Use of IoT in Evaluating Content Digital Marketing and Optimization and Web Development. In *Global Applications of the Internet of Things in Digital Marketing* (pp. 141–160). IGI Global. doi:10.4018/978-1-6684-8166-0.ch008

Ajeng, N. J. D., & Marsasi, E. G. (2023). IoT-Based Integrated Marketing Communication in Closing Quality Agent Marketing Program. *Jurnal Informatika Ekonomi Bisnis*, 198-208.

Aliahmadi, A., Ghahremani-Nahr, J., & Nozari, H. (2023). Pricing decisions in the closed-loop supply chain network, taking into account the queuing system in production centers. *Expert Systems with Applications*, *212*, 118741. doi:10.1016/j.eswa.2022.118741

Aliahmadi, A., Nozari, H., & Ghahremani-Nahr, J. (2022). A framework for IoT and Blockchain Based on Marketing Systems with an Emphasis on Big Data Analysis. *International Journal of Innovation in Marketing Elements, 2*(1), 25-34.

Bhusan, B., Sharma, S. K., Unhelkar, B., Ijaz, M. F., & Karim, L. (Eds.). (2022). Internet of Things: Frameworks for Enabling and Emerging Technologies. Academic Press.

Cai, T., Wu, Y., Lin, H., & Cai, Y. (2023). Blockchain-empowered big data sharing for internet of things. In *Research Anthology on Convergence of Blockchain, Internet of Things, and Security* (pp. 278–290). IGI Global.

Jayadeva, S. M., Al Ayub Ahmed, A., Malik, R., Shaikh, A. A., Siddique, M. N. E. A., & Naved, M. (2022, June). Roles of Cloud Computing and Internet of Things in Marketing Management: A Critical Review and Future Trends. In *Proceedings of Second International Conference in Mechanical and Energy Technology: ICMET 2021, India* (pp. 165-173). Singapore: Springer Nature Singapore.

Joghee, S. (2021). RETRACTED ARTICLE: Internet of Things-assisted E-marketing and distribution framework. *Soft Computing*, *25*(18), 12291–12303. doi:10.1007/s00500-021-05920-0

Kumar, V., Sharma, N. K., Mittal, A., & Verma, P. (2023). The Role of IoT and IIoT in Supplier and Customer Continuous Improvement Interface. In *Digital Transformation and Industry 4.0 for Sustainable Supply Chain Performance* (pp. 161–174). Springer International Publishing. doi:10.1007/978-3-031-19711-6_7

Moedt, W., Bernsteiner, R., Hall, M., & Fruhling, A. (2023). Enhancing IoT Project Success through Agile Best Practices. *ACM Transactions on Internet of Things*, *4*(1), 1–31. doi:10.1145/3568170

Mohammed, A. B., & Syed, A. S. (2023). Applications and Impact of Internet of Things in Digital Marketing. In *Global Applications of the Internet of Things in Digital Marketing* (pp. 161–186). IGI Global. doi:10.4018/978-1-6684-8166-0.ch009

Nagaty, K. A. (2023). IoT Commercial and Industrial Applications and AI-Powered IoT. In *Frontiers of Quality Electronic Design (QED) AI, IoT and Hardware Security* (pp. 465–500). Springer International Publishing. doi:10.1007/978-3-031-16344-9_12

Naim, A., Muniasamy, A., Clementking, A., & Rajkumar, R. (2022). Relevance of Green Manufacturing and IoT in Industrial Transformation and Marketing Management. In *Computational Intelligence Techniques for Green Smart Cities* (pp. 395–419). Springer International Publishing. doi:10.1007/978-3-030-96429-0_19

Najafi, S. E., Nozari, H., & Edalatpanah, S. A. (2022). Investigating the Key Parameters Affecting Sustainable IoT-Based Marketing. In *Computational Intelligence Methodologies Applied to Sustainable Development Goals* (pp. 51–61). Springer International Publishing. doi:10.1007/978-3-030-97344-5_4

Niu, B., Zhang, J., & Mu, Z. (2023). IoT-enabled delivery time guarantee in logistics outsourcing and efficiency improvement. *International Journal of Production Research*, *61*(12), 4135–4156. doi:10.1080/00207543.2022.2117868

Nozari, H., Fallah, M., Szmelter-Jarosz, A., & Krzemiński, M. (2021). Analysis of security criteria for IoT-based supply chain: a case study of FMCG industries. *Central European Management Journal, 29*(4).

Nozari, H., Szmelter-Jarosz, A., & Ghahremani-Nahr, J. (2021). The Ideas of Sustainable and Green Marketing Based on the Internet of Everything—The Case of the Dairy Industry. *Future Internet*, *13*(10), 266. doi:10.3390/fi13100266

Nozari, H., Szmelter-Jarosz, A., & Ghahremani-Nahr, J. (2022). Analysis of the challenges of artificial intelligence of things (AIoT) for the smart supply chain (case study: FMCG industries). *Sensors (Basel)*, *22*(8), 2931. doi:10.3390/s22082931 PMID:35458916

Nozari, H., Tavakkoli-Moghaddam, R., Rohaninejad, M., & Hanzalek, Z. (2023, September). Artificial Intelligence of Things (AIoT) Strategies for a Smart Sustainable-Resilient Supply Chain. In *IFIP International Conference on Advances in Production Management Systems* (pp. 805-816). Cham: Springer Nature Switzerland. 10.1007/978-3-031-43670-3_56

Pizło, W., Kałowski, A., & Zarzycka, A. (2022). Internet of Things Applications in Marketing. In *Internet of Things* (pp. 149–162). CRC Press. doi:10.1201/9781003219620-8

Reis, J. L., Peter, M. K., Cayolla, R., & Bogdanovic, Z. (2021). Marketing and smart technologies. *Proceedings of ICMarkTech, 1.*

Remadna, A. (2023). Impact of IoT on Consumer Behaviour. *Management Dynamics, 23*(1), 7. doi:10.57198/2583-4932.1320

Sehgal, P., Kumar, B., Sharma, M., Salameh, A. A., Kumar, S., & Asha, P. (2022). Role of IOT in Transformation of Marketing: A Quantitative Study of Opportunities and Challenges. *Webology, 19*(1), 5838–5849.

Zhang, H. (2024). *Revolutionizing Digital Marketing Industrial Internet of Things-enabled Supply Chain Management in Smart Manufacturing*. Academic Press.

Chapter 10
Smart Marketing:
A Multi–Stakeholder Review of Implications for Sustainable Business Practice

Neda Abdolvnad
https://orcid.org/0000-0003-3623-1284
Department of Management, Faculty of Social Sciences and Economics, Alzahra University, Tehran, Iran

Nasim Ghanbar Tehrani
Kharazmi University, Iran

ABSTRACT

Smart marketing is a term that encompasses various forms of marketing that leverage artificial intelligence (AI) and the internet of things (IoT) to deliver personalized, relevant, and engaging experiences to customers. This research aims to provide a comprehensive literature review on smart marketing, covering its definitions, applications, advantages, disadvantages, and implications on sustainability. The chapter also discusses the benefits and challenges of smart marketing for both marketers and customers, such as improved efficiency, effectiveness, creativity, customer satisfaction, loyalty, and retention, as well as ethical, privacy, security, and social issues. Furthermore, the chapter examines the impact of smart marketing on sustainability, highlighting the potential opportunities and risks for environmental, social, and economic dimensions. The chapter concludes with some suggestions for future research directions and best practices for smart marketing.

INTRODUCTION

Businesses have been facing challenges and opportunities in the dynamic and competitive marketing environment, such as customer needs, market conditions, competitive advantage, and social welfare (Wang et al., 2021) Today, it has been made possible to handle those challenges and embrace the opportunities for advancement in digital technologies, such as artificial intelligence (AI), machine learning (ML), big data analytics, social media platforms, IoT devices, e-commerce platforms, and blockchain technology.

DOI: 10.4018/979-8-3693-1339-8.ch010

This is referred to as smart marketing which in turn improves various aspects of marketing, such as strategy, product, price, place, promotion, people, process, and culture (Kotler et al., 2020). Using smart marketing makes businesses able to create value for customers and stakeholders by delivering personalized, interactive, and responsive marketing campaigns that increase customer satisfaction, loyalty, and advocacy (Grönroos & Voima, 2013).

This chapter synthesize the previous studies which are mainly selected from the publications in the scholarly databases, such as Elsevier, Wiley web of science, SAGE, Springer and Emerald. Based on a deep literature review, this study aims to provide an overview of the current body of knowledge on smart marketing and to discuss its applications, advantages, and disadvantages for marketers and customers. Moreover, this study investigates the implications of smart marketing on sustainability and its dimensions. Sustainable business and marketing emphasize on considering the demands of current direct and indirect stakeholders, as current generation, and the future stakeholders, as next generations. For this, it is necessary that resource use, resource orientation of investments, and even technology dynamics to be compatible with current and future requirements (Harandi et al., 2023).

At first, the concept of smart marketing and its key features has been explained and defined. Then, several existing and emerging smart marketing applications in different sectors and contexts have been explored. Next, the benefits and drawbacks of smart marketing for both marketers and customers have been investigated. The rest of this study is focused on the impact of smart marketing on sustainability and social responsibility. Finally, several gaps and directions for future research on smart marketing have been extracted based on the reviewed literature.

SMART MARKETING AS AN UMBRELLA CONCEPT

By the advancement of technology, marketing discipline has been revolutionized in the past decades. ICT technologies enabled marketers to access vast amounts of data about their customers and use analytics tools to understand their target markets, customer and consumer behavior, market changes and return on marketing investments. This technology-based approach allows for more data gathering and analysis, which leads to improved decision-making, precise targeting, informed pricing strategies, and improved campaign effectiveness.

Various trends have emerged in marketing based on information and communication (ICT) technologies. While database marketing provides an infrastructure to store customer data for future use, other technologies are efficient tools in providing more channels for interacting with customers and delivering digital goods and services to customers.

Database marketing is the use of customer data to segment, target, and customize marketing campaigns, which allows marketers to understand customer behavior, preferences, and needs, in order to deliver relevant and timely messages that increase customer loyalty and retention (Ngai et al., 2014). Email marketing is a subset of digital marketing and focuses on the use of email as a communication channel with customers and prospects (Bharadiya, 2023), which allows marketers to deliver personalized and relevant messages that may produce leads, conversions, and sales, as well as build relationships and loyalty with customers (Bharadiya, 2023). E-commerce marketing can also be considered as a type of digital marketing. E-commerce is buying and selling products and services and handling customer interactions online. E-commerce marketing is the practice of promoting websites to increase the traffic of a website and sales to enhance customer loyalty. It is also called e-commerce website marketing and encompasses pay-per-click (PC) advertising, search engine optimization (SEO), email marketing and social media marketing (Jadhav et al., 2023). Mobile marketing aims at mobile devices and mobile apps because of their rapid growth and broad usage. In mobile marketing, mobile devices and mobile apps are considered as the current ultimate device to deliver marketing messages and offers to customers and prospects (Dacko, 2017). Mobile devices and apps enable marketers to gather more detailed data of customers lifestyle and behavior (though there is the privacy issue), provide more personalized and individualized services, also leverage the ubiquity, connectivity, and contextuality of mobile devices, and to engage customers in real-time and location-based interactions (Dacko, 2017; Stocchi et al., 2022). Social media marketing or social network marketing, which can be used interchangeably, refer to use of social media and network platforms to connect, reach and engage with a large and diverse audience, raise the brand awareness, and generate word-of-mouth to promote products and services (Kaplan & Haenlein, 2020; Hudders et al., 2021). Contents can be shared directly by the businesses, influencers which is referred to as influencer marketing, or co-creation of customers. Influence marketing is also a new trend of marketing which is empowered by social networks. Influencer marketing increases the power and credibility of influencers who can endorse products or services to their followers (Hudders et al., 2021)

Beside providing new channels, the main technologies in marketing practice can be utilized for data gathering and data analytics technologies. Data gathering techniques started by databases to store the data of customers which were mainly produced in enterprise information systems. Then, businesses got enabled by gathering more data using their-owned e-commerce websites, and mobile apps. Also, there is an opportunity to gather user-generated content in websites and social media. Today, businesses are enabled by gathering more details of their products, services and customers using internet-of-things (IoT) and Internet-of-every-things (IoE). IoT has been known as an advanced technology in wireless communication by which it is possible to achieve marketing goals (Najafi et al., 2022). In IoT, different things are enabled to connect and exchange data using sensors and software so that there is a network of physical devices such as vehicles, and appliances. In IoE, it is possible to extend this network so that it includes people, processes, machines, and things. The importance of IoT and IoE in marketing is because of the real-time data of customers (Saheb et al., 2022) which connects businesses to a huge new type of data that could be used in analytics. It is referred to as IoT-based marketing.

These data can be analyzed by the use of artificial intelligence and machine learning algorithms. These technologies enable marketers to analyze huge amounts of data, generate insights, which enables them to target the audience more precisely, improve the effectiveness of marketing campaigns, personalize services, and customize products for different segments and individuals (Bharadiya, 2023; Dacko, 2017). They also help marketers to optimize pricing, demand forecasting, and brand positioning (Bharadiya, 2023). Today, the growth of AI facilitates and accelerates the process of generating knowledge and intuition using knowledge. Moreover, this makes it possible to use intelligent agents and bots in automating front-office processes. This is referred to as AI-powered marketing which is "the process of leveraging artificial intelligence to create, deliver, and measure personalized and relevant marketing content and experiences across different channels and touchpoints" (Wang et al., 2021).

Using technologies in marketing emerged various strategies for marketing, such as relationship marketing, digital marketing, omnichannel marketing, interactive marketing, cognitive marketing, and smart marketing.

Relationship marketing refers to creating long-term and mutually beneficial relationships with customers and other stakeholders, such as suppliers, distributors, employees, and competitors (Grönroos & Voima, 2013). Relationship marketing helps marketers to create value for customers and stakeholders, enhance customer satisfaction and trust, and foster customer loyalty and advocacy (Grönroos & Voima, 2013). Relationship marketing is shaped based on the knowledge which is generated by data analytics. The earliest relationship marketing was based on databases and simple data mining techniques such as clustering, classification, and association rules. The progress of technology enabled marketers to gain deep knowledge and intuition using AI-powered marketing which in turn, empowered them to enhance their marketing practices.

Digital marketing is a broad concept which involves using digital channels and platforms, such as websites, social media, email, search engines, and mobile apps in a wide range of marketing activities (Chaffey & Ellis-Chadwick, 2019). Digital marketing enables marketers to reach a large and diverse audience, measure and optimize their performance, and create personalized and interactive experiences (Chaffey & Ellis-Chadwick, 2019). Various trends including email marketing, social media marketing, e-commerce marketing, mobile marketing, those can be considered as subsets of digital marketing.

Omnichannel marketing strategy is the result of the emergence of digital technologies. It involves integrating a plenitude of channels, both digital and physical to provide a seamless unified experience across multiple channels. As a result of elevated integration and coordination of marketing efforts across different touchpoints and platforms (Lehrer & Trenz, 2022), omnichannel marketing help businesses to shape a unified view of their customers for a better understanding of customer needs, behavior, and preferences which allow marketers to offer convenience, variety, and value to customers (Chaffey & Ellis-Chadwick, 2019; Verhoef et al., 2015).

Another marketing strategy shaped around the emergent digital technologies, is interactive marketing. It focuses on a customer-centric approach that creates two-way relationships with customers by engaging customers, providing relevant contents, creating personalized experiences which are integrated in different channels (Peltier et al., 2022).

Cognitive marketing is considered to be a combination of psychology, marketing, and digital technologies. Digital technologies made it possible to gather the data of customers' behavior and preferences. Based on the psychology theories, a variety of cognitive factors including perception, attention, emotions, and memory are understood which can help marketers to understand how customers process the related information and how they decide to purchase. Using cognitive marketing, businesses can monitor customer behavior and shape customized customer experience to create more competitive advantage (Plassmann et al., 2015).

Smart marketing is a broad concept which encompasses digital technologies such as databases, IoT and IoE to collect data about the customer needs, behavior, and preferences; and then AI and machine learning is used to analyze collected data to provide personalized services and customized goods based on the knowledge and intuitions. Intelligent agents and bots are also used to automate customer services and interaction with customers (Baeva et al., 2021). Smart marketing could support and enhance marketing practice in different ways such as improving customer satisfaction, enhancing customer engagement, increasing customer value, improving marketing performance, enhancing marketing efficiency, fostering innovation and differentiation (Chaffey & Ellis-Chadwick, 2019). Moreover, it may bring operational excellence for the businesses. Concludingly, smart marketing could serve as an umbrella concept that includes the application of a broader range of digital technologies and strategies in marketing, for instance AI and IoT technologies.

All the above-mentioned strategies agree that the presence of technology is dependent on the "use" or "application" that means "improvement" or "enhancement" of marketing activities or functions. As a result, the technology usage is not an advantage by itself, and a holistic approach could be used to define the systematic improvements driven by technological tools.

In the next section, applications, advantages, and disadvantages of smart marketing will be explored in more detail.

Applications of Smart Marketing and Its Related Technologies

Smart marketing utilizes different digital technologies including, data, algorithms, hardware, software, networks as a "process" (Wang et al., 2021) or "system" (Grewal et al., 2017) to evolve strategies, amplify channels, optimize tasks and operation, improve decision-making, and increase outcomes. However, the final goal of such a system or process is defined by marketing strategy which leads to the application of smart marketing in the business.

The main technologies in smart marketing can be categorized in five main groups: data management, social media and social networks, internet of things and internet of everything, machine learning and artificial intelligence, and intelligent agents and bots. This categorization does not mean that each of these technologies can be applied alone. Indeed, the implementation of a combination of these technologies is necessary to make smart marketing work. However, it can help to figure out different technologies and how they can apply in smart marketing. These categories of technology, their application in marketing and the explanation of technologies are listed in Table 1.

Smart marketing could perform as an integrative concept to leverage the use of digital technologies such as artificial intelligence, machine learning, big data analytics, IoT devices, social media platforms, e-commerce platforms, and blockchain technology makes smart marketing innovative and technologically advanced. Thus, it increasingly applied in various aspects of organizational marketing, and there are various examples of its application.

As a relatively new concept in the marketing discipline, researchers and practitioners are examining and validating the applications and examples of smart marketing in different fields. A brief review of applications mentioned by researchers in this field is summarized in Table 2. Five main applications of smart marketing are described which are: product-, service-, price-, place-, and promotion-related applications. As it is mentioned smart marketing can help businesses in better understanding of customers' needs. This can be a basis for better product development and introduction. Moreover, it can help them in customizing products, better product recommendation, and improving the quality of products. Moreover, having precise knowledge and intuition of customers' behavior, and expectations enables businesses to improve the quality of customer services, provide personalized services, and enhance customer engagement. In price-related applications, digital technologies facilitate dynamic pricing, segmented pricing, and individualized pricing. It offers flexible pricing options which can increase customer attraction and loyalty rate. Also, smart contracts make pricing transparent and secure on online platforms. Today, various technologies including mobile devices and apps, IoTs, and even e-commerce websites can provide information of customer location. This information can be analyzed to create a better customer experience of product/service delivery, and offer location-based services. It also gives businesses the capability or real-time monitoring of their products/services to improve its quality. Finally, smart marketing can be used to enhance the promotion process. Using artificial intelligent agents, companies can create content and communicate with customers and users on social media platforms. Moreover, technology can be

Table 1. Application of technology in smart marketing

Technology	Application	Explanation
Data Management	These technologies are used to collect, store, process, analyze, and visualize data for smart marketing purposes	• Big data: The use of cutting-edge techniques and tools to handle huge and complex data sets (Bharadiya, 2023). • Cloud computing: The use of remote servers and networks to maintain on-demand access to data and services (Ngai et al., 2014). • Blockchain: The use of a distributed ledger system to record and verify transactions and data (Dacko, 2017).
Social media and social networks	These technologies are used to connect to customers and interact with them as well as create and deliver content and experiences.	• Social media platforms: The use of online platforms that can facilitate communication and interaction among users (Kaplan & Haenlein, 2020). • Content marketing: The use of online content that can educate, entertain, or persuade customers (Kotler et al., 2017)
Internet of things (IoT) and internet of everything (IoE)	Application of Internet of Things (IoT) devices and technologies to gather, analyze, and act on customer data and behavior in real time" (Peltier et al., 2023). The collected data could be used for enhancing smart marketing activities.	• These technologies are used to connect and interact with physical objects and devices for smart marketing purposes. They include: • Smart sensors: The use of devices that can sense, measure, and transmit data. • RFID tags: The use of devices that can store and transmit identification data (Ng et al., 2009). • IoT platforms: The use of software and hardware that can manage and control IoT devices and data (Ray, 2018).
Machine Learning and artificial intelligence	These technologies are applied to learn from data, generate insights, and present solutions for smart marketing problems	• Machine learning: The use of algorithms and models to learn from data and make predictions (Kshetri et al., 2023). • Natural language processing: The use of techniques and tools to understand and generate natural language (Liu & Zhang, 2012). • Computer vision: using techniques and tools to understand and generate images and videos. • Big data analytics: outlines the process of discovering trends, hidden patterns, and intangible correlations in huge amounts of raw data to enable data-driven decisions.
Intelligent Agents and bots	AI-powered computer programs to interact with customers and automate customer services.	• Chatbots: using NLP to simulate human conversation. If these both are applied in social media to interact with customers and posting comments, they will be referred as social media bots. • Virtual assistant: using NLP and machine learning to implement intelligent agents for interacting with customers and performing repetitive tasks such as appointment scheduling, message sending and making phone calls. • Personal shopping assistant: bots that use machine learning to analyze customer behaviors and preferences to provide purchases' recommendations. • Robotic process automation (RPA): it is used to automate simple routine tasks. In marketing, it is used to enter product description, customized product description based on customer preferences, and customer services.

used for programmatic advertisement which is automated purchase and placement of online ads in both websites and apps which is done through real-time auctions. Customer data including user preferences and history and AI-technology can be used to improve the effectiveness of programmatic advertising (Todorova & Antonova, 2023). Another application of AI and sensory technologies promise the advancement of facial recognition and emotional recognition which can be used for tracking customers and promotion purposes for online and physical purchases (Haleem et al., 2022).

It is good to mention at this point that the applications of smart marketing are not limited to these five main applications or mentioned examples and also the progress of technologies extend its applications increasingly.

Table 2. Applications of smart marketing

Application	Description	Example
Product-related applications	Helping to design and develop products that meet customer needs and expectations by using data-driven insights, customer feedback, and prototyping tools.	Nike uses its Nike+ app to collect customer data and feedback, and then uses it to create personalized products and services (Kotler et al., 2017).
	Offering customized and personalized products to customers by using mass customization, product configuration, and recommendation systems.	Amazon uses its recommendation system to suggest products to customers based on their browsing and buying history (Grewal et al., 2017).
	Improving the quality and safety of products by using smart sensors, RFID tags, and blockchain technology.	Walmart uses RFID tags and blockchain technology to track the origin and quality of its food products (Dacko, 2017).
Service-related Applications	Improving the quality of customer services by using intelligent agents, chatbots, assistants, and so on. (Zhang and Zhang, 2022)	Shopify implemented a personal shopping assistant app, named Shop, which facilitates and accelerates finding new products, placing orders, and tracking packages for customers.
	Personalization of content and experiences to customers by using ML, AI, and natural language processing (NLP). (Zhang and Zhang, 2022)	Gmail uses AI, ML, and natural language processing to filter spam emails, suggest smart replies, and generate smart compose sentences
	Improving customer engagement and making communication with customers more efficient. (Zhang and Zhang, 2022)	Infosys has developed an AI-powered customer engagement platform that evolve contact center operations by analyzing collected data of customer support centers to provide insights and recommendations.
Price-related applications	Adjusting prices that reflect customer value and market conditions by using dynamic pricing, price optimization, and yield management techniques.	Uber uses dynamic pricing to adjust its fares based on the demand and supply of drivers based on data of traffic, demands, and supplies (Liang et al., 2018).
	Offering flexible and tailored pricing options to customers by using subscription models, pay-per-use models, and freemium models.	Netflix uses a subscription model to offer different plans to customers based on their preferences and usage (Maddodi, 2019).
	Improving the transparency and fairness of pricing by using smart contracts, digital currencies, and peer-to-peer platforms.	Airbnb uses smart contracts and digital currencies to facilitate secure and transparent transactions between hosts and guests (Lee & Kotler, 2011).
Place-related applications	Increasing the efficiency of product delivery by using e-commerce platforms, online marketplaces, and logistics systems	Alibaba uses its e-commerce platform and online marketplace to connect sellers and buyers from different countries, and its logistics system to deliver products faster and cheaper. (Marr, 2021).
	Increasing channel accessibility for customers by using mobile technologies, location-based services, and omnichannel strategies.	Starbucks uses its mobile app to allow customers to order, pay, and pick up their drinks from nearby stores (Kumar et al., 2019).
	Improving the traceability and sustainability of distribution and delivery by using IoT devices, big data analytics, and cloud computing.	DHL uses IoT devices, big data analytics, and cloud computing to monitor location, temperature, and condition of its shipments in real time (Aydınocak, 2021).
Promotion-related applications	Improving communication and interaction with customers using content marketing, chat bots, social media platforms and gamification techniques.	Zappos uses chatbots and virtual assistant to improve personalized services to its customers (Zhang and Zhang, 2022).
	Programmatic advertising by using customer history, preferences to provide more relevant ads, and automated advertisement bid in real-time auctions, and also automatically merchandise online ads space.	Albert.ai which is acquired by ZoomD has developed a cloud-based AI for bid management which claims to cover most of online bids (Todorova & Antonova, 2023).
	Automated customer tracking using facial recognition which is possible to link them to customer profile to provide real-time promotions (Haleem et al., 2022).	Using smart coolers' doors in store, Walgreen uses facial recognition to determine the age, gender and emotion of customers to target customer advertisement (Kuligowski, 2023)

Advantages and Disadvantages of Smart Marketing

In above-mentioned discussions, various benefits and advantages of smart marketing are stated for both customers and businesses. In this section, the focus is both advantages and disadvantages of smart marketing. For two main reasons, a single section is dedicated to advantages and disadvantages of smart marketing. First, the scope of the implications of smart marketing goes beyond customers and businesses and it has been expanded to society to assess how this rapidly growing field can influence our society and world. Second, although at the current moment most marketers positively describe smart marketing and use terms such as personalization, optimization, automation, augmentation, differentiation to highlight its benefits and advantages, its implications are double-edge and its strength can be its drawback, so various debates exist in the literature which are discussed in the following and summarized in Figure 1. By considering benefits, challenges, and drawbacks of applying smart marketing practices, it is obvious that there are different stockholders for each aspect. As a result, these implications could be sorted by the stakeholder who is impressed by the issue.

As it is mentioned, IoT, machine learning and artificial intelligence can assist businesses to achieve real-time feedback, analyze data to gain knowledge and intuitions, and implement bots to automate routine tasks. These can lead to an improvement in the performance and impact of marketing strategies and activities (Bharadiya, 2023). Najafi et al. (2022) indicated four benefits of IoT-based marketing which are better marketing influence, the capability to provide simultaneous and interoperable information, smart relationship management with customers, and ability to forecast social networks. Moreover, real-time feedback, precise knowledge and automated tasks can reduce costs, mistakes (particularly human errors), human workload, and wastes which in hence, enhance the efficiency and effectiveness of marketing processes and operations (Bharadwaj et al., 2013; Ngai et al., 2014; Haleem et al., 2022). Furthermore, those businesses who transform their business models based on the novel data, and analytics engine can gain new revenue sources (Marr, 2021), innovation and differentiation (Kshetri et al., 2023).

However, those mentioned technologies are complex, and expensive. Those businesses which demand for more benefits and innovation, should adopt digital transformation which evolves strategies, human resource, structure, processes, and even culture of the business. So, these kinds of changes are time-, money-, and labor-consuming. It is risky and most times faces strict resistance to change. Similarly, smart marketing is based on different technologies and platforms and it involves various stakeholders. Therefore, it increases the complexity and risk of marketing strategies, activities, and operation (Alalwan et al., 2017; Grewal et al., 2017). Demanding high-quality data which is the foundation of correct knowledge, advanced algorithm which is the basis of precise knowledge and intuitions, and skilled personnel who implement those technologies and algorithm and used them demands significant investments not also in implementation phase but also in maintenance phase (Chaffey & Ellis-Chadwick, 2019). However, these technologies are not mutually exclusive or static; they are constantly evolving and converging as technology advances and customer demands change. Therefore, marketers need to keep up with the latest developments and trends in these fields and adopt a flexible and adaptive mindset to leverage their potential. Besides, information technologies including data and business analytics have changed the nature of competition and now businesses are competing on analytics capabilities (Kshetri et al., 2023). Moreover, the data availability and transparency on social networks and e-commerce websites mean that businesses can easily access the customers' opinions and attitude against the products and services of their competitors. They can also imitate the innovation of technological leaders. These give them potentially the ability to offer better value proposition (Grewal et al., 2017).

Figure 1. Advantages and disadvantages of smart marketing

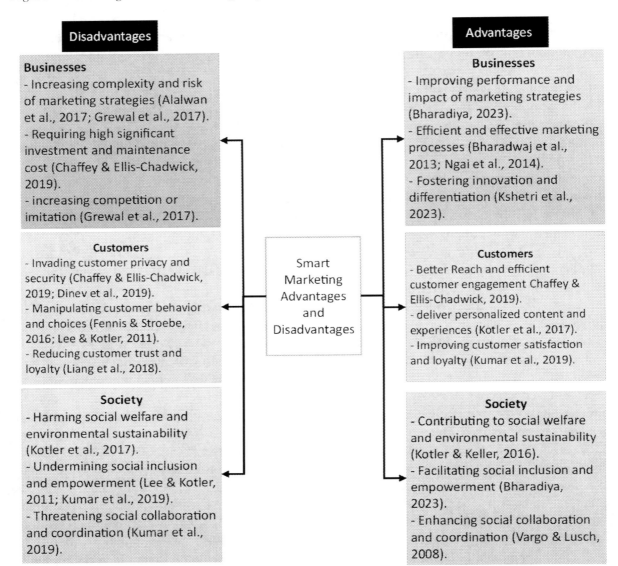

Smart marketing gives businesses and marketers the ability to customize, differentiate, and personalize products/services, and offer better value. These abilities stem from accurate recognition and understanding of customer needs, preferences, and behaviors. In this way, customers may be reached and engaged more effectively and efficiently using digital technologies and platforms (Chaffey & Ellis-Chadwick, 2019). In other words, services and products are easily available and accessible for customers who can easily give their feedback and interactively communicate with businesses and other customers. Moreover, personalization and customization make it possible for customers to receive relevant content and experience (Kotler et al., 2017). The improved customer experience, value-added services, more engagement, and interactive communication may lead to higher levels of satisfaction and loyalty of customers (Kumar et al., 2019).

However, all above-mentioned benefits for both businesses and customers derive from customers' data. Authority organizations such as the European Union have been regulating data access, process, transferring, and portability. Using data without the consent or awareness of customers may lead to heavy legal fines and public scandal (Chaffey & Ellis-Chadwick, 2019; Dinev et al., 2019). Additionally, it may have reverse influence on customers and cause that customer to lose their trust and loyalty and churn that business. As smart marketing may manipulate customer behavior and choices by using persuasive or deceptive techniques (Fennis & Stroebe, 2016; Lee & Kotler, 2011), and may suffer from information overload, or inconsistency and unreliability of information or services, customers may even lose more trust or loyalty (Liang et al., 2018).

Marketers believe that smart marketing has three main advantages for society. First, it can contribute to social welfare and sustainability, as it addresses social issues, promotes ethical values, and reduces resource consumption (Kotler et al., 2017). Second, it can provide access to information, education, and opportunities for all groups including underrepresented or marginalized groups; therefore, it can facilitate social inclusion and empowerment (Bharadiya, 2023). Finally, it enables communication and interaction among different stakeholders or agents, and hence, it can empower social collaboration and coordination (Vargo & Lusch, 2008).

The debating point is that the same three have been reversely mentioned as drawbacks of smart marketing for society. Smart marketing strategies can increase consumption and lead to consuming excessive resources, so it generates waste, and creates negative externalities. Therefore, it could be harmful for social welfare and sustainability (Kotler et al., 2017). Moreover, smart marketing may lead to the manipulation and exploitation of customers, particularly vulnerable or marginalized groups. Thus, it may lead to social exclusion and undermine social empowerment (Lee & Kotler, 2011; Kumar et al., 2019). And finally, smart marketing may create conflicts, inconsistencies, or redundancies among different stakeholders or agents, hence, it can threaten social collaboration and coordination (Kumar et al., 2019).

The debates surrounding smart marketing are still ongoing in the literature, as it is a relatively new trend and some of its long-term implications are still unknown and untested. Most researchers study these implications qualitatively or based on the perceived value for customers and society. It is important to note that new technologies are often exciting for users, and they may answer based on their emotions or based on short-term perceived values. Therefore, more studies are necessary to investigate the long-term implications of society for both customers and society. In the following, this study focuses more on the implications of smart marketing on sustainability to explore more aspects of debates and future research which will be explained in the last section.

IMPLICATIONS FOR SUSTAINABILITY

In the current situation of global warming and lack of water and other natural calamities, a pressure has been raised for sustainability worldwide. This pressure businesses should integrate sustainability to their business models and strategies including marketing strategies and activities to ensure robustness and stability of their operations and decrease the future uncertainty and risks.

The increasing use of smart marketing significantly results in both sustainability and unsustainability. Smart marketing is more sustainable than traditional marketing as it efficiently and effectively uses the resources. Moreover, there is a possibility that smart marketing leads to more sustainable goods and services. It also can increase the awareness of environmental and social issues and change customers' behaviors to a more eco-friendly one (Fallah Shayan et al., 2022).

However, greenwashing can be an outgrowth of smart marketing because the companies consider sustainable marketing and business as an advertising term and they do not really operate sustainably. Because of this, many customers do not trust the claims of businesses regarding their sustainable behaviors (Sama, 2013). Moreover, it can promote consumption culture because of efficient advertisement of selling products and services. Additionally, no one can deny the consequence of digital technologies including data servers, servers, and various devices on global carbon emissions (Harandi et al., 2023). Indeed, smart marketing promotes the use of these technologies.

In the following the implications and consequences of smart marketing on three dimensions of sustainability which is made up of environmental, social., and economic, which have been discussed in more detail.

Social

Social sustainability emphasizes on considering poverty, identity, and equity, social equality, protecting public space and human rights, and considers health and safety regulations, empowerment of people and communities, and maintenance of residents' rights to the city. It supports those practices which create a healthy, livable, and durable society for both current and future generations.

On one hand, smart marketing has several positive implications for the social dimension of sustainability. It can empower the customers by aligning the brand values with the customers' values, and by providing customers with personalized and customized solutions, and engaging them in co-creation and co-innovation processes which increase customer loyalty and satisfaction (Zhang and Chang, 2021). Smart marketing can increase the commitment of business to social causes and ethical standards which in turn improves the reputation and image of its brand (Smart Insights, 2022). Moreover, it can elevate consumer's awareness and preference for sustainable products and practices, and motivate them to adopt pro-environmental and pro-social behaviors (Fallah Shayan et al., 2022). It also can empower consumer's decision making by offering them more information, transparency, and feedback, and enabling them to compare and evaluate alternatives (Peighambari et al., 2016). Smart marketing may lead to social justice and human rights by supporting fair trade, diversity, inclusion, and empowerment of marginalized groups (Green Business Bureau, 2022).

It Is also possible that businesses adopt social innovation as a marketing strategy. In this case, sustainable marketing makes it possible to cultivate social innovation and collaboration by Interacting with different stakeholders and partners to solve social problems (Green Business Bureau, 2022). In the case of customers' demand for more transparency, accountability, and social responsibility from the monopolist, and potential antitrust actions, authorities may put in more monopoly regulation (Seyfang, 2009). Moreover, innovative, and differentiated products or services that appeal to the customers and meet their unmet needs can increase the competition and lower the prices or increase the quality of the products or services, which in turn decrease monopoly power (Dehghani et al., 2022).

However, smart marketing can create new monopoly opportunities by exploiting the network effects, economies of scale, and first-mover advantages of digital technologies and platforms (Guo et al., 2023). Particularly, AI-powered marketing which can improve customer engagement and loyalty through personalized marketing efforts, strengthen the monopolist's market position. (Kshetri et al., 2023; Guo et al., 2023).

Moreover, smart marketing may lead to greenwashing or cause-related marketing in the absence of a consistent sustainability strategy for a business, which in turn increases consumers' skepticism or distrust to exaggerated or misleading claims of business on sustainable strategies (Sama, 2013). Consumers' skepticism also will be increased if businesses cannot successfully deliver its promises or meet the expectations of its customers (Smart Insights, 2022).

Additionally, smart marketing has several negative social and environmental impacts, such as data breaches, cyberattacks, digital divide, consumer manipulation, information overload, resource depletion, algorithmic bias, and social exclusion (Gao & Liu, 2022). It can also subjugate consumers by making them confused or overloaded by exposing them to too much or conflicting information, or offering them too many or complex choices (Sama, 2013; Peighambari et al., 2016).

There are some ethical issues regarding smart marketing, as well. The first concern involved the threats to consumer's privacy or security concerns by collecting and using their personal data, or exposing them to potential cyberattacks or frauds. The second concern is caused by creating trade-offs or conflicts among different stakeholders particularly in complex social issues (Green Business Bureau, 2022). Last ethical concern raises when smart marketing challenges the consumers' values, beliefs, or norms.

Environmental

Environment dimension refers to the protection and conservation of natural resources and ecosystems which is both positively and negatively influenced by smart marketing:

Eco-friendly practices may adopt a green approach in designing, packaging, logistics, and disposal. These green practices may cause reducing the environmental impact of production and consumption (Dangelico & Vocalelli, 2022; Fallah Shayan et al., 2022). Communicating the environmental benefits and values of products and services can increase the environmental awareness and responsibility of consumers and businesses (Dangelico & Vocalelli, 2017; Fallah Shayan et al., 2022). Moreover, aligning the marketing objectives with the environmental objectives can contribute to the fulfillment of sustainable development goals (SDGs) and global environmental agreements (Dangelico & Vocalelli, 2017).

However, sustainable marketing adoption can be challenging for all stakeholders. Adoption of green products or practices can be faced by resistance from consumers or competitors who are not willing or able to adopt green or due to lack of awareness, trust, affordability, or convenience (Dangelico & Vocalelli, 2017). There may exist ethical issues or conflicts when balancing the interests of different stakeholders or addressing complex environmental issues that may involve trade-offs or uncertainties (Dangelico & Vocalelli, 2022; Springer Nature et al., n.d.). Another challenge can be related to legal risks or regulations that may limit or constrain the marketing activities or claims related to environmental aspects (Dangelico & Vocalelli, 2017; Fallah Shayan et al., 2022) As it is mentioned, digital technologies are considered as a significant source of carbon emissions. So, smart marketing can have a negative impact on global warming by increasing use of data servers and servers, and promoting use of digital technologies (Harandi et al., 2023).

Economic

Economic dimension of sustainability refers to stable and low inflation, economic growth, and equitable allocation of natural resources while considering both present and future generations. Economic growth involves investing in innovation and financial stability (Harandi et al., 2023). Economic sustainability can be effective on the well-being and prosperity of individuals, organizations, and communities.

Smart marketing may enhance customer satisfaction, loyalty, and retention; increase market share, revenue, and profitability; reduce costs and waste; improve efficiency and productivity; foster innovation and competitiveness; create social and environmental value (Kotler et al., 2021); and foster consumer's well-being by improving their quality of life, health, happiness, and social relationships (Sheth et al., 2011). Therefore, it has positive implications on economic sustainability.

However, requiring high investments in technology and infrastructure, maintenance expenses, market imbalances, and potential reductions in customer loyalty, facing legal and regulatory uncertainties, encountering ethical and social dilemmas, experiencing technical glitches and cyber threats, creating digital dependency and addiction, and disrupting traditional markets and industries are drawbacks of smart marketing on economic sustainability (Alalwan et al., 2017; Kotler et al., 2021; Vermanen et al., 2022). Also, by adopting green practices or initiatives that may not generate immediate or adequate returns or benefits and due to the innovative nature of these practices, smart marketing may lead to higher costs, risks, or investments (Belz & Peattie, 2022; Dangelico & Vocalelli, 2022; Sheth et al., 2011) which has negative implication on economic sustainability and even neutralize the one of the main benefits of smart marketing on environmental sustainability.

Considering implications and consequences of smart marketing on three dimensions of sustainability reveals that various stakeholders can be influenced differently as it is summarized in Table 3.

Indeed, smart marketing requires careful management and evaluation to balance its advantages and disadvantages, and to ensure that it is advantageous for the customers and the society, not only for the marketers (Bharadwaj et al., 2013). As shown in the advantages, smart marketing is suitable for marketing situations that require high levels of efficiency, effectiveness, personalization, and innovation, as it can leverage the capabilities and benefits of digital technologies to achieve these goals (Chaffey & Ellis-Chadwick, 2019; Kotler et al., 2017), although it is not appropriate for marketing situations that involve high levels of privacy, security, ethical., or social concerns, as it can pose challenges and risks related to the use and misuse of customer data and digital technologies (Bharadiya, 2023). Moreover, smart marketing should be aligned with social marketing to ensure that it is proficient for all stakeholders and it should be aligned with sustainability and its three dimensions.

DISCUSSION AND CONCLUSION

Based on the literature review, smart marketing as a multifaceted and evolving concept, involves various applications of digital technologies in marketing. Findings of previous research reveal that smart marketing has significant both advantages and disadvantages for various stakeholders including businesses, customers, and society. In this section, main findings, limitations, and implications of the associated literature to smart marketing will be discussed concisely.

Table 3. Implications and consequences of smart marketing on various stakeholders of sustainability

Stakeholder	Impact	Possible Advantage	Possible Disadvantage
Business	Global Reach	helping businesses reach potential customers across the world by means of digital channels, such as websites, social media, email, and online advertising.	
	Cost efficiency	helping businesses reduce their marketing expenses by using online tools and platforms that are cheaper and more effective than traditional media, such as print, radio, and TV.	Smart marketing can require significant investment and maintenance costs by demanding high-quality data, advanced algorithms, and skilled personnel (Chaffey & Ellis-Chadwick, 2019).
	Measurable results	helping businesses track and analyze marketing performance and ROI using online metrics and tools, such as web analytics, social media insights, email open rates, and conversion rates.	
	Effective targeting	helping businesses segment and target customers based on demographics, behaviors, preferences, and needs using online data and tools.	Smart marketing can face competition or imitation from other smart marketing systems that may offer similar or better value propositions (Grewal et al., 2017).
	Increased engagement	helping businesses engage and interact with their customers through online channels, which can help build trust, loyalty, and advocacy among customers.	Smart marketing can increase the complexity and risk of marketing activities and strategies by involving multiple technologies, platforms, and stakeholders (Alalwan et al., 2017; Grewal et al., 2017).
	Flexibility	helping businesses adapt and respond to altering customer needs and market dynamics by using online tools and platforms that allow them to test, modify, and optimize their marketing campaigns in real time.	
	Improved conversion rate	helping businesses increase their sales and revenue by using online tools and techniques that persuade and motivate customers to take action.	
Customers	Personalization	helping customers receive personalized and tailored offers and recommendations based on their preferences, needs, and behaviors using online data and tools	Smart marketing can reduce customer trust and loyalty by providing inconsistent or unreliable information or services (Liang et al., 2018).
	Convenience	helping customers access and purchase products and services anytime and anywhere through online channels.	Smart marketing can invade customer privacy and security by collecting and using customer data without their consent or awareness (Chaffey & Ellis-Chadwick, 2019; Dinev et al., 2019).
	Education	helping customers learn more about the products and services they are interested in or need through online channels in order to make informed and confident decisions.	
	Engagement	helping customers interact with the businesses they buy from or are loyal to through online channels, which makes them feel valued, satisfied, and loyal.	Smart marketing can manipulate customer behavior and choices by using persuasive or deceptive techniques (Fennis & Stroebe, 2016; Lee & Kotler, 2011)
	Feedback	helping customers to provide feedback and reviews to the businesses they buy from or are loyal to through online channels, to express their opinions, suggestions, and complaints.	

continues on following page

Table 3. Continued

Stakeholder	Impact	Possible Advantage	Possible Disadvantage
Society	Positive impact on society	Helping to create a better world for everyone. Businesses can help make society healthier, cleaner, and safer by focusing on social issues.	Smart marketing can undermine social inclusion and empowerment by excluding or exploiting vulnerable or marginalized groups (Lee & Kotler, 2011; Kumar et al., 2019).
	Improved public image	Increasing the public image of companies which may lead to increased social capital. They can demonstrate their social responsibility and ethical values to their customers and stakeholders which is dispersed in the society.	Smart marketing can threaten social collaboration and coordination by creating conflicts, inconsistencies, or redundancies among different stakeholders or agents (Kumar et al., 2019).
	Increased social well-being	Helping to increase the quality of life and happiness of people by providing them with goods and services that grant their needs and preferences. It can also help reduce social problems such as poverty, hunger, and inequality	Smart marketing can harm social welfare and environmental sustainability by consuming excessive resources, generating waste, and creating negative externalities (Kotler et al., 2017).
	Economic planning for society	Helping to promote economic development and growth by creating more jobs, income, and opportunities for people. It can also help foster innovation and creativity in various sectors	

Findings of this study could be displayed in 3 categories: First of all, researches are all agreed upon the concept of Smart marketing is a technology-driven artifact. It uses artificial intelligence, machine learning, big data analytics, IoT devices, social media platforms, e-commerce platforms, and blockchain technology which give business the ability to analyze big data to generate insights, and personalize goods and services (Bharadiya, 2023; Dacko, 2017). Second, aggregation of researches show smart marketing applications are holistic by its nature. In the other way, it covers all aspects of marketing including product introduction, pricing, positioning, promotion, targeting customers, demand forecasting, and customer services (Kotler et al., 2020; Bharadiya, 2023). It also enhances back-office operations such as strategy planning, and operational excellence. The third finding suggests that smart marketing is not just about the IT as a tool. As the new applications of technology in marketing makes businesses able to success-fully address marketing's challenges and opportunities such as customers' needs, market conditions, competitive advantage, and social welfare (Wang et al., 2021), its generated insights can be utilized to evolve traditional business models to data-centric business models, and add data-driven services. In other words, smart marketing can make possible monetizing from data and the generated insights. Moreover, it may cause an increase in revenue and profitability for businesses by improving customers' satisfaction, loyalty, and advocacy by creating value for customers and other stakeholders using delivering personal-ized, interactive, and responsive marketing campaigns (Grönroos & Voima, 2013).

The fourth finding is about the dual nature of opportunities and threats for smart marketing. Smart marketing can bring different advantages and disadvantages for various stakeholders including customers, businesses, and society.

For customers, smart marketing can *empower* them by offering convenience, variety, and value to customers in online or offline purchases across multiple channels (Chaffey & Ellis-Chadwick, 2019; Verhoef et al., 2015). It also helps customers by providing more information, choice, and control over their purchases (Chaffey & Ellis-Chadwick, 2019). As smart marketing can leverage the power and credibility of social media and influencer marketing, it can also improve customer *engagement* and *trust* (Kaplan & Haenlein, 2020). However, customers may face *ethical*, *privacy*, and *security threats*, and may be manipulated, deceived, or even cheated by some businesses or third-parties (Dacko, 2017; Wang et al., 2021) who have legal or illegal access to their data. Although some researches present approaches for elimination of these issues (Aliahmadi et al., 2022) *Information overload*, *paradox of choice*, or *loss of human touch* as the outgrowth of smart marketing, makes customers overwhelmed and alienated by the abundance and complexity of digital options (Chaffey & Ellis-Chadwick, 2019; Wang et al., 2021).

For businesses, smart marketing first helps them in acquiring *better recognition* of their customers, and their related segments, needs, and behaviors. So, they can design and provide *more value-added services* to increase the level of their *satisfaction, loyalty*, and *perceived value* to increase their lifetime value for businesses. It also makes it possible for businesses to continuously *improve their processes* to reduce waste, emissions, and costs by *optimizing resources*, processes, and supply chains (Belz & Peattie, 2012). Reducing human errors and decreasing workload are the visible impressions on human resources in this thread. Moreover, businesses can apply smart marketing applications in introducing *new products and services*, and evolving their business models, which can give them *better positioning* in a competitive environment, and new sources of revenue making (Fallah Shayan et al., 2022). Smart marketing can help businesses to *align* their strategies with sustainable goals, green strategies, and value of customers and society who may ask for more ethical, transparent, and green practices from them. It also gives this opportunity to businesses to *balance* the economic, social, and environmental objectives and impacts of their activities (Taiminen & Karjaluoto, 2015). However, businesses suffer from the *complexity* of the new technologies, fast emerging and disruptive technologies, and high increasing level of *investment* that the technological infrastructure needs. Moreover, businesses may face a *reputation scandal* because of their use of customers' data as it has happened to Meta, Spotify, and other companies in recent years. As a result of smart marketing applications, businesses face *ethical concerns*, conflicts, or controversies as they should balance profit and purpose, customer and stakeholder interests, or short-term and long-term goals (Fallah Shayan et al., 2022; Taiminen & Karjaluoto, 2015). Businesses should adopt some *ethical standards* and principles to address these ethical concerns. Then, they should also correctly implement those standards and principles. Ensuring ethical data management and governance, applying ethical algorithms and artificial intelligence techniques, engaging in ethical communication and education, and fostering ethical collaboration and co-creation are other necessary actions that businesses should take to guarantee the ethical use of data and successful smart marketing applications (Vermanen et al., 2022).

The main benefits of smart marketing for society are its implications on sustainability and social responsibility, because of the resulting opportunities which make the environment, society, and economy more sustainable (Belz & Peattie, 2012; Fallah Shayan et al., 2022). Compared to the benefits of smart marketing, however, it seems that it brings more threats to sustainability and social responsibility. Smart marketing increases *customers' demand*, stimulates impulse buying, and shortens product's lifetime (Belz & Peattie, 2012; Wang et al., 2021) As a result, the levels of the consumption, materialism, and disposability of products and services would be increased which has a negative effect on three dimensions of sustainability. Moreover, it brings more drawbacks such as *social inequalities*, *exclusion*, or *discrimination* by dividing customers and individuals to segments and labelling them favorable or unfavorable based on their data, preferences, or behavior (Wang et al., 2021). By addressing challenges (customer needs, market conditions) and opportunities (competitive advantage, social welfare) in marketing, smart marketing could demonstrate responsiveness and adaptability.

Research Gap and Future Research

Based on the reviewed literature, there are some theoretical implications which contribute in defining the smart marketing definition, and its related terms such as AI-powered marketing, and IoT-based marketing. The discussion of implications and consequences of smart marketing on different stakeholders contributes to the better perception of the concept and the field of research.

The main focus of the literature is on practical implications of smart marketing in different industries such as retailing (Dacko, 2017), healthcare (Bharadiya, 2023), tourism (Taiminen & Karjaluoto, 2015), education (Chaffey & Ellis-Chadwick, 2019), and banking (Grewal et al., 2020) to help businesses to have a better understanding of market responses regarding customers' behaviors. Moreover, it is studied in the literature how to improve data quality, how to keep ethical standards, how to increase the level of customers' engagement, and how to strategically plan for customer centricity. The success factors, risks and challenges of digital technologies adoption and implementation have been well studied in different sectors. However, the literature is more silent about factors that cause unsuccessful implementation or failure in utilization of the technologies. Based on the literature, it is not also to recommend to businesses particularly the small ones how to use or evaluate the smart marketing applications, as there are a few explanatory or prescriptive studies. Moreover, most of the big success stories refer to big companies and names and there is still less knowledge about how small enterprises can utilize these technologies considering the heavy investments that they need. Because of that, it cannot be said that society and governments are aware of all threats of smart marketing and particularly what can lead to monopoly.

Although customers' behavior and satisfaction now have been studied for decades, these topics are still suggested as the large amount of data, the AI-powered algorithms, and the emerging technologies can provide more detailed and exact insights. Particularly, these studies may lead to better insights which are necessary in cognitive marketing.

However, there are still more debates in the literature about the advantages and disadvantages of smart marketing for customers, businesses, and society. Therefore, more studies should be conducted to evaluate the outcomes of smart marketing in different dimensions. These kinds of studies can help authorities to regulate the use of AI, customer data and even the permitted use of cognitive marketing. Moreover, more studies should be focused on different technologies that smart marketing uses such as AI which should be investigated regarding policy making, privacy, bias, and ethics.

In spite of that current study does not cover all related literature, it seems that just a sample of the existing and emerging smart marketing applications have been studied and it does not cover different domains and industries. Therefore, it can be said that the literature review is more explorative and it is not comprehensive particularly in investigating other sides other than businesses such as customers and society. In the same way, the current literature review is not conclusive regarding the implications of smart marketing on sustainability as most of the studies conducted in a descriptive or evaluative way. Indeed, because of the lack of explanatory and prescriptive studies, the literature review cannot bring enough insights for society and authorities to understand and then take actions to alleviate the consequences of smart marketing applications.

Finally, this study categorizes and provides different research topics which are extracted of the literature review:

- **Smart marketing and customer behavior (Bharadiya, 2023; Dacko, 2017; Wang et al., 2021):** Researchers who are interested in this topic can study how the way customers perceive, evaluate, and respond to marketing campaigns, products, and services will be influenced by smart marketing. The main point is that in different contexts and cultures, customers may perceive and evaluate smart marketing applications differently. Moreover, these differences may lead to different responses of customers to smart marketing applications. So, more studies should be conducted to reveal these differences.

- **Marketing performance and innovation:** It is necessary to define measures to quantitatively measure the efficiency, effectiveness, and profitability of smart marketing. Moreover, other studies should evaluate those descriptive statements about the results of smart marketing in innovation, differentiation, and competitive advantage in marketing. Like other information systems and technologies, smart marketing applications can be influenced by organizational., environmental., and cultural factors. Therefore, another direction of study should aim to investigate moderating factors which are effective on marketing performance and innovation.

- **Sustainability and social responsibility:** One of the sub-themes in this topic is about how businesses can align their strategies and objectives with the sustainability goals and values of customers and stakeholders. Those researchers who are interested in this topic should be suggested to focus on the debates of smart marketing applications on environmental., social., and economic sustainability. For example, in the environmental dimension, Chaffey & Ellis-Chadwick (2019) believe that smart marketing has a positive implication by reducing resource consumption, waste generation, and greenhouse gas emissions. However, it is shown that technology has a convincing impact on carbon footprint and global warming (Harandi et al., 2023). Moreover, Peltier et al (2023) believes that smart marketing can result in excessive energy consumption, electronic waste, and negative externalities. Another debate that was mentioned in this study, is the "monopoly" which can be increased or decreased by smart marketing applications. So, it is necessary to investigate what conditions may lead to an escalation or decrease of monopoly and how monopoly can be avoided. In social sustainability, social inclusion (Chaffey & Ellis-Chadwick, 2019) and social exclusion (Gao & Liu, 2022) have been mentioned as implications and consequences of smart marketing applications as well as social sustainability, empowerment, networking, and diversity (Chaffey & Ellis-Chadwick, 2019) in one hand, and privacy invasion, security risks, potential harm to social welfare, and threats to collaborative efforts (Alalwan et al., 2017) in other hand. Finally, it is recommended to study the trade-offs and challenges of sustainability in marketing related to smart marketing applications (Belz & Peattie, 2012; Fallah Shayan et al., 2022; Taiminen & Karjaluoto, 2015).

REFERENCES

Alalwan, A. A., Rana, N. P., Dwivedi, Y. K., & Algharabat, R. (2017). Social Media in Marketing: A Review and Analysis of the Existing Literature. *Telematics and Informatics, 34*(7), 1177–1190. doi:10.1016/j.tele.2017.05.008

Aliahmadi, A., Nozari, H., & Ghahremani-Nahr, J. (2022). A framework for IoT and Blockchain Based on Marketing Systems with an Emphasis on Big Data Analysis. *International Journal of Innovation in Marketing Elements, 2*(1), 25-34.

Aydınocak, E. U. (2021). Internet of Things (IoT. In M. Logistics (Ed.), *Logistics 4.0 and Future of Supply Chains* (pp. 153–169). Springer Nature Singapore.

Baeva, L. V., Khrapov, S. A., & Azhmukhamedov, I. M. (2021). "Smart Technologies" in Education: Development Opportunities and Threats. In "Smart Technologies" for Society, State and Economy 13 (pp. 714-723). Springer International Publishing.

Belz, F. M., & Peattie, K. (2022). *Sustainability Marketing: A Global Perspective* (2nd ed.). Wiley.

Bharadiya, J. P. (2023). A Comparative Study of Business Intelligence and Artificial Intelligence with Big Data Analytics. *American Journal of Artificial Intelligence*, 7(1), 24–30.

Bharadwaj, A., El Sawy, O. A., Pavlou, P. A., & Venkatraman, N. (2013). Digital Business Strategy: Toward a Next Generation of Insights. *Management Information Systems Quarterly*, 37(2), 471–482. doi:10.25300/MISQ/2013/37:2.3

BrightEdge. (2019). *BrightEdge Research: The Future of Marketing Is Here - Are You Ready?* Retrieved at 20 Oct. 2023 from https://www.brightedge.com/resources/research-reports/future-of-marketing

Chaffey, D., & Ellis-Chadwick, F. (2019). *Digital Marketing: Strategy Implementation and Practice* (7th ed.). Pearson Education Limited.

Dacko, S. G. (2017). Enabling Smart Retail Settings via Mobile Augmented Reality Shopping Apps. *Technological Forecasting and Social Change*, 124, 243–256. doi:10.1016/j.techfore.2016.09.032

Dangelico, R. M., & Vocalelli, D. (2017). "Green Marketing": An Analysis of Definitions, Strategy Steps, and Tools Through a Systematic Review of the Literature. *Journal of Cleaner Production*, 165(1), 1263–1279. doi:10.1016/j.jclepro.2017.07.184

Dangelico, R. M., & Vocalelli, D. (Eds.). (2022). *Green Marketing: A Case Study-Based Approach*. Springer.

Dehghani, M., Abubakar, A. M., & Pashna, M. (2022). Market-Driven Management of Start-ups: The Case of Wearable Technology. *Applied Computing and Informatics*, 18(1/2), 45–60. doi:10.1016/j.aci.2018.11.002

Dinev, T., Hart, P., & Mullen, M. R. (2019). Internet Privacy Concerns and Beliefs About Government Surveillance–An Empirical Investigation. *The Journal of Strategic Information Systems*, 28(1), 66–83. doi:10.1016/j.jsis.2018.09.002

Fallah Shayan, N., Mohabbati-Kalejahi, N., Alavi, S., & Zahed, M. A. (2022). Sustainable Development Goals (SDGs) as a Framework for Corporate Social Responsibility (CSR). *Sustainability (Basel)*, 14(3), 1222. doi:10.3390/su14031222

Fennis, B. M., & Stroebe, W. (2016). *The Psychology of Advertising* (2nd ed.). Routledge.

Gao, Y., & Liu, H. (2022). Artificial intelligence-enabled personalization in interactive marketing: a customer journey perspective. *Journal of Research in Interactive Marketing*, (ahead-of-print), 1-18.

Green Business Bureau. (2022). *What Is Sustainable Marketing and why Is It Important in 2022.* Retrieved at 20 Oct. (2023) from https://greenbusinessbureau.com/business-function/marketing-sales/what-is-sustainable-marketing-and-why-is-it-important-in-2021/

Grewal, D., Roggeveen, A. L., & Nordfält, J. (2017). The Future of Retailing. *Journal of Retailing, 93*(1), 1–6. doi:10.1016/j.jretai.2016.12.008

Grönroos, C., & Voima, P. (2013). Critical service logic: Making sense of value creation and co-creation. *Journal of the Academy of Marketing Science, 41*(2), 133–150. doi:10.1007/s11747-012-0308-3

Guo, X., Song, X., Dou, B., Wang, A., & Hu, H. (2023). Can digital transformation of the enterprise break the monopoly? *Personal and Ubiquitous Computing, 27*(4), 1629–1642. doi:10.1007/s00779-022-01666-0

Haleem, A., Javaid, M., Qadri, M. A., Singh, R. P., & Suman, R. (2022). Artificial intelligence (AI) applications for marketing: A literature-based study. *International Journal of Intelligent Networks.*

Harandi, S. R., Boubereje, A., & Abdolvand, N. (2023). Platform economy implications for sustainability: Good, bad, unknown. In D. B. Sarıpek & V. Franca (Eds.), *Digital and Green Transition: New Perspectives on Work Organization* (pp. 73–104). Dora Publishing.

Hudders, L., De Jans, S., & De Veirman, M. (2021). The Commercialization of Social Media Stars: A Literature Review and Conceptual Framework on the Strategic Use of Social Media Influencers. *International Journal of Advertising, 40*(3), 327–375. doi:10.1080/02650487.2020.1836925

Jadhav, G. G., Gaikwad, S. V., & Bapat, D. (2023). A Systematic Literature Review: Digital Marketing and Its Impact on SMEs. *Journal of Indian Business Research, 15*(1), 76–91. doi:10.1108/JIBR-05-2022-0129

Kaplan, A., & Haenlein, M. (2020). Rulers of the World, Unite! The Challenges and Opportunities of Artificial Intelligence. *Business Horizons, 63*(1), 37–50. doi:10.1016/j.bushor.2019.09.003

Kotler, P., Kartajaya, H., & Setiawan, I. (2021). *Marketing 5.0: Technology for Humanity.* John Wiley & Sons.

Kotler, P., Kartajaya, H., Setiawan, I., & Hendratmoko, W. (2017). *Marketing 4.0: Moving from Traditional to Digital.* John Wiley & Sons.

Kotler, P., Keller, K. L., Brady, M., Goodman, M., & Hansen, T. (2020). *Marketing Management* (3rd ed.). Pearson.

Kshetri, N., Dwivedi, Y. K., Davenport, T. H., & Panteli, N. (2023). Generative Artificial Intelligence in Marketing: Applications, Opportunities, Challenges, and Research Agenda. *International Journal of Information Management, 102716,* 102716. Advance online publication. doi:10.1016/j.ijinfomgt.2023.102716

Kuligowski, K. (2023). *Facial Recognition Advertising: The New Way to Target Ads to Consumers.* Retrieved at 24 Dec. 2023 from https://www.businessnewsdaily.com/15213-walgreens-facial-recognition.html

Kumar, S., Tiwari, P., & Zymbler, M. (2019). Internet of Things is a revolutionary approach for future technology enhancement: A review. *Journal of Big Data, 6*(1), 1–21. doi:10.1186/s40537-019-0268-2

Lee, N., & Kotler, P. (2011). *Social Marketing: Influencing Behaviors for Good* (4th ed.). SAGE Publications.

Lee, N. R., & Kotler, P. (2011). *Social marketing: Influencing behaviors for good*. SAGE publications.

Lehrer, C., & Trenz, M. (2022). Omnichannel Business. *Electronic Markets*, *32*(2), 687–699. doi:10.1007/s12525-021-00511-1

Liang, L. J., Choi, H. C., & Joppe, M. (2018). Exploring the Relationship between Satisfaction, Trust and Switching Intention, Repurchase Intention in the Context of Airbnb. *International Journal of Hospitality Management*, *69*, 41–48. doi:10.1016/j.ijhm.2017.10.015

Liu, B., & Zhang, L. (2012). A Survey of Opinion Mining and Sentiment Analysis. In C. Aggarwal & C. Zhai (Eds.), *Mining Text Data*. Springer, doi:10.1007/978-1-4614-3223-4_13

Maddodi, & Krishna Prasad, K. (2019). Netflix Bigdata Analytics-The Emergence of Data Driven Recommendation. *International Journal of Case Studies in Business, IT, and Education (IJCSBE)*, *3*(2), 41-51.

Marr, B. (2021). *Data strategy: How to profit from a world of big data, analytics and artificial intelligence*. Kogan Page Publishers.

Najafi, S. E., Nozari, H., & Edalatpanah, S. A. (2022). Investigating the Key Parameters Affecting Sustainable IoT-Based Marketing. In J. L. Verdegay, J. Brito, & C. Cruz (Eds.), *Computational Intelligence Methodologies Applied to Sustainable Development Goals. Studies in Computational Intelligence* (Vol. 1036). Springer. doi:10.1007/978-3-030-97344-5_4

Ng, I. C. L., Scharf, K. A., Pogrebna, G., & Maull, R. S. (2009). Contextual Variety, Internet-of-Things and the Choice of Tailoring over Platform: Mass Customization Strategy in Supply Chain Management. *International Journal of Production Economics*, *159*, 76–87. doi:10.1016/j.ijpe.2014.09.007

Ngai, E. W., Xiu, L., & Chau, D. C. (2009). Application of Data Mining Techniques in Customer Relationship Management: A Literature Review and Classification. *Expert Systems with Applications*, *36*(2), 2592–2602. doi:10.1016/j.eswa.2008.02.021

Peighambari, K., Sattari, S., Kordestani, A., & Oghazi, P. (2016). Consumer Behavior Research: A Synthesis of the Recent Literature. *SAGE Open*, *6*(2), 1–9. doi:10.1177/2158244016645638

Peltier, J. W., Dahl, A. J., & Schibrowsky, J. A. (2022). Artificial Intelligence in Interactive Marketing: A Conceptual Framework and Research Agenda. *Journal of Research in Interactive Marketing*, *16*(4), 345–362.

Plassmann, H., Ramsøy, T. Z., & Milosavljevic, M. (2015). Branding the Brain: A Critical Review and Outlook. *Journal of Consumer Psychology*, *25*(1), 18–36. doi:10.1016/j.jcps.2011.11.010

Saheb, T., Cabanillas, F. J. L., & Higueras, E. (2022). The Risks and Benefits of Internet of Things (IoT) and Their Influence on Smartwatch Use. *Spanish Journal of Marketing-ESIC*, *26*(3), 309–324. doi:10.1108/SJME-07-2021-0129

Sama, R. (2013). Marketing Smart. In *Fast-tracking your Career: Soft skills for engineering and IT professionals*. Wiley-IEEE Press.

Seyfang, G. (2009). *The New Economics of Sustainable Consumption: Seeds of Change*. Palgrave Macmillan. doi:10.1057/9780230234505

Sheth, J. N., Sethia, N. K., & Srinivas, S. (2011). Mindful Consumption: A Customer-centric Approach to Sustainability. *Journal of the Academy of Marketing Science*, *39*(1), 21–39. doi:10.1007/s11747-010-0216-3

Smart Insights. (2022). *What Is Sustainable Marketing and How Should You Use It?* Retrieved at 20 Oct. (2023) from https://www.smartinsights.com/online-brand-strategy/brand-positioning/sustainable-marketing-how-should-you-use-it/

Stocchi, L., Pourazad, N., Michaelidou, N., Tanusondjaja, A., & Harrigan, P. (2022). Marketing Research on Mobile Apps: Past, Present and Future. *Journal of the Academy of Marketing Science*, *50*(2), 195–225. doi:10.1007/s11747-021-00815-w PMID:34776554

Taiminen, H. M., & Karjaluoto, H. (2015). The usage of digital marketing channels in SMEs. *Journal of Small Business and Enterprise Development*, *22*(4), 633–651. doi:10.1108/JSBED-05-2013-0073

Todorova, A., & Antonova, D. (2023, October). Smart Marketing Solutions: Applications with Artificial Intelligence to Increase the Effectiveness of Marketing Operations. In *2023 7th International Symposium on Multidisciplinary Studies and Innovative Technologies (ISMSIT)* (pp. 1-6). IEEE.

Vargo, S. L., & Lusch, R. F. (2008). Service-Dominant Logic: Continuing the Evolution. *Journal of the Academy of Marketing Science*, *36*(1), 1–10. doi:10.1007/s11747-007-0069-6

Verhoef, P. C., Kannan, P. K., & Inman, J. J. (2015). From Multi-Channel Retailing to OMNI-Channel Retailing: Introduction to the Special Issue on Multi-Channel Retailing. *Journal of Retailing*, *91*(2), 174–181. doi:10.1016/j.jretai.2015.02.005

Vermanen, M., Rantanen, M. M., & Harkke, V. (2022). Ethical Framework for IoT Deployment in SMEs: Individual Perspective. *Internet Research*, *32*(7), 185–201. doi:10.1108/INTR-08-2019-0361

Wang, Y., Deng, Q., Rod, M., & Ji, S. (2021). A Thematic Exploration of Social Media Analytics in Marketing Research and an Agenda for Future Inquiry. *Journal of Strategic Marketing*, *29*(6), 471–491. doi:10.1080/0965254X.2020.1755351

Wu, X., & Gereffi, G. (2018). Amazon and Alibaba: Internet Governance, Business Models, and Internationalization Strategies. In International Business in the Information and Digital Age (pp. 327-356). Emerald Publishing Limited.

Zhang, J. Z., & Chang, C.-W. (2021). Consumer Dynamics: Theories, Methods, and Emerging Directions. *Journal of the Academy of Marketing Science*, *49*(1), 166–196. doi:10.1007/s11747-020-00720-8

Zhang, Y., & Zhang, Y. (2022). Service-related Applications in Smart Marketing: A Review and Research Agenda. *Journal of Business Research*, *141*, 1–10.

ADDITIONAL READING

Dwivedi, Y. K., Hughes, L., Wang, Y., Alalwan, A. A., Ahn, S. J., Balakrishnan, J., & Wirtz, J. (2023). Metaverse marketing: How the metaverse will shape the future of consumer research and practice. *Psychology and Marketing, 40*(4), 750–776. doi:10.1002/mar.21767

Grand View Research. (2020). *Artificial Intelligence Market Size, Share & Trends Analysis Report by Solution (Hardware, Software, Services), By Technology (Computer Vision, Machine Learning, Natural Language Processing), By End Use, By Region, And Segment Forecasts, 2020 - 2030.* https://www.grandviewresearch.com/industry-analysis/artificial-intelligence-ai-market

Kshetri, N., Dwivedi, Y. K., Davenport, T. H., & Panteli, N. (2023). Generative artificial intelligence in marketing: Applications, opportunities, challenges, and research agenda. *International Journal of Information Management, 102716,* 102716. Advance online publication. doi:10.1016/j.ijinfomgt.2023.102716

Kumar, S., Tiwari, P., & Zymbler, M. (2019). Internet of Things is a revolutionary approach for future technology enhancement: A review. *Journal of Big Data, 6*(1), 1–21. doi:10.1186/s40537-019-0268-2

Peltier, J. W., Dahl, A. J., & Schibrowsky, J. A. (2022). Artificial intelligence in interactive marketing: A conceptual framework and research agenda. *Journal of Research in Interactive Marketing, 16*(4), 345–362.

Vermanen, M., Rantanen, M. M., & Harkke, V. (2022). Ethical framework for IoT deployment in SMEs: Individual perspective. *Internet Research, 32*(7), 185–201. doi:10.1108/INTR-08-2019-0361

Wang, Y., Deng, Q., Rod, M., & Ji, S. (2021). A thematic exploration of social media analytics in marketing research and an agenda for future inquiry. *Journal of Strategic Marketing, 29*(6), 471–491. doi:10.1080/0965254X.2020.1755351

KEY TERMS AND DEFINITIONS

AI-Powered Marketing: The process of leveraging artificial intelligence to create, deliver, and measure personalized and relevant marketing content and experiences across different channels and touchpoints (Wang et al., 2021).

Cognitive Marketing: Considered to be a combination of psychology, marketing and digital technologies. Based on the psychology theories, a variety of cognitive factors including perception, attention, emotions, and memory are understood which can help marketers to understand how customers process the related information and how they decide to purchase. Using cognitive marketing, businesses can monitor customer behavior and shape customized customer experience to create more competitive advantage (Plassmann et al., 2015).

Database Marketing: The use of customer data to segment, target, and customize marketing campaigns, which allows marketers to understand customer behavior, preferences, and needs, in order to deliver relevant and timely messages that increase customer loyalty and retention (Ngai et al., 2014).

Digital Marketing: A broad concept which involves using digital channels and platforms, such as websites, social media, email, search engines, and mobile apps in a wide range of marketing activities (Chaffey & Ellis-Chadwick, 2019).

E-Commerce Marketing: The practice of promoting websites to increase the traffic of a website and sales to enhance customer loyalty. It is also called e-commerce website marketing and encompasses pay-per-click (PC) advertising and search engine optimization (SEO), as well as email marketing and social media marketing (Jadhav et al., 2023).

Email Marketing: A subset of digital marketing and focuses on the use of email as a communication channel with customers and prospects (Bharadiya, 2023), which allows marketers to deliver personalized and relevant messages that may produce leads, conversions, and sales, as well as build relationships and loyalty with customers (Bharadiya, 2023).

Influence Marketing: Is also a new trend of marketing which is empowered by social networks. Influencer marketing increases the power and credibility of influencers who can endorse products or services to their followers (Hudders et al., 2021).

Interactive Marketing: Focuses on a customer-centric approach that creates two-way relationships with customers by engaging customers, providing relevant contents, creating personalized experiences which are integrated in different channels (Peltier et al., 2022).

IoT Marketing: The application of IoT technologies to collect, transmit, and transform data into knowledge. The marketing and sales sectors are capable of using data gathered through IoT to interact with customers on an individual basis.

Mobile Marketing: Aims at mobile devices and mobile apps because of their rapid growth and broad usage. In mobile marketing, mobile devices and mobile apps are considered as the current ultimate device to deliver marketing messages and offers to customers and prospects (Dacko, 2017).

Relationship Marketing: Refers to creating long-term and mutually beneficial relationships with customers and other stakeholders, such as suppliers, distributors, employees, and competitors (Grönroos & Voima, 2013).

Smart Marketing: A broad concept which encompasses digital technologies such as databases, IoT and IoE to collect data about the customer needs, behavior, and preferences; and then AI and machine learning is used to analyze collected data to provide personalized services and customized goods based on the knowledge and intuitions. Intelligent agents and bots are also used to automate customer services and interaction with customers (Baeva et al., 2022).

Social Media Marketing or Social Network Marketing: Which can be used interchangeably, refer to use of social media and network platforms to connect, reach and engage with a large and diverse audience, raise the brand awareness, and generate word-of-mouth to promote products and services (Kaplan & Haenlein, 2020; Hudders et al., 2021).

Chapter 11
Consumer Awareness and Perception of Online Services:
A Comparative Analysis of Brand Preferences and Decision-Making Processes

Meenu Kumari
Lalit Narayan Mithila University, India

Amit Dutt
Lovely Professional University, India

ABSTRACT

The advent of the digital age has brought about significant changes in consumer behavior, with online services becoming an integral part of everyday life. This chapter explores the consumer awareness and perception of online services, focusing on a comparative analysis of brand preferences and the decision-making process. By examining various studies and surveys, this chapter aims to shed light on the factors that influence consumer choices in the online service domain and understand how brands can enhance their strategies to attract and retain customers. The chapter concludes with actionable insights for businesses to better align their offerings with consumer expectations.

1. INTRODUCTION

The widespread digital revolution has profoundly reshaped the consumer landscape, facilitating an evolving inclination towards online services for a myriad of daily needs, ranging from banking and shopping to education and entertainment (Pappas, 2018). This seismic shift underscores the need for an in-depth understanding of consumer awareness, perception, and decision-making processes in the digital milieu (Lamberton & Stephen, 2016).

DOI: 10.4018/979-8-3693-1339-8.ch011

The current paper embarks on an expedition to scrutinize these pivotal aspects, placing particular emphasis on the comparison of brand preferences across a diverse array of online service providers. Grounded in a meticulous review of pertinent studies, surveys, and scholarly articles (Solomon, 2014; Verhoef, Kannan & Inman, 2015), this paper aims to illuminate the factors influencing consumer choices in the realm of online services, thereby offering strategic insights for brands to refine their approach towards customer attraction and retention. Additionally, this study responds to calls for more research in the field, particularly concerning the comparative analysis of brand preferences and the influence of various factors on the online decision-making process (Chen & Ann, 2016). By examining these dynamics, the paper seeks to contribute to both the academic literature and practical knowledge, providing vital guidance for businesses navigating the complexities of the digital marketplace. This study is guided by the research question: *"How are consumer perceptions and decision-making processes shaped in the digital age, and what are their preferences for different online service brands?"* The underlying hypothesis is that consumer awareness and perceptions of online services vary significantly across different brands, thereby exerting substantial influence on their decision-making processes (Schiffman, Kanuk, & Kumar, 2016).

2. CONSUMER BEHAVIOR IN THE DIGITAL AGE

2.1 Shift in Consumer Behavior in the Digital Era

The advent of the digital era has dramatically reshaped consumer behavior, fundamentally transforming how consumers interact with businesses and how they make purchasing decisions. The increased ubiquity of internet access, coupled with the widespread adoption of smartphones and other digital devices, has made online services more accessible and convenient than ever before (Morgan-Thomas & Veloutsou, 2013).

These developments have given rise to a new breed of consumers known as 'digital consumers.' Digital consumers are characterized by their heavy reliance on online platforms for information, communication, and transaction (Van Dijck, 2013). They are tech-savvy, informed, and demand convenience, personalization, and instant gratification (Huang & Benyoucef, 2013). Their behaviors are shaped by the abundance of information and choices available online, their interactions with brands and other consumers on social media, and their experiences with e-commerce and other online platforms (Lamberton & Stephen, 2016).

Furthermore, consumers in the digital era are increasingly relying on online reviews and recommendations from peers before making purchase decisions, a behavior known as 'social commerce' (Hajli, 2015). They also exhibit a high level of comfort and trust in online transactions, leading to increased online spending and loyalty towards online brands (Kumar & Reinartz, 2012).

As a result, businesses are required to adjust their strategies and practices to align with the behaviors and expectations of digital consumers. Understanding these shifts is crucial for businesses looking to succeed in the digital marketplace.

2.2 Impact of Online Services on Traditional Businesses

The emergence and growth of online services have had significant implications for traditional businesses. As consumers increasingly embrace the convenience, accessibility, and variety offered by online services, traditional brick-and-mortar businesses are experiencing intensified competition and are compelled to adapt to this changing landscape (Brynjolfsson, Hu & Rahman, 2013). The most immediate impact of online services on traditional businesses is the shift in customer expectations. Digital consumers demand a seamless shopping experience that integrates online and offline channels, known as the "omnichannel" experience (Verhoef, Kannan, & Inman, 2015). Consumers now expect to be able to browse products online, read reviews, compare prices, and make purchases at their convenience. This has forced traditional businesses to invest in their digital infrastructure and adopt new strategies to meet these expectations (Rigby, 2011). Moreover, the ubiquity of online services has increased market transparency and price competition. With just a few clicks, consumers can compare prices across multiple vendors, leading to downward pressure on prices and margins for traditional businesses (Brynjolfsson & Smith, 2000). Additionally, online platforms and e-commerce have also enabled businesses to reach a global audience, breaking down geographical barriers that previously limited the growth of traditional businesses (Goldmanis, Hortaçsu, Syverson & Emre, 2010).

However, the shift towards online services also presents new opportunities for traditional businesses. By integrating online services into their existing offerings, businesses can enhance customer engagement, improve customer service, and create additional revenue streams (Piotrowicz & Cuthbertson, 2014). The growth of online services represents both a challenge and an opportunity for traditional businesses. Success in this new environment depends on businesses' ability to adapt and innovate in response to changing consumer behaviors and expectations.

3. CONSUMER AWARENESS OF ONLINE SERVICES

3.1 The Role of Marketing and Advertising

In the digital age, marketing and advertising play a crucial role in shaping consumer awareness of online services. Consumers are exposed to a plethora of online services, and businesses use strategic marketing and advertising efforts to distinguish themselves and capture consumer attention (Armstrong et al., 2015).

Digital marketing strategies, such as search engine optimization (SEO), content marketing, email marketing, and social media marketing, have proven effective in increasing consumer awareness of online services (Chaffey & Ellis-Chadwick, 2019). For instance, SEO helps businesses to increase their visibility on search engine result pages, thus enhancing their reach to potential consumers (Patrutiu-Baltes, 2016). Advertising, particularly through online channels, is also a potent tool in raising consumer awareness. Online advertisements are capable of reaching a vast audience and can be personalized to target specific consumer groups based on their demographics, interests, and online behaviors (Lambrecht & Tucker, 2013). In recent years, the use of social media for marketing and advertising has skyrocketed. Social media platforms provide businesses with a direct line of communication to their consumers, facilitating real-time engagement and feedback (Hudson et al., 2015). They also enable businesses to leverage user-generated content, such as reviews and recommendations, to build trust and credibility with consumers (Kumar et al., 2016).

In conclusion, marketing and advertising play an instrumental role in promoting consumer awareness of online services. As consumers continue to spend more time online, businesses must harness the power of digital marketing and advertising tools to effectively reach and engage their target audiences.

3.2 Influence of Social Media on Consumer Perceptions

Social media has drastically changed the landscape of online services by reshaping the way consumers perceive and interact with brands. Social media platforms like Facebook, Twitter, Instagram, and LinkedIn have become essential tools for businesses to engage with consumers and influence their perceptions (Mangold & Faulds, 2009). These platforms offer businesses a venue to humanize their brands, share their stories, and build meaningful relationships with consumers, which can result in more positive consumer perceptions (Hajli, 2015). They also provide a channel for customers to share their experiences and opinions about the brands, impacting the perceptions of other consumers (Cheung & Thadani, 2012).

A significant element of social media's influence lies in the concept of social proof, wherein consumers' decisions are impacted by the actions and opinions of others. Online reviews, ratings, and testimonials have become powerful sources of social proof, influencing consumers' brand perceptions and purchase decisions (Hu, Zhang, & Pavlou, 2009). User-generated content (UGC), such as customer reviews, photos, videos, and social media posts about a product or service, also greatly influence consumer perception. UGC is viewed as more authentic and trustworthy than traditional advertising, and it significantly affects consumers' perceptions and decision-making (Smith, Fischer, & Yongjian, 2012). Moreover, the real-time and interactive nature of social media allows for immediate feedback and communication, which can enhance consumer satisfaction and strengthen brand perception (Labrecque, vor dem Esche, Mathwick, Novak, & Hofacker, 2013).

In conclusion, social media's influence on consumer perceptions is substantial. By strategically leveraging the power of social media, businesses can positively influence consumers' brand perceptions, fostering brand loyalty and increasing customer engagement.

4. CONSUMER PERCEPTION OF ONLINE SERVICE BRANDS

4.1 Factors Shaping Brand Image

The brand image of online service providers is largely influenced by a multitude of factors, each playing a critical role in shaping consumer perceptions. Several studies highlight the importance of service quality, trust, and reputation in establishing a strong and positive brand image (Sichtmann, 2007). Service quality is considered a key determinant of consumer perceptions and, consequently, brand image (Parasuraman, Zeithaml, & Berry, 1988). For online services, service quality extends beyond the core service to include aspects such as website design, ease of navigation, and transaction safety. A seamless and satisfying user experience can enhance the brand's perceived quality, leading to a positive brand image (Santos, 2003). Trust is another pivotal factor that shapes the brand image of online services (Kim, Ferrin, & Rao, 2008). Given the virtual nature of online transactions, consumers often face uncertainty and perceived risk. Trust in an online brand, therefore, can alleviate these concerns, positively influencing brand image. Factors that enhance online trust include website security, privacy protection, transparent information policies, and a proven track record of reliable service (Liu, Marchewka, Lu, & Yu, 2005).

Reputation is also a significant driver of brand image. The reputation of a brand is built over time based on past consumer experiences, word-of-mouth, and online reviews. A good reputation indicates that the brand is reliable and delivers on its promises, which can significantly enhance the brand image (Walsh & Beatty, 2007). User-generated content, like online reviews and social media conversations, also shapes the brand image. As consumers often trust peer reviews, these can significantly influence the perceived image of a brand (Lee & Youn, 2009).

The brand image in the online service context is shaped by a multitude of factors, including service quality, trust, reputation, and user-generated content. Understanding these drivers is crucial for businesses seeking to improve their brand image.

4.2 Importance of Reputation and Customer Reviews

In the digital era, a company's reputation and customer reviews significantly influence consumer perceptions and purchase decisions. A well-regarded reputation often serves as a signal of quality and trustworthiness for consumers, mitigating the uncertainties associated with online transactions (Walsh & Beatty, 2007). Research suggests that companies with good reputations are perceived as more trust-worthy and are more likely to attract and retain customers (Keh & Xie, 2009). A strong reputation can also lead to customer loyalty and advocacy, further enhancing the company's image and market position (Sirdeshmukh, Singh, & Sabol, 2002). On the other hand, customer reviews have emerged as a potent source of influence in the digital age. With platforms like Google, Yelp, and social media enabling users to easily share their experiences, these reviews often shape other consumers' perceptions and decisions about a brand (Chevalier & Mayzlin, 2006).

Reviews have been found to affect various consumer behaviors, including product consideration, choice, and post-purchase evaluation (Zhu & Zhang, 2010). Positive reviews can enhance the perceived quality of a brand and increase consumer trust, while negative reviews can significantly damage brand image and reduce sales (Lee, Park, & Han, 2008). Importantly, businesses that actively manage customer reviews, responding promptly and constructively to both positive and negative feedback, can influence consumer perceptions and build stronger relationships (Bolton, Keh, & Alba, 2010).Reputation and customer reviews are integral to the perceived value of online service brands. Businesses should care-fully manage these aspects to positively influence consumer perceptions and enhance their brand image.

4.3 User Experience and Customer Service

In the context of online services, user experience (UX) and customer service play critical roles in shaping consumer perceptions and, by extension, the brand's image. High-quality UX design and customer service contribute to the positive perception of a brand, leading to increased customer satisfaction, loyalty, and advocacy (Flavián, Guinalíu, & Gurrea, 2006; Homburg, Wieseke, & Hoyer, 2009). User experience, encompassing all aspects of the end-user's interaction with a company's online services, greatly influences how customers perceive the brand (Hassenzahl & Tractinsky, 2006). This experience is shaped by many factors, including ease of use, aesthetics of the website or application, personalization, and the ability to fulfill user needs effectively and efficiently. Studies have shown that a positive UX can lead to improved user satisfaction, higher conversion rates, and increased customer retention (Verhoef et al., 2009).Similarly, customer service is another crucial determinant of consumer perception in the online service context. Effective customer service in the digital age goes beyond resolving queries and issues.

It encompasses personalized communication, timely response, proactive service, and understanding customer needs (Dong, Evans, & Zou, 2008). Online service providers that excel in these aspects are often viewed more positively by consumers, enhancing their brand image and customer loyalty (Homburg et al., 2009). By focusing on user experience design and providing exceptional customer service, online service providers can significantly enhance their brand image and forge stronger relationships with their customers.

5. BRAND PREFERENCES IN ONLINE SERVICE SELECTION

5.1 The Role of Brand Loyalty

Brand loyalty plays a vital role in shaping customer preferences in online service selection. It is defined as a deeply held commitment to repurchase or patronize a preferred product or service consistently in the future, despite situational influences and marketing efforts having the potential to cause switching behavior (Oliver, 1999). The digital landscape's competitive nature means that building and maintaining brand loyalty is increasingly crucial for online service providers (Shankar, Smith, & Rangaswamy, 2003). Research indicates that loyal customers often show a higher likelihood to repurchase, less sensitivity to price, and greater willingness to recommend the brand to others (Reichheld & Schefter, 2000). Several factors contribute to the development of brand loyalty in the online environment. Trust, customer satisfaction, and perceived value have been identified as some of the primary drivers of online brand loyalty (Anderson & Srinivasan, 2003). Personalization of services and a strong online community can also lead to higher levels of loyalty (Casaló, Flavián, & Guinalíu, 2008).

Effective management of brand loyalty can lead to increased customer retention and profitability (Reinartz & Kumar, 2002). It has been shown that it costs much less to retain an existing customer than to acquire a new one, making brand loyalty a critical factor in online service selection and an essential component of a successful business strategy (Reichheld, 1996). Brand loyalty is a powerful tool in determining online service selection, with loyal customers providing a valuable source of recurring revenue and advocacy for the brand.

5.2 Building Trust With Consumers

Trust is a crucial element in the relationship between businesses and consumers, especially in online interactions where face-to-face communication is absent. Trust can significantly impact consumer behavior, brand preferences, and the decision to engage in transactions with an online service provider (Morgan & Hunt, 1994).Trust in the online context can be described as consumers' willingness to depend on the service provider in a situation characterized by uncertainty and vulnerability (Mayer, Davis, & Schoorman, 1995). Trust in online services is often built through factors such as perceived security, privacy protection, company reputation, quality of service, and the presence of familiar cues or seals of approval (Gefen, Karahanna, & Straub, 2003).

Building trust can lead to various positive outcomes. High trust levels have been associated with enhanced customer loyalty, increased likelihood of purchasing, and greater willingness to share personal information, all of which contribute to the success of online services (Srinivasan, Anderson, & Ponnavolu, 2002). Studies have also highlighted the role of trust in mitigating perceived risks in online transactions, thereby encouraging consumers to engage in e-commerce activities (Pavlou, 2003). Moreover, trust plays a crucial role in customer retention and the development of long-term relationships (Chaudhuri & Holbrook, 2001). Building trust is a key element in shaping brand preferences in the online service context. As digital technologies continue to evolve, businesses must adopt effective strategies to build and maintain trust with their consumers.

5.3 Perceived Value and Its Impact on Decision Making

Perceived value, in the context of consumer decision making, refers to the consumer's overall assessment of the utility of a product or service based on their perception of what is received and what is given (Zeithaml, 1988). It is a critical factor influencing consumer decision-making processes and brand preferences, particularly in the online services domain (Chen & Dubinsky, 2003). Perceived value is a multidimensional concept, encompassing elements such as perceived quality, monetary cost, time cost, and the psychological benefits derived from the purchase or use of the service (Sweeney & Soutar, 2001). Studies have shown that a positive perception of value can lead to higher levels of customer satisfaction, repeat purchase intention, and brand loyalty (Bolton & Lemon, 1999; Anderson, Fornell, & Lehmann, 1994). In the context of online services, factors such as the convenience of usage, the richness of information, personalized service, and security can significantly contribute to the perceived value (Parasuraman & Grewal, 2000). Service providers can enhance their perceived value by focusing on these aspects and communicating them effectively to consumers (Sweeney, Soutar, & Johnson, 1999). Perceived value is a powerful influencer of consumer decision making and brand preference. By providing superior perceived value, online service providers can attract and retain customers, build loyalty, and maintain a competitive advantage in the online marketplace.

6. DECISION-MAKING PROCESS IN SELECTING ONLINE SERVICES

6.1 Steps Involved in Decision Making

The process of making decisions in selecting online services is multifaceted, involving several steps derived from established consumer behavior models (Solomon, 2014). Understanding these steps can provide significant insights into consumers' cognitive processes and influence on online service selection.

1. **Need Recognition:** The first step in the decision-making process begins when consumers recognize a need or problem that can be satisfied or solved by a product or service (Kotler & Armstrong, 2010). In the context of online services, this could be the need for information, entertainment, purchasing a product, or any service that can be fulfilled online.
2. **Information Search:** After identifying the need, consumers engage in an information search to gather relevant data about potential solutions. Given the nature of the internet, this process can be extensive, involving search engines, social media, online reviews, and company websites (Peterson & Merino, 2003).
3. **Evaluation of Alternatives:** With the information gathered, consumers then evaluate different online service providers. This stage involves comparing various aspects such as price, quality, reputation, and features offered by different brands (Laroche, Zhang, & Dai, 2005).

4. **Purchase Decision:** Based on the evaluation, consumers make a purchase decision. This stage involves not just the selection of the brand but also other elements like payment method, and agreeing to terms and conditions (Kotler, Kartajaya, & Setiawan, 2016).

5. **Post-Purchase Evaluation:** After the purchase, consumers evaluate their experience with the online service. Satisfaction or dissatisfaction at this stage can influence future decisions and potentially result in word-of-mouth referrals or criticisms (Anderson, 1998).

6.2 Key Criteria for Service Selection

Choosing an online service involves evaluating multiple criteria that significantly influence the final decision. Understanding these criteria is crucial for online service providers to attract and retain customers.

1. **Price:** Price is a fundamental criterion for consumers when selecting a service. Competitive pricing strategies can significantly influence consumers' choice of online service providers (Völckner, 2008).

2. **Quality of Service:** Quality is another key criterion, encompassing elements such as the actual service provided, the website's user-friendliness, service delivery speed, and customer support (Parasuraman, Zeithaml, & Berry, 1985).

3. **Reputation:** The reputation of the online service provider plays a crucial role in the decision-making process. A well-regarded reputation can help build trust and decrease perceived risk among consumers (Gommans, Krishnan, & Scheffold, 2001).

4. **Security and Privacy:** In the digital age, concerns about data security and privacy significantly impact consumers' choices. Service providers with robust security measures are likely to attract more consumers (Culnan & Armstrong, 1999).

5. **Reviews and Recommendations:** Online reviews and recommendations can sway consumers' decisions significantly. Positive reviews can lead to increased trust and reduced uncertainty (Chevalier & Mayzlin, 2006).

Understanding these criteria can help online service providers focus their efforts on areas that consumers value most, ultimately leading to increased satisfaction and loyalty.

7. COMPARATIVE ANALYSIS OF BRAND PREFERENCES

7.1 Patterns and Trends Across Different Service Sectors

In the realm of online services, brand preferences vary significantly across different sectors, reflecting the diverse needs, expectations, and behaviors of consumers. In the e-commerce sector, brands that provide a wide range of products, competitive prices, quick delivery, and easy return policies are typically favored by consumers (Liu, He, Gao, & Xie, 2008). For example, Amazon has become a popular choice for online shopping due to its vast product selection, customer-friendly services, and reputation (Gupta, Su, & Walter, 2004). The online streaming sector shows a preference for brands providing high-quality content, user-friendly interfaces, and personalized recommendations. Netflix, with its vast library of content and personalized viewing recommendations, has emerged as a favored choice (Gomez-Uribe &

Hunt, 2016). In the online travel and accommodation sector, brands that offer comprehensive information, secure transactions, and reliable customer service are preferred. Brands like Airbnb and Booking.com have gained popularity due to their user-friendly platforms and transparent review systems (Xiang, Du, Ma, & Fan, 2017).

Online banking services are preferred based on security, ease of use, and the range of services offered. Banks that offer robust online services, such as JP Morgan Chase or Bank of America, have been successful in attracting and retaining customers (Srivastava, 2007). These patterns suggest that while consumers' brand preferences are shaped by sector-specific factors, some common themes—such as quality, convenience, security, and customer service—are prevalent across sectors. Understanding these trends can help businesses in different sectors develop strategies to enhance their appeal and gain a competitive edge.

7.2 Factors Influencing Consumer Choices

Understanding the factors that influence consumer choices is crucial for online service providers to develop strategies that effectively attract and retain customers. Various factors play a role in shaping consumer choices in the realm of online services.

1. **Quality of Service:** High-quality service, encompassing aspects like reliability, efficiency, and user-friendliness, significantly influences consumer choices (Parasuraman, Zeithaml, & Berry, 1985).
2. **Price:** Competitive pricing strategies can sway consumers' choices towards a particular online service (Völckner, 2008).
3. **Brand Reputation:** Brands that have built a strong reputation and gained consumers' trust are more likely to be preferred by consumers (Walsh & Beatty, 2007).
4. **Reviews and Recommendations:** Positive reviews and recommendations can reduce consumer uncertainty and lead to increased trust in an online service (Chevalier & Mayzlin, 2006).
5. **Customization:** Online services that offer personalized experiences tailored to individual consumers' needs and preferences are more likely to be chosen by consumers (Kumar & Reinartz, 2012).
6. **Security and Privacy:** Given increasing concerns about data privacy and security, consumers are likely to prefer online services that ensure robust data protection measures (Culnan & Armstrong, 1999).

8. FACTORS INFLUENCING CONSUMER PERCEPTION

8.1 Cultural Influences on Perception

Culture plays a significant role in shaping consumer perception of online services. It informs consumer attitudes, beliefs, and behaviors, which in turn impact their interaction with online brands.Cultural norms and values influence consumers' attitudes towards privacy, security, and trust, which are critical factors in the adoption and use of online services (Dinev, Bellotto, Hart, Russo, Serra, & Colautti, 2006). For instance, consumers in cultures that place a high value on privacy may show more concern about data privacy and security when using online services (Milberg, Smith, & Burke, 2000). Cultural preferences also influence the user interface and design of online services. For example, consumers from high-context cultures (such as many Asian cultures) prefer websites with more images and context, while those from low-context cultures (such as the US and Western Europe) prefer more direct and explicit information (Cyr & Trevor-Smith, 2004).Cultural factors can shape consumers' expectations and evaluations of service quality. Service attributes valued in one culture may not hold the same importance in another (Furrer, Liu, & Sudharshan, 2000). Understanding these cultural nuances can help online service providers cater to their diverse customer base effectively.

8.2 Socio-Economic Factors Affecting Perception

Socio-economic factors significantly influence consumer perception of online services. Variables such as income, education, and occupation can shape the preferences, decision-making, and overall perception of consumers in the digital marketplace. Income level can influence the perception of pricing and value, with higher-income consumers often willing to pay more for premium services or products online (Gupta, Su & Walter, 2004). In contrast, consumers with lower income may seek out online services offering better deals or discounts (Hsieh & Tsao, 2014).

Education level also affects the consumer's perception of online services. Highly educated consumers are likely to feel more comfortable using online services, value the convenience, and show greater concern about data privacy and security (Blank & Dutton, 2012). Occupation can influence the types of online services used and how these services are perceived. For instance, professionals might place more importance on efficiency and reliability of online services due to their time constraints, while students may focus more on price (Venkatesh & Morris, 2000).

8.3 Demographic Characteristics and Their Impact

Demographic characteristics, such as age, gender, and location, can have a significant impact on consumer perception of online services. These characteristics can shape the ways consumers perceive, interact with, and make decisions about online services. Age is a vital factor influencing consumer's technology acceptance and use. Younger consumers, often referred to as digital natives, are generally more comfortable with using online services and are more likely to adopt new online trends (Prensky, 2001). In contrast, older consumers might show less comfort with online services and place more importance on aspects like security and customer service (Choudrie & Vyas, 2014). Gender also plays a role in the perception and use of online services. Studies have found that men and women use online services differently, with men often showing a higher willingness to take risks online, while women tend to be more concerned about privacy and online security (Garbarino & Strahilevitz, 2004). Lastly, geographic location, especially in terms of urban versus rural, can greatly influence consumer's access to and perception of online services. Consumers in urban areas, where access to high-speed internet is more prevalent, might have a more positive perception of online services compared to those in rural areas (Salemink, Strijker, & Bosworth, 2017).

9. STRATEGIES TO ENHANCE BRAND PERCEPTION AND CONSUMER AWARENESS

9.1 Targeted Marketing Approaches

In the era of digital marketing, targeted marketing approaches have shown to significantly improve brand perception and consumer awareness. Using data analytics, businesses can segment their audience and deliver personalized content that is relevant to each segment, enhancing engagement and brand perception (Bleier & Eisenbeiss, 2015).

Targeted advertising through digital channels, such as social media and search engines, can effectively reach specific consumer groups. This approach allows businesses to curate messages that resonate with consumers' interests, needs, and preferences, thereby increasing the likelihood of engagement and conversion (Li & Kannan, 2014).Additionally, behavioral targeting, which involves tracking consumers' online activities to understand their behavior and preferences, can lead to more personalized and relevant marketing campaigns. This approach can increase click-through rates, improve conversion rates, and ultimately, enhance brand perception (Lambrecht & Tucker, 2013). Content marketing is another effective targeted approach that can drive consumer awareness and shape brand perception. By creating valuable, relevant, and consistent content, brands can establish themselves as thought leaders in their industry, build trust with consumers, and improve customer retention (Pulizzi, 2012).

9.2 Personalized Customer Experiences

Personalized customer experiences are fundamental for enhancing brand perception and consumer awareness in the realm of online services. By leveraging data analytics, AI, and machine learning technologies, businesses can offer highly tailored experiences to their customers (Huang & Rust, 2018). Personalization can be manifested in various ways, from product recommendations based on browsing history to customized email campaigns. It can significantly improve user engagement, increase customer satisfaction, and lead to higher conversion rates (Tam & Ho, 2006). For example, e-commerce giants like Amazon have seen great success with personalized recommendations (Smith & Linden, 2017).

Furthermore, personalized customer service, including responsive support through various digital channels (like chatbots, emails, and social media), can also enhance the customer experience. Timely, personalized customer service can help resolve issues effectively, build trust, and foster loyalty (Kumar & Reinartz, 2012). While implementing personalized experiences, businesses must carefully balance personalization and privacy concerns, as excessive personalization can lead to perceived privacy invasion, adversely affecting brand perception (Awad & Krishnan, 2006).

9.3 Customer Engagement Initiatives

Customer engagement initiatives are vital strategies for enhancing brand perception and awareness. These initiatives involve fostering a two-way interaction between the brand and its consumers, enabling a deeper connection and building a loyal customer base (Brodie, Hollebeek, Juric, & Ilic, 2011). One effective customer engagement initiative is social media engagement, where brands interact with their customers through likes, comments, shares, and direct messages on various social platforms. Active engagement on social media can enhance brand visibility, build community, and create a platform for real-time customer service (Kietzmann, Hermkens, McCarthy, & Silvestre, 2011). Another strategy is gamification, which involves incorporating game mechanics into non-gaming environments to motivate participation, engagement, and loyalty. Gamified experiences can increase user engagement, foster a sense of achievement, and ultimately enhance brand perception (Hamari, Koivisto, & Sarsa, 2014). Loyalty programs, such as points systems, membership benefits, and rewards for referrals, are also effective for increasing customer engagement. These programs incentivize repeat purchases, encourage positive word-of-mouth, and foster long-term customer loyalty (Liu & Yang, 2009). In sum, customer engagement initiatives can significantly enhance brand perception and consumer awareness by fostering interactive relationships between the brand and its customers.

10. FUTURE TRENDS IN CONSUMER BEHAVIOR AND ONLINE SERVICES

10.1 Anticipated Changes in Consumer Behavior

As we continue to advance in the digital era, several trends are expected to shape consumer behavior in the future. First, the rise of artificial intelligence and machine learning will continue to provide businesses with more comprehensive consumer insights. This will lead to even more personalized marketing strategies, offering products and services tailored to individual needs, preferences, and behaviors (Huang & Rust, 2018). Next, with the increasing popularity of voice-activated technology like Amazon's Alexa and Google Home, voice search and voice shopping are anticipated to become more prevalent. This shift will likely lead businesses to adjust their digital strategies to fit voice search optimization and offer voice-based shopping experiences (Lopatovska & Rink, 2018). The growing concern over data privacy will also significantly influence consumer behavior. Consumers are expected to become more cautious about their online activities and the information they share with businesses, potentially affecting online shopping behaviors and responses to digital advertising (Martin, 2018). Lastly, the trend towards socially responsible consumption is expected to grow, with consumers favoring brands that demonstrate a commitment to social, ethical, and environmental issues (Carrington, Neville, & Whitwell, 2014). Brands will need to address these concerns in their strategies to maintain customer loyalty and positive brand perception.

10.2 The Evolution of Online Services

With technological advancements and changing consumer behaviors, online services are expected to undergo several evolutions. *Firstly*, advancements in artificial intelligence (AI) and machine learning are expected to refine and expand online service offerings. From personalized product recommendations to AI-driven customer support, these technologies are enabling a new level of customization and efficiency in online services (Huang & Rust, 2018).

Secondly, the emergence of blockchain technology could significantly alter the landscape of online services. Blockchain could offer decentralized, secure platforms for transactions, leading to enhanced trust and transparency in areas like e-commerce and financial services (Mougayar, 2016). *Thirdly,* virtual and augmented reality (VR and AR) technologies will likely become more prevalent in online services. They provide immersive experiences that can enhance user engagement and satisfaction, particularly in sectors such as retail, entertainment, and real estate (Javornik, 2016). *Lastly*, 5G and future iterations of internet connectivity will enable quicker, more stable access to online services, transforming experiences especially in video streaming, online gaming, and teleconferencing, among others (CISCO, 2020).

11. CONCLUSION

The advent and continued evolution of the digital age have significantly transformed consumer behavior and the nature of online services. This review paper has endeavored to explore and analyze these changes, focusing particularly on brand preferences and decision-making processes.

Shifts in consumer behavior in the digital era have emphasized the importance of online services, impacting traditional businesses and necessitating adaptability. The key role of marketing, advertising, and social media in shaping consumer awareness and perceptions of online services has also been highlighted, demonstrating the profound influence of these channels on shaping brand image and reputation. Consumer loyalty and trust emerged as critical factors influencing brand preference, further emphasized by the importance of perceived value in the decision-making process. The analysis also uncovered that cultural, socio-economic, and demographic characteristics significantly affect consumer perceptions. Looking ahead, businesses must align with emerging trends such as increased personalization, voice-activated technologies, heightened data privacy concerns, and socially responsible consumption. With the expected evolution of online services, driven by AI, machine learning, blockchain, AR/VR, and enhanced internet connectivity, the landscape of online services is poised for substantial transformation.

Through this review, it is evident that understanding consumer behavior, maintaining brand loyalty, and adapting to digital advancements are crucial for businesses to thrive in the digital age. As consumer behavior and online services continue to evolve, further research is essential to keep abreast of these changes and provide relevant insights for businesses seeking to maximize their online potential.

In conclusion, the digital age has introduced a new era of consumer behavior and online services, driving businesses to adapt and innovate. By enhancing their understanding of consumer perceptions and aligning their strategies accordingly, businesses can successfully navigate this dynamic landscape.

REFERENCES

Anderson, E. W. (1998). Customer satisfaction and word of mouth. *Journal of Service Research, 1*(1), 5–17. doi:10.1177/109467059800100102

Anderson, E. W., Fornell, C., & Lehmann, D. R. (1994). Customer satisfaction, market share, and profitability: Findings from Sweden. *Journal of Marketing, 58*(3), 53–66. doi:10.1177/002224299405800304

Anderson, R. E., & Srinivasan, S. S. (2003). E-satisfaction and e-loyalty: A contingency framework. *Psychology and Marketing, 20*(2), 123–138. doi:10.1002/mar.10063

Armstrong, G., Adam, S., Denize, S., & Kotler, P. (2015). *Principles of Marketing*. Pearson Australia.

Awad, N. F., & Krishnan, M. S. (2006). The personalization privacy paradox: An empirical evaluation of information transparency and the willingness to be profiled online for personalization. *Management Information Systems Quarterly, 30*(1), 13–28. doi:10.2307/25148715

Blank, G., & Dutton, W. H. (2012). Age and trust in the Internet: The centrality of experience and attitudes toward technology in Britain. *Social Science Computer Review, 30*(2), 135–151. doi:10.1177/0894439310396186

Bleier, A., & Eisenbeiss, M. (2015). Personalized online advertising effectiveness: The interplay of what, when, and where. *Marketing Science, 34*(5), 669–688. doi:10.1287/mksc.2015.0930

Bolton, R. N., Keh, H. T., & Alba, J. W. (2010). How do price fairness perceptions differ across culture? *JMR, Journal of Marketing Research, 47*(3), 564–576. doi:10.1509/jmkr.47.3.564

Bolton, R. N., & Lemon, K. N. (1999). A dynamic model of customers' usage of services: Usage as an antecedent and consequence of satisfaction. *JMR, Journal of Marketing Research, 36*(2), 171–186.

Brodie, R. J., Hollebeek, L. D., Juric, B., & Ilic, A. (2011). Customer engagement: Conceptual domain, fundamental propositions, and implications for research. *Journal of Service Research, 14*(3), 252–271. doi:10.1177/1094670511411703

Brynjolfsson, E., Hu, Y. J., & Rahman, M. S. (2013). Competing in the Age of Omnichannel Retailing. *MIT Sloan Management Review, 54*(4), 23–29.

Carrington, M. J., Neville, B. A., & Whitwell, G. J. (2014). Lost in translation: Exploring the ethical consumer intention–behavior gap. *Journal of Business Research, 67*(1), 2759–2767. doi:10.1016/j.jbusres.2012.09.022

Casaló, L. V., Flavián, C., & Guinalíu, M. (2008). The role of satisfaction and website usability in developing customer loyalty and positive word-of-mouth in the e-banking services. *International Journal of Bank Marketing, 26*(6), 399–417. doi:10.1108/02652320810902433

Chaffey, D., & Ellis-Chadwick, F. (2019). *Digital Marketing*. Pearson UK.

Chaudhuri, A., & Holbrook, M. B. (2001). The chain of effects from brand trust and brand affect to brand performance: The role of brand loyalty. *Journal of Marketing, 65*(2), 81–93. doi:10.1509/jmkg.65.2.81.18255

Chen, Y. R. R., & Ann, B. S. (2016). Exploring online consumer behavior: The role of extrinsic and intrinsic motivation. *Telematics and Informatics, 33*(4), 1149–1160.

Chen, Z., & Dubinsky, A. J. (2003). A conceptual model of perceived customer value in e-commerce: A preliminary investigation. *Psychology and Marketing, 20*(4), 323–347. doi:10.1002/mar.10076

Cheung, C. M., & Thadani, D. R. (2012). The impact of electronic word-of-mouth communication: A literature analysis and integrative model. *Decision Support Systems, 54*(1), 461–470. doi:10.1016/j.dss.2012.06.008

Chevalier, J. A., & Mayzlin, D. (2006). The effect of word of mouth on sales: Online book reviews. *JMR, Journal of Marketing Research, 43*(3), 345–354. doi:10.1509/jmkr.43.3.345

Choudrie, J., & Vyas, A. (2014). Silver surfers adopting and using Facebook? A quantitative study of Hertfordshire, UK applied to organizational and social change. *Technological Forecasting and Social Change, 89*, 293–305. doi:10.1016/j.techfore.2014.08.007

CISCO. (2020). *Cisco Annual Internet Report (2018–2023) White Paper*. Retrieved from https://www.cisco.com/c/en/us/solutions/collateral/executive-perspectives/annual-internet-report/white-paper-c11-741490.html

Culnan, M. J., & Armstrong, P. K. (1999). Information privacy concerns, procedural fairness, and impersonal trust: An empirical investigation. *Organization Science, 10*(1), 104–115. doi:10.1287/orsc.10.1.104

Cyr, D., & Trevor-Smith, H. (2004). Localization of web design: An empirical comparison of German, Japanese, and United States web site characteristics. *Journal of the American Society for Information Science and Technology, 55*(13), 1199–1208. doi:10.1002/asi.20075

Dinev, T., Bellotto, M., Hart, P., Russo, V., Serra, I., & Colautti, C. (2006). Privacy calculus model in e-commerce–a study of Italy and the United States. *European Journal of Information Systems, 15*(4), 389–402. doi:10.1057/palgrave.ejis.3000590

Flavián, C., Guinalíu, M., & Gurrea, R. (2006). The role played by perceived usability, satisfaction and consumer trust on website loyalty. *Information & Management, 43*(1), 1–14. doi:10.1016/j.im.2005.01.002

Furrer, O., Liu, B. S. C., & Sudharshan, D. (2000). The relationships between culture and service quality perceptions: Basis for cross-cultural market segmentation and resource allocation. *Journal of Service Research, 2*(4), 355–371. doi:10.1177/109467050024004

Garbarino, E., & Strahilevitz, M. (2004). Gender differences in the perceived risk of buying online and the effects of receiving a site recommendation. *Journal of Business Research, 57*(7), 768–775. doi:10.1016/S0148-2963(02)00363-6

Gefen, D., Karahanna, E., & Straub, D. W. (2003). Trust and TAM in online shopping: An integrated model. *Management Information Systems Quarterly, 27*(1), 51–90. doi:10.2307/30036519

Goldmanis, M., Hortaçsu, A., Syverson, C., & Emre, O. (2010). E-commerce and the Market Structure of Retail Industries. *Economic Journal (London), 120*(545), 651–682. doi:10.1111/j.1468-0297.2009.02310.x

Gomez-Uribe, C. A., & Hunt, N. (2016). The Netflix recommender system: Algorithms, business value, and innovation. *ACM Transactions on Management Information Systems, 6*(4), 1–19. doi:10.1145/2843948

Gommans, M., Krishnan, K. S., & Scheffold, K. B. (2001). From brand loyalty to e-loyalty: A conceptual framework. *Journal of Economic and Social Research, 3*(1), 43–58.

Gupta, S., Su, B. C., & Walter, Z. (2004). An empirical study of consumer switching from traditional to electronic channels: A purchase-decision process perspective. *International Journal of Electronic Commerce, 8*(3), 131–161. doi:10.1080/10864415.2004.11044302

Hajli, M. (2015). Social commerce constructs and consumer's intention to buy. *International Journal of Information Management, 35*(2), 183–191. doi:10.1016/j.ijinfomgt.2014.12.005

Hamari, J., Koivisto, J., & Sarsa, H. (2014). Does gamification work? A literature review of empirical studies on gamification. In *2014 47th Hawaii International Conference on System Sciences* (pp. 3025-3034). IEEE.

Hassenzahl, M., & Tractinsky, N. (2006). User experience - a research agenda. *Behaviour & Information Technology, 25*(2), 91–97. doi:10.1080/01449290500330331

Homburg, C., Wieseke, J., & Hoyer, W. D. (2009). Social identity and the service-profit chain. *Journal of Marketing, 73*(2), 38–54. doi:10.1509/jmkg.73.2.38

Hsieh, J. K., & Tsao, W. C. (2014). Reducing perceived online shopping risk to enhance loyalty: A website quality perspective. *Journal of Risk Research, 17*(2), 241–261. doi:10.1080/13669877.2013.794152

Hu, N., Zhang, J., & Pavlou, P. A. (2009). Overcoming the J-shaped distribution of product reviews. *Communications of the ACM, 52*(10), 144–147. doi:10.1145/1562764.1562800

Huang, M. H., & Rust, R. T. (2018). Artificial intelligence in service. *Journal of Service Research, 21*(2), 155–172. doi:10.1177/1094670517752459

Huang, Z., & Benyoucef, M. (2013). From e-commerce to social commerce: A close look at design features. *Electronic Commerce Research and Applications, 12*(4), 246–259. doi:10.1016/j.elerap.2012.12.003

Hudson, S., Huang, L., Roth, M. S., & Madden, T. J. (2015). The influence of social media interactions on consumer–brand relationships: A three-country study of brand perceptions and marketing behaviors. *International Journal of Research in Marketing, 32*(1), 27–41. doi:10.1016/j.ijresmar.2015.06.004

Javornik, A. (2016). Augmented reality: Research agenda for studying the impact of its media characteristics on consumer behaviour. *Journal of Retailing and Consumer Services, 30*, 252–261. doi:10.1016/j.jretconser.2016.02.004

Keh, H. T., & Xie, Y. (2009). Corporate reputation and customer behavioral intentions: The roles of trust, identification and commitment. *Industrial Marketing Management, 38*(7), 732–742. doi:10.1016/j.indmarman.2008.02.005

Kietzmann, J. H., Hermkens, K., McCarthy, I. P., & Silvestre, B. S. (2011). Social media? Get serious! Understanding the functional building blocks of social media. *Business Horizons, 54*(3), 241–251. doi:10.1016/j.bushor.2011.01.005

Kim, D. J., Ferrin, D. L., & Rao, H. R. (2008). A trust-based consumer decision-making model in electronic commerce: The role of trust, perceived risk, and their antecedents. *Decision Support Systems, 44*(2), 544–564. doi:10.1016/j.dss.2007.07.001

Kumar, A., Bezawada, R., Rishika, R., Janakiraman, R., & Kannan, P. K. (2016). From social to sale: The effects of firm-generated content in social media on customer behavior. *Journal of Marketing, 80*(1), 7–25. doi:10.1509/jm.14.0249

Kumar, V., & Reinartz, W. (2012). *Customer Relationship Management: Concept, Strategy, and Tools.* Springer. doi:10.1007/978-3-642-20110-3

Labrecque, L. I., vor dem Esche, J., Mathwick, C., Novak, T. P., & Hofacker, C. F. (2013). Consumer power: Evolution in the digital age. *Journal of Interactive Marketing, 27*(4), 257–269. doi:10.1016/j.intmar.2013.09.002

Lamberton, C., & Stephen, A. T. (2016). A thematic exploration of digital, social media, and mobile marketing: Research evolution from 2000 to 2015 and an agenda for future inquiry. *Journal of Marketing, 80*(6), 146–172. doi:10.1509/jm.15.0415

Lambrecht, A., & Tucker, C. (2013). When does retargeting work? Information specificity in online advertising. *JMR, Journal of Marketing Research, 50*(5), 561–576. doi:10.1509/jmr.11.0503

Laroche, M., Zhang, Q., & Dai, M. (2005). Online consumer behavior: a review and agenda for future research. In Research Developments in Computer Vision and Image Processing: Methodologies and Applications (pp. 155-170). IGI Global.

Lee, J., Park, D. H., & Han, I. (2008). The effect of negative online consumer reviews on product attitude: An information processing view. *Electronic Commerce Research and Applications, 7*(3), 341–352. doi:10.1016/j.elerap.2007.05.004

Lee, M., & Youn, S. (2009). Electronic word of mouth (eWOM). *International Journal of Advertising, 28*(3), 473–499. doi:10.2501/S0265048709200709

Li, H., & Kannan, P. K. (2014). Attributing conversions in a multichannel online marketing environment: An empirical model and a field experiment. *JMR, Journal of Marketing Research, 51*(1), 40–56. doi:10.1509/jmr.13.0050

Liu, C., Marchewka, J. T., Lu, J., & Yu, C. S. (2005). Beyond concern—A privacy-trust-behavioral intention model of electronic commerce. *Information & Management, 42*(2), 289–304. doi:10.1016/j.im.2004.01.003

Liu, X., He, M., Gao, F., & Xie, P. (2008). An empirical study of online shopping customer satisfaction in China: A holistic perspective. *International Journal of Retail & Distribution Management, 36*(11), 919–940. doi:10.1108/09590550810911683

Lopatovska, I., Rink, K., Knight, I., Raines, K., Cosenza, K., Williams, H., Sorsche, P., Hirsch, D., Li, Q., & Martinez, A. (2018). Speak to me: Exploring user interactions with the Amazon Alexa. *Journal of Librarianship and Information Science, 51*(4), 984–997. doi:10.1177/0961000618759414

Mangold, W. G., & Faulds, D. J. (2009). Social media: The new hybrid element of the promotion mix. *Business Horizons, 52*(4), 357–365. doi:10.1016/j.bushor.2009.03.002

Martin, K. (2018). Privacy notices as tabula rasa: An empirical investigation into how complying with a privacy notice is related to meeting privacy expectations online. *Journal of Public Policy & Marketing, 37*(2), 236–248.

Mayer, R. C., Davis, J. H., & Schoorman, F. D. (1995). An integrative model of organizational trust. *Academy of Management Review, 20*(3), 709–734. doi:10.2307/258792

Milberg, S. J., Smith, H. J., & Burke, S. J. (2000). Information privacy: Corporate management and national regulation. *Organization Science, 11*(1), 35–57. doi:10.1287/orsc.11.1.35.12567

Morgan, R. M., & Hunt, S. D. (1994). The commitment-trust theory of relationship marketing. *Journal of Marketing, 58*(3), 20–38. doi:10.1177/002224299405800302

Morgan-Thomas, A., & Veloutsou, C. (2013). Beyond technology acceptance: Brand relationships and online brand experience. *Journal of Business Research, 66*(1), 21–27. doi:10.1016/j.jbusres.2011.07.019

Mougayar, W. (2016). *The Business Blockchain: Promise, Practice, and Application of the Next Internet Technology.* Wiley.

Oliver, R. L. (1999). Whence consumer loyalty? *Journal of Marketing, 63*(4_suppl1), 33–44. doi:10.1177/00222429990634s105

Pappas, I. O. (2018). User experience in personalized online shopping: A fuzzy decision-making model and empirical study. *Technological Forecasting and Social Change, 125,* 254–264.

Parasuraman, A., & Grewal, D. (2000). The impact of technology on the quality-value-loyalty chain: A research agenda. *Journal of the Academy of Marketing Science, 28*(1), 168–174. doi:10.1177/0092070300281015

Parasuraman, A., Zeithaml, V. A., & Berry, L. L. (1985). A conceptual model of service quality and its implications for future research. *Journal of Marketing, 49*(4), 41–50. doi:10.1177/002224298504900403

Parasuraman, A., Zeithaml, V. A., & Berry, L. L. (1988). SERVQUAL: A multiple-item scale for measuring consumer perceptions of service quality. *Journal of Retailing, 64*(1), 12.

Patrutiu-Baltes, L. (2016). Inbound Marketing - the most important digital marketing strategy. Bulletin of the Transilvania University of Brasov. *Economic Sciences. Series V, 9*(2), 61.

Pavlou, P. A. (2003). Consumer acceptance of electronic commerce: Integrating trust and risk with the technology acceptance model. *International Journal of Electronic Commerce, 7*(3), 101–134. doi:10.1080/10864415.2003.11044275

Peterson, R. A., & Merino, M. C. (2003). Consumer information search behavior and the Internet. *Psychology and Marketing, 20*(2), 99–121. doi:10.1002/mar.10062

Piotrowicz, W., & Cuthbertson, R. (2014). Introduction to the Special Issue Information Technology in Retail: Toward Omnichannel Retailing. *International Journal of Electronic Commerce, 18*(4), 5–16. doi:10.2753/JEC1086-4415180400

Prensky, M. (2001). Digital natives, digital immigrants part 1. *On the Horizon, 9*(5), 1–6. doi:10.1108/10748120110424816

Pulizzi, J. (2012). The rise of storytelling as the new marketing. *Publishing Research Quarterly, 28*(2), 116–123. doi:10.1007/s12109-012-9264-5

Reichheld, F. F. (1996). Learning from customer defections. *Harvard Business Review, 74*(2), 56–69.

Reichheld, F. F., & Schefter, P. (2000). E-loyalty: Your secret weapon on the web. *Harvard Business Review, 78*(4), 105–113.

Reinartz, W. J., & Kumar, V. (2002). The mismanagement of customer loyalty. *Harvard Business Review, 80*(7), 86–94. PMID:12140857

Rigby, D. (2011). The Future of Shopping. *Harvard Business Review, 89*(12), 65–76.

Salemink, K., Strijker, D., & Bosworth, G. (2017). Rural development in the digital age: A systematic literature review on unequal ICT availability, adoption, and use in rural areas. *Journal of Rural Studies*, *54*, 360–371. doi:10.1016/j.jrurstud.2015.09.001

Santos, J. (2003). E-service quality: A model of virtual service quality dimensions. *Managing Service Quality*, *13*(3), 233–246. doi:10.1108/09604520310476490

Schiffman, L. G., Kanuk, L. L., & Kumar, S. R. (2016). *Consumer behavior*. Pearson Education India.

Shankar, V., Smith, A. K., & Rangaswamy, A. (2003). Customer satisfaction and loyalty in online and offline environments. *International Journal of Research in Marketing*, *20*(2), 153–175. doi:10.1016/S0167-8116(03)00016-8

Sichtmann, C. (2007). An analysis of antecedents and consequences of trust in a corporate brand. *European Journal of Marketing*.

Sirdeshmukh, D., Singh, J., & Sabol, B. (2002). Consumer trust, value, and loyalty in relational exchanges. *Journal of Marketing*, *66*(1), 15–37. doi:10.1509/jmkg.66.1.15.18449

Smith, B., & Linden, G. (2017). Two decades of recommender systems at Amazon. com. *IEEE Internet Computing*, *21*(3), 12–18. doi:10.1109/MIC.2017.72

Smith, T., Fischer, E., & Yongjian, C. (2012). How Does Brand-related User-generated Content Differ across YouTube, Facebook, and Twitter? *Journal of Interactive Marketing*, *26*(2), 102–113. doi:10.1016/j.intmar.2012.01.002

Solomon, M. R. (2014). *Consumer behavior: Buying, having, and being*. Prentice Hall.

Srinivasan, S. S., Anderson, R., & Ponnavolu, K. (2002). Customer loyalty in e-commerce: An exploration of its antecedents and consequences. *Journal of Retailing*, *78*(1), 41–50. doi:10.1016/S0022-4359(01)00065-3

Srivastava, R. K. (2007). Managing brand performance: Aligning positioning, execution and experience. *Journal of Brand Management*, *14*(1-2), 129–140.

Sweeney, J. C., & Soutar, G. N. (2001). Consumer perceived value: The development of a multiple item scale. *Journal of Retailing*, *77*(2), 203–220. doi:10.1016/S0022-4359(01)00041-0

Tam, K. Y., & Ho, S. Y. (2006). Understanding the impact of web personalization on user information processing and decision outcomes. *Management Information Systems Quarterly*, *30*(4), 865–890. doi:10.2307/25148757

Van Dijck, J. (2013). 'You have one identity': Performing the self on Facebook and LinkedIn. *Media Culture & Society*, *35*(2), 199–215. doi:10.1177/0163443712468605

Venkatesh, V., & Morris, M. G. (2000). Why don't men ever stop to ask for directions? Gender, social influence, and their role in technology acceptance and usage behavior. *Management Information Systems Quarterly*, *24*(1), 115–139. doi:10.2307/3250981

Verhoef, P. C., Kannan, P. K., & Inman, J. J. (2015). From multi-channel retailing to omni-channel retailing: Introduction to the special issue on multi-channel retailing. *Journal of Retailing*, *91*(2), 174–181. doi:10.1016/j.jretai.2015.02.005

Verhoef, P. C., Lemon, K. N., Parasuraman, A., Roggeveen, A., Tsiros, M., & Schlesinger, L. A. (2009). Customer experience creation: Determinants, dynamics and management strategies. *Journal of Retailing*, *85*(1), 31–41. doi:10.1016/j.jretai.2008.11.001

Völckner, F. (2008). The dual role of price: Decomposing consumers' reactions to price. *Journal of the Academy of Marketing Science*, *36*(3), 359–377. doi:10.1007/s11747-007-0076-7

Walsh, G., & Beatty, S. E. (2007). Customer-based corporate reputation of a service firm: Scale development and validation. *Journal of the Academy of Marketing Science*, *35*(1), 127–143. doi:10.1007/s11747-007-0015-7

Xiang, Z., Du, Q., Ma, Y., & Fan, W. (2017). A comparative analysis of major online review platforms: Implications for social media analytics in hospitality and tourism. *Tourism Management*, *58*, 51–65. doi:10.1016/j.tourman.2016.10.001

Zeithaml, V. A. (1988). Consumer perceptions of price, quality, and value: A means-end model and synthesis of evidence. *Journal of Marketing*, *52*(3), 2–22. doi:10.1177/002224298805200302

Zhu, F., & Zhang, X. (2010). Impact of online consumer reviews on sales: The moderating role of product and consumer characteristics. *Journal of Marketing*, *74*(2), 133–148. doi:10.1509/jm.74.2.133

Chapter 12
Place–Based Strategies, Multichannel Merger, and Context–Driven Alerts for Engagement With Mobile Marketing

Anagha Kuriachan
Christ University, India

Reshma Rose Thomas
Christ University, India

R. Sukanya
https://orcid.org/0000-0002-4356-3407
Christ University, India

ABSTRACT

Mobile marketing is essential for timely, personalized communication in the digital world. Engagement is increased by location-based strategies like geofencing and context-driven notifications. Integrating social media improves ties with customers. In the digital age, multi-channel integration guarantees a smooth and personalized experience. As per the authors, this chapter explores how location-based suggestions, context-driven notifications, and multi-channel integration enhance client connections while highlighting the significance of geolocation data for targeted content. For context-driven notifications to be effective, helpfulness and privacy must be balanced. Companies create stronger relationships with their consumers and improve the customer experience, which motivates both present and new customers to engage and connect with their brand. An analysis is conducted on the changing field of mobile marketing, emphasizing the use of location-based tactics, multi-channel integration, and context-driven notifications to increase user engagement.

DOI: 10.4018/979-8-3693-1339-8.ch012

1. INTRODUCTION

Technological advancements have altered the way consumers behave, obtain information, and interact with one another and how businesses must communicate their marketing message to consumers is impacted by this change in behavior. Mobile phones have become increasingly important in consumers' daily lives in recent years, surpassing the internet, which is currently one of the most popular communication platforms. Therefore, the easiest way to get in touch with customers is by using a cell phone. In the current digital era, mobile marketing has become essential for companies to engage with their target customers. It provides customers with personalized location and time-sensitive information. Companies should continue developing and implementing strategies to achieve organizational goals, with marketing strategies being crucial for performance enhancement. Mobile marketing is centered on using mobile devices like smartphones and tablets to connect and engage with target audiences. The relevance of mobile marketing is undeniable. Due to their increasing necessity in today's world, people are using mobile devices more and more. This suggests that businesses must ensure the appropriate execution of mobile marketing strategies in order to reach their target populations.

It is essential in the digital age as mobile devices have become integral parts of people's lives, providing marketers new channels to connect with potential customers. Any firm that wishes to reach its target audience must invest in mobile marketing, a subject that is both complicated and constantly changing. The key aspects of mobile marketing includes mobile devices, mobile apps, mobile websites, SMS marketing, mobile advertising, location-based marketing, social media marketing, mobile SEO, mobile payment and wallet marketing, compliance with privacy regulations etc. Mobile phones provide valuable location data, allowing marketers to deliver targeted ads and offers based on users' current and past locations. Marketers need to be more mindful relating to privacy regulations and user consent to ensure effective mobile marketing. As technology advances, mobile marketing strategies evolve to meet mobile users' changing needs and preferences.

1.1 Engagement With Mobile Marketing

Engagement with mobile marketing is essential for success in the modern digital world. By understanding what drives consumer engagement and implementing those insights, brands can achieve their marketing goals and build enduring relationships with their target audience. When customers are more involved with the brand, they are more likely to make purchases, refer it to others, and stay loyal to the firm. Customer engagement marketing facilitates brand interaction with the intended audience. There are several ways for customers to communicate with businesses including email, social media, community forums, etc, where they can receive more individualized service and answers to their questions. Marketers' involvement not only improves sales and reputation but also fosters long-lasting relationships with customers. Instead of waiting for consumers to interact with material passively when using a computer or watching a TV commercial, businesses can use mobile marketing to design interactive marketing campaigns that reach their customers wherever they are and respond to their behavioral indications.

Methods like push notifications and in-app messaging, allow for direct communication and the dissemination of helpful information and promotions, resulting in a more smooth and engaging user experience. "In-app messaging" is a feature that lets users send and receive messages straight from a mobile or web application while they're using it. Among the many applications for in-app messaging are user-to-user communication, notifications, chat sessions with customer support representatives, and the sharing of news and updates. It is simple to keep consumers engaged, informed, and connected when they are actively using the programme, which enhances the user experience overall. Consumer behavior, the frequency with which they check their messages, and social media usage are some of the key elements that mobile marketers take into account when attempting to assess client engagement (Saurav, 2023). Among the many elements, the important elements of engagement are attracting users' attention in the deluge of mobile material, building strong relationships and trust, obtaining enlightening feedback and data, encouraging conversions and sales, and ensuring user retention and loyalty. Virality, word-of-mouth marketing, personalized marketing, and seamless adaptation to the distinct preferences and behaviors of mobile consumers are all advantages of effective engagement tactics. They also cover customer support and service, which enhances the user experience in general. Engagement metrics, such as website traffic and return on investment, can be used to evaluate a campaign's effectiveness and provide data for future improvement.

2. LOCATION-BASED STRATEGIES, MULTI-CHANNEL INTEGRATION, AND CONTEXT-DRIVEN NOTIFICATIONS

The three essential elements of contemporary marketing are context-driven alerts, multichannel integration, and location-based strategies. These strategies can also be utilized to increase engagement. They let companies communicate with clients in real time and relevantly, irrespective of their preferences, device, or location. Customers and content producers are coming to more and more agreement about them (Ceri et al., 2007). The combination of these several strategies is what makes mobile marketing so effective. Location-based strategies, which are commercial approaches, leverage geographic data and consumer location data to enhance operations, marketing, and customer experiences. These strategies employ mobile apps, beacons, and the Global Positioning System (GPS) to target customers with offers and content relevant to their past and current whereabouts. They enable businesses to maximize their physical presence by tailoring their products and services to certain locations or even specific businesses. Moreover, location-based strategies facilitate geo-targeted advertising and location-specific promotions, helping companies engage with their clientele more quickly and relevantly while also gaining valuable insights into localized consumer behavior and preferences. Context-driven alerts are another tactic which are different from standard notifications that are often issued independently of the user's context. In this age of mobile dominance, businesses are able to interact with clients in a more personalized and targeted manner by utilizing the power of context-driven notifications. As a result, customers will have a better overall experience and help businesses to develop strong brand loyalty. The technique of using numerous mobile channels to contact and engage with consumers is known as multi-channel integration in mobile marketing. Channels including social media, email, mobile apps, and SMS are a part of this and these channels can produce a smooth consumer experience if they are properly linked. It enables companies to connect with more people. By enabling customers to communicate with organizations over many channels, multi-channel integration can help firms increase customer engagement.

2.1 Mobile Marketing Landscape

With the increasing use of cellphones, consumer behavior has changed, which has had a big effect on the mobile marketing sector. Businesses use a variety of strategies, including location-based marketing, social media advertising, mobile-responsive websites, SMS marketing, and mobile apps, to connect with their target audience. Advanced targeting options are provided by social media platforms, and businesses provide clients with a more engaging experience. Businesses should give customers customized messages based on how close they are to their site. Mobile commerce and virtual reality are also popular. Without data and analytics, businesses are unable to track user behavior and make strategic improvements. Businesses will also prosper if they embrace user privacy and data protection, capitalize on emerging technologies, and adapt to changing customer needs.

In addition to serving as a link to other marketing media platforms, mobile has evolved into a marketing engine. Mobile marketing has become an increasingly important component of modern marketing strategies since it allows businesses to communicate with their target audience in a timely and customized way. Nowadays, consumers choose mobile marketing over physical storefronts because it is accessible to everyone, anywhere, at any time. They are able to use their phones while traveling, at home, or even at work. Based on condition, software availability, and location, people have become device agnostic, and they are able to switch between devices with ease. This considerably facilitates their capacity to purchase and explore new products and services. It can reach a global audience and is cost-effective, measurable, personalized, and convenient. This study explores crucial methods for increasing user engagement through mobile marketing, with a focus on location-based tactics, multi-channel integration, and context-driven alerts. These methods include location-based targeting that delivers pertinent content, multiple channel integrations like email and social media, and notifications that are pertinent to the current context.

Mobile marketing is constantly evolving and businesses are now able to personalize their communications to customers based on their location, requirements, and interests. It drives user engagement and improves the customer experience. The field of mobile marketing encompasses a dynamic and multifaceted ecosystem of strategies and platforms that are designed to connect with the intended audience via mobile devices. It centers on using tablets and smartphones to advertise goods, services, and brands. Businesses are able to contact clients directly, offer personalized experiences, and boost engagement through the use of mobile apps. Social media platforms, search engines, and influencer networks all play a big part in how companies tailor their services for mobile customers. Even more of an impact is made on the environment by emerging technologies like augmented reality (AR) and virtual reality (VR), which offer new dimensions for immersive mobile marketing experiences. To successfully engage with their mobile-savvy target consumers in the constantly changing mobile landscape, businesses must, in essence, adapt and innovate.

2.2 Current Trends and Challenges in Mobile Marketing

Mobile marketing is the process of connecting and interacting with potential customers via mobile devices. Mobile marketing has a big impact on every part of the marketing mix (Shankar & Balasubramanian, 2009). M_commerce is one trend that has grown in popularity recently as more and more individuals purchase online using their cellphones. Mobile videos are a significant new trend in mobile marketing. This pattern is being used by marketers, who are creating and disseminating more mobile video content. However, the problem with this is that about 70% of all mobile traffic comes from it. As more individuals use voice assistants and smart speakers for internet research, voice searches are currently an increasingly popular trend. The growth of visual search, which enables users to submit videos and images for information searches, is another trend. Lately, in-store experiences are being improved by the integration of mobile apps. Some retailers allow consumers to make restaurant reservations, scan product barcodes for additional information, and check out using their mobile applications instead of waiting in a queue. Customers are benefiting from a more seamless and convenient purchasing experience because of this development (Chang, 2023).

In addition to letting smartphone users browse their catalog, IKEA Place also lets users see how furniture will fit into its intended setting through an app. In order to accomplish this step, the smartphone app uses Augmented Reality (AR) to display a life-size picture of the object on top of the background that the camera has taken. IKEA Place is currently serving more than 370,000 monthly active users (MoEngage, 2023). As mobile marketing gets increasingly complex, privacy concerns are at the forefront. Customers are becoming more aware of the information that is being gathered about them via their mobile devices and the purposes for which it is utilized. When collecting and utilizing data, marketers need to be open and truthful about it. Giving clients control over their data is another requirement. Potential users will have a difficult time finding the necessary software in the millions of apps that are accessible in app stores. To really get their apps seen by the intended demographic, marketers must employ a range of techniques and approaches. Determining the efficacy of mobile marketing presents additional hurdles for marketers. As a result, companies must introduce a number of initiatives to gauge the success of the advertising. Despite these challenges, mobile marketing remains a useful instrument for businesses to engage with their customers.

3. LOCATION-BASED STRATEGIES

In recent times, location-based strategies have gained popularity as companies search for more specialized and individualized ways to connect with their customers. Consumers anticipate that businesses will comprehend their demands, envision them, and provide pertinent remedies to their issues. Therefore, it is essential to ascertain the preferences of the intended audience and adjust business strategies accordingly. Location-based marketing is an effective marketing strategy that is used by many businesses to reach customers and generate more sales. This kind of marketing is helpful for companies looking to connect with consumers since it targets clients based on location information. It has been proved that location-based marketing is an effective way to access client lifecycles. Furthermore, it helps users make purchases. They are also an effective way to reach the customers in a more personalized and targeted way. Perhaps businesses also strengthen their customer relationship by providing users with contextual experiences and relevant information.

Location-based strategies refer to the use of geographic information and location-specific data to inform and optimize various aspects of business operations, marketing, and decision-making. These strategies have gained significant importance in recent years due to advancements in technology and the growing availability of location-based data. One of the key important areas in which location based strategies are employed and utilized is in marketing. In order to create personalized and contextually appropriate experiences, location-based marketing tactics take advantage of users' actual locations. According to Rinner and Reisslein (2004), location-based services assist users in making decisions as they complete tasks in both space and time. Some strategies, like beacon technologies, go a step further by using Bluetooth beacons to send users push notifications or information based on their current position, thereby boosting interaction in a physical place. When a potential consumer is close by, a retail store employs beacon technologies to send them promotions or special deals. It not only boosts foot traffic in the physical sense but also makes marketing campaigns and messaging more pertinent. Local SEO entails optimizing online content to ensure businesses' exposure in local search results when consumers hunt for goods or services locally. Businesses are able to communicate and engage with individuals in particular geographic locations through the use of social media platforms that have location-based capabilities, which promotes community participation. These tactics foster a deeper and more meaningful relationship between businesses and their target market in addition to increasing the effectiveness of marketing initiatives.

3.1 Location-Based Marketing

Delivering appropriate material or services to a user based on their mobile device's location is known as location-based marketing, or LBM. It can be used to reach consumers with targeted ads, promotions, or information based on their physical location. In addition, it's an effective marketing tool that accomplishes a range of objectives, including increasing sales, enhancing customer loyalty, expanding brand awareness, and enhancing client understanding. Location based marketing is used to reach new customers and introduce them to a brand. In the case of retail stores it is used to encourage customers to visit a store or event that is nearby, where a clothing store sends push notifications to customers who have recently visited its website, offering them a discount on their next purchase if they visit a nearby store within the next week. This marketing also promotes special offers or discounts to customers who are near a store. For example, customers who are within a few blocks of the shop should receive a push notification, offering them a free coffee if they purchase a breakfast sandwich. LBM is used to provide customers with relevant information or offers based on their location and it is used to collect data about customer behavior, such as which stores they visit, what products they buy, and how often they make purchases. The development of new products and marketing strategies are benefitted from this data.

Location based marketing is a rapidly growing industry, and companies of all kinds are beginning to utilize its power. It is used in a number of different ways in which Geofencing allows marketers to create virtual boundaries around specific locations. When a user with a location-enabled mobile device enters or leaves a geofenced area, they receive a push notification or other message from the marketer. Next is the location targeting which allows marketers to exploit users' present locations to focus their adverts or past location history. Another one is the beacons which are the small devices that transmit signals, which are picked up by smartphones and tablets. Depending on the users' proximity to a beacon, beacons are utilized to give them targeted messages. Looking at location-based marketing statistics, it is obvious why location technology should be used in marketing, since according to eMarketer, over 94% of US millennials will own smartphones by 2022 (Marketing, 2023). LBM is a versatile and powerful marketing tool that is used to send customers targeted messages at the perfect time and place. It assists companies in achieving their marketing objectives and enhancing consumer happiness when applied successfully.

3.2 Benefits and Challenges

Location-based marketing is a valuable tool for improving customer retention. It helps companies to take one step closer towards generating more income and providing brand awareness at a less cost. So companies should effectively serve the customers and need to adhere to the standards and code of conduct of business since customers are voluntarily providing permission to disclose their location with other parties in order to serve them better. To ensure the success of businesses' efforts in location based marketing it is important to consider the benefits and challenges of them. LBM has become one of the dominating channels in the field of digital marketing. It is an efficient method of attracting clients because the majority of people own mobile devices and carry them everywhere (Location-based Marketing - Benefits & Effectiveness | Optimove, 2023). The ability to deliver customers relevant and personalized material depending on their location has many advantages for a company's brand.

LBM offers a number of benefits to both businesses and consumers. For businesses, it helps to increase brand awareness by helping businesses to reach potential customers who are already in their area. This is possible through geofencing, which allows businesses to send notifications to customers when they enter a specific geographic area. It is also used to help businesses to increase sales by delivering relevant and timely offers to customers and increasing foot traffic. It is nevertheless possible to use location-based marketing to target ideal customers in areas with minimal usual foot activity or in-person trade. Additionally, location-based marketing raises activity on this level by boosting online traffic and sales. As the digital presence expands, it will attract more internet traffic. It helps the consumers in different ways such as saving time and money, discovering new businesses and receiving personalized offers. LBM helps consumers to find the products and services they need at the best possible price. First, they assist customers in finding the goods and services they require more quickly and conveniently by providing them with appropriate adverts and offers. This saves customers time and helps them make better purchasing decisions by eliminating irrelevant advertisements. It is also used to help consumers find the nearest location of a business or service that they are looking for. This saves consumers time and money on travel costs. Secondly, LBM gives personalized offers to customers based on their preferences and geographical history. For instance, a nearby client receives a push notice from a coffee shop offering them a discount on their subsequent purchase. By assisting customers in locating the greatest offers on the goods and services they require, this helps consumers save money.

Location based marketing also helps consumers to discover new businesses in their area and receive personalized offers. It assists customers in locating establishments that are close by. Finding new eateries, stores, and other companies that are not well-known or that customers may not have otherwise considered is helpful in this situation. A customer might, for instance, notice a push notification for a new coffee shop that is only a few blocks away while they are walking down the street. Second, based on their interests, LBM assists customers in finding new businesses (Aliahmadi et al., 2023). For instance, a shopper interested in fashion uses a shopping app to discover brand-new businesses nearby. Another option is for a customer looking for new eateries that deliver near them to utilize a food delivery app. Location-based marketing has a big positive impact on business revenue. This marketing tactic is used to lower sales obstacles. Once they are inside your store, it is simple to persuade them to make a purchase, which is essential for boosting sales (Brisk, 2022).

LBM is further used to deliver personalized offers to consumers based on their interests and purchase history. It first assists companies in determining based on the requirements and interests of their clients where those customers are located. For instance, a company is able to examine the purchasing patterns of its clients in various areas to determine which goods and services are most in demand there. Based on the consumers' past location data, this information is then utilized to produce personalized offers for them. Later they assist companies in making personalized offers to clients at the appropriate moment and location. For instance, a company utilizes geofencing to notify a consumer via push notification when they are close enough to a store to receive a discount on their subsequent purchase or, a company sends a customized email to a customer using location information. A successful method for helping businesses reach their target customers and achieving their marketing objectives is location-based marketing. However, there are a number of difficulties with LBM, including privacy concerns, technical challenges, relevance, attribution, accuracy etc. Customers are becoming more and more concerned about their privacy, thus they are reluctant to provide access to their location data. In light of recent controversies concerning the abuse of personal data by organizations like Facebook and Cambridge Analytica, this is particularly true. Businesses must be open and honest with customers about how they use location data and provide them the choice to stop being tracked. Particularly when it comes to location data gathered from mobile devices, it becomes unreliable. Weather conditions, the type of device being used, and the number of satellites in view have an impact on GPS accuracy. Before employing location data for marketing, companies must use trustworthy data sources and confirm its accuracy.

LBM also faces a variety of technical difficulties, such as geofencing and beacon technology. Businesses should use geofencing to offer customers targeted messages when they enter or depart a particular area. Consumers receive notifications via Bluetooth when they are close to a specific device, such as a beacon in a store. Businesses must possess the expertise to use these technologies efficiently because their implementations are difficult and expensive. Businesses need to make sure that the LBM campaigns they are running are relevant to their target audience. Sending irrelevant offers to consumers is annoying and damages the brand's reputation. It will be challenging to assess the success of LBM efforts as it's hard to determine whether a customer was influenced by a LBM campaign to make a purchase or whether they would have made the purchase anyway. Businesses need to use a variety of methods to track the results ("Location-Based Mobile Marketing: Benefits & Challenges," 2022).

3.3 Case Studies of Successful Location-Based Campaigns

The paper "Toward the regulation of ubiquitous mobile government: a case study on location-based emergency services in Australia" explores the major issues faced by government, business, and society at large in the deployment of a fully fledged location-based emergency warning system for personal mobile devices in Australia. The paper presents a qualitative study that gathers data from the general public and key informants through open-ended survey questions and interviews. The study comes to the conclusion that regulation is ultimately the result of the intricate interactions between governmental organizations, telecommunications companies, and the Australian people. The paper provides a series of recommendations toward the successful deployment of mobile government applications, which should be applied by other nations considering similar initiatives. These recommendations include creating a thorough and well-defined regulatory framework for mobile government applications, forming a public-private collaboration, public education and awareness initiatives, and giving government entities technical and financial assistance in order to create and implement mobile government applications. By implementing these suggestions, governments foster the creation and implementation of mobile government applications, which have the potential to enhance citizens' lives (Aloudat & Michael, 2010).

The paper "Micro mobility marketing: Two cases on location-based supermarket shopping trolleys" explores the field of micro-mobility and explains how location-based shopping trolleys are used to promote different products. Micro-mobility marketing is a type of advertising that targets a specific area and uses mobile technology to advertise products or services. The paper presents two cases where location-based shopping trolleys were used to promote a new line of organic products and a new credit card. The ads were displayed to shoppers as they walked through the store, and the promotions were effective at boosting sales and sign-ups. Location-based supermarket shopping trolleys are just one example of how micro-mobility marketing is used to promote goods and services. Businesses should utilize micro-mobility marketing to connect with customers who are already considering their goods or services (Hosbond & Skov, 2007).

3.4 Tools and Technologies for Location-Based Marketing

Location-based techniques enable location-specific promotions and geo-targeted advertising, assisting businesses in connecting with their customers in a more timely and relevant way while also learning important details about consumer behavior and preferences related to particular regions. Geotargeting remedies are essential because they enable companies to send local customers specialized content or commercials. These technologies determine users' particular geographic locations using GPS technology, allowing for accurate targeting. With the help of the geofencing approach, businesses send customers appropriate notifications or promotions as they enter or leave certain geographic areas. Mobile apps with location-based capabilities enable businesses to interact with clients based on their current location, contributing to personalized user experiences. With the addition of an interactive component, augmented reality (AR) creates immersive experiences that are connected to actual places. Businesses connect with their audience in particular geographic areas via social media platforms with location-based features, which promotes community participation. Google My Business, enables businesses to control their profile on Google and offers accurate information for local searches. Google Maps and local business insights are examples of local SEO tools. Businesses should make sure their internet presence is effectively optimized for local search by working with Moz Local, which helps them manage and maintain consistent company listings across a variety of internet platforms, to increase visibility when customers search for products or services in their area (What Is Local SEO, and How Does It Work? | Mailchimp, n.d.).

4. MULTI CHANNEL INTEGRATION

Multi-channel integration is critical in today's world, because customers want a seamless, personalized experience from businesses regardless of the channel via which they choose to interact. Multi-channel integration is the process of merging numerous customer-facing systems and channels. This is applicable to call centers, websites, mobile applications, social media, and physical retail, among other online and offline venues. Because it allows businesses to reach customers on the channels they prefer. This helps to enhance the user experience and foster closer ties with their clients. By using multiple channels, companies are able to reach their customers where they are and make it easier for them to engage with them. It also provides a more personalized experience. When they interact with customers on multiple channels, they are able to collect more data about them and use that data to personalize the interactions. The creation of a seamless customer experience across all channels is the aim of multichannel integration. This implies that users shouldn't have to start over or repeat their information in order to complete a transaction that they started on one channel and finished on another. For instance, a consumer ought to be able to use a mobile app to check out after adding products to their cart on a website.

Multi-channel integration is very beneficial for businesses of all sizes. By integrating their channels, businesses are able to increase the sales, improve the customer experience and reduce the cost. Clients can communicate with companies in a way that suits them best and trust that the same information will be provided through all channels. By facilitating customers' purchases of goods and services, multi-channel integration assists firms in growing their sales. Multi-channel integration is implemented in a variety of ways. Using a Multi-Channel Integration Platform (MIP) is one popular strategy. MIPs offer a central hub for tying several channels and systems together. Data management and integration across all channels are facilitated by this. Another approach to implement multi-channel integration is by developing custom integrations between different systems and channels. This approach is more complex and expensive than using a MIP, but it will be necessary for businesses with complex needs.

Multi-channel integration is also used in various industries such as retail, education, healthcare etc. Multi-channel integration is used by retail companies to link its social media accounts, website, mobile app, and physical stores. Customers are able to buy, return, and exchange merchandise through all available channels (Verhoef et al., 2015). A bank could use multi-channel integration to connect its online banking platform, mobile app, and ATM network. This allows customers to access their accounts and perform transactions from any channel. A healthcare provider could link its patient portal, website, and Electronic Health Record (EHR) system together through multi-channel integration. Patients will be able to use any channel to make appointments, pay expenses, and view their medical records. Businesses of all sizes are able to use multi-channel integration as a valuable tool to streamline processes and enhance customer satisfaction (Hersh, 2009).

4.1 Significance of Multi-Channel Marketing

The process of reaching and interacting with customers through a variety of channels is known as multi-channel marketing. Both online and offline media platforms, including email, social media, search engine optimisation (SEO), pay-per-click (PPC) advertising, print advertising, and direct mail, are used for this. Smooth integration of multiple channels is necessary in order to deliver a comprehensive and consistent user experience and boost brand recall and engagement. These enable the investigation of the distribution of pertinent offers and material to users based on their location. This helps the company stay in the minds of both current and potential customers, encouraging interaction. By reaching a wider audience, building strong relations with customers and improving customer service, one can build a strong brand image that helps to grow revenue through bringing in new customers, keeping hold of existing ones, and both. Multi-channel marketing is significant because it allows businesses in various ways such as reaching a wider audience, sales boosting, increase in brand awareness, improving customer loyalty and satisfaction etc.

By using many channels, businesses are able to reach a wider range of potential customers, including those who are not active on a single channel. Then, it helps to increase brand awareness by exposing customers to the brand across different channels. When customers see a brand on multiple channels, they are more likely to remember it and trust it. By giving consumers additional options to research and buy goods and services, multi-channel marketing can boost sales. Multi-channel buyers spend more money than single-channel shoppers, according to a McKinsey study (Lindecrantz et al., 2020). It also allows businesses to deliver more personalized and relevant messages to customers by tracking their activity across different channels. For example, a business could send an email to a customer who has recently visited their website about a product they looked at. Furthermore, by giving consumers a more uniform and smooth experience across all channels, it can increase customer satisfaction and loyalty. Customers are more likely to be happy and devoted when they are able to engage with a business across their preferred channels and receive the same superior experience.

4.2 Strategies for Integrating Mobile Marketing With Other Channels

To integrate mobile marketing with other channels, businesses should use different strategies. First simple strategy should be creating a unified customer experience. This entails making certain that clients receive a consistent experience on all platforms, including mobile. Using consistent branding, messaging, and design across all platforms is one way to do this. Businesses should use cross-channel data and analytics to understand the ways in which consumers engage with their brand's different channels. This information is then used to create more personalized and relevant marketing campaigns. Another strategy is coordinating mobile campaigns with other channels because campaigns for mobile marketing should support and enhance existing marketing initiatives rather than function alone. Businesses should utilize offline media to generate leads for their SMS or push notifications, or use social media to advertise mobile contests or coupons. They also use email to increase traffic to their mobile app. Companies should make it simple for clients to move across channels in accordance with their requirements and preferences.

Businesses integrate mobile marketing with other channels under the following areas. An e-commerce company utilizes email marketing to advertise its mobile app, which it would then utilize to provide users with special deals and promotions. Retailers utilize social media to advertise their smartphone app, which enables users to scan barcodes to view product details and make purchases. A restaurant uses email marketing to send customers a coupon for their mobile app, then uses the mobile app to enable advance food ordering and payment for customers. Businesses should provide customers with a more smooth and interesting experience by integrating mobile marketing with other channels.

4.3 Leveraging Social Media, Email, and Web for Mobile Integration

In today's interconnected digital world, businesses must keep their brand's tone and messaging consistent across all different platforms, including social media, email, and mobile applications. The process of leveraging social media, email, and the web for mobile integration involves connecting with mobile consumers through these channels and ensuring a consistent experience across all platforms. There are several ways to accomplish this. Users follow businesses' social media accounts from within their app, contribute content from their app to social media, and make them log in to their mobile app using their social media accounts. Email correspondence gives users the option to read and manage their emails, receive push notifications when new emails arrive, and join their email list, all from within their mobile app. Integrating social media, email, and the web, create a more engaging and user-friendly experience. It also makes it easier for users to find and connect with a brand, and to learn more about their products and services.

With only one swipe, users of a social media app are able to publish content from the app to their social media feeds after logging in with their Facebook or Twitter accounts. Users of an e-commerce app are able to subscribe to the company's email list from within the app, after which they would get push alerts about any new deals and promotions. Users of a news app are able to access links to articles on the corporate website from within the app, which allow them to read the articles in the app's web view (Albrecht, 2023). Some of the major benefits of leveraging social media, email and the web are improved customer service, increased user engagement and enhanced brand awareness. Customer service is improved by allowing users who subscribe to their email list within their app, to receive push notifications for new emails. Businesses are able to post material from their websites to social media, making it easier for customers to find out more about a company, its goods, and services. The return on investment is increased by identifying the key influencers and providing them with additional incentives to serve as brand ambassadors (Ishwaran, 2017). All things considered, integrating social media, email, and the web with mobile is an ideal way to enhance user experience and expand a business.

4.4 Best Practices of Multi-Channel Integration

Multi-channel integration is a marketing strategy that combines different channels to reinforce the message, keep the brand top of mind, and amplify results. It is a viable practice in various industries, including healthcare, marketing, and education. By following best practices and learning from case studies, organizations are able to successfully implement multi-channel integration and achieve their marketing goals.

4.4.1 Case Study on Amazon

One of the best examples of how to seamlessly and customer-focusedly integrate many channels is Amazon. Its Multi Channel Integration helped them to become one of the biggest online retailers in the world. The company's two main pillars are delivering an exceptional customer experience and front-end and back-end channel integration. These are a few of Amazon's multi-channel integration best practices. a) Data Unification and Amazon Prime: Amazon Prime is a key element of their omnichannel strategy since it unites customer data across devices and channels, enabling responsive and personalized interactions. b) Amazon Echo and Channel Expansion: In order to reach customers where they are, Amazon keeps growing its channels, including its physical stores and online marketplaces. The business uses technology like Amazon Echo as well to improve the clientele's experience. c) Ecommerce Integrations: allow businesses to automate order fulfillment, optimize operations, and increase multi-channel sales by connecting its back-end systems with a variety of sales channels. Offering a better customer experience, consolidating customer data, growing channels, capitalizing on channel dominance, and leveraging eCommerce attachments to optimize fulfillment and streamline operations are the main aspects of Amazon's multi-channel integration strategy.

4.4.2 Case Study on Walmart

Walmart's multi-channel integration strategy has resulted in increased sales and improved customer experience, making it a popular choice for customers. Walmart offers various online and offline shopping options, including order pickup in-store, online returns to store, grocery delivery, and Walmart Pay mobile wallet. These services cater to customers' needs and preferences, making it easier for them to shop and save on shipping costs. Walmart's multi-channel integration strategy differentiates it from competitors and ensures convenience for customers. Walmart is also experimenting with new ways to integrate its online and offline channels, such as testing Walmart Go, which eliminates checkout lines. They are also using supply chain practices with a focus on mass merchandising and internet retailing. Walmart is continually attempting to integrate several channels in order to provide its customers with smooth experiences and increase sales. To achieve a successful multi-channel retailing strategy, the company is focusing on supply chain management, leveraging its foreign operations, and adjusting to changing formats.

5. CONTEXT DRIVEN NOTIFICATIONS

Context-driven notifications in mobile advertising constitute a pivotal evolution inside the way businesses have interaction with their audience, providing a profound shift from time-honored, mass verbal exchange to notably customized, actual-time interactions. In this chapter we focus on context-driven notifications and analyzing their context of advertising. Context-driven notifications are predicated on the precept of handing over timely and relevant messages to mobile users based on their precise context or occasions. Unlike traditional, indiscriminate notifications, context-driven notifications leverage a multitude of records resources, consisting of persons behavior, place, options, and actual-time environmental elements, to arrange the delivery of messages that aligns with the recipient's immediate needs. This technique recognizes that cellular devices are not mere verbal exchange devices but powerful extensions of people, intimately related to their everyday lives (Geum et al., 2011).

Context-driven notifications in mobile marketing are crucial because they have the ability to deepen customer engagement, improve user experiences, and ultimately drive desired actions, significance, demanding situations, and good practices for powerful implementation inside like increasing app usage, conversions, and brand loyalty. By utilizing contextual data, businesses can move away from a generic approach and deliver content that precisely aligns with a user's current activities, location, and interests. This personalized level of communication not only captures the user's attention but also creates value, reducing the chances of notifications being seen as irrelevant. Despite the clear benefits of such immersive mobile applications, device fragmentation is becoming a bigger problem for software developers. The large diversity of software platforms and hardware features encompassing the mobile ecosystem cannot be handled by the current application development solutions. To implement context-driven notifications, it is essential to have a deep understanding of the various sources of information that contribute to context. These include GPS location, Wi-Fi data, sensor readings, user preferences, and in-app behavior. To accomplish this, organizations need to invest in robust data analytics capabilities that process, interpret, and act upon large volumes of data in real-time. The integration of contextual information should seamlessly blend into mobile advertising platforms, enabling the dynamic coordination of notifications throughout the user's journey. In order to send personalized notifications depending on user context, artificial intelligence (AI) and machine learning are also essential. These technologies enable businesses to predict user behaviors and customize notifications accordingly.

Businesses should adjust their messages and products to the particular interests and behaviors of consumers in a given place by utilizing geolocation data. Users receive alerts or messages in the form of context-driven notifications based on their preferences, actions, or conditions at the time. These notifications give timely and pertinent information by taking into consideration a user's location, activity, or device status, among other contextual aspects. When a user's GPS indicates they are in a new city, for instance, a context-driven notification offers a weather update or it reminds them to finish a task when they approach a particular location. These notifications, which are frequently tailored, seek to improve the user's experience by providing them with the information that is most relevant to them at the time. When integrating context-driven notifications, it's crucial to strike a balance between helpfulness and privacy concerns, though, to make sure they work effectively. Marketing effectively captures attention and delivers value in a fast-paced digital landscape. The majority of newly developed mobile services are created by analyzing users' daily lives. As a result, knowing the context of the user can yield a wealth of information, such as the user's location, time, goal, and social environment, which offer crucial for creating new mobile application services.

5.1 Personalization and Relevance in Mobile Marketing

Personalization and relevance are at the forefront of mobile advertising in the virtual age, shaping the way businesses have interaction with their target audience on the private platform of cellular gadgets (Fritz et al., 2017). In a time when customers are updated with facts and selections, personalization serves as the medium to mass advertising, permitting agencies to craft messages that connect each individual. Relevance, intently intertwined with personalization, extends the concept further by making sure that the content and interactions are not personalized; however it is well timed and valuable to the recipient. It acknowledges that the mere act of personalization is not sufficient, the content material has to align with the user's current context and needs. Fundamentally, relevance serves as the structural foundation that converts personalization from an idle business into a dynamic and significant means of engagement. In order to increase relevance, ad campaigns usually get more targeted and personalized by utilizing context information gathered from user interactions and smartphone sensors (Hardt and Nath 2012). The importance of personalization and relevance in cellular advertising and marketing lies in their potential to beautify consumer studies, foster deeper purchaser relationships, and drive favored moves together with app engagement, conversions, and loyalty.

5.2 Tools and Technologies for Context-Driven Notifications

The landscape of context-driven notifications is constantly changing. Businesses now create individualized and relevant connections with their audience. These tools cover areas such as data analytics, artificial intelligence (AI), mobile app development, and notification orchestration. The foundation of context-driven notifications lies in data analytics platforms. These platforms let companies collect, examine, and get insightful information from a variety of user data sources and it includes information from mobile apps, websites, Internet of Things (IoT) devices, and location data. Advanced analytic tools enable real-time analysis, giving businesses a comprehensive understanding of user behavior, preferences, and context. With these insights at their disposal, businesses customize their notifications to be highly pertinent and timely for users. AI and machine learning technologies act as engines that power dynamic personalization in context-driven information. Machine learning algorithms have the ability to predict user behavior and preferences based on historical data, read natural language processing algorithms and it enables chatbots and virtual assistants to provide real-time and contextual answers to user questions. These AI-powered capabilities not only improve the user experience and development but contribute to the overall importance of the information. Frameworks and platforms for mobile app development are necessary for creating the mobile applications that give context-driven notifications.

By enabling the concurrent development of apps for many platforms, cross-platform development frameworks like React Native and Flutter help businesses expand their reach and ensure that a wider audience can take use of context-driven notifications. Context-driven notification shipping depends on notification management systems. These systems give businesses the ability to define notification rules and triggers depending on context, such as location, time, and customer behavior. By using these structures, businesses can guarantee that notifications are not only personalized but also delivered to customers on time. Push notification systems, such as Apple Push Notification Service (APNs) and Firebase Cloud Messaging (FCM), enable the smooth delivery of alerts to mobile devices, ensuring that users receive them in real-time. Within the context-pushed notification landscape, geofencing and region-based technologies are crucial tools, particularly for organizations looking to communicate with customers based on their physical proximity. Geofencing technologies enable the creation of virtual boundaries around actual locations, resulting in notifications whenever users enter or leave these boundaries. Geofencing and the delivery of hyper-localized notifications are made possible by the precise and real-time place records provided by technologies like beacon production and the Global Positioning System (GPS). The biggest beneficiaries of this feature are physical stores that want to drive foot traffic to their locations. Platforms for marketing automation offer greater capabilities for coordinating context-driven notifications across several channels. These solutions enable businesses to schedule tailored messages, automate person journeys, and capture customer interactions through music. Real-time location information provided by Location Based Strategic technologies like GPS, Wi-Fi, bluetooth, and beacon technology serves as the basis for area-based notifications. These services let businesses send customers communications that are contextually relevant to their location, such as promotions while they are close to a store (Durach et al., 2012).

5.2.1 Case Study on Starbucks

The international chain of coffee shops Starbucks makes excellent use of location-based notifications. Starbucks has implemented several effective context-driven notification campaigns. Here are some examples. a)Starbucks' Location-Based Offers: Based on location-based products, Starbucks generates personalized and location-specific notifications for its customers. The company uses beacon or GPS technology to find out where a customer is as they enter or approach a location. Starbucks is able to instantly alert customers to timely deals and menu items on their mobile device. For instance, customers are able to receive a discount on their chosen drink or a complimentary croissant if they visit a Starbucks shop within a specific amount of time. This encourages customers to make a purchase while also enhancing their in-store experience. b) Mobile app program: Customers who sign up for the Starbucks Rewards programme are eligible for exclusive offers and discounts, free products, and free in-store refills. Consumers can simply find a retail outlet and make an advance payment. To generate personalized discount offers later on, the app collects data on the preferences and purchasing habits of each user. The software also highlights the music that is playing in the store when a customer picks up a mobile order. c) Hashtags: Starbucks turns its patrons into content producers for the brand by utilizing hashtags to capture people' interest. For instance, "The HowWeMeet'' campaign invited users to share their tales of meeting their soulmates at Starbucks.

5.2.2 Case Study on Uber

Uber is a digital startup that uses its app to match drivers and passengers. Since its founding in 2009, the business has grown to offer freight transportation, package delivery, and meal delivery. Uber has improved the user experience by implementing efficient context-driven notification campaigns. Uber Ride Alerts (a): Uber is a ridesharing startup that provides customers with context-driven ride alerts based on their location and time of day. Uber will send an alert to a client who frequently requests trips to work in the morning, reminding them of the trip and the expected pick-up time. This proactive approach guarantees that customers' transit reservations are perfect and helps them stay on schedule. b) Push Notifications: UberEats notifies users about new restaurants, deals, and services using push notifications. Uber developed a system known as the Consumer Communication Gateway (CCG), which controls the frequency, timing, ranking, and quality of push notifications at the user level, in order to best arrange the timing of these alerts. Uber also employs linear programming and machine learning techniques to figure out when to deliver each user push messages. Uber's ability to execute these campaigns successfully is a result of its timely, relevant, and individualized notification strategy, which improves customer experience.

6. INCREASING ENGAGEMENT THROUGH INTEGRATION

Social media integration is another topic covered in this chapter as a means by which customers are able to quickly share their experiences. According to the survey, two strategies that will boost user engagement with mobile marketing include incorporating interactive content and providing avenues for user comments and reviews. This chapter also mentions social media integration as a way for consumers to easily share their experiences. Incorporating interactive content and creating opportunities for user comments and reviews are two methods highlighted by the study as that will lead to greater engagement in mobile marketing. To give clients a uniform and consistent experience, multi-channel integration is a business approach that entails seamlessly integrating numerous sales and communication channels. Social media is a great way to connect with customers on a personal level. Through many touchpoints, including physical stores, websites, mobile applications, social media, and customer support, this strategy enables customers to engage with a business while upholding a consistent brand image and messaging across all channels, highlighting the significance of personalisation as a vital component in mobile marketing that drives consumer engagement and conversion rates. Customer engagement is greatly increased through personalized messaging and experiences that cater to individual tastes. Moreover, smooth user interfaces and interactive elements promoted higher levels of interaction and better conversion rates (Daoud et al.2023). This promotes community and assists in establishing relationships with clients. Companies accelerate processes, share data and insights, and provide better customer service by integrating various channels, which helps to increase sales and improves customer satisfaction. These insights help them expand their customer base and improve their social media strategies.

6.1 Alliance of Location-Based, Multi-Channel, and Context-Driven Approaches

In the mobile-driven era, integrating location-based strategies, multi-channel integration, and context-driven alerts offers businesses a comprehensive framework for connecting with customers on a deeper level and developing brand loyalty. Marketing and consumer interaction tactics have undergone a substantial change as a result of the combination of location-based, multichannel, and context-driven approaches. The first pillar, location-based marketing, makes use of a customer's actual location as a source of data and a driver for customized engagement. By using this strategy, companies may provide customers hyper-localized information, promotions, and experiences that are targeted to their exact location. For instance, geofencing enables companies to create virtual boundaries around physical locations, then used to send customers personalized messages or promotions as they enter or leave these areas. As a result, clients receive information that is more relevant to their wants and environment. A multi-channel marketing approach entails using a variety of platforms and channels to connect with customers about businesses.

By facilitating a smooth transition between touchpoints including physical storefronts, internet, mobile apps, social media, and email, it guarantees consistency and ease for businesses. When carried out flawlessly, a well-executed multi-channel strategy delivers a smooth journey for customers, fostering engagement, building brand loyalty, and increasing conversions. The goal of context-driven marketing is to deliver products and services that are appropriate for each unique consumer engagement. This strategy takes into account variables including the time of day, consumer behavior, preferences, and mood. Advanced analytics and artificial intelligence are used by companies that excel at context-driven marketing to predict client demands and provide pertinent information. Businesses increase consumer happiness and encourage desirable activities, like making purchases or strengthening brand loyalty, by comprehending and adjusting to the context of each interaction. The alliance between location-based data and multi-channel techniques allows firms to combine localized promotions and information across several touchpoints, hence enhancing customer engagement. The harmony and high effectiveness of this strategy's customer engagement model fills the vacuum left by less effective conventional marketing strategies. To effectively capitalize on the alliance of location-based data sources and context-driven marketing, organizations must make investments in strong data analytics capabilities and technological infrastructure. Context-driven marketing depends on the integration of location-based data sources into the marketing stack, multi-channel platforms, cutting-edge algorithms, and machine learning models.

A customer-centric approach is important, as it is prioritizing data privacy and security. Successful implementation depends on knowing people's preferences and making sure that data collection and use are transparent. Staying competitive and responsive to changing consumer expectations requires regular monitoring and strategy adaptation based on customer feedback and market trends. The synergy of these strategies is a fundamental force in modern marketing, allowing companies to build stronger relationships with their clients and provide highly relevant experiences. Gaining control of this synergy can improve client satisfaction, stimulate revenue development, and provide businesses a competitive edge in a changing market.

6.2 Strategies for Enhancing User Engagement

This chapter focuses on the strategies, tactics, and factors that enable companies and marketers to excel at user engagement, emphasizing the significance of grabbing and holding users' attention in the fast-paced digital environment of today and the multifaceted nature of digital marketing. Understanding the user journey, which encompasses a sales funnel from awareness to action, is essential for effective user engagement. Adapting information and interactions to users' changing needs and expectations, effective engagement techniques address each stage. The core of engagement strategies is the use of user's personal data, which enable marketers to match messaging, content, and user experiences to users' preferences and behaviors. This user-centric strategy makes sure that engagement activities are noticed by the appropriate audience at the appropriate time. Content is crucial for user engagement, as it informs, entertains, and resonates emotionally with users. It should align with their journey, offering solutions and addressing their desires. Storytelling is also powerful in user engagement, capturing attention, evoking emotions, and making content memorable. Mastering storytelling can forge lasting connections with users, extending beyond transactional interactions and fostering deeper engagement. Businesses must utilize the potential of multi-channel marketing to maximize user engagement. Users are found on a wide range of digital platforms, including social media, email, search engines, and mobile apps (Hapsari et al., 2020).

A comprehensive strategy that incorporates numerous channels enables consistent messaging and enhances the brand's perception and message among users. This omnichannel strategy calls for flawless collaboration as well as knowledge of the specific traits and requirements of each platform. In the digital age, data-driven decision-making is crucial for businesses to understand user behavior and preferences. By analyzing user data, businesses can tailor their engagement strategies with precision. Machine learning and AI can predict user behaviors and recommend content and products. Segmentation is a fundamental strategy for enhancing user engagement, dividing the user base into distinct segments based on demographics, behaviors, or other criteria. This allows for highly targeted and personalized messaging, increasing conversion rates and loyalty. Further mobile optimization is essential for user engagement, with responsive design, mobile-friendly content, and user-friendly apps providing seamless experiences for on-the-go users. Using social media sites like Facebook, Instagram, Twitter, and LinkedIn, businesses can interact with customers in new and creative ways. These platforms provide influencer collaborations, paid advertising, community building, and content sharing.

Social listening tools allow businesses to monitor conversations, gather feedback, and respond to user sentiments in real-time. Influencer marketing is a powerful strategy for user engagement, as it extends a brand's reach and credibility. Email marketing, when executed strategically, remains a robust tool for user engagement. Personalized campaigns, triggers emails based on user behavior, and segmentation ensure relevance and timely delivery. Automation tools help nurture leads, onboard new customers, and re-engage lapsed users. Live streaming and real-time engagement on platforms like Twitch, YouTube Live, and Facebook allow businesses to connect with users in real-time, answer questions, conduct product demos, and foster a sense of community. Community building is a long-term strategy that fosters connections and sharing experiences among users through online forums, social media groups, and dedicated communities. User-generated content (UGC) uses authenticity to build trust and showcase real-world experiences, validating a brand's value and fostering a sense of belonging (Daoud et al., 2023). Personalization technologies are transforming user engagement by tailoring experiences to individual preferences, with dynamic content, product recommendations, and personalized messaging resonating more deeply with users. Machine learning algorithms refine personalization efforts to ensure relevance and timeliness. User engagement optimization requires experimentation since they help companies learn what appeals to their audience the most and inform iterative adjustments, enabling continual improvement of engagement methods. User feedback and sentiment analysis are crucial for refining user engagement strategies. They provide insights into user satisfaction allowing businesses to adjust their strategies and address concerns promptly. Enhanced user engagement strategies cover all user interactions, from initial touchpoints to post-purchase engagement. Prioritizing engagement tailored to user context and needs helps to capture attention, foster loyalty, and drive digital growth. This comprehensive exploration offers actionable insights, best practices, and innovative approaches for organizations.

6.3 Measuring Engagement and ROI

Digital marketing measurement of engagement and return on investment (ROI) is a multidimensional task that necessitates a thorough understanding of data analytics, customer behavior, and the complex interplay between multiple marketing channels and techniques. The ability to accurately assess engagement and ROI in today's data-driven environment, where every click, view, and interaction is able to be tracked, which is not only a competitive advantage but also a crucial part of a successful marketing plan. User involvement with a brand's content, goods, or services is measured by engagement. It comprises a variety of metrics, including click-through rates, conversion rates, likes, shares, and comments, along with website visits and page views. These measurements show how consumers react to marketing tactics and offer suggestions for enhancements. Precise targets must be specified, sometimes in the form of key performance indicators (KPIs), in order to measure engagement and ROI and evaluate the efficacy of marketing initiatives. These goals help to increase leads, increase social media followers, increase website traffic, and increase sales. An essential instrument for monitoring these goals is web analytics, like Google Analytics. These tools offer insights into user behavior on websites and other digital platforms.

Measuring demographics, traffic sources, time spent on sites, bounce rates, and conversion funnels helps marketers better understand user behavior and conversion rates. As it connects user interaction to revenue creation, conversion tracking is an essential tool for calculating ROI. It enables firms to calculate ROI by allowing them to link specific actions to their marketing initiatives (Lal et al., 2019). By using an advanced technique called attribution modeling, firms are able to better understand how various consumer touchpoints affect conversion rates and return on investment. As people interact with several marketing channels before deciding, this aids in more efficient resource allocation. Both approaches are necessary for comprehending and improving customer involvement. An insight into user involvement on websites like Facebook, Twitter, Instagram, and LinkedIn is offered by social media analytics. Social media analytics also provide information on the audience's interests and demographics, enabling the creation of more focused and pertinent content. Email marketing platforms provide detailed reporting and analytics, allowing marketers to track open rates, click-through rates, conversion rates, and unsubscribe rates. A/B testing allows experimentation with email elements to optimize engagement and ROI. Pay-per-click advertising platforms like Google Ads and Facebook Ads offer detailed metrics on ad performance, allowing for fine-tuning of ROI calculations considering advertising costs and revenue generated from ad-driven conversions. Content marketing efforts are assessed through content analytics, providing insights into user consumption and interaction, guiding content optimization and strategy refinement. Video analytics are crucial in today's digital environment given the rising popularity of video content.

Marketing professionals should better target their content to their audience's tastes by using platforms like YouTube, which offer data on views, watch time, audience demographics, and engagement metrics. These platforms keep track of customer and lead engagements, enabling targeted communication. By transforming raw data into aesthetically pleasing dashboards and reports, data visualization technologies like Tableau and Power BI enable marketers to spot trends and gain insights. Customer surveys and feedback are being used more frequently by businesses to measure engagement and return on investment. This qualitative data is further paired with quantitative data to provide a complete picture and offer insightful information on customer satisfaction and experience. Artificial intelligence is utilized to improve measurement efforts by analyzing massive datasets, finding trends, and even forecasting user behavior. Based on historical data, predictive analytics models predict future engagement and ROI, enabling proactive decision-making. Due to the fact that customers interact across numerous touchpoints, multi-channel marketing necessitates a holistic viewpoint. Multi-channel attribution modeling enables improved resource allocation by assisting firms in understanding how various channels affect conversions and ROI (Hoffman & Fodor, 2010).

In the digital age, real-time analytics are essential since it allows marketers to track the success of their campaigns and make quick changes. Alerts indicate trends or irregularities that require rapid attention. Marketers must comply with these rules when gathering and using customer data because doing so not only upholds the law but also fosters user trust. Digital marketing engagement and ROI measurement is a challenging endeavor that calls for a variety of tools, strategies, and knowledge. By defining clear objectives, using web analytics, conversion tracking, attribution modeling, and leveraging social media analytics, email marketing metrics, and content analytics, organizations obtains a thorough understanding of their marketing effectiveness. Data visualization, customer feedback, machine learning, and multi-channel attribution modeling further enhances measurement efforts. Real-time analytics, compliance with data privacy regulations, and a customer-centric approach are essential tools for effective measurement (Kumar et al., 2013).

6.4 Challenges and Pitfalls to Avoid

Some of the common pitfalls and challenges to avoid are privacy Issues, device and platform fragmentation, ignoring analytics and feedback. Finding a way to combine personalisation with user privacy is a difficult task. Consumers' concerns about the handling and collection of their data are growing. To keep consumers trust and avoid privacy-related problems, businesses need to be open and honest about their data practices, have user consent, and follow strict data protection laws like the CCPA which is California Consumer Privacy Act and GDPR which is General Data Protection Regulation. Over- Sending an overwhelming amount of emails, SMS messages, or notifications to users causes them to become weary and eventually opt out. To prevent overstimulation and user disengagement, it's imperative to determine the ideal message frequency and timing. Maintaining a consistent user experience is challenging due to the wide range of mobile devices, operating systems, and screen sizes availability. Companies need to spend money on comprehensive testing and responsive design in order to avoid problems with inconsistent performance and disgruntled users. Data security and cybersecurity is always a concern to secure user data and guard against data breaches. Users and the company need to suffer greatly as a result of a security breach. To prevent data security problems, it is imperative to implement strong cybersecurity measures and be informed about the current threats.

Ad-blocking software is becoming more and more common, which keeps companies from advertising to their target market on mobile devices. Companies must concentrate on delivering pertinent and discreet advertisements that users are less likely to block in order to lessen this difficulty (Donohue et al., 2009). Ineffective personalization of messages and content results in lower conversion rates and alienation from users. The efficacy of mobile tactics will be weakened by generic and irrelevant marketing that is produced when user data and preferences are ignored. Users become irritated and leave websites and applications that take too long to load. To keep users from giving up, businesses need to make their mobile experiences as fast as possible. If a firm ignores mobile Search Engine Optimization (SEO), it will have a low visibility ranking in mobile search results, which makes it more difficult for potential customers to find it. In order to not lose out on mobile visitors, mobile SEO must be prioritized. New technologies like voice-activated interfaces, virtual reality (VR), and augmented reality (AR) are causing a constant change in the mobile landscape. Companies who do not experiment and adapt to these technologies face the risk of becoming obsolete and missing opportunities for innovative ideas.

Businesses will be unable to determine the success of their mobile marketing campaigns if they fail to evaluate user data and get feedback. Utilizing analytics and user feedback is essential for improving strategy and preventing stagnation. Mobile marketing has a lot of promise for businesses, but it also has a lot of drawbacks and obstacles that impede progress and harm a company's reputation. Prioritizing privacy, avoiding excessive messages, addressing device fragmentation, maintaining data security, fighting ad blockers, emphasizing personalization and user experience are all necessary for organizations to effectively handle these problems. To avoid the dangers that affect the success of mobile marketing, it is crucial to remain flexible, adjust to new technology, and constantly review and enhance tactics.

7. BEST PRACTICES AND CASE STUDIES

In today's business world, organizations must implement strategies considering location, multiple channels and context. To thrive in this landscape, businesses must adopt an approach that combines these three vital elements seamlessly. To begin with, a location-based strategy involves utilizing data to customize marketing and operational efforts. By understanding the context of their customers, businesses can provide relevant and personalized experiences. Depending on the customer's vicinity, this could entail streamlining supply chain operations or introducing geofencing techniques. It could also involve offering promotions based on location. Also, it is essential to consider the ways consumers engage with brands, whether it is through a store, website, mobile app, social media platforms, or even voice assistants, customers expect a convenient experience across all channels. To achieve this, creating an omnichannel ecosystem that ensures a seamless and integrated customer journey at every touchpoint is crucial (Venkatesh, 2015).

Additionally, adopting a context-driven approach is critical. This means delivering content and services that match the circumstances of each interaction. It goes beyond location and channel; factors like the time of day, user behavior and preferences should also be considered. Businesses should anticipate client preferences by using analytics and artificial intelligence. Implementing location-based, multi-channel, and context-driven strategies is essential for businesses to enhance customer experiences, drive revenue development and acquire a competitive advantage in the changing industry. Contemporary marketing is a dynamic and highly individualized undertaking that is necessary for implementing location-based, multi-channel, and context-driven tactics. Businesses must follow a set of best practices covering data gathering, technology use, personalization, and ongoing adaptation to cross this landscape successfully. A concise and thorough approach is essential, first and foremost. This requires identifying the precise corporate goals, target market segments, and key performance indicators (KPIs) that will be used to measure the effectiveness of these strategies. It is crucial to align these three unique techniques with more general marketing objectives. For instance, if increasing foot traffic to physical stores is the goal, the location-based strategy should be adapted to use geofencing and targeted real-time offers. Businesses need robust records analytics tools capable of processing and decoding statistics from numerous assets, including GPS, WiFi, cell apps, and social media. Data privacy and regulatory compliance are critical concerns, necessitating meticulous interest in moral facts series and control practices.

A unified purchaser profile is the pillar of personalization. By consolidating information from various touch points into a novel view, companies are able to deliver extra context-aware and personalized experiences. Records platforms facilitate aggregating and effectively controlling these facts. Technology, especially Artificial intelligence (AI) and devices gaining knowledge, plays a necessary role (Schierholz, 2007). For instance, AI-powered chatbots provide immediate assistance based on consumer context and behavior, contributing to continuing and responsive purchaser enjoyment. Personalization lies at the heart of these techniques. Guidelines and content should be customized explicitly with the customer's location, behavior, and choices taken into account. AI-pushed algorithms ensure that content dynamically adapts in actual time, fostering relevance and engagement. Consistency and coherency in purchaser interactions throughout all channels, whether or not physically or digital, are pivotal. Mobile-friendly websites and apps, coupled with location-primarily based push notifications, allow agencies to interact with users efficiently even if they are in the process. Geofencing and region-primarily based advertising and marketing provide a robust way of personalization.

Customer feedback serves as a guiding light. Requesting and complying consumer entry via surveys, critiques, and social media interactions allows organizations to refine their strategies and continually fulfill customers needs. There are opportunities for innovation in emerging technologies including voice-activated interfaces, blockchain, augmented reality, and virtual reality. Businesses should explore and experiment with integrating those technologies to beautify engagement and live at the forefront of advertising and marketing traits. Finally, investment in schooling and improvement is essential to equip workers with the requisite skills and information for effective strategy execution. Training programs and workshops ensure that employees are proficient in leveraging region-based, multi-channel, and context-pushed tactics to their total capacity. In precise, the implementation of vicinity-primarily based, multi-channel, and context-driven strategies in current advertising and marketing necessitates a meticulous and complete method. By adhering to these satisfactory practices, corporations will be able to create a dynamic and customer-centric marketing ecosystem that leverages facts, era, and personalization to forge deeper connections with customers and drive a sustainable boom in the ever-evolving digital advertising panorama. These strategies are not simply competitive blessings; they constitute the destiny of advertising in an interconnected and personalized world.

7.1 In-Depth Case Studies of Companies With Successful Engagement Campaigns

7.1.1 Case Study of Netflix

Netflix is a global streaming company that has transformed how people consume content by emphasizing data-driven personalization and customization. Utilizing user data, the company's recommendation algorithm makes content recommendations based on personal tastes, increasing engagement and optimizing platform usage. Netflix's original programming demonstrates the potential of high-caliber, unique content by drawing in new viewers and keeping hold of current ones. A favorable customer experience is enhanced by the company's easy-to-use interface, simple categorization, and hassle-free streaming. In order to maintain client engagement, businesses should give priority to making their digital platforms user-friendly. Because Netflix is a subscription service, users are encouraged to explore its growing collection of material and maintain a relationship with the platform.Important Lessons of Give data-driven personalization top priority if you want to improve consumer satisfaction and promote continuous use. Invest in unique, high-quality material to draw in and keep clients.Make sure the interfaces on your digital platforms are easy to use and intuitive.To sustain long-term relationships with clients, take into consideration subscription-based models.The effectiveness of these tactics is demonstrated by Netflix's achievements in customer engagement. Netflix continues to be a leader in the digital streaming space because of its ongoing evolution and adaptation to changing customer tastes and technology improvements. Companies can learn a lot from Netflix's strategy to create longer-lasting and more robust consumer relationships (Arun, 2023).

7.1.2 Case Study of Amazon

Amazon's success as a global e-commerce giant demonstrates the importance of customer-centricity, offering exceptional value through programs like Amazon Prime and personalized recommendations. The company's success also highlights the importance of cultivating customer loyalty, as Amazon

Prime boosts customer retention and drives increased spending on the platform. The power of data and personalization is evident in Amazon's use of advanced algorithms to tailor product recommendations to individual shoppers, highlighting the impact of data-driven insights on engagement. In addition, by integrating offline and online experiences, Amazon is demonstrating the benefits of simplifying customer access to a variety of channels with its acquisition of Whole Foods and other seamless and convenient services. This approach underscores the importance of convenience and accessibility in customer engagement campaigns. Amazon's commitment to exceptional customer service is a testament to the importance of trust and satisfaction in building long-lasting customer relationships. The company's successful engagement campaigns demonstrate the significance of customer-centricity, loyalty programs, data-driven personalization, convenience, and exceptional customer service. These lessons are crucial for businesses to create effective engagement campaigns that foster trust and loyalty, highlighting the enduring importance of these principles in the ever-evolving e-commerce landscape (Goel, n.d.).

7.1.3 Case Study of Airbnb

Airbnb is a cutting-edge home-sharing company that has completely changed the travel and hospitality sectors with its own method of consumer interaction. The company's dedication to provide its customers with unique and unforgettable travel experiences is what drives its success. The focus that Airbnb has on community development is one of the main tactics that accounts for its amazing level of involvement. By encouraging personal connections between hosts and visitors, Airbnb promotes a feeling of community and trust. This community-driven strategy creates a base of devoted and devoted customers while also improving the user experience overall. Moreover, a notable aspect of Airbnb's engagement approach has been its referral program. With the help of referral bonuses, Airbnb has grown at an impressive rate. Referring new users to the platform earns users travel credits, which has caused the Airbnb network to grow virally. Personalized recommendations that are based on a user's past interactions and interests are another area in which Airbnb shines. In addition to improving the user experience, personalization promotes repeat reservations and higher levels of interaction. The reasons behind Airbnb's success in the travel and hospitality sector are its community-driven strategy, continual innovation, personalized suggestions, referral systems, and trust. More engaged and devoted consumers have resulted from establishing connections and encouraging a sense of belonging among users. Since referral programs encourage current users to recommend new clients, they can be an effective strategy for user engagement and growth. By using data and technology to customize recommendations and services to individual tastes, personalization can increase user engagement. The foundations of Airbnb's engagement approach are trust and transparency, and what makes it unique is its capacity for constant innovation and adaptation to shifting consumer demands and market trends. Other companies looking to improve their client interaction tactics can learn a lot from these lessons (Shastri, 2023).

7.1.4 Case Study of Nike

Nike, a renowned sportswear brand, has been a pioneer in product innovation and customer engagement. The company's success is attributed to its ability to connect with its audience on a personal and emotional level. Nike's commitment to promoting a healthy and active lifestyle is a key strategy. The company sponsors various athletes and sports events, inspiring consumers who share their interests. Nike has also embraced technology to drive engagement, using the Nike app and ecosystem to track fitness goals, connect with the brand, and access exclusive content. This integration not only enhances user experience but also fosters brand loyalty and engagement. Nike's marketing campaigns often feature compelling storytelling, fostering a strong emotional connection with customers. The "Just Do It" campaign, for example, has been a source of inspiration for millions and demonstrates the power of storytelling in driving engagement. Nike's success is attributed to its emotional connection with customers, leveraging technology to create unique opportunities for engagement. Authentic storytelling that reflects the brand's values and aligns with customers' aspirations is a powerful tool for fostering engagement. Community building encourages customers to join a broader community that shares their interests and values, driving engagement and brand loyalty. Collaborations with influencers, athletes, or events can also effectively engage a target audience with shared interests. These strategies have not only resulted in a strong customer base but also positioned Nike as a global leader in the sportswear industry. The lessons learned from Nike's success can guide businesses in creating lasting and meaningful customer engagement (Tamang, 2023).

8. FUTURE TRENDS AND EMERGING TECHNOLOGIES

It is essential to keep current with future trends and new technologies in the ever changing world of technology and innovation. This takes readers on a journey through the exciting world of technological growth as we examine the remarkable advancements that are reshaping our planet. Several revolutionary trends and cutting-edge technologies have emerged as a result of humanity's insatiable quest for advancement, and they promise to reshape several sectors, improve daily life, and tackle major global issues. Owing to the swift progress of technology and shifting consumer expectations, the marketing environment is undergoing a substantial transition. As a result of the digital revolution, social networking, e-commerce, and data analytics have changed how businesses interact with their customers (Narang & Shankar, 2019). The Internet of Things, blockchain technology, augmented and virtual reality, automation, machine learning, will all be disruptive breakthroughs in the future. These technologies will support data privacy, sustainability, and ethical behavior while enabling hyper-personalization, predictive analytics, and improved user experiences. Many companies use these new technologies and trends to stay on the cutting edge of marketing innovation. Mobile technologies and wearables offer numerous opportunities for data collection, including fine-grain location data and sensor data unique to the markets industry. According to Scharl et al (2005) the study analyzed Fortune Global 500 websites to understand mobile business models and technology adoption by area and industry. It found regional and sectoral variations in mobile marketing. The study revealed a strong presence among technology providers like telecommunications and electronics companies, as well as interest in implementing mobile services in automotive and financial sectors. The study proposed a conceptual model for successful SMS advertising based on industry experts' surveys.

8.1 Emerging Technologies in Mobile Marketing

Emerging innovations reimagines how organizations communicate with their customers in this digital age continuously transforming the landscape of mobile marketing. In this book chapter, we set out on a journey into the exciting world of mobile marketing to investigate the most significant new technologies that have the potential to completely alter how businesses interact with their customers. First and foremost, mobile marketing is seeing new possibilities because of the advent of 5G connection. 5G networks provide real-time interactions, high-definition video streaming, and augmented reality experiences because of their lightning-fast data rates and minimal latency. This allows marketers to deliver content and services with previously unparalleled richness and immediateness (Liébana-Cabanillas et al., 2020). Mobile marketing now relies heavily on artificial intelligence (AI) and machine learning (ML). Virtual assistants and chatbots powered by AI provide individualized customer care, while ML algorithms analyze massive datasets to forecast user behavior and create marketing campaigns that are relevant and engaging to the greatest extent possible. The way customers engage with goods and services is changing as a result of virtual and augmented reality (VR). With the use of augmented reality (AR), marketers are able to offer virtual try-ons, interactive product demos, and location-based advertising, resulting in immersive experiences that capture customers and increase conversion rates. By tying commonplace items to the digital world, the Internet of Things (IoT) has changed how mobile marketing is done. Marketers are now able to exploit information from smart devices to give hyper-targeted content and services. Examples include tailored product suggestions based on a user's activity tracker data and location-based offers triggered by connected home devices (Bragge et al., 2005).

Transparency and trust in mobile marketing are being improved by blockchain technology. As a result, ad fraud is decreased and consumers are given legitimate offers and incentives. It also enables safe and transparent transactions. Digital IDs built on blockchains also improve data security and user privacy. It is necessary to optimize for speech-driven inquiries and instructions since voice search and voice-activated gadgets are becoming more and more common. To appeal to the expanding user population that relies on voice assistants like Siri, Alexa, and Google Assistant, marketers must modify their approach. This chapter analyzes the uses, advantages, and difficulties of these cutting-edge technologies in mobile marketing, arming marketers and companies with the information and tactics required to keep up in the quickly developing field of mobile marketing (Simakova & Neyland, 2008).

8.2 Future of Mobile Marketing

Mobile marketing has evolved significantly over time, from simple SMS campaigns to sophisticated, data-driven strategies. The advent of smartphones and apps allowed marketers to reach users directly, enabling highly targeted and personalized marketing efforts. Today, mobile marketing encompasses various channels and tactics, including mobile websites, apps, social media advertising, and location-based marketing. The rise of data analytics, artificial intelligence, and machine learning has refined mobile marketing, enabling businesses to reach audiences more effectively and understand their behaviors. The future of mobile marketing is characterized by hyper-personalization, immersive technologies, 5G connectivity, inclusivity, and data privacy. A crucial component of mobile marketing is hyper-personalization, which has completely changed how firms interact with their customers. It entails developing customized customer experiences through the use of cutting-edge technology and data-driven insights. This method makes use of a sizable amount of data from mobile consumers to comprehend their purchasing patterns, preferences, and activities (Leppäniemi et al., 2006). This process is further improved by the incorporation of AI and machine learning algorithms, which enable marketers to recognize trends and forecast consumer behavior. This approach is further improved by predictive analytics, which enables marketers to precisely predict consumer wants and preferences.

By recognizing the unique demands of each customer, hyper-personalization advances user engagement and fosters brand loyalty. Mobile marketing is being revolutionized by Augmented Reality and

Virtual Reality, which provide immersive experiences that go beyond the limitations of conventional advertising. Users can engage with products and environments in ways that were previously unthinkable, which boosts confidence and lowers costs. Through interactive 3D advertisements or location-based AR experiences, AR/VR advertising offers advertisers an engaging canvas on which to engage their target audience. The use of AR and VR in mobile marketing is expected to increase as these technologies become more widely available through smartphones and wearable technology. This will give brands more chances to stand out from the competition and establish long-lasting relationships with customers who long for immersive, dynamic mobile interactions. Mobile marketing is undergoing a change because of 5G technology, which provides faster bandwidth and lower latency while enabling instantaneous connectivity (Pereira et al., 2021). This improves customer engagement and happiness by enabling the delivery of high-quality video content, live streaming, and virtual reality experiences to mobile devices without buffering or lag. The ability to give live polls, interactive games, and immersive AR/VR experiences in real time is a crucial characteristic of real-time interactivity. The quick reactions to user inputs made possible by 5G's reduced latency also improve the overall user experience. Its Internet of Things (IoT) connection creates new opportunities for location-based marketing, individualized suggestions, and data-driven insights. In the mobile marketing landscape, 5G promises to be a game-changer as technology continues to roll out internationally, reshaping how brands communicate with consumers. Mobile marketing is being revolutionized by voice search and smart speakers because they allow hands-free, speech-activated interactions between businesses and customers (Smail & Jia, 2017).

Voice search has become a standard part of daily life as smartphones and smart speakers grow more and more common. As a result, voice-activated campaigns offer a direct path to customers, which presents challenges as well as opportunities for marketers. Marketers must use natural language, optimize for local search, and give succinct, clear responses in order to optimize for voice Search engine optimization (SEO). Utilizing smart speakers like the Google Home and Amazon Echo can increase brand loyalty and engage customers. Mobile marketing is being revolutionized by new technologies, creating new chances for marketers. Blockchain, a decentralized ledger technology, can improve campaign trust and transparency, ensuring effective advertising expenditures and consumer ownership over data (Davenport et al., 2019). Smartwatches and fitness bands are only two examples of wearable technology's new interaction touchpoints. Faster data processing and real-time applications are made possible by edge computing, which processes data closer to the network. With the help of these technologies, brands are able to deliver data-driven campaigns to their target consumers with a competitive advantage.

The majority of the material is video, with short-form videos, live streaming, and compelling narratives being crucial. User participation in brand experiences is encouraged by interactive content like polls and quizzes. Real-time help is offered through chatbots and AI-powered assistants, improving client engagement. User-generated content (UGC) encourages users to contribute their experiences, which increases engagement and trust. These tactics give businesses innovative ways to interact, engage, and cultivate long-lasting connections with consumers in the mobile environment. The future of mobile marketing is expected to be a dynamic and transformative one, driven by rapid technological advancements, changing consumer behavior, and evolving industry trends. Key predictions include personalized experiences, augmented reality and virtual reality, 5G networks, inclusivity, voice search, and regulatory landscape. Personalized experiences will be key, as data analytics and artificial intelligence will enable marketers to craft highly individualized messages and offers, boosting engagement and conversion rates. AR and VR will revolutionize mobile marketing, allowing brands to create immersive brand experiences beyond traditional advertising. The rise of 5G networks will significantly impact mobile marketing, allowing marketers to deliver high-quality video content, live streams, and real-time interactive experiences to users on the go. Inclusivity and accessibility will be paramount, with brands needing to cater to diverse audiences, including those with disabilities. Voice search and smart speakers will reshape mobile marketing strategies, necessitating optimized content and voice-activated campaigns (Lamberton & Stephen, 2016). The evolving regulatory landscape will continue to impact mobile marketing practices, necessitating transparent data practices and user consent.

8.3 Preparing for the Next Wave of Mobile Engagement

Preparing for the next wave of mobile engagement requires a holistic approach, incorporating consumer behavior understanding, hyper-personalization, inclusivity, data privacy compliance, and strategic deployment of content formats and engagement strategies. Staying ahead of the curve in mobile engagement is not only a competitive advantage, it's a requirement as the unstoppable spread of smartphones and the incorporation of mobile gadgets into our everyday routines increases. Understanding the evolving consumer behavior within the mobile ecosystem is crucial for businesses to effectively engage with today's connected, informed, and discerning consumers. Mobile devices serve as gateways to information, entertainment, social interaction, and commerce (Persaud & Azhar, 2012). Businesses must comprehend the intricacies of this connected journey, including the micro-moments when consumers turn to their devices for specific needs. Identifying and catering to these micro-moments is central to effective mobile engagement strategies. A crucial idea in mobile engagement is hyper-personalization, which enables companies to design unique customer experiences.

Smartphone adoption is increasing exponentially, and present marketers have more chances to connect with clients. It helps to investigate consumers' willingness to accept marketing through their smartphones. It demonstrates that the main drivers of customers' participation in mobile marketing via their smartphones are their buying preferences, level of brand trust, and perceived value. This will demonstrate how consumers actually wish to interact with mobile marketing (Persaud and Azhar 2012b). With the help of analytics and artificial intelligence, this data-driven marketing enables companies to produce recommendations, offers, and content that profoundly resonate with consumers, promoting brand loyalty and increasing conversions. Beyond customization, this era of hyper-personalization enables firms to provide clients unparalleled value. The emergence of Augmented Reality and virtual reality technology has changed mobile engagement by allowing marketers to craft experiences that are both memorable and shareable. These technologies are used to create gamified marketing experiences, demonstrate products, and create virtual clothes. The deployment of 5G networks, offers faster speeds, lower latency, and greater connection, will further improve mobile engagement. In a congested digital market, this makes it possible for companies to stand out through the use of high-quality video content, live streaming, and interactive experiences that happen in real time. For businesses to be prepared for mobile engagement, inclusivity and accessibility are essential since they must serve a variety of customers, including those with disabilities. Making sure no potential customer is left behind is a moral and wise business move as the digital world grows more intertwined. Voice-search content and voice-activated campaigns are crucial for preserving exposure and relevance as voice search and smart speakers are changing consumer behavior.

Mobile engagement is a rapidly evolving field, with video content dominating the market, interactive materials like surveys, and chatbots providing instant support. Social media and influencer marketing are crucial channels for reaching target audiences. Location-based marketing offers real-time engagement opportunities, but businesses must navigate privacy concerns. Mobile payment and commerce are essential components, with mobile wallets and contactless payments. Secure mobile marketing practices, robust data protection measures, and ethical data handling are essential for businesses to thrive. Businesses that align with sustainable practices can earn trust and loyalty by incorporating eco-friendly campaigns and reducing carbon footprints. Key performance indicators need to reflect the complexity of mobile engagement, considering factors like user retention, app engagement, and mobile-specific conversion rates. Advanced analytics and attribution models provide insights to optimize campaigns and make data-driven decisions. Globalization and localization strategies are crucial for mobile engagement preparedness, as businesses must consider multilingual content, cultural sensitivities, and local SEO and ASO practices to resonate with diverse audiences. The recent global pandemic has accelerated digital transformation and brought lasting changes to consumer behavior, requiring mobile engagement strategies to adapt and embrace resilience.

9. DISCUSSIONS AND CONCLUSION

Location-based strategies, multi-channel integration, and context-driven notifications are effective tools for boosting mobile marketing engagement. By targeting customers based on their physical location, businesses are able to send relevant and timely messages. Through multi-channel integration, businesses are able to reach customers where they are and at the moments when they are most likely to be engaged by sending communications over various channels, including email, SMS, and push notifications. Context-driven notifications allow businesses to send messages relevant to their current situation or context, such as providing information about local attractions and restaurants. Combining these strategies helps businesses to create a more engaging and personalized mobile marketing experience, leading to increased app usage, customer loyalty, and sales. When used together it is a powerful way to increase engagement with mobile marketing. It is crucial to apply these tactics in a way that complements overall marketing goals and objectives to get the most out of them. Additionally, it's critical to maintain client privacy by only communicating with those who have given their consent to receive messages.

9.1 Summary

Context-driven notifications in mobile advertising are a shift from traditional mass verbal exchange to personalized, real-time interactions. These notifications use data resources like person behavior, place, and environmental elements to deliver timely and relevant messages to users. This technique deepens customer engagement, improves user experiences, and drives desired actions. Organizations need to understand various sources of context, such as GPS location, Wi-Fi data, sensor readings, user preferences, and in-app behavior, to implement context-driven notifications. Personalization and relevance are key in mobile advertising, allowing agencies to craft messages that resonate on a one-to-one level. Tools like data analytics platforms, AI, mobile app development, and notification orchestration enable businesses to create personalized interactions. In the mobile-driven era, businesses should leverage location-based, multi-channel, and context-driven approaches to connect with customers and build brand loyalty. Location-based marketing uses customers' actual location for customized engagement, while multi-channel marketing uses various platforms. Context-driven marketing uses advanced analytics and artificial intelligence to predict customer demands and provide relevant information. To effectively leverage these strategies, organizations must invest in strong data analytics capabilities, prioritize data privacy and security, and understand user preferences. Strategies for enhancing user engagement include understanding user journeys, content, storytelling, and personalization technologies. Digital marketing measurement of engagement and ROI requires understanding data analytics, customer behavior, and marketing channels. Metrics like click-through rates, conversion rates, and website visits are used. Advanced techniques like attribution modeling help understand consumer touchpoints. Organizations must address privacy, consent, data security, and mobile optimization. Mobile marketing has evolved significantly with the advent of smartphones and apps, enabling highly targeted and personalized campaigns. The future of mobile marketing is characterized by hyper-personalization, immersive technologies, 5G connectivity, inclusivity, and data privacy. Technologies like augmented reality, virtual reality, voice search, and smart speakers are revolutionizing the landscape. Voice search offers marketers opportunities to reach customers directly, while new technologies like blockchain, IoT, and edge computing provide faster data processing and real-time applications. Key predictions include personalized experiences, augmented reality, virtual reality, 5G networks, inclusivity, voice search, and regulatory landscape.

9.2 Conclusion

The importance of location-based strategies, multi-channel integration, and context-driven notifications in mobile marketing is emphasized. These strategies allow businesses to use geospatial data to target users with relevant content, transforming physical locations into valuable marketing touchpoints. This approach is particularly effective for traditional businesses bridging the online and offline worlds. Multi-channel integration is crucial in modern mobile marketing, ensuring a seamless brand experience across multiple devices and platforms. This approach enhances engagement, reinforces brand recognition, and drives conversions. Context-driven notifications, based on real-time data and user context, offer personalized engagement. Businesses should embrace advanced technologies like data analytics and artificial intelligence while respecting user privacy, prioritizing consent and transparency in data usage. The mobile revolution has made user engagement crucial for success in mobile marketing. Effective strategies like location-based, multi-channel integration, and context-driven notifications are essential. Businesses should incorporate these strategies to enhance user engagement, build customer relationships, increase conversions, and stay ahead in the dynamic digital landscape.

REFERENCES

Albrecht, M. G. (2023, January 25). *16.2 Social Media and Mobile Marketing - Principles of Marketing OpenStax.* https://openstax.org/books/principles-marketing/pages/16-2-social-media-and-mobile-marketing

Aliahmadi, A., Ghahremani-Nahr, J., & Nozari, H. (2023). Pricing decisions in the closed-loop supply chain network, taking into account the queuing system in production centers. *Expert Systems with Applications, 212,* 118741. doi:10.1016/j.eswa.2022.118741

Aloudat, A., & Michael, K. (2010). Toward the regulation of ubiquitous mobile government: A case study on location-based emergency services in Australia. *Electronic Commerce Research, 11*(1), 31–74. doi:10.1007/s10660-010-9070-0

Arun, R. (2023). *A case study on Netflix marketing strategy*. Simplilearn.com. https://www.simplilearn.com/tutorials/marketing-case-studies-tutorial/netflix-marketing-strategy

Bragge, J., Hengst, M. D., Tuunanen, T., & Virtanen, V. (2005). A repeatable collaboration process for developing a road map for emerging new technology business: Case mobile marketing. *Americas Conference on Information Systems, 198*. https://aisel.aisnet.org/amcis2005/198/

Brisk, G. (2022b, June 18). *How Location-Based Marketing Helps Businesses drive footfall and improve ROI*. PlotProjects. https://www.plotprojects.com/blog/location-based-marketing-drive-footfall-improve-roi/

Ceri, S., Daniel, F., Matera, M., & Facca, F. M. (2007). Model-driven development of context-aware Web applications. *ACM Transactions on Internet Technology, 7*(1), 2. doi:10.1145/1189740.1189742

Chang, J. (2023, September 20). *Mobile phones have become an indispensable part of today's digital lifestyle. With network speeds and coverage*. Financesonline.com. https://financesonline.com/mobile-marketing-software-trends/

Daoud, M. K., Al-Qeed, M. A., Ahmad, A. Y. B., & Al-Gasawneh, J. A. (2023). Mobile Marketing: Exploring the efficacy of User-Centric strategies for enhanced consumer engagement and conversion rates. *International Journal of Membrane Science and Technology, 10*(2), 1252–1262. doi:10.15379/ijmst.vi.1425

Davenport, T. H., Guha, A., Grewal, D., & Breßgott, T. (2019). How artificial intelligence will change the future of marketing. *Journal of the Academy of Marketing Science, 48*(1), 24–42. doi:10.1007/s11747-019-00696-0

Donohue, T. J., Ortiz, R., & Meyer, T. L. (2009). The challenges presented by the mobile phone market. *International Journal of Technology, Knowledge and Society, 5*(6), 19–28. doi:10.18848/1832-3669/CGP/v05i06/56048

Durach, S., Higgen, U., & Huebler, M. (2012). Smart Automotive Apps: An approach to Context-Driven Applications. In Springer eBooks (pp. 187–195). doi:10.1007/978-3-642-33838-0_17

Fritz, W., Sohn, S., & Seegebarth, B. (2017). Broadening the Perspective on Mobile Marketing: An Introduction. *Psychology and Marketing, 34*(2), 113–118. doi:10.1002/mar.20978

Geum, Y., Kim, S., & Park, Y. (2011). *Development of new mobile application services: An approach using context-driven morphology analysis*. IEEE Xplore. doi:10.1109/ICSSSM.2011.5959338

Goel, J. (n.d.). *Top 12 Commerce Project Topics & Ideas in 2023* [For Freshers]. upGrad blog. https://www.upgrad.com/blog/amazon-business-case-study-in-depth-analysis/

GroundTruth Marketing. (2023, June 16). *Location-Based Marketing: The Ultimate Guide*. GroundTruth. https://www.groundtruth.com/insight/location-based-marketing-101/

Hapsari, R., Hussein, A. S., & Handrito, R. P. (2020). Being Fair to Customers: A strategy in enhancing customer engagement and loyalty in the Indonesia mobile telecommunication industry. *Services Marketing Quarterly, 41*(1), 49–67. doi:10.1080/15332969.2019.1707375

Hardt, M., & Nath, S. (2012). *Privacy-aware personalization for mobile advertising.* ACM Digital Library. doi:10.1145/2382196.2382266

Hersh, W. R. (2009). A stimulus to define informatics and health information technology. *BMC Medical Informatics and Decision Making*, *9*(1), 24. Advance online publication. doi:10.1186/1472-6947-9-24 PMID:19445665

Hoffman, D. L., & Fodor, M. (2010). Can you measure the ROI of your social media marketing. *MIT Sloan Management Review*. https://labarce.files.wordpress.com/2010/10/mit.pdf

Hosbond, J. H., & Skov, M. B. (2007). Micro mobility marketing: Two cases on location-based supermarket shopping trolleys. Journal of Targeting. *Measurement and Analysis for Marketing*, *16*(1), 68–77. doi:10.1057/palgrave.jt.5750058

Ishwaran, A. (2017). 5 Benefits of social media Integration and the Ways to Achieve it I TO THE NEW blog. *TO THE NEW BLOG.* https://www.tothenew.com/blog/5-benefits-of-social-media-integration-and-the-ways-to-achieve-it/

Kumar, V., Chattaraman, V., Neghina, C., Skiera, B., Aksoy, L., Buoye, A., & Henseler, J. (2013). Data-driven services marketing in a connected world. *Journal of Service Management*, *24*(3), 330–352. doi:10.1108/09564231311327021

Lal, B., Ismagilova, E., Dwivedi, Y. K., & Kwayu, S. (2019). Return on Investment in Social Media Marketing: Literature review and suggestions for future research. In Advances in theory and practice of emerging markets (pp. 3–17). doi:10.1007/978-3-030-24374-6_1

Lamberton, C., & Stephen, A. T. (2016). A Thematic Exploration of Digital, Social Media, and Mobile Marketing: Research Evolution from 2000 to 2015 and an Agenda for Future Inquiry. *Journal of Marketing*, *80*(6), 146–172. doi:10.1509/jm.15.0415

Leppäniemi, M., Karjaluoto, H., Sinisalo, J., & Salo, J. (2006). Integrated marketing communications in mobile context. In DUV eBooks (pp. 397–415). doi:10.1007/3-8350-5702-2_21

Liébana-Cabanillas, F., Japutra, A., Molinillo, S., Singh, N., & Sinha, N. (2020). Assessment of mobile technology use in the emerging market: Analyzing intention to use m-payment services in India. *Telecommunications Policy*, *44*(9), 102009. doi:10.1016/j.telpol.2020.102009

Lindecrantz, E., Gi, M. T. P., & Zerbi, S. (2020). *Personalizing the customer experience: Driving differentiation in retail.* McKinsey & Company. https://www.mckinsey.com/industries/retail/our-insights/personalizing-the-customer-experience-driving-differentiation-in-retail

Location-based marketing - benefits & effectiveness. (2023, July 18). Optimove. https://www.optimove.com/resources/learning-center/location-based-marketing

Location-Based Mobile Marketing. Benefits & Challenges. (2022, October 27). Sekel Tech. https://sekel.tech/blog/location-based-mobile-marketing-benefits-challenges

MoEngage. (2023, July 26). *11 Awesome examples of mobile marketing campaigns done right.* https://www.moengage.com/learn/examples-of-mobile-marketing-campaigns

Narang, U., & Shankar, V. (2019). Mobile Marketing 2.0: state of the art and research agenda. In Review of marketing research (pp. 97–119). doi:10.1108/S1548-643520190000016008

Pereira, P., Cortez, P., & Mendes, R. (2021). Multi-objective Grammatical Evolution of Decision Trees for Mobile Marketing user conversion prediction. *Expert Systems with Applications*, *168*, 114287. doi:10.1016/j.eswa.2020.114287

Persaud, A., & Azhar, I. (2012). Innovative mobile marketing via smartphones. *Marketing Intelligence & Planning*, *30*(4), 418–443. doi:10.1108/02634501211231883

Rinner, C., & Reisslein, M. (2004). Personalized Multi-Criteria decision strategies in Location-Based decision support. *Annals of GIS*, *10*(2), 149–156. doi:10.1080/10824000409480666

Saurav, K. (2023, February 26). Adopting mobile marketing to increase consumer engagement in 2023-24. *Times of India Blog*. https://timesofindia.indiatimes.com/blogs/voices/adopting-mobile-marketing-to-increase-consumer-engagement-in-2023-24/

Scharl, A., Dickinger, A., & Murphy, J. (2005). Diffusion and success factors of mobile marketing. *Electronic Commerce Research and Applications*, *4*(2), 159–173. doi:10.1016/j.elerap.2004.10.006

Schierholz, R. (2007). Mobile customer relationship management: Foundations, challenges and solutions. *Business Process Management Journal*, *13*(6). Advance online publication. doi:10.1108/bpmj.2007.15713faa.001

Shankar, V., & Balasubramanian, S. (2009). Mobile Marketing: A synthesis and prognosis. *Journal of Interactive Marketing*, *23*(2), 118–129. doi:10.1016/j.intmar.2009.02.002

Shastri, A. (2023, April 10). *Extensive Marketing Strategy of Airbnb - Full case Study*. IIDE. https://iide.co/case-studies/marketing-strategy-of-airbnb/

Simakova, E., & Neyland, D. (2008). Marketing mobile futures: Assembling constituencies and creating compelling stories for an emerging technology. *Marketing Theory*, *8*(1), 91–116. doi:10.1177/1470593107086486

Smail, G., & Jia, W. (2017). *Techno-economic analysis and prediction for the deployment of 5G mobile network*. IEEE Xplore. doi:10.1109/ICIN.2017.7899243

Tamang, R. (2023, March 11). *UX and Gamification in Duolingo - UX Planet*. Medium. https://uxplanet.org/ux-and-gamification-in-duolingo-40d55ee09359

Venkatesh, R. (2015). *Mobile marketing From marketing strategy to mobile marketing campaign implementation*. https://www.semanticscholar.org/paper/Mobile-Marketing-From-Marketing-Strategy-to-Mobile-Venkatesh/8a626502264cca8316c1a99c95b3f9f92ed7cad3

Verhoef, P. C., Kannan, P., & Inman, J. J. (2015). From Multi-Channel retailing to Omni-Channel retailing. *Journal of Retailing*, *91*(2), 174–181. doi:10.1016/j.jretai.2015.02.005

What is Local SEO, and How Does It Work? (n.d.). Mailchimp. https://mailchimp.com/resources/what-is-local-seo/

Chapter 13
Unveiling the Advancements and Trends in Innovative Sustainable Marketing Strategies

N. V. Kavimayil
School of Law, SASTRA University, India

C. Vijayabanu
https://orcid.org/0000-0002-0125-4534
School of Management, SASTRA University, India

ABSTRACT

This chapter aims to bring a crystalline understanding of trends in marketing strategies with their origin of invention. Marketing, a significant component, was incorporated following the division of the section within the chapter that encompasses the management abstract. It brings out an ocean of information on the past viability of management and marketing alignment for performance by understanding the stiff competition and predicting recent trends based on the relevant strategies. Integration into e-commerce and engaging in technologies lead an organization to get itself well-developed and managed accordingly. The chapter will facilitate traders, academicians, research scholars, government, consultants, and practicing managers through the current trends in marketing strategies.

1. PRELUDE

The tertiary sector purchases and sells goods relatively in quantities, generally to ultimate consumers. A marketer is a person who portrays the goods and services of an organization. They serve as a vital link between the producers and final consumers in the distribution of products and services. Helping in distributing goods, personal selling, enabling large-scale operations, collecting market information, and helping promote are some of the services that marketers offer to manufacturers and wholesalers. Also,

DOI: 10.4018/979-8-3693-1339-8.ch013

making products available in the market regularly, providing information on new products, providing convenience in buying, selecting the products widely, providing customer services, and allowing credit facilities are some doings of marketers to end users.

Moreover, on the other hand, a few extraneous cons sometimes affect their performance. To tackle all the cons and improve their pros, a bunch of principles, insights, strategies, etc., would be used to ameliorate the marketing sector. There exist practices among marketers facing the competition, such as taking precautionary measures, introducing lucrative offers, etc., But these are insufficient to meet the competition persisting in this era. It requires strong and healthy ways to equip itself and host the trend.

The current chapter studies the various marketing techniques and principles required to overcome the competition and understand the essential strategies in managing the market sector amidst the amelioration. It also contains some fascinating notions on the management and the marketing fields of such sectors in which the desired results would be the development. The current chapter aims to bring a crystalline understanding of trends in marketing strategies with their origin of invention.

Though there are many strategies for amelioration and performance, marketers lack the implementation of these strategies effectively and efficiently. The implementation process does not only attract expert skills personnel but also management support and technological updates. The current chapter will have the following research questions.

- How could marketers face the competitive markets? How will they overcome these obstacles? Are there any specific aspects to be concentrated on?
- How do we unveil trends and keep ourselves updated? Are there any strategies to ameliorate the firm sustainably?

Likewise, there are many questions to be answered, and the chapter will concentrate on those perspectives of contemporary markets and their strategies.

2. REVIEW OF LITERATURE AND OBJECTIVES

A group of interdependent businesses making a good or service accessible for use or consumption is referred to as a marketing channel. Despite the challenges of evaluating actual circumstances, mid-century work on marketing channels was more prescriptive, creating management decision models that concurrently considered the information, revenue potential, and cost functions. A study in the middle of the 20th century more explicitly highlighted the presence of non-economic variables in marketing channels. The domain has become more diverse and mature, and e-commerce and internationalization have generated considerable disruptions, as evidenced by recent channel research (Watson IV et al., 2015). Digital communication is more focused and improves the perception and memory of the received information. Businesses easily obtain instant client feedback, and it may be responded to. Businesses use different tools in their digital marketing communication process.

Among them are tablets, smartphones, telephones, and personal computers—consoles for games, TV, etc. Nowadays, more than half of humanity uses the Internet. Additionally, most people now use smartphones, accounting for over two-thirds of all mobile phone users. The fact that the average internet user now uses internet-powered devices and services for almost six hours daily is noteworthy. The increasing use of digital technologies implies that marketers should broaden their perspective to include all platforms that enable a company to conduct business electronically, not just the Internet. Put another way, the three components that have combined to form the newest and fastest-growing online phenomenon are social (life), media (environment), and network (interconnections—technology and human). Digital media has the potential to help a business succeed in the marketplace. Digital media-supported marketing initiatives can potentially establish and improve a business's brand and line of products. Because digital media plays such a significant role in the lives of contemporary customers, it should be considered when organizing marketing communication initiatives (Slijepčević & Radojević, 2018).

So, the holy grail of the chapter is the target marketers who find one's feet in a predicament due to prevailing market competition in both domestic and international trade. Its grail is not just for the target marketers; the sole aim is to aid them in stewardship to regulate management and marketing, which would develop the whole business. The chapter not only concentrates on the development of business but also the development of society at large. As it centralizes society in the beneficiary list, the general public and the firms' stakeholders benefit from this information. Apart from the beneficiaries, the chapter flows like a river, crossing many concepts for the upliftment of entities and finally merging with the large ocean of development in society. The concentration towards GDP of the economy's growth and market growth of the countries was included to add more impact to the beneficiaries. People who practice as a managers, researchers, students, and others who desire management and marketing would enjoy witnessing this chapter. With the short cover on competition, the chapter continues with the marketing at first, then walks through the management pathway, and finally ends with the maneuver for its blossoming.

3. A GLIMPSE OF THE COMPETITION AND GROWTH

Rivalry exists everywhere, from the player's perspective in succeeding it. In the case of retail trade, the increase in competition was not new. Their competition not only persists with traders themselves; it varies from country to country. This is because of factors such as changes in taste and preferences of customers, lack of updates, supplier's bargaining power, purchasing power and pattern, frequency of buying and time concerns, promotional techniques, purchase methods, lack of flexibility, and wrong anticipations. All these loopholes need two mantras to first aid their wound: "the management and the marketing." Evolution happens in every sector, especially in a business organization. It shall seem a surprise only when such evolution does not happen. The economy underwent a major evolution during COVID-19 (Shetty et al., 2020). Such transformation converted the medium of sales to online. Online sales growth would impact positively, and in the Middle East, Africa, and Latin America, sales would increase by over 20%, and Asia is forecasted to increase by 12%. Global sales are anticipated to increase by 5%, but inflation would be 6%, flattening demand and reducing profits (Sergiu Iscu, 2022). Besides all those factors, customers' engagement with marketers continues and cannot be barred.

Figure 1. Trends in digital marketing
Source: https://blog.aweber.com/digital-marketing-2/digital-marketing-statistics.htm

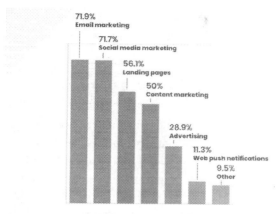

Which digital marketing strategies are you currently using to promote your business and/or communicate with your audience?

4. MARKETING STRATEGIES

The gathering and analyzing of the market information and the marketing process will continue until the firm's product reaches its storage or warehouse unit. Still, the saturation point of the marketing process is foggy per se. Marketers use all of these marketing strategies as they are the end sellers. The complex functions that help in marketing highlight the 4Ps – Product, Price, Physical Distribution, and Promotion (Bhasin, H, 2016).

4.1 Gathering and Analyzing Market Information

It is necessary to gather and analyze market information to successfully market goods and services and make major decisions on retail trade. Gathering means the collection of data on market trends and other statistics. The analysis here means the awareness of available opportunities and threats and the organization's strengths and weaknesses and helps decide the best opportunity for future pursuance (Itani et al.,2023). Market information relates to information on financial markets, market data, research, forecasts, trends, etc. (Xiao et al.,2023); for crystalline understanding, nothing would replace the popular brand 'THE NESTLE- THE GOOD FOOD GOOD LIFE' as an example. The present statistics state that the number of people working is increasing daily. This is reflected in the decrease in concentration on home life. The main cooking activity is expected to be quick, and the eating routine is fast. Nestle Pvt Ltd used the expected market trend of fast cooking, which came with introducing "2 minutes Maggi" into the market. Its market is still irreplaceable, though it faces some struggles. They covered all roots of markets benefitting the end users. The other instance where the collection and research on market information stand essential is the Departmental Stores, which make displays of products for sales that attract customers. When they plan to buy two products while preparing for shopping, the colorful showcase of products would willingly change their plan to buy four or five products. The increase in the percentage of sales is due to the strategy of exhibiting in the store.

4.2 Market Planning

Market planning is the strategy of forethought and preparation toward future commitments on the market (THIS, T. M. I. L, 2020). Anticipation and forecasting are the two main tools for this function. The market has a high demand for this planning as it realizes returns and assists in estimation. Planning implies adopting the environment, grasping opportunities, taking cautious steps against threats, etc., in the sense of the market. Marketers should be cautious regarding market plans, investigation of market trends, anticipation over future demand, eye on current supplies, contribution towards the sales, etc., are some key points aiding their plans (Wilson, 2010). Market planning is a continuation of the market information analysis process. Nowadays, many entities work on free market planning templates for other companies for their growth (Buchelt, 2011). Planning the market templates also makes entities depend on outsourcing. Let us take an example for a grip on the concept: the popular South Indian restaurant 'Adyar Anandha Bhavan fixed a goal that its presence should exist worldwide without any exception. Their objective was to facilitate South India's Vegetarians. To accomplish such a goal, they started planning the market. At first, they started preparations to establish themselves domestically, then slightly moved internationally. Some areas were given franchises, and some were owned by themselves. The recently trending tea shop 'The Black Pekoe' would also help us gain better knowledge of market planning. This shop's objective is to savor unique tea with exceptional quality. Once the goal was to savor unique tea, it planned to search for key ingredients. A good search for ingredients resulted in a unique taste in tea, and it also pushed the pekoe team to introduce varieties of tea, namely ginger tea, cardamom tea, green tea, etc. Here, market planning concentrated on the distinct quality of the product to meet the high competition and distraction for coffee lovers through the introduction of unique quality tea. It even increased its franchise system and plans to introduce its identity in London, United Kingdom.

4.3 Product Assortment

The marketing mix of the product is the collection of market supply inventories (Khan, 2014). Increasing and decreasing the stock level based on the demand in the market is the crucial role marketers play. For instance, when there is a low onion harvest, it is not easy to supply the customers with their everyday needs. Marketers plan to maintain a good stock of onions during the higher harvest, which would help in the lower harvest situation. Pre-planning is essential to meet the competition regarding trade as rivalry increases daily. Some durable products like automobiles, electronic accessories, etc., require services, and a concentration on customer services to retain them with satisfaction would help widen the market. An assortment of products occupies a unique position in a market. Marketers now face notable possibilities and challenges due to the development of electronic commerce (often known as e-commerce). The area of channel management may be where the impact is most noticeable. Channel conflict is currently the main problem for many business-to-business (B2B) companies (Webb, 2002).

4.4 Pricing Strategies

The manufacturer initially fixes the price of a product through the calculation of expenditure plus the profit percentage they need for them. They also fix the Maximum Retail Price(MRP), which is a limit for the price to restrict the retailers from selling it at higher. The price fixed for the product varies with the product assortment (Sun & Gilbert, 2019). The middle stage in marketing is fixing prices. The first aspect is to balance the expenditure, and the next is to make a profit. Expenditure refers to the expenses incurred for purchasing such a product and establishing such a retail shop (in the case of a new shop). The profit the marketer fixes will be based on a few factors, as the changes can only be made in the profit percentage and not on the expenditure side. Like two sides to a coin, the fixing of price needs two elements where one side (profit percentage) can be determined by analyzing some factors, and the other would fix itself as expenditure, which is what they spent (Niar, 2022). The determining factors of profit percentage are the market demand and competition for the product. Other than the two determining factors, some occupy a quarter portion of determination. They are credit terms, the retail firm's objective, positioning strategies, fixed and variable costs, discounts, and pricing policies that exist in the firm, etc. The reason for the brief information given on the pricing was to insist that pricing is also a refreshing mix to compete with the other firms. Sometimes, sales would increase when the product is offered at a lower price when compared to other firms or when the firm offers it at a discounted price.

4.5 Omni Channel and Physical Distribution

Through the mobile, online, or store medium, it is mandatory to provide the product to the customer for their necessity (Zhu & Gao, 2019). Customers usually jump to shops where the required products are readily available. It is advisable to use omni channels or multi-channel or single channels for sales based on the circumstances and location of their shop. Omni channel comprises three dimensions: stage, channel type, and channel agent (Saghiri et al., 2017). According to Nielsen, 86% of the population shop physically and online, 14% shop exclusively in physical mode, while less than 1% shop online. Take Amazon, a voguish online platform, and an American technology company. It proceeds the market with the use of the online methodology. Almost all the products are available on their website except the funeral or mortuary freezer boxes. Such service by them, that is, making every product available and having a timely delivery, makes customers addicted to buying.

4.6 Fostering Promotion

This marketing mix is very important as the main secret of facing the competition rests with it. This strategy refers to promoting the product that is kept to be sold. It may be through publicity, personal selling, sales promotion, or advertising. The most popular digital marketing channel in the industry being studied was social networks, and the most popular tool for evaluating the effectiveness of digital marketing was Google Analytics (Melović et al., 2020). Marketers, blind while implementing promotional tools, lack a hold to stand in the market. They must choose the more optimized technique; it should increase sales and create an identity for the shop for its future survival. An optimal selection of a modus operandi and identity creation connect marketing and management strategy (Mingione & Leoni, 2020). There can be a method of comparing many approaches towards Promotion to select the best one suitable for the entity's growth and not to narrowly stick to any promotional tool, which will sometimes affect the growth. For instance, a proprietor who aims to develop her store should consider advertising expenditures; if it increases the budget, she must look for an alternate, either publicity or personal selling, and not stick to advertising. Boosterism converts the proprietor's narrow intelligence to wide brilliance through serving many choices of techniques and makes her use a different practice that attracts customers at large. An essential part of Promotion depends on the nature of the products, place of selling, taste, and people's preferences (Dašić et al., 2019). The necessities of customers should be identified to make them buy and enhance customer satisfaction. The general ideology of the coverage place where the store is located as a café will flop in residential places. Rather, it would experience huge development in the town or highways where travelers require it. All these elements must be considered while boosting a shop in a locality.

4.7 Societal and Sustainable Marketing

Figure 2 depicts the link between society, consumers, and the company, which means to be the embryo of the societal marketing notion.

Figure 2. A diagram of societal marketing
Source:*https://marketingbasicconcept.blogspot.com/2011/10/societal-marketing-concept.html*

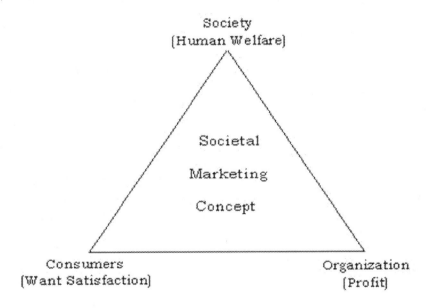

The social process of marketing is how different groups get what they need and want by making offers and trading valuable goods and services with one another (Istanti et al., 2020). Marketing orientation implies that focusing on satisfying customers' needs is the key to the success of any organization in the market. A comprehensive set of principles and ideas known as "social marketing" can strategically assess, deliver, plan, and evaluate a social program that aims to improve behavior (French & Gordon, 2019). This concept assumes that, in the long run, an organization can maximize profit by identifying the needs of its present and prospective buyers and effectively satisfying them. According to the marketing concept, customer satisfaction becomes the focal point of all marketing decision-making. If society changes greatly in its production and sales marketing concept, it slightly changes to a societal marketing concept. The dilemma between the two decides the survival of the organization. Any activity of the merchandise sector that satisfies human needs but is detrimental to the interests of society at large cannot be justified (business ethics). Corporate social responsibility stands as a companion for the societal marketing concept. Also, CSR plays a vital role in sustainable marketing (Shah & Khan, 2020). It survives as a responsibility for the business traders to rectify and contemplate large issues of long-term social welfare, such as environmental pollution, shortage of resources, deforestation, population explosion, and inflation. It might focus on marketing's social, ethical, and ecological facets in addition to client happiness. The following are two real-life examples projected to make the readers more realistic about the concept.

A firm that depends on returns (profit) must fulfill customer satisfaction and societal welfare. Based on the aforementioned real-life concept, 'Srimaan Trusts' in Tamil Nadu is an absolute example. Srimaan Trust (Helping those in need) works on education, health care, human welfare such as women empowerment, animal welfare, and protection of the environment, heritage, and culture. They are famous for their Ghosalai, where they protect nearly 30+ cows and sell cow products to make returns out of it. They believe that the protection of cows removes poverty and gives good health, wealth and prosperity, and financial stability. They engage in 'Cow Dhaanam,' which means donating cows to the farmers for their benefit. Their main aim is to protect the orphan cows who do not have people to take care of them. While analyzing the base of this trust, one could conclude that they concentrate on their expected returns and the social welfare strategy where they protect cows and, on the other hand, protect the environment. Also, the customers, the farmers, were satisfied as the cows were provided to them free of cost; in turn, they made a profit on the other side, where they sold the by-products of cows.

Another instance is the 'Bloom Box' invented by K.R. Sridhar, who started his journey as an advisor to NASA in the Surveyor Lander Mission on Mars in 2001. This project was based on the creation of oxygen via some energy. When the project got canceled without leaving hope, he reversed it and worked on it. Reversing the project gave him a new start-up for creating energy via oxygen and hydrogen. Through that invention, he co-founded Bloom Energy in 2001 and succeeded in "making clean, reliable energy affordable for everyone on the earth." The introduction of Bloom Box created a new trend in America, and many leading companies, namely Adobe Systems, eBay, Yahoo, Google, FedEx, Wal-Mart, Coco-Cola, and San Fransico International Airport, started using such boxes, especially for electric energy. When this invention is perceived as a retail lease, one could not escape saying it is the best example of societal marketing in the retail sector.

4.8 Plinth for Interactive Marketing

- **Opting for choosy Brands** – Branding is one of the vital decisions for marketers. A marketer should concentrate on branding for sales. Some brands of consumable products like Lifebuoy, Dabur, Himalaya, Colgate, Pepsi, Loreal shampoos, etc., and durable products like Life's Good (LG), Samsung, Prestige, etc., have a better space in the hearts of the customers. The regular supply of products should be identified for the occupation of the hearts of consumers.

- **Diversification** in sales refers to varieties in the product assortment. As large enterprises diversify in marketing, retail also has such a space to be filled with. Merchandisers should be capable of transporting and importing customers' required and desired products. Also, strategies for selecting diversification should be consistent and appropriate.

- **Pillars of the marketing mix – Packaging, Labeling, and Standardising**. The first taste almost coincides with vision (Stolle, 2019). So, marketers require the process of packing and labeling as their function is to sell products that should attract buyers per se and be a standardized good. Usually, customers seek International Organization for Standardised (ISO) certified products. So, marketers should confirm such certifications, packages, and labels. Likewise, retailers shall seek Food Safety and Standard Authority of India (FSSAI) licensed products in India for the sale of food and beverages.

- **Transportation** is also a strategy for marketers to keep stocks readily available for purchase by customers. It can be through roadways, waterways, or airways, depending on the location of purchase from wholesalers. For the city's residents, who frequently have a high level of mobility, online transport services are convenient. GO-JEK and GRAB are two active rival internet transportation service providers (Prabowo et al., 2019).

- When transportation is accomplished, **storage or warehousing** plays a crucial role. Some products fix a deadline for their consumption. If the deadline expires, it cannot be sold. This was handled by purchasing only the highly consumable products of large quantities from the wholesalers and then storing them and smaller quantities of vulnerable products for them to be sold soon.

- Once all was done and the products were sold, the process did not end. It has one more responsibility to be done - **"The Customer Support Services."** Customer Suppor Services are very effective in bringing repeat sales from consumers, considered one of the old concepts. The support services that marketers offer to their target clients to ensure their satisfaction and retention include after-sales care, managing customer complaints and adjustments, obtaining credit services, maintenance services, technical assistance, and consumer information. In India, a highly growing company is Dell, which has its online store and branches in every district with a specialized team appointed for home services. It got popularised only because of this strategy of service and maintenance as it was delighted by many customers whose positive reviews attracted other people to buy them.

- **Remarketing** is the strategy where marketers advise the customers to use the products optimally and minimally (Gerstner et al., 1993). The reason behind such advice was the lack of alternate resources for such products. The concept of demarketing is a discouraging notion in the perception of a layman, but it supports a firm when done with differentiation in the product. Examples of such products are refinery companies who advertise to use petroleum-based products optimally ("do not waste petrol"), water companies advertising "save water," etc.; these are tricks for retailers to attract customers by showing that they are more sustainable in their business.

5. TRENDS IN SUSTAINABLE MARKETING

"A little competition is good, and severe competition is a blessing." Following the sruti of Jacab Kindleberger, the remedy to the severe competition in the market is marketing, which stands as a way of blessing. The belief is that marketing is a blessing; every marketer should work hard and crush the minds of their stores to be placed in an irreplaceable, unique identity. All marketing strategies are to be considered as guidelines, and procedures implemented in those guidelines are in the hands of the merchandise sellers. Motivating customers to buy the products, customer satisfaction, etc., are the importance of marketing in the competition. Marketing and competition in the organization are interconnected. Changing the online marketing scenario increases sales and, similarly, the competition. When progress toward marketing happens, rivalry follows up. It should not be negatively thought that to handle the decreasing competition, and one should reverse, which is to decrease marketing quality. It is completely a wrong phenomenon. An update of the market and analysis of customer preferences using attractive ideas will take marketers to success (Shaw et al., 2001). It is not easy to judge every customer personally, but the idea that attracts most of the population is the matter here. A marketer who faces competition should not frame a rigid and opaque character towards marketing; she has to be flexible and updated (Lim, 2023).

A marketer should adopt the character of translucent objects when it comes to marketing because she should only adopt the needed changes in the store to market the goods and improve its performance or attain the goal, not the unnecessary things per se. When the character of translucency is adopted, a marketer must have the brain to divide the needy process and the waste process. She can acquire feedback from customers for the products sold, analyze the sales, and compare it with competitors, etc., but the decisions after acquiring results are to be taken by the marketer, and she has to be very, very cautious. Since many clients consider corporate reputation when determining whether to do business with a brand or firm, acting ethically has become increasingly crucial (Lim et al., 2023). The trial and error shall be combined with the cause and effect relationship and, if followed, shall increase the status of the market from the regular portion of survival (Morschett et al., 2006).

Table 1. Green technology and sustainable market size worldwide (2022-2023)

Year	Market Size (in Billions of U.S. Dollars)
2022	13.76
2023	16.5
2024	20.19
2025	24.24
2026	29.11
2027	34.95
2028	41.97
2029	50.4
2030	61.92

Source: Statista. (2023, July 21). Global green technology and sustainability market size 2022-203.https://www.statista.com/statistics/1319996/green-technology
-and-sustainability-market-size-worldwide/

It is anticipated that between 2022 and 2030, the worldwide market for green technology and sustainability will grow. In 2022, this market was estimated to be worth 13.76 billion US dollars, as shown in Table 1. Growth is expected to attain a compound annual growth rate of 20.8% between 2023 and 2030, when it is expected to reach its peak at around 62 billion US dollars.

6. DYNAMIC MANAGEMENT

Unlike manufacturers, marketers do not need effective managers or productions; they require only efficient sales planning in the market that would provide them with returns for survival. The efficacy of sales shall be achieved through effective management. The financial management plays quite an important role in the marketing sector. Analyzing the management scope is a process in which the goals are achieved effectively and efficiently; the marketing section of the firm should absorb the characteristics of going concern, cardinal relationships, intangible force, and dynamic mechanisms from the notion of management. When the procedures are implemented as planned, it makes the work completion successful. Success necessitates the adoption of management functions such as planning the market, organizing the assortment of necessary products, staffing personnel for personal selling, directing the physical distribution, and controlling the business environment. However, the only clarification is that all these functions should be done in a smaller circle, no - when it comes to digital sales, it can be wide in a sense. Therefore, the marketing management process, which attempts to maximize revenue by satisfying consumer demands, includes controlling the marketing components, setting corporate goals, organizing plans step-by-step, making decisions for the company, and putting those decisions into action (Naim et al., 2023). The main goal set in all enterprises is to help customers find products and satisfy them. Its implementation starts with organizing the goods, establishing hierarchies, and making decisions using the proper managerial tools. Continuing the organizing, staffing, which is a part of human resource management, comes into the role where the marketers recruit their servants or workers directly or indirectly. Staffing is followed by directing where the main stewardship happens. Controlling succeeds in directing the process, as standards measurement and comparison shall be made only at the final stage, which directly links with the planning – the first and foremost function. Stewardship, coordination and collaboration, financial management, business environment management, and sustainability are dealt with in detail in the following sections.

6.1 Leadership

Influence is the relationship that exists between a leader and those who follow them and wish to see real changes that represent their common objectives. Stewardship influences the servants who work under the management and sometimes the customers, too. For example, Woodland is a renowned brand of footwear whose parent company, Aero Group, commenced in America and waived it all over the world today. Therefore, a retailer should be the one who attracts customers and employees. Once the failure occurs, it will not be easy to retrieve the position. They may use autocratic, transactional, democratic, transformational, or Laissez-faire leadership in their management to establish identity and achieve the goal. Via stewardship, interpersonal skills were developed in pursuance of the achievement of goals. As leadership is a continuous process, relationships are maintained effectively. Sometimes, a small acquisition of feedback leads to a major change in an organization. A stewardship's base is learning; the lesson was the key to unlocking perspective. Employee perceptions of their organizations are shaped by leadership, and this affects how customers see the brand. Beyond personality, effective leadership is dependent on trust and a determination to assign tasks to people in order to completely realize their potential (O'Keeffe et al., 2016).

6.2 Coordination and Collaboration

Coordination, which is the essence of management, is a process of synchronization of activities of various departments. Here, an individual may be appointed to manage the organization at the middle level, and the position is named operation manager to coordinate the firm. Such sorts of managers are appointed only in the larger concerns and not in the smaller concerns, as owners themselves get it accomplished. The operation manager ensures efficient workflow, gives feedback on performance, improves performance by motivation, determines optimal stock level through inventory analysis, defines product quantity to be sold, monitors customer services, and reviews sales records to fulfill financial objectives. For proper administration and management, a firm needs an operation manager for its successful survival and growth.

Coordination does not only refer to internal coordination; it may also include external collaboration. The best example that broke the belief that "only two retailers can collaborate" is Walmart's partnership with Buzzfeed, an internet media company. They collaborated to promote food and drink recipes and related content. Their journey commenced in 2019, which collided with their notion of promotion. Although the collaboration was done with the motive of expansion, it promoted the organization's and the customers' benefits on larger levels.

6.3 Managing Finance

Financial management predominantly focuses on working capital management. Concentration on the primary and secondary market was low as they do not manufacture, produce, or process products. An initial investment of capital is very good enough for those marketers. In the current era, the omni channels cover the major part of the world where the initial investments are start-ups of their finance. They may require additional investments for other purposes, such as pledging for loans, collaborating with other companies, investing in shares, etc. However, the absolute concentration should be on operational finance management because working capital, that is, capital for day-to-day operations, is the backbone of every firm that runs for a long term. Budgeting, leverage management, asset management, inventory planning and organizing, profit planning, and optimum resource allocation are the weighty aspects of finance management (Bhat, 2008). Like companies' cash flow analysis, marketers also must avoid extensive cash shortages and conserve the balance between cash inflows and outflows. Merchandisers should act as owls in the darkness of credit facilities provided to customers. In the modern era, online marketers offer EMI facilities, which may sometimes result in an allocation of space for doubtful debt or bad debts in the network's financial statement (annual statement). This may seem risky, but it follows the concept of "more risk and more return." At the same time, the skill to meet the supplier's bill, employee expenses, taxes, and so on is an essential factor. Every marketer is poorly equipped and must appoint a financial manager who manages the entity's finances. By using an annual statement, a comparative analysis of the firm's position, growth, development, and cash flow analysis can be made. It would also help in making many investment decisions in the management, and the vulnerable areas in the firm are found so that they could be strengthened (Olayinka, 2022). The firm should always move in a smooth path where liabilities are less. However, at all times, it may not be smooth. To face the worst path, it may be advisable to go for outsourcing strategies where corporations usually hire professionals.

7. ASTUTES IN MARKETING

7.1 Digital Marketing

A business environment refers to the external forces that influence the organization. Similarly, atmospherics influence the environment, where shoppers are persuaded to enter into such atmospherics and adopt them for survival. The organization's cult was pervasive in which network links all. It is wrong to hope that such external forces only cause negative impacts. The environment intimates information about opportunities and caution towards the threats. Forces would not disclose such opportunities and threats directly, but marketers are responsible for probing through threats and using the opportunities to grow and shine in the competitive market. Even though the internal forces of an organization stand vital for decision-making, external forces influence such decisions because of their dynamic character. It would provide clearness when merchandisers use SWOT or PEST analysis for their environmental management. SWOT (Strength, Weakness, Opportunities, Threats) analysis refers to identifying existing organizational strengths and weaknesses and searching for opportunities for their shine and threats against their future success. PEST analysis analyzes political, economic, social, and technological factors that affect the organization (Sammut-Bonnici & Galea, 2014). Some of the biggest changes in the business landscape include the rise of "cyber consumers" and the world of online business-to-business; the reality of a world becoming more complex, dynamic, and chaotic; and the waves of entrepreneurship and innovation and the new business models that accompany them. It is possible to forecast that digital technology would reduce the influence held by corporations by giving consumers access to more "perfect" information. Research indicates that branding is becoming more and more important. Due to the abundance of options and lack of in-person relationships, consumers may turn to well-known brands as evidence of more ethereal qualities. Because it projects an image of the buyer in this setting, the Nike brand is still powerful. However, an airline brand that depends on affordable costs and on-time performance may undermine its reputation since its information about low rates and on-time service may be empirically assessed through conveniently executed online searches (Wind & Mahajan, 2002).

Table 2. Digital marketing growth – Forecast

Continent	Data (US Dollars)		Growth/Increase (%)
	2020	2025	
Asia	1703.2	2573.3	51
China	1343.5	1996.0	49
North America	588.4	794.6	35
Europe	460.5	655.6	42

Source: These are the world's biggest e-commerce markets. (2021, October 18). World Economic Forum;https://www.weforum.org/agenda/2021/09/e-commerce-fast-growth-online-sales-china-europe-america/

The Statista Digital Market Outlook reports that China has the largest e-commerce market. E-commerce sales in China were estimated to be worth $1.3 trillion in 2020, and by 2025, that amount is expected to rise to about $2 trillion. Over the next five years, e-commerce is predicted to expand at a rate of 47% on average across the globe. With growth rates of 42% and 35% in North America and Europe, respectively, the Asian market is predicted to expand at a rate of 51%.

7.2 Sustainability Growth in Marketing

Sustainability means the ability of people to maintain the environment for their successors. It is the responsibility of the current generations to protect the resources and provide them to the upcomers without any damage. The new 3Ps for sustainability in the fashion industry proposed here are Public, Performance, and Preservation, which are added to the current marketing mix. The public represents the 'who' of sustainability. The public may consist of management, personnel, and customer service representatives. One of the main forces behind sustainability marketing strategies is consumers. Human capital should be included in the public face of fashion sustainability marketing at every stage of the fashion supply chain. Since sustainability in fashion depends on embracing diversity, inclusive refers to policies and organizations that have the overall impact of including all groups and cultural traditions fairly and equally. The public has a connection between materialistic concerns and the environment and is aware that changing fashion marketers' priorities is necessary to keep the ecological system in balance. Sustainable marketing and digital marketing are closely connected in their work these days. Popular companies integrate both concepts to increase their reputation and to attract consumers' attention (Fuxman et al.,2022).

7.3 Internet Social Spaces

The introduction of social media and other new technologies has had an impact on many families and altered the way that buyers research products before making a purchase. As the number of people using social media increases, businesses are advised to take advantage of this emerging marketing channel and successfully interact with customers. The discipline of increasing website traffic or attention through social media platforms is known as "social media marketing." Social networking websites foster communities and partnerships by facilitating online interactions between individuals and organisations. E-word of mouth, or electronic social networking, is spread through social networking sites. Marketers can identify buying signals by utilizing emerging semantic analysis technologies, such as information shared online and online queries. Because mobile phones contain social networking features that enable instant web browsing and access to social networking sites, they are also useful for social media marketing (Kaur, 2016).

7.4 Post COVID-19 Impact

Since the COVID-19 pandemic is affecting lifestyles and supply chains worldwide, the public aspect of consumer purchasing decisions is crucial as customers witness how the pandemic affects those who work in the fashion supply chain. However, the global pandemic of COVID-19 has effects on sustainability beyond economics. While the environmental effects of the virus are mostly focused on the air pollution features brought about by the virus's proliferation, the social effects of the virus include the uneven spread of infections across social groups. Increasing supply chain transparency will enable customers to comprehend, perceive, and, if feasible, personally experience the effects of their sustainable purchasing. Although the empowered and involved consumer is crucial in this situation, it should not be confined to businesses that interact with customers. By closely collaborating with supply chain partners, brands could facilitate information exchange to give consumers a better understanding of how people who contribute to the creation of the clothing that they consume are treated in their workplace and, ultimately, how their decision to buy is affected. Access to reliable information results in feeling good, eliminating shame and doubt, and eventually changing one's purchasing habits to favor more environmentally friendly clothing use (Fuxman et al., 2022).

Table 3. Development of e-commerce share in the retail market after COVID-19 (country-wise)

Country	E-Commerce as a Share of Total Retail (in Percentage %)
United Kingdom	24.1
Germany	9.9
Italy	5
France	10.9
Russia	7
India	5
Australia	9
Canada	15
United States	17
Mexico	6.2
Brazil	7
Argentina	7

Source: Stephanie Chevalier, Statista. (2023, August 29). Development of e-commerce shares pre and post COVID-19, by country;https://www.statista.com/statistics/1228660/e-commerce-shares-development-during-pandemic/

E-commerce's percentage of overall retail sales reached previously unheard-of levels during the peak of the COVID-19 epidemic in March and April 2020, when lockdown measures were enacted in various countries throughout the globe. In the UK, a developed market, the percentage of e-commerce peaked at 31.3 percent and then steadily declined in the years that followed. With respective percentages of 24, 17, and 15 percent, the United States, Canada, and the United Kingdom ranked first through third in terms of e-commerce's proportion of global retail as of January 31, 2021.

8. AI'S EFFECT ON MARKETING

AI is defined as "programs, algorithms, systems, and machines that demonstrate intelligence," is "manifested by machines that exhibit aspects of human intelligence," and entails machines imitating "intelligent human behavior," according to researchers. First, AI algorithms automate business processes by completing well-defined tasks without human involvement. Examples include transferring data from email or call centers into recordkeeping systems (updating customer files), replacing lost ATM cards, carrying out straightforward market transactions, or "reading" documents to extract crucial clauses using natural language processing. Second, AI can learn from enormous amounts of transaction and consumer data, including numerical data and text, voice, image, and facial expression data. Companies can then estimate what customers will buy using AI-enabled analytics, detect credit fraud before it occurs, or use real-time targeted digital advertising (Davenport et al., 2020).

Figure 3. Sustainable marketing and digital marketing
Source: https://www.kub-uk.net/insights/sustainable-marketing-b2b-selling/

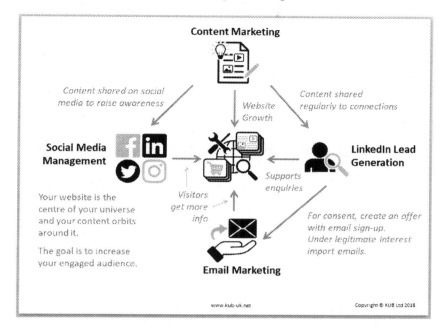

9. GLOBAL MARKET PLACES: STRATEGIES

Due to the world's economic boom and the impact of globalization, organizations started to set up marketing units of their own. Social media and internet access gave them the confidence to shine over the marketers. Market competition increased regularly, and firms slightly decreased their sales concentration. When it comes to international marketing, there is a good chance that the controllable factors—like cost and price structures, advertising opportunities, and distribution infrastructure—will also differ significantly from market to market in addition to the uncontrollable factors, which vary greatly. These kinds of distinctions are what make international marketing so challenging. The Internet has transformed international marketing strategies and access to the World Wide Web. From small businesses with a few employees to large multinational corporations, companies have seen the potential of global web marketing and have developed the ability to purchase and sell their products and services worldwide. The advantages of promoting products and services online have wide-ranging effects on all businesses. Thanks to the Internet, consumers now have access to abundant information, allowing them to buy goods from the most affordable suppliers worldwide. As a result, prices are becoming more uniform across borders, or, at the very least, price differences are closing as customers become more aware of costs in various countries and purchase various goods online (Doole & Lowe, 2012).

Across global marketplaces, wealthy nations are facing intense competition from rising economies and less developed nations, which are utilizing cutting-edge technology and their low labor costs to compete in markets that are no longer as well-protected by tariff walls.

The intentional use of international component sourcing by multinational corporations and global enterprises to gain competitive advantage further adds to the complexity of the market. Nine deficiencies in cross-cultural management skills were highlighted by Perlmutter in 1995. Core deficiencies are "the collection of managerial and business activities inappropriate in a wide range of countries where firms operate." The first three are connected and have to do with the lack of market-drivenness.

- They are failing to identify the appropriate market niches.
- Reluctant to modify and upgrade items to meet regional requirements.
- They did not have distinctive goods that local consumers considered high enough added value.
- A tentative dedication. Learning to live and work in places like Japan takes time.
- Choosing the incorrect personnel. Selecting the incorrect top team or individuals for an affiliate.
- It is choosing the incorrect partners. There are many obstacles to forming alliances; one major one is choosing partners that do not have the correct combination of skills to assist in entering the local market.
- Failure to control local stakeholders. This includes a failure to establish effective working relationships with unions and governments.
- Mistrust and a lack of respect between the Head office and the affiliates at various management levels.
- The inability to transfer innovations from one nation to others around the world.

It is crucial to ensure the business has a comprehensive and rigorous approach to its international marketing planning processes if you do not want to make such errors in your marketing strategy (Doole & Lowe, 2012).

10. CONCLUSION

Starting a business is like a snowball effect – starting with little significance, growing slowly, and finally establishing a catastrophic atmosphere. Considering all the strategies, a marketer must apply the right strategy at the right place without delay. It is difficult to analyze a strategy's merits and demerits and determine that it fulfills the appropriate requirements. Exercising responsibilities, maintaining discipline, and successful survival in the market are the outcomes of a retail marketer's decisions. A good decision leads to a good administration. Therefore, the marketer must be well-skilled to make a good decision, or outsourcing should be appointed for such a function. Decision-making, managing, and marketing were detailed in this chapter to facilitate the changes in the contemporary world. A marketer should act as a leader for the employees and an inspirer who causes them to buy more products than planned. Different dominant roles like problem-solving, decision-making, motivating, customer services, promoting the products, etc., played by the marketers get themself fulfillment when they reach profit margin or increase customer support over their shop. In addition, a marketer could manage the two eyeball-to-eyeball sides that attract each other through the abovementioned strategies. The strategies meeting the dynamic business of PESTLE (Political, Economical, Social, Technological, Legal, and Environmental) would be simple. With the inclusion of marketers in the packet, the market holds many responsibilities of deciding demand and supply with invisible hands, price determination, etc. Since this chapter concentrates on marketing, which is a continuation of its management, market determination and support are impliedly added. Therefore, in the list of beneficiaries of this chapter, the market was also added. The other recipients are academicians, research scholars, government consultants, and practicing managers.

11. SCOPE FOR FURTHER STUDIES: SUGGESTIONS

In the ever-changing world of digital marketing, consistency and flexibility are essential. Assess and modify the strategy regularly in response to shifts in the market and performance indicators. Establishing real connections with your audience should be your priority if you want to promote engaging, sustainable marketing. Provide material that speaks to the needs and problems of the target audience. By using social media, forums, and other channels for two-way communication, actively reply to remarks and criticism. Use environmentally friendly campaigns or socially conscious projects as examples of sustainable marketing strategies. Encourage engagement and user-generated content to build a sense of community. To keep the customers interested, use interactive content formats like surveys, quizzes, and live sessions. Stress openness and moral business conduct are also important since customers are becoming more and more drawn to companies that share their beliefs. To guarantee long-term success, continuously evaluate and improve the strategy in light of audience insights and shifting market conditions. The current chapter will provide insights to economists, academicians, researchers, market practitioners, and other learned audiences. Future research and study could be considered from the perspectives of different consumer cultures, consumer personality emotions, other behavior dimensions of consumers, and strategies.

REFERENCES

Ahmed, I., Mehta, S. S., Ganeshkumar, C., & Natarajan, V. (2023). Learning from failure to enhance performance: A systematic literature review of retail failure. *Benchmarking, 30*(2), 532–561. doi:10.1108/BIJ-04-2021-0189

Bhasin, H. (2016). *Service marketing mix–7 P's of marketing*. Marketing91. http://www. marketing91. com/service-marketing-mix

Bhasin, H. (2018). *Service Marketing Mix-7P's of marketing*. Access mode: http://www. marketing91. com/service-marketingmix

Bhat, S. (2008). *Financial management: Principles and practice*. Excel Books India.

Blaettler, L. (2021). *Identifying essential data to evaluate and monitor energy performance* [Doctoral dissertation]. North-West University.

Blut, M., Teller, C., & Floh, A. (2018). Testing retail marketing-mix effects on patronage: A meta-analysis. *Journal of Retailing, 94*(2), 113–135. doi:10.1016/j.jretai.2018.03.001

Buchelt, B. (2011). Performance management as modern approach to employees' appraisal in healthcare entities. *Edukacja Ekonomistów i Menedżerów, 22*(4), 75–92. doi:10.5604/01.3001.0009.5540

Christina, S., & Munishamappa, P. (2014). Caveat Emptor To Caveat Venditor In The Process. *International Research Journal of Management Sociology & Humanity*, 430-436.

Dašić, G., Radosavac, A., Knežević, D., & Đervida, R. (2019). Preferences of customers and improvement of production and sales of organic products in Serbia. *Ekonomika Poljoprivrede, 66*(1), 127–142. doi:10.5937/ekoPolj1901127D

Davenport, T., Guha, A., Grewal, D., & Bressgott, T. (2020). How artificial intelligence will change the future of marketing. *Journal of the Academy of Marketing Science, 48*(1), 24–42. doi:10.1007/s11747-019-00696-0

Doole, I., & Lowe, R. (2012). *International marketing strategy* (Vol. 7). Cengage Learning.

Frei, F. X. (2008). The four things a service business must get right. *Harvard Business Review, 86*(4), 70–80. PMID:18435008

French, J., & Gordon, R. (2019). Strategic social marketing: For behavior and social change. *Sage (Atlanta, Ga.).*

Fuxman, L., Mohr, I., Mahmoud, A. B., & Grigoriou, N. (2022). The new 3Ps of sustainability marketing: The case of fashion. *Sustainable Production and Consumption, 31*, 384–396. doi:10.1016/j.spc.2022.03.004

Gerstner, E., Hess, J., & Chu, W. (1993). Demarketing as a differentiation strategy. *Marketing Letters, 4*(1), 49–57. doi:10.1007/BF00994187

Hart, C., Doherty, N., & Ellis-Chadwick, F. (2000). Retailer adoption of the Internet–implications for retail marketing. *European Journal of Marketing, 34*(8), 954–974. doi:10.1108/03090560010331441

Istanti, E., Sanusi, R., & Daengs, G. S. (2020). Impacts of price, Promotion and go food consumer satisfaction in faculty of economic and business students of Bhayangkara University Surabaya. *Ekspektra: Jurnal Bisnis dan Manajemen, 4*(2), 104-120.

Itani, O. S., Badrinarayanan, V., & Rangarajan, D. (2023). The impact of business-to-business salespeople's social media use on value co-creation and cross/up-selling: The role of social capital. *European Journal of Marketing, 57*(3), 683–717. doi:10.1108/EJM-11-2021-0916

Jones, P., Comfort, D., & Hillier, D. (2007). What's in store? Retail marketing and corporate social responsibility. *Marketing Intelligence & Planning, 25*(1), 17–30. doi:10.1108/02634500710722371

Kaufinger, G. G., & Neuenschwander, C. (2020). Retail Apocalypse? Maybe blame accounting. Investigating inventory valuation as a determinant of retail firm failure. *American Journal of Business, 35*(2), 83–101. doi:10.1108/AJB-07-2019-0050

Kaur, S. (2016). Social media marketing. *Asian Journal of Multidimensional Research, 5*(4), 6–12.

Khan, M. T. (2014). The concept of 'marketing mix' and its elements. *International Journal of Information, Business and Management, 6*(2), 95–107.

Li, S., Leszczyc, P. T. P., & Qiu, C. (2023). International retailer performance: Disentangling the interplay between rule of law and culture. *Journal of Retailing, 99*(2), 193–209. doi:10.1016/j.jretai.2023.01.001

Lim, W. M. (2023). Transformative marketing in the new normal: A novel practice-scholarly integrative review of business-to-business marketing mix challenges, opportunities, and solutions. *Journal of Business Research, 160*, 113638. doi:10.1016/j.jbusres.2022.113638

Lim, W. M., O'Connor, P., Nair, S., Soleimani, S., & Rasul, T. (2023). A foundational theory of ethical decision-making: The case of marketing professionals. *Journal of Business Research, 158*, 113579. doi:10.1016/j.jbusres.2022.113579

Melović, B., Jocović, M., Dabić, M., Vulić, T. B., & Dudic, B. (2020). The impact of digital transformation and digital marketing on brand promotion, positioning, and electronic business in Montenegro. *Technology in Society, 63*, 101425. doi:10.1016/j.techsoc.2020.101425

Mingione, M., & Leoni, L. (2020). Blurring B2C and B2B boundaries: Corporate brand value co-creation in B2B2C markets. *Journal of Marketing Management, 36*(1-2), 72–99. doi:10.1080/0267257X.2019.1694566

Morschett, D., Swoboda, B., & Schramm-Klein, H. (2006). Competitive strategies in retailing—An investigation of the applicability of Porter's framework for food retailers. *Journal of Retailing and Consumer Services, 13*(4), 275–287. doi:10.1016/j.jretconser.2005.08.016

Mulhern, F. J. (1997). Retail marketing: From distribution to integration. *International Journal of Research in Marketing, 14*(2), 103–124. doi:10.1016/S0167-8116(96)00031-6

Naim, A., Alqahtani, H., Muniasamy, A., Bilfaqih, S. M., Mahveen, R., & Mahjabeen, R. (2023). Applications of Information Systems and Data Security in Marketing Management. In Fraud Prevention, Confidentiality, and Data Security for Modern Businesses (pp. 57-83). IGI Global. doi:10.4018/978-1-6684-6581-3.ch003

Niar, H. (2022). Examining Linkage of Product Selling Prices on Profitability. *Golden Ratio of Marketing and Applied Psychology of Business, 2*(1), 12–25. doi:10.52970/grmapb.v2i1.82

O'Keeffe, A., Ozuem, W., & Lancaster, G. (2016). Leadership marketing: An exploratory study. *Journal of Strategic Marketing, 24*(5), 418–443. doi:10.1080/0965254X.2014.1001867

Olayinka, A. A. (2022). Financial statement analysis as a tool for investment decisions and assessment of companies' performance. *International Journal of Financial, Accounting, and Management, 4*(1), 49–66. doi:10.35912/ijfam.v4i1.852

Prabowo, H., Hamsal, M., & Simatupang, B. (2019, August). E-Marketing and Service Quality on Repurchase Intention of Online Transportation. In *2019 International Conference on Information Management and Technology (ICIMTech)* (Vol. 1, pp. 324-329). IEEE.

Quinones, M., Gomez-Suarez, M., Cruz-Roche, I., & Díaz-Martín, A. M. (2023). Technology: A strategic imperative for successful retailers. *International Journal of Retail & Distribution Management, 51*(4), 546–566. doi:10.1108/IJRDM-03-2022-0088

Saghiri, S., Wilding, R., Mena, C., & Bourlakis, M. (2017). Toward a three-dimensional framework for omni-channel. *Journal of Business Research, 77*, 53–67. doi:10.1016/j.jbusres.2017.03.025

Sammut-Bonnici, T., & Galea, D. (2014). *SWOT analysis*. Academic Press.

Sen, R., Yu, H. F., & Dhillon, I. S. (2019). Think globally, act locally: A deep neural network approach to high-dimensional time series forecasting. *Advances in Neural Information Processing Systems, 32*.

Sergiu Iscu. (2022). *Retail industry outlook - 2023, Pimics*. Available at: https://www.pimics.com/en/Blog/Retail-industry-outlook-2023

Shah, S. S. A., & Khan, Z. (2020). Corporate social responsibility: A pathway to sustainable competitive advantage? *International Journal of Bank Marketing*, *38*(1), 159–174. doi:10.1108/IJBM-01-2019-0037

Shaw, M. J., Subramaniam, C., Tan, G. W., & Welge, M. E. (2001). Knowledge management and data mining for marketing. *Decision Support Systems*, *31*(1), 127–137. doi:10.1016/S0167-9236(00)00123-8

Shetty, G., Nougarahiya, S., Mandloi, D., & Sarsodia, T. (2020). COVID-19 and global commerce: An analysis of FMCG, and retail industries of tomorrow. *International Journal of Current Research and Review*, *12*(17), 23–31. doi:10.31782/IJCRR.2020.121715

Slijepčević, M., & Radojević, I. (2018). *Current trends in digital marketing communication*. Faculty of Management, Belgrade Metropolitan University.

Stolle, M. (2019). Labeling and packaging: The first taste is almost always with the eye! *Wine & Viticulture Journal*, *34*(2), 59–60.

Sun, H., & Gilbert, S. M. (2019). Retail price competition with product fit uncertainty and assortment selection. *Production and Operations Management*, *28*(7), 1658–1673. doi:10.1111/poms.13005

THIS, T. M. I. L. (2020). *Strategic Marketing Planning. Hashtags and Headlines: Marketing for School Leaders*. Academic Press.

Vaja, M. B. R. (2015). Retail management. *International Journal of Research and Analytics Reviews*, *2*(1), 22–28.

Wang, Z., Ye, C., Liu, X., Ma, R., Sun, Z., & Ruan, J. (2023). Optimal retail sales strategies for old and new products in monopoly and horizontal competition scenarios. *Journal of Retailing and Consumer Services*, *71*, 103218. doi:10.1016/j.jretconser.2022.103218

Watson, G. F. IV, Worm, S., Palmatier, R. W., & Ganesan, S. (2015). The evolution of marketing channels: Trends and research directions. *Journal of Retailing*, *91*(4), 546–568. doi:10.1016/j.jretai.2015.04.002

Webb, K. L. (2002). Managing channels of distribution in the age of electronic commerce. *Industrial Marketing Management*, *31*(2), 95–102. doi:10.1016/S0019-8501(01)00181-X

Wilson, R. M. (2010). *Strategic marketing planning*. Routledge. doi:10.4324/9780080912127

Wind, J., & Mahajan, V. (2002). Digital marketing. Symphonya. *Emerging Issues in Management*, (1), 43–54.

Wu, Z., Qian, X., Huang, M., Ching, W. K., Wang, X., & Gu, J. (2023). Recycling channel choice in closed-loop supply chains considering retailer competitive preference. *Enterprise Information Systems*, *17*(2), 1923065. doi:10.1080/17517575.2021.1923065

Xiao, Y., Zhu, Y., He, W., & Huang, M. (2023). Influence prediction model for marketing campaigns on e-commerce platforms. *Expert Systems with Applications*, *211*, 118575. doi:10.1016/j.eswa.2022.118575

Zhu, G., & Gao, X. (2019). Precision retail marketing strategy based on digital marketing model. *Science Journal of Business and Management*, *7*(1), 33–37. doi:10.11648/j.sjbm.20190701.15

Chapter 14
Acceptance of Digital Technologies:
Empirical Evidence From Sport Marketing (or Industry)

Alireza NazemiBidgoli
University of Tehran, Iran

Ehsan Mohamadi Turkmani
University of Tehran, Iran

Hamid Reza Irani
ⓘ https://orcid.org/0000-0003-4103-9975
University of Tehran, Iran

ABSTRACT

This study investigated the intention to use wearable sports technologies using a social-psychological approach, namely technophobia. This study was applied and correlational. The statistical population of this study included all athletes who had been insured in the current year. A non-probability sampling method was used, and 394 people were selected as the study sample using the Morgan table. The results of the study showed that expected performance and social influence have a positive and direct effect on the attitude to use. No significant negative effect of technophobia was found for the relationship between expected effort and expected performance on the attitude to use. Based on the results, it is suggested to launch different campaigns with rich content to highlight the capabilities of these technologies and the power of these devices in increasing the effectiveness of sports activities and motivating people to lead a healthier life.

DOI: 10.4018/979-8-3693-1339-8.ch014

INTRODUCTION

Acceptance is a perceptual phenomenon involving the evaluation of novel experiences and the formation of a final judgment regarding their advantages and disadvantages. Acceptance outcomes are the result of attitudes or actions. The emergence of acceptance is contingent on the interaction of three factors: subjective acceptance, objective acceptance, and the surrounding environment. Acceptance is an unpredictable concept because altered perceptions or general circumstances can result in varying degrees of acceptance. The decision to embrace or reject a particular technology is influenced by multiple factors (Safi et al., 2018). The Vodafone Institute's Tech Divide Report on the adoption of new technologies reveals that there are significant regional differences in the acceptance and popularity of technological innovations. While well over 80% of those surveyed in countries such as China and Japan are optimistic about digitalization and new technologies, only 54% of those surveyed in the United States, the birthplace of the digital revolution, are optimistic. In European nations such as Germany and the United Kingdom, even less than half of those polled hold positive views on the topic (merckgroup, 2023).

One of the technologies and innovations of the digital age is the Internet of Things, which aims to create a dynamic network around the world that can sense, collect, share, and exchange information anytime and anywhere. With the rapid development of the Internet of Things (Al-Fuqaha et al., 2015; Haight et al., 2016) and cloud computing in the last few decades, the field of sports has also been affected and has seen revolutionary changes (Luo et al., 2021). This technology has accelerated the ability to assess fitness and monitor exercise (Chaabene et al., 2018) understand athletes' conditions and performance adaptations over time (Weston, 2018) and improve safety (Wilkerson et al., 2018) as well as athletes' performance and progress in sports (Passos et al., 2021). Sports wearables are becoming a fundamental part of IoT technology, with research showing that they account for 50% of wearable technology unit sales worldwide (Insight, 2016). The sports industry is a vast and diverse sector, encompassing a wide range of companies, organizations, and individuals. It includes manufacturers of sports equipment and apparel, sports event organizers, sports media entities, and other stakeholders involved in sports. As of 2022, the global sports market is estimated to be valued at 624billion, and it is projected to reach 940 billion by the year 2027 (Research, 2023). However, it should be noted that the use of sports wearables is still in its early stages, and more than 30% of users abandon them after a period of time (Moore, 2016). This usage pattern may lead to companies not being able to obtain enough data from users to improve their products (Ledger,). On the other hand, users may not be able to benefit from the results of exercises and health if these devices are not used for a long time. Therefore, having a better understanding of the acceptance and continuous use of sports wearables can have significant effects on management methods and even the quality of life of athletes (Lee et al., 2016). Acceptance of technology by users is one of the important factors of success that should be taken into account. It should be considered that this does not happen instantaneously, but is a process that develops over time. In case of continuous use and addiction, successful acceptance brings benefits (Mollahosseini & Foroozanfar, 2019).

While these technologies bring many benefits, they can also create barriers to challenge and continued acceptance. Concerns about privacy and security issues are particularly important in this context and highlight the potential negative aspects of these devices (De Cremer et al., 2017). According to some psychologists, new technologies should not be solely managed by engineers and marketers, as these products can have significant psychological effects on the buyer's mind (Clegg, 1994). The relationship between technology, humans, and society can be categorized into two extremes: technophilia and technophobia. Technophilia refers to the attraction towards technology, while technophobia refers to the fear of technology (Khasawneh, 2018). Technophobia is currently being studied as a research field, and although its impact on sports wearables has not yet been investigated in Iran, it is crucial to evaluate people's perceptions and concerns. These concerns reflect people's fear of advanced technology and complex devices, which can prevent them from using or purchasing related technology and lead to unfavorable outcomes for businesses (Milani & Franklin, 2017). Due to the complexities of human behavior and limitations of researchers, no single theory or framework can examine all or several existing factors for predicting human behavior in the decision-making process for innovation adoption. Therefore, many efforts have been made to combine and integrate diverse models and theories. The integrated model of technology acceptance and application is a result of integrating the main elements of eight famous models, including rational action theory, technology acceptance, motivational theory, theory of planned behavior, combined model of technology acceptance and planned behavior, computer exploitation model, innovation diffusion theory, and theory of social cognition (Venkatesh et al., 2003). This model, due to its simple structure, has been able to account for 70% of the variations in willingness to use and 50% of the variations in behavior related to technology usage (Guo, 2022). This model essentially aims to comprehend individuals' rationales and justifications for accepting or rejecting technology, and predicts their behavior regarding the desire to use technology (Azami, 2020).

According to the UTAUT model, there are four primary factors that directly determine technology acceptance and willingness: expected performance, expected effort, social influence, and facilitating conditions. Expected performance pertains to the extent to which an individual believes that using a particular system will enhance their job performance. Expected effort is defined as the level of ease of use of the system. Social influence refers to the degree to which significant others, friends, and family believe that the use of the system is necessary for the individual. Finally, facilitating conditions refer to the degree of belief associated with the fact that the individual will receive support or assistance from an organizational and technical infrastructure when using the system . There have been numerous studies investigating the impact of expected performance, expected effort, social influence, and facilitating conditions on attitude, behavioral intention, and technology use. Among these factors, expected performance is widely regarded as the most influential predictor of attitude and behavioral intention (Venkatesh et al., 2003). This variable has been extensively studied across various fields, including artificial intelligence devices (Kim & Shin, 2015), augmented reality smart cameras (Kalantari & Rauschnabel, 2018), and smart clothing (Hwang et al., 2016). The research consistently demonstrates the significant impact of this variable on desired outcomes, as well as its influence on attitudes towards wearable technologies and the intention to use them.

However, it should be noted that some recent studies suggest that the perceived effort of others is not a hindrance to the adoption of technology by today's users, as they already have sufficient experience with technology (Wang et al., 2014). However, the use of sports wearables is a bit more complex. Other studies have investigated the direct effects of social influence and facilitating conditions on attitudes and willingness to use technology (Aksoy et al., 2020; Tan et al., 2014). These studies demonstrate that understanding the factors that affect attitudes and intentions to use wearable technology can be crucial. Attitude is considered a determinant of behavioral intention, which is influenced by people's beliefs (Venkatesh et al., 2003). This situation can be even more important for wearable devices equipped with IoT technology in sports, as it is one of the ways to observe people's behavior that has not yet been translated into action. Therefore, examining attitudes towards wearable technology can be a valuable approach (Holbrook et al., 2005). In a study titled "Wearable Fitness Technology: A Structural Investigation of Acceptance and Perceived Fitness Outcomes," researchers found that individuals who have a positive attitude towards wearable fitness devices are more likely to use the technology (Lunney et al., 2016). In another study, researchers investigated the relationship between the acceptance of multi-functional health and fitness features of wearable wristbands and their actual use. The results of this study showed that when users learned to use the fitness functions and found them useful for physical activity without causing any problems, they were more inclined to use those functions that provide more health benefits in the digital interactive environment (Hahm et al., 2023). Most of the constructs examined in research have shown positive effects on attitude and propensity to use wearable fitness devices. However, since negative views can also be influential, significant progress can be made in this area by studying and examining them more closely. To address this, the technophobia model has been added to the research model. This psychologically-based construct may not be related to internal system factors, such as facilitating conditions, or external social and environmental factors, such as social influence (Aksoy et al., 2020). We examined the moderating effects of technophobia on the relationship between expected performance and expected effort on attitude, using a psychological approach to analyze individuals' expectations. Our focus was on how a socio-psychological theory influences individuals' attitudes, particularly in the presence of negative structures. In a separate study, researchers investigated the moderating effect of technophobia in the field of online banking in Pakistan. They found that technophobia moderated the relationship between perceived credit, perceived usefulness, social risk, and customer acceptance (Agha & Saeed, 2015). Furthermore, a study on people's intention to use sports wearables with the moderating role of technophobia found that technophobia did not have a significant effect on the relationship between expected effort and attitude (Aksoy et al., 2020). Based on the aforementioned cases, the following hypotheses are proposed:

H1: Facilitating conditions significantly affect the attitude towards the use of IoT technology in sports.
H2: Social influence significantly affects the attitude towards the use of IoT technology in sports.
H3: Expected effort significantly affects the attitude towards the use of IoT technology in sports.
H4: Expected performance significantly affects the attitude towards the use of IoT technology in sports.
H5: Technophobia has a negative and significant effect on both expected effort and attitude towards the use of IoT technology in sports.
H6: Technophobia has a negative and significant effect on both expected performance and attitude towards the use of IoT technology in sports.
H7: Attitude significantly affects the willingness to use IoT technology in sports.

Figure 1. Research model

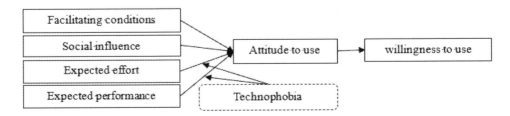

METHOD

The purpose of this study was to examine the impact of technophobia on the willingness to use sports wearable technologies, making it an applied-descriptive research. The statistical population consisted of all athletes who obtained sports insurance this year, and a non-probability sampling method was utilized to select 394 participants based on Morgan's table. To test the research model, digital forms were employed to create an online questionnaire, and the questionnaire questions were adapted and refined based on previous literature and the study's context (Aksoy et al., 2020; Kim & Shin, 2015; Shin & Lee, 2014; Tan et al., 2014). The questionnaire consisted of a total of 39 questions, covering seven variables: facilitating conditions (four questions), social influence (five questions), expected effort (four questions), attitude (four questions), willingness to use (four questions), and technophobia (thirteen questions). The questionnaire utilized a five-point Likert scale ranging from "completely disagree" (1) to "completely agree" (5), and its reliability was evaluated using Cronbach's alpha. To assess face validity, the questionnaire was reviewed by 10 sports management professors. Structural equation modeling (SEM) was employed to analyze the data and test the research hypotheses, using SmartPLS version 3 and SPSS software version 22.

RESEARCH FINDINGS

In Table 1, the demographic status of the research samples is reported.

Table 1. Description of the demographic characteristics of the research samples

Cumulative Frequency Percentage	Relative Abundance Percentage	Abundance	Demographic Variables of the Research	
39/1	39/1	154	Men	Gender
100	60/9	240	Women	
46/4	46/4	183	for up to 20 years	Age
70/8	24/4	96	21 to 30 years	
89/1	18/3	72	31 to 40 years	
97/0	7/9	31	41 to 50 years	
100	3/0	12	Over 51 years old	

The results of the demographic description of this study showed that most of the research participants were female (240 people) and under the age of 20 (183 people). Cronbach's alpha index and composite reliability were used to assess the internal consistency of the questionnaire constructs, and the extracted mean variance index was used to assess convergent validity. According to the researchers, the measurement model is considered homogeneous if the absolute values of the factor loadings of the observable variables are at least 0.7, although some researchers suggest that factor loadings of at least 0.4 are sufficient and that variables with factor loadings below 0.4 should be removed. The results in Table 2 show that the variables have sufficient usefulness.

Table 2. factor loading, reliability coefficients, convergent validity, and Cronbach's alpha of research variables

Factor Load	Alpha ≥ 0.7	CR ≥ 0.7	AVE ≥ 0.5	Variable
0.781				
0.754				
0.825	0.817	0.879	0.645	Expected Effort
0.848				
0.781				
0.812				
0.843	0.845	0.896	0.683	willingness to use
0.861				
0.787				
0.634				
0.593				
0.706				
0.674				
0.681				
0.786				
0.764				
0.796	0.940	0.945	0.555	Technophobia
0.793				
0.844				
0.773				
0.781				
0.803				
0.753				
0.825				
0.850	0.821	0.879	0.645	Facilitating conditions
0.742				
0.792				
0.778				
0.811	0.833	0.888	0.666	Expected performance
0.877				
0.796				
0.667				
0.786				
0.500	0.723	0.816	0.475	Social influence
0.724				
0.732				

continues on following page

Table 2. Continued

Factor Load	Alpha ≥ 0.7	CR ≥ 0.7	AVE ≥ 0.5	Variable
0.835				
0.762	0.821	0.882	0.651	Attitude to use
0.848				
0.780				

To also check divergent validity, the Fornell and Larcker indices were extracted. Fornell and Larcker state that divergent validity is at an acceptable level when the average variance extracted (AVE) for each construct is greater than the shared variance between that construct and other constructs in the model. Based on the results in Table 3, the divergent validity of the research variables is also confirmed.

Table 3. Divergent validity of research variables

(7)	(6)	(5)	(4)	(3)	(2)	(1)	Variable
-	-	-	-	-	-	0.803	(1) Expected effort
-	-	-	-	-	0.826	0.524	(2) Willingness to use
-	-	-	-	0.745	-0.168	-0.093	(3) Technophobia
-	-	-	0.803	0.125	0.345	0.649	(4) Facilitating conditions
-	-	0.816	0.380	-0.155	0.565	0.567	(5) Expected performance
-	0.689	0.544	0.371	-0.084	0.447	0.437	(6) Social influence
0.807	0.436	0.722	0.258	-0.225	0.527	0.477	(7) Attitude to use

The basic evaluation metric for endogenous variables is the coefficient of determination (R-squared), with values of 0.25, 0.5, and 0.75 indicating small, medium, and large effect sizes, respectively. The R-squared values for the variables of willingness to use and attitude to use are 0.277 and 0.566, respectively, indicating a good fit for the structural model. The structural model quality index also assesses the model's ability to make predictive insights. Q2 values greater than zero indicate that the model has predictive ability. The Q2 values obtained for the variables of willingness to use and attitude to use in this study are 0.174 and 0.336, respectively, indicating that the structural model has good predictive ability.

Table 5 shows the results of path coefficient analysis and significance level of this research.

Table 4. Evaluation indices of the structural model

R Square	Q2	Variable
0.277	0.174	Willingness to use
0.566	0.336	Attitude to use

Table 5. Evaluation indices of the structural model

Direction	Path Coefficient	Standard Deviation	T Level	Significance Level	Result
Expected effort - attitude to use	0.106	0.056	1.885	0.059	Rejection
Expected effort - Technophobia - Attitude to use	-0.046	0.057	0.799	0.424	Rejection
Expected Performance - Technophobia - Attitude to Use	-0.109	0.064	1.690	0.091	Rejection
Facilitating conditions of - attitude to use	-0.022	0.049	1.440	0.660	Rejection
Expected performance - Attitude to use	0.606	0.048	12.680	0.000	confirmation
Social influence of - attitude to use	0.043	0.045	0.937	0.349	confirmation
Attitude to use - willingness to use	0.527	0.039	13.351	0.000	confirmation

Based on the results presented in Table 5, it can be concluded that the expected effort variable does not have a significant level of influence on attitude towards use (p=0.059). Additionally, the results indicate that technophobia does not moderate the relationship between expected effort and expected performance variables (p=0.424, p=0.091). Furthermore, the relationship between facilitating conditions and attitude towards the use of IoT technology in sports does not reach an acceptable level of significance (p=0.660). The expected performance variable has a significant impact on attitude towards the use of IoT technology in sports (p=0.00, β=0.606). The study also confirms the positive and direct effect of social influence on attitude towards the use of IoT technology in sports (p=0.349, β=0.043). Furthermore, the study confirms the positive and direct effect of attitude towards the use of IoT technology in sports on willingness to use it (p=0.000, β=0.527).

DISCUSSION

The sports industry is a major and dynamic sector that exerts significant social and economic influence in today's fiercely competitive world. Marketing strategies can profoundly impact the performance of Internet of Things (IoT) technology in sports. Hence, it is crucial to possess knowledge and awareness of how consumers respond to the product, while also providing solutions and features that differentiate the performance of goods and services. This understanding is both apparent and essential. This approach is essential to ensure the success of IoT technology in sports. This research investigates the desire to use sports wearable technologies, which represents a rapidly growing market. Understanding people's attitudes towards these new generation consumer products is critical in terms of consumer behavior, as attitudes can predict actual behavior. Therefore, gaining insights into people's attitudes towards sports wearable technologies can be of significant importance (Venkatesh et al., 2003). The results of this research indicate that attitude has a significant impact on the willingness to use sports wearable technologies. The obtained path coefficient was 0.527, which means that if an athlete's attitude towards using a unit increases, their willingness to use sports wearable technologies increases by 0.527 units. Furthermore, a review of the research literature revealed that this result is consistent with the findings of other studies conducted by scientists in the field (Hahm et al., 2023; Lunney et al., 2016). The findings of this study provide evidence for the positive impact of expected performance and social influence on attitudes towards sports wearables. The expected performance structure has been identified as the most influential predictor of the desire to use sports wearable technologies (Hwang et al., 2016; Kalantari & Rauschnabel, 2018; Venkatesh et al., 2003). The results of this research also demonstrate that a one-unit change in this variable can lead to a 0.606 unit change in the attitude towards using sports wearable technologies. People develop a positive attitude towards wearable sports equipment when they perceive it to be useful, stable, and efficient. Therefore, if an innovation is deemed to have higher performance from the athletes' perspective, it is more likely to be adopted. Venkatesh (Venkatesh et al., 2003) also suggested that expected performance is the extent to which an individual believes that the innovation will assist them in achieving their desired outcome. Therefore, highlighting the performance benefits of these devices for athletes can be crucial in improving their attitude towards using them. In addition, the research results indicate that the variable of social influence has an impact on the attitude towards and desire to use this technology, which is consistent with findings from other studies (Aksoy et al., 2020; Tan et al., 2014). The authors of the article on understanding the continuous intentions of users to use smart sports products investigated the prominent factors based on the theory of planned behavior. The results of this research indicate that the three main factors - attitude, social influence, and perceived behavioral control - significantly influence the continuous intentions of users (Aksoy et al., 2020). The significant and positive impact of social influence on attitudes towards the use of wearable technologies suggests that individuals with high social influence in sports, such as famous athletes and coaches, can be utilized to promote new technologies and increase athletes' willingness to use them.

The results of this research indicate that facilitating conditions do not reach an acceptable level of significance (p=0.660). However, in a study that employed a framework based on the integrated theory of acceptance and use of technology in the field of sports wearables, it was found that facilitating conditions do have an impact on attitudes towards sports wearables, as well as attitudes towards the intention to use them (Aksoy et al., 2020). Furthermore, the findings of an experimental study on the factors influencing consumers' initial trust in the wearable business indicate that all five proposed factors - concern about privacy, willingness to trust, expected performance, facilitating conditions, and hedonic motivation - have significant effects on attitudes towards and acceptance of technology in the wearable business (Gu et al., 2016). The results of this research differ from previous studies. Facilitating conditions are typically defined as an individual's belief in receiving help or support from an organizational infrastructure while using a system. In the context of new technologies, facilitating conditions may include training and support provision (Venkatesh et al., 2003). Satisfaction with support teams and receiving appropriate and sufficient training can be important factors in motivating individuals to use sports wearable technologies. The research results also indicated that the expected effort did not have a significant effect on the attitude towards technology use (p=0.059). Previous studies in the field of new technology acceptance, including (Aksoy et al., 2020; Guo, 2022; Lunney et al., 2016), have examined the expected effort variable and found positive and significant relationships between expected effort and attitude and willingness to use technology, which is not consistent with the results of this study. Expected effort refers to the ease of using the system, which Venkatesh introduced as the ease of using innovation and technology (Venkatesh et al., 2003).

However, recent studies suggest that expected effort is not a barrier to technology adoption for today's users (Wang et al., 2014) because they already have sufficient experience with technology. The research results showed that the expected effort had no significant effect on the attitude towards technology use (p=0.059). Previous studies in the field of new technology acceptance have investigated the expected effort variable, and all of these studies have observed positive and significant relationships between expected effort and attitude and willingness to use technology, which is not consistent with the results of the present study (Guo, 2022; Lunney et al., 2016). Expected effort refers to the ease of use of a system, which Venkatesh introduced as the ease of using innovation and technology (Venkatesh et al., 2003). However, some recent studies suggest that expected effort is not a significant barrier to technology adoption for today's users (Wang et al., 2014), as they already have sufficient experience with technology. The rapid expansion of the internet on a global scale has brought about fundamental changes across generations. It's worth noting that 46.4% of the participants in this research were under 20 years old. This generation is known as 'Internet natives' as they are the first to have easy access to internet technology. They have a unique set of characteristics when it comes to using technology, and it's a part of their lifestyle (Song et al., 2018). Therefore, using and learning from technology may come naturally to them. On the other hand, the results of this research did not find any significant negative effect of technophobia on the relationship between expected effort and expected performance towards attitude to use ($p=0.424$ and $p=0.091$). In a study titled 'People's Intention to Use Sports Wearables with the Moderating Role of Technophobia' (Aksoy et al., 2020), it was found that technophobia does not moderate the effect of expected effort on attitude, which is consistent with the results of this research. However, technophobia does moderate the relationship between expected performance and attitude, which is not consistent with the results of this research. Although expected performance has a positive, direct, and significant effect on attitude to use, the results indicate that technophobia cannot moderate this relationship. Athletes may need to overcome their fear of technology to improve their productivity and performance.

Sports marketers can highlight the benefits of sports wearables and how easy they are to use and integrate into everyday life. They can emphasize the devices' ability to enhance the effectiveness of sports activities and motivate people towards a healthier lifestyle. Additionally, emphasizing that these products are socially acceptable can also yield positive results. To bring attention to these issues, a range of digital campaigns with rich content can be created to serve as educational tools for these complex products. These campaigns can emphasize how intelligent, accelerating, interactive, and supportive sports wearables can be. In addition to highlighting the strengths and benefits of these devices, negative perceptions and fears can be challenged and overcome to encourage people to use them. Experience rooms can be created in stores where people can try out these products in a real-life setting. These rooms provide athletes with the opportunity to closely examine and interact with the products. Moreover, they can enhance the positive impact of social influence by providing an environment where people can interact with others and experience the products with their friends and family. Future research should consider examining the differences in intentions and attitudes between different generations, as their thoughts and approaches can vary significantly. Additionally, while the current study investigated technophobia as a negative and moderating construct, exploring technophilia could reveal the effects of a powerful positive construct towards wearable technologies and determine whether these effects are significant. Furthermore, other constructs could be included in this model to explore the potential negative aspects of such markets.

REFERENCES

Agha, S., & Saeed, M. (2015). Factors influencing customer acceptance of online banking in Pakistan and the moderating effect of technophobia. *Technology, 12*(1).

Aksoy, N. C., Alan, A. K., Kabadayi, E. T., & Aksoy, A. (2020). Individuals' intention to use sports wearables: The moderating role of technophobia. *International Journal of Sports Marketing & Sponsorship*, *21*(2), 225–245. doi:10.1108/IJSMS-08-2019-0083

Al-Fuqaha, A., Guizani, M., Mohammadi, M., Aledhari, M., & Ayyash, M. (2015). Internet of things: A survey on enabling technologies, protocols, and applications. *IEEE Communications Surveys and Tutorials*, *17*(4), 2347–2376. doi:10.1109/COMST.2015.2444095

Azami, H. (2020). Application of the integrated model of acceptance and use of technology to accept innovations among the farmers of Delfan city. *Agricultural Education Management Research, 12*(52), 157-76.

Chaabene, H., Negra, Y., Bouguezzi, R., Capranica, L., Franchini, E., Prieske, O., Hbacha, H., & Granacher, U. (2018). Tests for the assessment of sport-specific performance in Olympic combat sports: A systematic review with practical recommendations. *Frontiers in Physiology*, *9*, 386. doi:10.3389/fphys.2018.00386 PMID:29692739

Clegg, C. (1994). Psychology and information technology: The study of cognition in organizations. *British Journal of Psychology*, *85*(4), 449–477. doi:10.1111/j.2044-8295.1994.tb02535.x

De Cremer, D., Nguyen, B., & Simkin, L. (2017). The integrity challenge of the Internet-of-Things (IoT): On understanding its dark side. *Journal of Marketing Management*, *33*(1-2), 145–158. doi:10.1080/0267257X.2016.1247517

Gu, Z., Wei, J., & Xu, F. (2016). An empirical study on factors influencing consumers' initial trust in wearable commerce. *Journal of Computer Information Systems*, *56*(1), 79–85. doi:10.1080/08874417.2015.11645804

Guo, J. (2022). Influencing Factors of College Students' Use of Sports Apps in Mandatory Situations: Based on UTAUT and SDT. *BioMed Research International*.

Hahm, J., Choi, H., Matsuoka, H., Kim, J., & Byon, K. K. (2023). Understanding the relationship between acceptance of multifunctional health and fitness features of wrist-worn wearables and actual usage. *International Journal of Sports Marketing & Sponsorship*, *24*(2), 333–358. doi:10.1108/IJSMS-08-2022-0163

Haight, R., Haensch, W., & Friedman, D. (2016). Solar-powering the Internet of Things. *Science*, *353*(6295), 124–125. doi:10.1126/science.aag0476 PMID:27387939

Holbrook, A. L., Berent, M. K., Krosnick, J. A., Visser, P. S., & Boninger, D. S. (2005). Attitude importance and the accumulation of attitude-relevant knowledge in memory. *Journal of Personality and Social Psychology*, *88*(5), 749–769. doi:10.1037/0022-3514.88.5.749 PMID:15898873

Hwang, C., Chung, T.-L., & Sanders, E. A. (2016). Attitudes and purchase intentions for smart clothing: Examining US consumers' functional, expressive, and aesthetic needs for solar-powered clothing. *Clothing & Textiles Research Journal*, *34*(3), 207–222. doi:10.1177/0887302X16646447

Insight, C. (2016). *Wearables momentum continues*. Online verfügbar unter: http://www.ccsinsight.com/press/company-news/2516-wearables-momentum-continues

Kalantari, M., & Rauschnabel, P. (2018). *Exploring the early adopters of augmented reality smart glasses: The case of Microsoft HoloLens. Augmented reality and virtual reality.* Springer.

Khasawneh, O. Y. (2018). Technophobia: Examining its hidden factors and defining it. *Technology in Society, 54*(1), 93–100. doi:10.1016/j.techsoc.2018.03.008

Kim, K. J., & Shin, D.-H. (2015). An acceptance model for smart watches: Implications for the adoption of future wearable technology. *Internet Research, 25*(4), 527–541. doi:10.1108/IntR-05-2014-0126

Ledger, D. (2014). A look at the uncertain future of smart wearable devices, and five industry developments that will be necessary for meaningful mass market adoption and sustained engagement. *Inside Wearables-Part.*, 2.

Lee, J., Kim, D., Ryoo, H.-Y., & Shin, B.-S. (2016). Sustainable wearables: Wearable technology for enhancing the quality of human life. *Sustainability (Basel), 8*(5), 466. doi:10.3390/su8050466

Lunney, A., Cunningham, N. R., & Eastin, M. S. (2016). Wearable fitness technology: A structural investigation into acceptance and perceived fitness outcomes. *Computers in Human Behavior, 65*, 114–120. doi:10.1016/j.chb.2016.08.007

Luo, J., Gao, W., & Wang, Z. L. (2021). The triboelectric nanogenerator as an innovative technology toward intelligent sports. *Advanced Materials, 33*(17), 2004178. doi:10.1002/adma.202004178 PMID:33759259

merckgroup. (2023). https://www.merckgroup.com/en/the-future-transformation/acceptance-digital-technologies-worldwide-literacy-key.html

Milani, R. V., & Franklin, N. C. (2017). The role of technology in healthy living medicine. *Progress in Cardiovascular Diseases, 59*(5), 487–491. doi:10.1016/j.pcad.2017.02.001 PMID:28189614

Mollahosseini, A., & Foroozanfar, M.H. (2019). Development and localization of technology acceptance model (TAM) in small and medium-sized enterprises (SMEs). *Quarterly Journal of Industrial Technology Development, 16*(34), 39-48.

Moore, S. (2016). *Gartner survey shows wearable devices need to be more useful.* Gartner. Available online at: https://www. gartner. com/en/newsroom/press

Passos, J., Lopes, S. I., Clemente, F. M., Moreira, P. M., Rico-González, M., Bezerra, P., & Rodrigues, L. P. (2021). Wearables and Internet of Things (IoT) technologies for fitness assessment: A systematic review. *Sensors (Basel), 21*(16), 5418. doi:10.3390/s21165418 PMID:34450860

Research AM. (2023). *Global Sports Equipment and Apparel Market Size, Share & Trends Analysis Report by Product (Athletic Shoes, Apparel, Equipment), by Geography (North America, Europe, Asia Pacific, Middle East & Africa, South America), and Segment Forecasts, 2022-2031.* Academic Press.

Safi, S., Thiessen, T., & Schmailzl, K. J. (2018). Acceptance and resistance of new digital technologies in medicine: Qualitative study. *JMIR Research Protocols, 7*(12), e11072. doi:10.2196/11072 PMID:30514693

Shin, S., & Lee, W. (2014). The effects of technology readiness and technology acceptance on NFC mobile payment services in Korea. *Journal of Applied Business Research, 30*(6), 1615–1626. doi:10.19030/jabr.v30i6.8873

Song, J., Kim, J., & Cho, K. (2018). Understanding users' continuance intentions to use smart-connected sports products. *Sport Management Review*, *21*(5), 477–490. doi:10.1016/j.smr.2017.10.004

Tan, G. W.-H., Ooi, K.-B., Chong, S.-C., & Hew, T.-S. (2014). NFC mobile credit card: The next frontier of mobile payment? *Telematics and Informatics*, *31*(2), 292–307. doi:10.1016/j.tele.2013.06.002

Venkatesh, V., Morris, M. G., Davis, G. B., & Davis, F. D. (2003). User acceptance of information technology: Toward a unified view. *Management Information Systems Quarterly*, *27*(3), 425–478. doi:10.2307/30036540

Wang, T., Jung, C.-H., Kang, M.-H., & Chung, Y.-S. (2014). Exploring determinants of adoption intentions towards Enterprise 2.0 applications: An empirical study. *Behaviour & Information Technology*, *33*(10), 1048–1064. doi:10.1080/0144929X.2013.781221

Weston, M. (2018). Training load monitoring in elite English soccer: A comparison of practices and perceptions between coaches and practitioners. *Science & Medicine in Football*, *2*(3), 216–224. doi:10.1080/24733938.2018.1427883

Wilkerson, G. B., Gupta, A., & Colston, M. A. (2018). Mitigating sports injury risks using internet of things and analytics approaches. *Risk Analysis*, *38*(7), 1348–1360. doi:10.1111/risa.12984 PMID:29529346

Compilation of References

Abdulla, A., & Hussain, O. B. (2023). Use of IoT in Evaluating Content Digital Marketing and Optimization and Web Development. In *Global Applications of the Internet of Things in Digital Marketing* (pp. 141–160). IGI Global. doi:10.4018/978-1-6684-8166-0.ch008

Abdulwahid, A. H., Pattnaik, M., Palav, M. R., Babu, S. T., Manoharan, G., & Selvi, G. P. (2023, April). Library Management System Using Artificial Intelligence. In *2023 Eighth International Conference on Science Technology Engineering and Mathematics (ICONSTEM)* (pp. 1-7). IEEE.

Abrokwah-Larbi, K., & Awuku-Larbi, Y. (2023). The impact of artificial intelligence in marketing on the performance of business organizations: evidence from SMEs in an emerging economy. *Journal of Entrepreneurship in Emerging Economies*.

Adams, M. (2017). Big data and individual privacy in the age of the internet of things. *Technology Innovation Management Review*, *7*(4), 12–24. doi:10.22215/timreview/1067

Afrina, M., Samsuryadi, Hussin, A. R. C., & Miskon, S. (2020, December). Derivation of a Customer Loyalty Factors Based on Customers' Changing Habits in E-Commerce Platform. In *International Conference of Reliable Information and Communication Technology* (pp. 879-890). Cham: Springer International Publishing.

Agha, S., & Saeed, M. (2015). Factors influencing customer acceptance of online banking in Pakistan and the moderating effect of technophobia. *Technology*, *12*(1).

Ağlargöz, F. (2021). Enforcing Brands to Be More Sustainable: The Power of Online Consumer Reviews. *Social and Sustainability Marketing: A Casebook for Reaching Your Socially Responsible Consumers through Marketing Science*, 387.

Agrawal, S., & Joshi, M. (2020). Internet of Things (IoT) in customer engagement: A comprehensive review of the literature. *International Journal of Information Management*, *54*, 102000.

Agustini, D. H., Athanasius, S. S., & Retnawati, B. B. (2019). Identification of green marketing strategies: Perspective of a developing country. *Innovative Marketing.*, *15*(4), 42–56. doi:10.21511/im.15(4).2019.04

Ahmed, A. A. A., & Ganapathy, A. (2021). Creation of automated content with embedded artificial intelligence: A study on learning management system for educational entrepreneurship. *Academy of Entrepreneurship Journal*, *27*(3), 1–10.

Ahmed, E., Yaqoob, I., Abaker, I., Hashem, T., Khan, I., Ibrahim, A., Ahmed, A., Imran, M., & Vasilakos, A. V. (2017). The role of big data analytics in internet of things. *Computer Networks*, *129*, 459–471. doi:10.1016/j.comnet.2017.06.013

Ahmed, I., Mehta, S. S., Ganeshkumar, C., & Natarajan, V. (2023). Learning from failure to enhance performance: A systematic literature review of retail failure. *Benchmarking*, *30*(2), 532–561. doi:10.1108/BIJ-04-2021-0189

Ahmed, W., Wu, D., & Mukathie, D. (2022). Blockchain-Assisted Trust Management Scheme for Securing VANETs. *KSII Transactions on Internet and Information Systems*, *16*(2), 609–631.

Ajeng, N. J. D., & Marsasi, E. G. (2023). IoT-Based Integrated Marketing Communication in Closing Quality Agent Marketing Program. *Jurnal Informatika Ekonomi Bisnis*, 198-208.

Akhter, S. H. (2014). Privacy concern and online transactions: The impact of internet self-efficacy and internet involvement. *Journal of Consumer Marketing*, *31*(2), 118–125. doi:10.1108/JCM-06-2013-0606

Akhunova, S., & Abdusattorova, M. (2023). Digital Marketing: Near Future and Perspectives. *European Journal of Economics. Finance and Business Development*, *1*(2), 18–25.

Akroush, M. N., & Al-Debei, M. M. (2015). An integrated model of factors affecting consumer attitudes towards online shopping. *Business Process Management Journal*, *21*(6), 1353–1376. doi:10.1108/BPMJ-02-2015-0022

Aksoy, N. C., Alan, A. K., Kabadayi, E. T., & Aksoy, A. (2020). Individuals' intention to use sports wearables: The moderating role of technophobia. *International Journal of Sports Marketing & Sponsorship*, *21*(2), 225–245. doi:10.1108/IJSMS-08-2019-0083

Aladayleh, K. (2020). A framework for integration of artificial intelligence into digital marketing in Jordanian commercial banks. *Journal of Innovations in Digital Marketing*, *1*(1), 32–39. doi:10.51300/jidm-2020-10

Alalwan, A. A., Rana, N. P., Dwivedi, Y. K., & Algharabat, R. (2017). Social Media in Marketing: A Review and Analysis of the Existing Literature. *Telematics and Informatics*, *34*(7), 1177–1190. doi:10.1016/j.tele.2017.05.008

Alanazi, T. M. (2022). Marketing 5.0: An Empirical Investigation of Its Perceived Effect on Marketing Performance. *Marketing and Management of Innovations*, *13*(4), 55–64. doi:10.21272/mmi.2022.4-06

Alawaad, H. A. (2021). The role of artificial intelligence (AI) in public relations and product marketing in modern organizations. *Turkish Journal of Computer and Mathematics Education*, *12*(14), 3180–3187.

Albrecht, M. G. (2023, January 25). *16.2 Social Media and Mobile Marketing - Principles of Marketing OpenStax.* https://openstax.org/books/principles-marketing/pages/16-2-social-media-and-mobile-marketing

Al-Fuqaha, A., Guizani, M., Mohammadi, M., Aledhari, M., & Ayyash, M. (2015). Internet of Things: A survey on enabling technologies, protocols, and application issues. *IEEE Communications Surveys and Tutorials*, *17*(4), 2347–2376. doi:10.1109/COMST.2015.2444095

Al-Hitmi, H. K. (2020). A Transition from Brick-and-Mortar to Online Stores and Its Role in Shifts in Consumer Buying Patterns. *Psychology and Education*, *57*(6), 375–381.

Aliahmadi, A., Movahed, A. B., & Nozari, H. (2024). Collaboration Analysis in Supply Chain 4.0 for Smart Businesses. In Building Smart and Sustainable Businesses With Transformative Technologies (pp. 103-122). IGI Global.

Aliahmadi, A., Nozari, H., & Ghahremani-Nahr, J. (2022). A framework for IoT and Blockchain Based on Marketing Systems with an Emphasis on Big Data Analysis. *International Journal of Innovation in Marketing Elements, 2*(1), 25-34.

Aliahmadi, A., Ghahremani-Nahr, J., & Nozari, H. (2023). Pricing decisions in the closed-loop supply chain network, taking into account the queuing system in production centers. *Expert Systems with Applications*, *212*, 118741. doi:10.1016/j.eswa.2022.118741

Ali, I., Balta, M., & Papadopoulos, T. (2022). Social media platforms and social enterprise: Bibliometric analysis and systematic review. *International Journal of Information Management*, 102510.

Ali, W., Danni, Y., Latif, B., Kouser, R., & Baqader, S. (2021). Corporate social responsibility and customer loyalty in food chains—Mediating role of customer satisfaction and corporate reputation. *Sustainability (Basel)*, *13*(16), 8681. doi:10.3390/su13168681

Allal-Chérif, O., Simón-Moya, V., & Ballester, A. C. C. (2021). Intelligent purchasing: How artificial intelligence can redefine the purchasing function. *Journal of Business Research*, *124*, 69–76. doi:10.1016/j.jbusres.2020.11.050

AL-Najjar, D., Al-Rousan, N., & AL-Najjar, H. (2022). Machine learning to develop credit card customer churn prediction. *Journal of Theoretical and Applied Electronic Commerce Research*, *17*(4), 1529–1542. doi:10.3390/jtaer17040077

Aloudat, A., & Michael, K. (2010). Toward the regulation of ubiquitous mobile government: A case study on location-based emergency services in Australia. *Electronic Commerce Research*, *11*(1), 31–74. doi:10.1007/s10660-010-9070-0

Al-Shaer, H., & Hussainey, K. (2022). Sustainability reporting beyond the business case and its impact on sustainability performance: UK evidence. *Journal of Environmental Management*, *311*, 114883. doi:10.1016/j.jenvman.2022.114883 PMID:35287071

Altameem, A. A., & Hafez, A. M. (2022). Behavior Analysis Using Enhanced Fuzzy Clustering and Deep Learning. *Electronics (Basel)*, *11*(19), 3172. doi:10.3390/electronics11193172

Alyoshina, I. V. (2019). Artificial intelligence in an age of digital globalization. In *International Conference Technology & Entrepreneurship in Digital Society* (pp. 26-30). Academic Press.

Anderson, E. W. (1998). Customer satisfaction and word of mouth. *Journal of Service Research*, *1*(1), 5–17. doi:10.1177/109467059800100102

Anderson, E. W., Fornell, C., & Lehmann, D. R. (1994). Customer satisfaction, market share, and profitability: Findings from Sweden. *Journal of Marketing*, *58*(3), 53–66. doi:10.1177/002224299405800304

Anderson, R. E., & Srinivasan, S. S. (2003). E-satisfaction and e-loyalty: A contingency framework. *Psychology and Marketing*, *20*(2), 123–138. doi:10.1002/mar.10063

Andronie, M., Gârdan, D. A., Dumitru, I., Gârdan, I. P., Andronie, I. E., & Uță, C. (2019). Integrating the principles of green marketing by using big data. Good practices. *Amfiteatru Economic*, *21*(50), 258–269. doi:10.24818/EA/2019/50/258

Anggraeni, T., Gaffar, V., Disman, D., Dirgantari, P. D., & Handayani, T. (2023). Tourist satisfaction in era Society 5.0 as a marketing strategy. *Journal of Eastern European and Central Asian Research*, *10*(6), 877–887. doi:10.15549/jeecar.v10i6.1509

Anghelinu, M., Niță, L., Veres, D., Hambach, U., Händel, M., Cordoş, C., Ilie, M., & Murătoreanu, G. (2021). Break vs. continuity: Techno-cultural changes across the LGM in the Eastern Carpathians. *Quaternary International*, *581*, 241–257. doi:10.1016/j.quaint.2020.08.002

Antoniadis, I., Spinthiropoulos, K., & Kontsas, S. (2020). Blockchain applications in tourism and tourism marketing: A short review. *Strategic innovative marketing and tourism*, 375-384.

Antoniadis, I., Spinthiropoulos, K., & Kontsas, S. (2020). Blockchain applications in tourism and tourism marketing: A short review. *Strategic Innovative Marketing and Tourism: 8th ICSIMAT. Northern Aegean, Greece, 2019*, 375–384.

Antons, D., & Breidbach, C. F. (2018). Big data, big insights? Advancing service innovation and design with machine learning. *Journal of Service Research*, *21*(1), 17–39. doi:10.1177/1094670517738373

Aphirakmethawong, J., Yang, E., & Mehnen, J. (2022, September). An overview of artificial intelligence in product design for smart manufacturing. In *2022 27th International Conference on Automation and Computing (ICAC)* (pp. 1-6). IEEE. 10.1109/ICAC55051.2022.9911089

Armstrong, R. M., & Grobbelaar, S. S. S. (2022). Sustainable business models for social enterprises in developing countries: a conceptual framework. *Management Review Quarterly*, 1-54.

Armstrong, G., Adam, S., Denize, S., & Kotler, P. (2015). *Principles of Marketing*. Pearson Australia.

Arun, R. (2023). *A case study on Netflix marketing strategy*. Simplilearn.com. https://www.simplilearn.com/tutorials/marketing-case-studies-tutorial/netflix-marketing-strategy

Asker, J., Fershtman, C., & Pakes, A. (2022, May). Artificial intelligence, algorithm design, and pricing. *AEA Papers and Proceedings. American Economic Association, 112*, 452–456. doi:10.1257/pandp.20221059

Attia, Y. A. E. M. (2018). A Proposed Model for applying sustainable marketing strategy as a tool to improve the marketing performance Field study: Egypt air training academy. *Journal of Association of Arab Universities for Tourism and Hospitality, 15*(2), 29–44. doi:10.21608/jaauth.2018.47934

Auger, A., Exposito, E., & Lochin, E. (2018). Towards the internet of everything: Deployment scenarios for a QoO-aware integration platform. In *2018 IEEE 4th World Forum on Internet of Things (WF-IoT)* (pp. 499-504). IEEE.

Au-Yong-Oliveira, M., & Sousa, M. J. (2022). Sustainable Marketing and Strategy. *Sustainability (Basel), 14*(6), 3642. doi:10.3390/su14063642

Awad, N. F., & Krishnan, M. S. (2006). The personalization privacy paradox: An empirical evaluation of information transparency and the willingness to be profiled online for personalization. *Management Information Systems Quarterly, 30*(1), 13–28. doi:10.2307/25148715

Aydınocak, E. U. (2021). Internet of Things (IoT. In M. Logistics (Ed.), *Logistics 4.0 and Future of Supply Chains* (pp. 153–169). Springer Nature Singapore.

Azami, H. (2020). Application of the integrated model of acceptance and use of technology to accept innovations among the farmers of Delfan city. *Agricultural Education Management Research, 12*(52), 157-76.

Azzari, V., & Pelissari, A. (2021). Does brand awareness influence purchase intention? The mediation role of brand equity dimensions. *BBR. Brazilian Business Review, 17*(6), 669–685. doi:10.15728/bbr.2020.17.6.4

Bader, V., & Kaiser, S. (2019). Algorithmic decision-making? The user interface and its role for human involvement in decisions supported by artificial intelligence. *Organization, 26*(5), 655–672. doi:10.1177/1350508419855714

Baeva, L. V., Khrapov, S. A., & Azhmukhamedov, I. M. (2021). "Smart Technologies" in Education: Development Opportunities and Threats. In "Smart Technologies" for Society, State and Economy 13 (pp. 714-723). Springer International Publishing.

Bag, S., Gupta, S., Kumar, A., & Sivarajah, U. (2021). An integrated artificial intelligence framework for knowledge creation and B2B marketing rational decision making for improving firm performance. *Industrial Marketing Management, 92*, 178–189. doi:10.1016/j.indmarman.2020.12.001

Bakator, M., Vukoja, M., & Manestar, D. (2023). Achieving competitiveness with marketing 5.0 in new business conditions. *UTMS Journal of Economics (Skopje), 14*(1).

Bamberger, V., Nansé, F., Schreiber, B., & Zintel, M. (2017). Logistics 4.0–Facing digitalization-driven disruption. *Prism, 38*, 39.

Bandyopadhyay, D., & Sen, J. (2011). Internet of Things: Applications and challenged in technology and standardization. *Wireless Personal Communications*, *58*(1), 49–69. doi:10.1007/s11277-011-0288-5

Banholzer, V. M. (2022). From Industry 4.0 to Society 5.0 and Industry 5.0: Value-and Mission-Oriented Poli-cies. *Technological and Social Innovations–Aspects of Systemic Transformation. IKOM WP*, *3*(2), 2022.

Baranidharan, & Yuvarani, Sthapit, & Thiyagarajan. (2020). Customer Satisfaction with Special Reference to E-Business. *Ilkogretim Online*, *19*(4), 6481–6489.

Barnaghi, P., Sheth, A., & Henson, C. (2019). From the Internet of Things to the Internet of Everything. *Future Generation Computer Systems*, *91*, 993–997.

Barreto, L., Amaral, A., & Pereira, T. (2017). Industry 4.0 implications in logistics: An overview. *Procedia Manufacturing*, *13*, 1245–1252. Advance online publication. doi:10.1016/j.promfg.2017.09.045

Barrios, M., Guilera, G., Nuño, L., & Gómez-Benito, J. (2021). Consensus in the Delphi method: What makes a decision change? *Technological Forecasting and Social Change*, *163*, 120484. doi:10.1016/j.techfore.2020.120484

Bassano, C., Barile, S., Saviano, M., Pietronudo, M. C., & Cosimato, S. (2020). *AI technologies & value co-creation in luxury context*. Academic Press.

Bauer, J., & Jannach, D. (2018). Optimal pricing in e-commerce based on sparse and noisy data. *Decision Support Systems*, *106*, 53–63. doi:10.1016/j.dss.2017.12.002

Bechtold, J., Lauenstein, C., Kern, A., Bernhofer, L. (2011). Industry 4.0: The capgemini consulting view. *Capgemini Consult. Digit. Transform. Supply Chain*, 1–36.

Becker, J. C., Hartwich, L., & Haslam, S. A. (2021). Neoliberalism can reduce well-being by promoting a sense of social disconnection, competition, and loneliness. *British Journal of Social Psychology*, *60*(3), 947–965. doi:10.1111/bjso.12438 PMID:33416201

Belhadi, A., Mani, V., Kamble, S. S., Khan, S. A. R., & Verma, S. (2021). Artificial intelligence-driven innovation for enhancing supply chain resilience and performance under the effect of supply chain dynamism: An empirical investigation. *Annals of Operations Research*, 1–26. doi:10.1007/s10479-021-03956-x PMID:33551534

Belz, F. M., & Peattie, K. (2022). *Sustainability Marketing: A Global Perspective* (2nd ed.). Wiley.

Berger, J., Humphreys, A., Ludwig, S., Moe, W. W., Netzer, O., & Schweidel, D. A. (2020). Uniting the tribes: Using text for marketing insight. *Journal of Marketing*, *84*(1), 1–25. doi:10.1177/0022242919873106

Berkowitz, S. A., & Orr, C. J. (2023). Three Lessons About Diabetes and the Social Determinants of Health. *Diabetes Care*, *46*(9), dci230045. doi:10.2337/dci23-0045 PMID:37354315

Bernarto, I., Berlianto, M. P., Meilani, Y. F. C. P., Masman, R. R., & Suryawan, I. N. (2020). The influence of brand awareness, brand image, and brand trust on brand loyalty. *Jurnal Manajemen*, *24*(3), 412–426. doi:10.24912/jm.v24i3.676

Bešić, S. (2019). The Application of Contemporary Marketing Concept in the Sense of the Improvement of Business Subject Competitiveness. *Tehnicki Vjesnik (Strojarski Fakultet)*, *26*(2), 441–448.

Bharadiya, J. P. (2023). A Comparative Study of Business Intelligence and Artificial Intelligence with Big Data Analytics. *American Journal of Artificial Intelligence*, *7*(1), 24–30.

Bharadwaj, A., El Sawy, O. A., Pavlou, P. A., & Venkatraman, N. (2013). Digital Business Strategy: Toward a Next Generation of Insights. *Management Information Systems Quarterly*, *37*(2), 471–482. doi:10.25300/MISQ/2013/37:2.3

Bhasin, H. (2016). *Service marketing mix–7 P's of marketing.* Marketing91. http://www. marketing91. com/service-marketing-mix

Bhasin, H. (2018). *Service Marketing Mix-7P's of marketing.* Access mode: http://www. marketing91. com/service-marketingmix

Bhat, S. (2008). *Financial management: Principles and practice.* Excel Books India.

Bhattacharjee, S. (2019). Metamorphic transformation: Critically understanding Artificial Intelligence in marketing. Bhattacharjee, Sandeep.(2019)."Metamorphic Transformation: Critically Understanding Artificial Intelligence in Marketing. *Asia Pacific Journal of Multidisciplinary Research, 7,* 61.

Bhusan, B., Sharma, S. K., Unhelkar, B., Ijaz, M. F., & Karim, L. (Eds.). (2022). Internet of Things: Frameworks for Enabling and Emerging Technologies. Academic Press.

Bjelak, A., & Selimović, A. (2023, June). Emotion Detection Using Convolutional Neural Networks. In *International Symposium on Innovative and Interdisciplinary Applications of Advanced Technologies* (pp. 263-279). Cham: Springer Nature Switzerland.

Björck, F., Henkel, M., Stirna, J., & Zdravkovic, J. (2015). Cyber resilience–fundamentals for a definition. In *New Contributions in Information Systems and Technologies* (pp. 311–316). Springer. doi:10.1007/978-3-319-16486-1_31

Blaettler, L. (2021). *Identifying essential data to evaluate and monitor energy performance* [Doctoral dissertation]. North-West University.

Blank, G., & Dutton, W. H. (2012). Age and trust in the Internet: The centrality of experience and attitudes toward technology in Britain. *Social Science Computer Review, 30*(2), 135–151. doi:10.1177/0894439310396186

Bleakley, D. O., Demmler, L. M., Desai, A. A., Etgen, M. P., & Kenna, S. (2020). *U.S. Patent Application No. 16/681,798.* US Patent Office.

Bleier, A., & Eisenbeiss, M. (2015). Personalized online advertising effectiveness: The interplay of what, when, and where. *Marketing Science, 34*(5), 669–688. doi:10.1287/mksc.2015.0930

Blut, M., Teller, C., & Floh, A. (2018). Testing retail marketing-mix effects on patronage: A meta-analysis. *Journal of Retailing, 94*(2), 113–135. doi:10.1016/j.jretai.2018.03.001

Blythe, J., & Martin, J. (2019). Essentials of marketing. Academic Press.

Bojanova, I., Hurlburt, G., & Voas, J. (2014). Imagineering an internet of anything. *Computer, 47*(6), 72–77. doi:10.1109/MC.2014.150

Bolton, R. N., Keh, H. T., & Alba, J. W. (2010). How do price fairness perceptions differ across culture? *JMR, Journal of Marketing Research, 47*(3), 564–576. doi:10.1509/jmkr.47.3.564

Bolton, R. N., & Lemon, K. N. (1999). A dynamic model of customers' usage of services: Usage as an antecedent and consequence of satisfaction. *JMR, Journal of Marketing Research, 36*(2), 171–186.

Boone, T., Ganeshan, R., Jain, A., & Sanders, N. R. (2019). Forecasting sales in the supply chain: Consumer analytics in the big data era. *International Journal of Forecasting, 35*(1), 170–180. doi:10.1016/j.ijforecast.2018.09.003

Borden, N. H. (1964). The concept of the marketing mix. *Journal of Advertising Research, 4*(2), 2–7.

Boz, H., & Kose, U. (2018). Emotion extraction from facial expressions by using artificial intelligence techniques. BRAIN. *Broad Research in Artificial Intelligence and Neuroscience, 9*(1), 5–16.

Bragge, J., Hengst, M. D., Tuunanen, T., & Virtanen, V. (2005). A repeatable collaboration process for developing a road map for emerging new technology business: Case mobile marketing. *Americas Conference on Information Systems, 198.* https://aisel.aisnet.org/amcis2005/198/

Breur, T. (2015). Big data and the internet of things. *Journal of Marketing Analytics, 3*(1), 1–4. doi:10.1057/jma.2015.7

BrightEdge. (2019). *BrightEdge Research: The Future of Marketing Is Here - Are You Ready?* Retrieved at 20 Oct. 2023 from https://www.brightedge.com/resources/research-reports/future-of-marketing

Brisk, G. (2022b, June 18). *How Location-Based Marketing Helps Businesses drive footfall and improve ROI.* PlotProjects. https://www.plotprojects.com/blog/location-based-marketing-drive-footfall-improve-roi/

Brobbey, E. E., Ankrah, E., & Kankam, P. K. (2021). The role of artificial intelligence in integrated marketing communications. A case study of Jumia Online Ghana. Inkanyiso. *Journal of the Humanities and Social Sciences, 13*(1), 120–136.

Brodie, R. J., Hollebeek, L. D., Juric, B., & Ilic, A. (2011). Customer engagement: Conceptual domain, fundamental propositions, and implications for research. *Journal of Service Research, 14*(3), 252–271. doi:10.1177/1094670511411703

Brooks, R., Nguyen, D., Bhatti, A., Allender, S., Johnstone, M., Lim, C. P., & Backholer, K. (2022). Use of artificial intelligence to enable dark nudges by transnational food and beverage companies: analysis of company documents. *Public Health Nutrition, 25*(5), 1291-1299.

Brown, Z. Y., & MacKay, A. (2021). *Competition in pricing algorithms (No. w28860).* National Bureau of Economic Research. doi:10.3386/w28860

Brychko, M., Bilan, Y., Lyeonov, S., & Streimikiene, D. (2023). Do changes in the business environment and sustainable development really matter for enhancing enterprise development? *Sustainable Development (Bradford), 31*(2), 587–599. doi:10.1002/sd.2410

Brynjolfsson, E., Hu, Y. J., & Rahman, M. S. (2013). Competing in the Age of Omnichannel Retailing. *MIT Sloan Management Review, 54*(4), 23–29.

Buchelt, B. (2011). Performance management as modern approach to employees' appraisal in healthcare entities. *Edukacja Ekonomistów i Menedżerów, 22*(4), 75–92. doi:10.5604/01.3001.0009.5540

Bui, M., & Namin, A. (2019). Digital technology disrupting health: Reviewing key components of modern healthcare. In A. S. Krishen & O. Berezan (Eds.), *In Marketing and Humanity: Discourses in the Real World* (pp. 148–169). New Castle.

Buswari, M., Setiawan, M., & Khusniyah, N. (2021). The Effect between Green Product Innovation and Green Marketing on Competitive Advantage and Business Performance. *PalArch's Journal of Archaeology of Egypt/Egyptology, 18*(2), 47-63.

Cabato, M. G., Macadat, Y., & Bronola, F. B. (2020). Green marketing: A study on the perception of CBA students in PUP Manila. Polytechnic University of the Philippines, College of Business Administration.

Cai, T., Wu, Y., Lin, H., & Cai, Y. (2023). Blockchain-empowered big data sharing for internet of things. In *Research Anthology on Convergence of Blockchain, Internet of Things, and Security* (pp. 278–290). IGI Global.

Calvano, E., Calzolari, G., Denicolo, V., & Pastorello, S. (2020). Artificial intelligence, algorithmic pricing, and collusion. *The American Economic Review, 110*(10), 3267–3297. doi:10.1257/aer.20190623

Calvo-Porral, C. (2019). The role of marketing in reducing climate change: an approach to the sustainable marketing orientation. In *Climate Change and Global Development* (pp. 261–283). Springer. doi:10.1007/978-3-030-02662-2_13

Cao, S., Powell, W., Foth, M., Natanelov, V., Miller, T., & Dulleck, U. (2021). Strengthening consumer trust in beef supply chain traceability with a blockchain-based human-machine reconcile mechanism. *Computers and Electronics in Agriculture*, *180*, 105886. doi:10.1016/j.compag.2020.105886

Carey, D., Dumaine, B., Useem, M., & Zemmel, R. (2018). *Go long: Why long-term thinking is your best short-term strategy*. University of Pennsylvania Press. doi:10.2307/j.ctv2hdrfdx

Carrington, M. J., Neville, B. A., & Whitwell, G. J. (2014). Lost in translation: Exploring the ethical consumer intention–behavior gap. *Journal of Business Research*, *67*(1), 2759–2767. doi:10.1016/j.jbusres.2012.09.022

Casaló, L. V., Flavián, C., & Guinalíu, M. (2008). The role of satisfaction and website usability in developing customer loyalty and positive word-of-mouth in the e-banking services. *International Journal of Bank Marketing*, *26*(6), 399–417. doi:10.1108/02652320810902433

Cavalcante, I. M., Frazzon, E. M., Forcellini, F. A., & Ivanov, D. (2019). A supervised machine learning approach to data-driven simulation of resilient supplier selection in digital manufacturing. *International Journal of Information Management*, *49*, 86–97. doi:10.1016/j.ijinfomgt.2019.03.004

Ceri, S., Daniel, F., Matera, M., & Facca, F. M. (2007). Model-driven development of context-aware Web applications. *ACM Transactions on Internet Technology*, *7*(1), 2. doi:10.1145/1189740.1189742

Chaabene, H., Negra, Y., Bouguezzi, R., Capranica, L., Franchini, E., Prieske, O., Hbacha, H., & Granacher, U. (2018). Tests for the assessment of sport-specific performance in Olympic combat sports: A systematic review with practical recommendations. *Frontiers in Physiology*, *9*, 386. doi:10.3389/fphys.2018.00386 PMID:29692739

Chaffey, D., & Ellis-Chadwick, F. (2019). *Digital Marketing*. Pearson UK.

Chaffey, D., & Ellis-Chadwick, F. (2019). *Digital Marketing: Strategy Implementation and Practice* (7th ed.). Pearson Education Limited.

Chang, J. (2023, September 20). *Mobile phones have become an indispensable part of today's digital lifestyle. With network speeds and coverage*. Financesonline.com. https://financesonline.com/mobile-marketing-software-trends/

Chang, I. C., Chou, P. C., Yeh, R. K. J., & Tseng, H. T. (2016). Factors influencing Chinese tourists' intentions to use the Taiwan Medical Travel App. *Telematics and Informatics*, *33*(2), 401–409. doi:10.1016/j.tele.2015.09.007

Chaudhuri, A., & Holbrook, M. B. (2001). The chain of effects from brand trust and brand affect to brand performance: The role of brand loyalty. *Journal of Marketing*, *65*(2), 81–93. doi:10.1509/jmkg.65.2.81.18255

Chen, H., & Chen, T. J. (2002). Asymmetric strategic alliances: A network view. *Journal of Business Research*, *55*(12), 1007–1013. doi:10.1016/S0148-2963(02)00284-9

Chen, S. W., Gu, X. W., Wang, J. J., & Zhu, H. S. (2021). AIoT Used for COVID-19 Pandemic Prevention and Control. *Contrast Media & Molecular Imaging*, *2021*. doi:10.1155/2021/3257035 PMID:34729056

Chen, W., He, Y., & Bansal, S. (2023). Customized Dynamic Pricing when Customers Develop a Habit or Satiation. *Operations Research*, *71*(6), 2158–2174. doi:10.1287/opre.2022.2412

Chen, X., & Zhang, Y. (2009). Uncertain linear programs: Extended affinely adjustable robust counterparts. *Operations Research*, *57*(6), 1469–1482. doi:10.1287/opre.1080.0605

Chen, Y. R. R., & Ann, B. S. (2016). Exploring online consumer behavior: The role of extrinsic and intrinsic motivation. *Telematics and Informatics*, *33*(4), 1149–1160.

Chen, Y.-S., & Xu, Z. (2020). Sustainable marketing in the era of Internet of Everything (IoE): Opportunities, challenges, and strategies. *Journal of Business Research*, *117*, 535–546.

Chen, Z., & Dubinsky, A. J. (2003). A conceptual model of perceived customer value in e-commerce: A preliminary investigation. *Psychology and Marketing*, *20*(4), 323–347. doi:10.1002/mar.10076

Cheung, C. M., & Thadani, D. R. (2012). The impact of electronic word-of-mouth communication: A literature analysis and integrative model. *Decision Support Systems*, *54*(1), 461–470. doi:10.1016/j.dss.2012.06.008

Chevalier, J. A., & Mayzlin, D. (2006). The effect of word of mouth on sales: Online book reviews. *JMR, Journal of Marketing Research*, *43*(3), 345–354. doi:10.1509/jmkr.43.3.345

Chhabra, D. (2009). Proposing a Sustainable Marketing Framework for Heritage Tourism. *Journal of Sustainable Tourism*, *17*(3), 313–320. doi:10.1080/09669580802495758

Chintalapati, S., & Pandey, S. K. (2022). Artificial intelligence in marketing: A systematic literature review. *International Journal of Market Research*, *64*(1), 38–68. doi:10.1177/14707853211018428

Chiramel, S., Logofătu, D., Rawat, J., & Andersson, C. (2020). Efficient Approaches for House Pricing Prediction by Using Hybrid Machine Learning Algorithms. In Intelligent Information and Database Systems: 12th Asian Conference, ACIIDS 2020, Phuket, Thailand, March 23–26, 2020 [Springer Singapore.]. *Proceedings*, *12*, 85–94.

Chiu, T. C., Shih, Y. Y., Pang, A. C., Wang, C. S., Weng, W., & Chou, C. T. (2020). Semisupervised distributed learning with non-IID data for AIoT service platform. *IEEE Internet of Things Journal*, *7*(10), 9266–9277. doi:10.1109/JIOT.2020.2995162

Choi, H., & Sirakaya, E. (2006). Sustainability Indicators for Managing Community Tourism. *Tourism Management*, *27*(6), 1274–1289. doi:10.1016/j.tourman.2005.05.018

Choudrie, J., & Vyas, A. (2014). Silver surfers adopting and using Facebook? A quantitative study of Hertfordshire, UK applied to organizational and social change. *Technological Forecasting and Social Change*, *89*, 293–305. doi:10.1016/j.techfore.2014.08.007

Chouk, I., & Mani, Z. (2019). Factors for and against resistance to smart services: Role of consumer lifestyle and eco-system related variables. *Journal of Services Marketing*, *33*(4), 449–462. doi:10.1108/JSM-01-2018-0046

Chow, V. (2020). Predicting auction price of vehicle license plate with deep recurrent neural network. *Expert Systems with Applications*, *142*, 113008. doi:10.1016/j.eswa.2019.113008

Christina, S., & Munishamappa, P. (2014). Caveat Emptor To Caveat Venditor In The Process. *International Research Journal of Management Sociology & Humanity*, 430-436.

Cisco. (2015). *The internet of everything*. Available at: https:// newsroom.cisco.com/ioe

CISCO. (2020). *Cisco Annual Internet Report (2018–2023) White Paper*. Retrieved from https://www.cisco.com/c/en/us/solutions/collateral/executive-perspectives/annual-internet-report/white-paper-c11-741490.html

Clegg, C. (1994). Psychology and information technology: The study of cognition in organizations. *British Journal of Psychology*, *85*(4), 449–477. doi:10.1111/j.2044-8295.1994.tb02535.x

Cloarec, J., Meyer-Waarden, L., & Munzel, A. (2022). The personalization–privacy paradox at the nexus of social exchange and construal level theories. *Psychology and Marketing*, *39*(3), 647–661. doi:10.1002/mar.21587

Coita, D. C., Abrudan, M. M., & Matei, M. C. (2019). Effects of the blockchain technology on human resources and marketing: an exploratory study. In Strategic Innovative Marketing and Tourism: 7th ICSIMAT, Athenian Riviera, Greece, 2018 (pp. 683-691). Springer International Publishing. doi:10.1007/978-3-030-12453-3_79

Colabi, A. M. (2020). Modeling Factors Affecting the Sustainability of Business model. *Public Management Researches*, *13*(47), 111–134. doi:10.22111/jmr.2020.32518.4901

Crnovrsanin, T., Muelder, C., Correa, C., & Ma, K. (2009). *Proximity-based visualization of movement trace data. In 2009 IEEE symposium on visual analytics science and technology*. IEEE.

Cui, H., Nie, Y., Li, Z., & Zeng, J. (2022). Construction and Development of Modern Brand Marketing Management Mode Based on Artificial Intelligence. *Journal of Sensors*, *2022*, 1–11. doi:10.1155/2022/9246545

Cui, H., Shen, L., & Li, H. (2021). IoE-enabled supply chain management for transparency and sustainability. *Journal of Cleaner Production*, *280*, 124387.

Culnan, M. J., & Armstrong, P. K. (1999). Information privacy concerns, procedural fairness, and impersonal trust: An empirical investigation. *Organization Science*, *10*(1), 104–115. doi:10.1287/orsc.10.1.104

Cyr, D., & Trevor-Smith, H. (2004). Localization of web design: An empirical comparison of German, Japanese, and United States web site characteristics. *Journal of the American Society for Information Science and Technology*, *55*(13), 1199–1208. doi:10.1002/asi.20075

Dacko, S. G. (2017). Enabling Smart Retail Settings via Mobile Augmented Reality Shopping Apps. *Technological Forecasting and Social Change*, *124*, 243–256. doi:10.1016/j.techfore.2016.09.032

Dangelico, R. M., & Vocalelli, D. (2017). "Green Marketing": An Analysis of Definitions, Strategy Steps, and Tools Through a Systematic Review of the Literature. *Journal of Cleaner Production*, *165*(1), 1263–1279. doi:10.1016/j.jclepro.2017.07.184

Dangelico, R. M., & Vocalelli, D. (Eds.). (2022). *Green Marketing: A Case Study-Based Approach*. Springer.

Daoud, M. K., Al-Qeed, M. A., Ahmad, A. Y. B., & Al-Gasawneh, J. A. (2023). Mobile Marketing: Exploring the efficacy of User-Centric strategies for enhanced consumer engagement and conversion rates. *International Journal of Membrane Science and Technology*, *10*(2), 1252–1262. doi:10.15379/ijmst.vi.1425

Dašić, G., Radosavac, A., Knežević, D., & Đervida, R. (2019). Preferences of customers and improvement of production and sales of organic products in Serbia. *Ekonomika Poljoprivrede*, *66*(1), 127–142. doi:10.5937/ekoPolj1901127D

Daskou, S., & Mangina, E. E. (2003). Artificial intelligence in managing market relationships: The use of intelligence agents. *Journal of Relationship Marketing*, *2*(1-2), 85–102. doi:10.1300/J366v02n01_06

Davenport, T. H. (2018). From analytics to artificial intelligence. *Journal of Business Analytics*, *1*(2), 73–80. doi:10.1080/2573234X.2018.1543535

Davenport, T., Guha, A., Grewal, D., & Bressgott, T. (2020). How artificial intelligence will change the future of marketing. *Journal of the Academy of Marketing Science*, *48*(1), 24–42. doi:10.1007/s11747-019-00696-0

David, J. V., Ana, M. R., Santiago, F. B., & Faustino, A. V. (2021). Aspects of industrial design and their implications for society. Case studies on the influence of packaging design and placement at the point of sale. *Applied Sciences (Basel, Switzerland)*, *11*(2), 517. doi:10.3390/app11020517

Davis, F. D. (1989). Perceived usefulness, perceived ease of use, and user acceptance of information technology. *Management Information Systems Quarterly*, *13*(3), 319–340. doi:10.2307/249008

De Cremer, D., Nguyen, B., & Simkin, L. (2017). The integrity challenge of the internet-of-Things (IoT) on understanding its dark side. *Journal of Marketing Management, 33*(1-2), 145–158. doi:10.1080/0267257X.2016.1247517

de Regt, A., Plangger, K., & Barnes, S. J. (2021). Virtual reality marketing and customer advocacy: Transforming experiences from story-telling to story-doing. *Journal of Business Research, 136*, 513–522. doi:10.1016/j.jbusres.2021.08.004

Deggans, J., Krulicky, T., Kovacova, M., Valaskova, K., & Poliak, M. (2019). Cognitively enhanced products, output growth, and labor market changes: Will artificial intelligence replace workers by automating their jobs? Economics. *Management and Financial Markets, 14*(1), 38–43.

Dehghani, M., Abubakar, A. M., & Pashna, M. (2022). Market-Driven Management of Start-ups: The Case of Wearable Technology. *Applied Computing and Informatics, 18*(1/2), 45–60. doi:10.1016/j.aci.2018.11.002

Dekimpe, M. G. (2020). Retailing and retailing research in the age of big data analytics. *International Journal of Research in Marketing, 37*(1), 3–14. doi:10.1016/j.ijresmar.2019.09.001

Deng, S., Tan, C. W., Wang, W., & Pan, Y. (2019). Smart generation system of personalized advertising copy and its application to advertising practice and research. *Journal of Advertising, 48*(4), 356–365. doi:10.1080/00913367.2019.1652121

Dhir, S., & Dhir, S. (2015). Technology Penetration and its Impact on Information Access by Customers: An Exploratory Study. *Advances in Global Business Research, 12*(1), 361.

Dimitrov, D., & Zhelev, C. (2020). Internet of Things (IoT) technologies for waste reduction and enhanced shopping experience in the retail sector. *Sustainability, 12*(24), 10355.

Dinev, T., Bellotto, M., Hart, P., Russo, V., Serra, I., & Colautti, C. (2006). Privacy calculus model in e-commerce–a study of Italy and the United States. *European Journal of Information Systems, 15*(4), 389–402. doi:10.1057/palgrave.ejis.3000590

Dinev, T., Hart, P., & Mullen, M. R. (2019). Internet Privacy Concerns and Beliefs About Government Surveillance–An Empirical Investigation. *The Journal of Strategic Information Systems, 28*(1), 66–83. doi:10.1016/j.jsis.2018.09.002

Dinev, T., Xu, H., Smith, J. H., & Hart, P. (2013). Information privacy and correlates: An empirical attempt to bridge and distinguish privacy-related concepts. *European Journal of Information Systems, 22*(3), 295–316. doi:10.1057/ejis.2012.23

Dong, B., Shi, Q., Yang, Y., Wen, F., Zhang, Z., & Lee, C. (2021). Technology evolution from self-powered sensors to AIoT enabled smart homes. *Nano Energy, 79*, 105414. doi:10.1016/j.nanoen.2020.105414

Dong, S., Abbas, K., & Jain, R. (2019). A survey on distributed denial of service (DDoS) attacks in SDN and cloud computing environments. *IEEE Access : Practical Innovations, Open Solutions, 7*, 80813–80828. doi:10.1109/ACCESS.2019.2922196

Donohue, T. J., Ortiz, R., & Meyer, T. L. (2009). The challenges presented by the mobile phone market. *International Journal of Technology, Knowledge and Society, 5*(6), 19–28. doi:10.18848/1832-3669/CGP/v05i06/56048

Doole, I., & Lowe, R. (2012). *International marketing strategy* (Vol. 7). Cengage Learning.

Durach, S., Higgen, U., & Huebler, M. (2012). Smart Automotive Apps: An approach to Context-Driven Applications. In Springer eBooks (pp. 187–195). doi:10.1007/978-3-642-33838-0_17

Dwesar, R., & Kashyap, R. (2022). IOT in marketing: Current applications and future opportunities. *Internet of things and its applications*, 539-553.

Dwesar, R., & Kashyap, R. (2022). IOT in Marketing: Current Applications and Future Opportunities. In *Internet of Things and Its Applications* (pp. 539–553). Springer. doi:10.1007/978-3-030-77528-5_29

Dwivedi, Y. K., Hughes, L., Ismagilova, E., Aarts, G., Coombs, C., Crick, T., Duan, Y., Dwivedi, R., Edwards, J., Eirug, A., Galanos, V., Ilavarasan, P. V., Janssen, M., Jones, P., Kar, A. K., Kizgin, H., Kronemann, B., Lal, B., Lucini, B., ... Williams, M. D. (2021). Artificial Intelligence (AI): Multidisciplinary perspectives on emerging challenges, opportunities, and agenda for research, practice and policy. *International Journal of Information Management, 57*, 101994. doi:10.1016/j.ijinfomgt.2019.08.002

Ekramifard, A., Amintoosi, H., Seno, A. H., Dehghantanha, A., & Parizi, R. M. (2020). A systematic literature review of integration of blockchain and artificial intelligence. *Blockchain Cybersecurity, Trust and Privacy*, 147-160.

El Koufi, N., Belangour, A., & Sdiq, M. (2022). Research on Precision Marketing based on Big Data Analysis and Machine Learning: Case Study of Morocco. *International Journal of Advanced Computer Science and Applications, 13*(10). Advance online publication. doi:10.14569/IJACSA.2022.0131008

El Sawy, O. A., Gomaa, M. H., & Kamel, M. S. (2020). Internet of Things (IoT) for corporate social responsibility: A comprehensive review of the literature. *International Journal of Information Management, 55*, 102091.

Eliakis, S., Kotsopoulos, D., Karagiannaki, A., & Pramatari, K. (2020). Survival and growth in innovative technology entrepreneurship: A mixed-methods investigation. *Administrative Sciences, 10*(3), 39. doi:10.3390/admsci10030039

Elshaiekh, N. E., Al-Hijji, K., Shehata, A., & Alrashdi, S. M. A. (2023). An Empirical Analysis of Factors Motivating Unemployed Individuals to Engage in Digital Entrepreneurship in Oman: Focus on Technological Infrastructure. *Sustainability (Basel), 15*(17), 12953. doi:10.3390/su151712953

Enholm, I. M., Papagiannidis, E., Mikalef, P., & Krogstie, J. (2022). Artificial intelligence and business value: A literature review. *Information Systems Frontiers, 24*(5), 1709–1734. doi:10.1007/s10796-021-10186-w

Epstein, M. J. (2018). Adapting for digital survival. *Strategic Finance, 99*(8), 26–33.

Ersoy, N. (2022). The Influence of Statistical Normalization Techniques on Performance Ranking Results: The Application of MCDM Method Proposed by Biswas and Saha. *International Journal of Business Analytics, 9*(5), 1–21. doi:10.4018/IJBAN.298017

Esposito, C., De Santis, A., Tortora, G., Chang, H., & Choo, K. K. R. (2018). Blockchain: A panacea for healthcare cloud-based data security and privacy? *IEEE Cloud Computing, 5*(1), 31–37. doi:10.1109/MCC.2018.011791712

Eze, O., & Cherish, O. C. (2019). Achieving customer satisfaction through sustainable marketing strategies: A Qualitative analysis of three bread industries in Abakaliki Ebonyi State. Nigeria. *American Journal of Multidisciplinary Research & Development, 1*(4), 1-7.

Ezrachi, A., & Stucke, M. E. (2016). *Is Your Digital Assistant Devious?* Oxford Legal Studies Research Paper No. 52/2016, University of Tennessee Legal Studies Research Paper No. 304. Available at https://ssrn.com/abstract=2828117 doi:10.2139/ssrn.2828117

Fallah Shayan, N., Mohabbati-Kalejahi, N., Alavi, S., & Zahed, M. A. (2022). Sustainable Development Goals (SDGs) as a Framework for Corporate Social Responsibility (CSR). *Sustainability (Basel), 14*(3), 1222. doi:10.3390/su14031222

Fang, C., Lu, H., Hong, Y., Liu, S., & Chang, J. (2020). Dynamic pricing for electric vehicle extreme fast charging. *IEEE Transactions on Intelligent Transportation Systems, 22*(1), 531–541. doi:10.1109/TITS.2020.2983385

Faraji, A., Khodadadi, M., Nematpour, M., Abidizadegan, S., & Yazdani, H. R. (2021). Investigating the positive role of urban tourism in creating sustainable revenue opportunities in the municipalities of large-scale cities: The case of Iran. *International Journal of Tourism Cities*, 7(1), 177–199. doi:10.1108/IJTC-04-2020-0076

Farias da Costa, V. C., Oliveira, L., & de Souza, J. (2021). Internet of everything (IoE) taxonomies: A survey and a novel knowledge-based taxonomy. *Sensors (Basel)*, 21(2), 568. doi:10.3390/s21020568 PMID:33466895

Farrokhi, A., Shirazi, F., Hajli, N., & Tajvidi, M. (2020). Using artificial intelligence to detect crisis related to events: Decision making in B2B by artificial intelligence. *Industrial Marketing Management*, 91, 257–273. doi:10.1016/j.indmarman.2020.09.015

Fatima, S., Alqahtani, H., Naim, A., & Alma'alwi, F. (2022). E-CRM Through Social Media Marketing Activities for Brand Awareness, Brand Image, and Brand Loyalty. In *Building a Brand Image Through Electronic Customer Relationship Management* (pp. 109–138). IGI Global. doi:10.4018/978-1-6684-5386-5.ch006

Febriyantoro, M. T. (2020). Exploring YouTube Marketing Communication: Brand awareness, brand image, and purchase intention in the millennial generation. *Cogent Business & Management*, 7(1), 1787733. doi:10.1080/23311975.2020.1787733

Feng, C. M., Park, A., Pitt, L., Kietzmann, J., & Northey, G. (2021). Artificial intelligence in marketing: A bibliographic perspective. *Australasian Marketing Journal*, 29(3), 252–263. doi:10.1016/j.ausmj.2020.07.006

Fennis, B. M., & Stroebe, W. (2016). *The Psychology of Advertising* (2nd ed.). Routledge.

Fishman, A., Hellman, Z., & Weiss, A. (2023). Habit forming consumers and firm dynamics. *Journal of Economic Dynamics & Control*, 154, 104704. doi:10.1016/j.jedc.2023.104704

Fitzsimmons, A. B., Qin, Y. S., & Heffron, E. R. (2022). Purpose vs mission vs vision: persuasive appeals and components in corporate statements. *Journal of Communication Management*, (ahead-of-print).

Flavián, C., Guinalíu, M., & Gurrea, R. (2006). The role played by perceived usability, satisfaction and consumer trust on website loyalty. *Information & Management*, 43(1), 1–14. doi:10.1016/j.im.2005.01.002

Floridi, L., Cowls, J., Beltrametti, M., Chatila, R., Chazerand, P., Dignum, V., ... & Vayena, E. (2021). An ethical framework for a good AI society: Opportunities, risks, principles, and recommendations. *Ethics, Governance, and Policies in Artificial Intelligence*, 19-39.

Fonseca, L. M., & Azevedo, A. L. (2020). COVID-19: Outcomes for global supply chains. *Management & Marketing. Challenges for the Knowledge Society*, 15(s1), 424–438. doi:10.2478/mmcks-2020-0025

Fosso Wamba, S., Queiroz, M. M., Wu, L., & Sivarajah, U. (2020). Big data analytics-enabled sensing capability and organizational outcomes: assessing the mediating effects of business analytics culture. *Annals of Operations Research*, 1-20. doi:10.1007/s10479-020-03812-4

Fosso Wamba, S., Gunasekaran, A., Dubey, R., & Ngai, E. W. (2018). Big data analytics in operations and supply chain management. *Annals of Operations Research*, 270(1-2), 1–4. doi:10.1007/s10479-018-3024-7 PMID:36687515

Fowler, M. D. (2017). Linking the public benefit to the corporation: Blockchain as a solution for certification in an age of do-good business. *Vand. J. Ent. & Tech. L.*, 20, 881.

Fredette, J., Marom, R., Steinert, K., & Witters, L. (2012). *The promise and peril of hyperconnectivity for organizations and societies*. The Global Information Technology Report. World Economic Forum. https://www3.weforum.org/docs/GITR/2012/ GITR_Chapter1.10_2012.pdf

Fredström, A., Parida, V., Wincent, J., Sjödin, D., & Oghazi, P. (2022). What is the market value of artificial intelligence and machine Learning? The role of innovativeness and collaboration for performance. *Technological Forecasting and Social Change, 180*, 121716. doi:10.1016/j.techfore.2022.121716

Frei, F. X. (2008). The four things a service business must get right. *Harvard Business Review, 86*(4), 70–80. PMID:18435008

Frempong, M. F., Mu, Y., Adu-Yeboah, S. S., Hossin, M. A., & Amoako, R. (2022). Corporate sustainability and customer loyalty: The role of firm's green image. *Journal of Psychology in Africa, 32*(1), 1–7. doi:10.1080/14330237.2021.2017153

French, J., & Gordon, R. (2019). Strategic social marketing: For behavior and social change. *Sage (Atlanta, Ga.).*

Fritz, W., Sohn, S., & Seegebarth, B. (2017). Broadening the Perspective on Mobile Marketing: An Introduction. *Psychology and Marketing, 34*(2), 113–118. doi:10.1002/mar.20978

FTC. (2015). *IoT privacy & security in a connected world*. FTC Staff Report.

Furrer, O., Liu, B. S. C., & Sudharshan, D. (2000). The relationships between culture and service quality perceptions: Basis for cross-cultural market segmentation and resource allocation. *Journal of Service Research, 2*(4), 355–371. doi:10.1177/109467050024004

Fuxman, L., Mohr, I., Mahmoud, A. B., & Grigoriou, N. (2022). The new 3Ps of sustainability marketing: The case of fashion. *Sustainable Production and Consumption, 31*, 384–396. doi:10.1016/j.spc.2022.03.004

Gabisch, J. A., & Milne, G. R. (2014). The impact of compensation on information ownership and privacy control. *Journal of Consumer Marketing, 31*(1), 13–26. doi:10.1108/JCM-10-2013-0737

Gao, Y., & Liu, H. (2022). Artificial intelligence-enabled personalization in interactive marketing: a customer journey perspective. *Journal of Research in Interactive Marketing*, (ahead-of-print), 1-18.

Garbarino, E., & Strahilevitz, M. (2004). Gender differences in the perceived risk of buying online and the effects of receiving a site recommendation. *Journal of Business Research, 57*(7), 768–775. doi:10.1016/S0148-2963(02)00363-6

Garber, J., & Downing, D. (2021). Perceptions, Policy, and Partnerships: How Pharmacists Can Be Leaders in Reducing Overprescribing. *The Senior Care Pharmacist, 36*(3), 130–135. doi:10.4140/TCP.n.2021.130 PMID:33662235

Garg, P., Gupta, B., Chauhan, A. K., Sivarajah, U., Gupta, S., & Modgil, S. (2021). Measuring the perceived benefits of implementing blockchain technology in the banking sector. *Technological Forecasting and Social Change, 163*, 120407. doi:10.1016/j.techfore.2020.120407

Gautier, A., Ittoo, A., & Van Cleynenbreugel, P. (2020). AI algorithms, price discrimination and collusion: A technological, economic and legal perspective. *European Journal of Law and Economics, 50*(3), 405–435. doi:10.1007/s10657-020-09662-6

Gburova, J., & Fedorko, R. (2018). Online shops and online shopping from the point of view of the Slovak consumer. *Economic And Social Development: Book of Proceedings*, 134-140.

Gefen, D., Karahanna, E., & Straub, D. W. (2003). Trust and TAM in online shopping: An integrated model. *Management Information Systems Quarterly, 27*(1), 51–90. doi:10.2307/30036519

Gelter, J., Lexhagen, M., & Fuchs, M. (2021). A meta-narrative analysis of smart tourism destinations: Implications for tourism destination management. *Current Issues in Tourism, 24*(20), 2860–2874. doi:10.1080/13683500.2020.1849048

Geng, Y., Liu, Y., Zhang, J., Xue, B., & Chu, K. W. (2017). Internet of Things (IoT) applications in a circular economy: A review. *Journal of Cleaner Production, 168*, 591–604.

Gerstner, E., Hess, J., & Chu, W. (1993). Demarketing as a differentiation strategy. *Marketing Letters, 4*(1), 49–57. doi:10.1007/BF00994187

Geum, Y., Kim, S., & Park, Y. (2011). *Development of new mobile application services: An approach using context-driven morphology analysis.* IEEE Xplore. doi:10.1109/ICSSSM.2011.5959338

Ghahremani-Nahr, J., & Nozari, H. (2021). A Survey for Investigating Key Performance Indicators in Digital Marketing. *International Journal of Innovation in Marketing Elements, 1*(1), 1-6.

Giddens, A. (1977). *Studies in social and political theory.* Basic Books.

Giddens, A. (1984). *The constitution of society: Outline of the theory of structuration.* Polity Press.

Giri, A., Chatterjee, S., Paul, P., & Chakraborty, S. (2019). Determining the impact of artificial intelligence on'developing marketing strategies' in organized retail sector of West Bengal, India. *International Journal of Engineering and Advanced Technology, 8*(6), 3031–3036. doi:10.35940/ijeat.F9030.088619

Giroux, M., Kim, J., Lee, J. C., & Park, J. (2022). Artificial intelligence and declined guilt: Retailing morality comparison between human and AI. *Journal of Business Ethics, 178*(4), 1027–1041. doi:10.1007/s10551-022-05056-7 PMID:35194275

Gitarja, W. S., & Hariyati, R. T. S. (2023, November). The Influence of Marketing 5.0 and Creating Share Value on Wound Care Quality and Purchased Intention among Wound Care Professional. *Journal of International Conference Proceedings, 6*(4), 188–199. doi:10.32535/jicp.v6i4.2609

Goel, J. (n.d.). *Top 12 Commerce Project Topics & Ideas in 2023* [For Freshers]. upGrad blog. https://www.upgrad.com/blog/amazon-business-case-study-in-depth-analysis/

Golalizadeh, F., Ranjbarian, B., & Ansari, A. (2023). Impact of customer's emotions on online purchase intention and impulsive buying of luxury cosmetic products mediated by perceived service quality. *Journal of Global Fashion Marketing, 14*(4), 468–488. doi:10.1080/20932685.2023.2205869

Goldmanis, M., Hortaçsu, A., Syverson, C., & Emre, O. (2010). E-commerce and the Market Structure of Retail Industries. *Economic Journal (London), 120*(545), 651–682. doi:10.1111/j.1468-0297.2009.02310.x

Gomez-Uribe, C. A., & Hunt, N. (2016). The Netflix recommender system: Algorithms, business value, and innovation. *ACM Transactions on Management Information Systems, 6*(4), 1–19. doi:10.1145/2843948

Gommans, M., Krishnan, K. S., & Scheffold, K. B. (2001). From brand loyalty to e-loyalty: A conceptual framework. *Journal of Economic and Social Research, 3*(1), 43–58.

González-Ferriz, F. (2022). Marketing 5.0 and new technologies before and after the COVID-19 pandemic. *Estudios de Economía Aplicada, 40*(3). Advance online publication. doi:10.25115/eea.v40i3.7885

Gordon, R., Carrigan, M., & Hastings, G. (2011). A framework for sustainable marketing. *Marketing Theory, 11*(2), 143–163. doi:10.1177/1470593111403218

Goyal, M. (2019). Artificial intelligence: A tool for hyper personalization. International Journal of 360. *Management Review, 7*(01).

Green Business Bureau. (2022). *What Is Sustainable Marketing and why Is It Important in 2022.* Retrieved at 20 Oct. (2023) from https://greenbusinessbureau.com/business-function/marketing-sales/what-is-sustainable-marketing-and-why-is-it-important-in-2021/

Gretzel, U. (2018). From smart destinations to smart tourism regions, Investigaciones Regionales. *Journal of Regional Research, 42*, 171–184. https://investigacionesregionales.org/wp-content/uploads/sites/3/2019/01/10-GRETZEL.pdf

Grewal, D., Roggeveen, A. L., & Nordfält, J. (2017). The Future of Retailing. *Journal of Retailing, 93*(1), 1–6. doi:10.1016/j.jretai.2016.12.008

Grönroos, C., & Voima, P. (2013). Critical service logic: Making sense of value creation and co-creation. *Journal of the Academy of Marketing Science, 41*(2), 133–150. doi:10.1007/s11747-012-0308-3

Grossmeier, J. (2018). The Art of Health Promotion: Ideas for improving health outcomes. *American Journal of Health Promotion, 32*(4), 1145–1156. doi:10.1177/0890117118765037 PMID:29667500

GroundTruth Marketing. (2023, June 16). *Location-Based Marketing: The Ultimate Guide*. GroundTruth. https://www.groundtruth.com/insight/location-based-marketing-101/

Grover, P., Kar, A. K., & Dwivedi, Y. K. (2022). Understanding artificial intelligence adoption in operations management: Insights from the review of academic literature and social media discussions. *Annals of Operations Research, 308*(1-2), 177–213. doi:10.1007/s10479-020-03683-9

Güngör, H. (2020). Creating value with artificial intelligence: A multi-stakeholder perspective. *Journal of Creating Value, 6*(1), 72–85. doi:10.1177/2394964320921071

Guo, J. (2022). Influencing Factors of College Students' Use of Sports Apps in Mandatory Situations: Based on UTAUT and SDT. *BioMed Research International*.

Guo, H., Woodruff, A., & Yadav, A. (2020, April). Improving lives of indebted farmers using deep learning: Predicting agricultural produce prices using convolutional neural networks. *Proceedings of the AAAI Conference on Artificial Intelligence, 34*(08), 13294–13299. doi:10.1609/aaai.v34i08.7039

Guo, T., Yu, K., Aloqaily, M., & Wan, S. (2022). Constructing a prior-dependent graph for data clustering and dimension reduction in the edge of AIoT. *Future Generation Computer Systems, 128*, 381–394. doi:10.1016/j.future.2021.09.044

Guo, X., Song, X., Dou, B., Wang, A., & Hu, H. (2023). Can digital transformation of the enterprise break the monopoly? *Personal and Ubiquitous Computing, 27*(4), 1629–1642. doi:10.1007/s00779-022-01666-0

Gupta, P., & Malhotra, N. K. (2021). Internet of Things (IoT) and marketing: A review of opportunities and challenges. *Journal of Business Research, 129*, 122–138.

Gupta, S., Su, B. C., & Walter, Z. (2004). An empirical study of consumer switching from traditional to electronic channels: A purchase-decision process perspective. *International Journal of Electronic Commerce, 8*(3), 131–161. doi:10.1080/10864415.2004.11044302

Gurau, C., Ranchhod, A., & Gauzente, C. (2003). To legislate or not to legislate': A comparative exploratory study of privacy/personalisation factors affecting French, UK and US web sites. *Journal of Consumer Marketing, 20*(7), 652–664. doi:10.1108/07363760310506184

Gursoy, D., Lu, L., Nunkoo, R., & Deng, D. (2023). Metaverse in services marketing: An overview and future research directions. *Service Industries Journal, 43*(15-16), 1140–1172. Advance online publication. doi:10.1080/02642069.2023.2252750

Gutierrez, N. (2006). *Demystifying market basket analysis*. DM Review Special Report.

Gu, Z., Wei, J., & Xu, F. (2016). An empirical study on factors influencing consumers' initial trust in wearable commerce. *Journal of Computer Information Systems, 56*(1), 79–85. doi:10.1080/08874417.2015.11645804

Hafez, M. (2023). The nexus between social media marketing efforts and overall brand equity in the banking sector in Bangladesh: Testing a moderated mediation model. *Journal of Internet Commerce*, 22(2), 293–320. doi:10.1080/1533 2861.2022.2042968

Hahm, J., Choi, H., Matsuoka, H., Kim, J., & Byon, K. K. (2023). Understanding the relationship between acceptance of multifunctional health and fitness features of wrist-worn wearables and actual usage. *International Journal of Sports Marketing & Sponsorship*, 24(2), 333–358. doi:10.1108/IJSMS-08-2022-0163

Hahn, G. J. (2020). Industry 4.0: A supply chain innovation perspective. *International Journal of Production Research*, 58(5), 1425–1441. doi:10.1080/00207543.2019.1641642

Haight, R., Haensch, W., & Friedman, D. (2016). Solar-powering the Internet of Things. *Science*, 353(6295), 124–125. doi:10.1126/science.aag0476 PMID:27387939

Hajli, M. (2015). Social commerce constructs and consumer's intention to buy. *International Journal of Information Management*, 35(2), 183–191. doi:10.1016/j.ijinfomgt.2014.12.005

Haleem, A., & Javaid, M. (2019). Additive manufacturing applications in industry 4.0: a review. *Journal of Industrial Integration and Management, 4*(4), 1930001.

Haleem, A., Javaid, M., Qadri, M. A., Singh, R. P., & Suman, R. (2022). Artificial intelligence (AI) applications for marketing: A literature-based study. *International Journal of Intelligent Networks*.

Haleem, A., Javaid, M., Qadri, M. A., Singh, R. P., & Suman, R. (2022). Artificial intelligence (AI) applications for marketing: A literature-based study. *International Journal of Intelligent Networks*.

Hamari, J., Koivisto, J., & Sarsa, H. (2014). Does gamification work? A literature review of empirical studies on gamification. In *2014 47th Hawaii International Conference on System Sciences* (pp. 3025-3034). IEEE.

Hamid, S., & Jameel, S. T. (2020). A Study of Green Marketing Practices in the Selected Ayurvedic Resorts of Kerala. In *Global Developments in Healthcare and Medical Tourism* (pp. 176–187). IGI. doi:10.4018/978-1-5225-9787-2.ch010

Hamizan, M., Abu, N. H., Mansor, M. F., & Zaidi, M. A. (2023). An Analysis of the Effect of Price and Quality on Customer Buying Patterns: An Empirical Study of iPhone Buyers. *International Journal of Interactive Mobile Technologies*, 17(18).

Hamoudia, M., & Vanston, L. (2023). Machine Learning for New Product Forecasting. In *Forecasting with Artificial Intelligence: Theory and Applications* (pp. 77-104). Cham: Springer Nature Switzerland.

Handler, I., & Chang, W. (2015). Social Attributes of a Smartphone and their importance to young Taiwanese consumers: An explorative study. *source. International Journal of Arts and Commerce*, 4, 16–29.

Hanifah, I. A., & Ismawati, I. (2022). The effect of business strategy, innovation, organizational culture on the performance of micro small medium enterprises (MSMES) moderated by financial literature. *Fair Value: Jurnal Ilmiah Akuntansi dan Keuangan, 4*(10), 4416-4426.

Han, R., Lam, H. K., Zhan, Y., Wang, Y., Dwivedi, Y. K., & Tan, K. H. (2021). Artificial intelligence in business-to-business marketing: A bibliometric analysis of current research status, development and future directions. *Industrial Management & Data Systems*, 121(12), 2467–2497. doi:10.1108/IMDS-05-2021-0300

Hansen, K. T., Misra, K., & Pai, M. M. (2021). Frontiers: Algorithmic collusion: Supra-competitive prices via independent algorithms. *Marketing Science*, 40(1), 1–12. doi:10.1287/mksc.2020.1276

Hapsari, R., Hussein, A. S., & Handrito, R. P. (2020). Being Fair to Customers: A strategy in enhancing customer engagement and loyalty in the Indonesia mobile telecommunication industry. *Services Marketing Quarterly*, *41*(1), 49–67. doi:10.1080/15332969.2019.1707375

Harandi, S. R., Boubereje, A., & Abdolvand, N. (2023). Platform economy implications for sustainability: Good, bad, unknown. In D. B. Sariipek & V. Franca (Eds.), *Digital and Green Transition: New Perspectives on Work Organization* (pp. 73–104). Dora Publishing.

Hardt, M., & Nath, S. (2012). *Privacy-aware personalization for mobile advertising*. ACM Digital Library. doi:10.1145/2382196.2382266

Harmel, R. D., Kleinman, P., Eve, M., Ippolito, J. A., Beebout, S., Delgado, J., Vandenberg, B., & Buser, M. (2021). The Partnerships for Data Innovations (PDI): Facilitating data stewardship and catalyzing research engagement in the digital age. *Agricultural & Environmental Letters*, *6*(4), e20055. doi:10.1002/ael2.20055

Hart, C., Doherty, N., & Ellis-Chadwick, F. (2000). Retailer adoption of the Internet–implications for retail marketing. *European Journal of Marketing*, *34*(8), 954–974. doi:10.1108/03090560010331441

HarveyC. R.MoormanC.ToledoM. (2018). How blockchain will change marketing as we know it. *Available at* SSRN 3257511. doi:10.2139/ssrn.3257511

Hasan, O., Brunie, L., & Bertino, E. (2022). Privacy-Preserving Reputation Systems Based on Blockchain and Other Cryptographic Building Blocks: A Survey. *ACM Computing Surveys*, *55*(2), 1–37. doi:10.1145/3490236

Hassenzahl, M., & Tractinsky, N. (2006). User experience - a research agenda. *Behaviour & Information Technology*, *25*(2), 91–97. doi:10.1080/01449290500330331

Hastig, G. M., & Sodhi, M. S. (2020). Blockchain for supply chain traceability: Business requirements and critical success factors. *Production and Operations Management*, *29*(4), 935–954. doi:10.1111/poms.13147

Hatamifar, P., Ghaderi, Z., & Nikjoo, A. (2021). Factors affecting international tourists' intention to use local mobile apps in online purchase. *Asia Pacific Journal of Tourism Research*, *26*(12), 1285–1301. doi:10.1080/10941665.2021.1983626

Helberger, N., Huh, J., Milne, G., Strycharz, J., & Sundaram, H. (2020). Macro and exogenous factors in computational advertising: Key issues and new research directions. *Journal of Advertising*, *49*(4), 377–393. doi:10.1080/00913367.2020.1811179

Hermina, N., Rahma, Y. D., & Gusnia, A. R. (2022). Marketing 5.0 and consumer behavior of the millennial (GEN Z) Generation as business performance boosting in COVID-19 pandemic (case study: SMEs in West Java). *Central Asia & the Caucasus, 23*(1).

Hernández-Nieves, E., Hernández, G., Gil-González, A. B., Rodríguez-González, S., & Corchado, J. M. (2020). Fog computing architecture for personalized recommendation of banking products. *Expert Systems with Applications*, *140*, 112900. doi:10.1016/j.eswa.2019.112900

Hersh, W. R. (2009). A stimulus to define informatics and health information technology. *BMC Medical Informatics and Decision Making*, *9*(1), 24. Advance online publication. doi:10.1186/1472-6947-9-24 PMID:19445665

Heskiano, H., Syah, T. Y. R., & Hilmy, M. R. (2020). Social Media Marketing Relations, Brand Awareness to Brand Loyalty Through The Brand Image. *Journal of Multidisciplinary Academic*, *4*(4), 208–214.

Hildebrand, C. (2019). The machine age of marketing: How artificial intelligence changes the way people think, act, and decide. *NIM Marketing Intelligence Review*, *11*(2), 10–17. doi:10.2478/nimmir-2019-0010

Hoffman, D. L., & Fodor, M. (2010). Can you measure the ROI of your social media marketing. *MIT Sloan Management Review*. https://labarce.files.wordpress.com/2010/10/mit.pdf

Hohenberg, S., & Taylor, W. (2022). Measuring customer satisfaction and customer loyalty. Handbook of Market Research, 909.

Holbrook, A. L., Berent, M. K., Krosnick, J. A., Visser, P. S., & Boninger, D. S. (2005). Attitude importance and the accumulation of attitude-relevant knowledge in memory. *Journal of Personality and Social Psychology*, *88*(5), 749–769. doi:10.1037/0022-3514.88.5.749 PMID:15898873

Homburg, C., Wieseke, J., & Hoyer, W. D. (2009). Social identity and the service-profit chain. *Journal of Marketing*, *73*(2), 38–54. doi:10.1509/jmkg.73.2.38

Hopkins, J. L. (2021). An investigation into emerging industry 4.0 technologies as drivers of supply chain innovation in Australia. *Computers in Industry*, *125*, 103323. doi:10.1016/j.compind.2020.103323

Hopkinson, P. J., Singhal, A., Perez-Vega, R., & Waite, K. (2022, May). The Transformative Power of Artificial Intelligence for Managing Customer Relationships: An Abstract. In *Academy of Marketing Science Annual Conference* (pp. 307-308). Cham: Springer Nature Switzerland.

Hosbond, J. H., & Skov, M. B. (2007). Micro mobility marketing: Two cases on location-based supermarket shopping trolleys. Journal of Targeting. *Measurement and Analysis for Marketing*, *16*(1), 68–77. doi:10.1057/palgrave.jt.5750058

Hossain, M. S., & Rahman, M. F. (2022). Machine Learning and Artificial Intelligence: The New Move for Marketers. In Developing Relationships, Personalization, and Data Herald in Marketing 5.0 (pp. 215-241). IGI Global.

Howell, S., Yin, P. T., & Robinson, J. C. (2021). Quantifying The Economic Burden Of Drug Utilization Management On Payers, Manufacturers, Physicians, And Patients: Study examines the economic burden of drug utilization management on payers, manufacturers, physicians, and patients. *Health Affairs*, *40*(8), 1206–1214. doi:10.1377/hlthaff.2021.00036 PMID:34339243

Hsieh, J. K., & Tsao, W. C. (2014). Reducing perceived online shopping risk to enhance loyalty: A website quality perspective. *Journal of Risk Research*, *17*(2), 241–261. doi:10.1080/13669877.2013.794152

Huang, J. Y., & Liu, J. H. (2020). Using social media mining technology to improve stock price forecast accuracy. *Journal of Forecasting*, *39*(1), 104–116. doi:10.1002/for.2616

Huang, L., Zhen, L., Wang, J., & Zhang, X. (2022). Blockchain implementation for circular supply chain management: Evaluating critical success factors. *Industrial Marketing Management*, *102*, 451–464. doi:10.1016/j.indmarman.2022.02.009

Huang, M. H., & Rust, R. T. (2018). Artificial intelligence in service. *Journal of Service Research*, *21*(2), 155–172. doi:10.1177/1094670517752459

Huang, M. H., & Rust, R. T. (2021). A strategic framework for artificial intelligence in marketing. *Journal of the Academy of Marketing Science*, *49*(1), 30–50. doi:10.1007/s11747-020-00749-9

Huang, M. H., & Rust, R. T. (2022). A framework for collaborative artificial intelligence in marketing. *Journal of Retailing*, *98*(2), 209–223. doi:10.1016/j.jretai.2021.03.001

Huang, Z., & Benyoucef, M. (2013). From e-commerce to social commerce: A close look at design features. *Electronic Commerce Research and Applications*, *12*(4), 246–259. doi:10.1016/j.elerap.2012.12.003

Hudders, L., De Jans, S., & De Veirman, M. (2021). The Commercialization of Social Media Stars: A Literature Review and Conceptual Framework on the Strategic Use of Social Media Influencers. *International Journal of Advertising, 40*(3), 327–375. doi:10.1080/02650487.2020.1836925

Hudson, S., Huang, L., Roth, M. S., & Madden, T. J. (2015). The influence of social media interactions on consumer–brand relationships: A three-country study of brand perceptions and marketing behaviors. *International Journal of Research in Marketing, 32*(1), 27–41. doi:10.1016/j.ijresmar.2015.06.004

Humphreys, A., & Wang, R. J. H. (2018). Automated text analysis for consumer research. *The Journal of Consumer Research, 44*(6), 1274–1306. doi:10.1093/jcr/ucx104

Hu, N., Zhang, J., & Pavlou, P. A. (2009). Overcoming the J-shaped distribution of product reviews. *Communications of the ACM, 52*(10), 144–147. doi:10.1145/1562764.1562800

Hutson, J. (2023). *Shared cinematic experience and emerging technologies: Integrating mixed-reality components for the future of cinema.* Arts & Commuication.

Huynh, L. D., Duong, P. T., Bach, K. D., & Hung, P. D. (2023, February). Potential Customers Prediction in Bank Tele-marketing. In *Proceedings of International Conference on Data Science and Applications: ICDSA 2022,* Volume 2 (pp. 43-50). Singapore: Springer Nature Singapore. 10.1007/978-981-19-6634-7_4

Hwang, C., Chung, T.-L., & Sanders, E. A. (2016). Attitudes and purchase intentions for smart clothing: Examining US consumers' functional, expressive, and aesthetic needs for solar-powered clothing. *Clothing & Textiles Research Journal, 34*(3), 207–222. doi:10.1177/0887302X16646447

Hysa, B., Karasek, A., & Zdonek, I. (2021). Social media usage by different generations as a tool for sustainable tourism marketing in society 5.0 idea. *Sustainability (Basel), 13*(3), 1018. doi:10.3390/su13031018

Iacobucci, D., Petrescu, M., Krishen, A., & Bendixen, M. (2019). The state of marketing analytics in research and practice. *Journal of Marketing Analytics, 7*(3), 152–181. doi:10.1057/s41270-019-00059-2

Iafrate, F. (2018). *Artificial intelligence and big data: The birth of a new intelligence.* John Wiley & Sons. doi:10.1002/9781119426653

Ilyas, M. (2019). Determining Critical Success Factors for Quality and Accreditation through Delphi Technique. *International Journal of Higher Education, 8*(3), 148–158. doi:10.5430/ijhe.v8n3p148

İnan, Ü. S. E. (2023). Evaluation Of Digital Marketing From A Bibliometric Analysis Perspective. *Socialis Series in Social Science, 4,* 45–58. doi:10.20319/socv4.4558

Indiani, N. L., Sudiartini, N. W. A., & Utami, N. K. A. T. (2022). Pengaruh Brand Image, Awareness Dan Trust Terhadap Keputusan Pembelian Melalui Digital Marketing Pada Produk Dupa Harum Grosir. *Jurnal Valuasi: Jurnal Ilmiah Ilmu Manajemen dan Kewirausahaan, 2*(1), 152-163.

Insight, C. (2016). *Wearables momentum continues.* Online verfügbar unter: http://www ccsinsight com/press/company-news/2516-wearables-momentum-continues

Ishwaran, A. (2017). 5 Benefits of social media Integration and the Ways to Achieve it | TO THE NEW blog. *TO THE NEW BLOG.* https://www.tothenew.com/blog/5-benefits-of-social-media-integration-and-the-ways-to-achieve-it/

Istanti, E., Sanusi, R., & Daengs, G. S. (2020). Impacts of price, Promotion and go food consumer satisfaction in faculty of economic and business students of Bhayangkara University Surabaya. *Ekspektra: Jurnal Bisnis dan Manajemen, 4*(2), 104-120.

Itani, O. S., Badrinarayanan, V., & Rangarajan, D. (2023). The impact of business-to-business salespeople's social media use on value co-creation and cross/up-selling: The role of social capital. *European Journal of Marketing*, *57*(3), 683–717. doi:10.1108/EJM-11-2021-0916

Jadhav, G. G., Gaikwad, S. V., & Bapat, D. (2023). A Systematic Literature Review: Digital Marketing and Its Impact on SMEs. *Journal of Indian Business Research*, *15*(1), 76–91. doi:10.1108/JIBR-05-2022-0129

Jain, A., Kushwah, R., Swaroop, A., & Yadav, A. (2021). Role of Artificial Intelligence of Things (AIoT) to Combat Pandemic COVID-19. In Handbook of Research on Innovations and Applications of AI, IoT, and Cognitive Technologies (pp. 117-128). IGI Global.

Jaiwant, S. V. (2023). The Changing Role of Marketing: Industry 5.0-the Game Changer. In Transformation for Sustainable Business and Management Practices: Exploring the Spectrum of Industry 5.0 (pp. 187-202). Emerald Publishing Limited.

Jarek, K., & Mazurek, G. (2019). Marketing and Artificial Intelligence. *Central European Business Review*, *8*(2), 46–55. doi:10.18267/j.cebr.213

Jarrahi, M. H. (2018). Artificial intelligence and the future of work: Human-AI symbiosis in organizational decision making. *Business Horizons*, *61*(4), 577–586. doi:10.1016/j.bushor.2018.03.007

Jatobá, M., Santos, J., Gutierriz, I., Moscon, D., Fernandes, P. O., & Teixeira, J. P. (2019). Evolution of artificial intelligence research in human resources. *Procedia Computer Science*, *164*, 137–142. doi:10.1016/j.procs.2019.12.165

Javaid, M., Haleem, A., Singh, R. P., & Suman, R. (2022). Artificial intelligence applications for industry 4.0: A literature-based study. *Journal of Industrial Integration and Management*, *7*(01), 83–111. doi:10.1142/S2424862221300040

Javornik, A. (2016). Augmented reality: Research agenda for studying the impact of its media characteristics on consumer behaviour. *Journal of Retailing and Consumer Services*, *30*, 252–261. doi:10.1016/j.jretconser.2016.02.004

Jayadeva, S. M., Al Ayub Ahmed, A., Malik, R., Shaikh, A. A., Siddique, M. N. E. A., & Naved, M. (2022, June). Roles of Cloud Computing and Internet of Things in Marketing Management: A Critical Review and Future Trends. In *Proceedings of Second International Conference in Mechanical and Energy Technology: ICMET 2021, India* (pp. 165-173). Singapore: Springer Nature Singapore.

Jennings, R. (2019). *TikTok, explained*. Vox. Retrieved from https://www.vox.com/culture/2018/12/10/18129126/tiktok-app-musically-meme-cringe

Joghee, S. (2021). RETRACTED ARTICLE: Internet of Things-assisted E-marketing and distribution framework. *Soft Computing*, *25*(18), 12291–12303. doi:10.1007/s00500-021-05920-0

Johnson, J. P., Rhodes, A., & Wildenbeest, M. (2023). Platform design when sellers use pricing algorithms. *Econometrica*, *91*(5), 1841–1879. doi:10.3982/ECTA19978

Jo, J. W. (2020). Case Studies for Insurance Service Marketing Using Artificial Intelligence (AI) in the InsurTech Industry. *Journal of Digital Convergence*, *18*(10), 175–180.

Jones, P., Comfort, D., & Hillier, D. (2007). What's in store? Retail marketing and corporate social responsibility. *Marketing Intelligence & Planning*, *25*(1), 17–30. doi:10.1108/02634500710722371

Joshi, D. A., & Masih, D. J. (2023). Enhancing employee efficiency and performance in industry 5.0 organizations through artificial intelligence integration. *European Economic Letters*, *13*(4), 300–315.

Jung, S. Y., & Yoon, S. J. (2021). Augmented reality and virtual reality in the Internet of Things (IoE) for marketing: Opportunities and challenges. *Technological Forecasting and Social Change*, *172*, 120994.

Kaiyp, K., & Alimanova, M. (2020). Improving indicators of digital marketing using artificial intelligence. *Suleyman Demirel University Bulletin: Natural and Technical Sciences, 52*(1). Available at: https://journals.sdu.edu.kz/index.php/nts/article/view/71

Kajale, P. A., & Joshi, S. (2021). Gearing up for marketing 5.0 in the digital economy: Moving from traditional to digital. *IBMRD's. Journal of Management Research, 10*(2), 79–81.

Kakatkar, C., & Spann, M. (2019). Marketing analytics using anonymized and fragmented tracking data. *International Journal of Research in Marketing, 36*(1), 117–136. doi:10.1016/j.ijresmar.2018.10.001

Kalantari, M., & Rauschnabel, P. (2018). *Exploring the early adopters of augmented reality smart glasses: The case of Microsoft HoloLens. Augmented reality and virtual reality.* Springer.

Kandemir, H. K. (2021). Duties and Responsibilities of Directors of Joint Stock Companies on Corporate Social Responsibility: An Evaluation with Respect to Turkish Company Law. *Selcuk Universitesi Hukuk Fakultesi Dergisi, 29*, 2209.

Kaplan, A., & Haenlein, M. (2020). Rulers of the World, Unite! The Challenges and Opportunities of Artificial Intelligence. *Business Horizons, 63*(1), 37–50. doi:10.1016/j.bushor.2019.09.003

Karimova, G. Z., & Goby, V. P. (2021). The adaptation of anthropomorphism and archetypes for marketing artificial intelligence. *Journal of Consumer Marketing, 38*(2), 229–238. doi:10.1108/JCM-04-2020-3785

Kashif, M., & Udunuwara, M. (2022). Guest editorial: Socially responsible marketing: a transformative agenda. *Asia-Pacific Journal of Business Administration, 14*(2), 161–165. doi:10.1108/APJBA-05-2022-566

Kaufinger, G. G., & Neuenschwander, C. (2020). Retail Apocalypse? Maybe blame accounting. Investigating inventory valuation as a determinant of retail firm failure. *American Journal of Business, 35*(2), 83–101. doi:10.1108/AJB-07-2019-0050

Kaur, S. (2016). Social media marketing. *Asian Journal of Multidimensional Research, 5*(4), 6–12.

Keh, H. T., & Xie, Y. (2009). Corporate reputation and customer behavioral intentions: The roles of trust, identification and commitment. *Industrial Marketing Management, 38*(7), 732–742. doi:10.1016/j.indmarman.2008.02.005

Keys, C. (2021). Social Polarization and Ghettoization: Economic and Policy-Driven Causes. In *Reduced Inequalities* (pp. 789–798). Springer International Publishing. doi:10.1007/978-3-319-95882-8_88

Khan, S. A. (2023). E-Marketing, E-Commerce, E-Business, and Internet of Things: An Overview of Terms in the Context of Small and Medium Enterprises (SMEs). *Global Applications of the Internet of Things in Digital Marketing*, 332-348.

Khandai, S., Mathew, J., Yadav, R., Kataria, S., & Kohli, H. (2022). Ensuring brand loyalty for firms practising sustainable marketing: a roadmap. *Society and Business Review*, (ahead-of-print).

Khan, M. T. (2014). The concept of 'marketing mix' and its elements. *International Journal of Information, Business and Management, 6*(2), 95–107.

Khasawneh, O. Y. (2018). Technophobia: Examining its hidden factors and defining it. *Technology in Society, 54*(1), 93–100. doi:10.1016/j.techsoc.2018.03.008

Khokhar, P. (2019). Evolution of artificial intelligence in marketing, comparison with traditional marketing. *Our Heritage, 67*(5), 375–389.

Khrais, L. T. (2020). Role of artificial intelligence in shaping consumer demand in E-commerce. *Future Internet, 12*(12), 226. doi:10.3390/fi12120226

Khvoynitskaya, S. (2019). *Internet of everything vs internet of things: what is the difference?* Available at: www.itransition. com/blog/internet-of-everything-vs-internet-of-things-what-is-the-difference

Kibria, M. G., Ali, S., Jarwar, M. A., & Chong, I. (2017, October). A framework to support data interoperability in web objects based IoT environments. In *2017 International Conference on Information and Communication Technology Convergence (ICTC)* (pp. 29-31). IEEE. 10.1109/ICTC.2017.8190935

Kietzmann, J. H., Hermkens, K., McCarthy, I. P., & Silvestre, B. S. (2011). Social media? Get serious! Understanding the functional building blocks of social media. *Business Horizons, 54*(3), 241–251. doi:10.1016/j.bushor.2011.01.005

Kietzmann, J., & Pitt, L. F. (2020). Artificial intelligence and machine learning: What managers need to know. *Business Horizons, 63*(2), 131–133. doi:10.1016/j.bushor.2019.11.005

Kilani, Y. (2020). Cyber-security effect on organizational internal process: Mediating role of technological infrastructure. *Problems and Perspectives in Management, 18*(1), 449–460. doi:10.21511/ppm.18(1).2020.39

Kim, D. J., Ferrin, D. L., & Rao, H. R. (2008). A trust-based consumer decision-making model in electronic commerce: The role of trust, perceived risk, and their antecedents. *Decision Support Systems, 44*(2), 544–564. doi:10.1016/j.dss.2007.07.001

Kim, H.-M., Lee, I., & Kaminsky, P. (2021). Regulatory frameworks for the Internet of Everything (IoE): A review of opportunities and challenges. *Journal of Business Research, 126*, 101–113.

Kim, K. J., & Shin, D.-H. (2015). An acceptance model for smart watches: Implications for the adoption of future wearable technology. *Internet Research, 25*(4), 527–541. doi:10.1108/IntR-05-2014-0126

Klein, T. (2021). Autonomous algorithmic collusion: Q-learning under sequential pricing. *The RAND Journal of Economics, 52*(3), 538–558. doi:10.1111/1756-2171.12383

Koroglu, O. (2023). AI and XR (AIXR) Marketing in Industry 5.0 or Society 5.0. In Digitalization, Sustainable Development, and Industry 5.0: An Organizational Model for Twin Transitions (pp. 83-100). Emerald Publishing Limited.

Kotler, P., Kartajaya, H., & Setiawan, I. (2021). *Marketing 5.0: Technology for humanity*. John Wiley & Sons.

Kotler, P., Kartajaya, H., & Setiawan, I. (2021). *Marketing 5.0: Technology for Humanity*. John Wiley & Sons.

Kotler, P., Kartajaya, H., Setiawan, I., & Hendratmoko, W. (2017). *Marketing 4.0: Moving from Traditional to Digital*. John Wiley & Sons.

Kotler, P., Keller, K. L., Brady, M., Goodman, M., & Hansen, T. (2020). *Marketing Management* (3rd ed.). Pearson.

Kotler, P., & Zaltman, G. (1971). Social marketing: An approach to planned social change. *Journal of Marketing, 35*(3), 3–12. doi:10.1177/002224297103500302 PMID:12276120

Kousiouris, G., Tsarsitalidis, S., Psomakelis, E., Koloniaris, S., Bardaki, C., Tserpes, K., Nikolaidou, M., & Anagnostopoulos, D. (2019). A microservice-based framework for integrating IoT management platforms, semantic and AI services for supply chain management. *Ict Express, 5*(2), 141–145. doi:10.1016/j.icte.2019.04.002

Krishen, A. S., Raschke, R. L., & Kachroo, P. (2011). A feedback control approach to maintain consumer information load in online shopping environments. *Information & Management, 48*(8), 344–352. doi:10.1016/j.im.2011.09.005

Krishen, A. S., Raschke, R. L., & Mejza, M. (2010). Guidelines for shaping perceptions of fairness of transportation infrastructure policies: The case of vehicle mileage tax. *Transportation Journal, 49*(3), 24–38. doi:10.2307/40904902

Krishna, Sheoliha, Ghildiyal, Reddy, Manoharan, & Purohit. (2022). An overview of exploring the potential of artificial intelligence approaches in digital marketing. *The British Journal of Administrative Management*. https://tbjam.org/vol58-special-issue-06/

Kshetri, N., Dwivedi, Y. K., Davenport, T. H., & Panteli, N. (2023). Generative Artificial Intelligence in Marketing: Applications, Opportunities, Challenges, and Research Agenda. *International Journal of Information Management*, *102716*, 102716. Advance online publication. doi:10.1016/j.ijinfomgt.2023.102716

Kuligowski, K. (2023). *Facial Recognition Advertising: The New Way to Target Ads to Consumers*. Retrieved at 24 Dec. 2023 from https://www.businessnewsdaily.com/15213-walgreens-facial-recognition.html

Kulkarni, G., Kannan, P. K., & Moe, W. (2012). Using online search data to forecast new product sales. *Decision Support Systems*, *52*(3), 604–611. doi:10.1016/j.dss.2011.10.017

Kulkul, C. (2020). Public Space and Social Polarization: A case study of the New Wave Turkish Migrants with a comparative analysis of Berlin, İstanbul & Ankara. *The Journal of Public Space*, *5*(1), 111–128. doi:10.32891/jps.v5i1.1128

Kumar, P., Tomar, P. K., Bharti, S., Naredla, S. K., Ibrahim, R. K., & Bader Alazzam, M. (2023). Maximizing the Potential of Artificial Intelligence in Digital Marketing. *2023 3rd International Conference on Advance Computing and Innovative Technologies in Engineering (ICACITE)*, 2736-2741.

Kumar, A., Bezawada, R., Rishika, R., Janakiraman, R., & Kannan, P. K. (2016). From social to sale: The effects of firm-generated content in social media on customer behavior. *Journal of Marketing*, *80*(1), 7–25. doi:10.1509/jm.14.0249

Kumar, A., Gawande, A., & Brar, V. (2020). Neuro-Marketing: Opportunities and Challenges in India. *Vidyabharati International Interdisciplinary Research Journal*, *10*(2), 214–217.

Kumar, D. T. S. (2020). Data mining based marketing decision support system using hybrid machine learning algorithm. *Journal of Artificial Intelligence and Capsule Networks*, *2*(3), 185–193. doi:10.36548//jaicn.2020.3.006

Kumari, Dawra, Jaiswal, Raj, Manoharan, & Singh. (2022). An evaluation of machine learning techniques and how they affect human resource management and sustainable development. *The British Journal of Administrative Management*. https://tbjam.org/vol58-special-issue-06/

Kumari, S., Kumar, V., Sharmila, A., Murthy, C. R., Ahlawat, N., & Manoharan, G. (2023, August). Blockchain-Based E-Analysis of Social Media Forums for Crypto Currency Phase Shifts. In *2023 5th International Conference on Inventive Research in Computing Applications (ICIRCA)* (pp. 1222-1225). IEEE.

Kumar, S., Chawla, C., Yadav, A. K., Udaipure, P. A., & Chatley, P. (2022). Altered Consumer Behavior Paradigms and Novel Trends of Sustainable Marketing in the Next Normal. *Korea Review of International Studies*, *15*(3).

Kumar, S., Tiwari, P., & Zymbler, M. (2019). Internet of Things is a revolutionary approach for future technology enhancement: A review. *Journal of Big Data*, *6*(1), 1–21. doi:10.1186/s40537-019-0268-2

Kumar, V., Chattaraman, V., Neghina, C., Skiera, B., Aksoy, L., Buoye, A., & Henseler, J. (2013). Data-driven services marketing in a connected world. *Journal of Service Management*, *24*(3), 330–352. doi:10.1108/09564231311327021

Kumar, V., Rajan, B., Venkatesan, R., & Lecinski, J. (2019). Understanding the role of artificial intelligence in personalized engagement marketing. *California Management Review*, *61*(4), 135–155. doi:10.1177/0008125619859317

Kumar, V., & Reinartz, W. (2012). *Customer Relationship Management: Concept, Strategy, and Tools*. Springer. doi:10.1007/978-3-642-20110-3

Kumar, V., Sharma, N. K., Mittal, A., & Verma, P. (2023). The Role of IoT and IIoT in Supplier and Customer Continuous Improvement Interface. In *Digital Transformation and Industry 4.0 for Sustainable Supply Chain Performance* (pp. 161–174). Springer International Publishing. doi:10.1007/978-3-031-19711-6_7

Kummitha, R., Krishna Reddy, M., & Rao, S. S. (2021). Internet of Things (IoT) for sustainable city planning: Opportunities and challenges. *Journal of Cleaner Production*, *286*, 125592.

Kurniawan, G. (2022). Social Marketing and Corporate Social Responsibility on the Brand Image of Lifebuoy Bath Soap Products. *Enrichment: Journal of Management*, *12*(2), 1275–1279.

Labrecque, L. I., vor dem Esche, J., Mathwick, C., Novak, T. P., & Hofacker, C. F. (2013). Consumer power: Evolution in the digital age. *Journal of Interactive Marketing*, *27*(4), 257–269. doi:10.1016/j.intmar.2013.09.002

Lal, B., Ismagilova, E., Dwivedi, Y. K., & Kwayu, S. (2019). Return on Investment in Social Media Marketing: Literature review and suggestions for future research. In Advances in theory and practice of emerging markets (pp. 3–17). doi:10.1007/978-3-030-24374-6_1

Lamberton, C., & Stephen, A. T. (2016). A thematic exploration of digital, social media, and mobile marketing: Research evolution from 2000 to 2015 and an agenda for future inquiry. *Journal of Marketing*, *80*(6), 146–172. doi:10.1509/jm.15.0415

Lambrecht, A., & Tucker, C. (2013). When does retargeting work? Information specificity in online advertising. *JMR, Journal of Marketing Research*, *50*(5), 561–576. doi:10.1509/jmr.11.0503

Langert, B. (2019). *The battle to do good: Inside McDonald's sustainability journey*. Emerald Group Publishing. doi:10.1108/9781787568150

Laroche, M., Zhang, Q., & Dai, M. (2005). Online consumer behavior: a review and agenda for future research. In Research Developments in Computer Vision and Image Processing: Methodologies and Applications (pp. 155-170). IGI Global.

Leal Filho, W., Levesque, V., Sivapalan, S., Salvia, A. L., Fritzen, B., Deckert, R., Kozlova, V., LeVasseur, T. J., Emblen-Perry, K., Azeiteiro, U. M., Paço, A., Borsari, B., & Shiel, C. (2022). Social values and sustainable development: Community experiences. *Environmental Sciences Europe*, *34*(1), 1–13. doi:10.1186/s12302-022-00641-z PMID:35967983

Le, D., Nguyen, T. M., Quach, S., Thaichon, P., & Ratten, V. (2021). The Development and Current Trends of Digital Marketing and Relationship Marketing Research. In *Developing Digital Marketing*. Emerald Publishing Limited. doi:10.1108/978-1-80071-348-220211001

Ledger, D. (2014). A look at the uncertain future of smart wearable devices, and five industry developments that will be necessary for meaningful mass market adoption and sustained engagement. *Inside Wearables-Part.*, 2.

Lee, E. J. (2016). Empathy can increase customer equity related to pro-social brands. *Journal of Business Research*, *69*(9), 3748–3754. doi:10.1016/j.jbusres.2015.05.018

Lee, J. G., Schleicher, N. C., & Henriksen, L. (2019). Sales to minors, corporate brands, and assurances of voluntary compliance. *Tobacco Regulatory Science*, *5*(5), 431–439. doi:10.18001/TRS.5.5.3

Lee, J., Kim, D., Ryoo, H.-Y., & Shin, B.-S. (2016). Sustainable wearables: Wearable technology for enhancing the quality of human life. *Sustainability (Basel)*, *8*(5), 466. doi:10.3390/su8050466

Lee, J., Kim, H., & Kaminsky, P. (2020). Internet of Everything (IoE) for sustainability: A review of opportunities and challenges. *Journal of Cleaner Production*, *253*, 119994.

Lee, J., Park, D. H., & Han, I. (2008). The effect of negative online consumer reviews on product attitude: An information processing view. *Electronic Commerce Research and Applications*, *7*(3), 341–352. doi:10.1016/j.elerap.2007.05.004

Lee, M., & Youn, S. (2009). Electronic word of mouth (eWOM). *International Journal of Advertising*, *28*(3), 473–499. doi:10.2501/S0265048709200709

Lee, N. R., & Kotler, P. (2011). *Social marketing: Influencing behaviors for good*. SAGE publications.

Lee, N., & Kotler, P. (2011). *Social Marketing: Influencing Behaviors for Good* (4th ed.). SAGE Publications.

Lehrer, C., & Trenz, M. (2022). Omnichannel Business. *Electronic Markets*, *32*(2), 687–699. doi:10.1007/s12525-021-00511-1

Leppäniemi, M., Karjaluoto, H., Sinisalo, J., & Salo, J. (2006). Integrated marketing communications in mobile context. In DUV eBooks (pp. 397–415). doi:10.1007/3-8350-5702-2_21

Lerch, M. (2020). *Green marketing* [Doctoral dissertation]. Masarykova univerzita, Ekonomicko-správní fakulta.

Lewis, N., Huang, Q., Merkel, P., Rhee, D. K., & Sylvetsky, A. C. (2020). Differences in the sugar content of fast-food products across three countries. *Public Health Nutrition*, *23*(16), 2857–2863. doi:10.1017/S136898002000110X PMID:32576300

Liang, L. J., Choi, H. C., & Joppe, M. (2018). Exploring the Relationship between Satisfaction, Trust and Switching Intention, Repurchase Intention in the Context of Airbnb. *International Journal of Hospitality Management*, *69*, 41–48. doi:10.1016/j.ijhm.2017.10.015

Li, C., McMahon, C., & Newnes, L. (2009, January). Annotation in product lifecycle management: a review of approaches. In *International Design Engineering Technical Conferences and Computers and Information in Engineering Conference* (Vol. 48999, pp. 797-806). 10.1115/DETC2009-86624

Liébana-Cabanillas, F., Japutra, A., Molinillo, S., Singh, N., & Sinha, N. (2020). Assessment of mobile technology use in the emerging market: Analyzing intention to use m-payment services in India. *Telecommunications Policy*, *44*(9), 102009. doi:10.1016/j.telpol.2020.102009

Li, H. (2019). Special section introduction: Artificial intelligence and advertising. *Journal of Advertising*, *48*(4), 333–337. doi:10.1080/00913367.2019.1654947

Li, H., & Kannan, P. K. (2014). Attributing conversions in a multichannel online marketing environment: An empirical model and a field experiment. *JMR, Journal of Marketing Research*, *51*(1), 40–56. doi:10.1509/jmr.13.0050

Lim, W. M. (2023). Transformative marketing in the new normal: A novel practice-scholarly integrative review of business-to-business marketing mix challenges, opportunities, and solutions. *Journal of Business Research*, *160*, 113638. doi:10.1016/j.jbusres.2022.113638

Lim, W. M., O'Connor, P., Nair, S., Soleimani, S., & Rasul, T. (2023). A foundational theory of ethical decision-making: The case of marketing professionals. *Journal of Business Research*, *158*, 113579. doi:10.1016/j.jbusres.2022.113579

Lindecrantz, E., Gi, M. T. P., & Zerbi, S. (2020). *Personalizing the customer experience: Driving differentiation in retail*. McKinsey & Company. https://www.mckinsey.com/industries/retail/our-insights/personalizing-the-customer-experience-driving-differentiation-in-retail

Li, R., Cao, Z., Ye, H., & Yue, X. (2021, April). Application and development trend of artificial intelligence in enterprise marketing. *Journal of Physics: Conference Series*, *1881*(2), 022032. doi:10.1088/1742-6596/1881/2/022032

Li, S., Leszczyc, P. T. P., & Qiu, C. (2023). International retailer performance: Disentangling the interplay between rule of law and culture. *Journal of Retailing*, *99*(2), 193–209. doi:10.1016/j.jretai.2023.01.001

Liu, B., & Zhang, L. (2012). A Survey of Opinion Mining and Sentiment Analysis. In C. Aggarwal & C. Zhai (Eds.), *Mining Text Data*. Springer, doi:10.1007/978-1-4614-3223-4_13

Liu, C., Marchewka, J. T., Lu, J., & Yu, C. S. (2005). Beyond concern—A privacy-trust-behavioral intention model of electronic commerce. *Information & Management*, *42*(2), 289–304. doi:10.1016/j.im.2004.01.003

Liu, D., Alahmadi, A., Ni, J., Lin, X., & Shen, X. (2019). Anonymous reputation system for IIoT-enabled retail marketing atop PoS blockchain. *IEEE Transactions on Industrial Informatics*, *15*(6), 3527–3537. doi:10.1109/TII.2019.2898900

Liu, L., Li, S., & Opara, M. (2018). Corporate social responsibility and strategic company behaviour: CVS Health's discontinuation of tobacco products. *Corporate Social Responsibility and Environmental Management*, *25*(6), 1293–1305. doi:10.1002/csr.1639

Liu, X., He, M., Gao, F., & Xie, P. (2008). An empirical study of online shopping customer satisfaction in China: A holistic perspective. *International Journal of Retail & Distribution Management*, *36*(11), 919–940. doi:10.1108/09590550810911683

Liu, Y., & Chen, W. (2021). Optimization of brand marketing strategy of intelligent technology under the background of artificial intelligence. *Mobile Information Systems*, *12*, 1–8. doi:10.1155/2021/9507917

Liu, Y., Li, Y., & Yu, S. (2019). Internet of Things (IoT) for sustainable agriculture: A case study of precision irrigation. *Computers and Electronics in Agriculture*, *163*, 104831.

Liu, Y., Tang, Z., Chandu, T., & Joghee, S. (2021). Risk Handling and Vulnerability Assessment in IoT-Enabled Marketing Domain of Digital Business System. *Arabian Journal for Science and Engineering*, 1–13.

Li, W. (2022). Big Data precision marketing approach under IoT cloud platform information mining. *Computational Intelligence and Neuroscience*, *2022*. doi:10.1155/2022/4828108 PMID:35069719

Location-based marketing - benefits & effectiveness. (2023, July 18). Optimove. https://www.optimove.com/resources/learning-center/location-based-marketing

Location-Based Mobile Marketing . Benefits & Challenges. (2022, October 27). Sekel Tech. https://sekel.tech/blog/location-based-mobile-marketing-benefits-challenges

Lo, F. Y., & Campos, N. (2018). Blending Internet-of-Things (IoT) solutions into relationship marketing strategies. *Technological Forecasting and Social Change*, *137*, 10–18. doi:10.1016/j.techfore.2018.09.029

Lopatovska, I., Rink, K., Knight, I., Raines, K., Cosenza, K., Williams, H., Sorsche, P., Hirsch, D., Li, Q., & Martinez, A. (2018). Speak to me: Exploring user interactions with the Amazon Alexa. *Journal of Librarianship and Information Science*, *51*(4), 984–997. doi:10.1177/0961000618759414

Loureiro, S. M. C., Guerreiro, J., & Tussyadiah, I. (2021). Artificial intelligence in business: State of the art and future research agenda. *Journal of Business Research*, *129*, 911–926. doi:10.1016/j.jbusres.2020.11.001

Lourens, M., Sharma, S., Pulugu, R., Gehlot, A., Manoharan, G., & Kapila, D. (2023, May). Machine learning-based predictive analytics and big data in the automotive sector. In *2023 3rd International Conference on Advance Computing and Innovative Technologies in Engineering (ICACITE)* (pp. 1043-1048). IEEE. 10.1109/ICACITE57410.2023.10182665

Low, S., Ullah, F., Shirowzhan, S., Sepasgozar, S. M., & Lin Lee, C. (2020). Smart digital marketing capabilities for sustainable property development: A case of Malaysia. *Sustainability (Basel)*, *12*(13), 5402. doi:10.3390/su12135402

Lu, H., Ma, X., Huang, K., & Azimi, M. (2020). Carbon trading volume and price forecasting in China using multiple machine learning models. *Journal of Cleaner Production, 249*, 119386. doi:10.1016/j.jclepro.2019.119386

Lukin, E., Krajnović, A., & Bosna, J. (2022). Sustainability Strategies and Achieving SDGs: A Comparative Analysis of Leading Companies in the Automotive Industry. *Sustainability (Basel), 14*(7), 4000. doi:10.3390/su14074000

Lunney, A., Cunningham, N. R., & Eastin, M. S. (2016). Wearable fitness technology: A structural investigation into acceptance and perceived fitness outcomes. *Computers in Human Behavior, 65*, 114–120. doi:10.1016/j.chb.2016.08.007

Luo, J., Gao, W., & Wang, Z. L. (2021). The triboelectric nanogenerator as an innovative technology toward intelligent sports. *Advanced Materials, 33*(17), 2004178. doi:10.1002/adma.202004178 PMID:33759259

Lupak, R., Kunytska-Iliash, M., Berezivskyi, Y., Nakonechna, N., Ivanova, L., & Vasyltsiv, T. (2021). Information and analytical support system of enterprise competitiveness management. *Accounting, 7*(7), 1785–1798. doi:10.5267/j.ac.2021.4.018

Lu, W., & Wei, L. (2018). Internet of Things (IoT) for sustainable development: A review on enabling technologies, applications, and challenges. *Journal of Cleaner Production, 174*, 442–458.

Maddodi, & Krishna Prasad, K. (2019). Netflix Bigdata Analytics-The Emergence of Data Driven Recommendation. *International Journal of Case Studies in Business, IT, and Education (IJCSBE), 3*(2), 41-51.

Maedche, A., Legner, C., Benlian, A., Berger, B., Gimpel, H., Hess, T., Hinz, O., Morana, S., & Söllner, M. (2019). AI-based digital assistants: Opportunities, threats, and research perspectives. *Business & Information Systems Engineering, 61*(4), 535–544. doi:10.1007/s12599-019-00600-8

Makarius, E. E., Mukherjee, D., Fox, J. D., & Fox, A. K. (2020). Rising with the machines: A sociotechnical framework for bringing artificial intelligence into the organization. *Journal of Business Research, 120*, 262–273. doi:10.1016/j.jbusres.2020.07.045

Makvandi, P., Zarrabi, A., Ashrafizadeh, M., & Samarghandian, S. (2020). Technological complexity and integration challenges: Metal-based nanomaterials in biomedical applications: antimicrobial activity and cytotoxicity aspects. *Advanced Functional Materials, 30*(28), 2000459.

Malik, R., & Aggarwal, R. (2022). Innovative Marketing and Consumer Behavior: A Systematic Literature Review. *SAMVAD, 23*(0), 87–93. doi:10.53739/samvad/2021/v23/165188

Malthouse, E. C., & Copulsky, J. R. (2022). Artificial intelligence ecosystems for marketing communications. *International Journal of Advertising, 42*(1), 128–140. doi:10.1080/02650487.2022.2122249

Mamza, E. S. (2021). Use of AIOT in Health System. *International Journal of Sustainable Development in Computing Science, 3*(4), 21–30.

Mangold, W. G., & Faulds, D. J. (2009). Social media: The new hybrid element of the promotion mix. *Business Horizons, 52*(4), 357–365. doi:10.1016/j.bushor.2009.03.002

Manoharan, G., Durai, S., Ashtikar, S. P., & Kumari, N. (2024). Artificial Intelligence in Marketing Applications. In Artificial Intelligence for Business (pp. 40-70). Productivity Press.

Manoharan, G., Durai, S., Rajesh, G. A., & Ashtikar, S. P. (2023) A Study on the Application of Natural Language Processing Used in Business Analytics for Better Management Decisions: A Literature Review. *Artificial Intelligence and Knowledge Processing*, 249-261.

Manoharan, G., Durai, S., Rajesh, G. A., & Ashtikar, S. P. (2024). A Study on the Application of Expert Systems as a Support System for Business Decisions: A Literature Review. *Artificial Intelligence and Knowledge Processing*, 279-289.

Manoharan, D. S., & Sathesh, A. (2020). Geospatial and social media analytics for emotion analysis of theme park visitors using text mining and gis. *Journal of Information Technology and Digital World*, 2(2), 100–107. doi:10.36548/jitdw.2020.2.003

Manoharan, G., & Ashtikar, S. P. (2023). A review on the role of statistical tools in effective functionality of data science. *Journal of Pharmaceutical Negative Results*, *14*(2).

Manoharan, G., Durai, S., Rajesh, G. A., Razak, A., Rao, C. B., & Ashtikar, S. P. (2023a). An investigation into the effectiveness of smart city projects by identifying the framework for measuring performance. In *Artificial Intelligence and Machine Learning in Smart City Planning* (pp. 71–84). Elsevier. doi:10.1016/B978-0-323-99503-0.00004-1

Manoharan, G., Durai, S., Rajesh, G. A., Razak, A., Rao, C. B., & Ashtikar, S. P. (2023b). A study of postgraduate students' perceptions of key components in ICCC to be used in artificial intelligence-based smart cities. In *Artificial Intelligence and Machine Learning in Smart City Planning* (pp. 117–133). Elsevier. doi:10.1016/B978-0-323-99503-0.00003-X

Mansouri, S. A., Jordehi, A. R., Marzband, M., Tostado-Véliz, M., Jurado, F., & Aguado, J. A. (2023). An IoT-enabled hierarchical decentralized framework for multi-energy microgrids market management in the presence of smart prosumers using a deep learning-based forecaster. *Applied Energy*, *333*, 120560. doi:10.1016/j.apenergy.2022.120560

Maranchak, N. (2023). The Use of Artificial Intelligence in Digital Marketing of the Library Industry in Ukraine: Foreign Experience and Prospects. *Digital Platform: Information Technologies in Sociocultural Sphere*.

Mariani, M. M., Perez-Vega, R., & Wirtz, J. (2022). AI in marketing, consumer research and psychology: A systematic literature review and research agenda. *Psychology and Marketing*, *39*(4), 755–776. doi:10.1002/mar.21619

Márquez, G., & Taramasco, C. (2023). Barriers and Facilitators of Ambient Assisted Living Systems: A Systematic Literature Review. *International Journal of Environmental Research and Public Health*, *20*(6), 5020. doi:10.3390/ijerph20065020 PMID:36981929

Marr, B. (2021). *Data strategy: How to profit from a world of big data, analytics and artificial intelligence*. Kogan Page Publishers.

Martin, K. (2018). Privacy notices as tabula rasa: An empirical investigation into how complying with a privacy notice is related to meeting privacy expectations online. *Journal of Public Policy & Marketing*, *37*(2), 236–248.

Mayer, R. C., Davis, J. H., & Schoorman, F. D. (1995). An integrative model of organizational trust. *Academy of Management Review*, *20*(3), 709–734. doi:10.2307/258792

McDowell, R. M., & Goldstein, G. M. (2016, October 25). The authoritarian internet power grab: The internet of things will be worth trillions by 2025. China wants centralized control. *The Wall Street Journal*. Retrieved from http://www.wsj.com/ articles/the-authoritarian-internet-power-grab-477436573?mod5rss_opinion_main

McKee, K. M., Dahl, A. J., & Peltier, J. W. (2023). Gen Z's personalization paradoxes: A privacy calculus examination of digital personalization and brand behaviors. *Journal of Consumer Behaviour*, cb.2199. doi:10.1002/cb.2199

McKinsey. (2022). *The state of AI in 2022—and a half decade in review*. https://www.mckinsey.com/capabilities/quantumblack/our-insights/the-state-of-ai-in-2022-and-a-half-decade-in-review

Mehdizadehrayeni, M., Hamidmohammadi, H., & Dehdashti, M. (2022). Welfare effects of increasing competition in the market of export products (Case study: Saffron product). *Saffron Agronomy and Technology*, *10*(3), 287–302.

Melović, B., Jocović, M., Dabić, M., Vulić, T. B., & Dudic, B. (2020). The impact of digital transformation and digital marketing on brand promotion, positioning, and electronic business in Montenegro. *Technology in Society*, *63*, 101425. doi:10.1016/j.techsoc.2020.101425

merckgroup. (2023). https://www.merckgroup.com/en/the-future-transformation/acceptance-digital-technologies-worldwide-literacy-key.html

Miah, M. R., Rahman, A. A. M. S., Parisa, J. T., Hannan, M. A., Khan, M. S., Samdany, A. A., ... Chowdhury, S. H. (2021). Discovery of Coronavirus with Innovative Technology. *Science and Technology*, *11*(1), 7–29.

Miedema, T. E. (2018). Consumer protection in cyberspace and the ethics of stewardship. *Journal of Consumer Policy*, *41*(1), 55–75. doi:10.1007/s10603-017-9364-x

Miklós-Thal, J., & Tucker, C. (2019). Collusion by algorithm: Does better demand prediction facilitate coordination between sellers? *Management Science*, *65*(4), 1552–1561. doi:10.1287/mnsc.2019.3287

Milani, R. V., & Franklin, N. C. (2017). The role of technology in healthy living medicine. *Progress in Cardiovascular Diseases*, *59*(5), 487–491. doi:10.1016/j.pcad.2017.02.001 PMID:28189614

Milberg, S. J., Smith, H. J., & Burke, S. J. (2000). Information privacy: Corporate management and national regulation. *Organization Science*, *11*(1), 35–57. doi:10.1287/orsc.11.1.35.12567

Miller, R. P. (2015). Virtua and CVS Health: Partnering Within a Population Health Delivery Model. *Frontiers of Health Services Management*, *31*(3), 32–37. doi:10.1097/01974520-201501000-00004 PMID:26495552

Milman, A. (2022). Attraction Marketing Strategies. In *Managing Visitor Attractions* (pp. 271–288). Routledge. doi:10.4324/9781003041948-19

Milne, G. R., Bahl, S., & Rohm, A. J. (2008). Toward a framework for assessing covert marketing practices. *Journal of Public Policy & Marketing*, *27*(1), 57–62. doi:10.1509/jppm.27.1.57

Milne, G. R., Labrecque, L. I., & Cromer, C. (2009). Toward an understanding of the online consumer's risky behavior and protection practices. *The Journal of Consumer Affairs*, *43*(3), 449–473. doi:10.1111/j.1745-6606.2009.01148.x

Mingione, M., & Leoni, L. (2020). Blurring B2C and B2B boundaries: Corporate brand value co-creation in B2B2C markets. *Journal of Marketing Management*, *36*(1-2), 72–99. doi:10.1080/0267257X.2019.1694566

Mishra, Pant, Pant, Kumar, Kundu, & Manoharan. (2022). Integrating the principle of strategic human resource management to improve organisational performance. *The British Journal of Administrative Management*. https://tbjam.org/vol58-special-issue-06/

Mithas, S., Chen, Z. L., Saldanha, T. J., & De Oliveira Silveira, A. (2022). How will artificial intelligence and Industry 4.0 emerging technologies transform operations management? *Production and Operations Management*, *31*(12), 4475–4487. doi:10.1111/poms.13864

Modgil, S., Singh, R. K., & Hannibal, C. (2022). Artificial intelligence for supply chain resilience: Learning from Covid-19. *International Journal of Logistics Management*, *33*(4), 1246–1268. doi:10.1108/IJLM-02-2021-0094

Moedt, W., Bernsteiner, R., Hall, M., & Fruhling, A. (2023). Enhancing IoT Project Success through Agile Best Practices. *ACM Transactions on Internet of Things*, *4*(1), 1–31. doi:10.1145/3568170

MoEngage. (2023, July 26). *11 Awesome examples of mobile marketing campaigns done right*. https://www.moengage.com/learn/examples-of-mobile-marketing-campaigns

Mohamed, K. (2013). Evaluation of societal marketing (sustainable marketing) in maintaining ethics in marketing goods or services to the customers. *International Journal of Management Research and Reviews*, *3*(11), 3703.

Mohammed, A. B., & Syed, A. S. (2023). Applications and Impact of Internet of Things in Digital Marketing. In *Global Applications of the Internet of Things in Digital Marketing* (pp. 161–186). IGI Global. doi:10.4018/978-1-6684-8166-0.ch009

Mohanraj, G., & Karthikeyan, P. (2016). Green Marketing-New Opportunities and Challenges. *Asian Journal of Research in Social Sciences and Humanities*, *6*(7), 1238–1244. doi:10.5958/2249-7315.2016.00508.6

Mohanty, S., & Vyas, S. (2018). Decentralized autonomous organizations= blockchain+ AI+ IoT. In *How to Compete in the Age of Artificial Intelligence* (pp. 189–206). Apress. doi:10.1007/978-1-4842-3808-0_9

Mollahosseini, A., & Foroozanfar, M.H. (2019). Development and localization of technology acceptance model (TAM) in small and medium-sized enterprises (SMEs). *Quarterly Journal of Industrial Technology Development, 16*(34), 39-48.

Montero, A. R., Álvarez, A. C., & Rubio, R. S. (2023). Inbound marketing in the hospitality industry: A systematic review in the last 12 years. *Enlightening Tourism. A Pathmaking Journal, 13*(1), 86-125.

Montgomery, N. (Ed.). (2019). *Perspectives on Purpose: Leading Voices on Building Brands and Businesses for the Twenty-first Century*. Routledge. doi:10.4324/9781351173568

Moore, S. (2016). *Gartner survey shows wearable devices need to be more useful*. Gartner. Available online at: https://www. gartner. com/en/newsroom/press

Moraes, D. P., de Oliveira, F. R., & da Silva, V. A. (2021). Consumer skepticism towards data collection by IoT devices: A systematic review. *Journal of Business Research, 135*, 1–17.

Morgan, R. M., & Hunt, S. D. (1994). The commitment-trust theory of relationship marketing. *Journal of Marketing*, *58*(3), 20–38. doi:10.1177/002224299405800302

Morgan-Thomas, A., & Veloutsou, C. (2013). Beyond technology acceptance: Brand relationships and online brand experience. *Journal of Business Research*, *66*(1), 21–27. doi:10.1016/j.jbusres.2011.07.019

Morschett, D., Swoboda, B., & Schramm-Klein, H. (2006). Competitive strategies in retailing—An investigation of the applicability of Porter's framework for food retailers. *Journal of Retailing and Consumer Services*, *13*(4), 275–287. doi:10.1016/j.jretconser.2005.08.016

Mougayar, W. (2016). *The Business Blockchain: Promise, Practice, and Application of the Next Internet Technology*. Wiley.

Mukendi, A., Davies, I., Glozer, S., & McDonagh, P. (2020). Sustainable fashion: Current and future research directions. *European Journal of Marketing*, *54*(11), 2873–2909. doi:10.1108/EJM-02-2019-0132

Mulhern, F. J. (1997). Retail marketing: From distribution to integration. *International Journal of Research in Marketing*, *14*(2), 103–124. doi:10.1016/S0167-8116(96)00031-6

Muninger, M. I., Mahr, D., & Hammedi, W. (2022). Social media use: A review of innovation management practices. *Journal of Business Research*, *143*, 140–156. doi:10.1016/j.jbusres.2022.01.039

Murgai, A. (2018). Transforming digital marketing with artificial intelligence. International Journal of Latest Technology in Engineering, Management &. *Applied Sciences (Basel, Switzerland)*, *7*(4), 259–262.

Murugan, S., Assi, S., Alatrany, A., Jayabalan, M., Liatsis, P., Mustafina, J., ... & Al-Jumeily OBE, D. (2022, December). Consumer Behavior Prediction During Covid-19 Pandemic Conditions Using Sentiment Analytics. In *The International Conference on Data Science and Emerging Technologies* (pp. 209-221). Singapore: Springer Nature Singapore.

Mysakova, A. G., & Zakharcheva, K. S. (2023). The Impact of ESG Strategy on Brand Perception of Fuel and Energy Companies. In *Smart Green Innovations in Industry 4.0 for Climate Change Risk Management* (pp. 277–285). Springer International Publishing. doi:10.1007/978-3-031-28457-1_29

Nagaty, K. A. (2023). IoT Commercial and Industrial Applications and AI-Powered IoT. In *Frontiers of Quality Electronic Design (QED) AI, IoT and Hardware Security* (pp. 465–500). Springer International Publishing. doi:10.1007/978-3-031-16344-9_12

Nahr, J. G., Nozari, H., & Sadeghi, M. E. (2021). Green supply chain based on artificial intelligence of things (AIoT). *International Journal of Innovation in Management. Economics and Social Sciences*, *1*(2), 56–63.

Naim, A., Alqahtani, H., Muniasamy, A., Bilfaqih, S. M., Mahveen, R., & Mahjabeen, R. (2023). Applications of Information Systems and Data Security in Marketing Management. In Fraud Prevention, Confidentiality, and Data Security for Modern Businesses (pp. 57-83). IGI Global. doi:10.4018/978-1-6684-6581-3.ch003

Naim, A., Muniasamy, A., Clementking, A., & Rajkumar, R. (2022). Relevance of Green Manufacturing and IoT in Industrial Transformation and Marketing Management. In *Computational Intelligence Techniques for Green Smart Cities* (pp. 395–419). Springer International Publishing. doi:10.1007/978-3-030-96429-0_19

Najafi, S. E., Nozari, H., & Edalatpanah, S. A. (2022). Investigating the Key Parameters Affecting Sustainable IoT-Based Marketing. In *Computational Intelligence Methodologies Applied to Sustainable Development Goals* (pp. 51–61). Springer International Publishing. doi:10.1007/978-3-030-97344-5_4

Nalini, M., Radhakrishnan, D. P., Yogi, G., Santhiya, S., & Harivardhini, V. (2021). Impact of artificial intelligence (AI) on marketing. *International Journal of Aquatic Science*, *12*(2), 3159–3167.

Narang, U., & Shankar, V. (2019). Mobile Marketing 2.0: state of the art and research agenda. In Review of marketing research (pp. 97–119). doi:10.1108/S1548-643520190000016008

Nasajpour, M., Pouriyeh, S., Parizi, R. M., Dorodchi, M., Valero, M., & Arabnia, H. R. (2020). Internet of Things for Current COVID-19 and Future Pandemics: An Exploratory Study. *Journal of Healthcare Informatics Research*, *4*(4), 325–364. doi:10.1007/s41666-020-00080-6 PMID:33204938

Nazemi Bidgoli, A., Mohamadi Turkmani, E., & Irani, H. R. (2023). Investigating the Effect of Social Influence and Gender on the Willingness to use IOT Technology in Sports: From Consumer Perspective. *Research in Sport Management and Marketing*, *4*(4), 28–41.

Neck, C. P., Houghton, J. D., & Murray, E. L. (2018). *Organizational behavior: A skill-building approach*. Sage Publications.

Nedelea, A., Çanakcı, M., & Arslan, A. (2021). Social Polarization And Its Effects On Public Investments. *The USV Annals of Economics and Public Administration*, *21*(1 (33)), 153–166.

Nematpour, M., Khodadadi, M., Makian, S., & Ghaffari, M. (2022). Developing a competitive and sustainable model for the future of a destination: Iran's tourism competitiveness. *International Journal of Hospitality & Tourism Administration*, 1–33. doi:10.1080/15256480.2022.2081279

Nematpour, M., Khodadadi, M., & Rezaei, N. (2021). Systematic analysis of development in Iran's tourism market in the form of future Study: A new method of strategic planning. *Futures*, *125*, 102650. doi:10.1016/j.futures.2020.102650

Neuhofer, B., Magnus, B., & Celuch, K. (2021). The impact of artificial intelligence on event experiences: A scenario technique approach. *Electronic Markets*, *31*(3), 601–617. doi:10.1007/s12525-020-00433-4

Ngai, E. W., Xiu, L., & Chau, D. C. (2009). Application of Data Mining Techniques in Customer Relationship Management: A Literature Review and Classification. *Expert Systems with Applications*, *36*(2), 2592–2602. doi:10.1016/j.eswa.2008.02.021

Ng, I. C. L., Scharf, K. A., Pogrebna, G., & Maull, R. S. (2009). Contextual Variety, Internet-of-Things and the Choice of Tailoring over Platform: Mass Customization Strategy in Supply Chain Management. *International Journal of Production Economics*, *159*, 76–87. doi:10.1016/j.ijpe.2014.09.007

Ng, I. C. L., & Wakenshaw, S. Y. L. (2017). The Internet-of-Things: Review and research directions. *International Journal of Research in Marketing*, *34*(1), 3–21. doi:10.1016/j.ijresmar.2016.11.003

Nguyen, B., & Simkin, L. (2017). The Internet of Things (IoT) and marketing: The state of play, future trends and the implications for marketing. *Journal of Marketing Management*, *33*(1-2), 1–6. doi:10.1080/0267257X.2016.1257542

Nguyen, L. (2021). *Developing sustainable marketing plan for plant-based products*. LAB University of Applied Sciences.

Niar, H. (2022). Examining Linkage of Product Selling Prices on Profitability. *Golden Ratio of Marketing and Applied Psychology of Business*, *2*(1), 12–25. doi:10.52970/grmapb.v2i1.82

Nielsen, A. (2019). *Natural' Rise in Sustainability around the World*. Nielsen. Available online: https://www.nielsen.com/insights/

Nieuwenhuijsen, M. J. (2016). Urban and transport planning, environmental exposures and health-new concepts, methods and tools to improve health in cities. *Environmental Health*, *15*(S1), 161–171. doi:10.1186/s12940-016-0108-1 PMID:26960529

Ni, G., Xu, H., Cui, Q., Qiao, Y., Zhang, Z., Li, H., & Hickey, P. J. (2020). Influence mechanism of organizational flexibility on enterprise competitiveness: The mediating role of organizational innovation. *Sustainability (Basel)*, *13*(1), 176. doi:10.3390/su13010176

Niu, B., Zhang, J., & Mu, Z. (2023). IoT-enabled delivery time guarantee in logistics outsourcing and efficiency improvement. *International Journal of Production Research*, *61*(12), 4135–4156. doi:10.1080/00207543.2022.2117868

Nizam, N. Z., AlKaabi, M. R. A. Z., & Husseini, S. A. (2022). Customer service quality assessment and customers' satisfaction in food and beverage in McDonald's restaurant in United Arab Emirates. *Journal of Positive School Psychology*, *6*(3), 4684–4693.

No, E., Kelly, B., Devi, A., Swinburn, B., & Vandevijvere, S. (2014). Food references and marketing in popular magazines for children and adolescents in New Zealand: A content analysis. *Appetite*, *83*, 75–81. doi:10.1016/j.appet.2014.08.013 PMID:25128834

Nosratabadi, S., Mosavi, A., Shamshirband, S., Zavadskas, E. K., Rakotonirainy, A., & Chau, K. W. (2019). Sustainable business models: A review. *Sustainability (Basel)*, *11*(6), 1663. doi:10.3390/su11061663

Novera, C.N., Ahmed, Z., Kushol, R., Wanke, P. and Azad, M.A.K. (2022). Internet of Things (IoT) in smart tourism: a literature review. *Spanish Journal of Marketing - ESIC, 26*(3), 325-344. doi:10.1108/SJME-03-2022-0035

Nozari, H., Fallah, M., Szmelter-Jarosz, A., & Krzemiński, M. (2021). Analysis of security criteria for IoT-based supply chain: a case study of FMCG industries. *Central European Management Journal, 29*(4).

Nozari, H., Ghahremani-Nahr, J., Fallah, M., & Szmelter-Jarosz, A. (2022). Assessment of cyber risks in an IoT-based supply chain using a fuzzy decision-making method. *International Journal of Innovation in Management, Economics and Social Sciences, 2*(1).

Nozari, H., Tavakkoli-Moghaddam, R., Rohaninejad, M., & Hanzalek, Z. (2023, September). Artificial Intelligence of Things (AIoT) Strategies for a Smart Sustainable-Resilient Supply Chain. In *IFIP International Conference on Advances in Production Management Systems* (pp. 805-816). Cham: Springer Nature Switzerland. 10.1007/978-3-031-43670-3_56

Nozari, H., & Aliahmadi, A. (2023). Analysis of critical success factors in a food agile supply chain by a fuzzy hybrid decision-making method. *Iranian Journal of Management Studies*, 16(4).

Nozari, H., Fallah, M., Kazemipoor, H., & Najafi, S. E. (2021). Big data analysis of IoT-based supply chain management considering FMCG industries. *Бизнес-информатика*, 15(1, 1 (eng)), 78–96. doi:10.17323/2587-814X.2021.1.78.96

Nozari, H., & Szmelter-Jarosz, A. (2024). An Analytical Framework for Smart Supply Chains 5.0. In *Building Smart and Sustainable Businesses With Transformative Technologies* (pp. 1–15). IGI Global.

Nozari, H., Szmelter-Jarosz, A., & Ghahremani-Nahr, J. (2021). The Ideas of Sustainable and Green Marketing Based on the Internet of Everything—The Case of the Dairy Industry. *Future Internet*, 13(10), 266. doi:10.3390/fi13100266

Nozari, H., Szmelter-Jarosz, A., & Ghahremani-Nahr, J. (2022). Analysis of the challenges of artificial intelligence of things (AIoT) for the smart supply chain (case study: FMCG industries). *Sensors (Basel)*, 22(8), 2931. doi:10.3390/s22082931 PMID:35458916

O'Keeffe, A., Ozuem, W., & Lancaster, G. (2016). Leadership marketing: An exploratory study. *Journal of Strategic Marketing*, 24(5), 418–443. doi:10.1080/0965254X.2014.1001867

OECD. (2020). *OECD Tourism Trends and Policies 2020*. OECD Publishing. doi:10.1787/6b47b985-

Olayinka, A. A. (2022). Financial statement analysis as a tool for investment decisions and assessment of companies' performance. *International Journal of Financial, Accounting, and Management*, 4(1), 49–66. doi:10.35912/ijfam.v4i1.852

Oliver, R. L. (1999). Whence consumer loyalty? *Journal of Marketing*, 63(4_suppl1), 33–44. doi:10.1177/00222429990634s105

Ordóñez, M. D., Gómez, A., Ruiz, M., Ortells, J., Niemi-Hugaerts, H., Juiz, C., Jara, A., & Butler, T. (2021). *IoT Technologies and Applications in Tourism and Travel Industries*. https://www.riverpublishers.com

Orea-Giner, A., Fuentes-Moraleda, L., Villacé-Molinero, T., Muñoz-Mazón, A., & Calero-Sanz, J. (2022). Does the implementation of robots in hotels influence the overall TripAdvisor rating? A text mining analysis from the industry 5.0 approach. *Tourism Management*, 93, 104586. doi:10.1016/j.tourman.2022.104586

Owolabi, A. O., & Okegbade, I. Y. (2015). The impact of promotional tools on the sale of insurance products in Nigeria. *International Journal of Management. IT and Engineering*, 5(6), 26–44.

Palagiri, Mogre, Rawa, Manoharan, Singh, & Jaiswal. (2022). An investigation on the use of machine learning methods for predicting employee performance. *The British Journal of Administrative Management*. https://tbjam.org/vol58-special-issue-06/

Pangkey, F. M., Furkan, L. M., & Herman, L. E. (2019). Pengaruh artificial intelligence dan digital marketing terhadap minat beli konsumen. *Jurnal Magister Manajemen Unram*, 8(3), 21–25. doi:10.29303/jmm.v8i3.448

Pappas, I. O. (2018). User experience in personalized online shopping: A fuzzy decision-making model and empirical study. *Technological Forecasting and Social Change*, 125, 254–264.

Parasuraman, A., & Grewal, D. (2000). The impact of technology on the quality-value-loyalty chain: A research agenda. *Journal of the Academy of Marketing Science*, 28(1), 168–174. doi:10.1177/0092070300281015

Parasuraman, A., Zeithaml, V. A., & Berry, L. L. (1985). A conceptual model of service quality and its implications for future research. *Journal of Marketing*, 49(4), 41–50. doi:10.1177/002224298504900403

Parasuraman, A., Zeithaml, V. A., & Berry, L. L. (1988). SERVQUAL: A multiple-item scale for measuring consumer perceptions of service quality. *Journal of Retailing, 64*(1), 12.

Paschen, J., Kietzmann, J., & Kietzmann, T. C. (2019). Artificial intelligence (AI) and its implications for market knowledge in B2B marketing. *Journal of Business and Industrial Marketing, 34*(7), 1410–1419. doi:10.1108/JBIM-10-2018-0295

Paschen, J., Paschen, U., Pala, E., & Kietzmann, J. (2021). Artificial intelligence (AI) and value co-creation in B2B sales: Activities, actors and resources. *Australasian Marketing Journal, 29*(3), 243–251. doi:10.1016/j.ausmj.2020.06.004

Pasha, F. M. (2022). Increasing Generalizability: Naïve Bayes Vs K-Nearest Neighbors. *J Robot Auto Res, 3*(2), 178–188. doi:10.21203/rs.3.rs-1578985/v1

Passos, J., Lopes, S. I., Clemente, F. M., Moreira, P. M., Rico-González, M., Bezerra, P., & Rodrigues, L. P. (2021). Wearables and Internet of Things (IoT) technologies for fitness assessment: A systematic review. *Sensors (Basel), 21*(16), 5418. doi:10.3390/s21165418 PMID:34450860

Patrutiu-Baltes, L. (2016). Inbound Marketing - the most important digital marketing strategy. Bulletin of the Transilvania University of Brasov. *Economic Sciences. Series V, 9*(2), 61.

Pavlou, P. A. (2003). Consumer acceptance of electronic commerce: Integrating trust and risk with the technology acceptance model. *International Journal of Electronic Commerce, 7*(3), 101–134. doi:10.1080/10864415.2003.11044275

Pedersen, I., & Duin, A. (2022). AI agents, humans and untangling the marketing of artificial intelligence in learning environments. *Conference: 55th Hawaii International Conference on System Sciences.* 10.24251/HICSS.2022.002

Peighambari, K., Sattari, S., Kordestani, A., & Oghazi, P. (2016). Consumer Behavior Research: A Synthesis of the Recent Literature. *SAGE Open, 6*(2), 1–9. doi:10.1177/2158244016645638

Pellegrin, K. L. (2017). CVS Health: Checking the Vital Signs of the Largest Pharmacy Company in the US. In SAGE Business Cases. SAGE Publications.

Peltier, J. W., Dahl, A. J., & Schibrowsky, J. A. (2022). Artificial Intelligence in Interactive Marketing: A Conceptual Framework and Research Agenda. *Journal of Research in Interactive Marketing, 16*(4), 345–362.

Peppet, S. R. (2014). Regulating the internet of things: First steps toward managing discrimination, privacy, security and consent. *Texas Law Review, 93*, 85.

Pereira, P., Cortez, P., & Mendes, R. (2021). Multi-objective Grammatical Evolution of Decision Trees for Mobile Marketing user conversion prediction. *Expert Systems with Applications, 168*, 114287. doi:10.1016/j.eswa.2020.114287

Persaud, A., & Azhar, I. (2012). Innovative mobile marketing via smartphones. *Marketing Intelligence & Planning, 30*(4), 418–443. doi:10.1108/02634501211231883

Peterson, M. (2021). Sustainable marketing: A holistic approach. *Sustainable Marketing*, 1-100.

Peterson, R. A., & Merino, M. C. (2003). Consumer information search behavior and the Internet. *Psychology and Marketing, 20*(2), 99–121. doi:10.1002/mar.10062

Petrescu, M., & Krishen, A. S. (2018). Analyzing the analytics: Data privacy concerns. *Journal of Marketing Analytics, 6*(2), 41–43. doi:10.1057/s41270-018-0034-x

Peyravi, B., Nekrošienė, J., & Lobanova, L. (2020). Revolutionised technologies for marketing: Theoretical review with focus on artificial intelligence. *Business: Theory and Practice, 21*(2), 827–834. doi:10.3846/btp.2020.12313

Phanga, G., Chanb, J. K. L., Limc, T. Y., & Fresnidod, M. B. R. (n.d.). Key Success Factors, Marketing Opportunities and Challenges: A Case Study of Bonco Virgin Coconut Oil. *Journal of Agribusiness*, 9(1), 57–71.

Phan, M., Thomas, R., & Heine, K. (2011). Social media and luxury brand management: The case of Burberry. *Journal of Global Fashion Marketing*, 2(4), 213–222. doi:10.1080/20932685.2011.10593099

Pietronudo, M. C., Croidieu, G., & Schiavone, F. (2022). A solution looking for problems? A systematic literature review of the rationalizing influence of artificial intelligence on decision-making in innovation management. *Technological Forecasting and Social Change*, 182, 121828. doi:10.1016/j.techfore.2022.121828

Piotrowicz, W., & Cuthbertson, R. (2014). Introduction to the Special Issue Information Technology in Retail: Toward Omnichannel Retailing. *International Journal of Electronic Commerce*, 18(4), 5–16. doi:10.2753/JEC1086-4415180400

Pizło, W., Kałowski, A., & Zarzycka, A. (2022). Internet of Things Applications in Marketing. In *Internet of Things* (pp. 149–162). CRC Press. doi:10.1201/9781003219620-8

Plassmann, H., Ramsøy, T. Z., & Milosavljevic, M. (2015). Branding the Brain: A Critical Review and Outlook. *Journal of Consumer Psychology*, 25(1), 18–36. doi:10.1016/j.jcps.2011.11.010

Polak, M., Kolić Stanić, M., & Togonal, M. (2022). Artificial Intelligence in Communication with Music Fans: An Example from South Korea. *ENTRENOVA-ENTerprise REsearch InNOVAtion*, 8(1), 48–63. doi:10.54820/entrenova-2022-0006

Ponte, S. (2020). Green capital accumulation: Business and sustainability management in a world of global value chains. *New Political Economy*, 25(1), 72–84. doi:10.1080/13563467.2019.1581152

Popova, E. A. (2018). Using artificial intelligence in marketing. *Современные научные исследования и разработки*, 2(11), 31-32.

Porter, M. E., & Heppelmann, J. E. (2014). How smart, connected products are transforming competition. *Harvard Business Review*, 92(11), 64–88.

Prabowo, H., Hamsal, M., & Simatupang, B. (2019, August). E-Marketing and Service Quality on Repurchase Intention of Online Transportation. In *2019 International Conference on Information Management and Technology (ICIMTech)* (Vol. 1, pp. 324-329). IEEE.

Prabowo, S. H. W., Murdiono, A., Hidayat, R., Rahayu, W. P., & Sutrisno, S. (2019). Digital marketing optimization in artificial intelligence era by applying consumer behavior algorithm. *Asian Journal of Entrepreneurship and Family Business*, 3(1), 41–48.

Pradhan, M. K., Oh, J., & Lee, H. (2018). Understanding travelers' behavior for sustainable smart tourism: A technology readiness perspective. *Sustainability (Basel)*, 10(11), 4259. doi:10.3390/su10114259

Prensky, M. (2001). Digital natives, digital immigrants part 1. *On the Horizon*, 9(5), 1–6. doi:10.1108/10748120110424816

Pulizzi, J. (2012). The rise of storytelling as the new marketing. *Publishing Research Quarterly*, 28(2), 116–123. doi:10.1007/s12109-012-9264-5

Purwanto, P., Kuswandi, K., & Fatmah, F. (2020). Interactive applications with artificial intelligence: The role of trust among digital assistant users. *Форсайт*, 14(2, 2 (eng)), 64–75. doi:10.17323/2500-2597.2020.2.64.75

Qin, X., & Jiang, Z. (2019). The impact of AI on the advertising process: The Chinese experience. *Journal of Advertising*, 48(4), 338–346. doi:10.1080/00913367.2019.1652122

Quinones, M., Gomez-Suarez, M., Cruz-Roche, I., & Díaz-Martín, A. M. (2023). Technology: A strategic imperative for successful retailers. *International Journal of Retail & Distribution Management, 51*(4), 546–566. doi:10.1108/IJRDM-03-2022-0088

Quint, M. (2019). Measuring purpose: From organizational commitments to social impact. In *Perspectives on Purpose* (pp. 35–47). Routledge. doi:10.4324/9781351173568-5

Quynh, T. D., & Dung, H. T. T. Prediction of customer behavior using machine learning: A case study. In *Proceedings of the 2nd International Conference on Human-centered Artificial Intelligence (Computing4Human 2021)* (pp. 168-175). Academic Press.

Rabby, F., Chimhundu, R., & Hassan, R. (2022). Blockchain technology transforms digital marketing by growing consumer trust. *Transformations Through Blockchain Technology*, 265-289.

Rabby, F., Chimhundu, R., & Hassan, R. (2021). Artificial intelligence in digital marketing influences consumer behaviour: A review and theoretical foundation for future research. *Academy of Marketing Studies Journal, 25*(5), 1–7.

Rai, Y., Raj, A., Sah, K. S., & Sinha, A. (2020). AIRUYA-A Personal Shopping Assistant. In *International Conference on Innovative Computing and Communications: Proceedings of ICICC 2019*, Volume 1 (pp. 435-442). Springer Singapore. 10.1007/978-981-15-1286-5_37

Rainey, D. L. (2015). A Holistic Model for Linking Sustainability, Sustainable Development, and Strategic Innovation in the Context of Globalization. In *Handbook of Research on Sustainable Development and Economics* (pp. 222–247). IGI Global. doi:10.4018/978-1-4666-8433-1.ch010

Raiter, O. (2021). Segmentation of bank consumers for artificial intelligence marketing. *International Journal of Contemporary Financial Issues, 1*(1), 39–54.

Rajaguru, R. (2023). Effects of contemporary technologies, such as blockchain and artificial intelligence (AI) in enhancing consumers' trustworthiness of online reviews. *Journal of Hospitality Marketing & Management*, 1–9. Advance online publication. doi:10.1080/19368623.2023.2258522

Ramachandran, K. K., Mary, S. S. C., Painoli, A. K., Satyala, H., Singh, B., & Manoharan, G. (2022). Assessing the full impact of technological advances on business management techniques. *The British Journal of Administrative Management*. https://tbjam.org/vol58-special-issue-06/

Ramazonovma, M. D. (2022). Development of Marketing in the Context of A Tourism Pandemic in Uzbekistan. *Indonesian Journal of Innovation Studies, 17*, 10–21070. doi:10.21070/ijins.v17i.577

Ransbotham, S., Gerbert, P., Reeves, M., Kiron, D., & Spira, M. (2018). Artificial intelligence in business gets real. *MIT Sloan Management Review*. Retrieved from: https://sloanreview.mit.edu/projects/artificial-intelligence-in-business-gets-real/

Raschke, R., Krishen, A. S., & Kachroo, P. (2014). Understanding the components of information privacy threats for location-based services. *Journal of Information Systems, 28*(1), 227–242. doi:10.2308/isys-50696

Rathore, B. (2020). Predictive Metamorphosis: Unveiling the Fusion of AI-Powered Analytics in Digital Marketing Revolution. *International Journal of Transcontinental Discoveries, 7*(1), 15–24.

Rayna, T., Darlington, J., & Striukova, L. (2015). Pricing music using personal data: Mutually advantageous first-degree price discrimination. *Electronic Markets, 25*(2), 139–154. doi:10.1007/s12525-014-0165-7

Razak, A., Nayak, M. P., Manoharan, G., Durai, S., Rajesh, G. A., Rao, C. B., & Ashtikar, S. P. (2023). Reigniting the power of artificial intelligence in education sector for the educators and students competence. In *Artificial Intelligence and Machine Learning in Smart City Planning* (pp. 103–116). Elsevier. doi:10.1016/B978-0-323-99503-0.00009-0

Reichheld, F. F. (1996). Learning from customer defections. *Harvard Business Review*, *74*(2), 56–69.

Reichheld, F. F., & Schefter, P. (2000). E-loyalty: Your secret weapon on the web. *Harvard Business Review*, *78*(4), 105–113.

Reimsbach, D., Hahn, R., & Gürtürk, A. (2018). Integrated reporting and assurance of sustainability information: An experimental study on professional investors' information processing. *European Accounting Review*, *27*(3), 559–581. doi:10.1080/09638180.2016.1273787

Reinartz, W. J., & Kumar, V. (2002). The mismanagement of customer loyalty. *Harvard Business Review*, *80*(7), 86–94. PMID:12140857

Reis, J. L., Peter, M. K., Cayolla, R., & Bogdanovic, Z. (2021). Marketing and smart technologies. *Proceedings of ICMarkTech, 1*.

Rejeb, A., Keogh, J. G., & Treiblmaier, H. (2020). How blockchain technology can benefit marketing: Six pending research areas. *Frontiers in Blockchain*, *3*, 3. doi:10.3389/fbloc.2020.00003

Rejeb, A., Simske, S., Rejeb, K., Treiblmaier, H., & Zailani, S. (2020). Internet of Things research in supply chain management and logistics: A bibliometric analysis. *Internet of Things : Engineering Cyber Physical Human Systems*, *12*, 100318. doi:10.1016/j.iot.2020.100318

Rekha, A. G., Abdulla, M. S., & Asharaf, S. (2016). Artificial intelligence marketing: An application of a novel lightly trained support vector data description. *Journal of Information and Optimization Sciences*, *37*(5), 681–691. doi:10.1080/02522667.2016.1191186

Remadna, A. (2023). Impact of IoT on Consumer Behaviour. *Management Dynamics*, *23*(1), 7. doi:10.57198/2583-4932.1320

Research AM. (2023). *Global Sports Equipment and Apparel Market Size, Share & Trends Analysis Report by Product (Athletic Shoes, Apparel, Equipment), by Geography (North America, Europe, Asia Pacific, Middle East & Africa, South America), and Segment Forecasts, 2022-2031*. Academic Press.

Retnawati, B. B., Leong, H., & Irmawati, B. (2022). The Study of Natural Material Crafts MSMEs in Optimizing Digital Marketing: Opportunities and Challenges. *Sustainable Competitive Advantage (SCA), 11*(1).

Ribeiro, L. W., & Teixeira, J. M. (2021, October). *The creative industry and design 5.0: The relationship of the creative industry with proposed new execution models based on Design 5.0. 6 CIDAG*.

Rigby, D. (2011). The Future of Shopping. *Harvard Business Review*, *89*(12), 65–76.

Rinner, C., & Reisslein, M. (2004). Personalized Multi-Criteria decision strategies in Location-Based decision support. *Annals of GIS*, *10*(2), 149–156. doi:10.1080/10824000409480666

Rizvi, A. T., Haleem, A., Bahl, S., & Javaid, M. (2021). Artificial intelligence (AI) and its applications in Indian manufacturing: a review. *Current Advances in Mechanical Engineering: Select Proceedings of ICRAMERD 2020*, 825-835.

Roblek, V., Meško, M., Bach, M. P., Thorpe, O., & Šprajc, P. (2020). The interaction between internet, sustainable development, and emergence of society 5.0. *Data*, *5*(3), 80. doi:10.3390/data5030080

Rocha, A., Silva, V. A., & Oliveira, F. R. (2019). Internet of Things for sustainable marketing: A systematic review of opportunities and challenges. *Journal of Cleaner Production, 220,* 862–872.

Roden, S., Nucciarelli, A., Li, F., & Graham, G. (2017). Big data and the transformation of operations models: A framework and a new research agenda. *Production Planning and Control, 28*(11-12), 929–944. doi:10.1080/09537287.2017.1336792

Rodgers, W., & Nguyen, T. (2022). Advertising benefits from ethical artificial intelligence algorithmic purchase decision pathways. *Journal of Business Ethics, 178*(4), 1043–1061. doi:10.1007/s10551-022-05048-7

Rosário, A. T., & Dias, J. C. (2023). How has data-driven marketing evolved: Challenges and opportunities with emerging technologies. *International Journal of Information Management Data Insights, 3*(2), 100203. doi:10.1016/j.jjimei.2023.100203

Rowan, N. J., & Galanakis, C. M. (2020). Unlocking challenges and opportunities presented by COVID-19 pandemic for cross-cutting disruption in agri-food and green deal innovations: Quo Vadis? *The Science of the Total Environment, 748,* 141362. doi:10.1016/j.scitotenv.2020.141362 PMID:32823223

Rroy, A. D., Gulati, U., Sagi, S. G. K., & Gowda, K. R. (2022). Sustainability for Businesses: Marketing and Finance Perspective. *Academy of Marketing Studies Journal, 26,* 1–7.

Rust, R. T. (2020). The future of marketing. *International Journal of Research in Marketing, 37*(1), 15–26. doi:10.1016/j.ijresmar.2019.08.002

Rust, R. T., & Huang, M. H. (2014). The service revolution and the transformation of marketing science. *Marketing Science, 33*(2), 206–221. doi:10.1287/mksc.2013.0836

Rüütmann, A., Perens, R., & Raud, K. (2019). Internet of Things for optimizing business operations: A review of opportunities and challenges. *Journal of Business Research, 109,* 101–114.

Ryan, C. (2004). *High Performance Interactive Marketing.* Viva Books Private Limited.

Ryan, T. A. (2012). Understanding green marketing and advertising in consumer society: An analysis of method cleaning products. *Journal of Research for Consumers, 22,* 18–24.

Sachdev, R. (2020, April). Towards security and privacy for edge AI in IoT/IoE based digital marketing environments. In *2020 fifth international conference on fog and mobile edge computing (FMEC)* (pp. 341-346). IEEE.

Safi, S., Thiessen, T., & Schmailzl, K. J. (2018). Acceptance and resistance of new digital technologies in medicine: Qualitative study. *JMIR Research Protocols, 7*(12), e11072. doi:10.2196/11072 PMID:30514693

Saghiri, S., Wilding, R., Mena, C., & Bourlakis, M. (2017). Toward a three-dimensional framework for omni-channel. *Journal of Business Research, 77,* 53–67. doi:10.1016/j.jbusres.2017.03.025

Sahai, S., & Goel, R. (2021). Impact of artificial intelligence in changing trends of marketing. *Applications of Artificial Intelligence in Business and Finance: Modern Trends,* 221.

Saheb, T., Cabanillas, F. J. L., & Higueras, E. (2022). The Risks and Benefits of Internet of Things (IoT) and Their Influence on Smartwatch Use. *Spanish Journal of Marketing-ESIC, 26*(3), 309–324. doi:10.1108/SJME-07-2021-0129

Sajid, S., Haleem, A., Bahl, S., Javaid, M., Goyal, T., & Mittal, M. (2021). Data science applications for predictive maintenance and materials science in context to Industry 4.0. *Materials Today: Proceedings, 45,* 4898–4905. doi:10.1016/j.matpr.2021.01.357

Salemink, K., Strijker, D., & Bosworth, G. (2017). Rural development in the digital age: A systematic literature review on unequal ICT availability, adoption, and use in rural areas. *Journal of Rural Studies*, *54*, 360–371. doi:10.1016/j.jrurstud.2015.09.001

Sama, R. (2013). Marketing Smart. In *Fast-tracking your Career: Soft skills for engineering and IT professionals*. Wiley-IEEE Press.

Sammut-Bonnici, T., & Galea, D. (2014). *SWOT analysis*. Academic Press.

Santos, J. (2003). E-service quality: A model of virtual service quality dimensions. *Managing Service Quality*, *13*(3), 233–246. doi:10.1108/09604520310476490

Santoso, R. K., Dewi, N. F., & Anindita, C. P. (2023, October). Social Media Marketing using Buzzer on Brand Awareness at PT Telkomsel. In *The 6th International Conference on Vocational Education Applied Science and Technology (ICVEAST 2023)* (pp. 680-693). Atlantis Press. 10.2991/978-2-38476-132-6_58

Santos, R. S., & Lousã, E. P. (2022). Give Me Five: The Most Important Social Values for Well-Being at Work. *Administrative Sciences*, *12*(3), 101. doi:10.3390/admsci12030101

Sardjono, W., Cholidin, A., & Johan, J. (2023). Applying Digital Advertising in Food and Beverage Industry for McDonald's with Marketing 5.0 Approach. In E3S Web of Conferences (Vol. 426, p. 02009). EDP Sciences.

Sari, N. N. P., Paramitha, A. I. I., & Putri, N. L. P. N. S. (2023). Augmented Reality as the Implementation of Digital Marketing 5.0 (Study Case: LPK Bali Aviation Tourism Center). *ProBisnis: Jurnal Manajemen*, *14*(1), 97–107.

Sarıoğlu, C. İ. (2023). Industry 5.0, Digital Society, and Consumer 5.0. In Handbook of Research on Perspectives on Society and Technology Addiction (pp. 11-33). IGI Global.

Sasisuriyaphoom, P., & Choompolsathien, A. (2021). Marketing 5.0: how to improve user experience with digital solutions (No. 306535). Thammasat University. Faculty of Journalism and Mass Communication.

Saura, J. R., Palos-Sanchez, P., & Rodríguez Herráez, B. (2020). Digital marketing for sustainable growth: Business models and online campaigns using sustainable strategies. *Sustainability (Basel)*, *12*(3), 1003. doi:10.3390/su12031003

Saurav, K. (2023, February 26). Adopting mobile marketing to increase consumer engagement in 2023-24. *Times of India Blog*. https://timesofindia.indiatimes.com/blogs/voices/adopting-mobile-marketing-to-increase-consumer-engagement-in-2023-24/

Scharl, A., Dickinger, A., & Murphy, J. (2005). Diffusion and success factors of mobile marketing. *Electronic Commerce Research and Applications*, *4*(2), 159–173. doi:10.1016/j.elerap.2004.10.006

Schierholz, R. (2007). Mobile customer relationship management: Foundations, challenges and solutions. *Business Process Management Journal*, *13*(6). Advance online publication. doi:10.1108/bpmj.2007.15713faa.001

Schiffman, L. G., Kanuk, L. L., & Kumar, S. R. (2016). *Consumer behavior*. Pearson Education India.

Schlegel, M., Zavolokina, L., & Schwabe, G. (2018, January). Blockchain technologies from the consumers' perspective: What is there and why should who care? *Proceedings of the 51st Hawaii international conference on system sciences*. 10.24251/HICSS.2018.441

Sehgal, P., Kumar, B., Sharma, M., Salameh, A. A., Kumar, S., & Asha, P. (2022). Role of IoT in transformation of marketing: A quantitative study of opportunities and challenges. *Webology*, *18*(3), 1–11.

Sehgal, P., Kumar, B., Sharma, M., Salameh, A. A., Kumar, S., & Asha, P. (2022). Role of IOT in Transformation of Marketing: A Quantitative Study of Opportunities and Challenges. *Webology*, *19*(1), 5838–5849.

Sen, R., Yu, H. F., & Dhillon, I. S. (2019). Think globally, act locally: A deep neural network approach to high-dimensional time series forecasting. *Advances in Neural Information Processing Systems*, 32.

Seretny, M., & Gaur, D. (2020). The model of sustainable marketing as a responsible approach to marketing in the era of industry 4.0. *Advances in Science. Technology and Innovation*, 1.

Sergiu Iscu. (2022). *Retail industry outlook - 2023, Pimics*. Available at: https://www.pimics.com/en/Blog/Retail-industry-outlook-2023

Seyfang, G. (2009). *The New Economics of Sustainable Consumption: Seeds of Change*. Palgrave Macmillan. doi:10.1057/9780230234505

Shabbir, J., & Anwer, T. (2018). *Artificial intelligence and its role in near future*. arXiv preprint arXiv:1804.01396.

Shafiee, S., Jahanyan, S., Ghatari, A. R., & Hasanzadeh, A. (2023). Developing sustainable tourism destinations through smart technologies: A system dynamics approach. *Journal of Simulation*, *17*(4), 477–498. doi:10.1080/17477778.2022.2030656

Shah, D., & Shay, E. (2019). How and why artificial intelligence, mixed reality and blockchain technologies will change marketing we know today. Handbook of advances in marketing in an era of disruptions: Essays in honour of Jagdish N. Sheth, 377-390. doi:10.4135/9789353287733.n32

Shahid, M. Z., & Li, G. (2019). Impact of artificial intelligence in marketing: A perspective of marketing professionals of Pakistan. *Global Journal of Management and Business Research*, *19*(2), 27–33.

Shah, S. S. A., & Khan, Z. (2020). Corporate social responsibility: A pathway to sustainable competitive advantage? *International Journal of Bank Marketing*, *38*(1), 159–174. doi:10.1108/IJBM-01-2019-0037

Shaikh, I. A. K., Kumar, C. N. S., Rohini, P., Jafersadhiq, A., Manoharan, G., & Suryanarayana, V. (2023, August). AST-Graph Convolution Network and LSTM Based Employees Behavioral and Emotional Reactions to Corporate Social Irresponsibility. In *2023 Second International Conference on Augmented Intelligence and Sustainable Systems (ICAISS)* (pp. 966-971). IEEE. 10.1109/ICAISS58487.2023.10250754

Shameem, A., Ramachandran, K. K., Sharma, A., Singh, R., Selvaraj, F. J., & Manoharan, G. (2023, May). The Rising Importance of AI in Boosting the Efficiency of Online Advertising in Developing Countries. In *2023 3rd International Conference on Advance Computing and Innovative Technologies in Engineering (ICACITE)* (pp. 1762-1766). IEEE. 10.1109/ICACITE57410.2023.10182754

Shankar, V., & Balasubramanian, S. (2009). Mobile Marketing: A synthesis and prognosis. *Journal of Interactive Marketing*, *23*(2), 118–129. doi:10.1016/j.intmar.2009.02.002

Shankar, V., Smith, A. K., & Rangaswamy, A. (2003). Customer satisfaction and loyalty in online and offline environments. *International Journal of Research in Marketing*, *20*(2), 153–175. doi:10.1016/S0167-8116(03)00016-8

Shanmuganathan, H., & Mahendran, A. (2021, September). Current trend of IoT market and its security threats. In *2021 International Conference on Innovative Computing, Intelligent Communication and Smart Electrical Systems (ICSES)* (pp. 1-9). IEEE. 10.1109/ICSES52305.2021.9633850

Sharma, R. R., Kaur, T., & Syan, A. S. (2021). *Sustainability Marketing: New directions and practices*. Emerald Group Publishing. doi:10.1108/9781800712447

Sharmin, F., Sultan, M. T., Badulescu, D., Badulescu, A., Borma, A., & Li, B. (2021). Sustainable destination marketing ecosystem through smartphone-based social media: The consumers' acceptance perspective. *Sustainability (Basel)*, *13*(4), 2308. doi:10.3390/su13042308

Shastri, A. (2023, April 10). *Extensive Marketing Strategy of Airbnb - Full case Study*. IIDE. https://iide.co/case-studies/marketing-strategy-of-airbnb/

Shaw, M. J., Subramaniam, C., Tan, G. W., & Welge, M. E. (2001). Knowledge management and data mining for marketing. *Decision Support Systems*, *31*(1), 127–137. doi:10.1016/S0167-9236(00)00123-8

Shenoy, V., & Rao, R. (2020). E-Word of Mouth and Buying Patterns of Consumers: A Thematic Analysis. *Drishtikon: A Management Journal, 11*(2), 15.

Sheth, J. N., & Parvatiyar, A. (2021). Sustainable marketing: Market-driving, not market-driven. *Journal of Macromarketing*, *41*(1), 150–165. doi:10.1177/0276146720961836

Sheth, J. N., Sethia, N. K., & Srinivas, S. (2011). Mindful Consumption: A Customer-centric Approach to Sustainability. *Journal of the Academy of Marketing Science*, *39*(1), 21–39. doi:10.1007/s11747-010-0216-3

Shetty, G., Nougarahiya, S., Mandloi, D., & Sarsodia, T. (2020). COVID-19 and global commerce: An analysis of FMCG, and retail industries of tomorrow. *International Journal of Current Research and Review*, *12*(17), 23–31. doi:10.31782/IJCRR.2020.121715

Shigeta, R., Kawahara, Y., Goud, G. D., & Naik, B. B. (2018). *Capacitive-touch-based soil monitoring device with exchangeable sensor probe. In 2018 IEEE SENSORS*. IEEE.

Shin, S., & Kang, J. (2022). Structural features and Diffusion Patterns of Gartner Hype Cycle for Artificial Intelligence using Social Network analysis. *Journal of Intelligent Information Systems*, *28*(1), 107–129.

Shin, S., & Lee, W. (2014). The effects of technology readiness and technology acceptance on NFC mobile payment services in Korea. *Journal of Applied Business Research*, *30*(6), 1615–1626. doi:10.19030/jabr.v30i6.8873

Sholihin, M., Sari, R. C., Yuniarti, N., & Ilyana, S. (2020). A new way of teaching business ethics: The evaluation of virtual reality-based learning media. *International Journal of Management Education*, *18*(3), 100428. doi:10.1016/j.ijme.2020.100428

Shukla, A., Gullapuram, S. S., Katti, H., Kankanhalli, M., Winkler, S., & Subramanian, R. (2020). Recognition of advertisement emotions with application to computational advertising. *IEEE Transactions on Affective Computing*, *13*(2), 781–792. doi:10.1109/TAFFC.2020.2964549

Siau, K. L., & Yang, Y. (2017). Impact of artificial intelligence, robotics, and machine learning on sales and marketing. *Conference: MWAIS*.

Sichtmann, C. (2007). An analysis of antecedents and consequences of trust in a corporate brand. *European Journal of Marketing*.

Sığırcı, Ö. (2021). Artificial Intelligence in Marketing: A Review of Consumer-AI Interactions. Handbook of Research on Applied Data Science and Artificial Intelligence in Business and Industry, 342-365. doi:10.4018/978-1-7998-6985-6.ch016

Sima, E. (2021). Managing a brand with a vision to marketing 5.0. In *MATEC Web of Conferences* (Vol. 343, p. 07015). EDP Sciences.

Simakova, E., & Neyland, D. (2008). Marketing mobile futures: Assembling constituencies and creating compelling stories for an emerging technology. *Marketing Theory*, *8*(1), 91–116. doi:10.1177/1470593107086486

Simões, D., Filipe, S., & Barbosa, B. (2019). An overview on IoT and its impact on marketing. *Smart marketing with the internet of things*, 1-20.

Simões, D., Barbosa, B., & Filipe, S. (Eds.). (2018). *Smart marketing with the Internet of Things*. IGI Global.

Singh, J., Flaherty, K., Sohi, R. S., Deeter-Schmelz, D., Habel, J., Le Meunier-FitzHugh, K., & Onyemah, V. (2019). Sales profession and professionals in the age of digitization and artificial intelligence technologies: Concepts, priorities, and questions. *Journal of Personal Selling & Sales Management, 39*(1), 2–22. doi:10.1080/08853134.2018.1557525

Singh, L. P., & Challa, R. T. (2016). Integrated forecasting using the discrete wavelet theory and artificial intelligence techniques to reduce the bullwhip effect in a supply chain. *Global Journal of Flexible Systems Managment, 17*(2), 157–169. doi:10.1007/s40171-015-0115-z

Singh, T., & Hill, M. E. (2003). Consumer privacy and the internet in Europe: A view from Germany. *Journal of Consumer Marketing, 20*(7), 634–651. doi:10.1108/07363760310506175

Singireddy, M. (2020). Mcdonald's: Global Marketing. *International Journal of Health and Economic Development, 6*(2), 16–27.

Sirdeshmukh, D., Singh, J., & Sabol, B. (2002). Consumer trust, value, and loyalty in relational exchanges. *Journal of Marketing, 66*(1), 15–37. doi:10.1509/jmkg.66.1.15.18449

Skrbina, D., Heikkurinen, P., & Ruuska, T. (2021). *Sustainability Beyond Technology*. Academic Press.

Slijepčević, M., & Radojević, I. (2018). *Current trends in digital marketing communication*. Faculty of Management, Belgrade Metropolitan University.

Smail, G., & Jia, W. (2017). *Techno-economic analysis and prediction for the deployment of 5G mobile network*. IEEE Xplore. doi:10.1109/ICIN.2017.7899243

Smart Insights. (2022). *What Is Sustainable Marketing and How Should You Use It?* Retrieved at 20 Oct. (2023) from https://www.smartinsights.com/online-brand-strategy/brand-positioning/sustainable-marketing-how-should-you-use-it/

Smith, B., & Linden, G. (2017). Two decades of recommender systems at Amazon. com. *IEEE Internet Computing, 21*(3), 12–18. doi:10.1109/MIC.2017.72

Smith, P., Watson, J., & Geuens, M. (2020). Technological complexity and integration challenges: Marketing in the Internet of Everything era. *Journal of Marketing Management, 36*(11-12), 916–937.

Smith, T., Fischer, E., & Yongjian, C. (2012). How Does Brand-related User-generated Content Differ across YouTube, Facebook, and Twitter? *Journal of Interactive Marketing, 26*(2), 102–113. doi:10.1016/j.intmar.2012.01.002

Sobb, T., Turnbull, B., & Moustafa, N. (2020). Supply chain 4.0: A survey of cyber security challenges, solutions and future directions. *Electronics (Basel), 9*(11), 1–31. doi:10.3390/electronics9111864

Sohrabpour, V., Oghazi, P., Toorajipour, R., & Nazarpour, A. (2021). Export sales forecasting using artificial intelligence. *Technological Forecasting and Social Change, 163*, 120480. doi:10.1016/j.techfore.2020.120480

Soleimani, S. (2018). A perfect triangle with: Artificial intelligence, supply chain management, and financial technology. *Archives of Business Research, 6*(11). Advance online publication. doi:10.14738/abr.611.5681

Soliman, A. M. (2021). Governance and Sustainability Transitions in Urban Informality. In *Urban Informality* (pp. 51–83). Springer. doi:10.1007/978-3-030-68988-9_2

Solomon, M. R. (2014). *Consumer behavior: Buying, having, and being*. Prentice Hall.

Song, J., Kim, J., & Cho, K. (2018). Understanding users' continuance intentions to use smart-connected sports products. *Sport Management Review, 21*(5), 477–490. doi:10.1016/j.smr.2017.10.004

Sookhak, M., Gani, A., Shiraz, M., & Buyya, R. (2019). Energy efficiency and renewable energy in the Internet of Things: A review. *IEEE Communications Surveys and Tutorials, 21*(2), 1718–1747. doi:10.1109/COMST.2018.2867288

Sorokina, E., Wang, Y., Fyall, A., Lugosi, P., Torres, E., & Jung, T. (2022). Constructing a smart destination framework: A destination marketing organization perspective. *Journal of Destination Marketing & Management, 23*, 100688. doi:10.1016/j.jdmm.2021.100688

Spiller, L., & Baier, M. (2005). *Contemporary Direct & Interactive Marketing.* Pearson Education Inc.

Srinivasan, S. S., Anderson, R., & Ponnavolu, K. (2002). Customer loyalty in e-commerce: An exploration of its antecedents and consequences. *Journal of Retailing, 78*(1), 41–50. doi:10.1016/S0022-4359(01)00065-3

Srivastava, R. K. (2007). Managing brand performance: Aligning positioning, execution and experience. *Journal of Brand Management, 14*(1-2), 129–140.

Stallone, V., Wetzels, M., & Klaas, M. (2021). Applications of Blockchain Technology in marketing systematic review of marketing technology companies. *Blockchain: Research and Applications*, 100023.

Stocchi, L., Pourazad, N., Michaelidou, N., Tanusondjaja, A., & Harrigan, P. (2022). Marketing Research on Mobile Apps: Past, Present and Future. *Journal of the Academy of Marketing Science, 50*(2), 195–225. doi:10.1007/s11747-021-00815-w PMID:34776554

Stolle, M. (2019). Labeling and packaging: The first taste is almost always with the eye! *Wine & Viticulture Journal, 34*(2), 59–60.

Stone, M. D., & Woodcock, N. D. (2014). Interactive, direct and digital marketing: A future that depends on better use of business intelligence. *Journal of Research in Interactive Marketing, 8*(1), 4–17. doi:10.1108/JRIM-07-2013-0046

Suchanek, M., & Szmelter-Jarosz, A. (2019). Environmental aspects of generation Y's sustainable mobility. *Sustainability (Basel), 11*(11), 3204. doi:10.3390/su11113204

Su, M., Fang, M., Kim, J., & Park, K. S. (2022). Sustainable marketing innovation and consumption: Evidence from cold chain food online retail. *Journal of Cleaner Production, 340*, 130806. doi:10.1016/j.jclepro.2022.130806

Sun, H., & Gilbert, S. M. (2019). Retail price competition with product fit uncertainty and assortment selection. *Production and Operations Management, 28*(7), 1658–1673. doi:10.1111/poms.13005

Sun, Z., Zhu, M., Zhang, Z., Chen, Z., Shi, Q., Shan, X., Yeow, R. C. H., & Lee, C. (2021). Artificial Intelligence of Things (AIoT) Enabled Virtual Shop Applications Using Self-Powered Sensor Enhanced Soft Robotic Manipulator. *Advancement of Science, 8*(14), 2100230. doi:10.1002/advs.202100230 PMID:34037331

Sweeney, J. C., & Soutar, G. N. (2001). Consumer perceived value: The development of a multiple item scale. *Journal of Retailing, 77*(2), 203–220. doi:10.1016/S0022-4359(01)00041-0

Syam, N., & Kaul, R. (2021). *Machine Learning and Artificial Intelligence in Marketing and Sales: Essential Reference for Practitioners and Data Scientists.* Emerald Publishing Limited. doi:10.1108/9781800438804

Syam, N., & Sharma, A. (2018). Waiting for a sales renaissance in the fourth industrial revolution: Machine learning and artificial intelligence in sales research and practice. *Industrial Marketing Management, 69*, 135–146. doi:10.1016/j.indmarman.2017.12.019

Tabroni, I., Husniyah, H., Sapitri, L., & Azzahra, Y. (2022). Impact of Technological Advancements on The Establishment of Characteristics of Children. *East Asian Journal of Multidisciplinary Research, 1*(1), 27–32. doi:10.54259/eajmr.v1i1.453

Taiminen, H. M., & Karjaluoto, H. (2015). The usage of digital marketing channels in SMEs. *Journal of Small Business and Enterprise Development, 22*(4), 633–651. doi:10.1108/JSBED-05-2013-0073

Tamang, R. (2023, March 11). *UX and Gamification in Duolingo - UX Planet.* Medium. https://uxplanet.org/ux-and-gamification-in-duolingo-40d55ee09359

Tam, K. Y., & Ho, S. Y. (2006). Understanding the impact of web personalization on user information processing and decision outcomes. *Management Information Systems Quarterly, 30*(4), 865–890. doi:10.2307/25148757

Tan, T. F., & Ko, C. H. (2016, November). Application of artificial intelligence to cross-screen marketing: a case study of AI technology company. In *2016 2nd International Conference on Artificial Intelligence and Industrial Engineering (AIIE 2016)* (pp. 517-519). Atlantis Press.

Tanase, G. C. (2018). Artificial intelligence: Optimizing the experience of digital marketing. *Romanian Distribution Committee Magazine, 9*(1), 24–28.

Tan, G. W.-H., Ooi, K.-B., Chong, S.-C., & Hew, T.-S. (2014). NFC mobile credit card: The next frontier of mobile payment? *Telematics and Informatics, 31*(2), 292–307. doi:10.1016/j.tele.2013.06.002

Tan, Z., Sadiq, B., Bashir, T., Mahmood, H., & Rasool, Y. (2022). Investigating the impact of green marketing components on purchase intention: The mediating role of brand image and brand trust. *Sustainability (Basel), 14*(10), 5939. doi:10.3390/su14105939

Tariq, B., Taimoor, S., Najam, H., Law, R., Hassan, W., & Han, H. (2020). Generating marketing outcomes through Internet of things (Iot) technologies. *Sustainability (Basel), 12*(22), 9670. doi:10.3390/su12229670

Tchelidze, L. (2019). Potential and skill requirements of artificial intelligence in digital marketing. *Calitatea, 20*(S3), 73–78.

Teixeira, G. F. G., & Junior, O. C. (2019). How to make strategic planning for corporate sustainability? *Journal of Cleaner Production, 230*, 1421–1431. doi:10.1016/j.jclepro.2019.05.063

Thakur, A., & Kumar, A. (2022). Role of Artificial Intelligence-Based Technologies in Healthcare to Combat Critical Diseases. In *Digital Health Transformation with Blockchain and Artificial Intelligence* (pp. 195–218). CRC Press. doi:10.1201/9781003247128-11

Theodoridis, P. K., & Gkikas, D. C. (2019). How artificial intelligence affects digital marketing. In Strategic Innovative Marketing and Tourism: 7th ICSIMAT, Athenian Riviera, Greece, 2018 (pp. 1319-1327). Springer International Publishing. doi:10.1007/978-3-030-12453-3_151

Thiraviyam, T. (2018). Artificial intelligence marketing. *International Journal of Recent Research Aspects, 4*, 449–452.

THIS, T. M. I. L. (2020). *Strategic Marketing Planning. Hashtags and Headlines: Marketing for School Leaders.* Academic Press.

Thomassey, S., & Zeng, X. (2018). *Introduction: artificial intelligence for fashion industry in the big data era.* Springer Singapore.

Thontirawong, P., & Chinchanachokchai, S. (2021). Teaching artificial intelligence and machine learning in marketing. *Marketing Education Review, 31*(2), 58–63. doi:10.1080/10528008.2021.1871849

Tiwari, V., Mishra, A., & Tiwari, S. (2023). Role of data safety and perceived privacy for acceptance of IoT-enabled technologies at smart tourism destinations. *Current Issues in Tourism*, 1–16. doi:10.1080/13683500.2023.2247534

Tjepkema, L. (2019). *What Is Artificial Intelligence Marketing & Why Is It So Powerful.* Emarsys: https://www.emarsys.com/resources/blog/artificial-intelligence-marketing-solutions/03.05

Todorova, A., & Antonova, D. (2023, October). Smart Marketing Solutions: Applications with Artificial Intelligence to Increase the Effectiveness of Marketing Operations. In *2023 7th International Symposium on Multidisciplinary Studies and Innovative Technologies (ISMSIT)* (pp. 1-6). IEEE.

Topley, M. (2020). Keeping up with patient expectations. *BDJ In Practice, 33*(2), 23–25. doi:10.1038/s41404-020-0298-7

Torbica, A., Fornaro, G., Tarricone, R., & Drummond, M. F. (2020). Do social values and institutional context shape the use of economic evaluation in reimbursement decisions? An empirical analysis. *Value in Health, 23*(1), 17–24. doi:10.1016/j.jval.2019.11.001 PMID:31952668

Tripathi, M. A., Tripathi, R., Effendy, F., Manoharan, G., Paul, M. J., & Aarif, M. (2023, January). An In-Depth Analysis of the Role That ML and Big Data Play in Driving Digital Marketing's Paradigm Shift. In *2023 International Conference on Computer Communication and Informatics (ICCCI)* (pp. 1-6). IEEE. 10.1109/ICCCI56745.2023.10128357

Tripathy, A. K., Tripathy, P. K., Ray, N. K., & Mohanty, S. P. (2018). iTour: The future of smart tourism: An IoT framework for the independent mobility of tourists in smart cities. *IEEE Consumer Electronics Magazine, 7*(3), 32–37. doi:10.1109/MCE.2018.2797758

Tsai, W.-H., Wang, Y.-F., & Chen, Y.-C. (2020). Data ownership, governance, and rights in Internet of Things (IoT) ecosystems: Complexities, conflicts, and legal issues. *Telecommunications Policy, 44*(6), 101938.

Tsourela, M., & Nerantzaki, D. M. (2020). An internet of things (Iot) acceptance model. Assessing consumer's behavior toward iot products and applications. *Future Internet, 12*(11), 191. doi:10.3390/fi12110191

Tucker, K., Bulim, J., Koch, G., North, M., Nguyen, T., Fox, J., & Delay, D. (2018). Internet industry: A perspective review through internet of things and internet of everything. *International Management Review, 14*(2), 26–38.

Vaja, M. B. R. (2015). Retail management. *International Journal of Research and Analytics Reviews, 2*(1), 22–28.

Valentino, R. B. (2022). Developing Relationships, Personalization, and Data Herald in the Pandemic. In Developing Relationships, Personalization, and Data Herald in Marketing 5.0 (pp. 69-78). IGI Global.

Van Dijck, J. (2013). 'You have one identity': Performing the self on Facebook and LinkedIn. *Media Culture & Society, 35*(2), 199–215. doi:10.1177/0163443712468605

Vargo, S. L., & Lusch, R. F. (2008). Service-Dominant Logic: Continuing the Evolution. *Journal of the Academy of Marketing Science, 36*(1), 1–10. doi:10.1007/s11747-007-0069-6

Varma, P., Nijjer, S., Kaur, B., & Sharma, S. (2022). Blockchain for transformation in digital marketing. In *Handbook of Research on the Platform Economy and the Evolution of E-Commerce* (pp. 274–298). IGI Global.

Varmavuo, E. (2020). *Factors affecting the success of AI campaigns in marketing: data perspective.* Academic Press.

Varsha, P. S., Akter, S., Kumar, A., Gochhait, S., & Patagundi, B. (2021). The impact of artificial intelligence on branding: A bibliometric analysis (1982-2019). *Journal of Global Information Management, 29*(4), 221–246. doi:10.4018/JGIM.20210701.oa10

Venkatesh, R. (2015). *Mobile marketing From marketing strategy to mobile marketing campaign implementation.* https://www.semanticscholar.org/paper/Mobile-Marketing-From-Marketing-Strategy-to-Mobile-Venkatesh/8a626502264cca8316c1a99c95b3f9f92ed7cad3

Venkatesh, V., & Morris, M. G. (2000). Why don't men ever stop to ask for directions? Gender, social influence, and their role in technology acceptance and usage behavior. *Management Information Systems Quarterly, 24*(1), 115–139. doi:10.2307/3250981

Venkatesh, V., Morris, M. G., Davis, G. B., & Davis, F. D. (2003). User acceptance of information technology: Toward a unified view. *Management Information Systems Quarterly*, 27(3), 425–478. doi:10.2307/30036540

Vera-Martínez, J., Alvarado-Herrera, A., & Currás-Pérez, R. (2022). Do consumers really care about aspects of corporate social responsibility when developing attitudes toward a brand? *Journal of Global Marketing*, 35(3), 193–207. doi:10.1080/08911762.2021.1958277

Verchere, A. (2022). Is social polarization bad for the planet? A theoretical inquiry. *Bulletin of Economic Research*, 74(2), 427–456. doi:10.1111/boer.12303

Verhoef, P. C., Kannan, P. K., & Inman, J. J. (2015). From Multi-Channel Retailing to OMNI-Channel Retailing: Introduction to the Special Issue on Multi-Channel Retailing. *Journal of Retailing*, 91(2), 174–181. doi:10.1016/j.jretai.2015.02.005

Verhoef, P. C., Lemon, K. N., Parasuraman, A., Roggeveen, A., Tsiros, M., & Schlesinger, L. A. (2009). Customer experience creation: Determinants, dynamics and management strategies. *Journal of Retailing*, 85(1), 31–41. doi:10.1016/j.jretai.2008.11.001

Verhoef, P. C., Stephen, A. T., Kannan, P. K., Luo, X., Abhishek, V., Andrews, M., Bart, Y., Datta, H., Fong, N., Hoffman, D. L., Hu, M. M., Novak, T., Rand, W., & Zhang, Y. (2017). Consumer connectivity in a complex, technology-enabled, and mobile-oriented world with smart products. *Journal of Interactive Marketing*, 40(1), 1–8. doi:10.1016/j.intmar.2017.06.001

Vermanen, M., Rantanen, M. M., & Harkke, V. (2022). Ethical Framework for IoT Deployment in SMEs: Individual Perspective. *Internet Research*, 32(7), 185–201. doi:10.1108/INTR-08-2019-0361

Verma, S., & Rai, A. (2019). Internet of things (IoT) for marketing: A review of opportunities and challenges. *Journal of Business Research*, 116, 598–613.

Verma, S., Sharma, R., Deb, S., & Maitra, D. (2021). Artificial intelligence in marketing: Systematic review and future research direction. *International Journal of Information Management Data Insights*, 1(1), 100002. doi:10.1016/j.jjimei.2020.100002

Vinuesa, R., Azizpour, H., Leite, I., Balaam, M., Dignum, V., Domisch, S., Felländer, A., Langhans, S. D., Tegmark, M., & Fuso Nerini, F. (2020). The role of artificial intelligence in achieving the Sustainable Development Goals. *Nature Communications*, 11(1), 1–10. doi:10.1038/s41467-019-14108-y PMID:31932590

Voegtlin, C., Scherer, A. G., Stahl, G. K., & Hawn, O. (2022). Grand societal challenges and responsible innovation. *Journal of Management Studies*, 59(1), 1–28. doi:10.1111/joms.12785

Völckner, F. (2008). The dual role of price: Decomposing consumers' reactions to price. *Journal of the Academy of Marketing Science*, 36(3), 359–377. doi:10.1007/s11747-007-0076-7

Von Pape, T., Trepte, S., & Mothes, C. (2017). Privacy by disaster? Press coverage of privacy and digital technology. *European Journal of Communication*, 32(3), 189–207. doi:10.1177/0267323117689994

Vyas, P. G., & Priya, S. (2023). Social Media and Gen Y at Work: The Uses and Gratifications of Technology. In 5G, Artificial Intelligence, and Next Generation Internet of Things: Digital Innovation for Green and Sustainable Economies (pp. 123-142). IGI Global.

Walsh, G., & Beatty, S. E. (2007). Customer-based corporate reputation of a service firm: Scale development and validation. *Journal of the Academy of Marketing Science*, 35(1), 127–143. doi:10.1007/s11747-007-0015-7

Wamba, S. F., Bawack, R. E., Guthrie, C., Queiroz, M. M., & Carillo, K. D. A. (2021). Are we preparing for a good AI society? A bibliometric review and research agenda. *Technological Forecasting and Social Change, 164,* 120482. doi:10.1016/j.techfore.2020.120482

Wamba-Taguimdje, S. L., Wamba, S. F., Kamdjoug, J. R. K., & Wanko, C. E. T. (2020). Impact of artificial intelligence on firm performance: exploring the mediating effect of process-oriented dynamic capabilities. In Digital Business Transformation: Organizing, Managing and Controlling in the Information Age (pp. 3-18). Springer International Publishing. doi:10.1007/978-3-030-47355-6_1

Wang, D., Li, X., & Li, Y. (2013). China's "smart tourism destination" initiative: A taste of the service-dominant logic. *Journal of Destination Marketing & Management, 2*(2), 59–61. doi:10.1016/j.jdmm.2013.05.004

Wang, H., Chen, K., & Xu, D. (2016). A maturity model for blockchain adoption. *Financial Innovation, 2*(1), 1–5. doi:10.1186/s40854-016-0031-z

Wang, H., Jing, G., Bohan, K., Peng, L., & Shi, Y. (2022). Analysis and Research on the Marketing Strategy of Agricultural Products Based on Artificial Intelligence. *Mathematical Problems in Engineering.*

Wang, I., Liao, C. W., Lin, K. P., Wang, C. H., & Tsai, C. L. (2021). Evaluate the Consumer Acceptance of AIoT-Based Unmanned Convenience Stores Based on Perceived Risks and Technological Acceptance Models. *Mathematical Problems in Engineering, 2021,* 2021. doi:10.1155/2021/4416270

Wang, T., Jung, C.-H., Kang, M.-H., & Chung, Y.-S. (2014). Exploring determinants of adoption intentions towards Enterprise 2.0 applications: An empirical study. *Behaviour & Information Technology, 33*(10), 1048–1064. doi:10.1080/0144929X.2013.781221

Wang, W., & Zhang, J. (2019). Internet of Everything (IoE) for supply chain sustainability: A review of opportunities and challenges. *Sustainability, 11*(9), 2508.

Wang, Y., Deng, Q., Rod, M., & Ji, S. (2021). A Thematic Exploration of Social Media Analytics in Marketing Research and an Agenda for Future Inquiry. *Journal of Strategic Marketing, 29*(6), 471–491. doi:10.1080/0965254X.2020.1755351

Wang, Z., Ye, C., Liu, X., Ma, R., Sun, Z., & Ruan, J. (2023). Optimal retail sales strategies for old and new products in monopoly and horizontal competition scenarios. *Journal of Retailing and Consumer Services, 71,* 103218. doi:10.1016/j.jretconser.2022.103218

Ward, C. B., Roy, D. P., & Edmondson, D. R. (2016). Is CVS Just 'Blowing Smoke?': Evaluating the CVS Decision to Ban Tobacco Products. *Case Studies in Strategic Communication, 5*(1), 249–264.

Watson, G. F. IV, Worm, S., Palmatier, R. W., & Ganesan, S. (2015). The evolution of marketing channels: Trends and research directions. *Journal of Retailing, 91*(4), 546–568. doi:10.1016/j.jretai.2015.04.002

Webb, K. L. (2002). Managing channels of distribution in the age of electronic commerce. *Industrial Marketing Management, 31*(2), 95–102. doi:10.1016/S0019-8501(01)00181-X

Weinberg, B. D., Milne, G. R., Andonova, Y. G., & Hajjat, F. M. (2015). Internet of things: Convenience vs privacy and secrecy. *Business Horizons, 58*(6), 615–624. doi:10.1016/j.bushor.2015.06.005

Wen, X., Wang, S., Taveira, T. H., & Akhlaghi, F. (2021). Required warfarin dose and time in therapeutic range in patients with diagnosed Nonalcoholic Fatty Liver Disease (NAFLD) or Nonalcoholic Steatohepatitis (NASH). *PLoS One, 16*(9), e0251665. doi:10.1371/journal.pone.0251665 PMID:34525124

Wescott, R. F., Fitzpatrick, B., & Phillips, E. (2015). *McDonald's–Alliance for a Healthier Generation Partnership: Clinton Global Initiative Commitment to Action.* Academic Press.

Weston, M. (2018). Training load monitoring in elite English soccer: A comparison of practices and perceptions between coaches and practitioners. *Science & Medicine in Football*, 2(3), 216–224. doi:10.1080/24733938.2018.1427883

What is Local SEO, and How Does It Work ? (n.d.). Mailchimp. https://mailchimp.com/resources/what-is-local-seo/

Wierenga, B. (2010). Marketing and artificial intelligence: Great opportunities, reluctant partners. In *Marketing intelligent systems using soft computing: Managerial and research applications* (pp. 1–8). Springer Berlin Heidelberg. doi:10.1007/978-3-642-15606-9_1

Wijayanto, S., & Putra, J. C. P. (2021). The Effectiveness of a Virtual Reality Marketing Video on the People Desire to Buy a Product. *JOIV: International Journal on Informatics Visualization*, 5(4), 360–365. doi:10.30630/joiv.5.4.483

Wilkerson, G. B., Gupta, A., & Colston, M. A. (2018). Mitigating sports injury risks using internet of things and analytics approaches. *Risk Analysis*, 38(7), 1348–1360. doi:10.1111/risa.12984 PMID:29529346

Wilkinson, R., Black, J., Agnew, A., Arnold, J., Francolini, A., Gardner, M., & Harder, A. (2015). Rethinking the value chain. *Consum. Goods Forum*, 1, 48.

Wilson, R. M. (2010). *Strategic marketing planning*. Routledge. doi:10.4324/9780080912127

Wind, J., & Mahajan, V. (2002). Digital marketing. Symphonya. *Emerging Issues in Management*, (1), 43–54.

Wirth, N. (2018). Hello marketing, what can artificial intelligence help you with? *International Journal of Market Research*, 60(5), 435–438. doi:10.1177/1470785318776841

Woodside, A. G., & Sood, S. (2017). Vignettes in the two-step arrival of the internet of things and its reshaping of marketing management's service-dominant logic. *Journal of Marketing Management*, 33(1-2), 98–110. doi:10.1080/0267257X.2016.1246748

Wright, L. W. L. (2016, July 15). *5 ways the Internet of Things is already affecting you*. Retrieved October 17, 2023, from https://www.saga.co.uk/magazine/technology/Internet/communications/5-ways-theInternet-of-things-affects-yo

Wu, X., & Gereffi, G. (2018). Amazon and Alibaba: Internet Governance, Business Models, and Internationalization Strategies. In International Business in the Information and Digital Age (pp. 327-356). Emerald Publishing Limited.

Wu, D., & Liu, J. (2022). Involve Humans in Algorithmic Fairness Issue: A Systematic Review. In *International Conference on Information* (pp. 161-176). Springer. 10.1007/978-3-030-96957-8_15

Wu, F., Lu, C., Zhu, M., Chen, H., Zhu, J., Yu, K., Li, L., Li, M., Chen, Q., Li, X., Cao, X., Wang, Z., Zha, Z., Zhuang, Y., & Pan, Y. (2020). Towards a new generation of artificial intelligence in China. *Nature Machine Intelligence*, 2(6), 312–316. doi:10.1038/s42256-020-0183-4

Wu, G. (2021, March). Research on the development path of logistics management innovation in e-commerce environment. *IOP Conference Series. Earth and Environmental Science*, 714(4), 042022. doi:10.1088/1755-1315/714/4/042022

Wu, S. X., Wu, Z., Chen, S., Li, G., & Zhang, S. (2021). Community detection in blockchain social networks. *Journal of Communications and Information Networks*, 6(1), 59–71. doi:10.23919/JCIN.2021.9387705

Wu, Z., Qian, X., Huang, M., Ching, W. K., Wang, X., & Gu, J. (2023). Recycling channel choice in closed-loop supply chains considering retailer competitive preference. *Enterprise Information Systems*, 17(2), 1923065. doi:10.1080/17517575.2021.1923065

Xiang, Z., Du, Q., Ma, Y., & Fan, W. (2017). A comparative analysis of major online review platforms: Implications for social media analytics in hospitality and tourism. *Tourism Management*, 58, 51–65. doi:10.1016/j.tourman.2016.10.001

Xiao, F., & Ke, J. (2021). Pricing, management and decision-making of financial markets with artificial intelligence: Introduction to the issue. *Financial Innovation*, 7(1), 1–3. doi:10.1186/s40854-021-00302-9 PMID:35024295

Xiao, Y., Zhu, Y., He, W., & Huang, M. (2023). Influence prediction model for marketing campaigns on e-commerce platforms. *Expert Systems with Applications*, 211, 118575. doi:10.1016/j.eswa.2022.118575

Xu, L. D., He, W., & Li, S. (2014). Internet of things in industries: A survey. *IEEE Transactions on Industrial Informatics*, 10(4), 2233–2243. doi:10.1109/TII.2014.2300753

Xu, Z., Lv, Z., Li, J., & Shi, A. (2022). A novel approach for predicting water demand with complex patterns based on ensemble learning. *Water Resources Management*, 36(11), 4293–4312. doi:10.1007/s11269-022-03255-5

Xu, Z., Lv, Z., Li, J., Sun, H., & Sheng, Z. (2022). A novel perspective on travel demand prediction considering natural environmental and socioeconomic factors. *IEEE Intelligent Transportation Systems Magazine*, 15(1), 136–159. doi:10.1109/MITS.2022.3162901

Yadav, J., Misra, M., & Goundar, S. (2021). Autonomous agriculture marketing information system through blockchain: a case study of e-NAM adoption in India. In Blockchain Technologies, Applications and Cryptocurrencies: Current Practice and Future Trends (pp. 115-138). Academic Press.

Yan, C., Zhu, J., Ouyang, Y., & Zeng, X. (2021). Marketing method and system optimization based on the financial blockchain of the internet of things. *Wireless Communications and Mobile Computing*, 2021, 1–11. doi:10.1155/2021/9354569

Yang, L. T., Di Martino, B., & Zhang, Q. (2017). Internet of everything [editorial]. *Mobile Information Systems*, 1–3.

Yang, Y., Liu, Y., Lv, X., Ai, J., & Li, Y. (2022). Anthropomorphism and customers' willingness to use artificial intelligence service agents. *Journal of Hospitality Marketing & Management*, 31(1), 1–23. doi:10.1080/19368623.2021.1926037

Yap, D. (2018). CVS Pharmacy rolls out new prescription management system. *Pharmacy Today*, 24(5), 46–47. doi:10.1016/j.ptdy.2018.04.027

Yeğin, T. (2020). The place and future of artificial intelligence in marketing strategies. *Ekev Akademi Dergisi*, (81), 489–506.

Yılmaz, M. B., & Baybars, B. (2022). A Critical Perspective on Greenwashing Under the Roof of Corporate Environmentalism. In *Green Marketing in Emerging Economies* (pp. 119–140). Palgrave Macmillan. doi:10.1007/978-3-030-82572-0_6

Yoon, S.-J. (2002). The antecedents and consequences of trust in online-purchase decisions. *Journal of Interactive Marketing*, 16(2), 47–63. doi:10.1002/dir.10008

Yoo, S., Lee, S., Kim, S., Hwang, K. H., Park, J. H., & Kang, N. (2021). Integrating deep learning into CAD/CAE system: Generative design and evaluation of 3D conceptual wheel. *Structural and Multidisciplinary Optimization*, 64(4), 2725–2747. doi:10.1007/s00158-021-02953-9

York, J., Lugo, K., Jarosz, L., & Toscani, M. (2021). CVS health faces a new wave of disruption. *International Journal of Pharmaceutical and Healthcare Marketing*, 15(3), 333–353. doi:10.1108/IJPHM-01-2020-0008

Yudhiasta, S., & Mijiarto, J. (2023). Digitalization of tourist attractions: Increasing the capacity of Sunrise Land Lombok tourism workers through digital marketing. *Journal of Community Service and Empowerment*, 4(1), 95–103.

Yu, J., Park, J., Lee, K., & Han, H. (2021). Can environmentally sustainable development and green innovation of hotels trigger the formation of a positive brand and price premium? *International Journal of Environmental Research and Public Health*, 18(6), 3275. doi:10.3390/ijerph18063275 PMID:33809991

Yulianti, Y., & Saifudin, A. (2020, July). Sequential feature selection in customer churn prediction based on Naive Bayes. *IOP Conference Series. Materials Science and Engineering, 879*(1), 012090. doi:10.1088/1757-899X/879/1/012090

Zahay, D., Peltier, J. J., & Krishen, A. S. (2012). Building the foundation for customer data quality in CRM systems for financial services firms. *Journal of Database Marketing & Customer Strategy Management, 19*(1), 5–1. doi:10.1057/dbm.2012.6

Zaman, M. M. U. (2021). A Critical Review and Directions for the Use of Eco-Friendly Products in Bangladesh. *International Journal of Progressive Sciences and Technologies, 27*(1), 67–75.

Zaman, R., Jain, T., Samara, G., & Jamali, D. (2022). Corporate governance meets corporate social responsibility: Mapping the interface. *Business & Society, 61*(3), 690–752. doi:10.1177/0007650320973415

Zeithaml, V. A. (1988). Consumer perceptions of price, quality, and value: A means-end model and synthesis of evidence. *Journal of Marketing, 52*(3), 2–22. doi:10.1177/002224298805200302

Zhang, H. (2024). *Revolutionizing Digital Marketing Industrial Internet of Things-enabled Supply Chain Management in Smart Manufacturing*. Academic Press.

Zhang, S. (2022). Artificial intelligence and marketing intersection post-COVID-19: A conceptual framework. *International Journal of Innovative Technologies in Social Science.*

Zhang, J. Z., & Chang, C.-W. (2021). Consumer Dynamics: Theories, Methods, and Emerging Directions. *Journal of the Academy of Marketing Science, 49*(1), 166–196. doi:10.1007/s11747-020-00720-8

Zhang, J., & Wang, Y. (2020). Quantifying the impact of IoE-based sustainable marketing initiatives on environmental and social goals. *Journal of Cleaner Production, 259*, 120740.

Zhang, T. H., & Chen, Y. (2021). The role of Internet of Things (IoT) in empowering consumers to participate in sustainable movements and advocate for responsible business practices. *Journal of Cleaner Production, 280*, 124385.

Zhang, Y., Sotiriadis, M., & Shen, S. (2022). Investigating the Impact of Smart Tourism Technologies on Tourists' Experiences. *Sustainability, 14*(5), 30–48. doi:10.3390/su15010030

Zhang, Y., Zhang, X., & Zhao, C. (2018). Environmental impact of internet of things devices: A review. *Journal of Cleaner Production, 198*, 1222–1237.

Zhang, Y., & Zhang, Y. (2022). Service-related Applications in Smart Marketing: A Review and Research Agenda. *Journal of Business Research, 141*, 1–10.

Zhang, Z., Wang, R., Zheng, W., Lan, S., Liang, D., & Jin, H. (2015, November). Profit maximization analysis based on data mining and the exponential retention model assumption with respect to customer churn problems. In *2015 IEEE International Conference on Data Mining Workshop (ICDMW)* (pp. 1093-1097). IEEE. 10.1109/ICDMW.2015.84

Zhao, H., Lyu, F., & Luo, Y. (2022). Research on the effect of online marketing based on multimodel fusion and artificial intelligence in the context of big data. *Security and Communication Networks, 2022*, 1–9. doi:10.1155/2022/1516543

Zhao, R., & Cai, Y. (2021). Research on online marketing effects based on multi-model fusion and artificial intelligence algorithms. *Journal of Ambient Intelligence and Humanized Computing*, 1–17.

Zhu, F., & Zhang, X. (2010). Impact of online consumer reviews on sales: The moderating role of product and consumer characteristics. *Journal of Marketing, 74*(2), 133–148. doi:10.1509/jm.74.2.133

Zhu, G., & Gao, X. (2019). Precision retail marketing strategy based on digital marketing model. *Science Journal of Business and Management, 7*(1), 33–37. doi:10.11648/j.sjbm.20190701.15

Zhu, H., Tiwari, P., Ghoneim, A., & Hossain, M. S. (2021). A collaborative ai-enabled pretrained language model for aiot domain question answering. *IEEE Transactions on Industrial Informatics.*

Zhu, Y., Zhou, L., Xie, C., Wang, G. J., & Nguyen, T. V. (2019). Forecasting SMEs' credit risk in supply chain finance with an enhanced hybrid ensemble machine learning approach. *International Journal of Production Economics, 211,* 22–33. doi:10.1016/j.ijpe.2019.01.032

About the Contributors

Hamed Nozari is a research assistant in Industrial engineering at the Iran university of science and technology. He holds a Ph.D. in Industrial Engineering with a focus on Production Management and Planning and PostDoc in Industrial Engineering from the Iran University of Science and Technology. He has taught various courses in the field of Industrial Engineering and has published many books and papers as well. Now he is a researcher in the field of digital developments and smart systems and optimization.

* * *

Neda Abdolvnad is an associate professor in Alzahra University in Iran. She is interested in multi-disciplinary research with a strong background in different business sectors. She has applied her research in various industrial settings and gained hands-on experience in the application of information technology and systems. The role of machine learning and AI in e-business and social media has been her research focus in the past few years. She studies the implications of new digital technologies on sustainability and society.

Sunitha Ashtikar is pursuing her Ph.D. at SR University.

Mohd Azhar is currently working as Assistant Professor at the School of Business, Woxsen University, India. He received his Ph.D. in Marketing from Faculty of Commerce, Aligarh Muslim University, India. He has published research papers in reputed national and international journals. His five research papers have been recognized by the World Health Organization (WHO) and have been listed under the global literature on COVID-19.

Subhashini Durai is working as faculty at Bharathiar University.

Mohammad Ghaffari is an assistant professor and a faculty member of marketing at University of Tehran, Iran. His research focuses on marketing and tourism marketing.

Nasim Ghanbar Tehrani received her PhD in Industrial Engineering from the Tarbiat Modaress University, Tehran, Iran in 2011. In 2013 she became a faculty member of Industrial Engineering department of Kharazmi University, Tehran, Iran. Her research interest is mainly Knowledge Management, and she is active as an industry consultant in the field of KM system design. She has also translated many books in this field, from English into Persian, her mother language.

Atrij Jadon is a strategic and result-oriented marketing representative with a proven track record of success in growing businesses. Proven ability to develop and execute marketing plans that align with business goals. Strong understanding of the B2B market and how to reach decision-makers. Expertise in using a variety of marketing channels, including digital, social media, and content marketing. Excellent communication and presentation skills.

Anagha Kuriachan is currently pursuing MCOM in Christ Deemed to be University. I am a member of Business plan event in Utchrista which is a PG level Business Fest. My area of interest in research is marketing and artificial intelligence.

Pratap Chandra Mandal is an Assistant Professor (Marketing) at Indian Institute of Management, Shillong, India. He has completed graduate degree from the reputed Indian Institute of Technology, Kharagpur (IIT Kharagpur), India (Bachelor of Technology in Mechanical Engineering), post-graduate degree from Vinod Gupta School of Management, IIT Kharagpur (Masters in Business Adminstration), PhD (Marketing) from Vinod Gupta School of Management, IIT Kharagpur. His research concerns customer relationship management, customer satisfaction, services marketing, marketing intelligence, and qualitative methods in management. He is the editor-in-chief of two international journals and is on the editorial board of journals like Journal of Global Marketing. Pratap has won several prestigious scholarships and awards throughout his academic career.

Geetha Manoharan is currently working in Telangana as an assistant professor at SR University. She is the university-level PhD programme coordinator and has also been given the additional responsibility of In Charge Director of Publications and Patents under the Research Division at SR University. Under her tutelage, students are inspired to reach their full potential in all areas of their education and beyond through experiential learning. It creates an atmosphere conducive to the growth of students into independent thinkers and avid readers. She has more than ten years of experience across the board in the business world, academia, and the academy. She has a keen interest in the study of organizational behavior and management. More than forty articles and books have been published in scholarly venues such as UGC-refereed, SCOPUS, Web of Science, and Springer. Over the past six-plus years, she has participated in varied research and student exchange programs at both the national and international levels. A total of five of her collaborative innovations in this area have already been published and patented. Emotional intelligence, self-efficacy, and work-life balance are among her specialties. She organizes programs for academic organizations. She belongs to several professional organizations, including the CMA and the CPC. The TIPSGLOBAL Institute of Coimbatore has recognized her twice (in 2017 and 2018) for her outstanding academic performance.

Jayanthi Mohan is working for CIT as an assistant professor.

Mohammad Nematpour is a PhD in Marketing Management at the University of Tehran, Iran. He is also a tourism scholar whose research focuses on tourism-related studies of consumer behavior, marketing research, long-range planning, and foresight.

T. Priya is working as Assistant Professor in Department of Management Studies at Coimbatore Institute of Technology, Coimbatore.

Abdul Razak is working for Entrepreneurship Development Institute of India as an associate professor.

Harsh Sethia is currently pursuing a Master's degree in Business Administration at Woxsen University, where he has developed a strong foundation in key business concepts and strategies. His academic background has equipped him with a deep understanding of finance and marketing principles, including financial analysis, investment strategies, and market research.

Agnieszka Szmelter-Jarosz is an assistant professor at the Department of Logistics, Faculty of Economics, University of Gdansk, Poland. She is the author of over 80 scientific papers. She has been a principal investigator in two national projects and a co-investigator and team member in 14 international and national projects. Her major scientific interests are urban logistics and urban mobility. She is a Lean Six Sigma Black Belt, SAP Certified Application Associate and Design Thinking Moderator. She runs her own consulting company.

Reshma Thomas is currently pursuing MCOM in Christ Deemed to be University in Bangalore. I am a member of Team Influent which is a personality skill development club. My area of interest in research is Artificial Intelligence, marketing and accounting.

C. Vijayabanu is currently a Professor at the School of Management, SASTRA University in India. She obtained her Ph.D. in Commerce-Human Resource Management in 2000 at Bharathidasan University, India. Her current research interests focus on the areas of behavioral studies –Personality, Perception: attitudes & values. She handles courses such as Human Resource Management, organizational behaviour, and specialization courses such as Change Management, Training & Development, etc. She brings to her classes enriched knowledge of 5 years of Research & 16 years of academic experience. She has produced 5 doctoral scholars successfully and currently Guiding 2 Ph.D. scholars. She has presented papers at international and national level conferences and seminars. She has published several research articles and case studies in referred Scopus-indexed journals. She has served on the Editorial Review Boards of several academic journals, including Business theory and practice, the Journal of Management Social Science and Humanities and the Journal of Business Economics and Management.

Index

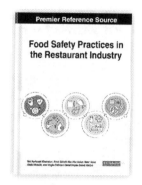

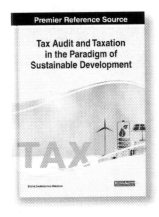

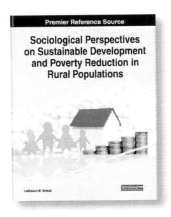

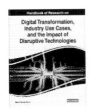